Worlds Made by Words

Worlds Made by Words

SCHOLARSHIP AND COMMUNITY IN THE MODERN WEST

Anthony Grafton

HARVARD UNIVERSITY PRESS

Cambridge, Massachusetts, and London, England · 2009

Library of Congress Cataloging-in-Publication Data

Grafton, Anthony.
    Worlds made by words : scholarship and community in the modern West / Anthony
Grafton.
        p.   cm.
    Includes bibliographical references and index.
    ISBN 978-0-674-03257-6 (alk. paper)
    1. Learning and scholarship—Europe, Western—History.   2. Learning and
scholarship—United States—History.   3. Europe—Civilization.   4. Europe—
Intellectual life.   I. Title.
CB245.G65   2009
940.1—dc22   2008041248

To the memory of Joseph Levine

Contents

Acknowledgments

I owe a special debt to Lindsay Waters, without whom this book would not exist, and to Phoebe Kosman, both of Harvard University Press, as well as to their frank and perceptive referees, whose reports reshaped my work in vital ways. My thanks, also, to Alex Bick, Leo Carey, Joseph Epstein, Ann Fadiman, Nicholas Jahr, Jordan McIntyre, David Remnick, Robert Silvers, and John Sturrock, all of whom provided editorial aid and counsel that went beyond any possible call of editorial duty, and to Ann Blair, Christopher Celenza, Anne Goldgar, Donald Kelley, Jill Kraye, Suzanne Marchand, Peter Miller, Martin Mulsow, William Newman, Richard Serjeantson, Nancy Siraisi, and Jacob Soll, with all of whom I have discussed the issues raised here many times. Finally, I want to thank Barb Leavey for faultless technical support and Amy Haley and Nick Popper for indispensable help and criticism in the final stages of revision. Joseph Levine gave me—as he gave to so many others—decades of friendship and encouragement, as well as the example of his own extraordinary scholarship. This book is dedicated to his memory.

Introduction

A single printed leaf, glued into the binding of a Greek dictionary in the Vatican Library, records the founding of a learned society—the Venetian publisher Aldo Manuzio's "New Academy." Probably printed around 1502, the text describes a compact made by seven of the erudite scholars who prepared editions of classical Greek texts for the Aldine Press. They agreed to speak only Greek in one another's company, to pay fines when they slipped, and to use the money (once enough had accumulated) to hold a symposium: a lavish common meal that was required to be better than the food usually distributed to Aldo's workers. Other "philhellenes" would be admitted to the circle over time.[1]

Like other learned societies of the time—for example, the Platonic Academy of Marsilio Ficino (the very existence of which has been called into doubt)—the New Academy hovers in a gray zone of historical uncertainty.[2] We do not know how often it met, how successful its experiments in spoken Greek proved, or even, in any detailed way, whether it ever existed as more than an idealistic plan. However, we do know that Aldo's "flying leaf"—to use a traditional term for such printed broadsides—can show us which way the intellectual winds blew in early modern Europe. Long before the age of the Enlightenment "public sphere," long before Immanuel Kant identified the work of the scholar who addressed the entire reading public as the preeminent example of the public use of reason, learned Europeans used the systems of communication at their disposal—above all, letter writing and print—to bring new public worlds into existence.

Citizens of the early modern Republic of Letters published manuals designed to transform history, philology, and other fields into disciplines as formal as law or medicine; held formal and informal meetings, in libraries and palaces as well as printing houses; and staged formal discussions of everything from proper Latin usage to the upcoming reformation of the world. They pursued these institutional concerns at every level, from the very local, like the New Academy, to the international—the "res publica litterarum," which supposedly stretched across the world of learning. Some of their projects offered utopian alternatives to the mean conditions of scholarly life, some provided the infrastructure that made research and publication possible, and still others did both. Meanwhile, every aspect of the social and institutional organization of learning, from formal patronage structures to the proper role and conduct of friendship, aroused sharp debate. The social imaginaries and social lives of early modern scholars were, in some ways, equally rich, and each helped to shape the other.[3]

Looking backward from the social, collaborative world of the modern laboratory, historians of science have long argued that the new scientific societies of the sixteenth and seventeenth centuries created and fostered new kinds of research for the natural world. Historians of scholarship, by contrast, have usually looked backward from the cluttered, solitary study of the modern philologist and historian, seeking comparable levels of what Wilhelm von Humboldt called "loneliness and freedom." Like the history of philosophy, the history of scholarship more often has been a story of great individuals than a study of a common project sustained by shared ideals, practices, and institutions.

Consider a classic example of this approach: Mark Pattison's unforgettably vivid biography of the Huguenot Hellenist Isaac Casaubon (1559–1614). Based on imaginative research into Casaubon's ways of reading and taking notes, as well as his correspondence and his commentaries, this pioneering work long shaped readers' understanding of its subject. Pattison set out to show that Casaubon had fashioned himself as a scholar through a strenuous, ascetic, and solitary regime. Lacking teachers on his own level and treated badly by his erudite father-in-law, the publisher Henri Estienne, Casaubon retired into his books and made himself from what he found in them. Happiness, for him, lay in detachment and concentration: loneliness and freedom. "When Casaubon is in his studies, and has made his orisons, shut up alone with God and with his books, then he is in fruition."

True, the lengthy diary in which Casaubon recorded his formation in minute, vivid detail was not a song of triumph but "a complaint, a groan, a record of unhappiness." What made Casaubon wretched, though, were not the endless hours he spent alone, hunched over a book, pen in hand, so intent on study that he paid no attention to the calls of nature, but instead the hours that he had to spend with others: "We find no complaint in the diary of the weariness of study, but much of those unkind friends who broke in upon study. It is not the search for truth which exhausts him, it is the being called off from it."[4] While Pattison admitted that Casaubon shared his own taste for learned company,[5] he concluded as he read the record that Casaubon found very little of this, even in what should have been centers of erudition. In Oxford, for example, where Casaubon spent two busy weeks in May 1613, "men of learning, who could venture to challenge him to discourse of books, were but few."[6] What Casaubon learned in Pattison's university came chiefly from the books and manuscripts in the Bodleian Library, and from a young Jew named Jacob Barnet, who happened to be working in Oxford, and with whom he read Judaica. The unique store of learning that Casaubon partly decanted into his commentaries on Diogenes Laertius's *Lives of the Philosophers* and Strabo's *Geography,* his Latin translation of Polybius, and his critique of Cesare Baronio's church history came from vintages that he himself had trampled out.

Casaubon had his doubts about Oxford. He found the colleges too splendid, the fellows' meals too lavish, and the undergraduates' lives too privileged. Accordingly, he refused all offers of honorary degrees and considered sending his son Meric to study abroad at the more disciplined and austere Leiden University. Still, Casaubon appreciated much of what he saw and a number of those whom he met. In particular, he admired the Bodleian Library, which had opened as recently as 1602. Its treasures did not rival those he had seen on the Continent. Casaubon wrote to Jacques-Auguste de Thou, the official in charge of the French royal library and a great collector in his own right: "You mustn't imagine that the manuscripts to be found here are comparable in quantity with those in the royal library." But the Bodleian's up-to-date holdings of new scholarship impressed him deeply: "The stock of printed books is remarkable, and it will grow every year, for [Thomas] Bodley left yearly revenues to pay for this." What pleased him most, though, was the fact that the library's books were not circulated. Casaubon saw immediately that the founder's technical decision about library rules had not only preserved the collections he endowed, but also created a new and delightful kind of academic community: "So long as I was in Oxford, I spent all day in the library, for the books cannot be taken out, but the library is open for scholars seven or eight hours a day. You would see many scholars there, eagerly enjoying the feasts spread before them. This gave me no little pleasure."[7]

No wonder Casaubon liked what he found in the Bodleian. He himself came to England to work on a massive project on the history of the early church, a rebuttal of Cesare Baronio's great Catholic Church history, the *Annales*. The Bodleian, as Paul Nelles has shown, was created to serve as an arsenal of erudition for the Protestant side in the great intellectual war that raged over the Christian past.[8] Bodley's first librarian, the Calvinist Thomas James, believed that Catholic scholars had deliberately corrupted the texts of the church fathers to make them support their theological positions. He systematically collected all the relevant materials he could, from medieval manuscripts—hundreds of which he acquired for the library, while he catalogued many more in other collections—to contemporary works of Catholic scholarship. In the years just before Casaubon's visit, James spent six hours a day attending to his readers and four more working with a team of younger scholars to produce meticulous collations of the British manuscripts of the church fathers. He hoped, quite wrongly, that these would reveal the perfidy of their Catholic editors. When Casaubon entered Duke Humfrey's library, he found himself exploring an enchanted palace of Protestant learning that could have been built to order for him: not only a superb collection of books he needed to read but also a resort of learned men whose interests he shared and whose philological practices were more precise and systematic than his own.

Even the presence of the Jew Jacob Barnet was more than a happy accident. Casaubon held that one could not understand the world of the early church without knowing a great deal about the traditions of ancient Israel and the life and customs of Palestine in the time of Jesus and his disciples. In Casaubon's eyes, this conviction, which he shared with Joseph Scaliger, formed one of the principal differences between the critical scholarship of the Protestants and the unhistorical methods of Catholic scholars like Baronio. Such men imagined Jesus and his disciples as Catholics like themselves, rather than as Jews creating a new religion.[9] English scholars—many of whom had just collaborated in the production of King James's Bible—shared Casaubon's belief in the vital importance of Hebrew. He enjoyed discussions and correspondence with men like Richard Kilbye, the Oxford professor of Hebrew, and

wrote with special excitement about the chronological scholarship of the recently deceased Cambridge Hebraist Edward Lively. No wonder, then, that
Casaubon took the time to describe the practices of Bodley's new library to his
sympathetic old friend in Paris. Whatever his complaints about the British
mandarins' edifice complexes, he recognized their prowess as scholars. More
important, he saw that the British had created institutions in which the studies
that mattered most to him could flourish. At once he wanted to tease out which
rules and practices had enabled them to achieve this.

The point here is simple. As A. D. Nuttall has shown, Casaubon had a far
livelier mind and led a much happier life than Pattison realized.[10] He was also
a great deal less solitary than Pattison believed. Learned friendships—some
carried on entirely by letter, like his relationship with Scaliger—helped to
shape his scholarship. Friendship, for Casaubon as well as for his contemporaries, embraced a wide variety of relationships, from the comradeship between equals that he felt with Scaliger to the more formal but still rewarding
ties that bound him to erudite grandees like de Thou and Lancelot Andrewes
(who enjoyed telling him ghost stories). Casaubon was less worldly than his
friend, the jurist Conrad Rittershusius. But he understood as clearly as Rittershusius that young men who needed to make their way in the world could
profit by studying texts—like the letters of Joachim Camerarius—from which
they could learn the proper formulas to use with those of higher rank.[11] After
all, Casaubon paid his own keep in Britain by dining with King James—that
is, standing behind the king as he sat at table and ate—and discussing learned
matters with him.[12] He did not regard the time and effort he spent on such
thoughts as a mere indignity or distraction from his true work. Casaubon
knew that friendship in all its senses, like the institutions of learning, shaped
his life and scholarship.

In fact, Casaubon regularly reflected on the social norms of scholarship.
He firmly believed that as a scholar, he had a duty to state the truth, even if
doing so might bring him into contention with friends and allies, and many
of his opponents recognized his adherence to this principle. Most Catholics
approved of his appointment as one of the commissioners in the conference
convoked at Fontainebleau in 1600 to judge the use of quotations in a Protestant treatise on the Eucharist—admittedly, some hoped that he might convert.[13] Though Casaubon deeply respected Joseph Scaliger, whom he saw as
the strongest of allies in his fight to cleanse Christianity of forged texts and

spurious authorities, he noted that Johannes Kepler had arrived at more plausible views than Scaliger on the chronology of Caius Caesar's expedition to the East. This in turn had implications for the more central question of dating Christ's birth.[14] Though Casaubon was unhappy when Jacob Barnet caused a scandal in Oxford by refusing to convert (a story to which we return in Chapter 1), he could not accept the authorities' harsh way of dealing with so learned a man: "Though I detest his perfidy with all my heart," Casaubon explained in a letter meant to reach the eyes of King James himself, "I cannot avoid feeling some sympathy for him, because of his remarkable learning."[15] In other words, Casaubon self-consciously located himself in a range of social networks and sometimes struggled to make his conduct fit their conflicting requirements. He felt personal warmth for learned Anglicans like Andrewes and Huguenot humanists like Scaliger, but he also felt a larger, transconfessional commitment to the pursuit of learning, which connected him to disaffected Lutherans like Kepler and even to a Jew like Barnet—and these loose ties had their impact on his ways of thinking and reading.

For all the differences between them, Casaubon and Aldo shared an understanding that humanists, like scientists, rarely create themselves. We learn first as students and then as practitioners of disciplines, members of communities, users of libraries, habitués of archives, apprentices, and friends—as lurkers in particular intellectual, social, and institutional corners from which we look out at the wide world. We see only one corner of the past or of the artistic or literary tradition, but we see it vividly, in color and perspective, because we know our set of sources so well and can study them in the particular ways into which we have been initiated by teachers and by the keepers of libraries and archives. Our choices of topics, our uses of sources, and our ability to publish all of these results all hinge on our relations with others as much as on our own abilities. This apparent limitation has been a feature of humanistic knowledge, not a bug, for centuries. The studies collected in this volume—which are, like the older forms of scholarship studied in it, the product of an individual conditioned by training, associations, and local habitation—use that condition as a lens through which to contemplate and understand the work of scholars.

The first nine chapters in this volume concern themselves with the particular mosaic of scholarly communities that I have studied since the early 1970s: the early modern Republic of Letters. In the introductory chapter, which maps the Republic as a whole, I argue that this interdisciplinary, international community of scholars existed as both a number of utopian projects and a set of labile but consequential rules for the conduct of scholarly life and debate. Individual citizens tried both to grasp and to revise the Republic's norms of scholarly exchange and debate. Unstated but powerful principles framed by collective discussion helped in their turn to shape the way individuals studied and wrote about the past and the present. A series of case studies follows the Republicans of Letters as they engage in their favorite collective pursuits: developing a new common language—Latin; crossing intellectual, cultural, and religious boundaries to devise new disciplines; negotiating disputes that threatened to hinder their passionate pursuit of knowledge; and envisioning and framing new institutions carefully designed to foster the pursuit of truth and peace.

Like Casaubon, the other protagonists of these studies, from Leon Battista Alberti to Francis Bacon and beyond, knew that intellectual communities shape, and are shaped by, their members. They worked hard to understand the dynamics of this complicated dialectical process on every level, from language itself to the analysis of complex sources. By setting these thinkers and writers back into the corners they occupied—and by attending, so far as possible, to their own reports about the ways that points of view, resources, and relationships shaped their work—we can describe their intellectual world in a way that is neither prettily hagiographical nor emptily sociological. Their ferocious articulateness about the conditions of inquiry and debate, as well as the nature of scholarly relationships and institutions, shows how large a space these issues occupied in actors' maps of the intellectual field.

The Republic of Letters reached its natural end in the late eighteenth century, but the life of scholarship did not. Three case studies, in Chapters 10–12, focus on the development of a preeminently modern subdiscipline, the history of ideas, and examine the ways in which two very different institutional worlds—Oxford University on the one hand, the Warburg Institute on the other—shaped the work of brilliant individuals. Chapters 13–15, finally, offer portraits of two prominent American intellectuals of the twentieth century and a broad-gauged investigation of the ways that books and media are changing in the twenty-first. These chapters argue that even in the age of mass media, electronic databases, and search engines, local conditions still enable us to know certain things—and prevent us from knowing others.

Most of the chapters in this volume are previously published essays that have been revised to eliminate overlapping sections and to take account of subsequent publications, but I have made no attempt to eliminate inconsistencies in tone. While some of these variations result from the long time span over which these essays were first published, most of them derive from my own experience as a teacher and writer. More than three decades spent grappling with the work of scholars in older generations have left me filled with respect for their erudition, their audacity, and their ability to couch the results of intricate and demanding jobs of research in lucid, elegant Latin, Thirty years and more spent living within the modern university—as well as the larger media and publishing worlds outside it—have sometimes left me shaken, even despairing. Times have been, and are, dark. But even in dark times, the social worlds of scholarship provide room for human warmth and the desire and pursuit of the truth and promote deep scholarship and intelligent writing. And these abide.

1

A Sketch Map of a Lost Continent

The Republic of Letters

The first nine chapters in this volume are a historical traveler's reports on a strange, imaginary land that had few of the distinctive marks by which we usually identify a state. It did have a distinctive name: *Respublica literarum,* or the Republic of Letters. Its citizens agreed that they owed it loyalty, and almost all of them spoke its two languages—Latin, which remained the language of all scholars from 1500 to about 1650 and still played a prominent role thereafter, and French, which gradually replaced Latin in most periodicals and in almost all salons. But the Republic had no borders, no government, and no capital. In a world of sharp and well-defined social hierarchies—in which men and women wore formal costumes that graphically revealed their rank and occupation—its citizens insisted that they were all equal, and that any special fame that one of them might enjoy had been earned by his or her own efforts. As one observer put it in 1699, "The Republic of Letters is of very ancient origin . . . It embraces the whole world and is composed of all nationalities, all social classes, all ages and both sexes . . . All languages, ancient as well as modern, are spoken. The arts are joined to letters, and artisans also have their place in it . . . Praise and honor are awarded by popular acclaim."[1] The Republic of Letters imagined itself as Europe's first egalitarian society, even if it did not always enact these high ideals in the grubby reality of its intellectual and professional practices.

Citizens of the Republic were the last Europeans who could plausibly claim that they were masters of their entire civilization. We live in a world of specialists. From engineering and mathematics to philosophy and criticism, success means something specific: defining a problem precisely and solving it in a formal, definitive way. We believe that only other specialists can or should tell us if such problems have been solved. We find ourselves baffled and worried

A sixteenth-century vision of the Republic of Letters, from Angelo Decembrio, *Politiae literariae . . . libri septem* (Augsburg, 1540). Courtesy of Princeton University Library.

when, as has recently happened in the superspecialized realms of mathematics and physics, the specialists do not seem to agree about who proved the Poincaré conjecture or whether string theory will ever reveal something about the real world.

For the most part, specialists and professionals are recent creations: they are the denizens of modernity, a world in which every highly educated man or woman has a particular function and has obtained a formal license to practice it.[2] Specialists existed in premodern Europe, but even those who proudly described themselves as "mathematicians" or "critics" practiced their arts in a broad context. The whole system of formal education was geared to produce generalists. Every learned person became a classicist at school. Specialists in the ancient higher faculties—medicine, law, and theology—imported their humanistic training into these fields and changed the humanities by bringing medical, legal, and theological perspectives to bear on them.[3] Specialists in a more modern sense often did the same. Even the most gifted mathematicians studied Greek, Latin, and history in school, and logic and philosophy in college, before they turned to numbers. Nowadays we remember Leibniz and Newton as scientists, the great men who created the calculus and modern physics, and Leibniz as a philosopher as well. Though the two men took justified pride in their extraordinary achievements in what now seem central fields, they also pursued their interests into many neighboring ones. Leibniz was a productive, critical historian and a penetrating student of the origin and development of human languages. Newton spent years of his life performing alchemical experiments, reworking the history of the ancient world, reconstructing the Temple of Solomon, and trying to interpret the prophecies of Daniel and the Book of Revelation. Thousands of pages of tightly written notes record Newton's efforts in these multiple fields, each of which he apparently took as seriously as the rest. Both men wrote Latin as easily as the modern languages, and often chose to use it—or French, in Leibniz's case—when addressing issues of importance to a wide audience.

One way to imagine the Republic, then, is as a sort of Pedantic Park—a world of wonders, many of them man-made, inhabited by scholarly dinosaurs. The Republicans haunted the massive, classical libraries that patrons preferred, where busts of the heroes of letters stared down from the laden shelves; gazed politely at the rhinoceros horns, skis, and Etruscan weapons artfully heaped on the walls and shelves of cabinets of curiosity; and

A seventeenth-century *Kunst- und Wunderkammer,* from Ole Worm, *Museum Wormianum* (Leiden, 1655). Courtesy of Princeton University Library.

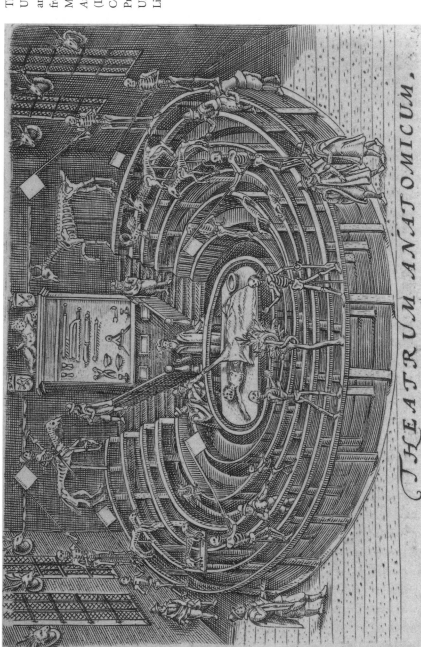

The Leiden University anatomy theatre, from Johannes Meursius, *Athenae Batavae* (Leiden, 1625). Courtesy of Princeton University Library.

THEATRUM ANATOMICUM.

savored the circular spectacle of the anatomy theater—at least in the winter, when the corpses did not stink.[4] Each of these preferred habitats reflected their eclectic tastes. Each one was an encyclopedia—designed to teach material or visual lessons about man and nature, science and history—and a laboratory, in which new forms of knowledge took shape. Leiden University's celebrated anatomy theater, for example, bristled with human and animal skeletons, neatly arrayed to teach comparative anatomy. The articulated bones of men and horses held up banners with Latin devices, designed to impress on visitors the moral lessons of mortality as well as the technical ones of zoology. Skeletal figures of Adam and Eve drove home the theological moral. The university's equally celebrated library offered visitors books and manuscripts, city views, globes, atlases, and learned conversation during its few weekly hours of opening.[5]

The dinosaurs themselves came in many forms. Most of them were mild plant eaters, but the gentle savants were flanked by vast lumbering monsters of erudition like Athanasius Kircher, who lived a life of adventure—physical and intellectual—that Indiana Jones himself might have envied. Kircher climbed into the crater of Vesuvius in pursuit of understanding volcanoes, helped Bernini design the Fountain of the Four Rivers, amused himself working out the magic tricks of the conjurers who performed next to the Fountain in the Piazza Navona, played football against the Dominicans—and speculated, in ways that frightened and angered the religious authorities, about heliocentric astronomy and the antediluvial history of Egypt and China. He preserved his complex thoughts on all of these subjects in a vast array of massive, heavily illustrated Latin folios—more than any modern scholar could possibly read, much less write. While his books reportedly found few buyers, they won generous support from patrons and widespread interest—as well as considerable ridicule—from readers.[6]

The Republicans of Letters were not uniformly distinguished for integrity and generosity. Noel Malcolm has compellingly argued that Kircher's pursuit of secrecy—not to mention his unfounded claims to mysterious knowledge about ancient Egypt and much else—put him in conflict with the Republic's principles of openness, transparency, and full citation of evidence. But Kircher's aggressive pursuit of knowledge, patronage, and fame was not unusual in this world. Under the feet of the giants, swift, vicious little raptors fought and tore their way to prominence with equal energy: for example,

The Leiden University library, from Johannes Meursius, *Athenae Batavae* (Leiden, 1625). Courtesy of Princeton University Library.

Justus Lipsius, the brilliant textual critic, who offered to recite the text of Tacitus with a knife held to his throat, to be plunged in if he made a mistake. Lipsius's moral writings made him the widely respected prophet of high Stoicism,
the preferred moral code for scholars in an age of absolutism and religious war.
Scholars have more recently emphasized his sophisticated pursuit of the lessons of Tacitus and Polybius and his ability to codify the results of sixteenth-
century antiquarianism for a new readership, which he reconfigured so
successfully that they proved indispensable for the practical purposes of military reform. Some have assumed that Lipsius—and his Stoical philosophy—
can stand as a kind of moral counter for the early Republic of Letters as a whole.
But he ensured his reputation as a textual critic by snitching other scholars'
clever emendations, which he recorded in a working copy of Tacitus now held
in Leiden. Sadly, his efforts to erase the evidence did not succeed.[7]

Yet Kircher and Lipsius, for all their idiosyncrasies, offer what still seem
to be powerful models for the conduct of intellectuals. They devised ways to
conduct research with rigor, even when its results were uncomfortable; to
publicize their results without fear or favor; and to rise above their prejudices
again and again, without losing their convictions—both men maintained
friendships that spanned ideological and political borders. They also both
collaborated, to spectacular effect, with artists who gave their books a radically new visual form and, in Kircher's case, realized his vision of ancient
Egypt in the piazzas of modern Rome. They still, I now believe, have much to
teach us about the forgotten premodern intellectual worlds that they inhabited and explored, and also, perhaps, about how modern intellectuals could
and should serve the public good in our own poisoned public sphere.

We must remember, first of all, that the period in which the Republic of
Letters flourished most was no golden age for Old Europe. The phrase *Respublica literarum* appeared in the fifteenth century as a euphonious way to
describe "the literary enterprise" or "the cause of letters." The Republic itself,
however, really began to take shape in the consciousness of scholars around
1500, as Erasmus became the leader of a self-conscious avant-garde of scholars bent on reforming the church and the universities.[8] This process unrolled
only a few years before Martin Luther and his Reformation split the Catholic
Church, which had been unified for more than a thousand years.

The Republic barely survived the years from 1550 onward, when militant
Catholics and Calvinists in France and the Low Countries created what

amounted to the first national revolutionary parties—organized by cells and inspired by absolutist ideologies—and fought civil wars of terrifying brutality. These years were marked by such terrible events as the Massacre of Saint Bartholomew and the assassinations of Kings Henry III and IV of France and William of Orange—made easier, as Lisa Jardine has shown, by the rise of the handgun, a curse then as now.[9] Yet the Republic staggered onward, and even flourished, during the first half of the seventeenth century, while almost all the European powers found themselves drawn into the Thirty Years' War, which turned Germany, then known as the Holy Roman Empire, into an impoverished and backward set of principalities.

All this is to say nothing of such horrors as the witch trials of the same period, which deprived thousands, mostly women, of life itself on the grounds that they had performed intercourse with devils, called up storms to destroy crops, and stolen men's penises, which they hid in birds' nests; or of the imposition of censorship in much of the Catholic world; or of the systematic oppression of Jews. It was a harsh world, as one might expect, because the men who ruled it generally cherished absolute convictions and all too often acted on them. As Brad Gregory has shown in a stunning book, hundreds of men and women died for their religious beliefs, willingly and bravely, after the Reformation began. Not a single one of the officers who imposed these punishments and watched them carried out, whether Catholic or Protestant, Lutheran or Calvinist, seems to have felt any qualms about inflicting martyrdom—to say nothing of converting to the martyrs' faith.[10]

Yet across this ocean of darkness—so historians have learned over the past half century and more—small bands navigated in fragile craft: little communities of scholars, whose members did their best to maintain a different kind of society, with its own rules and its own values. Many of the Republicans of Letters held official positions in universities, courts, or academies, and some used their skills to express imperial and national visions.[11] Others managed to hold official positions and to still work for the Republic's own vague but vital ideals of peace and tolerance.[12] However, some were barred from most such posts by their conviction that they could not serve the state or the institutional church without being swallowed up by it and forced to violate the teachings of their consciences.

Whether the Republicans belonged to an establishment or were hunted by one, they lived lives characterized by movement and distance. Protestants and Catholics alike crossed nations, borders, and sometimes whole worlds. The distinguished older literature on the Republic of Letters—the books and articles of Annie Barnes, Erich Haase, and Paul Dibon—concentrated on the Huguenot Refuge. They treated it, as Hugh Trevor-Roper summed up in a brilliant, overgeneralized article, as the refuge not only of Protestant intellectuals and artisans but also of an Erasmian ideal of tolerance.[13] More recently, students of the Catholic world have placed the Jesuits, always in purposeful motion, on the same imaginary map, and shown that they and the Huguenots—even as they denounced one another—cultivated the same fields of study, from natural science to the art of reading history, and sometimes even pursued the same ideals of civility and collaboration. The network of correspondents that linked José de Acosta, writing on the natural and moral history of the New World in Peru, to fellow Jesuits from Rome to China—and the knowledge transmission belts that, as Paula Findlen has shown, brought the results of Kircher's Egyptology from Rome to the cloister of Sor Juana in New Spain—were as global as those that brought the Samaritans in Palestine and the Jacobite patriarch Ignatius Na'matallah in Rome into productive contact with the Huguenot Joseph Scaliger in France.[14] The Republic of Letters existed, first and foremost, as a kaleidoscope of people, books, and objects in motion.

Motion, of course, was always difficult and sometimes dangerous in the premodern world, but it also had much to offer. Travel—as we have learned from Justin Stagl, Joan-Pau Rubiés, and Paola Molino—became an art in the sixteenth and seventeenth centuries.[15] The Republicans of Letters drew up for each city they visited a questionnaire with spaces for geographical setting and urban form, natural resources and crafts, and literary and religious life. They used this as a hermeneutic, which enabled them to read urban spaces as if they were texts (just as the antiquaries knew how to read texts so as to set them back into the three-dimensional cities where they had originally been produced). As they traveled, they learned about the diverse characters of nations, but at the same time they followed the thinnest capillaries of the Republic of Letters, seeking out their fellow Republicans in their local habitats. In city after city they performed the homosocial rituals of their kind, offering the respects of friends elsewhere and entering signatures, epigrams, and rebuses into one another's *alba amicorum*.[16] By doing so, they made deposits in a bank of social and cultural capital that served them throughout their lives.

Distance and motion had other functions as well. Above all, distance lent prestige—especially to such apparently glittering centers of new intellectual life as Louvain in the early sixteenth century, Leiden and Prague a century later, and Amsterdam and London later still—not to mention Paris and Rome, the eternal beacons of erudition and antiquity. By contacting a dominant figure in one of these brilliant galaxies of talent and receiving a testimonial of warm approval, one could win credit in one's own local, competitive environment. That is why, as Mario Biagioli has recently taught us, Galileo set such store by Johannes Kepler's approval of the findings that he announced in the *Sidereal Messenger*. Beleaguered by local critics and competitors in northern and central Italy, Galileo was bathed in a glowing nimbus of support from the detailed letter sent by the Imperial Mathematician from far-off Prague.[17]

The stars that glittered most brightly across distance were usually cities. The Republicans often had to spend time and provide services at courts. But they liked cities that enjoyed a certain measure of autonomy, and whose governors did not share the general belief that torture and execution were the appropriate tools for reducing religious and intellectual dissidents to order and submission. Citizens of the Republic also needed to perch near certain urban institutions, such as libraries and the printing presses that gave men and women of letters their only power—publicity. Their favored places—the capitals of their imagined state—included Strasbourg, a cosmopolitan and tolerant border town; Leiden and Amsterdam, the Dutch trading centers in which Catholics and Calvinists, Anabaptists and Jews rubbed elbows in mutual tolerance, and where all joined to reject what they called "the Genevan Inquisition" when doctrinaire preachers tried to carry out an ideological cleansing; and, of course, Basel, where Erasmus and other irenic souls found a spiritual home in a city ever hospitable to Christian refugees from oppression in their native countries (Jews, by contrast, were firmly excluded, except when they were needed to print texts in Hebrew, Aramaic, or Yiddish). London and Berlin also figured on the imaginary maps of the Republic because both cities harbored many of the refugee French Protestants who made up a major share of the Republic's population.

Cities, after all, offered unique intellectual resources. In such forcing houses of talent and research as the Lime Street community in Elizabethan London, reconstructed with great skill by Deborah Harkness in *The Jewel*

House, clusters of artisans and apothecaries, Paracelsians, and natural historians made their shops and gardens into a vast collective laboratory—something
like an embodiment of Bacon's supposedly utopian New Atlantis, in which
intellectual workers of very different kinds coordinated their efforts to force
nature to reveal her secrets. Yet this local world had foreign as well as British
inhabitants and was closely connected—by contacts made in travel and correspondence networks that passed through the Low Countries to the rest of
Europe—with a vast range of impressive foreign contacts who appreciated its
lively, fertile culture.[18] The active, engaged, and sometimes quarrelsome form
of collaboration between artisans and scholars that Harkness has turned up
in London had become a standard feature of cultural life in Renaissance Italy
and characterized the Republic throughout its history.

Cities were also the habitats of most of the learned women—beneficiaries,
as Sarah Ross and April Shelford have taught us, of surprisingly ardent support from the Latin-speaking patriarchy—who created such salons as that of
the Dames des Roches in Poitiers, and who, in the later seventeenth and eighteenth centuries, entered such once-male preserves as the realm of classical
philology.[19] Yet country houses, with their alluring mannerist gardens, also
offered islands of civility, many of them superbly stocked with books and antiquities, and historians of the Republic of Letters in the German and Austrian lands have emphasized the role of these aristocratic enclaves.[20]

Wherever they found jobs or refuge, the Republicans continued to respond
to changes in the world outside the scholarly enclaves. Gradually they ditched
backward-looking Latin for the up-to-date language of civilization, French,
and took their campaigns against persecution and oppression to a wider public, even as the wars of Louis XIV turned much of northern Europe into a
wasteland and systematic oppression and abuse almost destroyed France's
own Protestant communities.[21]

Citizens of the Republic carried no passports, but they could recognize one
another by certain marks (not wealth, of course—then, as now, scholar did
not rhyme with dollar). They looked for learning, for humanity, and for generosity, and they rewarded those who possessed these qualities. Any young
man, and more than a few young women, could pay the price of admission. If
they mastered Latin and, ideally, Greek, Hebrew, and Arabic; became proficient at what now seem the unconnected skills of mathematics and astronomy, history and geography, and physics and music; visited any recognized

scholar—from John Locke in London to Giambattista Vico in Naples—bearing a letter from a senior scholar, and greeted their host in acceptable Latin or French, they were assured of everything a learned man or woman could want: a warm and civilized welcome, a cup of chocolate (or, later, coffee), and an hour or two of ceremonious conversation on the latest editions of the classics and the most recent sightings of the rings of Saturn.[22]

If this state had no maps, no administrative officials, and no borders, how do we know it existed at all? And how can we define it more precisely? We know the Republic, initially, from what its citizens tell us about it. The documents in which they discussed it form the primary archive from which we can draw both descriptions and evaluation. Not all contacts were informal. Traditional historiography has emphasized the scientific societies that took shape over the course of the seventeenth century and whose officers and members did their best to establish new criteria and methods for the proper study of nature: the Accademia del Cimento, the Lincei, the Académie des Sciences, and the Academia Naturae Curiosorum.[23] More recent studies have taught us to see these as one particularly vital species within a larger genus. The Republicans of Letters created many local communities of savants, dedicated to the search for religious or secular truths, or both at once. In some cases, as in the sixteenth-century Neapolitan academies that dedicated themselves to hunting out the secrets of nature or the seventeenth-century utopian brotherhoods that took shape in Tübingen or elsewhere, individuals or groups drew up formal rules for membership and elaborate protocols for the proper pursuit of intellectual life.[24] In others, like the Cabinet of the brothers Dupuy or Théophraste Renaudot's Bureau d'Addresse, membership and activities formed more spontaneously.[25] In any number of cases, only a textual record remains, raising questions that are difficult to resolve about whether a given society functioned in the material and social world.[26] Nonetheless, these organizations clearly played vital roles. They made clear that intellectual life needed a social foundation—and needed it all the more as Europe's age of religious war progressed. And they helped to create the epistolary networks that gave the Republic its true circulatory system.

Above all, it is in the thousands of surviving letters—which combined the official and professional with the personal in a way that in the premodern world seemed entirely natural—that the outlines, highways, and capitals of the Republic can be glimpsed most vividly. Tucked into letters were the reports on barometric experiments and the movements of falling bodies; the specimens of Egyptian mummy and New World flora; the drawings of rhinoceros horn and Roman feet; the descriptions of newly discovered manuscripts of ancient texts; and the historical and political information that enabled men and women to know what was happening in the great world outside their little town and to compile the great syntheses of political, historical, philosophical, and scientific information that we still read: the work of Grotius on natural law, Galileo on natural philosophy, and Locke on the nature of property. To a world that has largely abandoned letters except when asking for money in a good cause, these epistles—with their formal Latin salutations and intimate details of urinalysis and kidney stones, astrological predictions, and monstrous births—may seem quaint. In their day, however, they constituted the fragile but vital canals that connected and animated intellectual commerce in the far-flung parts of the Republic. The strands of long-term correspondence formed a capillary system along which information could travel from papal Rome to Calvinist strongholds in the north, and vice versa—so long as both (as they did) had inhabitants who wished to communicate.[27]

The constant writing and sending of letters was more than a system for collecting and exchanging information. Many citizens of the Republic saw it as a moral duty: at once the only way to show their sympathy and affection for those from whom they were separated by political and religious borders and the only way to enter into a regular relationship with the greats who glittered far away. Consider just one instance: Erasmus, the great teacher and letter writer, whose textbooks dominated the schools and universities of northern Europe until the middle of the seventeenth century and whose own correspondence fills twelve volumes in the great modern edition published by the Clarendon Press. Erasmus treated the letter as a literary genre in its own right and set down rules for the composition of effective, eloquent letters. In one of his textbooks—the aptly named *On Copiousness in Words and Ideas*—he went farther, listing hundreds of ways to say "As long as I live, I shall remember you" and "Thank you for the letter" in elegant, correct Latin. The effort seems disproportionate to the task, until we realize that, as Kathy Eden has made clear, Erasmus deeply believed both in the community of intellectual and literary property ("all the property of friends is held in common," he liked to say, quoting the ancient Greek thinker Pythagoras) and in the connection between the language one used and the state of one's mind and soul.[28]

For Erasmus, the scholar must school himself or herself to write, over and over again, professing friendship and concern to critics as well as supporters, to enemies as well as friends. By doing so, he or she would knit the raveled sleeves of particular relationships, but would also become a true friend, one genuinely devoted to and concerned for others. The vast series of letters that fill dozens of volumes in every great European library are the relics of a great effort, inspired by Erasmus and many others after him, to create a new kind of virtual community that was sustained not by immediate, direct contact and conversation so much as by a decades-long effort of writing and rewriting.[29]

As Anne Goldgar and Brian Ogilvie have taught us, these exchanges followed—or were supposed to follow—a strict code. Write to another scholar and you engaged yourself to reply to future letters in reasonable time, to give credit to your correspondent for information received and suggestions accepted, and to call him or her a friend—a term that had a strong formal meaning.[30] Yet for all the coded formality of their Latin and French, for all their authors' desperate efforts to create *personae* on paper, and for all the breaches of epistolary etiquette that fused the circuits of this vast mechanism of exchange, many of them remain very moving.[31]

As this example suggests, some of the Republic's qualities give it a genuine contemporary relevance. Like us, its citizens made conscious efforts to create communities—both of people and of information—that crossed political, linguistic, and religious borders. Like us, they did their best to manage the vast amounts of information to which they had access. As Ann Blair, Richard Yeo, Daniel Rosenberg, and Noel Malcolm have shown, the early modern period witnessed multiple efforts to capture, organize, and make available to readers the turbid streams of information loosed on Europe by travelers, compiled by scientific observers, and excavated by historians—a flood not only reproduced but magnified by the printing press. The tools they forged included not only scholarly correspondence of a personal sort but also both technical and literary models for stockpiling information and making it available: the bibliography, the filing cabinet, the compilation of "historia litteraria," and the journal.[32] From the 1660s onward, a swarm of new printed publications, in both Latin and the modern languages, compiled new information, reviewed new books, and for the first time made it possible for intellectuals across Europe to have reliable, regular information on the doings of scholars—and kings—in every other corner of the European world.[33]

Trade became global again in the fifteenth century. Information also joined the global flow, as Huguenots in exile in Berlin and Potsdam informed the European world about recent science and scholarship in French. Kircher, admired and envied in Rome, used reports from fellow Jesuits around the world as he charted the underground movements of rivers and lava flows and the ancient migrations of peoples. Vico, isolated in Catholic, southern Naples, but well informed, used Dutch journals published in Latin as his primary sources for the new theories of Spinoza and Locke. Like the blogs that have accelerated the movement of facts and ideas in recent years, the new journals and publishing houses had a profoundly unsettling effect on political and social authorities. The Republic of Letters stood, initially, for a kind of intellectual market—one in which values depended not on a writer's rank but, at least in theory, on the quality of his or her work.

The Republic was more than a sprawling series of social and intellectual networks loosely linked by curiosity about nature and history. It would be wrong to suggest that it had a single ideology or an official set of beliefs—even that of the Radical Enlightenment recently reconstructed with such brio by Jonathan Israel.[34] Its citizens, after all, included Catholics of different sorts, Protestants of every flavor, and a few Sephardic and an even smaller number of Ashkenazi Jews—in addition, as time went on, to Unitarians and others who abandoned all the established churches. Patriotic Dutch scholars presumably felt a shiver of pride—and patriotic British ones just a shiver—when a Dutch fleet sailed up the Medway and burned much of the English navy.

Also, and more important, many of the most erudite scholars—Catholic, Calvinist, and Lutheran—pursued their research largely, or even primarily, for partisan reasons: in order to ensure the triumph of a religion or a ruling house. Jesuits in China and elsewhere showed a deep interest in alien systems of belief and practice, yet their primary goal was the conversion of the world to Catholicism. Even Matteo Ricci found it easy to draw the line between Chinese beliefs that he saw as compatible with Christianity and those that were not.[35] The large-scale research enterprises mentioned in this book—the teams of scholars assembled to study the history of the church—found patrons because they promised to supply weapons to be used in confessional strife. Even those who consciously tried to see the merits in others' programs and practices were still driven, much of the time, by theological convictions. Isaac Casaubon's demonstration that the philosophical Hermetica were late rested on his mastery of the language and technical philology. But it was motivated by an absolute conviction that neither Cardinal Baronio, whose work he dissected at enormous length, nor a pagan like Hermes, who supposedly anticipated Christian truths, could possibly have written in good faith.[36]

Yet certain views, shared in greater and lesser degree by the Republicans, ran counter to the confessionalism of the time. Some of them, for a start, believed that it was simply wrong—morally and intellectually—to break off communications with those who did not share their religious beliefs or their political views. Knowledge and sociability mattered most, and restrictions could only hamper the flow of information and ideas. That helps to explain why a long series of Vatican librarians, in the heart of papal Rome, admitted Protestant scholars as freely as Catholic ones.

A fair number went farther. In an age of brutal persecution, when torture was the standard legal method on the Continent for extracting information and confessions, scholarly citizens of the Republic of Letters pointed out, forcibly and clearly, that torture could make people confess not only crimes they had not committed but also crimes that no one could commit—a thesis that is anything but quaint or antiquated today. They also became the first to argue in detail that the vast, tottering structure of dogma that underpinned the persecution of witches was far too rickety to bear so great a weight. An early citizen of the Republic, Johannes Reuchlin, dared the disapproval of influential men and women across Germany when he wrote a powerful legal defense of the right of Jews to retain their own books, which influential Catholics wanted to burn.[37] Another citizen of the Republic, Sebastian Castellio, first elaborated an even more radical idea, which flew in the face of religious authority from Saint Augustine on. Castellio, once a great admirer of John Calvin's, was horrified by Calvin's part in the arrest and execution of the heretic Michael Servetus in 1553. He took action—the sort of action that the citizens of the Republic took. Working with local eminences like Bonifacius Amerbach and Thomas Platter as well as émigrés from Holland and France, all of whom shared his loathing of coercion and violence, Castellio compiled excerpts from early Christian and contemporary works to show that the state had no right to persecute those who did not accept the beliefs of its established church. The Basel printer Joannes Oporinus, whose list included authors of every conceivable ideology and religion, published this work—as subversive in import as it was mild in form—under a false imprint.

Each piece of the mosaic Castellio assembled added a distinctive color to his argument. Writing under the pseudonym Martin Bellius, Castellio argued that persecution was literally un-Christian. Those who executed heretics seemed to think that Jesus had been a "Moloch or a god of the sort," who commanded human sacrifice. Writing as Basilius Montfort, he mounted a more tightly defined political argument. Secular rulers had no right to punish anyone on grounds of belief: "He who suffers persecution on account of his faith stands either in the truth or in error. If he is right he must not be harmed. If he is wrong he must be forgiven. Christ asked God to forgive those who crucified him, for they knew not what they were doing. Would this not apply more greatly to those who allow themselves to be crucified for him?"[38] Castellio's arguments were hardly rigorous. In the end, he argued, one should judge people by their conduct—a theologically naive view that could not be reconciled with any Protestant understanding of grace and salvation. His convictions stemmed partly from his wide reading in the early, more radical writings of Martin Luther and the great polemics against persecution by Sebastian Franck, and in part from the lived experience of Basel, where Castellio had seen that men and women of different religions could manage and negotiate their differences—as, some years later, the Hebraist Johannes Buxtorf managed to publish important editions of Hebrew texts, even though the Jewish printers refused to work on Saturdays and the Christians on Sundays.

Castellio's book won few adherents at first, yet his ideas percolated into the minds of writers like Montaigne and, so it seems, even a few rulers—notably William of Orange and Elizabeth of England.[39] Other citizens of the Republic carried his enterprise onward, using the literary tools at their disposal because they lacked political ones. Of course, the battle against religious prejudice and persecution did not end during this period, any more than it has ended since. A later citizen of the Republic, Pierre Bayle—a brilliant, bitter critic of absolutism in state and church who lived in Holland and tormented the authorities with his dazzling pamphlets—shocked many readers when he argued that a society of atheists could live together in peace. And the great *philosophes* of the eighteenth century—men like Voltaire, who famously left his refuge near Geneva in order to confront the forces of darkness over the Calas case—argued cases like Castellio's, casting them in a far more radical light. Such characteristic Enlightenment attitudes grew from the speculations of learned men, forced into exile for their beliefs and instructed in the bitter school of political and religious experience that compulsion should never play a role in matters of belief.

Belief in such challenging principles as the free communication of ideas, tolerance in principle if not always in practice, open contact with those of other faiths, and publication of results even when they raised theological difficulties manifested themselves not only in such famous and controversial cases as that of Servetus but also in the everyday life and work of scholars, many of them less courageous—and stiff-necked—than Castellio. Here I pass from cartography to chorography. Like most of those who study the Republic, I have examined only one corner of this vast realm at close range, and in the course of this more limited and detailed scrutiny I have come to see just how the Republicans of Letters used their general canons of conduct to regulate particular technical forms of inquiry. Starting out in the 1970s, I wanted to understand how men and women could master the whole range of period disciplines and texts, from astronomy to philology; to learn what it felt like to be as skillful at interpreting ancient history as at reading the movements of the planets. So I set out to reconstruct a single discipline that nowadays has largely been forgotten: technical chronology, the formal study of the dates at which events happened in ancient and medieval history. Even in the early modern period, the field was known to be obscure—Johannes Kepler, who knew and loved the subject, noted that books with "chronology" in their titles did not sell.[40]

Still, chronology was a hot field in its day.[41] Leiden University, the most innovative institution of higher learning in early modern Europe, paid the French scholar Joseph Scaliger a higher salary than the law professors and allowed him to forego lecturing and devote himself to research because of the worldwide reputation he had earned as the leading expert on chronology. Like other hot fields, chronology was difficult. It demanded—and still demands—extraordinary skills: you had to be able to interpret ancient texts, decipher ancient inscriptions, and even plot the dates of the eclipses and other astronomical events mentioned in ancient texts, which provide the only potentially absolute confirmation for historical dates. Chronology posed problems that remain extremely difficult, and to some extent unsolved: for example, how to reconcile the dynasty lists and dates of the Old and New Testaments with one another and with those preserved in secular texts. Accordingly, its practitioners had to walk fine lines. In theory, they could not force or falsify any of the evidence, but as soon as they chose one biblical datum to rely on, they laid themselves open to the charge of neglecting others that contradicted it.

A great many early modern scholars wielded this rather daunting palette of technical skills with ease and dexterity. Scaliger and his Jesuit critic Denis Petau were probably the best known experts in the field. But chronology also fascinated great astronomers like Copernicus and Kepler, the important composer and musical theorist Seth Calvisius, the erudite Anglican churchman James Ussher, and the most original historical thinker of the whole premodern period, Giambattista Vico. These men did extraordinary, wrenchingly difficult work with meticulous care. By 1700 they had crafted the basic armature of dates on which modern scholars still hang the flesh and blood of ancient and medieval history. Yet they also had begun to study data from other cultures—such as the dynasty lists of the Chinese—which called their basic assumptions into question; in the end, they could not save their beautiful theories from the impact of these obdurate facts.[42]

Scaliger and Kepler, Calvisius and Petau turned out to be as phenomenally learned and analytical, as wide-ranging in their interests and as precise and prophetic in their results as I had believed before I ventured into the labyrinths of their books and manuscripts. However, these toiling giants had many human failings. They misreported one another's ideas, failed to give credit where credit was clearly due, and ripped each other's work apart with a zeal that would have been better spent on other pursuits.

Academic gossip described chronology as rife with extravagant and willful hypotheses: chronologers, like clocks, never agreed; and some chronologers lived up to these clichés. For example, the erudite Jesuit numismatist and textual critic Jean Hardouin decided after decades of chronological and philological study that pretty much all the Greek and Latin classics—except for Pliny's *Natural History,* which he had edited, and a few other texts—had been forged in the thirteenth century by an "atheistic sect" led by Frederick II of Hohenstaufen. He drew these conclusions partly from an exhaustive study of ancient coins, and partly from the texts, which he subjected to the kind of endlessly skeptical scrutiny that adherents of the Baconian theory inflict on the texts of Shakespeare. Protestants and Catholics alike were shocked by Hardouin's radicalism, which provoked bitter debates and unsettled all practitioners of chronology. Too many of them responded by making the

Jesuit order as a whole collectively guilty for his individual fancies.[43] More important—and more generally—it became clear that chronologers, like so many other Republicans of Letters, were hypersensitive to slights. Any letter that showed insufficient respect, any publication of a fact or utterance of a word that might reflect badly on them, and they turned on their discussion partners and rent them—even when, as Kepler haplessly tried to convince Seth Calvisius, the offended party had simply misunderstood the offender's use of German.

Yet even as I realized that my chronologers were not such consistent models of scholarly and human virtue as I had hoped, I also found them working hard and effectively to raise bridges across the most profound ideological and theological gaps. Scaliger—a fierce Calvinist who believed, as did many of his coreligionists, that the pope was the Antichrist—told his students to view the great Catholic Church history by Cardinal Baronio with respect because "every history is good." He explained that all information matters, and that you can learn far more from a great scholar whose opinions you do not share than from a charlatan with whom you go to church.[44]

Chronology could be brutally polemical, but it also could provide an ideal public stage for demonstrations of tolerance. The chronologer was constantly required to negotiate agreement between sources of radically different origin and nature—a delicate operation at best, and sometimes impossible. To study the Christian past, you had to understand the Jewish calendar—not just the sequence of years and months but also the nature of religious holidays and observances. Scaliger and his close friend, Isaac Casaubon, realized in the last decades of the sixteenth century that they could not reconstruct the sequence of events or understand the meaning of individual episodes in the Gospels themselves without mastering Jewish scholarship. The Last Supper—as Scaliger pointed out in his first chronology, to the astonishment of erudite theologians—was an adaptation of the Jewish Passover seder. To understand this primal Christian event, one must read a Passover Haggadah.[45]

But the Haggadah did not clear up all the problems—for example, how Jesus apparently had been condemned and executed on days when Jews were prohibited from appearing in court. How were Christians to gain this esoteric knowledge? Scaliger and Casaubon were masters of language, steeped in the Bible. Initially, learning to read Hebrew had only required them to work out which words were which in the Hebrew Old Testament, because they already knew it by heart in Latin and French. However, the Bible offered nowhere near all the information they needed. To understand exactly the world in which Jesus preached, they had to explore all the nooks and recesses of Jewish learning—chronicles, rabbinical commentaries, even the Talmud. For guidance through these labyrinths, they turned to Jews: Scaliger worked for six months with a very learned convert, Philippus Ferdinandus, who helped him to see that many of Jesus's precepts in the Gospels did not contradict but actually reflected Jewish moral teachings. Casaubon invited a learned Jew from Italy, Jacob Barnet, to stay with him for a month at his lodgings on Drury Lane in London. At every meal—one would love to know what they ate—the two men eagerly discussed Jewish texts. Barnet showed Casaubon discussions of Jewish burial practices—which revealed to the brilliant Calvinist that Jesus had been buried in a normal Jewish fashion rather than, as Cardinal Baronio maintained, in a new way that became the basis of Catholic burial practice.[46]

Neither Scaliger nor Casaubon was especially philo-Semitic in everyday life, but the ethics of scholarship as they understood it brought them into intimate contact with Europe's local Others; and this contact had a tremendous effect on both of them. Scaliger, the most arrogant of scholars in an age when scholarly arrogance flourished, admitted after Ferdinandus died that no Christian could hope to understand the Talmud and other Jewish texts as had his friend. He wept, in a very human way, for his personal and intellectual loss. Jacob Barnet, whom the Oxford authorities had destined for public conversion in Saint Mary's Church, rebelled, ran away, and wound up confined in miserable conditions at the university jail, Bocardo. Casaubon—a mild man, bent with age and unremitting study—intervened. He denounced Barnet's treatment as a violation of Christian ethics. In fact, he went so far as to appeal to King James I—himself an erudite man—on Barnet's behalf, and his pleas succeeded. A king's man brought a warrant to Oxford, removed Barnet from prison, and put him on the next ship to France. He soon turned up again, man of parts that he was, as an expert on Jewish matters at the French royal court, where he and Giulio Cesare Vanini enjoyed passing gossip about the stinginess of British patrons. The openness that men like Scaliger and Casaubon showed to others whose faith and culture they definitely did not share offered them no practical advantages and could have caused them endless difficulties. That these men behaved as they did is a tribute to the regulative principles of the Republic—and a sign of their historic impact.

In the course of their work, both Casaubon and Scaliger took on board ideas and ways of doing things that shocked some of their contemporaries. Neither went so far as those seventeenth-century Amsterdam Jews who appalled their coreligionists by adopting a form of Karaism that was not based on contact with actual Karaites, but on the descriptions given by Christian Hebraists.[47] Still, during Casaubon's years of biblical study and his intensive work with Barnet, he sometimes even prayed in Hebrew. After even longer years of historical study, Scaliger made a chronological discovery so profound that even his brilliance could not cope with it: Manetho's list of the Egyptian dynasties, according to which history had begun not only before the Flood, but before the Creation. Both men saw that in many ways, Christianity represented less a break with the Judaism of the time of Jesus than a new development within it. Historical research was supposed to rear and trim neat, tidy structures that showed the hand of Providence working to bring Christianity into being. Instead, Scaliger's and Casaubon's dangerous ideas and destructive practices undermined the authorities they were expected to support. Yet both men published what they learned—and by doing so disturbed and irritated more orthodox thinkers across the whole European world.

Finally, chronology has a chronology of its own—one that helps us to understand the larger chronology of the Republic of Letters. In the late 1650s, Isaac Vossius—whose father, Gerardus, had brought him up within the formidable learned tradition of Dutch humanism—shocked the world of learning. He helped to arrange the reprinting in Amsterdam of the Jesuit Martino Martini's history of China, which set the beginning of the Middle Kingdom so early that only the Greek Old Testament, with its longer chronology, could fit it in after the Flood. And then he published a pamphlet, first in Latin and then in Dutch, in which he insisted that the longer chronology of the Greek Bible deserved credence over the shorter one of the Hebrew. In doing this, Vossius did not forge a new thesis. Ever since Scaliger, chronologers had weighed the difficulties of early history and the virtues of the different biblical versions, and admitted the impossibility of arriving at firm results—in the privacy of their letters and conversations or in the relative privacy of vast Latin treatises. But Vossius—to borrow a term from my late friend and colleague

Gerald Geison—turned what had been private science into public science—so public that it provoked a series of pamphlet-sized refutations, which did nothing to soothe the scholarly waters.[48] A few years later, Vossius literally made the private public by printing Joseph Scaliger's table talk—which showed that in his chimney corner, talking to his students in a pithy mixture of Latin and French, Scaliger had entertained similarly bold ideas about the duration of history and the incompleteness of the Hebrew Bible.[49]

In these middle years of the seventeenth century, fissures and cracks opened up in many of the fields that mattered to the Republicans. Science and scholarship underwent dramatic transformations in key and tone, as great treatises in Latin gave way to pamphlets in the vernacular, and detailed arguments in dark libraries became lively debates in public venues—and as the practices of erudition revealed what could be a powerful potential to call ancient authorities into question. Traditional histories of the Enlightenment, often centered on France, have tended to treat the eighteenth century in almost Hegelian terms—as the time when the world spirit turned from erudition to philosophy, and scholars became marginal figures in the world of learning.[50] In chronology—as in other fields—older traditions of exegesis and newer methods of historical scholarship, both designed to clarify and confirm traditional structures, ended by destroying them.[51]

Citizens of the early modern Republic of Letters created a virtual community not of those who shared beliefs, but of those who differed. They made up rules for civility that could be used to judge the conduct of all those who offered their intellectual wares for sale in the new, largely free market. They developed new tolerances—for thinkers who disagreed with them on fundamental matters and for facts that challenged their most basic verities. These efforts were unified by a shared, if inchoate and incomplete, respect for truth, civility, and the integrity of the human being—a respect perhaps not founded on deep philosophical or theological arguments, and often violated in practice, but solid enough to make them bold when they confronted what they saw as superstitions. One of the most prominent citizens of the Republic, Jean Le Clerc—a Swiss, born in Geneva, who moved to Amsterdam to enjoy intellectual freedom—put it well: "If a thing is bad in itself, the example of the ancients does not make it better. Nothing should stop us from improving on them. The Republic of Letters has finally become a land of reason and light, and not of authority and blind faith, as it was for too long. Nowadays

Joseph Scaliger with his pupils around him, from *Scaligerana* (Amsterdam, 1695).
Courtesy of Princeton University Library.

numbers prove nothing, and there are no more cabals."[52] True, in this case Le Clerc was defending not freedom of speech or religion but the use of footnotes in historical texts, but he and his contemporaries wrote with equal clarity and power about religious and political oppression.

Naturally, practices were always more complex than precepts—and sometimes much darker and more oppressive. Citizens of the Republic of Letters who violated its rules, like Vossius, could change them—but only at the cost of suffering abuse and exclusion. The same fate awaited those who parodied its customs too radically—for example, those who devised erotic readings of the story of the Fall, and took the eating of the apple as an allegory for sexual intercourse. As Kristine Haugen and Martin Mulsow have shown, these rash young men found themselves deprived of their jobs, hunted from their homes, and forced into poverty and obscurity by the very fellow scholars who would have defended them if they had not breached the Republic's codes of decorum.[53] Senior academics, then as now, often showed less tolerance for their junior colleagues than for almost anyone else.

Still, the Republic of Letters provided a stage where free exchange of opinions could sometimes be proclaimed and performed in a new way. Though its story has often been treated as coextensive with that of the eighteenth-century Enlightenment, these accounts foreshorten the traditions of scholarship, debate, and sociability that connect the humanist sodalities of Renaissance Florence and Rome to the academies, public libraries, Masonic lodges, and salons of the seventeenth and eighteenth centuries. This complex and inspiring history remains to be written.

2

A Humanist Crosses Boundaries

Alberti on "Historia" and "Istoria"

One day in 1446, as the Benedictine Girolamo Aliotti made his way toward Arezzo, he encountered a new "religio" taking shape. Men dressed as penitents, women trudging on foot, boys and girls followed cruciform banners through a cleft in the hills. Joining them, Aliotti learned that the Virgin Mary had just appeared "in the body" to the citizens of a small town, where she had made believers out of the atheists and reconciled enemies divided by ancient lawsuits and feuds. Inquiring more closely, Aliotti learned that four teenaged girls had taken shelter in the local church during a heavy rain. They prayed to the Virgin to stop the downpour, which was causing serious floods, and to put an end to the civil strife that was doing even worse damage to their town. In answer to their prayers, the image of the Virgin painted on the wall of the church was "transfigured into the true mother of the Lord our Savior, no longer represented, but in the flesh, but breathing, but alive."

Once transformed into its prototype, the image exhibited miraculous powers. Mockers, brought into its presence, "began to feel the immense and terrible power of God." Trembling, stricken, they fell helpless to the ground, like the apostle Paul. Spectacular visions appeared to them: one saw the Virgin shooting arrows into his heart, another felt the most severe pains he had ever experienced. Contact with the image brought about conversion—immediate, irresistible, and awe-inspiring. Aliotti, deeply impressed, remembered his professional responsibilities. An icon's metamorphosis into its own holy subject would constitute a miracle. Accordingly, Aliotti consulted experts on the theology of the supernatural for help in assessing what he had seen and heard. He sent a detailed account to a friend in Rome, asking for the authoritative opinions of Cardinal Turrecremata, "the most expert theologian of our time," and Giovanni Mattiotti, the priest in Santa Maria in Trastevere who had served as

confessor to Santa Francesca Romana, "a man characterized by special apti-
tude for the precise discernment of spirits."[1]

Aliotti's social and intellectual worlds were very large—sizable enough, in
fact, to accommodate thinkers who had a very different way of looking at the
power of images. He took a serious interest in the new humanistic literature
of the 1430s and 1440s. Aliotti copied texts, wrote critiques, and at one point
even set out to create a public library entirely composed of modern Latin
texts, beginning with the complete works of Poggio Bracciolini.[2] Like many
other citizens of the humanist Republic of Letters, he eagerly collected and
read texts that dealt with the arts—for example, an anonymous work in Italian, *De arte fusoria*. Aliotti hoped that the painters and sculptors of Florence
might be able to provide him with a more correct text of the treatise, if possible in Latin. He also made a revealing conjecture about its authorship: perhaps, he thought, "Messer Baptista de Albertis" might have written it.[3] Aliotti's
guess suggests that he already knew, or knew of, a similar work by Alberti: his
treatise *On Painting*, the Italian and Latin versions of which both reached
completion before Aliotti saw the miraculous icon.[4] This is not surprising: as
we see later in this chapter, Aliotti knew and admired Alberti.

If Aliotti had decided to treat the phenomena he saw as natural rather than
supernatural, he might well have consulted Alberti rather than Turrecremata,
asking him to explain how a painting could so strongly affect those who encountered it. In *On Painting*, after all, Alberti had examined in detail the
means by which a painting of the highest excellence—a "historia," or "istoria," as he termed it in Latin, or a "storia" or "istoria" in Italian—could "move
the hearts of those who see it."[5] One can only imagine how Alberti would have
gone about analyzing the emotional effects wrought by the Virgin's image on
the church wall. One can, however, make a more systematic effort than has yet
been tried to establish exactly what Alberti had in mind when he described the
"historia" as "the consummate work of the painter."[6]

Scholarly interest in Alberti's text and terminology goes back to the very
origins of systematic art history. The Strasburg scholar Hubert Janitschek, a
distinguished student of the social and cultural history of Renaissance art,
translated Alberti's *Della pittura* into German more than a century ago. He
also equipped the work with notes, in which he identified some of the classical and postclassical sources on which Alberti drew and the ancient and
modern works of art on which he commented. Janitschek's work retains

considerable value. But when he confronted Alberti's discussion of the "historia," he read the relevant passages through a veil composed of the characteristic interests and assumptions of a connoisseur of painting in the 1870s. What the term "historia" called to his mind was, naturally enough, "history painting." He translated it accordingly, as "das Geshichtsbild"—a word that brings to mind heroic images of oaths and cavalry charges, represented with minute, even historicist attention to the details of costume and setting.[7]

By contrast, John Spencer, who translated *Della pittura* into English eighty years later, contented himself with a transcription of the term: "The *istoria*," he made Alberti write, "is the greatest work of the painter."[8] But in his introduction, he made clear that the term required an elaborate gloss. "The concept of *istoria*," he explained, "dominates the whole treatise and it is developed at length in the last half of the work." By weaving together several of the passages in which the word occurred, moreover, Spencer produced a detailed account of what it referred to. In essence, he held, neither size nor the materials used had much to do with the meaning of a "historia"; rather, the term referred to a work of art that met certain formal and substantive criteria: "It is to be built upon ancient themes with human gestures to portray and project the emotions of the actors."[9] A "historia," in other words, was an artistic treatment of a theme from classical history or mythology cast in such a way as to have a powerful effect on the emotions of anyone who saw it.

Spencer was one of the first scholars to open up what has revealed itself to recent generations as a highly productive way of examining Alberti's work. Spencer himself summed it up in the title of what has become a classic article, "Ut rhetorica pictura." He and others argued that Alberti set out to model the art of the painter on those of the humanist poet and orator. Taking the literary treatises and textbooks of Horace, Cicero, and Quintilian as his chief sources, if not as his exact models, Alberti envisioned painting as a learned art. It drew its subject matter, like the orations and poems that the humanists learned to write in the schools of Vittorino da Feltre and Guarino da Verona, from the realm of ancient myth and history. The painter hoped to produce the same sublime emotional effects as humanist oratory and poetry by delighting and moving, as well as by instructing, his audience.[10]

History, in the thought of the humanists as well as the ancients, belonged to the art of rhetoric. Seen above all as a narrative designed to embody the principles of morality and prudence in the form of well-told stories about great men, history—so humanist after humanist proclaimed, echoing the sentiments of ancient historians and rhetoricians—was *magistra vitae* (life's teacher). Its worked examples of good and evil, effective and ineffective conduct moved readers more rapidly and more profoundly than statements of general principle.[11]

By identifying the "historia" as the core of the painter's enterprise—as Spencer and others after him, notably Kristine Patz, have shown—Alberti strengthened his argument that painting itself was a liberal art, comparable in function and value to rhetoric, which formed the core of the entire humanistic curriculum. Alberti himself stated, in his later work *De re aedificatoria,* that when he applied the term "historia" to the arts, he meant to imply that one could draw precise analogies between literature and painting: "I look at a good painting (to paint a bad picture is to disgrace a wall) with as much pleasure as I take in reading a good 'historia.' Both are the work of painters: one paints with words, the other tells the story with his brush. They have other things in common: both require great ability and amazing diligence."[12] In both painting and history, as the context shows, Alberti prized above all the capacity to instruct and improve the reader or onlooker.[13]

Scholars have disagreed, however, about both the wider historical significance of Alberti's terminology and its precise interpretation. While most scholars have seen "historia" as primarily a formal term, one that denoted paintings of a particular kind, Jack Greenstein has argued that Alberti saw histories as also possessing a particular kind of substance, a higher sense that they expressed in a figural way as traditional, even "medieval," because their formal qualities were simultaneously classical and up-to-date.[14] But the connection between Alberti's painted histories and the ones written by humanists seems established.[15]

How then does one gain a fuller and more precise sense of what Alberti had in mind when he chose "historia" as the central term of *On Painting*—a work in which, as he declared, he self-consciously set out to write something that had no apparent counterpart in classical or modern literature? One way is simply by expanding the range of passages—and texts—taken into account. Scholars interested in Alberti's writing on the arts have tended to assume that one can properly elucidate *On Painting* and *On Sculpture* without investigating those of Alberti's works that do not deal explicitly with these fields.

The founding figures of Albertian studies may have unintentionally encouraged later scholars to adopt this point of view. When Janitschek translated what he described as Alberti's "shorter art-theoretical writings," and
when Julius von Schlosser later compiled his classic reference work on "the
literature of art," they created a canon of works that historians of Renaissance art needed to study. In Alberti's case, this included his works on painting, sculpture, and architecture.[16] It seems most unlikely that either of them
meant to suggest that scholars could confine themselves to those works that
addressed the arts explicitly: certainly neither of them did so, any more
than did Janitschek's pupil Aby Warburg. But this working assumption has
nonetheless governed—and limited—much of what has been written about
Alberti since their time. Scholars have scrutinized *On Painting* and *On
Sculpture* with imagination and care: advances have come about, usually
when these works were closely compared either with their classical sources
or with the work of other "humanistic observers of painting"—to quote the
subtitle of a particularly original and influential book by Michael Baxandall,
Giotto and the Orators. Only in the realm of city planning, where Manfredo
Tafuri demonstrated the vital importance of Alberti's *Momus* and *De porcar-
iana coniuratione* to understanding his role in the Rome of Nicholas V, has
this unofficial rule been broken.[17]

In fact, however, an ancient principle of philology suggests that the scholar
should "use Homer to interpret Homer" that is, that an author's complete
corpus should serve as the first port of call for those seeking parallel passages
and elucidations for any given text.[18] Alberti himself—as scholars have repeatedly argued—regularly attacked the same themes and questions in multiple works, revising his ideas as his situation changed, but remaining faithful
to certain problems that preoccupied him. Other texts produced by members of his immediate circle, like Aliotti, can also shed light on Alberti's usage. So can the ancient texts on which he drew—and to which he normally
referred in an oblique, emulative way that requires readers not simply to recognize, but also to decipher, his allusions.[19] In fact, passages drawn from a
wide range of sources can shed light on what Alberti usually meant when he
referred to "historiae" (histories) in *On Painting*. No single definition can exhaust the word's multiple meanings and functions. A haze of sources now
hangs about the text, transmitted by a series of editions with useful footnotes,
but nowhere is it analyzed in full. Only when some future scholar has provided

On Painting with a full commentary will we know for certain the sources from which Alberti drew his terminology, which terms he created himself, and how his usage in this text compares, detail by detail, with that in his other works and in the writings of his contemporaries. However, existing resources can be explored to some effect.

No one can exaggerate the ferocious ambition and creativity of the writer who set out to invent a terminology for discussing the arts—to claim a kind of discursive monopoly over the realm of the visual—and did so in two languages at once. But Alberti was only one of many highly articulate individuals in Tuscany who discussed and wrote about publicly commissioned works of art. A rudimentary terminology existed before Alberti wrote, and he drew on it, as we see later in this chapter. Sometimes, Albertian technical terms that scholars have singled out for their originality and profundity derived directly from the existing language of the artists' ateliers.[20]

At the same time, however, it would be wrong to assume that the range of meanings ascribed to "historia"—or any term—in Alberti's other works, in his identifiable sources, and in the language of the ancients and his contemporaries includes all the senses in which Alberti himself could have used the word. Alberti was a self-consciously innovative writer. He regularly appropriated passages from ancient texts, deliberately assigning to them a meaning that their author had not had in mind, as he cited them. Moreover, he wrote in a linguistically supercharged environment in which small linguistic errors cold cause large problems for an ambitious scholar. All humanists of the early fifteenth century wanted to write a Latin that would pass muster as classical. All of them knew, in addition, that the waters of literary life swarmed with sharks ready and eager to devour them—with critics, that is, like Lorenzo Valla, who might seek to humiliate them and destroy their literary reputations by showing that they had committed errors of grammar, syntax, or semantics. When Valla decided to slay Alberti's friend and patron Poggio Bracciolini, he composed a dialogue in which the cook and stable boy of the great teacher Guarino of Verona joined their master in examining and condemning Poggio's Latin prose. "Culinaria vocabula" ("Latin for the kitchen") passed into proverbial usage as a term for especially slovenly efforts at classical prose.[21]

Alberti himself could be a sharp critic of the misuse of language. He dismissed Vitruvius, for example, in part because his prose swarmed with stylistic errors of many kinds—especially the Greek terms of which he had made wildly excessive use:

> What he handed down was in any case not refined, and his speech such that the Latins might think that he wanted to appear a Greek, while the Greeks would think that he babbled Latin. However, his very text is evidence that he wrote neither Latin nor Greek, so that as far as we are concerned he might just as well have not written at all, rather than write something that we cannot understand.[22]

Alberti worked in two connected intellectual environments whose inhabitants registered the symbolic meaning of apparently small choices in wording with the precision and sensitivity to shock of earthquake meters. As a writer on painting, Alberti set out to discuss what he saw as the recent flowering of Florentine culture that he had witnessed on first visiting his ancestral city. But Florence was also the home of the savagely critical scholar Niccolò Niccoli, who notoriously despised the writings of such great moderns as Dante, Petrarch, and Boccaccio, and who considered the works of his contemporaries more suited for use in the outhouse than for publication.[23] Like many others, Alberti clashed with Niccoli—so sharply that he satirized the great book collector more than once in his densely ironic Latin dialogues, the *Intercenales*.[24] Bitterly conscious that Tuscans tended to be hypercritical, Alberti knew to his cost that small errors in taste and usage could damage a literary reputation beyond repair.

As a papal secretary, Alberti belonged to the Curia, where he and his colleagues labored to find classical ways of asserting the majesty and power of the papal monarchy. In 1453, for example, Pope Nicholas V became the first pope since the fourth century to describe himself officially as "pontifex maximus." By reviving this title he claimed a new kind of authority over the church, the city of Rome, and the Papal States, as sensitive observers did not fail to note. Moreover, Nicholas did so in highly visible contexts, no doubt chosen with great care—for example, the inscription in which he celebrated his own building of the Trevi Fountain, which offered a supply of fresh water to inhabitants of central Rome and thus revived a central function of the ancient Roman state. Alberti was very probably connected with this project; indeed, he may have designed the inscription in question.[25] Since the Curia spent much of the 1430s in Florence, Alberti had to find niches in two dangerous literary ecosystems at the same time.

Precision in diction requires sensitivity—especially to the reactions that violation of norms could provoke. Alberti's sensitivity to criticism emerges clearly, not only from the texts of the *Intercenales,* which he composed in the same period as *On Painting,* but also from the numerous letters in which he asked friends to edit and correct major and minor works—ranging from *On Painting* itself to the *Intercenales* and his dialogues *On the Family.*[26] These requests, moreover, were not mere commonplaces, but genuine demands for help: like Poggio and many other humanist writers, Alberti clearly incorporated many of the corrections provided by friends like Leonardo Dati into ambitious works like *Della famiglia,* which he revised and emended at their behest.[27] Like his colleagues, in other words, Alberti chose his words with painstaking care, seeking help from expert writers and critics. Like his colleagues, too, when Alberti used a Latin term in a sense that classical authority did not legitimate, he did so deliberately, in the full expectation that his readers would notice and seek to understand his choice of words. How then did he use "historia" and "istoria"?

In classical Latin, "historia" can refer both to events *(res gestae)* and to narrative accounts of them *(narrationes):* both to stories in general and to formal historical narratives.[28] Alberti regularly employed the word in these basic senses. At the age of twenty, for example, he wrote a Latin comedy about the human desire for fame. It represented so coherent and successful an imitation of a Roman comedy, at least in the eyes of its first readers, that Alberti gave in and ascribed it to a Roman poet named Lepidus. Some years later, however, he took back the false ascription and claimed authorship of the piece, which he wanted to dedicate to Leonello d'Este, a student of Guarino and patron of letters. In the short commentary that he wrote to introduce the work, he insisted that the hero's name—Philodoxeus, the lover of glory—perfectly fitted a Roman hero, "since all histories vouch for the fact that Rome was always the capital of fame."[29] In this case, "histories" means nothing more than an account or *narratio* of *res gestae,* such as the standard narrative of early Roman history by Livy, a work much loved and read in Leonelline Ferrara.[30] The word figures in an even more conventional way in the *Vita anonyma,* the third-person account of Alberti's life that he himself seems to have written around 1437. This text remarks that "he liked histories of anything so much that he considered even poor writers admirable."[31]

Many humanists, however, used "history" in a more precise and loaded way: to refer specifically to the sort of high, instructive account of past politics and war that retired statesmen and generals had written in ancient times. In this elevated sense, history referred to narratives of the sort written by Thucydides or Polybius, which provided exemplary stories of successful and unsuccessful conduct. Readers were meant to analyze these in order to equip themselves with the prudence needed in the active life and then to emulate, or avoid emulating, the actions they depicted when faced with similar circumstances.

On 8 April 1437, for example, Alberti's friend Lapo da Castiglionchio the Younger wrote to Flavio Biondo, who had sent him the first four books of his pioneering history of medieval Italy, the *Decades,* and asked for a critical assessment of the text.[32] Lapo found Biondo's text so eloquent and truthful that it needed no "emendation"—perhaps a misplaced act of editorial charity, since Pius II and other readers later criticized Biondo's prose as unpolished.[33] However, he took the opportunity to explain the value of history, for his friend and no doubt for a wider readership. He made clear that history was "varied, multifarious and wide-ranging, and based on a great many arts and disciplines."[34] Moreover, he identified one of its central functions as the provision of models for imitation by those involved in difficult political and military decision making:

> Precepts can be drawn from history, as from the richest imaginable source, for every area of life: the best way to govern one's household, the method of ruling the state, the reasons for undertaking wars, how they should be waged, and how far they should be prosecuted, how friendships are to be handled, treaties are to be made, alliances to be forged, how popular disturbances are to be calmed and revolutions put down. In history we may choose some great and wise man, all of whose sayings, actions, plans, and counsel we may imitate.[35]

Alberti used "history" in this more capacious and exacting sense of "philosophy teaching through examples" when he conceded, in his bitter Latin work *On the Advantages and Disadvantages of Letters,* that he was too young to write a real history. Only men of full maturity and true learning could "write histories, which would offer fitting analyses of the characters of kings and of great political events and wars."[36]

But producing instructive narrative was not altogether simple. Like Lapo, Alberti knew that writing history could present technical problems. Lapo noted that Biondo, writing the history of his own time, had successfully followed Cicero's "laws for historians," avoiding falsehood and telling the whole truth: "For you yourself were present, I think, at many events, and where you were not, you learned about them by going into the matter and interrogating those who were there. And you accepted as true those accounts that rested on the most reliable witnesses, and rejected as falsehoods and fictions those that derived from popular gossip and rumor."[37] Critical problems arose with special frequency when the historian had to write an account of events that had taken place before his own time, and had to decide which of the older reports he considered credible before composing his own work. Lapo's praise of Biondo—like the classical sources on which he drew—insisted that a history must be truthful as well as instructive, and tacitly admitted that the historian might not always find it easy, or possible, to pursue these two goals at once.[38]

An episode that took place early in Alberti's career in the papal Curia ensured his awareness of this point. Eugenius IV's chancellor Biagio Molin engaged him to write the biography of an early Christian martyr, Potitus, who had been put to death in the time of the pagan emperor Julian. Adopting a method often followed by humanist historians, Alberti set out to impose a proper rhetorical form on a narrative provided by Molin, presumably in the form of short medieval texts in Latin or Italian.[39] These told him that Potitus, a Christian soldier in the best spirit of Monty Python, suffered beatings and worse at the hands of the Romans: they also tore out his eyes and tongue. Yet he continued, even without his tongue, to confess the true God, and by doing so impressed the animals in the arena so deeply that they refused to eat him. Alberti was confronted with the task of retelling these stories in a way that was suitably modern—that is, classical.

Unlike Aliotti, Alberti had little love for miracles. In a letter to his friend Leonardo Dati, on whose literary judgment he regularly relied, Alberti confessed that he found the historical status of Potitus's martyrdom problematic:

> I was a bit worried, since, like you, I feared that scholars might entertain the doubt that this history [*istoriam*] of Potitus of ours is a childish, invented tale [*fabulam*]. For I knew what men of learning usually seek in history [*in istoria*]: they expect a full account of the event in

question, the places, the times, and the quality of the actors. And I saw that the ancients had given clear and full accounts of the acts of the apostles and the lives of the popes and other martyrs. But I saw that this history [*istoriam*] of Potitus was transmitted so carelessly that I could easily infer that ignorant men, rather than those scholars of great learning, produced it.[40]

Simply using the traditional, crude narratives first placed at his disposal, which left him stuck, in Alison Frazier's words, with "a handful of incompatible facts about three different Potituses," Alberti felt that he could not fix the chronology or geography of Potitus's heroic end precisely.[41] Bad historians and worse scribes had scrambled the entire account beyond recognition. Accordingly, Alberti collected all the works by early Christian writers he could find in the Curia that might shed light on Potitus's life, and used these primary documents to establish what he considered a plausible identity and date for his protagonist. He also amused himself by putting into the mouth of the emperor Julian a phosphorescent denunciation of the antisocial habits and idleness of the Christians.

In this case, Alberti treated history as something more than a well-turned narrative about events already known to the author: it was, or should be, a reflexive, scholarly genre that required its practitioners to be deft at research, honest with themselves and others, and able to assemble and compare multiple sources for a single event. Not even the precision of the critical procedures Alberti applied allayed all his doubts about Potitus. By stating them, however, he could at least make clear his own sense of what the genre demanded, wrapping his argument up with an apposite quotation from *De oratore*: "But as to what scholars think about the carelessness of the scribes or some historians, we can speak elsewhere."[42] Alberti's situation here was delicate. He cared sincerely about historical accuracy—so much that in the end he called his life of Potitus not a "historia" but a "laus," an unhistorical but improving text (though it was hardly a success from that standpoint either).[43]

Later in life, writing on the supremely delicate subject of Stefano Porcari's conspiracy against Nicholas V, Alberti seems to have given a highly accurate version of the speech in which Porcari denounced the pope for having deprived the Romans of their ancient rights of citizenship.[44] In the case of Potitus, however, he could only indicate—by including the letter in which he described his critical techniques with the life itself—what he saw as a contradiction between the historian's two obligations: to be truthful and to be instructive. Alberti's unusual work evidently found some admiring readers. It must have been his success with Potitus that made Aliotti see him as the ideal biographer of Ambrogio Traversari—a man not only erudite but also one so holy that lilies miraculously sprouted on his grave. As soon as Traversari died, Aliotti began to agitate for Alberti to be appointed his official biographer: once again, he would have worked with a set of documents provided him by the sponsors of the life in question.[45] Yet Alberti declined or evaded the commission—perhaps because he would have found it difficult to discharge in a way both principled and effective. Even within the classical senses of history, in other words, difficulties lurked.

Alberti, moreover, sometimes employed the term in one of its classical senses, but to an unclassical—or at least unconventional—end. When he dedicated the Italian form of *On Painting* to Filippo Brunelleschi, he remarked regretfully that "so many excellent and divine arts and science, which we know from their works and from historical accounts [*per le istorie*] were possessed in great abundance by the talented man of antiquity, have now disappeared and are almost entirely lost."[46] Here—as elsewhere—"storia" meant only an authoritative narrative about the past (perhaps, quite precisely, Livy's history of Rome). In other passages, however, Alberti manipulated the well-worn terms in ways that showed his characteristic independence of received views. Book 35 of the elder Pliny's encyclopedic *Natural History* treated painting not only as the object of aesthetic analysis but also as a historical subject, the development of which could be reconstructed olympiad by olympiad and artist by artist. This erudite work, based on elaborate research described in a well-known letter by the younger Pliny, clearly represented a scholarly effort to tell the truth about the past—and, by doing so, to offer serious lessons about the way that human efforts had perfected the arts. Pliny, moreover, built his critical "history" from little "histories," using a series of stories about the most proficient ancient artists—Zeuxis, Apelles, and the rest—to embody the central morals of his tale.

In doing so, Pliny followed well-established precedent. Ancient chroniclers and historians regularly included in their works information about the history of culture, usually in the form of remarks about inventors—identifications of the individuals or communities responsible for the invention or first use of a weapon or other device. Lapo wrote appreciatively of the usefulness and pleasure of history, which taught not only moral lessons but also "who founded the great cities, who devised the arts, who first began to educate the human race, which was rough and uncultivated, who assembled men in cities, who gave them laws, who introduced the worship of the gods, who first instructed them in sailing, agriculture, and letters, and who began to deal with military affairs."[47]

Although Alberti occasionally made one of Pliny's stories fit his own, quite different ends, he showed that he did not mean to emulate the Roman scholar's way of talking about the arts.[48] He maintained, in the Italian text, that he did not want "to tell stories like Pliny, but to write an original, systematic treatment of the art of painting."[49] In the Latin version, he stated that unlike Pliny, "he did not want to review the history of painting."[50] In each version of his remark, Alberti criticized the standard ancient text on painting. In other words, although Alberti used the terms "storia" and "historia" here in a classical sense, he did so only in order to declare himself free to depart from classical precedent whenever he liked. Accordingly, there is no reason to assume that he always had the classical model of rhetorical history in mind when he discussed painted and sculpted histories. Moreover, the rhetorical tradition as Alberti understood it included not only the Greek and Roman classics but also Byzantine texts in which the term "historia" meant simply "a painting" or "a representation" as it also did in the Latin and Italian of Alberti's day. Even when Alberti conformed to what he saw as the canons of the pure classical style, in other words, he could use the term "historia" in a sense not attested in ancient literature.[51]

At times, Alberti deliberately departed even further from classical norms. Cicero had made clear, in his *Brutus,* that orators normally applied the term "historia" to true events, not to myths. A "historia" could be a tale of many kinds—but not the false one properly known as a *fabula.*[52] Alberti certainly knew this newly discovered work by Cicero, which he cited at the conclusion of *On Painting,* and he referred to it directly when he noted the fabulous nature of the story of Potitus.[53] But he deliberately flouted Cicero's distinction when he referred to the story of the Calumny of Apelles as an ideal "historia" or "istoria," and even more directly when he described the story of Narcissus's metamorphosis into a flower in Latin as a "fabula" and in Italian as a "storia."[54] A history, in other words, might be the sort of high rendering of individuals in action that humanists liked to deliver in perfect Latin; but paradoxically, it might also be a myth. Alberti's readers had to think twice each time the word occurred before knowing for certain what it referred to.

What then was a history for Alberti, most of the time? In the first place, it seems to have been not only a painting but also, in most cases, a large-scale painting executed in a public place. At times, to be sure, Alberti writes as if absolute size and placement played no role in identifying a painting as a "historia." Early in *On Painting,* for example, he describes the picture plane in general terms that would fit anything from a panel painting to a panorama: "First of all, on the surface of which I am going to paint, I draw a rectangle of whatever size I want, which I regard as an open window through which the *historia* is to be seen: and I decide how large I want the human figures in the painting to be."[55] But in book 3, where Alberti gives his most detailed account of the process of composing a "historia," he recommends that the painter work out his entire "invention" in advance, before he sets brush to surface. Otherwise, he cannot be sure "that nothing at all will crop up in the work, the proper position of which we do not precisely know."[56] Here Alberti provides the painter with precise instructions on how to carry out this task:—he must lay out his entire work in detailed sketches, and then he must transfer his designs directly from these to the surface he intended to adorn: "In order that we may know this with greater certainty, it will help to divide our models into parallels, so that everything can then be transferred, as it were, from our private papers and put in its correct position in the work for public exhibition."[57] Alberti's terminology is suggestive: a "publicum opus" or "publico lavoro" must normally be a large-scale work meant to be displayed in a public building—exactly the sort of work that required the procedures Alberti had described. This helps to explain why Alberti so strongly emphasized that the painter "should not adopt the common habit of painting on very small panels. For I want you to become used to working on large-scale images, which indeed come as close as possible in size to the objects you wish to represent"—clear evidence that he saw paintings with life-size or near life-size figures as the chief work of the painter.[58]

The nature of the public work in question, or one form of it at least, is easy enough to establish. Paolo Uccello used exactly the technique Alberti recommended, squaring off a sketch of the monument to Sir John Hawkwood, now preserved in the Uffizi, before he transferred his design to the wall of the Florentine Cathedral, to serve as the basis for his fresco. Moreover, he did so in the summer of 1436—exactly at the same time that Alberti seems to have finished *Della pittura*.[59] Elsewhere, Alberti advised painters that if they included the face of a well-known individual in their "historia" or "storia," it would "attract the eyes of all onlookers."[60] He asked the artists who read *On Painting*, if they valued his advice, to include his portrait "in suis historiis [in their histories]."[61] Florentine fresco painters—notably Massaccio—regularly included portraits of famous men, including scholars like Alberti in their frescoes.[62] Finally, when Alberti wanted to give an example of a good modern history, he cited the *Navicella* of Giotto—a mosaic in the Vatican that no longer survives, and which represented Jesus and the apostles on the Sea of Galilee.[63] There seems every reason to infer, then, that Alberti, for all his interest in and knowledge of written histories, used the term initially in a deliberately up-to-date sense, to refer to large-scale works of art that included a number of figures engaged in a complex action and that were meant for public display. In his later work on architecture, Alberti claimed to prefer removable panel paintings to frescoes, and clearly considered that the term "historia" could apply to both.[64] For the most part, however, Alberti must have envisioned painted "historiae" as frescoes, the context of which—as the example of the *Navicella* shows—could be biblical as well as mythological or historical.

The qualities that Alberti ascribed to the ideal "historia" are too well known to require detailed discussion. It should contain no more than nine or ten characters, varied in age, gender, dress, and attitude. Most of them should be playing parts in a single story, but one chosen individual could be looking out at and gesturing toward the onlooker, inviting him or her to examine the action more closely. All of them should have bodies, clothing, and attitudes that fit their sexes, stations, and ages. Copiousness without chaos, variety without indiscipline, and decorum above all—these characteristics clearly fit a painting designed on the grand scale and intended for public display, like the frescoes of Massaccio, whom Alberti explicitly praised in his dedicatory letter to Brunelleschi.[65]

Yet by Alberti's own account, not all "historiae" were painted. He made clear in his critique of older "historiae" that the term embraced the work of "the ancient *sculptors and painters*." He complained, in *De pictura*, that "You will hardly find any 'historia' by one of the ancients that is properly composed, in painting or modeling or sculpture."[66] It is not clear whether Alberti had in mind here the work of ancient artists, as Greenstein holds, or that of medieval Italian painters, as seems more likely (in *On the Family,* after all, Alberti described earlier members of the Alberti family as "the ancients"). But it is clear that a "historia," in Alberti's sense, could be a work of sculpture as well as painting. A "historia" in this sense—a sculpted work that included, like a painted "historia," multiple figures carrying out a single action—would have to be a relief. Indeed, Alberti singled out for praise, along with Giotto's *Navicella,* what he called a "*historia* [or *storia*] at Rome which represents the dead Meleager"—a stone sarcophagus relief.[67] In *De re aedificatoria,* Alberti regularly used the term to refer to the sort of reliefs that encrusted the Arch of Constantine and the columns of Hadrian and Trajan.[68] Alberti did not mean, by his choice of title, to restrict his theories to the single artistic genre of painting.[69]

Moreover, Alberti did not create a critical language out of whole cloth. The vocabulary of art in Florence was already well developed and widely diffused long before he wrote. The thirty-four members of the jury empanelled to decide who should fashion the first set of doors for the Florentine Baptistery presumably discussed in some detail the relative merits of Brunelleschi and Ghiberti, not to mention other contestants. If Alberti hoped to find an audience ready to accept and use his own terminology, he was more or less bound to adapt terms that already existed to his purposes. The art language that existed when Alberti set to work, in other words, provided the resisting medium that he chiseled and polished until it took on a coherent new form.

As established terms for works of art in late fourteenth- and fifteenth-century Italy, "historia" and "storia" belonged to this language; both words could—and often did—refer to narrative paintings. But they also very often denoted sculpted reliefs—more particularly reliefs that represented a fairly large numbers of individuals at once.[70] Dante used "storia," in a celebrated passage in canto 10 of *Purgatorio,* to refer to panels cut from the living rock.[71] And many Florentines, both writers and artists, employed the term regularly in this specific, technical sense. Leonardo Bruni, when he proposed his plan for the second new set of doors for the baptistery in 1424, insisted that the twenty "storie" to appear on the new doors must be both meaningful and brilliantly executed. To that end, he argued, an adviser should be hired who was in a position to advise Ghiberti on the various "storie" he would represent (Ghiberti made the same play on the meaning of storia in his

Commentaries).[72] Matteo degli Organi, who built and rebuilt organs for the Florentine Cathedral, wrote to the Operai of the Cathedral of Prato in 1434 to urge that they cease complaining because Donatello was taking so long to execute his reliefs for the outdoor pulpit of the Chapel of the Girdle of the Blessed Virgin. The sculptor, he explained, had just finished "quella storia di marmo," and all connoisseurs had agreed that he had created something uniquely beautiful.[73] The official documents in which the Operai of the Florentine Cathedral discussed the monies paid to Luca Della Robbia for his reliefs for the Cantoria referred to the panels consistently as "storiae marmoris [histories in marble]."[74]

Ancient reliefs, also called "historiae" and "storie," fascinated the artists of the early fifteenth century. The first systematic sketches from the antique, now usually attributed to the workshop of Pisanello, include a good many figures drawn from Roman reliefs. True, these were usually pulled from context and redrawn in a way more decorative than precise by Pisanello's pupils, who showed little interest in the qualities of depth and composition that most interested Alberti.[75] But ancient reliefs also powerfully attracted Ghiberti and Donatello, and these artists—the ones whom Alberti explicitly praised—recovered and improved on the principles of composition, anatomy, and perspective that their ancient counterparts had employed.[76] Bacchic sarcophagi struck the most original artists of Alberti's time as an aesthetic revelation. In the Florentine "horizon of expectation" of the 1430s, "relief sculpture" was prominent among the senses that would have come to the mind of a reader of *De pictura* or of *Della pittura.*

Why then, when Alberti set out to characterize the ideal form of painting, did he use as his central term one charged with nonclassical senses strongly established in normal practice? Why suggest that ancient and modern reliefs embodied the ideal qualities that painters, as well as sculptors, should strive to attain? Alberti set out, in *On Painting,* to create an aesthetic language that was not only descriptive but also prescriptive. He wanted to convey a particular set of aesthetic ideals about the characteristics that a truly excellent work of art should possess. The artists whom Alberti admired most—to judge from his letter to Brunelleschi—were sculptors. Three of the five individuals he mentioned in that famous text—Ghiberti, Donatello, and Luca Della Robbia—were at work in the 1430s on relief panels that embodied some of Alberti's aesthetic preferences to a greater extent than any paintings then being created. They employed sophisticated systems of perspective; represented anatomically plausible bodies in solid, well-balanced poses; and attained considerable variety of expression and gesture. In Ghiberti's case, and sometimes in Donatello's, the relief panels used these formal devices to tell a single coherent story.

The sculptors achieved all of these effects not by the deployment of rich, decorative materials, which displeased Alberti in the 1430s, but by the application of their skilled hands.[77] In his doctoral dissertation, Aby Warburg notoriously connected Alberti's evocation of the expressive power of "bewegtes Beiwerk" [moving accessories], like hair and clothing, with Botticelli's mythologies, as well as to the somewhat earlier reliefs of Matteo de' Pasti and Agostino di Duccio in the Tempio Malatestiano at Rimini and elsewhere: "The concern . . . with capturing the transitory movements of hair and garments, corresponds to a tendency prevalent among Northern Italian artists, which finds its most telling expression in Alberti's *Libro della pittura*."[78] In fact, however, Alberti's description also corresponds closely to Della Robbia's reliefs for the Cantoria and Donatello's for Prato, both of which were at least in part being carved in Florence as he wrote his book. Many scholars have observed that the relief sculpture of the 1430s was far more "Albertian" than the paintings carried out in Florence during the same period.[79] Alberti presumably chose the term "historia" at least in part because he wanted to make that point clear, both to the patrons who would read his book in order to find out which artists they should choose to support and to the artists themselves.[80] By using a term at once classical and nonclassical, and by giving enough clues that an alert contemporary could grasp what he was doing, Alberti created something that had both the authority of antiquity and the luster of modernity—exactly as he did when he transformed medieval churches in Rimini and Florence by wrapping them in facades that adapted classical forms to new functions.

At the same time, however, Alberti did something more: he revealed to the literati who would read the Latin text of his work that the term "history" was not just polysemous but also unstable. The humanists, as we have seen, followed ancient precedent in defining history as a genuine set of facts attested by the best sources or witnesses available. They also insisted, however, that the study of history should serve an affective and moral purpose. Historical accounts taught their readers the principles of morality and prudence, correct behavior decorously carried out—and they did so in the most effective possible way, presenting them not as arid, abstract statements but as concrete, moving embodiments of the truth. But these two views of history could exist only in a tight state of tension. Faced with evil or indecorous conduct, the historian had to violate either the commandment to tell the complete truth or the commandment to provide reliable moral guidance couched in the most attractive form—a point Alberti himself felt keenly, as we have seen, when he was forced to play the hagiographer.[81]

A generation after Alberti, Lorenzo Valla returned to this point. Stimulated by a reading of Aristotle's *Poetics,* a text that proclaimed poetry superior to history because it did not strive for completeness and accuracy, Valla insisted that historians too were artful writers who deliberately omitted and shaped their materials and crafted their characters' speeches as lessons in good rhetoric and good morality. He thus admitted that the historian had to serve not one but two Muses, whose demands sometimes contradicted one another; and he cast his lot with the Clio who demanded truth to the established principles of morality and decorum.[82] In effect, however, Alberti had already made the same point in *On Painting.* When he insisted that the painter's "historia" could have the same beneficial effects on its audience as a written history—whether its contents came from the realm of myth, that of fact about the ancients, or sacred history—he implied that only style and execution, not the correspondence of the content to truth, determined the emotional effectiveness of a "history."

Here too Alberti opposed ancient authority. Sallust, in his widely read history of the war against Jugurtha, noted that:

I have often heard Quintus [Fabius] Maximus, Publius Scipio, and other outstanding Roman citizens say that when they contemplated the images of their ancestors, they were inflamed with desire for virtue. And it was not the wax used in those images, nor their appearance, but the memory of the events, that made this flame grow so strongly in the hearts of virtuous men that they could not rest until their virtue equaled their reputation and their glory.[83]

Alberti agreed with Sallust about the relative insignificance of the artist's material, but disagreed about the formal qualities of his work. These—not the verbal tradition that was passed on with it—made a visual history work.

Alberti's friend Lapo seems to have been very struck by the novelty of this argument.[84] In fact, his letter of spring 1437 to Biondo—a friend of both men—seems to have represented in part his response to *De pictura.* Lapo insisted, forcefully, that true histories would have even more effect on their readers than the finest images—just because they were truthful:

> When we hear or read of some great effort or risk, undertaken not for gain or profit but for the freedom of the country, for the safety of its citizens, for security, we all praise it to the skies, we are struck with admiration for it, and if possible we want to imitate it. This is clear from fables and pictures. Even if the affairs shown in them are invented, they still affect us by the various senses so that we feel the warmest affection for those of whose outstanding deeds we have heard, or seen depicted in a painting. If these things are so powerful, imagine how effectively virtue will be instilled by a history which represents real, not imaginary, characters, and real, not invented, events, and speeches not brought forth to show off the author's skill but set out as they were held.[85]

Lapo's insistence on the affective and educative value of truth was most unusual, as Mariangela Regoliosi has pointed out, in humanist writing about history.[86] And he made his argument in the context of an extended analogy between the effects of written histories and those of myths of paintings. It seems highly likely that he advanced this view so forcefully because he had read Alberti's text and became concerned at what he saw as an injudicious exaggeration of only the expressive and inspiring side of history. It is also possible that Lapo's praise of cultural history, quoted above, represents a response to Alberti's slighting remark about Pliny. Alberti's work on painting—as many scholars have pointed out—was aimed chiefly at an audience of literati. It seems all the more appropriate that one response to it came in a text on written "historiae."

It remains unclear why Alberti compared the "historia" to the "colossus," insisting that the former, rather than the latter, constituted the painter's chief and highest work. And it is equally uncertain exactly how Alberti's earliest readers understood his arguments—though at least one of them, Angelo Decembrio, who incorporated parts of *On Painting* directly into his own *De politia literaria,* seems to have had Alberti's classical, Mantegnaesque notion of the consistent, relief-like "historia" in mind when he made his hero, Leonello d'Este, condemn the anachronisms seen on Flemish tapestries that represented stories from ancient history.[87]

It does seem certain, however, that Alberti hoped to persuade both artists and patrons that they should continue to collaborate in the creation of a new kind of large-scale art—brought into being by the painter's brush, but ruled by the disciplined, austere aesthetic code of relief sculpture, ancient and modern. Alberti never meant to strip the artist's "historia" of its association with the high, dramatic narratives of the Old and New Testaments, nor to alter its goal—traditional for religious art—of inspiring the proper emotions. He saw the "historia" as rhetoric in paint, and rhetoric as the art of expressing and inspiring emotions. But he wanted the "historia" to be cast in rhetoric of a particular, humanistic kind, and executed in the most up-to-date modes of Florentine art and craft. Like the miraculous image conjured into being by the pious girls admired by Aliotti, Alberti's "historia" inspired emotions. However, unlike the irresistible, transfixing sorrows and pains injected into onlookers by wonder-working icons, these were disciplined by the ancient aesthetic and ethic of decorum. The term itself applied to allegorical paintings later created by Botticelli to represent Alberti's ideal "historia," the *Calumny of Apelles,* as well as to frescoes of the traditional religious kind. All motions, attitudes, and gestures represented by the artist followed the code of appropriateness to person and place. And the experience of looking at the completed work in situ took place, as its creation had, on a high aesthetic plane, as the onlooker painstakingly identified and examined the means the painter had used to obtain his effects.[88] Like a stone relief rather than a wonder-working icon, the "historia" remained at a distance from its viewer. The emotions it inspired were not only recollected but also experienced in tranquility. And the semantic range of the term itself, as Alberti used and reused it, would have suggested as much to a contemporary reader. Perhaps it is not so surprising after all that Aliotti turned for advice not to his iconoclastic friend, the Florentine critic, but to the Roman experts in the discernment of spirits.

3

A Contemplative Scholar

Trithemius Conjures the Past

The strongest emotion scholars normally feel is neither hate nor love, but what Germans call *Schadenfreude*—the pleasure we experience watching someone else suffer. And no great Renaissance scholar evokes this feeling more effectively than the Benedictine abbot and bibliophile Johannes Trithemius.[1] By his twenties, Trithemius had become a great man in the Benedictine order and the famous builder of a great library, but in his forties, his monastery expelled him and he had to leave his books behind. By his thirties, Trithemius had become one of the most innovative historians in Europe. In his fifties, however, colleagues accused him of inventing sources, and he had to fob off those who wanted to see the manuscripts—including the Holy Roman Emperor Maximilian—with the suggestion that his former monastic colleagues had sold the books in question. A famous abbot and spiritual counselor, Trithemius spent the last fifteen years of his life dealing with the accusation that he was a magician who employed diabolic help. Even posterity has joined the game and continued degrading the poor man. During most of his lifetime, Trithemius was a high lord of print culture. But like the legendary children who shouted, "Get a horse!" at the first cars that passed down their dusty main streets, the Benedictine abbot and bibliophile has gone down in book history as the technophobe par excellence. In 1492, at the request of a fellow abbot, he wrote a treatise *In Praise of Scribes*. Trithemius denounced the new printed books of his age as fragile and worthless: "The printed book is made of paper and, like paper, will quickly disappear. But the scribe working with parchment ensures lasting remembrance for himself and for his text."[2]

Like Federico da Montefeltro, the book-collecting condottiere whose favorite dealer, Vespasiano da Bisticci, recalled that he refused to have a single printed work in his collection, Trithemius has won a reputation as the perfect example of the new technology refusenik, doomed to irrelevance by his loyalty to an old way of doing things.[3] Learned adherents of the electronic word regularly cited his example, a few years ago, in support of their apocalyptic claims about those who resisted the upcoming disappearance of the printed book. Those stick-in-the-muds who defended books and print magazines, and even fought to preserve their independent bookshops, were as misguided as the defenders of the horse and buggy in 1900—or as Trithemius in 1500. The electronic word has taken a protean variety of forms and has come to dominate a vast range of activities. But the printed book and Trithemius are still with us.

Who was he? Historians have differed, from Trithemius's age to our own. The outline of his life is simple enough. Born in 1462 at Trittenheim on the Moselle, he managed to leave the family that frustrated his aspirations while still in his teens and study at Heidelberg. There he did not take a degree, but became acquainted with the new scholarship of the humanists. Heading homeward from the university, he found himself forced—by a miraculous snowstorm that threatened his life in a mountain pass—to stop at the Benedictine house of Sponheim, near Kreuznach. Like Martin Luther, he decided to become a monk—and not only carried out his decision, but found himself elected abbot after only eighteen months, early in his twenties. From 1483 to 1505, he ruled his house and participated in a massive effort to reform the Benedictine order as a whole. Trithemius often gave general addresses to the meetings of the general congregation of Bursfeld, to which Sponheim belonged. He wrote lives of the saints, from which he culled the miracles in the best humanistic fashion—and published them separately so as not to annoy the "simple." He advised monks and nuns on how to avoid the besetting sins of the monastic life—not an easy task in a time when monasteries, rather like universities today, had become extraordinarily rich, and entry into them was often a mark of social privilege. In the later Middle Ages, the budget of Mont Saint Michel included 1,700 crowns for food, 2,200 for wine, ample provision for lights and clothing—and, far down at the bottom of the accounts, 200 crowns for the poor on Shrove Tuesday.[4] Trithemius, by contrast, insisted that "idle monks should either not eat or be aware that they are acting against the injunctions of the apostle"—and he set them to copying manuscripts as their predecessors had done for centuries.[5] Yet he was not only stern: no one could explain more precisely what monks should do to keep themselves active, cheerful, and occupied, or why nuns should not have windows in their convents through which they could communicate with the outside world.[6] His *De triplici regione claustralium,* printed in an edition of a thousand copies in 1498, became a standard work for novices in the reformed Benedictine world.[7]

Trithemius built a great library, attracted learned visitors, and made Sponheim famous, both in the Benedictine order and outside it. He also wrote massive literary histories of the Catholic Church, of his own and other orders, and of Germany itself. But after some twenty-two years of successful administration, he left Sponheim, denouncing his former colleagues. For much of 1505 and 1506, he wandered, spending time at Speyer and Cologne, meeting the Holy Roman Emperor Maximilian, and adorning the court of the Brandenburg elector Joachim I at Berlin. Much affected by the experience, Trithemius never explained exactly what went wrong. But he did gather his correspondence from those years in a manuscript, now in the Vatican library, under the Ciceronian and Petrarchan title *Epistolae familiares*—clear evidence that he saw his departure as a crisis and wished to buttress his reputation.[8] Soon, however, an offer from the Cloister of Saint James at Würzburg arrived, and he returned to the Benedictine life. Trithemius spent the remainder of his days at Würzburg, where he built a second library and completed the works for which he is best remembered: his chronicle of the Abbey of Hirsau, his brief history of the Franks, and his massive work on cryptography, the *Polygraphia*. He died there in 1516.

The complex contours of Trithemius's reputation—in his own time and since—contrast sharply with the relative simplicity of his life. Many of his contemporaries admired and praised him. The Holy Roman Emperor Maximilian asked Trithemius to join his court and relied on his counsel about such vital matters as the powers of witches and demons.[9] At a time when even faithful Catholics saw their church as deeply, perhaps fatally corrupt, the abbots of Benedictine houses asked him to collect and edit the customs of their houses, to explicate their histories, and to counsel their monks. Yet others denounced him as a fantast, a forger, and a magician who invoked the help of the devil. Some asked his intercession with the saints; others told stories of the diabolic feasts at which he conjured plates of cooked pike from the air. Even now, Trithemius appears in modern secondary literature as both the inventor of technical bibliography and a prominent forger of historical texts.

By examining some specimens of his work as a scholar, by setting them into context, and by asking some precise hermeneutical questions, we may be able, if not to understand the abbot completely, at least to gain some purchase over one of the slipperiest figures in Western intellectual history—and to set him back into the contexts and communities that actually shaped him.

As James O'Donnell pointed out in an important article, Trithemius actually took a rather complex view of both manuscripts and print.[10] Manuscripts had qualities that print lacked; they were durable: "The word written on parchment will last a thousand years. The printed book is on paper. How long will it last?"[11] Printed books, moreover, often displayed errors in spelling and appearance, while manuscript books reflected the craftsmanlike precision of the individual scribes who wrote them. The low price and large number of printed books could never compensate for their technical and aesthetic defects. Most important, the making of printed books—so Trithemius held—could never amount to a sacred calling. Trithemius explained that he had known a Benedictine brother who spent his life on his duties in the choir and on copying the lives of the saints. When the brothers exhumed his body, many years after his death, they discovered that "the three fingers of his right hand, with which he had written so many books, were as preserved and fresh as if he had been buried the day before."[12] Fresh flesh and the odor of sanctity showed that a given body was that of a saint. In this case, the partial preservation of the hand revealed the holiness of the brother's occupation.

Trithemius, moreover, surfed the new wave of printing with the most skillful authors of his day. He had his text on the virtues of scribes printed by Peter von Friedberg of Mainz in a handsome roman font, relatively unusual in Germany, which clearly reflected his own humanistic tastes. In fact, Trithemius wrote no fewer than thirteen of the twenty-four incunabula printed by Friedberg, whose list amounted to one big advertisement for the abbot's work as a monastic reformer and scholar—at a time when, as Erasmus wrote to Aldo Manuzio, a printer whose fonts were especially attractive could make his authors uniquely famous.[13] Trithemius fervently praised the art of printing more than once. He conceded that his predecessor as abbot of Sponheim had not been able to reconstruct the abbey's library, as he himself did, because books were too expensive in the age before print. He even admitted—in practice, if not explicitly—that printed books could last. Peter Friedberg printed special copies of no fewer than eight of Trithemius's works on vellum—presumably for presentation to special patrons, but also perhaps to ensure that even the printed word could survive for a millennium. Trithemius, who denounced print, also exploited it as skillfully as any writer of his time. The figure of fun, the *retardataire* and hater of the new, was actually preoccupied with the present and the future.

Furthermore, Trithemius's career shows a similar seamless movement from the world of manuscripts to that of print. At first, he cast himself as an exemplary monastic writer who lacked all personal ambition, and he set his earliest literary work in this modest, pious key. True, he began writing as a young man on the day of St. Matthew the Evangelist (21 September) in 1484. But his first efforts took the traditional Benedictine form of compilation: "A master without much skill, I just wanted to make progress on my own, starting to collect in one work, but without any embellishment, passages from the holy fathers on all kinds of subject matter." In other words, Trithemius produced a florilegium: "plain, rather brief excerpts from the holy fathers on all kinds of subject matter as it would occur," designed for use in future sermons. Only gradually, as "this collection grew and grew and seemed like a wall set up without mortar, lacking all evenness," did Trithemius begin "to insert the mortar of [his] own words," turning his collection of texts into orations and treatises. Even then, he insisted that "nothing has been said by me which has not been said before in a better way by" the church fathers.[14]

To some extent, Trithemius followed a standard theological line in this traditionalist age. Catholic preachers insisted—in the words of the popular Viennese preacher Nikolaus von Dinkelsbühl—that "I will say nothing on the basis of my own intellect . . . but everything that I will say is the gift of almighty God and the teaching of holy learned Catholics. All I did was to collect it."[15] Trithemius saw sacred reading as an ascetic exercise in its own right. He believed that by copying holy texts one could take on their spirit. The monk's life, he explained, was dangerous. Monks could easily fall into errors, even while on the path to mystical contemplation. Idleness could corrupt. But the monk who spent his time on copying holy books "will not be burdened by vain and pernicious thoughts, will speak no idle words, and is not bothered by wild rumors . . . As he is copying the approved texts he is gradually initiated into the divine mysteries and miraculously enlightened."[16] In other words, Trithemius envisioned the monastic discipline of copying as more than the best way to preserve sacred texts. It formed a uniquely powerful hermeneutic tool that ensured the reader would extract the right message from his text, receive it in the proper spirit, and make it his own: "Every word we write is imprinted more forcefully on our minds since we have to take our time while writing and reading."[17] The reform of the Benedictines, in short, depended on their devoting themselves to copying, in silence and alone, the Bible and the classics of patristic and medieval spirituality. When Trithemius denounced printing, he highlighted the virtues of the special monastic world of few words and few books that he wanted to restore—the old Benedictine world in which, as he told the Bursfeld congregation in a speech in 1493, "the brothers did not spend their time in idleness, but after their prayers they systematically practiced the work of their hands, as the rules prescribe. Those capable of doing so wrote books to adorn the library, and working from the drafts of others made them publicly available. Others elegantly bound the written codices; still others corrected them; and others rubricated them. All burned with eagerness to take part in the holy labor."[18] The making of many books also made many men into saints.

Trithemius's practices as a spiritual master matched his words. When Franciscus Hofyrer from Kerzenheim, a novice, finished copying the letters of Saint Boniface on 17 August 1497, he noted that he did so "at the command of the reverend father and great scholar of the Scriptures Joannes Trithemius"— and asked readers to pray for both men's salvation.[19] Brother John of Bingen, already both priest and monk, was less effusive but just as precise when he recorded copying the chronicle of Robert the Premonstratensian in August 1494.[20] Trithemius himself copied a good many manuscripts—including a text of John's Gospel in Greek, which is now in the Bodleian Library, Oxford. The abbot did not hesitate to undertake, or order others to undertake, the proverbial "Benedictine labor."

Yet the same Trithemius who insisted on the need to read and copy the Bible over and over also burned with a passion for other books of every kind: "whatever can be known in the world," he admitted, "I always desired to know, and it was my chief delight to have and read every book I had ever seen or heard of in print, however childish or low in quality."[21] When Trithemius arrived at Sponheim, he found the monastery in a condition of bibliographical catastrophe, more like the fictional one of *A Canticle for Leibowitz* than that of *The Name of the Rose*. In 1459, when Sponheim was reformed, it had "scarcely ten books, in addition to the bible, and those not very useful." The monastery remained poor, moreover, and books remained rare and expensive in the early years of printing. Hence, Trithemius's predecessor had been able to buy only thirty more printed books, "and these were common ones for making sermons to the people, and the like"—such as the *Dormi secure,* which enabled its readers to do exactly what its title recommended.[22] They could sleep well the night before they had to deliver a sermon, and then simply read aloud one of the model texts contained in the book.

Trithemius, by contrast, set about building an encyclopedic, universal collection that included massive holdings in the liberal arts, as well as in theology and biblical studies. He visited the cloisters of his order in many provinces, buying or swapping for duplicate manuscripts. In addition, he often found manuscripts in fields like astronomy, music, mathematics, history, and medicine, which "the good fathers who possessed them either did not understand, or feared that they might violate their sacred observance."[23] In 1496, for example, when he traveled to a number of libraries "for love of books," Trithemius found a manuscript of the Tyronian notes, neglected and dusty, in a Benedictine library:

> I asked the abbot, a doctor of law, how much he thought it was worth. He answered: "I would rather have the edition of St. Anselm's shorter works that was just printed." I went to the bookshops, since this took place in a large city, and when I asked for the works of Anselm, I got the book for one sixth of a florin. I gave it to the abbot and monks, who were delighted, and freed the book from its near-death condition. For they had decided to shave it [and erase the text] for love of the parchment.[24]

Finally, he ordered books from printers and booksellers all around the empire and beyond: his hundred Greek manuscripts and printed books, for example, came mostly from Italy. By the time he left Sponheim, he had spent 1,500 florins—in addition to the expenses of copying incurred in his own abbey—and acquired a library of some 2,000 volumes, "in every faculty and science," and in Greek and Hebrew as well as Latin. By his own estimate, it was the greatest library in Germany—though he had seen many others "which have a vast stock of rare books, and secret and marvelous ones that are hardly to be found elsewhere."[25]

Trithemius did not exaggerate the scale and quality of his collection. Like other great Renaissance collectors, moreover, he saw to it that his polyglot books were housed in architectural conditions worthy of their rarity and age. A visitor, Mattheus Herbelin, described the Sponheim library in luminous detail:

> When we had the chance to take a walk he led me about, and then brought me into his admirable library, where I saw a great number of books in Hebrew and Greek. The stock of Latin writers in every art, science and discipline was immense. I was amazed at the diligence shown by one man in obtaining and establishing so many sources, since I would not have thought so many foreign volumes existed in all of Germany. For I found books in five languages, different from one another in language and in alphabet, there in ancient manuscripts, which Trithemius had obtained through constant effort, not without much sweat. This is how I found the library in Sponheim stocked. And I saw not only that, but the walls of the abbot's house, which is substantial, and the ceilings of its rooms, appropriately adorned with Greek, Hebrew and Latin verses and characters.[26]

Great men like Joannes Dalberg, bishop of Worms, the poet Conrad Celtis, and Johannes Reuchlin repeatedly visited Sponheim to see the books, as Trithemius enjoyed pointing out. Florentine humanists boasted of their magnificent collection at San Marco. They liked to report on the lively scholarly dialogues that had taken place there—from the time that Poggio Bracciolini entered it, early in its existence, to find Niccolò Niccoli and Cosimo de' Medici examining a splendid manuscript of Ptolemy's geography, to the discussions that Pico della Mirandola and Angelo Poliziano held there half a century later. Similarly, Trithemius's collection developed the reputation of being something more than a library. As Herbenus put it, "if there is in our Germany any sacred or Greek academy, it is the monastery at Sponheim, where you can draw more learning from the walls than you can from many other dusty libraries that have no books."[27]

Trithemius's tales of how he won the bibliographical war have that eerie vividness that makes one wonder if they have any factual content at all. Happily, a fair number of manuscripts from the Sponheim collection have survived, and the evidence of the material texts confirms at least the core of Trithemius's picaresque acquisition techniques. Consider his copy of the world chronicle of Freculf of Lisieux—a splendid eleventh-century manuscript on parchment, now in the Herzog August Bibliothek, Wolfenbüttel.[28] On the first blank, two notes in different colors tell the whole story: "Liber sancti heriberti Tuicii" (This book belongs to The Heribertkloster in Deutz), in black, followed by "nunc mutatus ad spanheym pro alio" (now moved to Sponheim in return for another), in red.[29] Similarly, his copy of the Carolingian Benedictine Hrabanus Maurus, made up of two originally separate manuscripts on parchment, bears, over an erasure, the note "Codex monasterii in Spanhem ordinis sancti benedicti" (This manuscript belongs to the Benedictine monastery in Sponheim).[30] Trithemius, in other words, really did sift the monasteries of the Benedictine order for their treasures. He swapped something—whether later manuscripts or bright new printed texts—for their Carolingian and twelfth-century manuscripts on parchment. And he assembled hundreds of his finds in Sponheim. On the spectrum of Renaissance book finding, his methods fall somewhere between the efforts of humanists like Zanobi della Strada and Poggio Bracciolini to "discover" the classical texts lurking in monastic libraries and those of John Leland and John Bale to catalogue the larger range of texts thrown into circulation by Henry VIII's dissolution of the monasteries.

Furthermore, just as Herbenus said, Trithemius made his collection a center not only of monastic learning but also of humanistic erudition. The German humanists—men like Conrad Celtis and Jacob Wimpheling—set out to redefine learning itself in the years when Trithemius built up his collection. Like the Italian humanists, they argued that learned men must study grammar, rhetoric, and poetics until they could write Latin prose and verse that sounded satisfyingly classical. Like the Italians, they insisted that the scholar must read Greek texts—and, ideally, Hebrew ones—in the original. And, like the Italians, they set out to discover forgotten texts and publicize them. The *Germania* of Tacitus, for example, delighted them with its vivid portrait of the fighting spirit of their ancestors. They did their best to argue from it, in the teeth of Italian condescension, that Germany, too, could boast of an ancient past.[31]

Self-conscious scions of a people whose greatest power and richest cultural achievements lay in the Middle Ages, many of the Germans—like the Italian humanists of the later fifteenth century—represented humanism and scholasticism, eloquence and encyclopedism, and natural and moral philosophy as complementary. They traced genealogies of knowledge that connected the ancient sages of Egypt and Babylon, as well as the great writers of Greece and Rome, to the old druids and newer scholastics who had made Germany a great center of philosophy and magic. Trithemius's great new library, with its vast holdings of both classical and medieval books, glowed before them like a grail-shaped beacon, and they naturally frequented it and—in the best humanist manner—deposited some of their own treasures there for what they fondly hoped would be safekeeping. Celtis left with Trithemius, for a time, the manuscript of Hroswitha of Gandersheim's sacred comedies. Wimpheling—who loved his manuscript of Statius's *Thebais* so much that he threatened anyone who stole it with hellfire—eventually presented it to Trithemius. He carefully noted that he meant the book to form part "of the library at Sponheim that is not private"—a sensible precaution, since Trithemius could take years to return a book he had borrowed, as the great collector Hartmann Schedel bitterly complained.[32] As the new printed editions flowed in and the gifts piled up, Trithemius's library came to seem the *locus classicus* of polished humanist civility—a place where even the abbot's pet dog understood commands in classical Greek.

"Books do furnish a room," but what matters most about a collection is, of course, what readers do with it. Recent work in the field awkwardly known as the history of books and reading has shown that the art and act of reading has its period styles and devices—for example, the hurried skimming characteristic of our own harassed, Taylorite world, which finds its virtual embodiment in the hot link. From the fifteenth to the seventeenth century, erudite readers worked through the arcane texts that mattered most to them in a particular, precisely defined way. They read extensively, comparing texts from many sources, and used the most elaborate, up-to-date equipment to do so. But they also read any particular work as intensively as possible, with pen in hand. Representations of work in the library during this period consistently show the most learned readers defacing the books in front of them, with a zeal that would horrify any modern librarian, as part of a systematic effort to excavate every bit of marrow from what now look like the dry bones of Latin erudition.[33]

Trithemius went through his books in a particular, precisely directed way. By 1492, in fact, he had drafted a massive work of scholarship, which reached print two years later: the *Liber de scriptoribus ecclesiasticis*. This described the lives and works of almost a thousand writers from Alexander of Cappadocia to Trithemius himself.[34] Each entry followed a set form: a short life, followed by a list of works with their incipits, and then a discussion of bibliographical problems and uncertainties. For example, in a brief note on Theodoric Ulsenius, Trithemius remarked that the learned medical man had written a number of elegies and epigrams, "and many other works that will reach posterity."[35] In his note on Hartmann Schedel, he accurately characterized Schedel's Chronicle as adapted from the world chronicle of Jacopo Foresti of Bergamo, with some additions "especially on German matters," and concluded "for the rest, I have seen nothing."[36] A more complex list on Augustine, which had some 277 entries, ended with detailed explanations of why Trithemius had omitted works ascribed to Augustine by others (as he explained, works that "echoed the style of Gregory the Great," or "seem to have the spirit and the language of the blessed Bernard," or that cited Augustine as an authority, could hardly belong in the saint's bibliography).[37]

The *Liber de scriptoribus ecclesiasticis* was not innovative in every respect. More than a millennium before, St. Jerome and Gennadius of Marseille had written books *De viris illustribus* (On Illustrious Men) in which they concentrated not on curious anecdotes about the lives of their subjects, but on providing lists of their works. Medieval writers like Vincent of Beauvais had accumulated long bibliographies for great men (on which Trithemius freely drew) and so had world chroniclers like Jacopo Foresti, who not only assembled bibliographies but also added the incipits of the works he listed. When Trithemius claimed that he followed "a new method in writing, so that the reader himself can obtain knowledge more easily from the incipits, so I put the incipits across from the titles," he exaggerated.[38]

In a deeper sense, too, the *Liber de scriptoribus ecclesiasticis* depended on existing models of scholarly work. Medieval librarians regularly catalogued the books in their possession, listing the individual titles in a given manuscript and collecting all the titles they possessed into lists. Even when these enterprises went beyond the local—as happened in the thirteenth century when Franciscans drew up a union listing of all books available in English libraries—they rested on local knowledge drawn from specific material objects.[39] Trithemius clearly worked in the same way; when he obtained a new book, he entered a list of its contents at the start. His manuscript of Hrabanus Maurus, for example, has the entry:

codex sancti martini in spanhem, qui continet
    Rabanum in iohannem   li. I   li. X in toto
    Eundem in genesin   li. iiii
    Eundem in machabeorum   li. i
    Eiusdem interpretacionum   li. I
    Eundem in paralippomenon   li. I

Trithemius's bibliographies of individuals represented the sum of listings like these. And he repeatedly insisted that his work rested on firsthand knowledge of this kind. Discussing Freculf of Lisieux, he acknowledged that "He is said to have written some outstanding works," but he had to admit, "I have read only a great and splendid volume, which contains history from the Creation of the world down to the birth of our Lord Jesus Christ"—a precise description of a particular book, now in Wolfenbüttel.[40] When Trithemius described the work of Hildegard of Bingen, he noted that he had read 135 of her letters—in a manuscript now preserved in the British Library (MS Add. 15, 102).[41] Trithemius himself had the letters copied from the original holograph in Bingen, with undue haste, by a monk of Sponheim in 1487.[42]

Trithemius did more than catalogue the works he added to his libraries. He also did his best to establish their authenticity and judge their quality, and the critical remarks he entered in an individual manuscript often filtered, in altered form, into his published bibliographies. In *De scriptoribus,* Trithemius noted that Rufinus had translated from Greek, among other works, that of Sixtus the philosopher.[43] Here he boiled down a long bibliographical argument that he had entered at the end of his manuscript of the work in question, the *Enchiridion* of Sixtus: "Note that this work is not by pope Sixtus, to whom it is ascribed, but by a certain other Sixtus the philosopher. On him see the *Lives of the Philosophers,* chapter 110: Sixtus the Pythagorean was a philosopher who flourished in the time of the Emperor Octavian. He wrote a book of moral maxims that he entitled *Enchiridion.* Rufinus translated this."[44] Similarly, Trithemius noted in the "commendation" that he entered at the start of his manuscript on Hildegard of Bingen that "In all her works, the blessed Hildegard works in a very mystical and obscure way, so that her works can barely be understood except by men in orders. This is not surprising. For everything that she wrote, she learned from revelation, both the sense and the words, which are mystical and precious and not to be cast before swine."[45] In *De scriptoribus,* perhaps intent on damping down controversy, Trithemius abbreviated and revised this assessment: "all her works give off the radiance of Catholic doctrine, which either confirms the faith or teaches good conduct. She never said or wrote anything that could be called into doubt. And though she was ignorant of Latin, she dictated everything in Latin, in good form, as the spirit of God revealed, and secretaries took it down."[46] Sometimes, moreover, Trithemius or his assistants added materials from his bibliographical works to the manuscripts. For example, his copy of Freculf of Lisieux contains a brief handwritten note on the author, which refers the reader to Trithemius's larger work on the Benedictine order.[47] Though only a few of Trithemius's thousands of books survive, it seems clear that he assembled and used them, initially, to carry out this massive project of bibliographical research and recycling—a process in which acquisition, cataloguing, and bibliography faded into one another, as they had for centuries. His ways of sifting, excerpting, and assessing texts were unusual only in scale.

Yet *De scriptoribus* did mark a milestone, and in more than one way. Trithemius recognized that the multiplication of texts and titles brought about by printing required scholars to create ordering and finding aids or they would suffer permanent bibliographical overload. By reviving the model of Jerome, which separated bibliography from history, he created exactly the form of technical literature that readers needed. No one contributed to this genre more tirelessly than Trithemius himself: in short order, he produced a massive bibliography of German writers, as well as further lists of the works of Carmelites and Benedictines and a survey of the literature of black magic. Later bibliographers acknowledged him as the head of all their tribe. John Leland modeled his journeys across the British Isles in search of information about British authors on those that Trithemius had undertaken in Germany, and the bibliography Leland produced served as the core of the first printed bibliography of British writers by John Bale. Similarly, Conrad Gesner saw his universal bibliography as an extension of Trithemius's work. In addition,

Trithemius set a new standard technically; he organized his entries chronologically, but added alphabetical indices as well, to make the contents easily accessible to readers.[48]

Still more innovative, though, was Trithemius's principle of selection. After reading the *Liber de scriptoribus ecclesiasticis* in draft, a priest named Albertus Morderer wrote to Trithemius to express his surprise that the work included "many professors of secular letters"—writers whom some people might now call "secular humanists."[49] After all, Morderer pointed out, Jerome and Gennadius had omitted worldly writers, since they did not contribute directly to the church. Trithemius admitted in his response, which he printed with the text, that he had done something innovative. "I'm not surprised," he wrote, "that you're surprised; others are surprised too."[50] But he defended his work passionately: "No one," he explained, "can be called sufficiently learned in divine scripture if he does not have a solid knowledge of secular letters."[51] Theologians could not confine themselves to learning the truth. They also had to "hold the minds of their listeners in their power."[52] Only oratory, the art of eloquence, could enable them to do this. "I wish," Trithemius wrote, "that all the theologians of our day studied rhetoric."[53] In making this argument, he did more than defend his practices as a collector—which, as we have seen, included massive acquisition of classical and other secular books. He also adumbrated the arguments put forward by his German humanist friends like Wimpheling, and those that would be made even more forcefully by Erasmus and Thomas More in the decades to come. Not just monastic life, but the church as a whole needed reform. The philological and rhetorical skills of the humanists—their knowledge of how to study and profit from texts, their ability to write eloquently and win support—would restore Christianity to its early luster. The border police who had separated secular from sacred studies suddenly lost their legitimacy in the abbot's mind. "Knowledge," Trithemius insisted, "has no enemy except the ignorant."[54] He made his bibliography of German writers a comprehensive demonstration of this point, and lavished praise on Charlemagne for the patronage of letters that had brought about a comprehensive revival of scholarship and the sciences. The Franciscans who compiled the British manuscript catalogue had also included classical texts along with religious ones. But they had not anticipated Trithemius's passionate effort to make bibliography part of a cultural program for the renewal of Christianity. Here, as in his bibliographical work more generally, Trithemius used his collection and the learned reference works he drew from it to strikingly novel ends.

Yet, even as Trithemius spun the gold of his collection into the platinum of new forms of scholarship, his work and life took a strange and decisive turn. Trithemius's publications had made him the leading expert on monastic history, and members of various orders consulted him regularly when controversies arose about the foundation date or privileges of a given house. Moving on from bibliography, accordingly, he began to draw up chronicles of great Benedictine houses—both his own house at Sponheim and the older and more important house of Hirsau, whose abbot, Blasius, asked him to undertake the project. These chronicles took their final form in the last fifteen years of the author's life, which he spent at Würzburg. They have some strange features. The Hirsau chronicle, for example, exists in two forms—the relatively compact *Chronicle* and the massive two-volume *Annals*, the holograph manuscript of which is in the Bayerische Staatsbibliothek in Munich (the 1690 printed edition of this monster fills some 1,300 folio pages).[55] In both works, Trithemius insisted at the outset on the high quality of the sources he had used. History, he wrote, followed two laws: it must be eloquent and it must be true. He acknowledged that he could make no claims to literary style, but he had done his best to pursue and acquire the facts, "since my monastic profession and my Christian faith force me to hate lies and be a friend of truth." And he could cite "many witnesses" for what he wrote, including "the annals, letters and privileges of the monastery of Hirsau"— which he actually used—and a slew of chroniclers, whom he named.[56] One of those not mentioned in the first version of his list of sources was Meginfrid of Fulda who, Trithemius remarked in the *Annals*, "wrote a great deal about the first foundation of the Monastery of Hirsau and the succession of the Abbots" in his twenty-four books *De temporibus*.[57] There was only one fly in the ointment—but it was big and buzzed loudly. No one but Trithemius mentions Meginfrid. No manuscript of his work has ever turned up. And the information Trithemius drew from him is worryingly inconsistent. In the first version of his Hirsau book, the *Chronicle*, Trithemius said that Abbot Rudolf died "in March 925, but Meginfrid did not note the day."[58] In the second version, the *Annals*, Rudolf died, "as Menfrid [sic] bears witness, on Wednesday, the alternate birthdate of our holy Father Benedict, 22 [normally 21] March,"

926.[59] Contradictions like these suggest that Meginfrid was not a real chronicler but the abbot's own invention—one that became fuller and more precise with time.

More troubling still—from the very moment of its appearance—was the abbot's compendium of the history of the Franks. From 1505, when he first met Maximilian, Trithemius felt himself drawn to that strange figure, the brilliant hunter and master of the arts of chivalry, haunted by the great emperors of the Middle Ages. Maximilian had no great castle, no capital city. But for propaganda he could capitalize on his ancestry—which, both his Habsburg and his Burgundian ancestors insisted, stretched all the way back to Troy. Albrecht Dürer underlined the emperor's claims with his magnificent *Gate of Honor*—a vast triumphal arch on paper that traced the emperor's roots back to ancient Egypt, and even praised his prudence in a hieroglyphic inscription drawn from the late antique writer Horapollo. So did historians like Hartmann Schedel, who fused medieval with Renaissance myths as they traced the Franks back to Priam and his descendants. The abbot's known special expertise lay in the history that mattered most to Maximilian—that of the German Middle Ages. Trithemius—who had the portraits of the ancient Frankish kings painted on the east wall of his new solarium in Würzburg—could spin exactly the webs of historical connectors that Maximilian needed.

Trithemius resisted the temptation simply to join the emperor's retinue. As he explained to the humanist Konrad Peutinger, a monk at court resembled a fish in a kitchen—as the fish was doomed to be cooked and eaten, so the monk was doomed to be corrupted by the pressures of city life.[60] In 1514, however, he published what he described as a brief summary of the history of the Franks, drawn from a writer named Hunibald, a "solid historian of the Franks who lived in the time of Clovis, in AD 500, and wrote, following the philosopher Doracus and the philosopher Wasthaldus and many others, the oldest historians, a splendid work in 18 books."[61]

It all made a dazzlingly attractive book. Trithemius promised to tell the stories of the 103 Frankish kings who succeeded one another from Marcomir to Maximilian—to say nothing of collateral lines. He hoped to cover 1,954 years, starting in 440 BCE, and to show that the Franks—far from erupting into Germany under the Roman Empire—actually arrived there, driven by the Goths, long before the birth of Jesus (in Bavaria, he argued in another work, they expelled an even older race, whose members lived, like animals, on acorns).[62] Though he did not complete the work, he told thrilling stories charged with wish fulfillment about the wise priests on whom the Franks, from the king on down, had depended for guidance in all matters. These included Heligast, who went into a frenzy, jerking his head and gesticulating—and then predicted the future, made the god Jupiter visible to his priests, publicized men's secret counsels, and revealed to his king, Basanus, all the secrets of his enemies—and Hildegast, who taught the Germans to make music and build splendid houses and temples.[63] Experts at astronomy, dream interpretation, and astrology, the priests showed a special love for the history of their ancient kings and fellow countrymen, which they preserved in histories and songs.[64] Heligast, for example, set out the deeds of the heroes in verse to educate the sons of rulers and noblemen. As Trithemius spun these tales, the abbot brought back to life an ancient Frankish kingdom whose priests had practiced all the arts he wanted to see flourish in the monasteries of his own day. He also managed to fulfill some of his own deepest wishes. Expelled from Sponheim by his fellow monks, he resented the attack on his authority for the rest of his life. As Ralph Trilipush, the protagonist of Arthur Phillips's novel *The Egyptologist,* invents a pharaoh in his own image, concocts and rediscovers his lost erotic poetry, and even paints his tomb, so Trithemius imagined a past in which all Germans had obeyed religious authority. Heligast, he explained, "had such a great reputation and authority, that all obeyed his rule at all times."[65] The book filled in the gaps in the historical record, the very ones that Maximilian and his court humanists had also set out to fill, but it did not quite make their case for the Trojan origin of the Habsburgs. And the tasty samples of early Frankish life that it offered left those who read it wanting a great deal more.

Suddenly, the learned abbot found himself sinking in quicksand that he himself had made. Even before the *Compendium* reached print, the emperor asked to see the original work of Hunibald, the feast from which Trithemius had snatched and displayed his bright flag of historical hors d'oeuvres. Maximilian dispatched a herald to ask for the book.[66] Trithemius could not produce it, and sent the herald off to Sponheim with a list of books to look for, nicely adorned with details to give some plausibility to what might otherwise have been a bare and unconvincing narrative. The first item was "Hunibaldus on the origin and deeds of the Franks, in parchment, it's a small volume and, if I remember correctly, it is bound in white pigskin." But Hunibald eluded the herald, and Maximilian inquired again. "Most serene king," Trithemius replied, his pen genuinely trembling, "I thought I should humbly point out that my successor in Sponheim, the current abbot, sold a good many volumes to the abbot of Hirsau." He recommended that "a most subtle inquiry be made at Hirsau"—but noted, dourly, that he had only too much experience with book collectors, especially those in monasteries, and that they usually proved reluctant to share their books with the good and the great.[67] Two and a half years later, in November 1515, he wrote again to assure the emperor that he had tried but failed to find Hunibald in Sponheim. He suspected the book had been sold, and in any event had not even been able to visit his former library, which the monks claimed had collapsed.[68] In 1516 he had to tell Frederick the Wise of Saxony that he had not been able to find either Hunibald or Wasthald, whose chronicle—he now claimed—had been bound with Hunibald's in the lost book. Never before or since has a great scholar been heard asserting so loudly or so often that his dog had eaten his homework.

By now, Trithemius's former friend Peutinger, who had been appointed to evaluate Trithemius's book before it appeared, was claiming that he had released it for publication only because he wanted the whole world to see how dishonest the abbot was.[69] Ioannes Stabius, another historian at the imperial court, compared the history of the Franks that Trithemius narrated in the *Compendium* to those the abbot had drawn up in other contexts. On the wall of his solarium at Würzburg, for example, Trithemius had noted in a sober inscription that the Franks left Sarmatia for Germany in AD 380. Furious with the abbot's twists and turns and self-contradictions, Stabius ranted that "everything that the abbot related from his Hunibald was false"—as well as everything he ascribed to Flodoard, Sigebert of Gembloux, and others (who were, in fact, genuine).[70] Scholars did not need to wait for Beatus Rhenanus to show, from the *Panegyrici latini,* that the Franks had arrived only in late antiquity.[71] There was nothing left for the abbot to do but die in a timely way. With the timing that had served him well through his life, he promptly expired.

How are we to explain Trithemius's metamorphosis? What made the bright butterfly of a forger finally emerge from the hardworking grub of the bibliographer? In the nineteenth-century heyday of source criticism, historians denounced him as a forger. In the twentieth-century heyday of theory, critics praised him as a storyteller. At the most prosaic level, contemporary models for Trithemius's behavior leap to mind. As a devout fan of the Carmelites, in praise of whose glorious traditions Trithemius wrote, he knew and showed sympathy for their way of writing history. Carmelite historians, as Andrew Jotischky has argued, tended "to turn the past inside out," offering an account of origins and continuity that depended for its cogency not on source criticism, but on typology, and which modeled the lost past on the known present.[72] A second mendicant model comes even closer to Trithemius. In 1498, a fellow member of a religious order, the Dominican Giovanni Nanni of Viterbo, published a set of twenty-four forged texts by Berosus the Chaldean, Manetho the Egyptian, Metasthenes the Persian, and other gentlemen unknown to fame. The texts were very short, so Nanni described them as a "defloratio" or compendium of a larger work. He also embedded them in a thick commentary, in which he showed that these texts—written by priests, on the basis of documents in the public archives—refuted the lying histories of the world drawn up by Greeks like Herodotus and Diodorus. From these materials he wove a genealogical web that connected antiquity to modernity, the Bible and Egypt to Greece and Rome. Medieval tradition had long identified the Gianicolo in Rome as the final resting place of Noah's ark, and Noah himself as Janus. But it took Nanni's inspired impudence to provide the etymological proof that the two were really one (Noah invented wine; and the Hebrew word for wine, *yayin*, was clearly the origin of Janus). No wonder that Nanni proved able to trace the genealogy of his patrons, the Borgia, back to Isis and Osiris—and to demonstrate, along the way, that his native Viterbo had been the center of ancient civilization.[73]

Even the sharpest critics—like Beatus Rhenanus—were amused by Nanni's presumption: "One milks the she-goat," wrote Beatus, using one of his friend Erasmus's adages to make apposite fun of the intertwined text and commentary, "while the other holds out the sieve."[74] Nanni's work was read intensively at Maximilian's court. As Trithemius recorded in a list of books that he offered to exchange, he owned a copy of "Berosum impressum de antiquitatibus latinum et ligatum"—Nanni's collection of texts, which was often referred to simply as "Berosus."[75] In at least one crucial way, Nanni offered the model that Trithemius followed, by taking care to ground his forgeries in scholarly argument. Priests, he maintained, deserved credence over lay writers, and public documents over private narratives. But Berosus, Manetho, and Metasthenes were priests who wrote on public authority. Hence, the rules of historical credibility supported his texts against their Greek opponents.[76]

Like Nanni, Trithemius decked out his forgeries in at least seven veils of camouflage—and like Nanni, he used the techniques of scholarship to make his fakes seem reliable. More than once, after retailing some especially miraculous tale from Hunibald, Trithemius noted that "these things seem remarkable to me, and are perhaps in part fabulous."[77] He commented that Hunibald must have invented the remarkable deeds of Heligast—unless, perhaps, the priest had carried them out through the arts of demons.[78] He cited genuine material texts—like the manuscript of Boniface that his obedient novice Franciscus once had copied for him—to make the existence of imaginary ones seem more plausible. And he larded his narrative not just with source citations and expressions of critical reserve, but even, unconventionally, with whole documents—like the rescript of Dagobert that he printed in full and that he argued must be a forgery since its date contained a technical error, it lacked a seal, and its testimony conflicted with that of other sources.[79] These are not the words of someone who is simply following the record, but of someone who is trying to buttress an invented one—and doing so in the manner already pioneered by an earlier monastic scholar. The man whose love of truth had led him, irresistibly, from ascetic, disciplined reading of the Bible to immersion in the *mare magnum* of world literature, deliberately betrayed his own ideals. Forgery, of course, is partly about *Schadenfreude:* perhaps, then, Trithemius deserves his place in the gallery of once-great scholars whose worlds were turned upside down by their own failings and the zeal of their enemies.

Nevertheless, it seems possible that Trithemius saw his creative efforts in a very different light. Nikolaus Staubach has offered a very suggestive reading of the episode, which tries to explain it using actors' categories. He points out that Trithemius took a passionate interest in the sort of knowledge that holy men and women obtained by revelation. Trithemius himself began his career with a vision about knowledge. A young man in bright raiment appeared to him at night as he slept, holding two tablets, "one written in letters, the other depicted with certain images," and told him to choose one. When Trithemius seized the written tablet, the youth told him that God had heard his prayers and would give him everything he asked for, and more.[80] Trithemius also reported at length in his monastic chronicles on earlier holy men whose knowledge had been obtained by revelation rather than study. Revelations played a vital role, moreover, in the transmission of the most sacred of all histories; after all, the prophet Esdras had "restored the books of Moses, which the Chaldeans had burned, using his memory as the original" (IV Ezra 14:21–41). False claims to such revelations, by contrast, infuriated him. In the presence of priests that Trithemius knew, the historical Faust supposedly insisted that he could reconstruct from his own mind the entire works of Plato and Aristotle—if they should perish—with their philosophy, in a new and improved form. Trithemius showed a special fury as he denounced the charlatan who thought himself "to be like another Hebrew Ezra."[81] Could Trithemius have thought that he, by contrast, was somehow restoring a true historical tradition from memory?

Trithemius himself suggests that this interpretation may be valid. He made clear that his two fields of activity—magic and scholarship—were linked. One kind of magic that Trithemius practiced and recommended supports the notion that his revelations came to him, in his view, from a supernatural source. He emphasized repeatedly that certain men could perform miracles, if they led a sufficiently austere and rigorous life and dedicated themselves intensively enough to contemplation—and, he admitted, so long as a good spirit aided them, since no human could attain knowledge except through the senses or through the help of a supernatural being. Trithemius told Maximilian that he had witnessed this way of doing miracles as a young man:

> When I was studying letters as a boy, four of us were sleeping in the same bed one night. One of my comrades rose from my side, as he regularly did when he dreamt, eyes closed, and walked about the house, as the full moon shone in. He climbed the walls more agilely than a cat. He also crossed the roof, a second and a third time. He stepped on us, but we didn't feel any more weight than if he had been a little mouse. Wherever his sleeping body moved, suddenly all the doors opened for him. With great speed, he passed to the highest part of the house, and perched on the roof like a sparrow.

"I am describing things that I have seen," Trithemius assured the emperor, "not things that I heard vaguely described." John Dee, the British scholar and magus who admired Trithemius unreservedly for his skills at cryptography and for conversing with angels, wrote "Mirandum" at this point in his copy of the book.[82] Though Trithemius warned that the enterprise was painfully difficult, he also encouraged ambitious readers to think that they too might achieve this form of enlightenment. Dee exclaimed, "May God grant me this someday" next to one such passage.[83]

Trithemius not only wrote his history at angelic dictation but also assigned the starring roles in his work to ancient forefathers who had written in the same way. His ancient models—the priestly historians of the ancient Franks—wrote what angel voices sang in their minds' ears. Is it possible that he sincerely believed his histories of ancient Franks and modern magi also came from angelic dictation and therefore had a credibility that histories transmitted by mere humans could not? After all, he did point out that only those "illuminated" by Hunibald could write the history of the Franks—and "illumination" was his technical term for the receipt of revelation from angels.[84]

One close encounter in particular may have played a crucial role. In 1487, close to the beginning of his learned career, Trithemius had one of his Sponheim Benedictines copy the correspondence of Hildegard of Bingen from the so-called Riesenkodex. In a note at the start of the new manuscript, now in the British Library, Trithemius recorded his order that the copy be made. He also reflected, "Everything that she wrote, she learned from revelation."[85] In one of her letters, Hildegard made clear her belief that the mathematics that ruled music also ruled the cosmos—very much the principle of Trithemius's numerological magic. Trithemius himself played a central role in promoting Hildegard's cult; I suspect that she provided him with both vital technical suggestions and an even more vital model—true knowledge derived from direct revelation. It seems likely that he would have explained himself, for the rest of his life, as doing what came naturally after he learned to do it from Hildegard—even as he turned visions from something to be studied historically into the source of history itself.

Of course, this explanation does not account for all the details in Trithemius's complex, intertwined tales of history and magic. But it does locate his inspiration in a place that he would have agreed was appropriate—in his contemplation of the inspired writing of a saintly woman, who wrote what the spirit dictated since she had no formal education. It seems only fair that Trithemius—who did so much to reform the monastic life of his time—also owed much of his approach to scholarship to the contemporary mendicants and the dead contemplative whom he so admired. A communal man by implication, he drew his scholarly methods and assumptions not only from the humanists whose passion for knowledge he shared but also from the real and imagined Christian communities to which he belonged. That helps to explain why the past, as he evoked it, proved so dangerously appealing to so many of his contemporaries.

4

The World in a Room

Renaissance Histories of Art and Nature

In *The City of the Sun,* Tommaso Campanella envisioned the ideal state as a visual encyclopedia of nature and culture. The Solarians' circular city on the hill has seven concentric walls that surround an enormous central temple. Covered with maps, diagrams, and specimens, the walls survey the natural world, realm by realm. Each of them provides full information, not just about the properties of the things or beings it portrays and the specimens in bottles in its niches but also on their relations to the cosmos as a whole. The outer wall of the third circuit, for example, shows "all manner of fish to be found in river, lake or ocean; their particular qualities; the way they live, breed, develop; their use; their correspondence to celestial and earthly things, to the arts, and to nature."[1] Outward appearances—that of the bishop-fish, for example—serve as signatures. They reveal each fish's place in a web of natural sympathies and antipathies that runs from the stars to the earth, and from the fish themselves to the bodily organs they resemble.

Campanella's fish stories—like those about stones and animals—involve not only cosmic correspondences but also human agents. Over the centuries, in and outside the City of the Sun, human effort has revealed natural virtues that would otherwise have remained hidden. The Solarians record the history of this collaboration between humanity and nature with special care and passion. Accordingly, the inner wall of the sixth circuit displays the mechanical arts "together with their inventors, their diverse forms, and their diverse uses in different parts of the world," and its outer wall celebrates not only the founders of laws but also the inventors of weapons—including the Chinese creators of firearms.[2]

These visual histories of crafts do more than celebrate the works of great men. The Solarians' children, exposed to the series of powerful images from birth, "come to know all the sciences pictorially before they are ten years old."[3] Unlike Europeans, they nurse no prejudices against the mechanical arts: "they laugh at us because we consider craftsmen ignoble and assign nobility to those who are ignorant of every craft and live in idleness."[4] Indeed, they require candidates for their highest official position, that of the Sun, to have mastered all the mechanical arts and their histories. In other words, a material history of the relations between art and nature was to play a vital role in the Utopia—a society with no idle members, no beggars, and no nobility—that Campanella hoped to create from the urban and rural poor of southern Italy after he overthrew their Spanish rulers.[5]

At the other end of late Renaissance Europe, Francis Bacon nourished similar hopes. He did not represent his *New Atlantis* as a single great museum of natural history. But Salomon's House, its central institution, closely resembles one, as many interpreters have pointed out. Along with its parks, orchards, "places for breed and generation of those kinds of worms and flies which are of special use," and "houses of deceits of the senses," it also includes "two very long and fair galleries." One of these contains "patterns and samples of all manner of the more rare and excellent Inventions," and the other "the statua's of all principal inventors." The member of Salomon's House who explains the institution to Bacon's narrator emphasizes that these twin galleries of invention are vital to its imaginative—and material— economy. His colleagues take special care to establish the identity of older inventors "by more certain tradition" than Europeans have, and to reward the creators of new mechanical arts with splendid brass, marble, jasper, quartz, or cedar statues of their own, as well as "a liberal and honourable reward."[6]

When Campanella and Bacon juxtaposed natural knowledge with the fine and mechanical arts, as many interpreters have pointed out, they built upon rich precedents, written and material. The courts and cities of sixteenth-century Europe harbored a number of *Kunst- und Wunderkammern,* where the marvels of nature flanked the most spectacular products of human industry. Samuel Quiccheberg surveyed many collections, most notably the spectacular one of the rulers of Bavaria, which he helped to create, before he offered his plan for displaying "artificial and miraculous things" in a "theatre" in 1565. Like the City of the Sun and Salomon's House, Quiccheberg's theatre sets out an inventory of nature and culture: pictures of rare animals and fish, skeletons of men and animals, seeds, fruits, metals, precious stones, and every imaginable product of human industry, from clothing to scalpels to weapons of war, as well as maps, city views, paintings, and prints.[7]

Bacon and Campanella drew on many models, including the working establishments of Giambattista della Porta, John Dee, and Cornelis Drebbel.[8] But it seems clear that both men had the sixteenth-century *Kunst- und Wunderkammer* primarily in mind as they sketched plans for what later generations, resolutely anachronistic, would see as modern laboratories and scientific states.[9] Their visions of the ideal site for study of nature resembled those of traditionalists like Jean Bodin, whose natural philosophy was a mosaic drawn mostly from books, but who imagined the Venetian house where seven wise men met to discuss the religions of the world as a "pantotheca" divided into 1,296 "capsulae," stuffed with specimens of metals, plants, fossils, and animals, as well as images of creatures too numerous or large to be accommodated, from insects to the rhinoceros.[10]

In one respect in particular, Bacon's and Campanella's state museums seem to break with long-standing cultural traditions. Both men portrayed nature as changing, gradually, because of human intervention. The Solarians use art, eugenics, and astrologically timed sex to improve the human stock of their city. After watching young men and women engaged, naked, in violent exercise, like the ancient Spartans, the elders pair them off in ways determined by their physical characteristics and temperaments: "Tall handsome women are not matched with any but tall brave men, while fat women are matched with thin men and thin women with fat ones, so as to avoid extremes in their offspring." Before intercourse, the young men digest their dinners and pray, while the young women examine "fine statues of illustrious men." Only then do they meet, at an astrologically determined time. The results are clear: this careful eugenic regime and the constant exercise required of girls has eliminated ugly women from the city—as opposed to Europe, where women's idleness "makes them pale, fragile, and short and creates a need for artificial coloring, high heels, and beauty care."[11]

The denizens of Salomon's House seek "the knowledge of Causes, and secret motions of things; and the enlarging of the bounds of Human Empire to the effecting of all things possible." They too can alter nature in crucial respects: for example, by changing the normal course of human life. The artificial metals that they create in their deep caves, for example, cure otherwise incurable diseases and prolong the lives of "some Hermits that choose to live there, well accommodated of all things necessary, and indeed live very long."[12] Similarly, their "subtle breads" nourish chosen individuals so well that they live long lives without taking any other nourishment. They can even create serpents, worms, flies, and fish that become "perfect Creatures, like beasts or birds, and have sexes and do propagate."[13] In their belief that humanity's relation with nature could be altered in a uniform way and could be steadily improved, both men seem to look forward to Descartes and other later writers, who would make the possibility of material and technical progress one of the most powerful slogans of the New Philosophy.

Some years ago, Horst Bredekamp connected these assertions to the *Kunst- und Wunderkammer*. Both collections and images of them, he pointed out, often juxtaposed stones, plants, and animals with statues—sometimes partially completed ones, half hewn from native rock. They often included automata—creatures crafted from inanimate materials to imitate the movements and qualities of living beings. Other scholars have made clear how productive these visions became. Lorraine Daston, Katherine Park, Martin Kemp, and others have shown how many objects in Renaissance collections deliberately challenged the onlooker to determine where nature left off and art began. And Thomas Kaufmann has revealed that Arcimboldo and other artists favored by the makers of *Kunst- und Wunderkammern* were fascinated by the historical development of arts and crafts.

Bredekamp brought his argument to a characteristically provocative close. Natural historians in the fifteenth and sixteenth centuries, following Pliny, saw natural history as a synchronic, not a diachronic, discipline. They mapped the variations of what they saw as a stable, natural world, not its transformation over time. Scholars believed that art could help, and even perfect nature—but only by drawing on nature's own resources, and within the narrow limits those resources imposed.[14] But artists and collectors came to see nature as changeable and human effort as a force constantly acting on it. They arranged collections and devised images to tell a visual story about the direction in which nature moved—a story that they literally could not have told in words, since they lacked both terminology and textual models. Two generations after *Kunst- und Wunderkammern,* botanical gardens, and grottos came into their full, strange flower, Campanella and Bacon finally found the words for an argument long made by assemblages of objects and pictures. What seem to be the most radical segments of their works thus express a view of nature that had long been literally embodied in specific sites of intellectual and artistic enquiry. More recently, Markus Popplow has argued, in a similar vein, that philosophers and humanists did not articulate a coherent vision of technological progress until they saw the one that engineers expressed, with dazzling theatricality, in the "Theaters of Machines" of the decades around 1600. These printed collections of designs—too general and inaccurate to serve as working drawings and sometimes impossible to carry out at all—advertised the prowess of inventors like Agostino Ramelli, Jacques Besson, and Salomon de Caus.[15]

These analyses have permanently altered our understanding of the great manifestos of *Science in Utopia*. They form a prism, read through which older works take on a radically new look. Quiccheberg, for example, explained that a "Theater" should include both real "miraculous and rare animals, such as rare birds, insects, fish, shells and the like" and, next to them, "sculpted animals of metal, plaster, clay, and any artificial material, so that art makes them all appear alive."[16] He also called for small-scale models of machines for drawing water, sawing wood, and pulling ships, so that "the examples of these little machines or structures might make it possible to create other, larger ones in the proper way, and gradually to invent better ones."[17] Nowhere does Quiccheberg argue explicitly that men change nature in a directed, consequential way, but the implication seems apparent.

Both Campanella and Bacon, however, cast their nets very widely. As much as the *Kunst- und Wunderkammern* mattered to them, other visual and textual sources also helped frame their visions of nature in directed motion. Consider, for example, the textual world of natural history as it developed in the sixteenth century. Even Marcello Virgilio Adriani, a dedicated humanist, boasted of his efforts to consult "doctors expert about herbs, who work in the fields," and to offer "eye-witness testimony about plants," though he had to import them expensively from other countries.[18] Adriani insisted that "nature's power extends widely, and its majesty is great; hence it can produce many things in different forms, and grant others what it has denied us and our world."[19] Just as crops improved when many worked together to plow and burn over fallow fields, so medicine would improve when many collaborated to bring textual knowledge and observation together—a program carried out largely by Pier Andrea Mattioli, whose edition of Dioscorides became a compendium of recent botanical research.[20] The textual natural histories that Campanella wished to transform into frescoes and cabinets already transmitted parts of the message that his imagined city was to preach with its very stones.

Other texts also helped to stimulate the utopian imagination. For example, Bacon began to imagine his ideal research center in the 1590s, as Kaufmann and others have shown. By 1608, in a set of notes on what he called "a place to command wytts and pennes" he expressed his disapproval of the denizens of existing institutions like Eton, Winchester, Trinity, and St John's. *"It must be the postnati,"* he wrote, not established scholars, who would create a new way of studying nature. And they would do so, ideally, in "a college for Inventors." This, in turn, must have "Galeries wth Statuas for Inventors past and spaces and bases for Inventors to come And a Library and an Inginary"—in other words, not just a material history of the previous development of the mechanical arts, but one designed to follow their growth and change over the year.[21]

Just before this passage, Bacon clarified the sort of subjects that the inhabitants of his new college would pursue. On the one hand, they would compile from ancient and modern sources, "wth Judgmt and without credulity," a "History of Marvailes, Historia naturae errantis aut variantis"—or, as he put it elsewhere, "Hystorie of all sorts for matters strange in nature told in serie temporum heare and there inter caetera." On the other hand, they would "procure an History mechanique," which would lay out "the experimts and observations of all Mechanical Arts." This would include materials, instruments, or engines, their uses, and "the woork it self and all the processe thereof," as well as "observacions, Axiomes, directions."[22]

Between the history of marvels and that of inventions, Bacon cited one near-contemporary source: "Pancarolus, de reb. Memorabilibus,"[23] a reference that suggests the range of sources on which he drew. Some decades before Bacon wrote, the Italian jurisconsult Guido Panciroli had published a short treatise in Italian on the lost inventions of the ancients and the new ones of the moderns. In 1603, Heinrich Salmuth republished this in a Latin translation, with an exhaustive commentary. This compendium made clear that the ancients had been able to create wonders that the moderns could not match, such as Egyptian obelisks and pyramids: to forget this, Salmuth pointed out, was to imitate the Greeks, whose ignorance of ancient history the Egyptians had ridiculed, calling Solon himself a mere child when he revealed that he did not know the history of Atlantis. In short, knowledge of the history of inventions was urgent and required careful reading of ancient texts. But it also required elaborate study of the postclassical world, which had devised such remarkable works of man as Greek fire and the compass, and had used the latter to discover the New World.

Panciroli and Salmuth showed, finally, that culture always mediated the ways in which men exploited nature. Panciroli argued that while the ancients did have sugar, they used it only for medicine; in recent times, however, new ways of making and purifying sugar had produced it in immense quantities. And human ingenuity had produced a world of things made up of this ancient substance, a new sort of sweet-tasting *Kunst- und Wunderkammer:* "Nowadays this art has reached such a pitch of subtlety, that rhubarb, pine nuts, pistachios, cinnamon and other species are candied in sugar, and thus preserved as if they were still fresh. Very pretty figures and little images are also fashioned from sugar, and every kind of fruit is represented, so that they seem natural and wild."[24] Salmuth developed the point more gloomily, pointing out that the new availability of sugar had produced addicts, who overheated their blood, developed a perpetual thirst, and contracted disgusting black marks on their teeth by their immoderate eating of sugar and "sugary confections."[25] Nature, evidently, could jump through any hoop that human inventiveness held up for it, including the apparent transmutation of metals, which both Panciroli and Salmuth described at length in their entry on alchemy. Bacon envisioned his collection of material on the arts as both a compilation, in the style of a commonplace book, much like the work of Panciroli and Salmuth, and a museum, in which statues would commemorate inventions and empty pedestals would stimulate others to emulate them. Thus he revealed his belief that he could draw on existing verbal and material sources to frame his vision of human agency on nature.

Existing literary and artistic traditions offered Bacon and Campanella rich resources to work from. Pliny himself suggested, for example, that the fine arts had developed over time. A long series of anecdotes, repeated *ad nauseam* and beyond by Renaissance writers, transmuted the histories of painting and sculpture into a series of problems that artists had posed and solved, first in antiquity and then after the arts revived in the fourteenth and fifteenth centuries. Artists did not need to be erudite in order to frame their own work in these terms. For instance, when Lorenzo Ghiberti examined an ancient statue of a hermaphrodite, he called special attention to the way "one of the legs was stretched out and the large toe had caught the cloth, and the pulling of the cloth was shown with wondrous skill."[26] Similarly, he pointed out that when he fashioned the Gates of Paradise for the Florentine baptistery, he "strove to imitate nature as closely as I could, and with all the perspective I could produce." He had set all his "histories" in frames, for example, "because the eye from a distance measures and interprets the scenes in such a way that they appear round."[27] In other words, from the beginning of the fifteenth century, the fine arts provided perfect examples of a human pursuit in which continued inventiveness revealed many—perhaps limitless—new possibilities.

Leon Battista Alberti took this argument a step further in his treatise *De statua*. This little work began, like Ghiberti's autobiographical *Commentaries*, with a history of the art of sculpture. But Alberti, here as elsewhere, told an idiosyncratic and revealing story. The first likenesses, he explained, had been images made by chance: "certain outlines," observed in tree trunks, clods of earth, and other inanimate objects, "in which, with slight alterations, something very similar to the real faces of Nature was represented." This view was not completely unprecedented. In a classic article, H. W. Janson collected other ancient and modern passages that referred to nature's ability to produce likenesses.[28] In fact, many believed that natural forces could stamp an exact likeness on stones. Writing around 1260, the Dominican philosopher Albertus Magnus noted that in certain conditions, the stars might impress a recognizable image on "precious stones and certain marbles," as they had impressed the image of a king's head on a cameo that he saw in the shrine of the Three Kings in Cologne Cathedral.[29]

Alberti, however, had a rather different point in mind. He described the natural images of faces as approximate and imperfect. Sculptors, he argued, "began by diligently observing and studying such things, to try to see whether they could not add, take away or otherwise supply whatever seemed lacking to effect and complete the true likeness." Correction and competition, new creations, and critical discussions ensued. "By emending and refining the lines and surfaces" produced by nature, sculptors "achieved their intention and at the same time experienced pleasure in doing so."[30] On this view, sculpture crystallized into an art only because humans collaborated with and corrected nature, and one another as well. Alberti intended his own treatment of statue making, as he indicated, to improve the art still more, by giving sculptors a "firm method" that would enable them to avoid mistakes.

Sculpture, Alberti claimed, needed only the means that nature itself provided in order to supply better likenesses than unaided nature could: "just as in a tree-trunk or clod of earth Nature's suggestions made men feel it possible to create something similar to her products, so in Nature herself there lies to hand something which provides you with a method and certain, exact means whereby you may with application achieve the highest excellence in this art."[31] When the sculptor studied the nature of likeness or resemblance, when he mastered the mathematical techniques that made it possible to measure and record human bodies in all their postures, he was only learning to apply "the convenient and necessary means . . . that Nature offers to sculptors to execute their work perfectly."[32] Human artistry could imitate *natura naturata* (the completed natural creation) more elegantly than *natura naturans* (nature in its active, creative sense) could.

Yet Alberti assigned the artist even more complex and demanding tasks than straightforward imitation of the natural world. In his treatise of the mid-1430s *On Painting*, he told the story of how the painter Zeuxis went about his task:

> The idea of beauty, which the most expert have difficulty in discerning, eludes the ignorant. Zeuxis, the most eminent, learned and skilled painter of all, when about to paint a panel to be publicly dedicated in the temple of Lucina at Croton, did not set about his work trusting rashly in his own talent as all painters do now; but, because he believed that all the things he desired to achieve beauty not only could not be found by his own intuition, but were not to be discovered even in Nature in one body alone, he chose from all the youth of the city five outstandingly beautiful girls, so that he might represent in his painting whatever feature of feminine beauty was most praiseworthy in each of them.[33]

In this case, Alberti took Zeuxis's efforts as directed toward perfect representation: "He acted wisely, for to painters with no model before them to follow, who strive by the light of their own talent alone to capture the qualities of beauty, it easily happens that they do not by their own efforts achieve the beauty they seek or ought to create; they simply fall into bad habits of painting, which they have great difficulty in relinquishing even if they wish."[34]

In *De statua*, however, Alberti cited the same passage to a radically different effect, in explaining why he had composed his own table of ideal human measurements:

> I proceeded accordingly to measure and record in writing, not simply the beauty found in this or that body, but, as far as possible, that perfect beauty distributed by Nature, as it were in fixed proportion, among many bodies; and in doing this I imitated the artist at Croton who, when making the likeness of a goddess, chose all remarkable and elegant beauties of form from several of the most handsome maidens and translated them into his work.[35]

Intensive study of nature and resemblance should yield the ability to create not only the likeness of an individual—such as Alberti's own famous self-portrait plaquette, with its unforgettably beaky profile—but also that of a type, which gives material embodiment to an ideal of beauty not found in any individual man or woman.

Over time, as Erwin Panofsky showed in *Idea*, artists and writers on the arts followed the Alberti of *De statua* in asserting that the artist must produce a higher beauty than nature could. Lodovico Dolce, for example, wanted the painter "not only to copy nature but also to surpass it . . . to show . . . in a single body all that perfection of beauty, that nature hardly chooses to reveal in a thousand." Raphael complained, in a famous letter to Baldesar Castiglione, that he could not find the beautiful models on whom Zeuxis had relied, while in any case Castiglione was not available to help him make a selection. "Since there are so few beautiful women and so few sound judges," he concluded, "I make use of a certain idea that comes into my head." Giorgio Vasari argued in his *Lives* that the artist could form his ideas only from experience: "Design is the imitation of the most beautiful things in Nature in all forms."[36] But he also argued that the greatest ancient artists had surpassed nature, and that Michelangelo had surpassed them.[37] As art developed, for these writers, it became not nature's ape, but nature's rival.[38]

As early as 1557, Julius Caesar Scaliger revealed in his famed attack on Girolamo Cardano what such a doctrine might imply. Cardano had argued that the human mind delights in false things, because they provoke wonder. Accordingly, only lesser intellects capable of wonder could experience the pleasure of the fake: the minds of boys and fools, not those of wise, mature men. Scaliger accepted this argument, but he also qualified it. Even wise men loved Homer's inventions, he pointed out, and kings loved fools. His argument was simple: The human mind, being infinite by nature, loves new things—especially those, like "pictures of monsters," that "surpass the common boundaries of truth." The wise man praises pictures, "even though he hardly fails to realize that they are feigned." Moreover,

> the wise man prefers a pretty image to one that resembles a particular natural being. For art surpasses nature in this respect. The symmetry [of the human form] has undergone many forms of corruption since the first man. But nothing prevents the artist from raising, lowering, adding, removing, twisting or pointing. In fact, this is my view: with two exceptions, that of the first man and that of the true man and true God, no human body was ever as skillfully made by nature as they are perfectly framed nowadays by the hands of craftsmen.[39]

In Scaliger's view, the contemporary artist approached divinity by creating forms so beautiful that they seemed exempt from the general corruption of nature introduced by the Fall. In the later sixteenth and early seventeenth centuries, a number of theorists of art drew the practical implications of Scaliger's thesis. Giovanni Paolo Lomazzo, for example, noted that the artist making a portrait of a woman "should use extreme diligence to achieve beauty, using art, so far as possible, to remove the errors of nature."[40] The most remarkable implication of Scaliger's view, however, was perhaps the historical thesis it implied: that high art could reverse the degenerative course of human and natural affairs.

The distinction between fine and mechanical arts, as Bredekamp points out in his book, took shape long after the early modern period. In the fifteenth and sixteenth centuries, many artificers now remembered primarily as painters, sculptors, or architects earned their living by what now looks like mere craft—as Jean Fouquet did when he made gunpowder for the Estensi.[41] Early in the 1480s, when Leonardo promised Ludovico Sforza that he could make moveable bridges, tanks, mortars, and mines, before he mentioned sculpture, he was promising not much more than Brunelleschi had offered his civic patrons half a century before.[42]

Humanist writers also paid close attention to the crafts and their results. The "Anonymous Life" of Alberti, written late in the 1430s, mentions that he interrogated skilled craftsmen about their techniques. He himself treated the sheer size of Brunelleschi's dome for the Florentine Cathedral, "vast enough to cover the entire Tuscan population with its shadow," as the clearest evidence that nature had not, as he himself once feared, "grown old and weary."[43] Alberti now realized that the power of engineering, as well as the artistry of Florentine sculptors and painters, showed that the Roman poet Lucretius, just rediscovered and an object of passionate interest to Florentine humanists, had been wrong. He had seen the absence of enormous creations in his time as evidence that nature was degenerating, but in fact, nature was as fertile as ever.[44] Brunelleschi outdid the ancients not because his building was more handsome than theirs but because his skills and knowledge enabled him to create an "artificio" that even the Greeks or Romans could not have pulled off. In this case, too, Alberti portrayed relations between human effort and nature as moving in a clear direction, not because art surpassed the beauty of nature, but because nature herself was still producing "ingegni" (intellects) on the grand scale, and they in turn exploited and revealed her hidden powers.

Not long after Alberti wrote his letter to Brunelleschi, the supreme humanist Lorenzo Valla confronted a related set of problems. The consummate master of classical Latin, Valla recognized that modern ingenuity had created devices unknown to the ancients: the bell *(campana),* the clock *(horologium),* and the compass *(pyxis nautica),* among others. He apparently took more than a casual interest in these matters. In discussing the clock, for example, he explained that the ancients had used sundials, hourglasses and water clocks. Even so, he insisted on the novelty of the modern device: "I mean the one that is truly a clock [*horologium*], in which one detects not only the numbers of their hours, but, so to speak, their speech . . . It does not only set out the hour to the eye, but also announces it to the ears of those far away and those at home, using the bell mounted on top of it to distinguish the numbers. Nothing could be more useful or more pleasant."[45] The great iron escapement clocks that rang the hours in Italian cities were something genuinely new in the world. "And it is certainly necessary," Valla wrote, "that the learned decide by what names we should refer to things that were invented not very long ago." Like Alberti, Valla took the existence of such devices as evidence of something fundamental about the order of things: "the minds of mortals are not yet exhausted." Also like Alberti, he argued that in some respects at least, the moderns "approached quite near to the high competence of the ancients."[46] Valla himself did not publish this text, but his friend Giovanni Tortelli inserted most of it into his famous lexicon, the *De orthographia.*[47] And the Florentine humanist Giannozzo Manetti, who, like Valla, spent time in Naples and Rome, and may well have taken part in discussions with Valla at Naples, cited the achievements of engineers and architects as powerful evidence for the dignity of man in the oration on the subject that he wrote for his and Valla's patron, Alfonso of Aragon, in 1452. Manetti cited the achievements of outstanding modern individuals, like Brunelleschi and Ghiberti; traced the history of navigation, which had opened up the whole world; and celebrated the architects and builders who had transformed the world itself into a human creation: "These creations are ours—that is human—since they are the work of men: all the houses, all the cities, and finally all the structures in the world, which are so great and so excellent, that they seem, because of their excellence, the work of angels rather than men. The paintings are ours, the sculptures are ours, the arts are ours, the sciences are ours."[48] In short, by the middle of the fifteenth century, the history of crafts was well established as an area of interest to scholars as well as artists— and one comparable, in its dignity, to the history of philosophy itself.

The craftsman's effective intelligence, moreover, had come to serve as a model of the divine mind at work. Marsilio Ficino saw the speaking statues of the ancient Egyptians not as automata but as stone sculptures animated by the proper incantations. He distinguished sharply between "the work of craft," which he defined as "the mind of the artist in disjunct matter," and "the work of nature," which he defined as "the mind of nature in conjunct matter": "The order of a work of nature . . . is more like the order in the art of nature than the order of a human artifact is like the art of man. This is to the degree that matter is closer to nature than to man and nature has greater sway over matter than man does."[49]

But Ficino also treated the work of especially skilled craftsmen as the best analogy for that of the Creator of the universe itself:

We saw recently in Florence a small cabinet made by a German craftsman in which statues of different animals were all connected to, and kept in balance by, a single ball. When the ball moved, they moved too, but in different ways: some ran to the right, others to the left, upwards or downwards, some that were sitting stood up, others that were standing fell down, some crowned others, and they in turn wounded others.

One single ball produced all these movements, he reflected, and the sounds of horns and trumpets and the songs of birds at the same time. "Thus God through His own being . . . has only to nod His head and everything which depends on him trembles."[50] Ficino also recommended contemplation of the mechanical clock in the Palazzo della Signoria as a way to gain deep understanding of the cosmos.[51]

In the course of the later fifteenth and sixteenth centuries, three separate developments finally dramatized and focused attention on the history of the arts. Artists such as Piero di Cosimo gave precise and powerful visual form to the primitive life evoked in different ways by Lucretius and Vitruvius. Fra Giocondo, Cesare Cesariano, and others, for example, offered visual commentaries on Vitruvius in the form of woodcuts. These images highlighted the ways in which the practical arts developed. Vitruvius described, following older sources, how civilization began when men had learned to use and control the fires made by branches rubbing against each other in the forest (2.1.2). The discovery of fire's uses stimulated the development of language and housing, and coexistence and collaboration led to the continual improvement of man's material condition. Sixteenth-century illustrators followed Vitruvius's lead by depicting the "life of the first men" in detail, in ways that showed increasing precision. Fra Giocondo, for example, imagined a group of clothed men and women sitting by a fire, equipped with vases (in the background, incongruously, he placed a Gothic city). He thus celebrated the crafts as essential to civic life, but suppressed what Vitruvius had said about their early development. Cesariano followed the text more closely, using the arts as a marker for the development of society. He depicted one group of humans, naked, as fleeing a fire in a clearing. The members of another group, some of them already wearing clothes, tended their common hearth and practiced crafts such as basket weaving. A single woodcut thus became a conjectural history of the origins of civilization.[52]

The exploration of Africa and the discovery of the New World confronted travelers, scholars, and illustrators with the practical problem of representing non-European peoples and the more refined difficulty of describing and assessing their level of cultivation. Occasionally someone met this with an open mind. Dürer, who examined jewelry, clothing, and weapons from the New World at Brussels in 1520, described them as "wonderful works of art" and "marveled at the subtle 'ingenia' (intellects) of men in foreign lands."[53] But most writers and artists saw primitive artifacts through a scrim of assumptions. Feather headdresses and facial jewelry, for example, came to be associated with societies that had no government, did not maintain European-style regulation over marriage, and ate human flesh. Royal entries, drawings, watercolors, and woodcuts—especially the famous works of Jacques Le Moyne and John White—popularized vivid images of tattooed men and women bearing primitive arms. The artists labeled their figures sometimes as Indians, sometimes as Picts or Germans. The latter step, though it rested on the ancient notion that time and space are convertible in ethnography, had a radical implication: it suggested that Europeans themselves had once gone naked, or largely so, had painted their bodies, and wielded simple, primitive tools and weapons.[54] These images reached a vast public, especially in the engravings and captions of Theodore de Bry's *America*. Well before Bacon and Campanella, scholars and artists had outlined the early segments of a revisionist "history mechanique."

The more recent segments of the mechanical history also took on sharper outlines. From the fourteenth century on, engineers like Giovanni Dondi began to highlight the novelty of their work more and more dramatically. Brunelleschi took extreme measures to protect his intellectual property. He carved model machines out of turnips, which would rot away after his workmen had used them and before his enemies could steal his ideas. And he warned the Sienese engineer Mariano Taccola never to reveal his new ideas to the public, since doing so meant courting insult or plagiarism—or both.[55]

Other engineers, however, adopted a different strategy. Dondi, Taccola, Georg Kyeser, Roberto Valturio, and others produced massive, splendidly illustrated compendia of their inventions. With these vast manuscripts they staked a double claim, to membership in the community of the learned and to authorship of new and valuable devices.[56] Up-to-date patrons like the Estensi recognized how much these claims meant to engineers, and offered specially gifted ones not only salaries and other privileges but also protection from competitors. In the sixteenth century, splendidly printed and illustrated books of inventions and the programmatic drawings of *Nova reperta* by Jan van der Straet, later engraved by Johannes Galle, defined a canon of modern inventions as specially dramatic and significant.

By the middle of the sixteenth century, some writers assimilated these views and gave them forceful expression.[57] Louis Le Roy argued as early as 1551 that early humans had lived in a barbarous state, mired in the "hard primitivism" described by the historian Diodorus Siculus and others.[58] In his 1575 synthetic work *De la vicissitude ou variété des choses en l'univers,* he also celebrated in phosphorescent rhetoric the invention of printing, the compass, and gunpowder: "antiquity," he stated baldly, "had nothing comparable to these three." No optimist, Le Roy recorded the appearance of syphilis and the degradation of morality among the "marvels" of his age. But he also predicted that "what is now hidden will come to light with time, and our successors will be amazed that we were ignorant of them."[59]

Le Roy's contemporary Jean Bodin went further; in his 1566 *Methodus ad facilem historiarum cognitionem,* he used the same three canonical inventions—printing, the compass, and the gun—to refute in formal terms the myth of the golden age. The earliest ancients had been little more than savages, he argued; they had not even understood that they should assess the death penalty for theft. And even the greatest ancient achievements in technology and warfare paled before the discoveries and inventions of the moderns. The ancients' catapults, Bodin scornfully pointed out, "might seem little more than toys if compared with modern cannon." The ancients had not known the "divine use" of the magnet for purposes of navigation, and printing "could easily compete on its own with all the inventions of all the ancients." Furthermore, additional startling discoveries about the "hidden secrets of nature," would be made in future years. For nature, Bodin insisted, "holds inexhaustible treasures of knowledge, which can never be exhausted."[60] Like Le Roy, Bodin expected the progress of the arts to cease at times, as the vicissitudes of the cosmos required, and he assumed that man could only learn what nature would teach. Nonetheless, he and Le Roy argued that, over time, the progressive work of human ingenuity had radically changed man's relation to the natural world.

At times, a still more radical attitude appeared—for example, in the world of what Francesco Zorzi and Henry Cornelius Agrippa christened "mathematical magic," whose practitioners operated by mixed mathematics and claimed that they could create automata, burning mirrors, submarines, and flying machines. Agrippa argued in both his *De occulta philosophia* and his oration *On the Vanity of the Arts and Sciences* that man's insatiable desire to build had led architects to attack and alter the face of nature itself:

> Thorowe whiche insatiable desire and studie of building, it is come to passe, that there is no measure or ende appointed herein: for this cause are hilles cut away, Vallyes filled up, Mountaines made plaine, stoanes perced thorowe, and the rockes of the sea discouered, the entrailes of the earthe digged, the riuers turned from their course, seas ioincd to scas, lakes consumed, marshes dried vp, armes of the sea barred out, the bottomes of the sea searched out, new Ilandes made, and againe other restoared to the maine lande. All which thinges, and more than these, albeit thei repugne against nature, yet oftentimes haue broughte verie greate commoditie to all the worlde.

Agrippa made similar claims about the power of mathematical magic to alter the face of the world—for example, by raising great stones, as the ancient builders of complexes like Stonehenge had done.[61] It is well known that Agrippa derived part of his optimism about man's ability to work on the cosmos from the vast range of magical, alchemical, and cabalistic works that he read, excerpted, and rewrote.[62] In this case, however, he drew on a different source. As an experienced military and mining engineer who had studied the Italian illustrated editions of Vitruvius, Agrippa learned from one of the most articulate Italian writers on the mechanical arts, Alberti himself, that architects could "cut down cliffs, cut through mountains, fill valleys, confine lakes and seas, dry out swamps, build ships, change the direction of rivers" and by doing so "make all the provinces of the world accessible."[63] Generations of mathematical practitioners repeated Agrippa's claims, adding new stories—like the one apparently created by Ramus about the mechanical fly and eagle created by Joannes Regiomontanus to welcome the Holy Roman Emperor to Nuremberg—but never radically changing his central thesis.[64] As late as the middle of the seventeenth century, Gaspar Schott used much the same set of anecdotes that Agrippa had—as well as descriptions of his own marvelous machines—to confirm the thesis, founded on Agrippa's fusion of magical and technological traditions, that magic of a particular sort was actually more powerful than nature: "This form of magic not only aids, and perfects nature, as the others do, but clearly overcomes her." The dazzling mechanical contrivances of the magicians, Schott insisted, involved the enhancement of natural powers and the imitation of every form of motion. He defined their art as "less a discipline that contemplates nature, than one that rules over her."[65] Here—and in other texts where traditions collided and sparks flew—the idea found expression that man's arts could not only provide increasing control over the natural world but actually transform it in radical ways.

Even those who set less store by human agency sometimes arrived at similar conclusions. Cardano and Campanella thought that all the inventions of their time, including such "stupendous" ones as the canonical three, had been caused by the action of the stars, which affected everything, if in different ways. "Hence," as Campanella put it, "the constellation that drew infectious vapors from Luther's cadaver drew fragrant exhalations of virtue from the Jesuits of that period and from Hernando Cortés."[66] But they no longer saw the heavens as stable and unchanging, since comets and the new star in Cassiopeia appeared there. They interpreted the radically new technologies of their day, accordingly, as evidence not only of what man could do to nature but also of an impending transformation of the entire natural and human order. "The conviction grows," Cardano wrote, "that as a result of these discoveries, the fine arts will be neglected and but lightly esteemed, and certainties will be exchanged for uncertainties. These things may be true sometime or other, but meanwhile we shall rejoice as in a flower-filled meadow. For what is more amazing than pyrotechnics? or than the fiery bolts man has invented so much more destructive than the lightning of the gods?"[67] The Christian world, Campanella predicted, would profit from the great changes that impended, "but first the world will be uprooted and cleansed, and then it will be replanted and rebuilt."[68] Meanwhile, the rise of new technologies confirmed other signs that the world was upside down: for example, the rise of women rulers in many parts of Europe and the growth of effeminacy among men, which made them call each other "Your Lordship" and resort, at least in Fez and Morocco, to male brothels.[69] The transformation of the arts thus accompanied—even if it did not cause—a transformation in the order of nature.

Conjectural histories of the arts, like material *Kunst- und Wunderkammern,* expressed powerful and innovative views about the relation between human inventiveness and the natural world. The verbal and the visual interfered with one another constantly as these texts and images took shape. Perfectionist optimism warred with fear and pessimism when scholars drew out their implications. Yet all of their authors saw the history of nature as substantially a history of culture, and many of them treated this as moving clearly in a forward direction. The City of the Sun and Salomon's House are porticos, with many entrances and many exits. Some of the paths that led to them began in craftsmen's shops, others in museums, still others in botanical gardens. But some had their origins in the overstuffed libraries where scholars cranked their desperate book wheels in the partly reasonable hope that reading books and studying pictures could help them to master a rapidly changing material universe.

5

Where Was Salomon's House?

Ecclesiastical History and the Intellectual Origins of Bacon's *New Atlantis*

No writer did more than Francis Bacon to found the seventeenth century's new style of intellectual life. Many thinkers of the late Renaissance argued that the ancients had not been omniscient: Jean Bodin, for example, found clear evidence for the superiority of modern culture in the fact that execution had replaced fines and imprisonment as the penalty for theft.[1] But no one matched the pithy brilliance with which Bacon stated, and generalized, the same point.[2] Many projectors wandered the schools and universities, offering royal methods by which the student could master any language or discipline. But none of them could rival the boldness and prescience of Bacon's call for a new kind of science: a collaborative, interdisciplinary enterprise designed to yield not theories of the traditional kinds, but operational knowledge: knowledge that afforded its possessors power over the natural world.[3]

Bacon stated this ideal most memorably in the description of Salomon's House, which concludes his incomplete utopia, the *New Atlantis*. In describing this "House or College," Bacon laid out the plan for what amounted to a scientific research institute. He used all the formidable resources of his rhetoric to evoke what natural philosophy could achieve, when pursued systematically, in a purpose-built environment. Methodical study of nature, he insisted, could enlarge "the bounds of Humane Empire to the Effecting of all Things possible."[4] The equipment of Salomon's House gave dramatic, vivid embodiment to Bacon's thesis. It included "large and deepe Caves" for "all Coagulations, Indurations, Refrigerations, and Conservations of Bodies," as well as the production of artificial metals.[5] Towers reaching as high as half a mile served for observation of the atmosphere and the heavens. "Great and Spatious Houses" enabled the members to "imitate and demonstrate Meteors, As Snow, Haile, Raine, some

Artificiall Raines of Bodies, and not of Water, Thunders, Lightnings; also Generations of Bodies in Aire, as Froggs, Flies and diverse Others"—to say nothing of "Furnaces," "Perspective-Houses," "Sound-Houses," "Perfume-Houses," "Engine-Houses," and even "Houses of Deceit of the Senses."

Bacon not only designed a new environment for intellectual work, but also imagined a new race of intellectuals to inhabit it—specialists who would each carry out one particular set of tasks among many. In fact, for the most part, their work could become meaningful only as part of a larger collaborative research program:

> For the severall Employments and Offices of our Fellowes Wee have Twelve that Sayle into Forraine Countries, under the Names of other Nations (for our owne wee conceale), Who bring us the Books, and Abstracts, and Patternes of Experiments of all other Parts. These wee call Merchants of Light.
>
> Wee have Three that Collect the Experiments which are in all Bookes. These wee call Depredatours.
>
> Wee have Three that Collect the Experiments of all Mechanicall Arts, And also of Liberall Sciences, And also of Practises which are not Brought into Arts. These we call Mystery-Men.
>
> We have Three that try New Experiments such as themselves thinke good. These wee call Pioners or Miners.
>
> Wee have Three that Drawe the Experiments of the Former Foure into Titles and Tables, to give the better light for the drawing of Observations and Axiomes out of them. These we call Compilers.
>
> We have Three that bend themselves, Looking into the Experiments of their Fellowes, and cast about how to draw out of them Things of Use and Practise for Mans life and Knowledge, as well for Works as for Plaine Demonstration of Causes, Meanes of Naturall Divinations, and the easie and cleare Discovery of the Vertues and Parts of Bodies. These wee call Dowry-men or Benefactours.
>
> Then after diverse Meetings and Consults of our whole Number to consider of the former Labours and Collections, wee have Three that take care out of them to Direct New Experiments of a Higher Light, more Penetrating into Nature than the Former. These wee call Lamps.

Wee have three others that doe Execute the Experiments so Directed, and Report them. These wee call Inoculatours.

Lastly, wee have Three that raise the former Discoveries by Experiments into Greater Observations, Axiomes and Aphorismes. These wee call Interpreters of nature.

Wee have also, as you must thinke, Novices and Apprentices, that the Succession of the former Employed Men doe not faile, Besides a great Number of Servants and Attendants, Men and Women. And this wee doe also: We have Consultations which of the Inventions and Experiences which wee have discovered shall be Published, and which not . . . [6]

This highly ramified intellectual program amounted to a radically new version of the scientific or philosophical enterprise. Unlike the subtly branching charts of the disciplines and their connections, rather like intellectual monkey puzzle trees, devised by so many philosophers of this period, Bacon drew up the table of organization for a new kind of institution.[7] His enterprise relied not on the intellectual brilliance of a single individual, but on the collaborative efforts of many teams; he demanded not solitary intellection but constant communication. And he envisioned his workers not as omnicompetent sages in the manner of Plato or Aristotle, but as specialized craftsmen of the mind and hand. Each of them would concentrate on culling materials from texts, observing natural phenomena, or drawing inferences.

As a design for intellectual living, Salomon's House hardly resembles most of the schools, learned academies, and universities of the sixteenth century, with their concentration on humanistic eloquence and scholastic logic—two pursuits that Bacon saw as impeding the study of nature, not promoting it, at least when carried to excess. Rather, it calls to mind the real and projected academies of the seventeenth- and eighteenth-century Republic of Letters, from the scientific societies that tried to put Bacon's method of natural philosophy into practice to the pan-Italian learned academy that, as Muratori hoped, would impose order on the pullulating, controverted records of medieval and modern history. Historians have often treated Salomon's House as one of the most radically new of Bacon's projects. They have pointed out that as Bacon came to see the need for large-scale public funding for his projects, Bacon dropped his insistence on communicating all new discoveries to an international public sphere. Only the economic value of discoveries—a value that depended on secrecy—could ensure that governments would finance them. Accordingly, he suggested that true advances must be kept secret, and in doing so adumbrated the torment of secrecy that proved to be one of the characteristics of late nineteenth- and twentieth-century Big Science. No wonder that the text often inspires future shock in its readers.[8]

Yet Salomon's House had its traditional elements too. The governor of the establishment describes it as having

> two very Long and Faire Galleries. In one of these wee place Patternes and Samples of all manner of the more Rare and Excellent Inventions; In the other wee place the Statua's of all Principall Inventours. There wee have the Statua of your Columbus, that discovered the West-Indies; Also the Inventour of Shipps; Your Monke that was the Inventour of Ordnance and of Gunpowder; The Inventour of Musicke . . . The Inventour of Silke of the Worme; the Inventour of Wine; the Inventour of Corne and Bread; the Inventour of Sugars; and all these by more certaine Tradition than you have.[9]

Here, as we have seen, Bacon's narrator evokes a scene that would have been familiar to any habitué of European courts in the later sixteenth century: a *Kunst- und Wunderkammer,* in which the display of natural objects altered by human effort revealed that nature developed over time.[10] Inventors were regularly honored in such spaces. The walls of the Salone Sistino, the late-sixteenth-century reading room of the Vatican Library, bristled with magnificent portraits of the creators of writing systems, from Thoth, who created the Egyptian hieroglyphs, to Ulfilas, who devised the Gothic alphabet. Bacon may have eerily adumbrated the Cavendish Laboratory of a Cambridge much later than his own, with its teams of researchers working in the public domain, its specialized research goals, and its sacred spaces set aside not for worship but for study. But he certainly evoked the Museo Aldrovandi, with its massed drawings of strange birds and fish—as well as the "goodly cabinet" of natural and human wonders described in his own *Gesta Grayorum* of 1594.[11]

Bacon, however, may have had a more particular model in mind as he created Salomon's House, one that was practical, not theoretical. A large-scale, collaborative intellectual enterprise had been famous throughout Europe for more than half a century before Bacon wrote the *New Atlantis*. Like Salomon's House, it consisted of scholars who worked in specialized teams, carrying out hierarchically connected functions and supported by endowments designed to enable them to do research. Like Salomon's House, too, it inspired both enthusiasm and discomfort. The identification of this model has broad implications. On the one hand, it locates one of the sources not only for Bacon's ideal of collaborative intellectual work but also for some of his most influential scholarly projects. On the other hand, it suggests that the seventeenth-century version of the Republic of Letters constituted itself in large part from the ideas and practices of erudite humanism.

From the 1510s onward, the history of the Christian church became a locus for scholarly controversy with precise practical applications. Protestants from Martin Luther to Thomas Münzer and beyond agreed that the arc of the church's history went downward after late antiquity, reaching a bottomless pit of iniquity in the later Middle Ages, when Antichrist ruled in Peter's chair. Even level-headed Protestant scholars like Joseph Scaliger firmly agreed: he told his students that anyone who managed to see the pope's tiara from close up would descry the word *Mysterium* written on it—clear evidence that the pope was the great beast of the apocalypse.[12] Catholics, by contrast, insisted that the new practices and doctrines of the Middle Ages did not reflect the intervention of human greed and corruption, but instead the continuity of divine inspiration. New prayers, new religious orders, and newly discovered relics revealed not the foul play of human entrepreneurs of the sacred, but instead the energizing presence of the Holy Spirit. Both sides drew on the history of the church as they tried to reform liturgical and sacramental practices, to work out the functions of priests and bishops, and to lay out the proper uses—if any—of church music. By the middle of the century, Catholics and Protestants alike saw that they needed a new kind of church history in order to fight fundamental theological and ecclesiological battles. Accordingly, they set out to revive the late antique discipline of ecclesiastical history—the heavily documented, highly polemical form of history, radically different from the political history written by Greeks and Romans, which had come into being in the fourth century.[13]

Matthias Flacius Illyricus, a South Slav born in 1520, devised the first well-defined project for filling this need; more remarkably still, he managed to turn the project into a working institution. Flacius studied in Venice, Basel, and Wittenberg before becoming professor of Hebrew at Wittenberg in 1544. In 1549 he moved to Magdeburg, where he worked out his plans in the next few years. Flacius saw at once that existing texts, such as the *Church History* of Eusebius and its many continuations, would not serve his need. As he explained to Pfalzgraf Ottheinrich in his *Consultatio de conscribenda accurata historia ecclesiae,* "The histories of the church that now exist are chiefly devoted to describing or praising individuals. They recall what a given person was like, how holy he was, what a marvelous life he led, how much he fasted and prayed, what miracles he did, alive or dead."[14] Eusebius and his followers had told implausible tales of wonder-workers, punctuated with pious ejaculations. And these, Flacius insisted, could not provide a firm basis for knowing what states the church had passed through or for judging what it should become in the future. Nevertheless, they would not be easy to replace.

Political history, Flacius explained, dealt with relatively simple matters: wars and their outcome. Ecclesiastical history, by contrast, must take on "the explication of the doctrines and religion which scholars, at different times, either corrupted or defended or obscured or illuminated, with true or false opinions and teachings"—that is, the history of theology, in all its incredibly diverse and contentious proliferation of opinion. But even theology did not exhaust the field: the historian of the church also had to take into account the devotions, the prayers, and even the church music used in the past. As Flacius told another correspondent,

> We want to show not only what doctrines existed in the church in each century, but also what sort of ceremonies and songs—though briefly, to be sure. For all these things are organically connected to one another. Therefore we will have to use those materials as well if we are to know or show others what the state of the church was at any given time.[15]

In other words, the historian of the church had to compile an exhaustive and varied collection of materials before he could even begin to work. Then he must recreate not only the institutions but also the spirit of the early church and follow both through time.

Flacius suited his action to his characteristically ambitious word. He plundered the existing bibliographical works of Johannes Trithemius and Conrad

Gesner in order to establish lists of texts, published and unpublished, that were relevant to his enterprise. He collected and edited a wide range of documents, including Waldensian documents and other testimonies to the existence, over the ages, of a hard core of 7,000 pious men. He wove a network of correspondents that stretched across central Europe. And he himself ransacked so many libraries and archives that his enemies gossiped, mendaciously, about the *culter flacianus*—the "Flacian razor" with which he supposedly slit from manuscripts the materials he needed but could not buy. By 1566, when Flacius published his massive survey of the literature he had studied, the *Catalogus testium veritatis,* he and his collaborators had a better command than anyone in Europe of the documents for the history of the church, some 430 of which they discussed at length.[16]

Flacius also devised—and discussed with other intellectuals across the empire—the best way to fuse these materials into the church history that pious Protestants so badly needed. He rapidly determined that a systematic rather than narrative order would work best for conveying what the church had been like, as a whole, in each period. Accordingly, as Heinz Scheible has shown, Flacius decided to use Melanchthon's system for retrieving materials from texts, the rhetorical *loci communes* or common places, as his basic tool for information analysis, storage, and retrieval. Century by century, the new church history would assemble and evaluate the materials that could enable moderns to know exactly when doctrines and practices had been pure, and when they became corrupt.[17]

At some point early in the 1550s, Flacius drew a vital inference from the mass of materials he had already turned up. One scholar, working alone in the traditional manner of the secular political historian, could not possibly master and deploy all the materials for a church history. Accordingly, Flacius floated a scheme before possible patrons and advisers alike, looking for both donors and collaborators:

> So far as my historical enterprise is concerned, I am now occupied above all with finding suitable men to carry it out, and that certain compensation be set up for them . . . I will need at least 500 florins or talers each year for a six-year period, to support four men: a writer who is a nice stylist and set down everything that needs to be written; two whose work will consist entirely of looking for materials and reading them,

and who will provide the writer with the materials, ready for use. The fourth, finally, will serve the enterprise as a copyist and by carrying out other lesser tasks.[18]

Over time, both Flacius's enterprise and his ambitions grew. By the mid-1550s, he and his colleagues, especially Caspar von Nidbruck, who did the lion's share of the actual work, had created a large-scale Institutum Historicum in Magdeburg. Its members soon began to turn out the massive period-by-period history of the church known ever since as the *Magdeburg Centuries*. It is well known that this soon inspired massive resistance from Catholic scholars; eventually, Cesare Baronio assembled an even larger cast of collaborators to produce his counterblast, the *Annales*. But Flacius also found himself under attack for corruption by his erstwhile Protestant colleagues in Wittenberg, like Justus Menius, with whom he had broken on theological grounds. They insisted that he had raised large sums for the enterprise under false pretenses from gullible Protestant rulers. Flacius defended himself, and the terms he used deserve close attention.

An elaborate polemical document laid out the goals and procedures of the Magdeburg Institutum in detail. Once again, Flacius and his collaborators insisted that they had far more in mind than producing another narrative of the lives and deaths of pious men. Rather, they intended to reconstruct "the idea of the church of Christ . . . using the best and oldest authors: the historians, the Fathers, and other writers as well."[19] To do so, they could not merely treat individuals, as Eusebius and other historians had done. Rather, they must also trace the development of doctrine, the evolution of ceremonies, the course of particular controversies, and the history of church government.[20] Flacius insisted that to carry out this ambitious plan, he had needed every penny his patrons provided, none of which had stuck to his own fingers.

A table of organization as elaborate as that of Salomon's House made clear—so the Magdeburgers hoped—that their enterprise was, in fact, no larger or more expensive than it had to be:

Men of judgment can easily see that one or two staffers would not be enough to collect and organize all this in the right way.

The handling of the materials, so to speak, is divided into four subsidiary processes. First of all, we support seven students, endowed with reasonable learning and judgment, with fixed grants. They carefully go through the authors assigned to them and make excerpts from them, paying close attention to the goals established with great care in our Method. They carry out what amounts to an anatomy of the authors, and copy everything out in its place, and do so always taking up one century at a time.

Next we support two Masters of Arts, men of outstanding maturity, learning and good judgment. They are presented with the materials that the hard-working little bees have already collected from flowers in various places. Their job is to assess, outline and arrange the materials that have already been assembled, which should form part of the text, and finally to work them up into a coherent historical narrative.

Thirdly, some of the gubernators (governors) of the enterprise have been selected as inspectors. They pass out the materials to the collectors, go over their reworkings of them, and help in making decisions about the contents and their arrangement (for nothing is finally written down until it has been subjected to this sort of assessment). Next they also give the written materials a further polish, and finally they themselves, when necessary, do some organizing and writing.

Fourth, we support a so-called amanuensis, who makes fair copies of the materials composed in this way.

Finally, there are in addition to these five governors and inspectors of the whole enterprise, men of the highest integrity. They take charge of formal discussions, hire suitable persons, fire unsuitable ones, and keep the accounts. One of them is responsible for keeping any contributions; he has the ledgers of income and expenses. Once a quarter, in the presence of the Consul, the accounts are balanced and recorded, with such care and precision that we believe that we can give a satisfactory account of every penny to any inquirer—and not only the honorable ones, but the malevolent as well.[21]

The Wittenbergers were not impressed by this formidable essay in the nascent German specialty of academic bureaucracy. To some extent, Flacius and his collaborators played into their opponents' hands. By using the metaphor of a public anatomy, they gave the Wittenbergers the chance to revive the charge that "Flacius' anatomies of historical books are well known, and much resented by those whose libraries have experienced them."

Worse still, by bringing bodily metaphors into play, Flacius and his allies unleashed the scatological imaginations of their opponents—never something in short supply in the German professoriate. The Wittenberg critics used an elaborate organic metaphor against the Institutum in Magdeburg. The seven inspectors, they joked, formed the belly of the beast. The inspectors, like the liver, separated chyme from blood, and sent the excrementary by-products along to the masters of arts, as if to the intestines. Flacius and the other inspectors must either be the brain or the heart of the enterprise: "Since Flacius is nothing in history, except the impresario of the money, we can more fittingly compare him to the heart. But clearly, if your heart is a great ass, it isn't very heartening to have it."[22] The college's elaborate table of organization, then, was nothing more than an adaptation of the human anatomy and physiology that its members had probably seen demonstrated for them on a chart. Like a human body, too, the college in the end produced nothing but excrement.

More was at issue, here, however, than heavy professorial wit. Flacius evidently deserves the honor of having set up the first endowed, full-time research institute in the history of modern Europe: the sixteenth-century counterpart to a modern Max Planck Institut für Kirchengeschichte, if there were one (sadly, none exists). But Flacius's critics also deserve credit for developing their organic analogy into the first sharp criticism of a scheme for grant-supported intellectual teamwork—a criticism that retains much of its validity today. After all, they pointed out, any errors made in the basic collection of material would eventually undermine the enterprise as a whole, since the scholar finally responsible for writing up the work, "who, we know, must be sweating a great sweat, especially in this heat, cannot construct something solid if the collectors have omitted the better things and assembled the worse ones." Only a scholar competent to compose the final text from the primary materials collected could really be competent to collect them in the first place. Flacius's application of *loci communes* could hardly ensure success in note taking on the part of what the Magdeburgers themselves described as "men of modest judgement." For the first, but not the last, time in modern Western history, senior scholars were forced to confront the sins of their

research assistants. One feels a certain sympathy with the Wittenberg scholars who pointed out that "it is a great matter, and one requiring perfect judgment, to see and excerpt what is useful from a great mass" and wondered if
the Masters of Arts would not make a better job of it than the students.[23]

There is every reason to think that Bacon knew about the Magdeburg Institutum. Flacius's history—and the institution that carried it out—remained
famous for the next century and more in Protestant circles. The seven stately
folio volumes of the *Magdeburg Centuries* formed a core possession of every
Protestant library. And the first one started out with detailed accounts, by
Flacius and his collaborators, of the scholarly and organizational methods
they had used, including the table of organization.[24] In other words, Flacius
supervised the creation of the first modern work of history to be produced by
grant-supported collaboration and to begin with a formal, detailed, self-
conscious account of its methodology. Bacon's own description of Salomon's
House begins in a way oddly reminiscent of Flacius's institutum, with
"Depredatours" and "Mystery-men"—specialists whose jobs, like those of
Flacius's students, involved making systematic notes on texts.

Bacon, moreover, took a considerable interest in ecclesiastical history. In
The Advancement of Learning, he discussed the subject at some length. General church history, he wrote, in words that Flacius would entirely have
approved—"describeth the times of the militant church, whether it be fluc-
tuant, as the Arke of Noah; or moueable, as the Arke in the Wildernes; or at
rest, as the Arke in the Temple; that is, the state of the Church in Persecution, in Remoue, and in Peace." As usual, Bacon did not find existing treatments perfect: "I would the vertue and sinceritie of it were according to the
Masse and quantitie."[25] But he clearly recognized ecclesiastical history as a
distinct historical genre with its own form and value. There is, accordingly,
every reason to think that Bacon knew about Flacius's institute and its
results.

In fact, the evidence suggests that Bacon found even more in ecclesiastical
history than his general model for a collaborative intellectual program. None
of Bacon's projects proved more influential in the next century and a half
than his call, first given concrete form in *The Advancement of Learning,* for
what he described as "a iust story of learning." Bacon admitted that "in di-
uers particular sciences, as of the Iurisconsults, the Mathematicians, the
Rhetoricians, the Philosophers, there are set down some small memorials of

the Schools, Authors and Bookes; and so likewise some barren relations touching the Inuention of Arts or usages." But these lists of disconnected facts did not amount to a history of "the generall state of learning . . . from age to age."[26] Without this history, Bacon proclaimed, "the history of the world seemeth to me to be as the statue of Polyphemus, with his eye out, the part being wanting which does the most show the spirit and life of the person." He urged the creation of a history of

> the Antiquities and Originalls of Knowledges and their Sects, their In-uentions, their Traditions, their diuerse Administrations and Managings, their Flourishings, their Oppositions, Decays, Depressions, Obliuions, Remoues, with the causes and occasions of them, and all other euents concerning learning, throughout the ages of the world.[27]

Bacon's ideal history would not only trace the development of the individual arts and sciences but also analyze the connections among them and identify the conditions that made them flourish or decay.

In *De augmentis scientiarum*, Bacon expanded on this program, laying out a whole palette of questions for the historian of the arts to raise—questions that began with the long-term influence of environment, passed to the shorter-term effects of different social forms, and only then dealt with the achievements of individuals:

> [The history] should include the nature of regions and peoples, their disposition, whether suited or unsuited to the various disciplines; the accidental qualities of the period which were harmful or favorable to the sciences; rivalries between and minglings of religions; the harmful and the favorable disposition of the laws; and finally the outstanding virtues and ability of certain individuals for promoting letters.[28]

All of these questions—as several scholars have shown in recent investigations—became canonical in the rich seventeenth- and eighteenth-century literature of the *Historia litteraria*, inspiring historians of philosophy like Thomas Stanley, historians of scholarship like Humphrey Hody, and historians of all branches of learning like Peter Lambeck and Daniel Georg Morhof.[29]

Bacon envisioned a cultural history of knowledge production that offered its readers not only the origins of a particular doctrine or craft, but the general conditions that made it possible to devise them. He portrayed this as an exacting and sophisticated discipline that could appeal to only a limited number of intellectual entrepreneurs like himself. The words with which he did this reveal, once more, that he had the model of ecclesiastical history on his mind:

> The use and end of which worke, I doe not so much designe for curiositie, or satisfaction of those that are the louers of learning, but chiefly for a more serious and grave purpose, which is this in fewe words, that it will make learned men wise in the vse and administration of learning. For it is not St. Augustines nor St. Ambrose workes that will make so wise a Diuine, as Ecclesiastical Historie thoroughly read and obserued; and the same reason is of Learning.[30]

Bacon's most detailed description of the form that the *historia litteraria* should take clearly alludes to *historia ecclesiastica* in the Magdeburg style—and, more particularly, to the form of chronological division by centuries that Flacius introduced into historiography:

> As to the method to be followed in constructing this history, let me say first of all that the materials for it should be drawn not only from historians and critics, but also that the chief books written in the period in question should be consulted, century by century or by shorter intervals, in order, starting at the earliest possible point. Not by reading through them, which would be an infinite task, but by tasting them, and observing their subjects, styles, and methods, we may call up the literary spirit of the period, as it were by an incantation, from the dead.[31]

In other words, Bacon proposed to organize the *historia litteraria* by chronological periods—perhaps by centuries. He took a multidisciplinary approach. And he set out to recreate the spirit of a culture at a given time.

In his ecclesiastical history, Flacius attacked exactly the sorts of historical questions that interested Bacon. Like Bacon, Flacius focused less on individual creative figures than on the general conditions within which they thought and worked. Like Bacon, Flacius envisioned a history that drew on a wide and varied range of evidence and canvassed a wide range of causal explanations. Like Bacon, Flacius believed that each period had a particular spirit or quality, a doctrinal character, which the historian must identify. And like Bacon, Flacius believed that a history of culture could achieve these goals only if its authors abandoned straightforward narrative for a topical, systematic organization. Odd though it may seem on the face of it, the erudite Flacius emerges on inspection as one of the influential ancestors from whom Bacon, that ardent defenestrator of traditional heroes, learned the most.

Flacius was certainly not Bacon's only source for the features of organization and argument common to their works. For example, a few years before Flacius began to work, Christopher Mylaeus argued for the creation of a collective, large-scale history of the arts—like the work of Flacius, organized topically and the product of collaboration.[32] The strange, rich tapestry of sixteenth-century scientific life contains some vignettes that offer striking parallels to Salomon's House: for example, the English research institute that, as William Sherman has shown, grew up around John Dee's famous library at Mortlake; the Danish observatories of Tycho Brahe, in which trained assistants, working with uniquely precise astronomical instruments, carried out a program of observation as systematic in character, and as carefully divided into parallel, systematic functions, as anything Bacon envisioned; and the alchemical laboratories that dotted the courts and cities of the Holy Roman Empire.[33] Such innovative specialized enterprises as Fuchs's *Herbal* and Reinhold's *Prutenic Tables* rested on collaborative, specialized labor of a strikingly Baconian kind. More recently, Deborah Harkness has demonstrated that London's communities of naturalists, alchemists, and medical men adumbrated many features of Bacon's ideal community—a fact that would have surprised no one more than Bacon himself.[34]

Of all these projects, however, the ones closest to Bacon himself in time and space, and which most closely resembled that of the *New Atlantis,* concerned themselves, like Flacius's *institutum,* with the study of the past, not of nature. Sir Robert Cotton's library, for example, amounted to a collaborative institute for the study of English antiquities and related subjects.[35] The Bodleian Library in Oxford approached Bacon's ideal even more closely. Founded at the end of the sixteenth century by Sir Thomas Bodley, with whom Bacon corresponded, it provided a handsome, purpose-built public space where scholars from Oxford and elsewhere could pursue their research. Like Salomon's House, the Bodleian was a very formal institution, ruled by precise statute, visits to which became formal and ceremonious in the extreme. Like the component parts of Salomon's House, the Bodleian formed only part of a massive complex dedicated to many kinds of learning, including the mathematical sort pursued by the Savilian Professor.[36]

Like Salomon's House, as we have seen, the Bodleian harbored in its early years a massive collaborative research enterprise—a project headed by Bodley's first librarian, Thomas James. He planned to collate manuscripts and editions of the works of the church fathers. By doing so, James hoped to prove that Catholic scholars based in Rome had falsified the texts that circulated in print. Bodley, who initially offered to support James's scheme, always held critical reservations on certain details and soon lost enthusiasm.[37] In 1610 the Archbishop of Canterbury chose twenty scholars to work in the Bodleian under James's direction, but they stopped after two years "for want of paiment."[38] Nonetheless, James managed to publish some of their results. And the enterprise provided another formidable example, this time local, of the systematic, hierarchical organization of inquiry—one connected to Flacius's in spirit and goals, about which Bacon must have known a good deal.[39] Church history was a collaborative discipline in antiquity, when Eusebius relied on assistants to collect and excerpt the sources he used.[40] It became so again—on an enormous scale—in the seventeenth century, when Oratorians, Benedictines, and Jesuits turned their orders into enormous institutes for the editing and study of documents for church history, and Protestant scholars rallied their students and assistants to produce massive replies. Historians have sometimes described these collaborative, document-based, research-driven historical enterprises as a new feature of the seventeenth-century intellectual landscape: a parallel, in the realm of human antiquities, to the new collaborative study of natural antiquities. They are certainly right to stress the new features of method—for example, the new emphasis on exact reporting about apparently insignificant objects—that connected Mabillon and Montfaucon to the experimentalists of the same period. But a natural enthusiasm for the scholarly society of Saint-Germain des Pres, like a natural enthusiasm for the scientific society of London, should not blind the modern historian to the continued existence, in both milieus, of practices created in the late Renaissance world of international humanism. Bacon's case suggests not only that the Lord Chancellor learned much from the earlier entrepreneur of Wissenschaft in Magdeburg but also that the intellectual traffic between modern historians of science and of ecclesiastical learning should not all move in one direction.

6

Chronology, Controversy, and Community in the Republic of Letters

The Case of Kepler

Kepler liked chronology, the dismal discipline that reconstructs calendars and establishes historical dates, and he studied it intensively throughout his life. During his student years at Tübingen, Michael Mästlin introduced him to the *De emendatione temporum* of Joseph Scaliger, the core chronological treatise of the late sixteenth century.[1] After Kepler left the university, he touched on chronological topics in two of his early works, the *Mysterium cosmographicum* and the *De stella nova*. He corresponded at length on chronological problems with Mästlin; with his patron, Herwart von Hohenburg; with the Calvinist master of the field, Scaliger, who apparently did not answer him; with the Jesuit revisionist Johannes Decker, who did; and with many others. From 1606 to 1620 he dedicated a series of publications to the subject, and he continued to take extensive notes on new publications like Jacobus Salianus's formidable *Annales ecclesiastici veteris testamenti*, a day-by-day history of the world that began to appear in 1619.

Yet Kepler's enthusiasm for the study of eras and calendars has rubbed off on few of his modern students. Christian Frisch devoted volume 4, part 1 of his edition of Kepler's *Opera omnia* to the astronomer's chronological studies.[2] Franz Hammer equipped volume 5 of Kepler's *Gesammelte Werke* with a detailed and penetrating commentary and useful, informative notes.[3] In 1944 the Reverend M. W. Burke-Gaffney, S.J. (1896–1979), a sound Latinist and "the well-loved astronomer" of St. Mary's University, Halifax, Nova Scotia, published an accurate and perceptive study of *Kepler and the Jesuits*. This deals at length and precisely with Kepler's encounter with Decker and his work on the chronology of the life of Jesus.[4] Yet these modest references exhaust the literature, older and younger, on Kepler's pursuit of his second-favorite subject. Keplerian scholarship has burgeoned in recent decades. The editors of the Munich edition of Kepler's works have continued to provide new source material. Judith Field, Bruce Stephenson, and James Voelkel have shed new light on the development of Kepler's cosmology.[5] Nick Jardine, Fernand Hallyn, Adam Mosley and others have taught us that, at many points in his career, Kepler worked within the traditions of humanism, usually in highly original ways.[6] But no one has done much to elucidate his chronology—even though the subject fascinated a multitude of humanistically schooled historians, cartographers, and natural philosophers in the late Renaissance and after, from Bodin and Mercator to Newton and Vico.

This is understandable; nowadays, chronology seems a difficult and intractable field of scholarship. The chronologer wields a wide range of tools, from the computation of eclipses to the analysis of texts, in order to establish the main epochs and reconstruct the varied calendar systems used in ancient and medieval, Eastern and Western history. In the end, however, this demanding, interdisciplinary form of inquiry produces what looks to most modern eyes like a dry and reductionist form of historical narrative. By a kind of reverse alchemy, the chronologer transmutes the golden histories of the Books of Kings, charged with memorable characters, into leaden lists of names and regnal years, and reduces the glorious prophecies of Isaiah and Jeremiah into a set of mind-bendingly technical problems about the dates on which Solomon built his temple, Nebuchadnezzar reduced it to rubble, and the Jews went into exile. Like the cliometrical histories of the 1970s, chronologies emit that distinctive cloud of pathos that smothers all great efforts to reduce the inevitable messiness of historical life to quantifiable data arranged in neat patterns, once the enthusiasm and grant support that brought them into being have dissipated.[7]

Chronologies, moreover, are long, and life is short. In February 1632 the medical man Isaak Habrecht wrote enthusiastically to the Tübingen Orientalist Wilhelm Schickard about Denys Petau's *De doctrina temporum*, which had come out in 1627. Full of admiration, Habrecht confessed that he thought Petau had solved all the major problems of the field. Habrecht confessed that he had kept the only copy of the book in Strasbourg in his house for almost a year, "for I never have my fill of reading it"—though he also admitted that he rapidly became exhausted studying a field so far outside his own, and did not fully trust his own judgment.[8] Almost a year later, in January 1633, he wrote again: "You didn't answer my discussion of Petavius.

I suspect this is because of the great size of the work. A year would hardly be enough for a man who is engaged in other tasks to read a book like this."[9] Apparently, even some of the polymaths of those polymathic decades around 1600 found chronology scarily complex and technical. When Kepler set out to publicize the chronological findings of a young Catholic scholar, he noted that he felt it was necessary to do so partly because "the title of this new author's book mentions chronology, a subject whose methods are cultivated by relatively few."[10]

Yet complexities never frightened Kepler, and the particular ones of chronology never lost their charm for him. Unlike Schickard, he read and took detailed notes on Petau's *De doctrina temporum,* and entered with pleasure into every debate on which this feisty Jesuit chronologer took a position.[11] One of the most striking pieces of evidence that Kepler was interested in time and history is the frontispiece of his *Rudolphine Tables.* This came out in 1627, the same year as Petau's book. Its opening illustration shows a magnificent, eclectic gazebo, populated by ancient and modern astronomers. The increasingly sophisticated styles of the pillars by which the various astronomers stand tell a story about their subject. At the back, an ancient Chaldean sights through his fingers, standing by a crude column that is really just a tree, its limbs lopped. Ptolemy and Hipparchus wield tables next to simple pillars. But Copernicus and Tycho are arguing between two elegant classical columns—the paradoxical symbols of their modernity and sophistication. Astronomy, Kepler's image shows, was not revealed by God to the patriarchs, but created over time by human industry.[12]

So much is well known. It is less well known that the *Tables* contain Kepler's most sustained pieces of work in technical chronology: a list of eras, a short but pregnant analysis of several calendars, and instructions for converting dates from one system to another with worked examples. Kepler told his readers that he had written "a particular commentary" in which he "demonstrated everything in this section with historical sources and suitable arguments," and promised that he would share this with them "on another occasion, if I live so long. For it seemed to me that this chronological matter would burst the bounds of an astronomical work like this one."[13] In this case, as in others, Kepler's reach exceeded his grasp. In 1628 Kepler explained to Paul Guldin that he still planned to draw up a substantial commentary on the list of eras that he had set out in the *Rudolphine Tables.* "Before I publish it," he remarked, "I have to read all of Petau, for we strike the same chord remarkably often." Like Kepler, Petau sharply criticized the chronological work of Joseph Scaliger. "You'll be surprised," Kepler wrote, "how often both of us answer Scaliger in the same way—unless you consider that only one answer is possible." Yet Kepler—who noted in the *Rudolphine Tables* that he had often departed from Scaliger—also remarked that Petau "sometimes criticizes Scaliger too sharply."[14]

To the end of his life, then, Kepler remained an engaged reader of chronological treatises and a committed student of the field, one who was still working out his views on contested problems. It was always one of the studies that could make him burn late-night oil. "Sed finem facere necesse habeo [I have to stop]," he wrote to Mästlin in January 1599, at the end of a three-page letter on chronology. He went on, switching into German: "Es hatt schon 11. geschlagen [the clock has already struck 11], and soon the 12th of January will be dawning."[15] And he meant it—as one can see from the start of his letter: "I greatly enjoyed reading your chronological essay. It's clear that you have carefully studied many notable passages, and you have made me aware of much that I had not sufficiently attended to. But hear the reasons why I don't agree on all points"—after which he was off and running.[16] When circumstances made Kepler's life really difficult, he escaped his troubles by turning to chronology. In 1611 and 1612, as his first wife, Barbara, and his son, Friedrich, fell ill and died, Kepler felt unable to work on the *Rudolphine Tables*. He turned to compiling a book on chronology, the *Eclogae chronicae*, which appeared in 1615. In 1626, when the city of Linz came under siege, Kepler escaped the bangs and smells of a city at war by turning back to his favorite study. Contemplating the mysterious numbers of the Hebrew kings and revealing the errors of his colleagues apparently brought Kepler a measure of serenity that nothing else could: as he wrote to Guldin, "This bellicose style of writing has really wiped away much of the misery I suffered because of the difficulties of the siege and the hindrances to my work."[17]

At least once—in his notes on the world history by the Jesuit Jacobus Salianus—Kepler made clear something of the strikingly broad range of feelings and interests that chronological studies could awaken in him. Salianus began his vast work by quoting John 1:1, "In the beginning was the Word, and the Word was with God, and the Word was God." He explained, "Before the world was created, then," God had existed for "innumerable centuries and eternal years," enjoying his own wisdom, beauty, and goodness, and planning the world that he would make.[18] Kepler notes,

> Salianus delighted me especially when he explicated the Gospel of John at the start of his account of the creator of time and the world. For this led me to the thought that John the Evangelist, as he proved the eternity of the son of God and his divine origin, also gave us a commentary on the Mosaic history of creation and brought forth a sort of Cabala, pregnant with venerable mysteries from Jewish tradition and designed to overcome the stubbornness of that people.[19]

By contrast, Salianus's complex, difficult account of how the earth was without form and void inspired Kepler to reflect on William Gilbert and his magnetic cosmology: "Clearly when Gilbert shows that the Earth is formed throughout by a magnetic form, this form was not imposed upon it in its first origin from nothing. It was rightly declared to be without form, and if the earth lacked minerals, it also lacked its magnetic form—that is, its true form. It was only mud submerged in water."[20] As in so many cases of early modern reading, the themes and problems Kepler picked out could not have been predicted from the text he read. As in many other cases, too, the text both shaped and was shaped by Kepler's approach to it. Chronology, as the mature Kepler saw it, was a vast and profound undertaking. It involved everything from the history of the earth to the determination of hundreds of minute technical questions, and its study was at once a spiritual and an intellectual exercise. It is no wonder that he could turn to this encyclopedic, demanding discipline for consolation.

The inspiration to scale Mount Chronology had a number of components. Like many of his contemporaries, including his teacher, Michael Mästlin, Kepler came to the field in part from astrology.[21] As he explained at the outset of the *Mysterium cosmographicum,* Kepler taught his students in July 1595 about the great conjunctions of Jupiter and Saturn that take place roughly every twenty years. Astrologers and astrological historians had seen these for centuries as a kind of ground bass to history, and the influential astrologer Cyprian Leowitz had correlated them with historical events in 1572.[22] Through Kepler's lifetime and beyond, chronologers continued to overlay the events of world history onto lists of the conjunctions, and to use the latter to predict that the end of time would soon arrive.[23] The patterns that the movement of the conjunction formed in Kepler's diagram inspired him as well, but in a characteristically distinctive way. He began thinking about the distances and sizes of the planetary spheres, and eventually he argued that these were determined by the interposition of the Platonic solids—a nice example of the ease with which, as always, Kepler could slide from one favorite branch of natural philosophy to another.[24] Later in the same work, Kepler tried to make time as evidently neat and symmetrical as he had already made space.[25] He looked for a date for the Creation that would yield an appropriately elegant planetary conjunction—and found it on April 27, 3977 BCE.[26]

Ten years later, in the *De stella nova,* Kepler tabulated the points at which the great conjunctions moved from one triplicity (group of three zodiacal signs) to another, and noted their connections, loose but unmistakable, to great historical events. Already he insisted—as he argued in more detail later in life—that individual conjunctions did not bring about radical changes. These took time, and came about through a complex interplay of local, human action and overarching providential guidance, as Kepler showed in a brilliant digression on technology, travel, and printing to which Nick Jardine called attention long ago.[27]

In his prognostications, Kepler drew more standard, precise correlations between events in the heavens and those on earth. Following the lead of the man he called "Cardanus/unser Lehrmaister,"[28] the influential Italian astrologer Girolamo Cardano, he noted similarities between the solar eclipse of 38 BCE, which had foreshadowed many disasters as well as the eventual triumph of the young Augustus, and another eclipse that took place in 1600 and predicted similar catastrophes for Rudolf, to be followed by triumphs for Ferdinand.[29] Moreover, even as Kepler gradually abandoned this mechanistic form of prediction in his own practice of astronomy and astrology, he found himself condemned to continue pursuing it for historical events. His friend and patron Herwart decided that he needed to know the exact nature and date of the threatening astrological configuration that, according to the Roman poet Lucan, had inspired the sage Nigidius Figulus to foresee the civil wars and the end of the Republic. As he often did, he asked Kepler to work out the details and to determine how they fit.

Kepler did the computing—so precisely and cleverly, as Patrick Boner has shown, that he won Herwart's lifelong interest and support. But he made his feelings clear when Mästlin passed on to him a second request from another friend, the Tübingen Greek professor Martin Crusius. Crusius had decided that the battles and love affairs of the gods in Homer represented oppositions and conjunctions of the planets. The hopeful philologist thought that if Mästlin or Kepler would compute these astrological configurations, it would be possible to fix the dates of the Trojan War. Kepler turned away this query with an adroit display of academic lifemanship. He suggested that if Mästlin could find the time to do the computations, he, Kepler, would happily provide an astrological analysis of the results—something he knew that his teacher would never do. After all, he explained, he already had to cope with the many requests with which Herwart was "tormenting" him.[30]

But Kepler's chief inspiration came from the field of chronology itself, which had taken shape in the last decades of the sixteenth century. From the 1530s to 1583, when Scaliger published his *De emendatione temporum,* a series of humanists and astronomers had established the basic rules of the chronological game. At its core—when it dealt with events in the first millennium BCE and later—chronology depended on combining astronomy with philology. Anyone who had mastered Ptolemaic planetary theory could compute the dates and, where necessary, establish the visibility of new and full moons, solar and lunar eclipses, and planetary conjunctions. All of these were reckoned in Egyptian years of 365 days—as astronomers had reckoned since antiquity—from the accession of Nabonassar to the throne of Babylon on February 26, 747 BCE. And any scholar who could connect such precisely computed celestial events with terrestrial ones could erect a framework of absolute, rather than relative, dates for such great historical landmarks as the Peloponnesian War (fixed by three lunar eclipses) and Alexander's defeat of Darius (fixed by a fourth). Ideally—so Scaliger argued—it would even be possible to connect these data with those of the ancient historians from Herodotus onward and with the Bible, and thus to create a single chronological system that linked and ordered all great events.

From the start, Kepler became and remained a true believer of these central points, an enthusiastic practitioner of technical chronology, as Scaliger had shaped it. When the Jesuit Decker, whose learning and perspicacity Kepler respected, tried to show that one could not correlate the regnal dates of the Roman emperors mentioned by Ptolemy, Trajan, and Hadrian, with their dates in the era of Nabonassar, Kepler gave him an uncharacteristically dusty answer: "Astronomy makes one thing certain: the years of the Roman emperors for which Ptolemy mentions certain celestial phenomena, connected to fixed times, can only have those years of Nabonassar that Ptolemy assigned them." Not everyone who shared Kepler's general approach believed in it so strongly.

Mästlin's chronology rested squarely, as he emphasized, on the astronomical evidence provided by Ptolemy, above all his eclipses dated from era Nabonassar.[31] But in 1612, Herwart produced a chronological treatise that rearranged all the central dates of world history. He did so, as a further, posthumous work later demonstrated, in order to show that from the time of King Solomon onward, all of ancient civilization had centered on the use of the compass to direct voyages to the New World (all ancient references to horses and other movers of people really referred to ships; all references to arrows and other pointy objects to magnetic compasses).[32] Herwart's chronology horrified Mästlin—who, like Kepler, had helped the learned chancellor by computing the dates and visibility of eclipses. But it also impressed him, even though Herwart's work contradicted his fundamental principles. "Er hatt mich recht irr gemacht," he wrote to Kepler. "If he is right, then a great deal of my Chronology must collapse."[33] He found himself paralyzed, unable either to refute or to accept the new theories. Kepler, by contrast, simply persisted in using the now traditional epoch dates that he had learned from Scaliger long before, and effectively dismissed Herwart's work.

To be sure, Kepler sharply criticized Scaliger on many technical questions. The *De emendatione temporum* actually begins not with a discussion of dates or eras but with a reconstruction of the ancient Attic calendar. With characteristic perversity, Scaliger decided, in the teeth of the sources, that the Attic year had not been lunar. His arguments—which are certainly wrong—are also couched in a hermetic form that makes the book inaccessible. Scaliger himself remarked that he had composed it as an intelligence test for his contemporaries, who had duly failed. In a long letter to Scaliger, Kepler described how hard he had struggled with this off-putting opening:

> I confess, that although there is no page which I have not skimmed, for the last ten years I have not been able to make myself read it in a systematic and precise way from beginning to end, collating the introductory material with what comes last. Perhaps this should have kept me

silent. But the method with which your book begins, and which builds a good bit of the later books on the first one, made me set this point aside. So long as I remain stuck at the beginning—and I am very stuck—my progress to the rest will remain blocked and sleepy.[34]

Prudently, Kepler excised these potentially irritating remarks from the letter he finally sent Scaliger. But he did tell the grand old man in Leiden that "all of the authorities that you cite in both editions of your book [1583/1593 and 1598] make one thing clear: the Attic year, which you reconstructed in your first book, was very different from your opinion of it."[35] Using the texts Scaliger had collected, Kepler proceeded to argue (correctly) that the Attic year was lunar. In later chronological debates, much of his attention went, as it did here, to the reconstruction of calendars—Jewish, Greek, and Roman—and his conclusions often differed starkly from Scaliger's. Yet here, too, he carried on Scaliger's enterprise, using the same textual resources to different ends.

The third major sector of Kepler's chronological interests had the least to do with his technical skills as an astronomer. Chronology, as practiced by everyone from Scaliger to Petavius, claimed completeness. The chronologer's default product was a single massive treatise that started with the Creation and devoted substantial attention to the earliest history of the human race. But ancient historians offered little precise information about the period before the twelfth century BCE, the traditional date for the fall of Troy. And the astronomical observations known to Europeans before the mid-seventeenth century began even later, with the Babylonian records preserved by Ptolemy, which dated back only to the eighth century BCE. Accordingly, chronologers had to rely heavily on the Bible, along with a few fragmentary and controversial texts on the ancient Near East. An assiduous and determined student of biblical chronology, Kepler devoted endless time and pains to sorting out problems such as the regnal years of the kings of Israel and Judah (a problem that, as a fellow chronologer, Seth Calvisius, remarked, no one of sound mind could hope to solve definitively). It is well known that Kepler and Mästlin discussed in detail the intricacies of planetary theory and the casting of Kepler's polyhedral model of the universe. It is less well known that they also discussed with precision and pertinacity the intervals between, for example, the Exodus from Egypt and the dedication of Solomon's Temple. This was only one of several problems they addressed for which astronomy afforded no help whatsoever. The two astronomers counted the years listed in various verses of the Bible, noted contradictions, and correlated the biblical narrative where possible with Herodotus or other pagan authors. In the end, one could support any given set of biblical numbers only by discounting another set. But this argument, whenever Kepler or Mästlin made it, inevitably prompted the other to warn, finger wagging almost visibly, against questioning the authority of the biblical text. As Mästlin put it in one contentious case, "it is hard to accuse Holy Scripture of error."[36] Here—as in his efforts to use Herodotus and other Greek historians to elucidate later sections of the biblical text—Kepler followed the road that Scaliger had laid down even when it took him straight out of the mathematical and quantitative domains that he normally preferred.

So far, Kepler looks like a fairly typical chronologer of the generations after Scaliger's—which grew up to inherit an interdisciplinary method that had already yielded powerful results. Seth Calvisius, the Thomaskantor (director of the choir school) at Leipzig, was born in 1556, Kepler in 1571.[37] Like Kepler, Calvisius learned his chronology from Scaliger's book. As he explained to a friend, he had become interested in chronology because he taught history, as well as music, at another great school, Schulpforta, and he had read widely in the field. But Calvisius had not been able to work out a full chronology until he bought and read Scaliger, from which time he devoted the rest of his life to producing and revising a more accessible introduction to Scaliger's work than the great man himself had composed. Calvisius's *Opus chronologicum* (1605), a work of great depth and clarity, was distinguished especially by its simple, lucid eclipse tables and the precise eclipse dates that formed its spine. But Calvisius also resolutely engaged with all the details of biblical narrative.[38] Kepler and Calvisius disagreed on many technical points. But they both believed absolutely in the solidity of era Nabonassar, the precision with which they could date eclipses, and the necessity of studying the Bible in the light of pagan sources. As one might expect, they had good fun swapping gossip about the technical incompetence of their critics.

One great difference remains. While Calvisius produced a comprehensive treatise, which went through a number of editions after it first appeared in 1605, Kepler never completed either what he called the "great Chronology of the Old Testament," for which he took extensive notes, or the promised full commentary on his list of eras.[39] Most of Kepler's work in the field ended up going into his extensive letters or into short, occasional publications. The most substantial of the latter, the *Eclogae chronicae* of 1615, was not a formal treatise, but an epistolary analysis of central questions in the life of Jesus and the history of the Jews in the century that stretched from the reign of Herod the Great to the Jewish War. Kepler battled through intricately technical data about the contested chronological ground in which the Jewish state came to an end and Christianity came into being. The book moves point by point, with many reverses of direction, as Kepler argues about tricky details with his Protestant critic and correspondent Calvisius, his Catholic friend and correspondent Decker, and a few others. Their letters, fragmented into excerpts and then put into new order as a complicated mosaic by Kepler, amount to one long and inconclusive conversation—less a coherent debate than a buzz of voices on an old-fashioned party line.[40]

At first I regretted the absence of a *Chronologia nova* or a *Great Chronology of the Old Testament*—especially as it made the task of expounding Kepler's technical views on any particular subject diabolically complex. But gradually it has become clear to me that Kepler saw chronology, as he and his contemporaries saw some other subjects, as particularly appropriate for treatment in letters—especially letters that exemplified William Blake's principle, "Opposition is true friendship." Kepler described chronology as a field that profited particularly from the open exchange of opinions and criticism, and his own practice as a chronologer exemplified this view at every point. In fact, Kepler's chronological work represented an effort not only to establish the truth about the past but also to set out, systematically, the proper conditions for doing so—conditions that, as Kepler formulated them, had to do with the canons of discussion, often among scholars who belonged to opposing ideological camps.

Kepler's chief public intervention in chronology began in 1605 and 1606. He hoped to work out the significance of the new star of 1604—in modern terms, the supernova in the foot of the constellation Ophiuchus, the serpent holder. The star's appearance followed a great conjunction of Jupiter and Saturn in 1603, in Sagittarius, one of the three signs of the Fiery Trigon (with Aries and Leo). This conjunction marked the beginning of the Trigon, a period of some 200 years during which all of the great conjunctions would take place in the same three signs. Kepler wondered if he could connect this new star in the heavens to another star that had appeared in the skies long before—the star of the Magi, which had led the wise men of the East to Bethlehem, and which had also accompanied the passage of the conjunctions from one trigon into another. The problem, as he explained, was simple: the conjunction that preceded the star of the Magi had taken place around 7 BCE—long before the standard date of the Incarnation and even of most efforts to revise it. If, he speculated, "it were established that Jesus Christ was born 4 or 5 years before the beginning of our era, which we wrongly date from the Incarnation, the new star I was discussing would have something in common with that of the Magi: each would coincide with a great conjunction of the superior planets, of the sort that takes place at the start of a new 800-year period, with the Fiery Trigon."[41]

Just at this point, the exact information that Kepler needed materialized in print.[42] In Graz, he came upon a set of printed theses that a Polish student named Laurentius Suslyga had defended at the local university, under the presidence of the Jesuit Decker.[43] Kepler did not approve of everything Suslyga had to say. When he came across a demeaning remark about the inutility of astronomy for the chronologer, he became so furious that he threw down the book and his pen and left his desk in a rage. But he admired the book's great learning—"What Hercules," he asked, "could oppose that prodigious heap of reading, from all of antiquity, which I embrace and which I would like both to be and to be considered the jewel of my library?"[44] Most important, he found Suslyga's thesis that Christ was born in 4 BCE very attractive. Suslyga laid out precise historical arguments, which Kepler admired. For example: Herod's son, Philip the Tetrarch, renamed the town of Bethsaida Bethsaida-Julias in honor of Augustus's daughter, Julia. But in 2 BCE Augustus exiled her from Rome for adultery. So Philip must have renamed the town before 2 BCE—and Herod must have died before Philip became Tetrarch. Yet Herod's death must have come after the birth of Jesus, since he massacred the Holy Innocents in a vain attempt to kill the King of the Jews prophesied by the Magi.[45] Hence Jesus must have been born several years before the conventional date. Inspired by precise, meticulous arguments like this, Kepler set out, as he explained to his readers, to publicize Suslyga's excellent dissertation, which might otherwise have remained in oblivion. Many readers, after all, were likely to be prejudiced against the author, and novel ideas always found support hard to win.

At the same time, though, Kepler attempted to improve on Suslyga's arguments, taking into account the astronomical data that the young man had neglected, and using them to push the birth of Christ still farther back in time. For instance, since the Jewish historian Josephus had noted that an eclipse of the moon had preceded Herod's death, Kepler computed the date of this eclipse, a partial one visible in Jerusalem, as 12/13 March 4 BCE. This astronomical datum, in turn, enabled Kepler to fix the death of Herod, which Josephus had connected with the spring festival of Passover, to that of 4 BCE, a month or so after the eclipse. The unblinking stars in their courses testified that Jesus must have been born in 6 BCE or even earlier. This neat solution was emblematic of Kepler's model of chronology: relying both on historical sources and on astronomical data, he insisted that the astronomical data could not be questioned. They were, so to speak, the period counterpart of DNA evidence today—the product of cutting-edge scientific inquiry and theoretically beyond question. When Herwart insisted that he had found evidence of error and corruption in Ptolemy's observations, Kepler replied to his friend and patron with unusual sharpness: "In my view, astronomers have more certain marks for dates in the uniform motion of the stars (unless you deny this) than historians do in their lists of consuls . . . For emperors are not the measure of the celestial motions, but the celestial motions of the emperors."[46] But unlike Herwart, he also insisted that one could not discount or dismiss the testimony of contemporary historians like Josephus. His historical acumen was so striking as to win the praise of Isaac Casaubon, even though Kepler corrected Casaubon's friend and ally Scaliger.[47]

Contemporaries found it remarkable that Kepler—the Lutheran imperial mathematician—decided to publicize and to build on a chronological pamphlet by any Catholic, much less a student of the Jesuits. They found it all the more remarkable when he continued to publicize the book even after he learned that its true author—following a practice common in the universities of the empire—had not been the innocent young student who had defended its theses, but the *praeses*, the Jesuit professor who had presided over the defense.

In other words, Kepler took the side of a Jesuit against the Calvinist hero Scaliger, who had set the Incarnation at 2 BCE, as well as Scaliger's sidekick Calvisius. And the Jesuits—as everyone in Europe knew—had made it one of their central aims to discredit Scaliger as a man and as a scholar. To achieve the former end, they helped Caspar Schoppe print the doctoral diploma proving that Scaliger's father had not really belonged to the princely della Scala family of Verona. To achieve the latter, they set up chronology workshops in Mainz, Munich, and elsewhere, where they reedited the Greek texts that Scaliger had used and excerpted in his books and attacked the details of his interpretations of the sources. This polemical edge in their collective response to Scaliger led the great nineteenth-century scholar Mark Pattison—who took Scaliger's partisan point of view—to characterize "Jesuit learning," influentially, as "a sham learning got up with great ingenuity in imitation of the genuine, in the service of the church."[48]

Kepler certainly found Decker's Latin text typically jesuitical—that is to say, mannerist—in its form: "the style is childishly elaborate, and he revels in allegories which seemingly should be postponed, since the points at issue are not proven."[49] Yet he not only took Decker's scholarship very seriously but also seemingly entered the ring on the Jesuits' side. Naturally, the Jesuits and their allies did their best to use Kepler in their campaign against the coryphaeus of Protestant erudition. Nicolaus Serarius, a Jesuit Hebraist in Mainz, had sharply disagreed with Scaliger about the early Jewish sects. He included a reference to Kepler's work in a subsequent polemical work, and he tried to persuade Kepler to let him publish his critical letter about Scaliger's reconstruction of the Attic calendar, which he had learned about from Herwart. The letter, after all, had never received an answer. Johannes Pistorius, a converted Protestant who served as the emperor's father confessor, went further, asking Kepler directly if he planned to convert.

These efforts at exploitation angered Kepler. He refused to let Serarius print his critique of Scaliger—which, as he explained, had been couched as a private letter, not a public document. And he told Pistorius that he had no intention of abandoning the great Reformation movement, which had freed the human intellect from subjection ("I wish you would cut out the theology," the Catholic replied. "Clearly you have absolutely no understanding of it.").[50] Kepler added even more marginal glosses praising Scaliger's fundamental work to the little treatise in which he argued for an earlier date for the Incarnation, and wrote again to Scaliger to assure him of his esteem and to reiterate, as he did in public, how much all serious students of chronology owed Scaliger.

Two points are central here. The first is that many of Kepler's readers found it genuinely shocking to suggest that Jesus was born at any date other than December 25, 1 BCE. The issue of the date of the Incarnation was typical of those that caused debate among chronologers: technical in its character but far more than technical in its implications. In their hermeneutics and homiletics, both Protestants and Jesuits in these years tended more and more to present the Bible as infallible—against the tradition of the medieval church. Pistorius, for example, tried to make himself believe Kepler and Decker—but then renounced their novel teaching when he decided he could not accommodate it with the Gospels: "To hell with Josephus [*pereat Josephus*]," he explained: "let us preserve the historical and divine truth of Scripture."[51] Dates mattered too. The Jesuits who studied chronology also, in their function as priests, taught children to act out pageants about the Holy Innocents—but only on the proper day.[52] The fabrics of sacred text and sacred time mattered—and the Protestant and the Jesuit were conspiring to tear them.

The second point worth noting is that in choosing Decker as an interlocutor, Kepler had hit upon a Catholic who shared his commitment to discussion across denominational borders. This too is remarkable. Decker, a highly cultured Jesuit trained in Antwerp, lived with Martin Del Rio, a Jesuit expert on witchcraft and a bitter enemy of Protestants in general and Scaliger in particular. Long before he came to Graz, Justus Lipsius—a brilliant historian and connoisseur of academic gossip, who was always happy to stab an old friend in the back—spread the news that Decker "is reciting against Scaliger in his public lectures and refuting his theses."[53] In fact, however, Decker resembled Kepler.[54] When Decker realized that Jesus must have been born much earlier than either Catholic or Protestant authorities believed, he communicated his results to both. Through the Augsburg scholar Markus Welser, he passed his arguments on to Scaliger; through the chain of command in his order, he sent them up to Cesare Baronio, cardinal, Vatican librarian, and author of the standard Catholic work on the history and chronology of the early church, the *Annales ecclesiastici*. Decker suffered the usual fate of an upright man in a time of ideological war. The extremes met: Scaliger denounced Decker and his ideas in two furious letters to Welser.[55] Baronio denounced Decker in a special appendix to volume 10 of the *Annales*. Worse, he went directly to the general of the Jesuit order, Claudio Acquaviva, and persuaded him to refuse Decker permission to publish his great work on chronology.[56] Apparently, not all Jesuits received Acquaviva's memo. Antonio Possevino, the great Jesuit bibliographer, continued to refer expectantly to the promising work of Decker. But in the end, Decker's supporters could not help him, and the book remained in manuscript, as it still does.

The relationship between this open-minded, tolerant Jesuit and Kepler was what Goethe would call a *Wahlverwandschaft* (an elective affinity). As their correspondence continued, moreover, and the areas of disagreement between them became apparent, each of them began to comment on the nature of their exchanges—and of fair exchange in general. Decker repeatedly insisted that just as it took the clash of flint and steel to produce sparks, so it took that of minds to produce new knowledge: "Against my will I must stop writing, so I break off our sweet conversation and come to a close. But let us not stop knocking, questioning, and praying." But he still tried to persuade Kepler of his own, slightly later date for the birth of Jesus, in very revealing terms: "Although it has always been permissible to have varied views in this area and keep one's friendship intact, nevertheless I can scarcely bear the fact that while we agree wonderfully on the dates of the Lord's baptism and passion, we have to divorce when it comes to the year of his birth."[57] Kepler's reply reveals that he too prized what Decker called their "dulce colloquium" (pleasant exchange): "Most learned of men, you have outdone me in humanity and generosity, and I cannot rival you in these virtues, save in the knowledge that I cannot win."

Both men distinguished carefully between what they could write to one another in private and what they thought it correct to publish. In 1607 Decker asked Kepler to return a polemical text "because I consider it better to play in this chronological field without causing anyone pain or bitterness."[58] Kepler not only obliged him, but when he printed their correspondence in the *Eclogae* in 1614, he omitted the relevant passage from Decker's letter, as well as the potentially hurtful material. Yet Kepler found himself repeatedly forced to remind the open-minded Decker that he was not being fair. In a passage he omitted from their printed correspondence, he urged:

> I beg you, your reverence, let me make one candid remark from the heart. Scaliger set out all the foundations for your argument, very prettily, and in a clearer and more elegant style than he usually managed elsewhere . . . Perhaps he is a heretic, an innovator, a defamer of the Fathers of the Church; perhaps he lied about his ancestors. What does any of that have to with the present question? Why can't it be handled without slandering him? . . . I don't object to your refuting the points with which you don't agree. I do the same. But when you mention that your

enemy has done something well, you make your own argument more credible.[59]

Kepler urged Decker to quote Scaliger's words in full, rather than summarizing them, before he subjected them to criticism. In another similar letter, Kepler actually brought himself up short, explaining that he had moved from the subject of chronology to that of ethics without noticing it, and needed to go back to his real theme.

Kepler exchanged letters about chronology with something like thirty separate interlocutors: some to the north in Görlitz, Bautzen, and Danzig; many in the intellectual centers of Lutheran Germany, Leipzig, and his own university of Tübingen; and some far to the west in Mainz and even in Alsace—most of them Lutheran or Reformed, but several Catholics as well. In many of these exchanges, though not all, he took great pains to ensure—as he did with Decker—that both parties explicitly agreed on the conditions of discussion and would take care not to injure one another, either in the course of the correspondence or through later publications.

At times, Kepler and his fellow chronologers oddly resemble Henry James's ideal author, "on whom," as James wrote in *The Art of Fiction*, "nothing is lost." Their extraordinarily powerful literary antennae picked up every reference that could possibly be taken as a slight and every argument that could possibly be rebutted on technical, rhetorical grounds, as out of place or unfair. This sensitivity was not abnormal. Kepler's Tübingen Greek teacher Martin Crusius, for example, became very excited when a friend notified him in 1598 that Scaliger had cited and praised him.[60] He immediately wrote to a well-informed friend, the Hellenist David Hoeschel in Augsburg, who had heard the same news but could not provide transcripts of the actual references since he did not yet have a copy of the book in question, the Leiden 1598 edition of Scaliger's *De emendatione temporum*.[61]

The Leipzig chronologer Calvisius also took a serious interest in the conditions of intellectual debate. Like Kepler, Calvisius spun a rich web of correspondence on chronological issues that reached from Leiden and Harderwijk in the Netherlands to Kepler's Prague. Like Kepler, too, Calvisius was sensitive to the value of free and open exchange of opinions. When he criticized Kepler's views on the Incarnation, life, and death of Jesus, he began by saying that he approached the astronomer "in a friendly spirit and with affection, and in the desire to learn the truth. If I go wrong, please teach me. If I speak too freely, please forgive me. And I am sure that you, in your humanity, will do this." And like Kepler, Calvisius drew careful distinctions between what others wrote in private letters and in the public prints. In 1600, the Jena history professor Elias Reusner published a chronology in which he remarked that Scaliger had thought the world began in 4712 BCE, a very odd date supported by neither the Hebrew nor the Greek text of the Old Testament. He also reiterated the old theories, refuted by Scaliger, that Nabonassar, the Babylonian king from whom ancient astronomers dated celestial events, was actually Salmanassar, king of Assyria, and that Nabopollassar, another Babylonian king mentioned by Ptolemy, was Nabuchodonosor, the conqueror of Jerusalem.[62] Calvisius corrected these mistakes privately. In a crisp letter, he explained to Reusner that the date in question—actually 4713 BCE—marked the beginning of Scaliger's artificial Julian Period, not of the Creation.[63] It was not a Creation date at all, but the start date for an arbitrary system that Scaliger had devised to give chronologers a framework for debate. He also set Reusner right on the kings of Babylon and Assyria, and pointed out that the fragments of the ancient historians Berosus and Megasthenes that Scaliger used were not the same as those forged in 1498 by Giovanni Nanni, which Reusner cited. Scaliger's fragments were genuine, Nanni's fake.[64]

Unlike Kepler, however, Calvisius suffered from a certain prestige deficit. As Thomaskantor in Leipzig, he held a job that the town council considered very important and whose incumbents—one of whom, more than a century later, was Bach—it paid well. But he worked in a school, not a university. Reusner, by contrast, was a university teacher. He replied to Calvisius in a letter whose snarkiness was clear before its recipient even began to read it. Calvisius's admirers addressed their letters "to Seth Calvisius, that man of extraordinary penetration, that most perceptive chronologer, that most excellent historian."[65] Reusner, by contrast, addressed his letter to "Seth Calvisius, the musician, my honorable friend." Haughtily, he explained that he had been so busy compiling his *Stratematographia,* a collection of examples of the art of warfare aimed at pupils of high birth, that he had thought of not replying at all, "especially since I was not certain if your letter was written in a friendly spirit."[66] He then proceeded to defend every one of his mistakes, showing that he had not understood a word of Calvisius's critique.

Yet Calvisius held his peace in public for ten years, until Reusner reprinted his book, its errors uncorrected, and added a new critique of Scaliger and Calvisius. Then and only then did Calvisius reply in a pamphlet, a printed open letter—and even there he noted that he had done so only under extreme provocation (from Reusner and from readers eager to have his opinion). Presumably Reusner, in his turn, thought that Calvisius should have played by other rules. In 1606 he published a Latin adaptation of Stefano Guazzo's work *On Civil Conversation,* in which he made it clear that "we should correct a friend in such a way that he likes the very correction, and it puts him even more in our debt."[67] In his view, Calvisius had broken the rules of civil conversation in chronology, and Reusner could punish him in public with a clear conscience. Calvisius, for his part, felt justified, for the same reasons, in flogging Reusner on the pillory of print, since Reusner had attacked him even though the two had established a private dialogue and Calvisius had never injured him.[68] Clearly the possession of criteria of civility, however precisely stated, was not enough.

For Kepler and many of his contemporaries, then, chronology was not a set discipline that they could take over from Scaliger and its other creators. Rather, it was a form of inquiry that they needed not only to master but also to free from its overly sectarian, polemical cast. It required not only mastery of both astronomy and philology but also adherence to a complex code of ethics—a deontology of scholarship. This standard was hard to meet— Calvisius thought that even Kepler sometimes failed to do so. First, it called for superhuman patience, not only in the solving of problems but also in the posing of questions, and even in the offering of compliments. Second, the very scholars who demanded that their colleagues reach these high standards of philological correctness were actually constructing them as they worked. As the great historians and Roman lawyers of these years, like Jacques-Auguste de Thou and Hugo Grotius, tried to find compromises in the big world of politics, the chronologers tried to do the same in the little world of scholarship and science. Over the last two decades, we have learned a great deal about the way that ancient rhetorical and traditional social canons about the trustworthiness of witnesses shaped the nature of scientific argument in early modern Europe.[69] In the case of chronology, the story looks somewhat different. The actors had to create new canons of civility even as they tested and relaid the technical foundations of their discipline. Kepler's epistolary form of chronological scholarship gives us a privileged access to this process—and to the many bumps and explosions that necessarily took place.[70]

Recent scholarship has taught us that specialists of many kinds created their own Republics of Letters, or their own specialized provinces of the larger one, in the late sixteenth and seventeenth centuries. Numismatists and epigraphers, as Peter Miller and William Stenhouse have shown, shared coins and inscriptions, building great collections on paper and in museums that represented essentially collaborative enterprises.[71] Paula Findlen and Brian Ogilvie have shown that botanists did the same with ancient texts and modern specimens.[72] Nick Jardine and Adam Mosley have taught us that astronomers turned the letter into a primary form of data publication and much more.[73] Arnoud Visser, Nancy Siraisi, and Gianna Pomata have demonstrated that medicine had its Republic of Letters—and so did alchemy, as Vera Keller argues in her dissertation.[74] In the same way, Kepler and other chronologers tried to construct a chronological Republic of Letters—a virtual realm where Calvinists, Lutherans, and Catholics could discuss the dates of Jesus's life in a calm and constructive way. To some extent, they managed it. Kepler's ability to build upon the work of Decker is a splendid case in point of the value of that distributed, collective intelligence that, these days, we all like to ascribe to networks. It also exemplifies the ways in which a shared humanistic training enabled many scholars—who belonged to the three competing confessions recognized in the Holy Roman Empire—to find intellectual common ground (a phenomenon on which Aviva Rothman's dissertation, which reconstructs the roles of learned friendship in Kepler's career, will shed light).[75]

However, in the Republic of Letters (as in the World Wide Web), level networks coexisted and collided with hierarchies of individuals, of loyalties, and of position.[76] If Kepler himself, a privileged Lutheran astronomer at the greatest of Catholic courts, could sometimes escape these structures and the pressures they exerted, others often could not. His remarkable ability to work across denominational lines represents a triumph of the spirit of the network over that of the hierarchy. The very explicitness of the commentary in which Kepler and his contemporaries engaged as they tried to work out the ethics of a new kind of scholarship shows how hard they found it to stage the conversations about the past that they most wanted to have. Ultimately, the tension between intellectual networks and institutional hierarchies of multiple kinds led to explosions in the garden of chronology, and to the demise of the enterprise as Kepler had conceived it.

In recent years, historians and historians of science have emphasized the broad geographical range of the Republic of Letters, and the ease with which its citizens and their letters traveled across it. From Nicolette Mout, who reconstructed the multiple roles played by scholars from the Netherlands at the imperial court in Prague, to Peter Miller, who traced the spiderwebs of correspondence by which Peiresc directed astronomical and antiquarian enquiries, physical experiments, and epigraphic expeditions around the Mediterranean world, the historians of the Republic have taught us to appreciate its cosmopolitanism.[77]

Chronology was as cosmopolitan, in theory, as almost any other discipline of the period. Since late antiquity, its practitioners had studied Chaldean and Egyptian, Jewish and Persian, and Greek and Roman traditions.[78] Early modern chronologers added the Islamic world, the Americas, and China to these established areas of inquiry. In practice, however, chronologers could be strikingly parochial—and to that extent, their work yields a different vision of the Republic, less a smooth fresco than a mosaic. For one thing, chronology required—as it had since antiquity—access to many books, some of them rare, puzzling, or both. But wars, journeys, censorship, and the sheer high cost of books meant that relatively few chronologers had reliable, long-term access to all the texts they needed. That great theorist of note taking, Jeremiah Drexel S.J., explained in his *Aurifodina* that no scholar could ever be sure that he would have continued access to vital texts:

> How lucky I was at Louvain, where I had all the old poets, all the most ancient historians, and all the works of Lipsius: where I had the theologians and philosophers of the better sort, and more, in my study. Now I am stuck, a fisherman on the rocks without a catch. I can hardly catch sight of a few historians, and those in bad editions. Lipsius is so mauled and discombobulated hereabouts that he seems to me to have turned into Pentheus. I find few of his works here, and those not in uniform editions. As to other good books, they are in short supply.[79]

Drexel offered scholars one solution to these problems: just take good notes, he urged, and carry them with you: "I emulate the bear and live on the fruits of my claws: that is, I use my excerpts."[80] But this advice could not help Mästlin, for example. He seems to have lacked regular access to Scaliger's *Thesaurus temporum* for several years after it appeared in Leiden in 1606. Accordingly, he went on fruitlessly trying to work out the chronology of the kings of Babylon without reference to the Ptolemaic list of them, which Scaliger had printed for the first time.[81] In fact, it is striking how often even Kepler or Mästlin was unable to lay his hands on a standard work.

Moreover, even those who read the same books often did so in dramatically different ways. Mästlin and Crusius lived near one another in Tübingen, taught the same students, and discussed everything from heavenly prodigies to calendar reform.[82] When Mästlin found himself worrying about a passage in Josephus, early one morning at the end of May 1596, he knew that he could knock at Crusius's door and obtain help. In fact, they had a good talk about chronology,[83] yet they differed radically on at least one fundamental point. Mästlin rejected the texts of Berosus, Manetho, and "Metasthenes" that first appeared in 1498 as "published by one Annius of Viterbo not that long ago, and confected in the time of our grandparents by some idle, or rather malicious, person, with malice aforethought."[84] Like Scaliger, he reposed his faith rather in the genuine fragments of Berosus and others that Josephus and Eusebius had preserved. Crusius, by contrast, had quoted the fake Berosus as genuine—as he recalled as he lay in bed two days after Mästlin came to see him, reading a letter from a friend who pointed out that Goropius Becanus and many others had branded those fragments as forgeries.[85] The next day, he perked up, and replied that the Annian texts were Latin epitomes of genuine works. The extant fragments, he admitted, were clearly distant from the originals, and perhaps corrupt, but not necessarily forgeries. After all, great scholars had drawn information from them.[86] Reusner, in short, was not the only well-known chronologer who never paid the full intellectual price of admission to the field. Mästlin and Crusius, colleagues and friends, both deeply interested in chronology, lived in the same material city. But in the virtual world of chronology they inhabited separate intellectual microclimates, where assumptions and approaches differed radically. Any account of the discipline and its development must somehow consider not only its cosmopolitan reach and breadth but also its microscopic—but distinctive—local cultures, and the multiple intermediate networks that sometimes connected and sometimes separated them.

Yet historians benefit from the very difficulties peculiar to chronology—the pressure exerted by the biblical text and its authority and the need to negotiate between texts and information that derived from radically different cultural traditions: Jewish, pagan, and Christian. They enable us to watch our actors trying to find ways to make intellectual exchange work across barriers that were often high and thick enough to prevent anyone from entering new territory—and they keep us from spinning fantasies that depict seventeenth-century intellectual life as all network and no hierarchy.

The creation of the Republic of Letters in these years, finally, matters most of all. For decades, historians of what we used to call the scientific revolution focused on the new scientific societies of the seventeenth century—those groups whose members agreed on explicit rules about giving credit to discoverers, sometimes ignored denominational differences, and often pretended that rank itself, in the traditional, social sense, did not matter. They have not always noticed that these societies were in fact so many special cases of a larger enterprise in the organization of knowledge.[87] Chronology, as Kepler practiced it, now seems curious, complex, and quaint. But it offers a privileged point of entrance into some of the central scenes in which intellectual life transformed itself, at that last moment when humanism and science were allied, and in which new, collective forms of inquiry took shape.

7

The Universal Language

Splendors and Sorrows of Latin
in the Modern World

Francis Bacon rarely found himself at a loss for words, as we have seen more than once. Yet at times he proved willing to borrow a comely phrase or two. In *The Advancement of Learning*, published in 1605, he set out to describe the new kind of inquiry practiced by contemporary historians of antiquity. Their experimental, innovative research was very much to his taste. The antiquaries collected and studied the material remains of the past: ruins, inscriptions, weapons, utensils, even clothing. They preferred reconstructing past beliefs and rituals to devising the eloquent narratives that had traditionally made up the core of the historian's art. To characterize their work, radically modern in method but eternally melancholy in its pursuit of endless, elusive fragments, Bacon quoted a Latin tag, taken from a source he did not name:

> Antiquities, or remnants of history, are, as was said, *tanquam tabula naufragii* [like a plank from a shipwreck]: [they are found] when industrious persons, by an exact and scrupulous diligence and observation, out of monuments, names, words, proverbs, traditions, private records and evidences, fragments of stories, passages of books that concern not story, and the like, do save and recover [them] somewhat from the deluge of time.

Not long ago, the great Italian historian Riccardo Fubini identified the work from which Bacon drew his fragment of Latin.[1] It was not an ancient text, as Bacon's manner in citing it might lead one to expect, but a Latin work by a fifteenth-century Italian scholar: *Italy Illuminated,* written by Flavio Biondo, master of Roman antiquities and close friend of Leon Battista Alberti, the brilliant Italian architect and theorist of art.

Biondo had ransacked texts and traveled through Italy in search of evidence about the locations of ancient communities. He then set out to compare what he had seen with the testimony of the ancient texts. He hoped to work out which modern place names corresponded to which places and peoples of Italian antiquity, to settle the authenticity of the new nomenclature, to revive and record the names that had been obliterated, and to shed some light upon the murkiness of Italian history. The task proved impossible to complete, but Biondo did write an informative and immensely readable book. At the start, he asked his reader "that I be thanked for having hauled ashore some planks from so vast a shipwreck, planks which were floating on the surface of the water or nearly lost to view, rather than be required to account for the entire lost ship." The modesty with which Biondo formulated his claims should not distract us—any more than it distracted Bacon—from the radical novelty of what he had written.

When Biondo chose the metaphor of hauling planks ashore from a shipwreck, he forcibly directed his readers' attention to the episode at the very center of his description of the district of Lazio, itself the center of Italy. In the 1440s, Alberti set out to raise one of the two Roman ships that lay on the bottom of the crystal-clear Lake Nemi in the Alban Hills, which belonged to Cardinal Prospero Colonna. Alberti had rows of empty wine barrels strung across the surface of the lake and fixed winches on either side of them. Divers from Genoa, "more like fish than men," attached thick ropes ending in iron hooks to one of the sunken vessels. As the entire papal Curia watched, the winches turned, the ropes strained—and the ship fell apart. Only a fragment came up. Undeterred by this catastrophic conclusion to their pioneering efforts as underwater archaeologists, Biondo, Alberti, and "all the fine minds of the Roman Curia" really began to have fun. Deprived of texts that could shed light on the ships—which were actually pleasure barges placed in the lake by Caligula—they scrutinized the planks that they had managed to bring ashore:

> The ship [they decided in a joint report] was entirely made of larchwood, braced by beams three inches thick and caulked on the outside with pitch. The pitch was covered and protected by a coating of yellow or red material, as can be seen even now, and the entire surface was clad with sheets of lead to protect the ship and the caulking from the waves

and rain. A mass of bronze nails (not iron as we use now) was driven into the sheets of lead to seal them.

Like modern archaeologists, the humanists set out to decipher the evidence in front of them: first to analyze its composition, layer by layer, and then to understand how each component had functioned in the ancient ship. When Biondo pointed to this episode, as a metaphor for his book as a whole, he did more than beg his readers to excuse his inability to bring ancient Italy back to life. He also highlighted the fact that he and his friends practiced an exciting, radically new discipline. Though Biondo himself concentrated on place names and other sorts of textual evidence, he and Alberti knew how to read objects, rather than books, using a method that had no clear ancient counterpart, and that would, over the centuries, split and transform itself into modern archaeology, as well as cultural history and the history of religion.

A marvelous publication project has made it easy, for the first time, to work out what Bacon learned from his unnamed source—and, more important, has made it easier than ever before to appreciate the Latin literature of the Italian Renaissance as a whole. The first volume of Biondo's *Italy Illuminated,* edited and translated by Jeffrey White, appeared in 2005. Like the first two volumes of Leonardo Bruni's *History of the Florentine People,* the six volumes of Marsilio Ficino's *Platonic Theology,* Boccaccio's *Famous Women,* Petrarch's *Invectives,* and Poliziano's *Silvae,* among many others, it forms part of a new series of books, the I Tatti Renaissance Library, sponsored by Harvard University's center for Renaissance studies, the Villa I Tatti, and handsomely published by Harvard University Press. Modeled on the long-established Loeb Classical Library, also published by Harvard, and designed to make the most important Latin works of the Italian Renaissance available to a wider audience, the I Tatti Renaissance Library offers readers both the original texts, in serviceable editions based on the best available sources, and facing translations, most of them new, into English.

Across the country, on the shelves of Borders and Barnes & Noble branches and in the stacks of small college libraries, the most ambitious and innovative writings of the Italian Renaissance, in prose and verse, in fields that range from comedy to metaphysics and beyond—works that for centuries only scholars have been able to read—have suddenly become accessible to readers who know only English. At least in translation, Renaissance Latin is back.

And as Biondo's case shows, it has a vast amount to offer us: a fascinating, often innovative literature, couched in a language of considerable elegance and surprising vividness.

The I Tatti series—with some thirty-six volumes published so far, and dozens more to come—has many historical lessons to teach. The first has to do with the variety, richness, and seductive beauty of the Latin language itself. Postclassical Latin, in a variety of forms, served as the medium of European learning for well over a thousand years. At the start of the Middle Ages, the creators of monastic culture used it for the liturgies and libraries of their houses. After the French Revolution, the great mathematician Johann Karl Friedrich Gauss still composed a fair amount of his cutting-edge work in Latin, to make it more widely accessible than it would have been in German. Yet the forms of Latin used in different contexts varied radically.

From the fourteenth to the seventeenth century, one kind of Latin—a revived classical language, purist and discriminating—played a special part in the drama of European culture. Italian humanists—scholars like Petrarch and Boccaccio—realized that the serviceable Latin used in their day for state documents and contracts; the liturgical Latin of the church; and the technical, precise Latin of the university-trained lawyers, medical men, and theologians all differed, in multiple ways, from the Latin used by such great ancient writers as Cicero and Virgil. In turning back to the ancients, they bucked some powerfully entrenched assumptions and practices.

Purists, especially in the mendicant orders, denounced any study of the classics as a stimulus to skepticism. "How many false stories," argued the Dominican Giovanni Dominici, "are told by the historians, when one tells a story this way, and the other in another! The great Livy himself bears witness to this. In this case the devil had only one thing in mind: to make the reader, while he sees celebrated writers appear as liars, feel similar doubts about the saints."[2] Habitués of universities in the north—and, from the mid-fourteenth century on, in Padua—preferred meticulous studies of logic and semantics, carried out in a remorselessly technical and specialized language, to Ciceronian prose or Virgilian verse. Four of these young sophisticates informed Petrarch—the first of the humanists to become known as grand master of an intellectual movement—that he was "a good man without learning." His scorching reply, a magnificent defense of the humanities, appears in the I Tatti volume of his *Invectives,* impeccably edited and translated by David Marsh.

Despite all opposition, the humanists triumphed—first in Italy and then across Europe. They hunted down and collected ancient books, bragging loudly every time they "rescued" or "restored" a lost classic—a process that sometimes amounted to filching a manuscript from the monastery whose members had preserved it for centuries, making some imperfect copies, and losing the original. They revived ancient genres, from epic and comedy to history and the personal letter, and found ways to make careers as writers of fine Latin. They even convinced hard-bitten mercenary captains like Federigo da Montefeltro and brilliant diplomats like Lorenzo de' Medici to build up libraries of classical texts, to send their sons (and even their daughters) to classical schools, and to hire classical scholars to serve as ambassadors and chancery secretaries. At their most ambitious, the humanists drew up sweeping surveys of the universe, of history, and of the world around them—works that had an immense impact on their contemporaries and that continued to find attentive readers in later ages among such connoisseurs of Latin as Thomas Browne, John Milton, and Samuel Johnson.

The I Tatti series helps us see what was so special, in a learned world that already spoke Latin, about the especially colorful varieties of the language that the humanists cultivated. A rich collection of *Humanist Educational Treatises,* edited and translated with great precision by Craig Kallendorf, lets us watch some of the most influential humanist teachers at work. Part of their success lay in the mastery of techniques for learning. Battista Guarino, for example, explained that the proper study of the classics had to be active, not passive—taking the form of a personal search for information, guidance, and stylistic models, carried out pen in hand:

> Let them look for new maxims with specific applications. Writing glosses in books is also extremely profitable, the more so if they have some hope of publishing them someday, for we are more careful with such things when we are in pursuit of praise. Writing of this kind wonderfully sharpens the wit, polishes the tongue, produces fluency in writing.

Only ceaseless study of this sort, based on close encounters with every kind of ancient writing, could have enabled humanists to wield a dead language with the snap and sparkle attained by Petrarch, when he dealt with an impudent doctor: "Facile se ipsum excusat, quem non pudet; facile consolatur alium, qui non dolet" [It is easy to defend yourself when you feel no shame, and easy to console others when you feel no grief]. Though Latin had never died, the Latin of the humanists—a language that set out to be classical in every detail, from spelling through syntax to the script in which it was recorded—was a new cultural force, a model of philological art for art's sake that caused Petrarch himself a lifetime of qualms.[3]

At times, the pursuit of perfect Latinity could become an obsession. Niccolò Niccoli, the fifteenth-century Florentine bibliophile and connoisseur, "took great delight in ancient painting and sculpture," which he collected with skill and taste. He knew ancient history and geography so well that "he could talk about every single province, city, locale, place—in short, about any region—better and in greater detail than people who had themselves lived in those places for long periods of time." A "glutton for books," he created a library of some 800 volumes, vast for the time, and after sharing it generously throughout his lifetime, he asked in his will that it become "a kind of public library which would be open to all scholars in perpetuity"—a secular, classical institution.[4]

Niccoli's taste in Latin was impeccable, and he set up shop as an adviser to those of his contemporaries who thought they had mastered the language: "He excelled all others in judging whether an author or an orator was polished or puerile." Writer after writer came to him, asking for criticism, only to learn that their work was suited not for publication but for the outhouse. An aesthete who "could not bear the noise of a braying donkey, a saw, or a mousetrap moving around," he loved and praised everything ancient. Yet Giannozzo Manetti, the Florentine humanist to whom we owe most of these vivid details, noted that Niccoli's hypercritical classicism silenced him: "Seldom or never did he undertake to speak or write in Latin, the reason being, in my opinion, that he approved of nothing unless it were full and perfect, and so feared that his own writings, like those of others, would fail to satisfy him completely." A way to solve this dilemma—studied to brilliant effect by Ingrid Rowland—became fashionable in High Renaissance Rome, where some of the best Latinists tried to use only words that appeared in the writings of Cicero. They composed dazzlingly classical speeches and poems, some of them gloriously elegant—but also, in the opinion of their northern contemporary, the satirical Erasmus, made themselves incapable of discussing the modern, Christian world around them.[5]

For the most part, though, the writers whose works the I Tatti series has brought to light wielded the new classical Latin to wonderful effect, and simply inserted unclassical words and terms whenever the need arose. Aeneas Sylvius Piccolomini, the Sienese humanist who became Pope Pius II, describes the election that brought him to the papal throne in a cold, mordant key that anticipates the Italian styles of Machiavelli and Guicciardini:

> The richer and more influential members of the college [of cardinals] summoned others to their presence. Seeking the papacy for themselves or their friends, they begged, made promises, even tried threats. Some threw all decency aside, spared no blushes and pleaded their own cases, claiming the papacy as their right. Among these were Guillaume, cardinal of Rouen; Pietro, cardinal of San Marco; and Giovanni, cardinal of Pavia; nor did the cardinal of Lerida neglect his interests. Each had a great deal to say for himself. Their rivalry was extraordinary, their energy unbounded. They neither rested by day nor slept at night . . . A large group of cardinals gathered in the latrines. Here, as if in a secret, private meeting place, they worked on a plan to elect Guillaume pope.

For all his severity, Pius had a delightful way of describing cities and countryside. He could mock himself charmingly, as when he described his stay among the barbarian inhabitants of the British borders, who had never seen wine or white bread, and whose eager young women he refused to sleep with, as he stayed up all night for fear of bandits "among the heifers and nanny goats, who kept him from sleeping a wink by stealthily pulling the straw from his pallet." Pius's *Commentaries,* presented in a most informative way by Margaret Meserve and Marcello Simonetta, may well be the most entertaining work in the whole series.

Even Pius did not lead so adventurous a life—or attain such precision and vividness as a descriptive writer—as Cyriac of Ancona, the merchant, adventurer, and self-taught student of antiquities who became, so to speak, the Patrick Leigh Fermor of the fifteenth century. As Cyriac crossed and recrossed the Mediterranean, catching rides on Venetian and Genoese naval ships as one might now take suburban commuter trains, and calmly examined gems with their captains, he pursued his lifelong effort "to speak with the dead"—a vocation that took him through the Aegean, down to Egypt, and into mainland Greece and led him to record his adventures in richly detailed letters as well as the notebooks in which he copied inscriptions. Cyriac documented his two stays at Cyzicus with characteristic care. He showed an equally characteristic nonchalance about the difficulties of surveying a site while Turkish and Christian forces battled one another across the Mediterranean and beyond. "But alas!" he wrote in 1444,

> How unsightly a structure we returned to, compared to the one we inspected fourteen years ago! For then we saw thirty-one surviving columns standing erect, whereas now I find that [only] twenty-nine columns remain, some shorn of their architraves. And the famous walls, almost all of which were [then] intact, now in great part lie ruined and dashed to the ground, evidently by the barbarians. On the other hand, those exceptional, glorious marble figures of the gods on the [temple's] outstanding, wondrous facade, remain unharmed in their nearly pristine glory, thanks to the protection of almighty Jove himself and the patronage of his exalted majesty.

Cyriac's prose becomes even more vivid when he describes the life around him: the "close-packed vineyards and trees and pleasant meadows" of Laconia, for example, where he watched the local youths run their ancient footrace, the *androdromon pentastadion,* and traced the remains of ancient custom in modern folkways:

> We discovered that they somehow preserve an ancient manner of speaking, for they say that their dead, no matter what their religion was, have gone off "to Hades," that is, to the lower world. Also, their meals consist of snapped beans seasoned generously with oil, and their loaves are made from barley.

For Cyriac and anyone who shared his belief that ancient customs and ways of speaking survived in the contemporary Mediterranean, it seemed only natural to revive classical Latin (as well as Greek, which Cyriac could also write).

The most elaborate and ambitious of the works so far presented in the I Tatti series are in prose: Leonardo Bruni's *History of the Florentine People,*

Marsilio Ficino's *Platonic Theology,* and Polydore Vergil's *On Discovery.* Each of them illustrates the range of ways in which these passionate classicists turned backward to antiquity, and by doing so found new ways to address central problems of the world around them. Bruni, in trying to demonstrate that Florence could trace its legitimate republican tradition back to deep antiquity, wrote a history of his city on the model of the ancient history of Rome by Livy. As he did so, he read Livy's eloquent, stagy book in a very imaginative, critical way. From the ancient historian's idealized account of virtuous Romans, Bruni reconstructed the virtuous and powerful world of their enemies, the Etruscans—from whom, he claimed, the modern Tuscans were descended. In Bruni's historical imagination, Livy's stories of Horatius, heroically defending the bridge across the Tiber, and Mucius Scaevola, thrusting his hand into the fire to show his contempt for death, metamorphosed into instances of Roman weakness, superstition, and dishonesty:

> It would have been more appropriate (if it is not irreverent to speak the truth) to honor the Tiber itself [rather than Horatius], for it was the river's swirling waters that saved the city when Roman valor could not. The Etruscans, who controlled the Janiculum and held all the areas on the north side of the Tiber, long held the other parts of the city in the grip of a siege. The besieged formed a plan to attack the person of the king. This was their sole remaining hope as they were unequal to open warfare. So they resorted to cunning tricks to lure him furtively away from the main body of his troops. Hence the murder of the secretary and the story of how Mucius Scaevola put his hand in the fire.

"Only my father and myself after him," wrote Zbigniew Herbert in his magnificent poem "Transformations of Livy,"

> read Livy against Livy
> carefully examining what is underneath the fresco
> this is why the theatrical gesture of Scevola awoke no echo in us.[6]

Like Herbert and his father, and long before, Bruni knew that "the empire will fall"—and wrote, in fine Livian Latin, a counterhistory that exalted the states that survived the collapse of the Roman Empire.

A generation and more after Bruni, and in the very different Florence of
Lorenzo de' Medici, Ficino set out to show that the ancient Neoplatonic philosophy embodied a "gentile theological tradition," one that complemented
the Mosaic revelation to the Jews and prepared its devotees for the final truths
of Christianity. Ficino worked in full knowledge of the internal complica-
tions of Neoplatonism. He wrote and argued in styles that ranged from the
logical and synthetic to the poetic and evocative, as he struggled to find ways
to prove that the universe was orderly and governed by a Creator and to lay
out the place within it of the immortal human soul. No optimist, Ficino suffered terribly from the attacks of Saturnian melancholy which, he argued, af-
flicted the great of soul as they did the most original artisans and artists. He
realized that newly available ancient texts—like the magnificent, frightening
Epicurean *On the Nature of Things* of the Roman poet Lucretius—challenged
his efforts to create a synthesis of Christianity and pagan philosophy. Yet Ficino found powerful and influential new ways to support his central thesis.
He praised the work of the most skillful artists and craftsmen—like the German who made a small cabinet in which a single ball somehow made automata move, trumpets blare, and birds sing—as a model of the cosmic order
as a whole: "Thus God through His own being . . . has only to nod His head
and everything which depends on Him trembles." Ficino, like so many of his
contemporaries, saw human artists as earthly counterparts to the divine Creator. Here he drew on the inventive work of a brilliant artisan to give the ancient argument from design a fine new analogical form, and at the same time
gave the lie to the ancient atomists and their dangerous critique of Platonic
metaphysics: "Let us hear no more from Lucretius the Epicurean, who wants
the world to come about and be borne along by chance."

Polydore Vergil, born in Urbino, spent much of his career in England. He
wrote a searingly critical history of his adopted land in which he demolished
many a medieval legend, not winning himself many friends in the process.
And he brought a keen sense of ambiguity to his breakthrough book—a vast
study of inventions that went through thirty Latin editions in his lifetime. As
Brian Copenhaver shows in the introduction to his superb edition of Vergil's
complex, learned compilation, *On Discovery*, some ancient authorities denounced human inventions as a source of corruption; others saw them as a
continual source of improvement in the human condition. The most reliable
sources Vergil had were the ancients, whom he revered; yet he knew that

modern men had invented "the time-piece that one often sees nowadays, made of metals, toothed wheels and weights, some pointing to the hours with pins, some announcing them with bells," as well as the printing press, thanks to which "in one day just one person can print the same number of letters that many people could hardly write in a whole year."

When Polydore's ancient sources conflicted or his modern ones remained silent, he had no way to decide who had invented the cannon, the stirrup, the mill, or the hat. So he concluded his massive and erudite book with a rather surly apology: "I would rather pass on reliable information in few words than use many to pursue uncertainties." Yet *On Discovery*, as Copenhaver shows, had a profound and lasting impact. It proved to be one of the principal channels through which the antiquarian methods of the fifteenth century reached the ethnographers and historians of religion over the next two centuries.

Renaissance Latin poetry—as one of its best students, John Sparrow, ruefully remarked long ago—is the sort of subject that hardheaded historians describe as "fundamentally piffle."[7] When Evelyn Waugh wanted to send a particularly hapless antihero on a picaresque journey into Communist Eastern Europe, he took as his main character a classics master at a public school, Granchester, one Scott-King, "slightly bald and slightly corpulent," who had become an expert on a seventeenth-century Neo-Latin poet, one Bellorius. The I Tatti volume *Humanist Comedies*, expertly edited and set into context by Gary Grund, does make harder reading than most of the others, and the two verse dramas it contains are less accessible than the three in prose. Yet Grund's edition nicely shows how Renaissance comedy mixed ancient motifs with Christian lessons, and offers fascinating information on the rapid development of comic performance in the Renaissance—from pantomimes carried out by characters while a single narrator read all the lines, to full-blown productions on stages, acted out before scenery painted in the new one-point perspective.

Even more revealing are Michael Putnam's edition of the shorter poems of Maffeo Vegio and Charles Fantazzi's edition of Angelo Poliziano's *Silvae*. A devout classicist, steeped in Ovid, Seneca, and Virgil, Vegio still found the ending of the *Aeneid* abrupt and disconcerting. Virgil's epic concludes with Aeneas, furiously angry, standing over the body of the enemy, Turnus, whom he has just killed, in order to avenge Turnus's killing of his own friend Pallas. Blood has called for blood, and the famously pious hero—that model of middle-aged endurance—winds up transported with rage. Vegio found this spectacle as unedifying as it was vivid. But he knew that Virgil had not completed the *Aeneid,* at least to his own satisfaction, and so he decided to round the poem out, smoothing off its jagged corners. He wrote a supplement, a thirteenth book, in which many of the happy events predicted earlier in the poem come true. After Aeneas marries Lavinia and rules the Latins and Trojans, he dies and becomes a star.

By meticulous comparisons between Vegio's book 13, Vergil's books 1–12, and the work of Ovid, on which Vegio also drew, Putnam teases out the ways in which Vegio transformed the mood of the work as a whole—how instead of Aeneas he made Turnus the one who rages, and managed to stage the hero's stellification, in Ovidian terms, not as a Christian rebirth to salvation but as the proper reward for a pagan's supremely virtuous life on earth. Vegio's scenes of festival and feasting have a nice Virgilian feel to them, as Aeneas and Latinus recall the struggles of the past in present tranquility—as well as a vivid period sense of the ways in which public ritual could seal and solidify a new community's identity:

> With such and other topics they stretched out night's length. Then shouts
> of joy rush rumbling through the lofty halls, and a mighty roar fills the
> whole palace. Torches bring their light and glisten with expensive glow.
> The Trojans jump to their feet, the Latins follow, as the cithara resounds.
> The applause intensifies as they merge together into a single assembly,
> vary the rhythms of their dance and yield to the frolic.

Putnam teaches us to appreciate Vegio's artistry—and his ability to reweave a troubling work of art until it clearly embodied the best pagan, but not Christian, morality. In his own way, Vegio glimpsed the incompleteness, the broken arch, that is a prominent feature of the epic's architecture.

As Fantazzi shows, Angelo Poliziano represents Italian humanism at its scholarly and artistic zenith. Like the critics of Hellenistic Alexandria, Poliziano practiced the crafts of scholarship as well as the arts of poetry, and at the very highest level. He rejected the hastily produced classical editions of his contemporaries as uncritical and incompetent, and devoted himself to studying the oldest manuscripts he could find, tracing the complex ways in which Latin poets had transformed Greek originals, and describing his most exciting results in the short essays that he entitled *Miscellanea* when he published some of them in 1489. From 1480 on, Poliziano taught at the University of Florence, where he lectured on authors who had not previously been included in the curriculum, such as Quintilian and Statius. He dismissed potential critics with a neat quotation from Tacitus: "We should not say that what is different is automatically worse."

He also chose the lonelier road when he declined to give the normal prose oration in praise of his author at the beginning of each course. Instead, he recited and printed the *Silvae:* metrical introductions in the manner of Statius, densely allusive in style. The *Rusticus* or *Countryman,* a charming introduction to his courses on Hesiod and Virgil's *Georgics,* evokes the Florentine countryside where Poliziano wrote as well as the imagined countrysides of his ancient poets. The *Nutricia* offers a comprehensive overview of Hebrew, Greek, and Latin poetry that is sharp and critical, richly informed about the Hellenistic poets on whom the Romans drew so heavily, and alert to the virtues of Lucretius and Lucan and to the faults of Ovid. The poem culminates, boldly, with the Florentine poets from Dante to Lorenzo himself and his son—a brilliant melding of history with panegyric, designed to show that the modern had a power all its own. Neo-Latin verse, in other words, could be very far indeed from piffle. Erudite, allusive, and polished to a high gloss, Neo-Latin poetry amounted to a subtle form of scholarship, dense with implicit interpretations of the ancients. But it could be something more as well. In the Latin verse of Poliziano, as Richard Aldington wrote long ago, "when the subtle flavours of innumerable reminiscences of earlier writers were deliberately enjoyed, when every line and phrase was drenched in older poetry, yet there was something new about it all, some expression of the poet's own personality."[8]

The I Tatti series is already beginning to transform the study and teaching of Renaissance culture. Consider just one example. In the 1920s and 1930s, Hans Baron, a brilliant German Jewish scholar, decided that the young Latinists of fifteenth-century Florence—above all Leonardo Bruni, the city's long-time chancellor—had created a new intellectual movement open to the urban world and committed to the active life, one that he eventually christened "civic humanism." These moderns, he argued, sought to revive not only classical texts but also classical values. They held that the best way to emulate the ancients, and the highest form of human achievement, was to lead an active life of republican citizenship. At the end of the 1930s, Baron moved to the United States, and his work, which began to appear in English, had a powerful impact there—especially after his synthetic *Crisis of the Early Italian Renaissance* was published in 1955 by Princeton University Press.

Ever since, the most erudite specialists in Renaissance culture—Gene Brucker, John Pocock, Quentin Skinner, James Hankins, William Connell, and many others—have debated the strengths and weaknesses of Baron's thesis. Advanced courses on Renaissance Florence and on Renaissance intellectual history have devoted weeks of study and discussion to the works of Baron, his critics, and his supporters. Yet until the late 1960s, students could find virtually no English translation of the key Latin documents on which Baron rested his case. Bruni's ambitious history, though much discussed, remained largely inaccessible. Thanks to the I Tatti Library, students can now examine firsthand the tapestry of the Florentine past that Bruni wove so deftly from ancient historians, medieval chronicles, and official documents—a key text for Baron and his critics alike.

The I Tatti series is not the first, or only, enterprise of its kind. True, the new historical scholarship of nineteenth-century Europe, powered by a fascination with national cultures and literatures, underplayed the Latin literatures of Northern Europe as well as Italy. But throughout the twentieth century, Neo-Latin has been rediscovered, again and again. Great editorial enterprises have restored to their central positions in Renaissance culture the works of those superbly original Northern Latinists, Erasmus and Thomas More. In recent decades, new editions and translations have restored and opened up such vastly influential Latin texts as the *De revolutionibus* of Copernicus, the *De humani corporis fabrica* of Vesalius, and the *Poetice* of Julius Caesar Scaliger, all from the middle of the sixteenth century, and the *Politica* of Justus Lipsius, from its end. Productive centers of Neo-Latin scholarship have been established in Messina, Rome, Florence, Louvain, Oxford, and elsewhere, and a few comparable series exist elsewhere—notably at the heroic French publishing house Les Belles Lettres.[9]

Over time, the library and related enterprises will help us to approach, in new ways, one of the great questions in the cultural history of early modern Europe: why the rise of a modern civilization was celebrated and articulated, not only by Petrarch and his followers, but for centuries, in a revived ancient language that set limits to some possibilities of expression even as it opened others.[10] Nowadays, of course, when Latin is spoken in public, it suggests the importance of tradition and the past. For example, every spring at Princeton's convocation, an undergraduate addresses the assembled students, parents, and faculty in Latin. Parents receive a plain copy of the text, which few of them can read. Most of the students cannot read it either, but they receive a different, annotated version. Footnotes, always written in Latin—"hic ridete"; "hic plaudite"—identify in-jokes and references to local and national events. By clapping, catcalling, and laughing, the graduating seniors delude their parents—as local tradition has it—into believing that their children have not only studied engineering, English, or chemistry but also learned Latin.

This curious form of public antiquarianism preserves a genuine academic tradition—one reared on the foundations laid by the Italian humanists. Thanks to their endless efforts both to use formal, classical Latin and to publicize its value, by the sixteenth century, mastery of this once-dead language had become the price of entrance to schools and universities. Learned Europeans savored the variety and distinctiveness of Latin styles, ancient and modern. Joseph Scaliger noted with amusement that his favorite pupil at the University of Leiden, Daniel Heinsius, would turn up "on some days drunk on Lipsius, on others drunk on Muret, and on others drunk on Erasmus, and would insist that all the rest are asses." Through the sixteenth and seventeenth centuries, savants composed Senecan tragedies and Catullan love poems, Tacitean histories and Ciceronian dialogues, and Plinian (Jr.) letters and Plinian (Sr.) treatises on every imaginable subject from astronomy to zoology. They even cracked Latin jokes. When a pedant irritated the poet Nicodemus Frischlin by addressing him with clumsy formality, "Tu, Frischline, vates [You, o Frischlin, the poet]," he replied, without missing a Latin beat, "Tu mihi lambe nates [You may lick my butt]." The story delighted generations of schoolboys—who, in those happy days, did not need to be told that the great scholar had told his interlocutor to kiss his arse.

Latin, in short, continued to play vital roles through the first modern age. From Prague to Peru, it served as the arena of literary artistry, the vehicle of scientific communication, and the medium of common room gossip. Individuals across Europe and beyond knew Latin as intimately, loved it as passionately, and rolled it off the tongue as easily as they did their native languages. Thereafter, apparently, something happened. By the beginning of the twentieth century, as A. E. Housman remarked more in anger than in sorrow, even professional Latinists revealed on every page of their work that they lived "in an age which is out of touch with Latinity." What trajectory did Latin follow between its heyday in the Renaissance and its slow death by a hundred bad conjectural emendations and a thousand cuts in curricula and budgets?

Traditional histories of modern Europe have treated Latin with some ambivalence. The humanists did more than make the ability to write obedient pastiches of Cicero and Catullus the outward sign of inward cultural grace. They wished to re-create something like ancient literary culture, not that they would have put the task in those terms—a culture based on grammar and rhetoric, history and moral philosophy, and designed to form an elite of generalists equipped to lead an active life in state or church. Petrarch and his immediate followers challenged the supremacy of scholastic philosophy and theology. Later humanists showed that they could find ways of tackling even the formidable technicalities of the scholastics. Eventually they forged a new Latinate public sphere in which the questions that mattered most could be accessibly, and eloquently, debated. Revolutionaries who looked backward, they ended up not only reviving lost skills but also creating a new world in which the doctrines and teaching authority of the church proved as vulnerable to challenge as the methods of the late medieval university. To that extent, the revival of classical Latin makes a logical beginning to the story of the modern age.

In the long term, however, the preservation of classical Latinity proved incompatible with the creation of a new intellectual world. Writers like Alberti and Montaigne, though steeped in the classics, used Italian and French to discuss contemporary issues and to reach a large public. The sixteenth-century Protestant Reformers were fluent Latinists—Luther gossiped with his pupils about his dream life and the apparitions of the devil as easily in Latin as in German. But they translated the Bible and the liturgy into German, French, and English, and they insisted that the medieval church had used Latin to keep the most precious religious truths inaccessible to ordinary laypeople. Natural philosophers like Galileo and Boyle argued that one could discuss the most recondite problems of astronomy and chemistry in Italian or English. French replaced Latin as the common language of the citizens of the Republic of Letters. By the eighteenth century, even the greatest compendia of knowledge—like Diderot's *Encyclopedia*—were normally written in French or other modern languages. Latin had lost its practical utility. Progress-minded *philosophes* attacked its persistent use in universities and other erudite circles as one more relic of the Old Regime. No wonder, then, that active command of Latin declined so radically, to become all but extinct in recent centuries. The language that had served as the banner of modernity in the Renaissance had turned into a symbol for traditionalism and intellectual sclerosis.

In *Latin, or the Empire of a Sign*, Francois Waquet has sketched a nuanced story of this lost language. From the start, she emphasizes that Latin was always as much a matter of ritual as of substance. True, from the sixteenth century on, the school was "Latin country." Boys were required to speak Latin in Renaissance classrooms, where spies, known as "foxes," informed on those who slipped into the vernacular. Masters lectured in Latin on Latin texts, and the most successful pupils learned to produce Latin prose and verse on demand. But many boys—perhaps a majority—found their entrance to this country blocked, not facilitated, by the traditions of Latin pedagogy. These confronted the young with towering complex grammatical structures, typographical monstrosities that they often had to memorize before they could really understand that they were studying a foreign language.

When Churchill began Latin, at the age of seven, he opened his grammar and found himself staring, bug-eyed, at the first declension, which his textbook exemplified but did not explain:

Mensa	a table
Mensa	o table
Mensam	a table
Mensae	of a table
Mensae	to or for a table
Mensa	by, with, or from a table

"What on earth did it mean?" he asked readers many years later. "Where was the sense in it? It seemed absolute rigmarole to me." Churchill managed to memorize "the acrostic-looking task," but inquired about the paradox that "mensa" could mean both "a table" and "o table." The master explained that one would use the vocative "mensa" when " 'addressing a table, in invoking a table.' And then seeing he was not carrying me [Churchill] with him, 'You would use it in speaking to a table.' " "But I never do," Churchill protested, even more baffled—only to be threatened with severe punishment for his impertinence. This form of pedagogy—which established itself in the Renaissance and survived until relatively recent times—turned the Latin school into a labyrinth, whose center many never reached.

Even schoolboys who managed to master Latin grammar read a limited canon, which changed little over the centuries: Cicero, Terence, and some poets and historians usually pulled from their contexts and presented without any of the background information that could have made them come alive. Miguel de Unamuno, for example, found himself tormented by boredom as he and a friend translated their way, word by word, though the "intolerably dry" works of Nepos, Sallust, and Caesar. Eventually, he became convinced that the Latin writers had first written down their thoughts straightforwardly, like the moderns. Then, he decided, they had amused themselves by "dissecting the phrases, dislocating the sentences, scattering the words here and there with capricious abandon, simply to annoy us, the children of future generations." Thomas Hughes vividly revealed in *Tom Brown's Schooldays* how Latin verses were composed, as boys desperately sewed shreds and patches drawn from the *Gradus ad Parnassum* into verses that could be scanned and more or less made sense. Even some great writers of Latin—like the historian Jacques-Auguste de Thou—could hardly speak the language: "It is said that some Germans and some Englishmen, having heard him speaking so badly at home, quaerebant Thuanum in Thuano ('sought for de Thou in de Thou')."

Critics of classical education and classical scholars agreed on at least one point: they deplored the low levels attained in most classical schools. Educational reformers like Jan Amos Comenius and Enlightenment thinkers like Helvétius held that schools based on drudgery and dead languages could have no other results. The professionals, for their part, insisted—generation after generation—that once upon a time, things had been better. But this pan-European golden age was a myth, as Waquet shows by tracing nostalgic evocations of it back through time, generation by generation, and by offering wonderful examples of classroom life. (For example, the young Verlaine, trying to conjugate *lego,* found himself stumped when asked for the perfect, guessed *legavi* and floundered until a would-be helpful friend whispered *"lexi."* The master howled, and threw his keys and a Latin dictionary. Fortunately, he missed. All of this was not in the barbarous twenty-first century but the disciplined and erudite nineteenth.) Even periods of local brilliance in Latin writing did not always reflect superb teaching in schools and universities. When James Boswell showed Samuel Johnson his Latin thesis, the doctor shook his head at the many solecisms and remarked, "Ruddiman is dead." He knew that the high quality of the Latin dissertations previously submitted to the Society of Advocates in Edinburgh resulted not from superior Scottish schooling but from the corrections provided by the great Neo-Latin scholar and editor Thomas Ruddiman.

True, the Catholic Church provided another forum where Latin was in constant, active use—a forum that now shows signs of revival. The medieval church staunchly resisted efforts by Slavs, Waldensians, Lollards, and others to translate the liturgy into vernacular languages. Sixteenth-century Protestant and Catholic reformers who demanded a vernacular Mass met with condemnation at the Council of Trent. A particular form of Latin thus came, over time, to symbolize and embody the traditions and majesty of Catholicism—and was charged with deep meaning by many prelates and intellectuals. At the Second Ecumenical Council of the Vatican (Vatican II), John XXIII himself dwelt lovingly on the universality, antiquity, and majesty of the Latin language, which Providence—so he argued—had led the church to adopt. Catholics, then, were bombarded every Sunday with a form of Latin. It came to be, in some ways, consubstantial with their religious beliefs, associated with them almost as tightly as Hebrew with Judaism, and often no better understood by those using it to pray.

Still, even in the centuries when priests performed the Mass in Latin alone, many of them had little or no idea what they were saying. Reformers complained that ignorant priests rattled off the words of the liturgy in absurdly corrupt forms. One friend of Erasmus, who notoriously reproved a priest for saying "Mumpsimus" rather than "Sumpsimus" received a revealingly dusty answer: the man had been doing it that way for twenty years and saw no reason to change his habits. Seminary administrators complained in later centuries that few priests voluntarily studied a wide range of Latin authors, and fewer still could express complex thoughts effectively in Latin. As to the congregations, most of their members had only a general understanding of what the priest said and the choir sang. When Bruni—who saw Latin, in the medieval way, as an artificial construct rather then a natural language—wanted to demonstrate that ordinary Romans could not have understood the oratory of Cicero and the plays of Plautus and Terence in detail, he compared them to modern Italians at the Mass: "Men of distinction could understand an orator speaking in learned Latin very well, but bakers and trainers of gladiators and riff-raff of that sort understood the orator's words as they now understand the liturgy of the mass"—that is, "they understand, but they cannot speak that way themselves, and could not do so, even if they understand."

Yet Latin pervaded the early modern world, and even the modern one, in multiple ways that began with the work of the Italian humanists but eventually grew far beyond their ken. Though vernacular books became more numerous than Latin ones in Paris by the 1570s, and English dominated the London book trade, Latin retained preeminence in Italy and the Holy Roman Empire until deep in the seventeenth century. In every country, moreover, most scholars who wished to address a public not limited to their own kingdom continued for centuries to write in Latin. The most radical prophets of modernity—Descartes, Grotius, Hobbes, and Newton, for example—cast at least some of their new thoughts about nature and nature's laws, scripture, and tradition, in Latin rather than in their native languages. Into the eighteenth century, diplomats continued to study Latin, and often used it in negotiations (a number of monarchs, like Queen Elizabeth I and King Philip II, also spoke it accurately and well). For the old, teleological story in which the vernaculars marched forward to a natural triumph, Waquet substitutes something much more complex: a dance in which every forward movement was complemented by a backward one, and which, she argues, took centuries to degenerate into a *Totentanz*.

Perfect command of the language of Catholic liturgy was reserved for clerical elites and a few highly educated laymen. But church Latin permeated local cultures and dialects. In the early nineteenth century, Tuscan dialects swarmed with strange beings like Santo Ficè (formed from Latin *sanctificetur*). In Lucca, "Homo natus de muliere" [man born of woman], the opening phrase from a reading from the book of Job, became a proverb, "omo nato deve morire" [man, who is born, must die]. Nineteenth-century congregants in Brittany eagerly assented to the "Dies Irae." *Diêz* means difficult in Breton, and they agreed: "All this is far from easy, we have every reason to repeat the word." Creative misunderstandings like these gave the Latin Mass a participatory feeling, and helped ordinary Catholics make the set liturgy, in some part, their own. The mysterious, half-understood, and wholly familiar Latin of the church often had a charm, a magical quality that translation would destroy after Vatican II, and Waquet evokes this brilliantly. Latin, in other words, was not a single language, but a congeries of dialects, each of which flourished in a particular locale and played a particular role—a fact underlined by the unintentional comedies that took place every time scholars from more than one country attempted to carry on a conversation in Latin. When the great Huguenot scholar Samuel Bochart asked permission to attend a public ceremony in Oxford in 1621, the Master of Arts to whom he addressed himself thought that he was begging.

Yet Latin fulfilled certain purposes almost everywhere in Europe. First and foremost, it made the gentleman (at least when it was not being used to say "Will work for food"). In the Renaissance, to be sure, using too much Latin identified one as no gentleman, but a player. Castiglione and Montaigne distinguished sharply between the pedant, who clumsily spouted Latin tags at every opportunity, and the adroit, supple gentleman, who used Latin sparingly and at the right moments. Noblemen studied arms and etiquette, not Cicero's speeches. But by the seventeenth century, everyone agreed that young noblemen should in fact study the classics for a time, in schools designed for them.

Over the next 200 years, however, Latin gradually lost its practical function. Modern textbooks, histories, and reference works replaced ancient ones for most practical purposes, French became the international language of ladies and gentlemen, and schools made less and less effort to produce real fluency in their pupils. At exactly the same time, Waquet shows, Latin became a necessary accomplishment for anyone who aspired to gentility. Or at least the study of Latin became necessary—though few were expected to retain it in adulthood. "Do you think Sir John Crake, the master of the harriers, knows Latin?" Tom Tulliver questions Philip Wakem in *The Mill on the Floss*. "He learned it as a boy, of course," replies his more sophisticated friend, "But I daresay he's forgotten it." In fact, the lack of practical utility made Latin all the more attractive as a pure mark of distinction. As Benjamin Franklin astutely remarked, it became the "chapeau bras" of high culture—the hat that a man of fashion carried under his arm even though his wig made it superfluous. It survived the fall of the Ancient Regime to become the accomplishment of the nineteenth- and early twentieth-century bourgeoisie, who enjoyed, in the words of Louis MacNeice, "the privilege . . . of learning a language that is incontrovertibly dead"—as well as the privilege of seeing others excluded from learning it.

For practitioners of the learned professions, Latin served another set of purposes, some of them richly contradictory. It could mystify and create authority—as it did for doctors, from Molière's Sganarelle, whose fake Latin amazes his bourgeois patients ("Aye," one remarks, "it's all so proper, I can't understand a word of it") to the doctors who infested the Piazza Navona at Rome, hefting big books in Latin and Greek that they quoted to justify the useless nostrums they proposed. It did the same for civil lawyers, as their clients and their critics regularly protested. Yet Latin could also express what otherwise could not be expressed; a learned man could properly discuss obscene and sexual matters, so long as he did so in Latin.

Latin, in other words, had a double power: it could conceal or reveal. It prevented the supposedly vulnerable young person from reading such potentially corrupting texts as Isaac Vossius's pioneering study of ancient brothels, J. H. Meibom's 1639 essay on sexual masochism, or Gibbon's discussions of the sexual proclivities of the empress Theodora. Yet, as Waquet shows in fascinating detail, it also made possible the production of the first modern literature on sexuality, enabling a male cultural elite to say what "the prevailing norms would not allow to be stated in everyday language." Indeed, Latin sometimes assumed an erotic or sexual flavor—especially when futile and obvious efforts at bowdlerization of school texts sent boys leaping into their paternal libraries to read, and never to forget, the full story of Catullus's love life and Horace's premature ejaculation.

There is one vital question, at least, that Waquet does not raise, much less answer: Why have most historians of modern culture paid relatively little attention to Latin? After Waquet's book appeared, Christopher Celenza—an American scholar who works across disciplinary borders in history, Italian, and Neo-Latin—put forward a compelling hypothesis. Jacob Burckhardt argued, in his brilliant, justly influential essay of 1860 on *The Civilization of the Italian Renaissance,* that the new culture of the Renaissance resulted not from the revival of ancient texts and ideas, but from the new national spirit that developed in Italy once the pope and the Holy Roman Emperor could no longer impose their power on the small, competitive Italian states. The humanists, he maintained, were for the most part deracinated intellectuals, whose cult of Latin revealed that they did not share fully in the intellectual life of their nation. Burckhardt made this case so compellingly that he even convinced his contemporary Georg Voigt, who had dedicated a pioneering book of his own in 1859 to the revival of classical antiquity. Voigt revised his work to integrate Burckhardt's antihumanist interpretation into his treatments of writers like Leon Battista Alberti. True, in the twentieth century, Baron and others argued that Burckhardt was wrong, and triumphantly demonstrated the modernity and freshness of the humanist movement. But even Baron found humanist Latin a bit of a stumbling block. He liked to emphasize the Italian writings of the civic humanists—and the way in which some of them insisted that Italian could be as cultivated a language as Latin.[11]

In the twenty-first century, the idea of Europe as a coherent group of nations with a common culture seems very compelling. This may help to explain why, in an age even farther from Latinity than the one whose tin ear Housman deplored, we have once again begun to cultivate Neo-Latin. More deracinated than any humanists in the past, deprived of any shared set of cultural markers on whose worth we can agree, we may understand better than our more self-confident scholarly forerunners just why an ancient language proved, for centuries, so alluring to writers whose thoughts could not have been more challenging and up to date.

8

Entrepreneurs of the Soul, Impresarios of Learning

The Jesuits

Deep in Peru, late in the sixteenth century, a Jesuit missionary wrote of his experiences during an expedition to the Chunchos. As he surveyed the jungles of the Amazon from a mountaintop, he felt that he could see as far as the Caribbean. His greatest desire was to visit the unknown peoples between, supported only by the hand of God and a companion, and bring them to Christianity. Clearly, he thought that a faithful Jesuit could penetrate any society, however strange. At the same time, at another border of the Christian world, another Jesuit was in fact moving steadily toward the heart of the greatest of all gentile kingdoms. Dressed in Chinese silks and reading the Chinese classics, Matteo Ricci would soon be the first Christian mandarin. His legendary mastery of Western cartography and written and spoken Chinese would win him imperial favor, enabling him to spend his last years in Peking. There he would explore the rich and virtuous classics of Chinese philosophy and try with occasional success to convince literati that the Christianity he taught represented not a rejection but the completion of their grand tradition.[1]

At the margins of the expanding Christian universe, in other words, some Jesuits showed a startling openness to other peoples and forms of society and belief. True, their passionate interest in Andean religion was motivated by a crusading zeal to stamp out its vestiges, and they rejected Buddhism as forcefully as they embraced Confucianism. But their undeniable faith in the unique value of a single Western message should not obscure their equally undeniable intellectual courage. They underwent transformations and felt their way over distances then unknown and now probably unimaginable.

Other Jesuits inhabited the center rather than the peripheries of the Catholic world, and dreamed less of finding common ground with the best pagans than of cleansing the earth of the worst heretics, inside and outside Europe.

The influential Jesuit Antonio Possevino was almost as cosmopolitan as Ricci; his career as a diplomat and polemicist took him as far from Italy as the Russia of Ivan Grozny and the Poland of Stephan Bathory, between whom he tried to make peace. Though his efforts as an ambassador failed, he became one of the first Westerners to describe Muscovite Russia from first-hand knowledge. But he saw the new worlds that Europeans had discovered in 1492 and after as a haunt of devils and their worshipers.

Even worse, Possevino reflected, they had become a source of corruption for Christendom. True, the conquistadors had destroyed the natives' temples and codices, and missionaries now preached the word of God in new lands. But Satan had responded by attacking Christian worship in its European home. One of his chief tools took the form of high Renaissance scholarship and art. The tempting nude bodies portrayed by the pagan sculptors whose works were recovered and collected in the fifteenth and sixteenth centuries and, worse still, by the Christian painters who imitated them, defiled the walls of the churches they decorated. The new Italian idolatry of white skin and straining limbs had to be rooted out as brutally as the old American idolatry of monstrous beings who demanded human flesh. Cooperation and extermination, respect and revulsion—Jesuits felt and showed every reaction human beings can muster for the victims and beneficiaries of their preaching and polemics.[2]

The diversity of Jesuit thought and action was only natural, for the order was as cosmopolitan as the new European colonial empires that it both served and resisted. By 1600, only sixty years after the official foundation of the Society of Jesus, Jesuits and their institutions could be found everywhere, from Prague to the Philippines. They denounced their opponents in formal theological treatises and in scabrous ad hominem polemics, gave exquisitely sensitive counseling to troubled spirits and provoked Catholic crowds to massacre Protestants, walked a knife-edge between orthodoxy and heterodoxy and helped impose censorship on publishers and philosophers. They hid in the country houses of the English Catholic gentry and educated (and converted) the children of Protestant squires in grand schools in Austria and Bohemia. They ran schools and set up printing presses, staged plays and held revivals, taught Latin rhetoric, and demonstrated the rules of ballistics.

By the end of the eighteenth century, when the Society of Jesus was suppressed by papal decree, it controlled a worldwide network of more than

800 colleges and seminaries. Some of its members were engaged participants in the philosophical controversies of the late Enlightenment. Others had only recently been forced to give up their roles as priests and patrons of the famous Utopian "reductions," or agricultural communes, in regions that now belong to Brazil, Argentina, and Paraguay. Jesuits, in short, were everywhere—especially under the beds of zealous Calvinists and skeptical philosophers. They were pervasively feared and loathed as no single group of priests and thinkers had ever been before—and as none would be again until the Bolshevik commissars of the 1920s.

Readers' long-established curiosity about the magnificence and malevolence of the Jesuit order has not yet been gratified by the production of a full-scale history worthy of the subject. No counterpart to David Knowles's magnificent study of the monastic orders of medieval England traces the development of the Society of Jesus from its formal foundation in 1540 to the present. The plentiful monographs naturally do not offer universal coverage of uniform quality. Hence, until recently, the order itself was misrepresented and misunderstood—as often, perhaps, by historians as by lay readers.

This sad situation has many causes. The Jesuits themselves have published profusely about their past. More than 125 volumes of primary sources, a long-running and excellent historical journal, biographies, and bibliographies attest to their industry and devotion. But from the late Renaissance to the mid-twentieth century, much of their work adopted the method and tone of a traditional genre of Catholic scholarship: ecclesiastical history. Writers in this vein meant to edify as well as inform and tended to be saccharine rather than analytical. Vast blocks of quotation from contemporary letters and pious biographies, interspersed with criticism of all opponents and adorned with the imprimi potest and imprimatur, marked their books as suitable only for Catholic consumption.

In the last few decades, admittedly, Jesuit archivists, historians, and archaeologists have explored the history of their predecessors with insight, sophistication, and objectivity in addition to their traditional craftsmanship and erudition. They have become increasingly open to new questions and forthright about old problems. Many of them—like François de Dainville and Walter Ong, who revolutionized the study of education in early modern Europe—rank with the most distinguished humanistic scholars anywhere. An imaginative exhibit held in the Vatican Library in 1990 summed up some of the results of this work for a larger public, setting Jesuit architecture and spirituality back into the streets where they were formed.[3]

The path these scholars followed was not always straight. Even as the old political correctness of the Index of Forbidden Books faded away in Rome, a new one of liberal right-mindedness arose to replace it. When the seventeenth-century chapel containing the tomb of Ignatius Loyola was restored and opened to the public, the bold black inscriptions showing that some of the sculptures found there were intended to condemn paganism and heresy seemed embarrassing. On orders, they were discreetly filled in with white wax, in the hope that gullible visitors would fail to notice that early Jesuits did not always share the ecumenism of their modern counterparts. (Since then, Jesuit and secular scholars have done their best, by discreet fingernail scraping, to restore the inscriptions to visibility.)

In American universities, moreover, the results of Jesuit scholarship—and even the periods they studied—long remained accessible mostly to professional scholars. Historians of art and music naturally introduced their pupils to mannerism and the baroque as well as the Renaissance. But most introductory history courses have skipped blithely from Renaissance to Reformation to absolutism and the Scientific Revolution, and literature courses have rarely paused to consider Catholic classics like the moral writings of Gracián or the autobiographies of saints Teresa and John of the Cross. The Catholic Reformation never established the right to a place in the curriculum like the one long enjoyed by the Protestant one.

In America, after all, Jesuits—like postmedieval Catholicism itself—have rarely, if ever, seemed a proper object of study for scholars in elite universities. Such time and energy as undergraduates devote to studying have often gone to the colorful, remote, and elevating history and literature of the (Catholic) Middle Ages. By contrast, modern Catholic culture—like most Catholics—was usually disdained as the province of lesser breeds, fit only for the legendary parochial schools where nuns told their charges never to order ravioli on a date, lest their boyfriends be reminded of pillows. Stereotypes and prejudices of this kind, as nasty as anything fastened upon Jews, persisted in American universities until an uncomfortably recent date.

In the 1970s and 1980s, scholars both in the United States and in Europe turned with new interest to the study of past forms of religious life. But they concentrated, for the most part, on the popular rather than the official: on the lost forms of thought and feeling of the anonymous many who built the great schools and churches rather than on the well-preserved views and emotions of the established few who lived and preached in them. Even those who examined the experience of the Jesuits tended to treat it in a schematic way. They provided one more clear example of the pervasive effort to establish social and cultural discipline that characterized sixteenth-and seventeenth-century Europe—the same social discipline that confined beggars in the name of virtue and madmen in the name of sanity, and put an end to traditional carnivals and forms of conjuring in the name of uniformity and orthodoxy. The gloomy, hierarchical religion that the Jesuits brought to city slums and country villages restricted—and largely replaced—the creatively anarchical religious forms of the Middle Ages. The Jesuit schools and churches, revival meetings, and missions mattered only as part of an effort to impose the hegemony of the written over the oral, the disciplined over the spontaneous, and the modern over the archaic.

More recently still, however, the Jesuits have at last begun to attract historians' attention without being reduced to mere symptoms. Many students of the history of Christianity have begun to insist on taking Catholic devotion and spiritual counseling seriously—as part of a coherent enterprise to change the feelings of individuals, not simply a repressive plot. Historians of science and of the expansion of the West have come to realize just how tenaciously and originally Jesuit intellectuals grappled with the philosophical and anthropological discoveries of their time. Brilliant monographs in these fields—like Pietro Redondi's wrongheaded but wonderfully stimulating study of Galileo's trial and the complementary (and in part contradictory) books of Jacques Gernet and Jonathan Spence on Ricci and the Jesuit China mission—have dramatized the interest of Jesuit history for a large public. The need for an up-to-date and open-minded synthesis has become almost palpable.

In 1993, John O'Malley—a Jesuit and a historian—produced a masterly account of the first generation, the period in which nine disheveled and somewhat disreputable men, some of them already middle-aged and none of them famous or powerful, transformed themselves into the core of an organization that spanned the world and helped to save the Roman church from the frightening challenge of the Protestant Reformation. O'Malley begins with the documents, which are staggeringly rich. He carefully reviews the basic texts of the order, including Ignatius's *Constitutions* and the *Spiritual Exercises,* which became the basis of their discipline and their great success as spiritual counselors; the twelve volumes of Ignatius's letters; and the mass of official correspondence and memoranda, mostly still unpublished, that maintained communication in this society of strong-minded individuals living thousands of miles apart.

Like the so-called New Monarchies, the newly powerful states built by the rulers of sixteenth-century Spain and England, the Society of Jesus decided early that control of the files meant control of the organization. Large numbers of documents were regularly summarized and circulated for digestion by the society as a whole and tenaciously docketed and preserved at its Roman core. Accordingly, historians find themselves confronted not only by old prejudices but also by mountain ranges of new material. Like the vast documentary echo chambers of the Stasi archives now being opened by German researchers, the sheer volume of this material challenges any normal scholar to muster the necessary patience to work through it—not to mention some even rarer qualities, like the insight to see what the documents do not make explicit and the objectivity to set them in context.

O'Malley carries out all these arduous jobs with an economy and insight that compel admiration. He begins, naturally, with Ignatius himself: the thirteenth son of a minor noble family from the Basque country, who chose a military career rather than an ecclesiastical or naval one, only to be forced to reconsider when a French cannonball smashed his legs at the battle of Pamplona in 1522. Ignatius found himself laid up for a long time and subjected more than once to the brutal surgery of the time. With nothing to read but medieval saints' lives and a vast fourteenth-century series of meditations on the life of Christ, he began to explore his own mental and devotional history. Gradually, he discovered that thoughts of a military and chivalrous career left him feeling desolate and dry. Religious thoughts and aspirations, by contrast, gave him "consolation," a combination of feelings, hard to describe but easy to identify, which lay, as O'Malley shows, at the center of the Jesuit experience and enterprise.

Ignatius's subsequent life combined religious growth with romantic adventure. A trip to the Holy Land confirmed his aspirations but left him without a clear career to follow; a long period of retreat and contemplation brought him vivid spiritual experiences. Eventually, he went back to school, first in Spain, at Barcelona and Alcalà, and then to the University of Paris, where he lived for a time at the Collège de Montaigu, a famous establishment whose austere living standards and rotten eggs had almost killed the famous scholar Desiderius Erasmus a few decades before. O'Malley, an expert in Renaissance intellectual history, calls back to life the lost Left Bank of the medieval colleges, a crowded city of bell towers and cloisters that resembled Oxford more than the Paris of today. He reconstructs Ignatius's theological education in as much detail as possible, and carefully traces Ignatius's spiritual development: his increasing prestige and attraction as a religious counselor, his personal austerity, and his emergence as the central figure in a close group of spiritual athletes in Paris.

The scene changes in the second half of the 1530s. O'Malley follows Ignatius and his first friends to Italy, which became their permanent home. Their efforts to go abroad as missionaries failed. Eventually, however, thanks in part to influential friends, they gained permission to organize themselves as a formal order, the Company of Jesus. A papal bull of 1540 ratified their status. O'Malley shows insight and objectivity as he describes Ignatius's visions, the growth of his support group, the papal deaths and elections that promised help or menaced destruction. The bulk of the book treats the Jesuit story as that of the collaborative efforts of a group rather than the exemplary achievement of a single hero, and emphasizes the wider context.

As O'Malley shows, from the 1490s to the 1530s, Italy underwent both a political and a religious crisis, which continually intersected with and reinforced each other but were not identical. Imperial and French armies, much larger than any Italian ones, battled repeatedly for control of the major cities. Prophets and reformers walked the streets and piazzas, predicting the end of the world, urging women to burn their cosmetics, or calling for a more personal and less mechanical kind of Christianity—or doing all three at once. New and radical ideas were stimulated by the printed Bibles and devotional literature, radical pamphlets and apocalyptic images that welled up from the printing presses into an irresistible flood. Radicals of new kinds—from rich urban illuminati to poor rural Anabaptists—challenged the existing order in society and church. Sometimes they were flanked by the remaining adherents of medieval heresies, and often they were identified by the authorities with the practitioners of forgotten rural cults or the Protestant creators of a revolutionary new theology. The Italian cities saw many experiments with new forms of individual and collective Christian life, carried out by women as well as men: for example, the nonmonastic group known as the Oratory of Divine Love, and the women's group founded by Saint Angela Merici, which eventually gave rise to the Ursuline order. All ran risks; many failed.

It is one of the many strengths of O'Malley's book that he keeps this background in the foreground. He shows that the first Jesuits were much less militant—and far less bent on change within the church or combat outside it—than traditional accounts suggest. The Jesuit rhetoric of organization, for example, was monastic rather than military. The often cited fact that a "general" headed the order, for example, reflected Ignatius's status as "praepositus generalis" [superior general], rather than an effort to organize an army of priests to combat Luther. True, the Jesuits' general had fewer powerful subordinates to deal with than his counterparts in other orders. But he remained firmly under the control of the "general congregation" of the order as a whole. Similarly, the order's intentions were far less radical than some of Ignatius's own language suggests—at least when taken out of context, as it often is. When Ignatius advised Jesuit spiritual directors, in a famous passage, that one should believe that black is white if the hierarchy of the church so instructed, he was not summoning Catholics to believe something new and unprecedented. Any sixteenth-century Catholic accepted that what appeared to be the bread and wine of the sacraments were really the body and blood of Jesus, whatever they might look like. (True, in relying exclusively on the authority of the church, as opposed to that of the scripture, Ignatius reacted against the claims of Catholic humanists as well as Protestant reformers that church doctrines needed biblical verification.)

Not only were the Jesuits less militant than has been thought but they were also far less clear about the direction in which they were marching. In their early years, as O'Malley shows, they mostly improvised. The first Jesuits—like many of their confreres in the 1960s and after—took their stand among the urban poor. Their Roman habitat lay in what is still the heart of the city, near the ghetto, where they were tormented by noisy neighbors who wanted to use their property to raise chickens. Much of their time went to helping people at the margins of urban society, or wholly outside it. They tried to help prisoners. They did their best to convince prostitutes—including the notoriously intractable Roman ones—to adopt better lives as servants, wives, or members of a monastery of Conversae, and founded innovative halfway houses where such women could stay for a time while deciding which course of action they should follow. They addressed themselves to ordinary crafts-people, to whom they became expert at preaching.

At the core of their enterprise lay the simple belief that Catholics should confess and take the sacraments more often. And much of their zeal expressed itself in negation rather than in action of any sort. They refused to yield to the temptations of property, power, and benefices, which, they thought, might corrupt their vocations and their enterprise. They also fought to avoid limiting their freedom of action—for example, by refusing to spend several hours together every day singing the liturgical hours in church, as the members of other religious orders did. But they hardly knew, for certain, why they so valued what they soon saw as their own peculiar ways.

In short, the early Jesuits were not the brilliant deceptive polemicists and spies of legend, but spiritual entrepreneurs who wanted to break open new markets, rather like the original mendicants of the thirteenth century. And they never adopted some forms of the spiritual hard sell that earlier orders had practiced. Even when the society became attractive, it remained selective. It was always hard to join, still harder to attain full membership. At Ignatius's death in 1556, there were more than 1,000 Jesuits worldwide. Only forty-three had taken the final vow of willingness to go as missionaries at a moment's notice on papal command.

Gradually, the central enterprises of the order crystallized. At the start of his career, Ignatius tried to live in the Holy Land, and he and his early followers hoped to preach Christianity in Muslim territory, a task at which they failed. But by 1542 one of his first followers, Francis Xavier, had established himself in Portuguese Goa, and the drama of the Jesuit missions had begun. By the time of Ignatius's death, Jesuit schools and churches, manuals of confession, and treatises on theology had spread from Japan to Africa. Experiments were being made—rarely with full success—to bring non-Europeans into the order and train them. At the same time, Jesuit missionaries to the lands of northern and eastern Europe that had turned Protestant in the last half century were beginning their long, lonely efforts—often at deadly personal risk—to outpreach the Calvinists in Europe's cities and to minister to Catholic aristocrats.

Both inside and outside Europe, moreover, the Jesuits were becoming masters of a particular intellectual trade: that of the schoolmaster. Ignatius and his friends had studied in Paris; they had a deep, if not always precisely defined, belief in the value of learning, and almost immediately began to set up small institutions near Catholic universities, where their novices could study theology more efficiently and safely. But it was another kind of education to which they really dedicated themselves.

The fifteenth and early sixteenth centuries witnessed an extraordinary spread, especially in Italy, of two kinds of school: the vernacular or "abacus" school, where boys learned to read and count, gaining the basic skills for life in a mercantile society; and the Latin or grammar school, where a smaller number learned to read and imitate the classic texts of Roman antiquity.[4] Schools of the first sort were obviously practical, but those of the second became fashionable, and then indispensable, as the taste for Latin and the classics spread. Renaissance rulers gave preferment to scholars, amassed spectacular libraries, and even sat through debates about the textual criticism of Roman historians.

For the Jesuits, humanist classicism turned out to have many uses. The classically educated soon proved that their training in the arts of speech and writing made them effective and articulate. The Jesuits greatly valued skill in preaching. The sermon and the lecture on biblical texts, after all, were their basic medium for reaching the masses in city and country and their only weapon for debating with Protestants. As O'Malley shows in some of his most interesting pages, they also seem to have felt a special affinity for the classical art of rhetoric. At the heart of classical rhetoric lay the precept that an effective speaker tailors every utterance to its immediate context, taking account of listeners' needs and desires. The Jesuits, who expertly "accommodated" their clothing, diet, and language to new circumstances, took naturally to a discipline that gave them systematic training in sizing up occasions and audiences.

Ignatius soon committed himself to providing classical literary training as well as theology for young Jesuits. Drawing on their experience in Paris, the Jesuits designed a curriculum based on small classes, carefully regulated progress through increasingly difficult subjects, and meticulously expurgated classical readings. Their efficiency won customers in astonishing numbers. After 1548, when a first experiment took place in Messina, cities and rulers across Catholic Europe asked the Jesuits to establish free Catholic colleges where the young, rich and poor alike, could learn to be articulate Latinists of the fashionable type. Jesuit education proved attractive: a heavy emphasis on writing and staging plays—normally in Latin, sometimes six hours long, and often visually spiced with collapsing idols and flying saints—gave their schools a special flair. It also proved flexible. When the Jesuits saw that young aristocrats needed practical as well as classical instruction to make their way as professional soldiers, they added fencing, drill, and artillery practice to their literary offerings. They thus established a Catholic military tradition that would still exist centuries later, during World War I. More to the point, the Jesuit humanists won a clientele that included many Protestant noble families—whose children learned Catholic theology as well as Ciceronian Latin. The splendid colleges that the Jesuits reared in Austria, Bavaria, and Bohemia probably did more than anything else to win the nobility of much of eastern Europe back to the church.

Finally, the Jesuits rapidly made a specialty of spiritual direction. Ignatius codified his own development in a vivid text, the *Spiritual Exercises,* which he intended not for the person who needed help but for the spiritual director who would give it. By disciplining his life; working to eradicate his besetting sins; and undergoing a carefully staged series of vivid, concretely described meditations and visitations, loosely keyed to the life of Christ, the practitioner of the exercises could find out what task God meant him to carry out in life. The *Exercises,* a delicately calibrated tool for self-analysis and a sophisticated manual for spiritual improvement—derived in part, as Pierre Hadot has argued, from a long premodern tradition of ascetic self-formation, with roots in classical philosophy—guided Jesuits into the order. The fantastically precise questionnaires with which the Jesuits interrogated themselves about their lives and methods show how effective a guide it was, and well-kept records show how low a rate of failure it permitted.[5] But the *Exercises* did more. Almost from the start, as O'Malley shows, powerful clerics and laymen also asked to make the exercises with Ignatius or another Jesuit.

Members of the order became known as experts in guiding the spiritual and emotional lives of individuals. They began to study and then to teach the best ways of counseling individuals on how to reconcile inclination with duty, on how to bridge—and how to judge—the gap that separated the humdrum details of everyday life and the inevitable humiliations of sin and the flesh from the unremitting commands of Christian morality. They devised the retreat—the pause from everyday life for systematic prayer and contemplation. And although they did not invent the branch of theology that dealt with sin and confession, they became its master practitioners. Casuistry—the meticulous examination of problems of conduct—became a prime subject of Jesuit writing and a central area of Jesuit teaching. Within a generation, the Jesuits had established themselves as specialists in confession and absolution. Lectures, using a case system, made their results available in every Jesuit college. For centuries to come, their position as the spiritual advisers of preference for Catholic kings did much to promote the order's reputation for intrigue, worldliness, and hidden political power.

In recent years, as O'Malley shows, Jesuit casuistry has lost much of its old reputation as a holy sham—a reputation that it owed largely to the brilliant but unfair attack launched against it by Pascal in his *Provincial Letters.* Jesuits in danger of their lives in Protestant countries stretched the possibilities of spiritual counseling to their limits, sometimes by taking refuge in the notorious doctrine of the mental reservation that could make an apparently false statement true. In one famous case, a Jesuit who had denied being a priest under interrogation later explained that he had meant "a priest of Apollo."[6] Such conduct was little better than ammunition for Calvinist guns. But it was hardly the norm. O'Malley affords impressive evidence of the Jesuits' central commitment to bringing common sense to bear on the basic problems of the Catholic life. To hear Ignatius's old friend, the troublesome but forthright Father Bobadilla, insisting that one should not entertain paranoid fears of taking communion after ejaculation if one confessed the sin frankly was to come into contact with a humane sensibility from which many later authorities in Catholic moral philosophy could have learned a great deal. "The reasons of the heart," as O'Malley says in a slightly different connection, "have primacy."[7]

Naturally, O'Malley's book does not fill every need. On the immediate historical setting, for example, he is immensely informative but necessarily incomplete. The Jesuits knew many rival innovators personally or by writing, and the extent to which they learned from them remains an open question. Ignatius's brand of Catholicism, with its insistence on the needs of each person, often reminds modern readers of the spirituality of the Dutch humanist Erasmus. But the relation between the two men is unclear. Though Erasmus's excellent textbooks established themselves in Jesuit schools, Ignatius expressed only distaste for his religious writing. In this case—as in the even more delicate case of the sources of *Spiritual Exercises*—O'Malley offers judicious comment and well-chosen references, but not a definitive treatment.[8]

Another book on the early Jesuits, W. W. Meissner's *Ignatius of Loyola: The Psychology of a Saint,* promises some help here. Both a Jesuit and a distinguished psychoanalyst, Meissner brings to his topic an erudition that psychohistorians have sometimes lacked, a commitment to the value of Ignatius's spirituality, and a welcome insistence that secular science should be able to elucidate the life of a saint. Unfortunately, his results are disappointing. *Spiritual Exercises* is a fascinating and unusual text, rich with concrete instructions on how to visualize scenes from the life of Christ, from hell, and from the Holy Land, and then to draw spiritual profit from them. It had obvious connections to the popular devotional literature of the later Middle Ages, which offered similar exercises in visualization to a large and unlearned public. But it also draws on the learned art of artificial memory—the art, used by Matteo Ricci to such brilliant effect in China, which enabled the orators of Renaissance Europe to master and retain the details of Cicero's Latin. And it harks back to medieval and patristic works on spiritual counseling and authority.[9]

The *Exercises'* sumptuous and lurid images and crisp techniques of analysis probably require the attentions of a professional student of the human mind—but of one who is willing to begin by isolating what was peculiar to Ignatius. No earlier text seems to have come close to rivaling Ignatius's in psychological effectiveness and insight. Meissner, however, largely ignores the richly worked surface of the text—to say nothing of its earlier and contemporary sources. Instead he correlates a number of Ignatius's images and preoccupations with modern models of human development. But the norms from which Ignatius's experience is shown to deviate are those of the twentieth century, not the sixteenth. For all the rich material he quotes and all the striking analytical suggestions that crop up along the way, Meissner leaves the richest Ignatian soil untilled.

O'Malley concentrates on the early Jesuits, the creators of something new rather than its mere inheritors. Yet as he points out more than once, the order continued to evolve and respond to circumstances for centuries to come. Some of the artistic forms with which we tend to associate the Jesuits nowadays—like elaborate church music and lavish, triumphalist art—were adopted only in the seventeenth century. But changes affected more than the expression of theological views; they also affected their content.

During the last third of the sixteenth century, many Jesuits hardened. Novices ate in refectories decorated with scenes from the martyrdoms of early Christians as they prepared to seek martyrdom themselves in Japan or England. Jesuit theology became less experimental and Jesuit scholarship more one-sided. The society had lost the openness to conversos and other non-Christian recruits that Ignatius had displayed and defended. The worst of the Jesuit Black Legend developed—and found its real, if partial, justifications—in this later age.

Since O'Malley's book appeared, the Jesuits' archives and churches, their writings and their actions, have attracted new cohorts of historians. Many spots on the imaginary map of the Jesuits' worldwide activities have now been filled in, at least in part. Carlo Ginzburg showed long ago that the history of the seventeenth-century Jesuits must take into account the countryside of southern Italy, where they were often the first to bring a recognizably Christian theology and set of practices. The fathers who came to Eboli—where, as Carlo Levi wrote three centuries later, Christ stopped—interrogated shepherds about the Holy Trinity. They laughed unkindly at the confused replies the men offered, as each shepherd tried to win favor by guessing that there were more gods than the last one had said. But then they held processions and preached, built bonfires and marched flagellants through the mountain roads, until they had brought a simple version of Christian doctrine to the Italian countryside—which became, for the first time, not the haunt of pre-Christian beliefs and practices but the faithful core of Catholic Christianity.[10] Recently, Jennifer Selwyn has taken up Ginzburg's pregnant suggestion and told the story of the Jesuits' mission to the "Indies of Europe," the Mezzogiorno, in a crisp, well-documented study.[11]

But the history of the order in this period must also be cosmopolitan enough to embrace the Jesuit mission in China—one member of which, Adam Schall von Bell, brought news of Galileo's telescope to the Far East and actually worked in the astronomical division of the imperial civil service. The work of the most celebrated Jesuits in China—men like Schall von Bell and Matteo Ricci—has been studied for decades. But recent studies have opened up a much wider world of Jesuit practices in China. In an erudite, wide-reaching study, Benjamin Elman has traced the many ways the Jesuits trafficked with their Chinese hosts, showing how much they felt they had to learn from this more sophisticated society. Liam Brockey has reconstructed in vivid detail the story of the Portuguese Jesuit mission to China. Concentrating on the rank and file rather than the few heroic figures described by most of his predecessors, Brockey shows how Jesuits were selected and trained for the mission—his pages on the Jesuits' method of learning Chinese are especially fascinating—and then follows them into the field, charting both their efforts as missionaries and the larger context of imperial rivalries that eventually put an end to their enterprise.[12]

Much has been learned as well about the lives and works of Jesuits in the order's European heartlands. Robert Bireley, himself a Jesuit, and Harro Höpfl have taught us to appreciate the diversity of Jesuit views on the central questions of political thought, from reason of state to tyrannicide—and have shown, in doing so, that the views of Jesuits in politics still current in the English-speaking world reflect Protestant polemics as much as, or more than, the real contents of the Jesuits' treatises and pamphlets.[13] Luciano Canfora and Evonne Levy have used diverse evidence to remind us how deft the Jesuits were at using artistic forms, spiritual counsel, and personal pressure to win groups and individuals to their cause.[14] Others, meanwhile, have revealed the range and originality of Jesuit scientific practices—and shown how men, reviled by some Protestants as the enemies of the human race, played humane and cosmopolitan roles in the world of intellectual exchange known as the Republic of Letters.[15]

It will not be easy for O'Malley's successor, when he or she materializes, to synthesize these diverse and sometimes conflicting perspectives.[16] Peripheries are fashionable nowadays, and the adventurous history of the Jesuits invites scholars to adopt global and non-European perspectives. But a full history will also have to embrace the view from the center, and cover in detail the intellectual and religious life of the order in its European core—the great, skyline-dominating buildings of the Collegio Romano and the Gesù. There the German Jesuit polymath Athanasius Kircher, who took as deep an interest in the mountains of Italy and the mechanics of volcanoes as he did in the culture of China, interpreted the books of nature and the books of men to large and fascinated audiences. Kircher's thick folios full of speculations about the hieroglyphs of ancient Egypt, which he regarded as the special language of a caste of ancient sages, now seem more quaint than scholarly. But they rested on new evidence as well as old Neo-Platonic ideas, and won extensive support from other scholars. Moreover, they helped to inspire one of baroque Rome's most memorable sculptures. Bernini's fountain in the Piazza Navona bears—and invites the onlooker to admire—an Egyptian obelisk that Kircher excavated and interpreted.[17] The future historian of the Jesuits and their world could do worse than to start work in this spectacular public space, where the crowds in the Roman street present their ongoing play before yellow and orange façades, and a Jesuit's profoundly Western effort to appreciate a non-Western tradition changes shape and color with the ambient light.

9

In No Man's Land

Christian Learning and the Jews

The fifteenth-century Italian philosopher Giovanni Pico della Mirandola loved nothing more than buying books—the costlier and the more outlandish the better. He built up a splendid library in the palace at Mirandola, decorated with a fresco by Cosimo Tura that depicted the Persian sage Zoroaster and the Egyptian Hermes, as well as the Greek and Roman philosophers. He firmly believed that his collecting was a philosophical enterprise. In his view, every major thinker offered readers a unique and valid slice of the vast, universal set of truths, and therefore each book represented one colorful tile in a magnificent, divinely ordained mosaic.

Whatever their provenance, whatever their content, none of Pico's books excited him more than the Latin ones provided by his major informant on the Kabbalah and other Jewish subjects, Flavius Mithridates, a learned Jew from Sicily who had become a Christian. These renderings of Hebrew texts previously unknown in the West revealed to Pico that—as the "old Talmud" clearly showed—the Jews had once been Trinitarians, or believers in the Father, the Son, and the Holy Spirit. They also revealed that the name of Jesus, spelled in Hebrew, formed the secret core of the Kabbalistic tradition. If the Jews of Pico's time denied the Trinity or the divinity of Jesus, they did so not because they sincerely believed in the integrity of their own tradition, but in order to spite the Christians, whose true religion they obstinately refused to accept.

Flavius's ancient texts sharply spiced the heady mixture of information and exhortation that Pico brewed in his so-called *Oration on the Dignity of Man*—the speech with which he planned to open a public disputation in Rome, to which he invited all the great scholars of Europe. Sadly, Flavius's texts were of dubious value. He earned his living in a Christian world as an expert on Hebrew, Aramaic, and Arabic. A sermon that he held in the papal

Curia on Good Friday, "although it lasted two hours, still pleased everyone, thanks to the variety of its contents and the sound of the Hebrew and Arabic words, which he pronounced like a native." On that occasion, too, Flavius had deftly welded genuine Jewish traditions and the inventions of medieval anti-Jewish polemicists into a form that the Christians wanted to hear.[1] Though Pico was a pioneering Greek scholar and a clever student of the ancient Near East, he was completely taken in, and eagerly coughed up every payment Flavius demanded.[2]

This story harbors many ironies. When Pico set out to unlock the secrets of Jewish exegesis and tradition, he had to depend on Jewish informants, some of whom, though steeped in genuine Jewish traditions, told him what he wanted to hear. Nonetheless, he helped to spark one of the most radical intellectual movements of a radical age. In the late fifteenth and sixteenth centuries, many Christian scholars followed Pico's lead. They decided that they could not master the sacred texts of their own religion, the Old and New Testaments, without taking into account the scholarship of the Jews who had transmitted and interpreted the Hebrew Bible. Christian scholars began to study Hebrew, usually working with Jewish or convert teachers. They printed editions of the Hebrew Old Testament and its ancient Aramaic translations, the Targums—even though one of them, Cardinal Ximenes, described the Latin Vulgate text, which formed a central column between the Hebrew and Greek versions of the Old Testament, as resembling Christ, crucified between two thieves. By doing this, they opened and began to explore what the Israeli scholar Moshe Idel has called a "third library," one as ancient and as precious as the libraries of the Greeks and the Romans—and one both newer and more central to Christian culture than the pagan ones, since it offered new insight into the origins of Christianity itself.

Christian scholars burst into the vast memory palace of the Jews at a time when it was dangerous to do so. Italian communes forced Jews to wear yellow stars; the Catholic kings expelled them from Iberia and southern Italy; and German cities staged ritual murder trials, their central testimony obtained by torture, in which Jews were condemned for allegedly killing Christian children to use their blood in the manufacture of matzoh. Powerful figures like Kunigunde, sister of the Holy Roman Emperor Maximilian, called for the burning of Hebrew books. Converts and Christian experts competed to write ethnographies that exposed the superstitious and magical practices of Jews.

Images of Jews carrying out purificatory rituals that involved dropping their sins into running water or whirling chickens around their heads decorated tracts. They confirmed the Jews' collective reputation as a people immersed in magic. Only the boldest Christian scholars—above all, the man whom Gershom Scholem revered as an imaginary ancestor, the jurist Johannes Reuchlin—actively defended the Jews' right to keep their traditions or described them as rich and profound. And even Reuchlin, like Pico, recast the Jewish mysteries he read about in Hebrew commentaries on the Bible to fit Christian needs, and hoped to see all Jews convert in the end to Christianity.[3] Still, the opening of the Jewish tradition caused an intellectual earthquake, and the tremors it sent out shook everything, from the structures of theological education to the practice of natural philosophy. Isaac Newton was only the most famous of the several influential thinkers who found inspiration in the Kabbalah for some of their most radical ideas about nature and society.

Two generations ago, few students of European intellectual history paid much attention to the Jews. European scholars—so it seemed—had concentrated their interest and attention on Christian and classical writers and ideas. It was well known that the irascible Luther, and other writers more renowned for their tolerance, such as Erasmus and Voltaire, plunged their bent nibs into the Jews as often as they could manage. Others—like Thomas Hobbes and Pierre Bayle—elaborately discussed the Old Testament, usually in contexts where they also seemed to be scoring polemical points off fellow Christians. But Jewish influence on Christian culture and Christian responses to Jewish thought and practice both seemed subjects of local and specialized interest. Only occasionally did a scholar—usually a Jew—pursue what now seem obvious historical questions: for example, why did the tolerance of the thinkers of the French Enlightenment slumber when Jews were persecuted? Even scholars deeply schooled in Jewish learning, like the late Frank Manuel, paid relatively little attention to the intellectual collisions of Jews and Christians.

During the last forty years or so, however, all students of the European past have come to see the Western tradition as much less unified, and its borders a great deal more labile, than they once realized. The study of Jewish history has blossomed. Specialists in the field like Scholem, Moshe Idel, Joseph Dan, Amos Funkenstein, Yosef Hayim Yerushalmi, Josef Kaplan, Elisheva Carlebach, and David Ruderman have found a wide readership among students of European thought—and they, in turn, have realized that European thinkers took a passionate interest in the Kabbalah, the rituals of Jewish worship, and the textual status of the Hebrew Bible. Experts on Christian Europe like Brian Pullan, Natalie Zemon Davis, William Chester Jordan, R. Po-chi Hsia, and Jonathan Israel have turned their attention to Jewish communities and individuals living in the European world. Very few scholars, like the Israeli historian David Katz, know both worlds firsthand.[4] Syntheses remain few and incomplete: one of the most stimulating is Frank Manuel's *The Broken Staff*, written in the 1980s, when that great historian returned late in his career to the Hebrew studies of his youth. But no historian of European culture can now ignore the prominent roles that Jews have played, over the centuries, in both European life and the European imagination. Some of the most exciting recent books in European history—such as David Nirenberg's *Communities of Violence* and Miri Rubin's *Gentile Tales*—have traced the fault lines that separated Jewish and Christian communities and delicately recorded, from the sources, the shocks created when each community rubbed against the other.

For all the new light that scholars have thrown upon this once dark border region, central questions nevertheless remain unsolved and obscure. For example, how typical was Pico's deep, engaged, passionate, mediated, and sometimes spurious experience of Christian contact with and thought about the Jews? How typical was Reuchlin's more direct immersion in the sources? Did Christians invent imaginary Jews, their hereditary enemies within Europe, as they invented other imaginary enemies, from Turks to cannibals, outside Europe? Or did they learn really to see Jews, in their full humanity? When, if ever, did Jews themselves find a voice within the European world? And what messages did they send to Christians?

Two recent books—both of them passionate, well informed, and eloquent—attack these problems in instructively different ways. Adam Sutcliffe, a pupil of the prolific and erudite historian Jonathan Israel, uses the role of Judaism in Enlightenment thought to develop his teacher's thesis that the most radical shifts in modern European culture took place in the decades just before and after 1700. His wide-ranging study starts in the seventeenth-century heyday of polymathy, when Christian scholars exhausted themselves trying to establish an absolutely reliable text of the Bible and an absolutely rigorous, coherent approach to world history—achingly difficult enterprises to begin with, and made more so by the dizzying new information about the Near East, the New

World, China, and India that filtered back to Europe. New versions of the Bible and new evidence about the antiquity of Eastern societies transmogrified the narrow, orderly mansions of history.

Traditional world chronicles laid out history as a neat sequence of names and dates that started with Adam and ended with the present. But the new accounts of the Americas and China broke time lines, defied traditions, and made the past a bizarre carnival fun house. Its shocking mirrors dramatically magnified the Egyptian and Chinese traditions, making them look older and more profound than the Jewish one. These debates grew hotter as the seventeenth century wore on—especially, as Sutcliffe shows, when they moved from the studies in which grave and learned scholars wrote Latin folios for a few peers into the journals and coffeehouses of the time. Suddenly, women and Grub Street writers could read about and join in debates that had once been the province of the erudite. Gradually, Sutcliffe argues, the old baroque disciplines like chronology lost their luster, and even their coherence.

Jewish tradition then became the object of sharp questions. Was it the source of all true knowledge about the origins of life, the universe, and everything else, as scholars had traditionally insisted? Or was it a parochial and self-serving body of stories that obscured the older and more vital civilizations whose culture and religion the Jews had rejected? Could the Calvinist thinker Isaac La Peyrère be right when he claimed that the biblical story of Creation did not describe the origin of the Jews, but that of humanity itself, thousands of years before Jewish history began? Or the Catholic thinker Richard Simon, when he insisted that the Hebrew scriptures had not been dictated by God, but assembled by fallible humans, long after the events they described? Neither man's ideas were so novel as modern historians generally believe, as Noel Malcolm has shown in a brilliant piece of scholarly detective work.[5] Yet if earlier divines provided the tools with which La Peyrère and Simon went about their tentative work of demolition, others had declared every word—and every mark of punctuation—in the Bible to be the product of direct divine inspiration. Both men were denounced and their books condemned and rebutted, yet even their opponents, like Bishop Bossuet, knew that they could no longer maintain with absolute confidence the old simple truths about history and tradition. The search for certainty in scholarship led only to controversy without end, as the vast constructs of the late humanists collapsed like the Old Man of the Mountains in New Hampshire.

Yet the failure of Christian Hebraism marked only the beginning of Enlightenment Europe's engagement with the Jews. Sutcliffe describes a new breed of thinkers—open-minded, revisionist scholars like Jacques Basnage and Pierre Bayle—who subjected the Jews to a new kind of scrutiny. Basnage, who wrote the first large-scale history of the Jews by a European, highlighted at many points the value and interest of Jewish thought—especially that of those almost-Protestant Jews, the Karaites, who rejected tradition and followed only scripture and reason. Yet Basnage also judged the Jews as a Calvinist, and made clear his hope that all of them would eventually convert.

Bayle, for his part, wittily exposed in his dictionary the immorality of great figures from the Jewish past, like David. He argued more generally that Jewish law was inferior to Christian ethics, since it imposed a single, absolute standard where Christianity schooled the individual conscience. Yet Bayle also praised the morality of Jewish customs—for example, he saw the prohibition against speaking during marital sex, which he found in a guide to proper conduct for Jewish women, as an excellent preventive remedy for lust. Judaism somehow remained outside ethics and exemplified it simultaneously.

Even as Christian thinkers struggled to define what Judaism meant and should mean to their fellows, Jews—of a sort—found a new voice. In the Sephardi community at Amsterdam, many of whose members had little traditional Jewish education, and all of whom were exposed to cultural influences of the most diverse kinds, Jewish thinkers like Isaac Morteira and Uriel da Costa challenged Jewish orthodoxy. Though their texts too were largely suppressed, they had an impact nonetheless—especially on the young Spinoza. When he, in turn, was expelled from the Jewish community, he developed the most radical of all assaults on biblical authority and tradition. Many of the Dutch had long seen their Calvinist state, created by a lengthy rebellion against Catholic Spain, as a modern Israel. Radical preachers and their followers wanted to dissolve Holland's republican institutions, since they distrusted the tolerant patricians who ran them and preferred to put their fate in the hands of the godly house of Orange.

In the *Tractatus Theologico-Politicus,* Spinoza engaged both with the long arc of Jewish tradition and with the short-term crisis of the Dutch Republic. He argued forcefully that the Bible was addressed to the primitive Jews whose actions it described—and thus could not offer moral rules or natural philosophy to the more sophisticated readers of his own time. That explained why it described impossible events and put forward errors about the physical world. The best chapters of Sutcliffe's book trace the complex ways in which Spinoza became a hero—perhaps *the* hero—of the Enlightenment, as radicals summarized, applied, developed, and travestied his ideas, sometimes combining them with strange notions from the Hermetic and other traditions. Throughout the seventeenth and early eighteenth centuries, critical thinkers continued their fight to understand, classify, and determine Europeans' duties toward the Jews.

Throughout the Enlightenment, Sutcliffe concludes, Jews proved a source of trouble and ambiguity. He nicely describes the increasing prominence of actual Jews on the urban scene in Amsterdam, London, and elsewhere; the continued vitality of anti-Jewish stereotypes; and the ambiguities of eighteenth-century thought. Thinkers repeatedly acknowledged the virtues of individual Jews, but nonetheless insisted that Jews as a race must drop their peculiar habits and customs if they hoped to join the civilized European world. Over the decades, as the din made by these colliding facts and theories battered the ears of the philosophes, Jews remained impossible to fix in any historical or religious pigeonhole. The Enlightenment's bequest to later periods was less Voltaire's harsh anti-Semitic rhetoric than a series of ambiguities, which left unclear both what category the Jews belonged in (race, religion, other?) and how public discourse or politics should treat them.

Like Adam Sutcliffe, Maurice Olender—the product of a Parisian training in classics and intellectual history—sees scholarly traditions as central to the modern fate of the Jews.[6] Where Sutcliffe emphasizes seventeenth-century scholars' efforts to show that the Jews had learned from the Egyptians, Olender highlights the late eighteenth- and nineteenth-century philological revolution, when scholars discovered Sanskrit and tried to redraw the family tree of nations by creating a history of the world's languages. The history and relations of languages mattered, in a new way, in this period. Philosophers in France and Germany, among them Montesquieu and Herder, argued that a people's language expressed—and even shaped—its culture. They systematically compared the Jews, who were located in the Bible at the beginnings of world history and established by comparative theology as the inventors of monotheism, with the Aryans, who were omitted from the Bible but identified by the new kind of comparative philology as the ancestors of modern Europeans and the most creative of all the races. From the late eighteenth to the late nineteenth centuries, as Olender convincingly argues, scholars of very different kinds envisioned the histories of Jews and Aryans as the two long backbones of a double helix. Between them, these traditions formed a body of complementary genetic materials that determined nothing less than the course of history itself.

History's two backbones—so argued thinkers from Herder onward—complemented each other in a neat and symmetrical way. Jews believed in one God, Aryans in many. Jews and other Semites created a stable, sterile, unchanging culture, which lasted over centuries and millennia. Aryans, by contrast, innovated endlessly. Both the imperfect language of the Jews, which lacked inflections and a proper system of tenses, and the perfect one of the Aryans, which had a past and a future tense, expressed (or defined) their cultural and racial abilities. From Herder to Pictet, as Olender eloquently shows, these categories framed and limited scholars' vision of the past. Occasional exceptions did not tear the tough but delicate screen of myths and prejudices that hung between scholars and sources. Only in the work of Ignaz Goldziher—a nineteenth-century Jew who worked in Hungary and Egypt, and was trained in but not imprisoned by the categories of modern scholarship—did they meet a full-scale refutation. Even then, the prejudices that lost ground on the battlefields of philology regained it in institutes of racial science, concentration camps, and even faculties of theology.

Olender's book has many virtues. Brief, intense, and often ironic, it rests on a deep foundation of learning. His ability to compress his material into sinuous chapters, concise and packed with material but never overly schematic or simplified, compels admiration. *The Languages of Paradise* is a little masterpiece of exposition as well as of analysis. One side of Olender's project is iconoclastic. He challenges one of the founding myths of nineteenth-century thought: that of philology itself. According to the standard tale, history lay sleeping for centuries until Herder and his crowd of attendant professors came and released it. No one before the great eighteenth-century innovators—Winckelmann, Heyne, and Herder—had real insight into the otherness of the past, into the sharp differences between one's own culture and all others. By contrast, the scholars of the late eighteenth and nineteenth centuries, inspired by Herder, shared his sharp historical sense and his ability to detect in language the clues that revealed the development of cultures.

The Languages of Paradise replaces these simple formulas with more complex readings of the texts. Olender demonstrates how deeply myth remained lodged in the mental structures of nineteenth-century history. When the mid-nineteenth century's most influential historian of Judaism and Christianity, Ernest Renan, described the Semites of Jesus's time as passive, superstitious creatures, unlike the more Hellenized and Westernized inhabitants of the Galilee, he was not recording history as it had been, but imposing a retrospective construction on the sources. The Galileans who populated Renan's *Life of Jesus* were historical straw men, imaginary figures. So, more generally, were the gifted, mercurial, and witty Aryans conjured up by the sober scientists of the past (and who, in Renan's vision, bizarrely included Jesus himself).

At a more basic level still, the project of historicism, which claimed to read cultures in their own terms, turned itself, as well as the past, into myth. Herder and Renan insisted that each culture had a particular nature, as independent of all others as a Leibnizian monad. Nonetheless, their belief in a providential and progressive order led them, time and again, to make qualitative judgments about the peoples and cultures of the past. They compared languages and literatures, arranging them in a hierarchical order that proved the upward movement of humanity—upward and away from the Jews. Historical analysis blended imperceptibly into comparative taxonomy. Historicism, which had been open to consideration of different traditions, metamorphosed into a philosophy of history as severe and stereotyped as those of the eighteenth-century philosophes; scholarship embodied racist notions and lived on in racist theories. Yet the heroes of nineteenth-century philology, the scholars who explored and criticized the textual sources of Christian belief, and who found the fault lines in every chronicle, did not recognize the contradictions that lay at the heart of their enterprise.

Olender, however, does not simply seek to expose the failings of the nineteenth century. He shows an ironic affection for the swelling richness of his subjects' language—the uncontrollable profusion of metaphors and images that gave their accounts of Semites and Aryans depth and drama. He appreciates their immediate response, so characteristic of their period, to landscape and local color: the ease with which they found the inspiration for Jehovah in a thunderstorm or recognized Mary Magdalene in a modern Arab woman glimpsed at a well.

In the end, Olender's intellectual sympathy obviously lies with Goldziher, who insisted on the permeability of racial and cultural borders and on the primacy of concrete evidence over abstract schemes. But all his actors have fully developed characters, and all of them are treated seriously and with respect. In his refusal to imprison past scholars in the iron cages of simple, coherent formulas, and in his careful tracing of their self-contradictions, self-betrayals, and self-transcendences, Olender shows that he himself is something of a nineteenth-century novelist. His book makes an instructive contrast to the banal simplicities of much modern historiography, and provides a model of historical analysis that does justice to the form, as well as the content, of complex intellectual systems. Like Sutcliffe, he shows that the history of scholarship is not only densely technical but also richly human.

Both of these books help us to see how Western intellectuals have imagined the Jews who lived among them. Both help us also to understand why the same categories—and the same ambiguities—framed Western understandings of other non-Western peoples, like those of the Middle East. Sutcliffe and Olender show that Edward Said, in *Orientalism,* described not a unique construct but one among many templates through which Western writers viewed, and with which they tried to describe, non-Western cultures and peoples.[7]

Yet the history of European views of Judaism in the early modern period is even more complex than these excellent books suggest. Sutcliffe and Olender both write as if early modern intellectuals envisioned the Jewish tradition as simple and uniform—a world of Jews who lived in similar communities, followed similar laws, and used the Hebrew language for divine service and biblical study. In fact, however, the Christian Hebraists of the sixteenth and seventeenth centuries knew perfectly well that this was not true. As early as the 1580s, Joseph Scaliger argued that the "Hellenists" mentioned in the New Testament Acts of the Apostles were not simply Jews who lived in the Greek and Roman lands of the Roman Empire, but Jews "who read the Bible in Greek in their Synagogues." Paul and the New Testament evangelists cited the Bible in Greek because, for the most part, they were addressing Hellenized Jews.

As evidence for this revisionist thesis, Scaliger cited a Jewish writer whom Christians had traditionally treated with respect: Philo, the Alexandrian philosopher who lived between approximately 20 BCE and 50 CE. He and his fellows were devout Jews, as committed as anyone to orthodox practice. They worshiped in a synagogue at Alexandria that rivaled the temple in Jerusalem for scale and splendor. Philo and the other Hellenists pursued a form of Judaism distinct in language and in other respects from that of Palestine. On the other hand, though ignorant of Hebrew, they knew much more than contemporary Hebrew speakers about the history and culture of the wider world the Jews inhabited.[8]

In the late sixteenth and seventeenth centuries, when Christian scholars discovered the existence of a Hellenistic phase in Jewish history, the Jews—or at least one learned Jew—did the same. Azariah de' Rossi, a Ferrarese Jew, produced an immense treatise entitled *The Light of the Eyes,* in which he systematically compared Jewish, Christian, and classical traditions about the past. He and other Jewish scholars, like David Provenzali, read Philo, whom Azariah called "Yedidyah the Alexandrian." Azariah was disturbed and fascinated by his encounter with a Jewish writer whose works were published and translated by Christian scholars. Like Scaliger, he recognized that although Philo "had expert knowledge of Greek and expressed himself fluently and lucidly in the language," he "never saw nor knew the original text of Torah." Azariah responded with a complex mixture of admiration and repulsion to the discovery of ancient Egyptian Jews who could articulate "beautiful" allegories on the scripture, but could not read it in the original: "I cannot pass an immediate and absolute verdict on him."[9] Many Christians read Azariah, in turn, and found rich material to add to Scaliger's insights into the culture of the Hellenists.

In the course of the seventeenth century, scholars developed and sharpened these analyses. Scaliger suggested that one could find parallels to many of Jesus's commandments in the Talmud, the great Jewish compilation of legal codes and commentaries. He even used the Passover Haggadah to reconstruct the full Last Supper, as Jesus had conducted it. The account given in the Gospels, Scaliger argued, described only the segments of the ritual that deviated from normal Jewish practice. Only a historical reconstruction—one that pieced together the original event by setting the Gospel accounts into their Jewish context—could reveal what actually happened at the Messiah's table. Scaliger's pupil Daniel Heinsius argued that the Jews had created a Greek dialect or language of their own, a "Hellenistic language," in which Greek words bore new, Semitic meanings. *Sarx,* for example, the medical term for "flesh" in classical Greek, corresponded in the Hellenistic language to the Hebrew term *basar,* which could bear a much wider sense, as in the biblical phrase "all flesh."[10]

Heinsius held that one could understand the New Testament only by learning the particular Jewish Greek in which it had been written. Others— especially his great enemy, Claude Saumaise—denounced these ideas, and argued that the Hellenists had used no special language. The Greek of the New Testament revealed unusual, Semitic usage because the texts had been translated from Hebrew and Aramaic originals. And the Hellenists, Saumaise insisted, had had no great synagogue of their own in Alexandria or elsewhere.

The learned controversy about the language of the Hellenists went on for centuries, until scholars much later reconstructed the history of the *koine* dialect of Greek that Jews and non-Jews alike spoke in the years of Christ's life. But throughout the seventeenth and eighteenth centuries, one point remained clear. No learned man could imagine that all Jews, in antiquity or later, had spoken the same language, read the same version of their holy books, or used the same liturgy. Some even speculated on the ways in which the special Judaism of the Hellenists had inflected the language and thought of the early Christians. The crisis of Christian humanism was not as sudden and total as Sutcliffe argues, and the stereotypes of Jews and their language not as confining as Olender suggests.

The authors of these short, packed, and cogent books have illuminated lost worlds of passionate and engaged discussion, demonstrated the central part that Judaism played in Christians' efforts at self-definition, and teased out the ambiguities of Enlightenment and historicism. Not least of all, they have shown how much we still do not know about the no man's land in which learned Jewish and Christian armies struggled over the centuries.[11]

10

The History of Ideas

Precept and Practice, 1950–2000 and Beyond

In the middle years of the twentieth century, the history of ideas rose like a new sign of the zodiac over large areas of American culture and education. In those happy days, Dwight Robbins, the president of a fashionable progressive college, kept "copies of *Town and Country,* the *Journal of the History of Ideas,* and a small magazine—a little magazine—that had no name" on the table in his waiting room. True, Robbins did not exist: he was the fictional president of Randall Jarrell's equally fictional Benton, a liberal arts dystopia where "half of the college was designed by Bottom the Weaver, half by Ludwig Mies van der Rohe."[1] But Jarrell's notation of the *Journal's* status was accurate nonetheless.[2]

In the twenty years or so after its foundation, the *Journal* attracted attention from many quarters, some of them unexpected. And it occupied a unique position between the technical journals of history and philology, each firmly identified with a discipline in which professional humanists normally published their results, and the quarterlies, often based not in disciplines but in liberal arts colleges and universities, which cultivated a mixed readership to which they offered fiction and poetry as well as essays. By contrast with both, fifty years ago the *Journal* ran on a rich mix of technical articles and wide-ranging essays that could easily have attracted the attention of a sophisticated administrator—or at least made a good impression on his coffee table. Bliss was it to be a subscriber in that happy day when the *Journal* glowed with something of the luster that haloed *Representations* in the 1980s and *Critical Inquiry* more recently.

The main reason for the *Journal's* prominence was that it represented a new field, as appealingly located between disciplines as it was between other sorts of periodicals. In its postwar heyday, the history of ideas was not a dim subdivision of history, itself a discipline whose luster has worn off with time, but an intellectual seismic zone where the tectonic plates of disciplines converged and rubbed against one another, producing noises of all sorts. In recent years, it has sometimes seemed impossible, even to the best informed observers, that intellectual history, or the history of ideas, ever enjoyed this sort of prestige. A quarter century ago, Robert Darnton surveyed the state of intellectual and cultural history in the United States in an informative and influential essay. Using a language more resonant of the historical President Carter than the fictional President Robbins, Darnton detected "malaise" everywhere he looked. In the 1950s, he noted, intellectual historians had seen "their discipline as the queen of the historical sciences. Today she seems humbled." True, desperate cries for help were not yet called for. Historians continued to write histories of ideas, and even to cast them in the technical languages of A. O. Lovejoy or Perry Miller: "One still finds 'unit-ideas' and 'mind' among the trendier terms." Moreover, the just-published *Dictionary of the History of Ideas* offered the reading public a vast selection of Lovejoyan formal analyses, systematically organized.[3]

Since the 1960s, Darnton argued, younger scholars, especially graduate students, had been scrambling over the gunwales of the good ship *History of Ideas,* abandoning the effort to converse abstractly with the mighty dead, and clambering in hordes over the side of a newer vessel, Social History, which boasted a Hogarthian passenger list of heretics, misfits, and military women. At the level of the dissertations written in history departments, social history was outpacing intellectual history by a proportion of three to one. At the level of the scholarly journal, too, social history had forged ahead, though by a smaller margin. In the murkier but no less significant world of opinion, finally, the decline of intellectual history appeared clearest. History of ideas no longer occupied the cutting edge in young scholars' mental vision of their discipline.

In the 1960s, after all, social history had captured the minds of a generation—or a large percentage of it—thanks both to the power of its own new method and vision and to the political conditions that inspired so many historians to dedicate themselves to recovering the experience of those who had not had power, voice, or privilege in the past. From the 1960s on, the study of core texts and writers underwent siege after siege, from the era when "irrelevance" formed the central charge against it to the later age of the culture wars, when tragedy repeated itself as farce. Even more important,

intellectual history had genuinely lost its edge and coherence in the same period. The collapse of a certain type of liberalism in the 1960s undermined the
Americanist pursuit of a unified "national mind," leaving the field open for
social historians who emphasized the varied experiences of those groups that
the older picture had omitted. Europeanists also found it impossible by the
1960s to draw the unified pictures of intellectual traditions and cultural periods that had occupied A. O. Lovejoy and Carl Becker. Instead they traced
what amounted to intellectual biographies of individuals or groups—studies
that were often erudite and insightful, but not methodologically distinct
from the work of cultural historians or historians of science.[4]

Darnton noted continued signs of life amid the ruins. Some practitioners—
like Carl Schorske and Dominick LaCapra—were determined to emphasize
direct reading of texts, works of art, even pieces of music. Though the two
men used very different methods, they agreed that intellectual historians must
confront the genres, styles, and local details of the works of art and literature
that they analyzed, rather than reducing them to instances of larger concepts.
Others, primarily historians of political thought like Bernard Bailyn and
Quentin Skinner, had set out to erect a new discipline in which context—the
local matrices within which texts were forged and read—and language—the
language of humble pamphlets and bold speeches, as well as that of canonical
texts—took center stage. Political thought mattered, Bailyn argued, when it
became part of a larger discussion carried on in newspapers and argued
through in taverns, as had happened in eighteenth-century America. Political
thought changed, Skinner claimed, when someone dared to use key terms,
with malice aforethought, in senses clearly different than their normal ones. If
Bailyn provided a new way to follow ideas into action, Skinner offered a new
version of intellectual history itself—one that traced its roots to Peter Laslett's
brilliant edition of Locke's *Second Treatise* and that challenged all traditional
ways of doing intellectual history. In a very influential article, Skinner himself
argued that no historian could write meaningfully of intellectual traditions,
interpret older texts as speaking to a modern context, or usefully construct an
intellectual biography.[5] Some older scholars experienced this crisply framed
critical exercise, directed at the removal of deadwood, as a form of clear-
cutting that left few trees where forests once loomed. Over time, Skinner's
method both yielded remarkable results and underwent major modifications,
but neither could easily have been predicted in the 1970s.

Other fields within the larger territory of intellectual history revealed on closer inspection that sharp debates, always a preeminent sign of life, were still being waged. For example, the history of science remained, as it had long been, a battlefield. Where Marxists had once struggled with sociologists, internalists now fought externalists. The tension between them, Darnton thought, "will continue to be creative . . . and even the most recondite scientific activity will be interpreted within a cultural context"—especially since this tension appeared within the work of particularly eminent and original scholars like Thomas Kuhn, as well as in the territory that seemed to be opening up between warring schools.[6] Moreover, a number of shared themes connected the projects that looked most promising: for example, the effort to locate even the most seemingly abstract of enterprises, from Harvard philosophy to Weimar physics, in institutional, social, and discursive contexts.

His appreciation for these writers and others notwithstanding, however, Darnton saw the scene as fragmented and rather depressing. Massive studies of intellectual traditions continued to appear, some of them masterly: for example, Frank Manuel and Fritzie Manuel's 1979 survey of *Utopian Thought in the Western World*. But few enterprises in intellectual history had the innovative character and compulsively readable quality of the work being done by the new cultural historians, with their passionate if still inchoate concern "for the study of symbolic behavior among the 'inarticulate.' "[7] Furthermore, many of the liveliest and most accomplished intellectual historians bent over their spades and hoes not in the long-cultivated gardens and borders of the Renaissance and the Enlightenment and the nineteenth-century age of evolutionary schemes, but in distant, gravel-strewn border zones where the history of ideas touched—or even passed over into—other forms of history. For Darnton, in the end, intellectual history could survive only if it became a basically social and cultural history of ideas and their bearers.

Darnton's observations were characteristically trenchant and mostly just. A striking number of the younger scholars in whom he saw special promise in the early stages of their careers have more than borne out his predictions, producing long series of influential books and articles. Many of the most original and significant intellectual histories of the late 1950s, 1960s, and 1970s—for example, H. Stuart Hughes's *Consciousness and Society* (1958), Fritz Stern's *The Politics of Cultural Despair* (1961), Fritz Ringer's *The Decline of the German Mandarins* (1969), and Martin Jay's *The Dialectical*

Imagination (1973)—offered new models for setting the life of ideas into institutional, social, and cultural contexts. The new cultural history that Darnton saw aborning in the late 1970s did come to occupy a special place in historical research and teaching, just as he predicted, in the 1980s and 1990s— the period when Darnton's own *Great Cat Massacre,* Carlo Ginzburg's *The Cheese and the Worms,* Natalie Zemon Davis's *The Return of Martin Guerre,* and Jonathan Spence's *Death of Woman Wang* and *Memory House of Matteo Ricci* captured a vast reading public and transformed the teaching of history across the country. This form of scholarship, which grasped, often successfully, for previously unrecorded and unplumbed worlds of experience, defined a growth sector of intellectual and cultural historiography for the decades ahead. Perhaps those historians of ideas who felt and showed malaise in the 1970s were right.[8]

Early in the new millennium, it seems reasonable to have another broad look at the way our field has developed. After all, we can now look back, and forward, with another twenty-five years' experience to guide us, and with all the charity and clarity that hindsight affords. If we do so—and especially if we survey the same scene not from within the discipline of history, as Darnton was asked to, but from the interdisciplinary space that the *Journal* has always occupied—we may see that matters were not as bleak as they seemed in the late 1970s. The humanistic disciplines were moving, in their glacial, irresistible way. And although it seemed, around 1980, that they were pulling apart, they were in fact meeting at new points and transforming one another in the process. The tremors they created soon reoriented intellectual history. And the residual strength that the field and the *Journal* displayed in the 1990s and after had everything to do with the roots from which it sprang.

From the beginning, the *Journal* and the enterprise it represented were never meant to be wholly or even partly owned subsidiaries of the discipline of history. Scholars who mention the name of A. O. Lovejoy these days often do so in order to lampoon his methods. Arnaldo Momigliano spoke for many before and after him when he compared Lovejoy and his vision of "unit-ideas" to the Oxford scholar Margoliouth, who believed that there were thirty Indo-European Ur-jokes from which all the rest were derived. "Lovejoy," Momigliano quipped, "did not believe that the number of Ur-ideas was much greater."[9] In fact, however, Lovejoy took as passionate an interest in institutions and their flesh and blood inhabitants as in abstract ideas—he was, after all, one of the creators of the American Association of University Professors.[10] He deliberately designed the history of ideas, as he explained in the first issue of the *Journal,* as a field that had to be interdisciplinary if it was to exist at all. And his program for the external organization of the field derived from his vision of its content and method.

Capsule summaries of Lovejoy's work usually portray him—and sometimes dismiss him—as one who wanted to reduce all works of literature and art to illustrations of particular philosophical doctrines. Lovejoy did set out to map the "unit-ideas" that, he believed, had originally framed and must now be reconstructed to explicate all great works of literature and art, as well as science and philosophy, in the Western tradition. It is not surprising that Lovejoy saw formal systems of ideas as the core object of his studies. He was a philosopher by training. So was Philip Weiner, executive editor of the *Journal* for forty-five years, and their joint vision helped to shape both the journal and the field it served over time. But although both men cherished a personal preference for studies of formal ideas, they also agreed that ideas had to be studied as expressed in the whole field of culture. Lovejoy believed that "in the history of philosophy is to be found the common seed-plot, the locus of initial manifestation in writing, of the greater number of the more fundamental and pervasive ideas." But he also acknowledged that these ideas manifested themselves in multiple and varied ways: to survey the life of any single idea, such as "evolution," would require expert knowledge of fields from geology to aesthetics, as well as a firm ability to distinguish the various meanings of particular words and phrases in the texts of a given period. The same held, even more strongly, for the study of larger and more confused categories like "Romanticism," to which Lovejoy devoted pages that since published have been as controversial as they have been influential.[11] Lovejoy argued from the start that in order to carry out this immense task, scrupulous scholars from every humanistic discipline would have to collaborate, since no individual with a normal, limited training in a single field could hope to exhaust the story of a single true unit-idea on his own—much less complete the analysis of any one of the massive works that embodied these abstract but powerful entities. Humanists, in fact, should emulate the sciences and work in collaboration. By doing so, Lovejoy suggested not without irony, they could create a commentary on Milton's *Paradise Lost,* at a level of precision and completeness that no individual, however learned and energetic, could hope to reach.[12]

For decades it has been normal to criticize Lovejoy on the grounds that he wanted to reduce art and literature to the expression of formal ideas. The critique has its merits—though it ignores his emphasis on the emotional power with which intellectuals charged an idea like that of *The Great Chain of Being.*[13] But Lovejoy regularly invited representatives of the other humanistic disciplines to collaborate in the plotting of the larger story—even though he must have suspected that they would bring their own priorities and practices with them, and find his wanting.

From the start, in other words, Lovejoy envisioned the history of ideas as a field in which scholars with varied disciplinary trainings and loyalties would meet. The *Journal* was to play a social as well as an intellectual role. This is exactly how the history of ideas had functioned at Lovejoy's own university, Johns Hopkins, for decades before the *Journal* came into existence. Not a charismatic teacher, Lovejoy attracted few graduate students to the Philosophy Department, of which he and George Boas were the only members. But the History of Ideas Club that he and Boas founded in 1923 became an extraordinarily successful, if sometimes "zoo-like," interdisciplinary enterprise—a regular meeting place where members of the erudite, articulate Hopkins humanities faculty could offer papers and dispute with one another at a very high level.[14] No prophet in his own country, Lovejoy found one of his sharpest critics at home, in the person of Leo Spitzer, who joined the Hopkins faculty as an exile in the 1940s and who argued, against Lovejoy, that only a combination of philological precision in the analysis of language and evocative *Geistesgeschichte* for the re-creation of contexts could provide a method adequate to the new discipline's needs. In his view, Lovejoy's history of ideas represented a slip backward from the Romantic method—on which, Spitzer thought, Lovejoy largely blamed the rise of the Nazis—to the superficial analysis of the Enlightenment: "It seems to me tragic that in inorganically detaching certain features from the whole of Romanticism in order to draw lines of continuity with our times, the historian of ideas has discarded the very method, discovered by the Romantics, which is indispensable for the understanding of the alternation of historical or cultural climates."[15] Lovejoy disagreed, with spirit and some asperity.[16] But since he treated the history of ideas not as a set doc-trine, but as a center for fruitful and passionate debate, the *Journal* printed Spitzer's critique as well as Lovejoy's reply. In a sense, Lovejoy's famously mixed reception at Harvard, where the philosophers stopped coming to the lectures that became *The Great Chain of Being* while the literary scholars re-mained, only confirms the larger point. In the prewar American university system, faculty taught many hours per week and young scholars took many years to complete their doctorates and struggled even longer to reach the bot-tom rung of the tenure track. The system boasted few of the lecture series, workshops, and postdoctoral fellowships that now bring young scholars from multiple disciplines into productive contact. Accordingly, the history of ideas served as one of the few virtual salons that encouraged conversations of the right sort. In the *Journal* and the fields it covered, disciplines that usually had little traffic with one another—English literature and history, for example—could meet and discuss texts of common interest in productive ways. So could the émigré scholars and their American colleagues and pupils who made the *Journal* one of the most cosmopolitan of scholarly periodicals.

By the 1950s, as the successive issues of the *Journal* established the interest and legitimacy of the field and graduate education in humanities expanded, the discipline showed its interdisciplinary appeal at a number of institutions. At Columbia University, for example, Rosalie Colie and Samuel Mintz—formally a literary scholar and a philosopher, respectively—founded a *Newsletter* for the history of ideas in 1954. This lively, even frenetic publica-tion gave graduate students and young scholars a venue where they could publish short primary sources, review books, and float their own ideas about the past and the discipline of intellectual history. It attracted eager participa-tion and provoked widespread interest. When Colie herself ventured to argue that the best way to teach the history of science was as social history, she re-ceived sharp, critical responses from distinguished historians and literary scholars around the country, including such eminences as Crane Brinton and Harcourt Brown—a historian and a literary scholar, respectively. Though Colie pronounced herself "well and truly drubbed" by their replies, she re-butted them with characteristic vigor and confidence.[17] In the age of the Web site and the blog, it is salutary to be reminded that the U.S. mail and the mimeograph machine could sustain a national, interdisciplinary network of this quality. Columbia continued to be a great center for intellectual history for decades to come. Evidently, then, the history of ideas, and the *Journal,* flourished in part because they provided something of what campus humanities centers do now—spaces between disciplines, where scholars can come together, master one another's tools, and apply them to their own objects.

In its first heyday, moreover, the history of ideas flourished in many contexts and for many reasons. It rested, in large part, on pedagogical foundations that had been reared quite independently of Lovejoy and the *Journal.* In the aftermath of World War I, urban universities like Columbia and Chicago created introductory courses on Western civilization. Administrators and professors saw these surveys as a vital way to impart a common background, or at least apply a shared veneer, to their ethnically varied and culturally unpolished students. After World War II, broad-gauged courses of this kind took on a new function, as they provided veterans who studied on the GI Bill with not only the elements of a humanistic education but also some acquaintance with texts that they could use to work through what they had experienced on Pacific islands and in the bomber stream over Berlin.[18] These courses attracted faculty from a variety of disciplines. They were often, perhaps usually, team taught, and they were enriched by formal presentations in which a member of the course staff presented particular texts or problems to his or her colleagues. The course on Western Civilization—or as Columbia called it, Contemporary Civilization—became something like a way of life. It also served, at Columbia, as the foundation for the Humanities Colloquium—an intensive, two-year study of great books, in which a staff that included Jacques Barzun and Lionel Trilling debated, before their students, the virtues of historical and nonhistorical approaches to texts. Crane Brinton's legendary course on Men and Ideas at Harvard pushed large numbers of students in another direction, toward the question of how ideas generated action. Thanks to these courses, students from many, though hardly all, of the better colleges and universities were prepared, even conditioned, to see intellectual history as a vital field—which they found easy to enter, and whose practices came to them with a feeling of naturalness. Historians whose own careers took radically different directions in the 1950s and 1960s more recently have paid eloquent tribute to the interdisciplinary surveys of Western civilization that set them on the path to scholarship.[19]

Moreover, the history of ideas was an established field of scholarly inquiry long before Lovejoy published his first articles on evolution in *Popular Science*

Monthly, or the first new historians began setting up their courses in the field. In a powerful and erudite book, Donald Kelley has traced the ancestry of the history of ideas—a chain of scholars, philosophers, scientists, and social reformers that leads all the way back from the new research universities of the nineteenth century to classical antiquity. Greek philosophers drew up doxographical histories of philosophy, painted polemical portraits of their predecessors, and occasionally pursued systematic inquiries into the growth of astronomy or anatomy. Medieval scholars constructed genealogies and—in the remarkable case of Roger Bacon—mounted formal inquiries into the reasons why certain older thinkers had produced solid and useful results. Renaissance humanists compiled what they called "literary histories"—rich, complex, and sometimes perversely polemical inquiries into the history of disciplines, from history itself to astronomy and mathematics. Francis Bacon found this form of humanistic scholarship so stimulating that he urged his readers to compile, working century by century, histories of the different arts and disciplines and the conditions that had made them flourish or decline. In the eighteenth and nineteenth centuries, finally, histories of philosophy, science, literature, and social thought became a central occupation of thinkers as influential as Victor Cousin and Hippolyte Taine, and the writing of proper histories often came to be seen as a prerequisite for the larger reform of intellectual life.[20]

These enterprises varied radically in character and method. Even in nineteenth-century Germany, traditionally regarded as the West's locus classicus for the development of historical approaches to all forms of knowledge, the formal history of philosophy took root only gradually, as university teaching began to adopt the seminar method of close collective reading of older texts, and flourished in a wild variety of forms, many of them devoid of the Hegelian inspiration once thought to have made philosophy historical. Much work in this field went on in lecture rooms rather than studies, moreover, as philosophers offered formal courses on the history of their subject, which has only begun to be studied.[21] The same is true for any number of other disciplines that became articulately self-conscious in the nineteenth century, from philology to physics, and whose disciplinary histories in many cases have not yet attracted their historians. Nonetheless it is striking to see how widely the history of ideas was written and taught, long before anyone thought of including it in the discipline of history.

In the last sunny decades of nineteenth-century liberal culture, histories of ideas—as well as histories of philosophy—flourished widely, especially in the English-speaking world. John Draper and Andrew Dickson White used history to examine the millennial conflict between science and religion, in massive books that retain a certain relevance now. As the liberal consensus neared its strange death, the history of ideas became a central concern of British intellectuals like the Carlyles, Leslie Stephen, and J. B. Bury, whose books had no rivals on the Continent. In the years when modernity seemed to have created a civilization and technology that would carry all before it, the history of the ideas that underpinned the modern world came to seem as urgent as the history of battles and constitutions—perhaps more so, for a wide, nonscholarly readership. Momigliano, writing in the 1970s, recalled that as a student in the 1920s, he had read the work of Flint, Buckle, Bury and others, all of them formed in the nineteenth century. Accordingly, he had regarded the history of ideas as a British specialty. He found it puzzling, therefore, that when he reached Oxford in 1939, "It was enough to mention the word 'idea' to be given the address of the Warburg Institute."[22] By the outbreak of World War II, the rise of new forms of political and economic history had left intellectual historians like Herbert Butterfield as isolated figures, at least among the British professionals. A generation earlier, the intellectual map had looked quite different. When reforming American advocates of a "new history" like Charles Beard began their campaign against the political narratives of an older, positivist historiography, after the First World War, they imported these excellent foreign products—as Beard did when he reprinted Bury's history of the idea of progress with a long, admiring introduction.[23]

The sense that the history of ideas formed part of a progressive approach to history and society—and the effort to use the method to work out not only, as Lovejoy did, the development of metaphysics and aesthetics, but also the paths by which ideas had shaped, and could reshape, the political and social order—did not dissipate with the reform currents of the early 1920s. Writers like Vernon Parrington and, later, the brilliant outsider Richard Hofstadter, used the history of ideas to understand where America's energies came from—and to trace the fault lines within the world of the American intellect. In the 1950s and early 1960s, courses on intellectual history at major American universities—for example, the famous survey courses offered by

George Mosse at the University of Wisconsin—served as primary rallying points for hundreds of students critical of the existing order in society and the state. Often they continued to play this role during the crisis of the later 1960s, even when, as in Mosse's case, the content of the course remained solidly in the realm of ideas, and the instructor resolutely intent on revealing to his students the flaws and contradictions that made their own programs useless. To that extent, the relation between intellectual history and social protest was not simple, or unidirectional, even in the heyday of social history.

Three more existing streams of thought and practice flowed into the history of ideas and helped to fertilize the soil its practitioners cultivated. One was decidedly foreign. From the middle of the nineteenth century onward, German scholars had experimented with a range of new models for the study of cultures. Jacob Burckhardt and his many disciples and critics devised new ways to portray past cultures as wholes, offering new contexts for the study of past ideas and thinkers. Aby Warburg and his followers created equally novel ways to trace traditions over the centuries of Western history, following the disappearances and reappearances of symbols and explicating their transformations, and their larger meanings, in a richly interdisciplinary way. In the same period, a range of medievalists in and outside Germany turned Burckhardt's weapons against him, creating histories of the medieval centuries that, like Burckhardt's history of the Renaissance, emphasized the realm of culture and ideas even as they argued that medieval men and women had been far more realistic, less shackled to authority, than Burckhardt realized.

Some of these traditions moved to North America and settled comfortably there even before the nineteenth century ended. Pioneering medievalists like Charles Homer Haskins and Lynn Thorndike attacked the same questions, wielding vast reserves of new material drawn from European libraries and archives. Of all American enterprises in the history of ideas, Thorndike's *History of Magic and Experimental Science* proved perhaps the largest in scale. It drew its intellectual inspiration directly from the European debate about the Middle Ages and the Renaissance. The *Journal* provided, among other things, a platform for the debate and pursuit of these already existing issues—one that soon came to be both crowded and turbulent.

Moreover, the stream of new methods and materials from abroad continued to grow during the early decades of Lovejoy's career, as European scholarship moved in new directions and then, more rapidly, as European scholars began to make their forced *translatio studii* to the United States. Friedrich Meinecke offered new models for understanding the history of major intellectual formations like historicism. Werner Jaeger showed how to write the biography of a great thinker, Aristotle, who had left no letters and the development of whose mind could be established only by internal analysis of his texts. In the 1950s and 1960s, younger members of these foreign schools, uprooted from their German homes by Hitler, transformed the humanities in America as they themselves were transplanted into them—or at least came to write in English. Erwin Panofsky made a version of Warburg's method elegantly accessible to generations of young scholars, by no means all of them in art history. His former colleagues at the Warburg Institute, now reestablished in London, developed their method in a whole series of different ways, not without engaging in polemics. Meanwhile, Felix Gilbert and other German émigrés offered a sharper, more archival form of Meinecke's method to students of both European and American ideas, and Hans Baron brilliantly deployed the methods of the Leipzig school of cultural history to transform the study of Renaissance humanism. Leo Spitzer and Erich Auerbach imparted different versions of German philology and hermeneutics to American graduate students. Jaeger's severely analytical method of intellectual biography, with its fierce concentration on finding the inconsistencies and fissures in apparently finished, coherent works, gave Gilbert, Baron, Hexter, and many others a new way to study Machiavelli, whose work became a seedbed for new methods. These scholars saw the redating and decomposition of classic and apparently coherent texts like *The Prince* and *The Discourses* as a way to transform what seemed to be fissures and contradictions—like the dramatic, brain-exploding contrast between the pragmatic absolutism and immoralism of *The Prince* and the republicanism of *The Discourses*—into the evidence for intellectual development, usually in response to particular biographical and political circumstances. Hexter famously applied the same method to Thomas More, and gradually the intellectual biography—an approach that fused a concentration on context and development with close attention to the texts that had formed the center of past intellectuals' lives—established itself as a standard approach, distinct from the straight biography of an intellectual and rooted in the study of texts.[24]

The stream of models and stimuli from abroad never dried up. Even Great Britain—which in the 1950s no longer saw itself as friendly to the history of ideas—harbored the brilliant Isaiah Berlin, who had more pupils and disciples in the United States than at home, as well as younger scholars like John Burrow, whose 1966 *Evolution and Society: A Study in Victorian Social Theory* became a model for American historians of social thought. In the same years, the massive programs of translation and paperback publication supported by the Bollingen Foundation and the new publishers of upscale paperbacks, primarily Harper, made the work of these scholars and some of their teachers accessible to a broad American public. Momigliano recalled that he realized, soon after arriving at University College London, that the most distinguished and penetrating intellectual historians within the institution were the historians of science—scholars like Michael Polanyi, whose insights did not derive from formal training as historians and who did not teach in the department of history. But he found it impossible to establish a connection with them. Disciplinary boundaries were lower in the United States than in Great Britain—low enough that students, as well as faculty members, could often see over them. No one could begin the study of European intellectual history in America in the 1950s or 1960s without realizing that some of the most distinctive and powerful minds in the field were art historians—Panofsky above all, whose modified version of Burckhardt continued to provide an intellectual agenda for Renaissance scholarship long after his death. But on his appearance in the American marketplace of ideas, Panofsky was flanked by such powerful exponents of different approaches to the same problems as Ernst Robert Curtius, Jean Seznec, and Edgar Wind.[25]

A second stream flowed from decidedly native springs. Nowadays, it is customary to look back with anger—or sometimes with pity—at the rise of American studies. Scholars nourished on Said, Foucault, and Bourdieu can all too easily detect the blindness that always accompanied insight, and sometimes overcame it, in founding historians of American thought like Perry Miller and F. O. Matthiesen. These men all too often took the text as a key to the whole society—and a few texts, chosen sometimes in advance of large-scale research, as keys to the whole universe. Their passion for finding the structure, the metaphor, or the trope that governed and expressed American culture as a whole seems naive in retrospect.

And yet, the pioneers of American studies were moved by a profound excitement that is hard to recapture in a time when no one doubts that American writers and philosophers deserve serious scholarly attention. In the early decades of the twentieth century, it took courage for a professor to declare his respect for Walt Whitman or Theodore Dreiser; more courage still for one to dedicate himself to the study of American literature or intellectual history. Furthermore, students of American thought soon began to reveal to astonished Europeanists the significance of texts and developments that the Europeanists themselves had neglected. Perry Miller and Samuel Eliot Morison, for example, first announced the vital importance that many Puritans ascribed to the reforms of dialectic and rhetoric demanded by the French humanist Petrus Ramus—at the time, a figure largely neglected in scholarship on British and European intellectual history.[26] Subsequent studies have taught us that Puritan Harvard also retained a very substantial interest, which Miller and Morison did not fully detect, in the traditions of scholastic philosophy, and to that extent have modified the structures reared by those toiling giants.[27] But the Americanists' rediscovery of Ramus has propelled important changes in the intellectual history of early modern Europe. So has Lewis Hanke's rediscovery of the use of Aristotle in early modern times to justify the imposition of slavery on the inhabitants of the New World. The opening up of American intellectual history, in a sense, created the possibility of studying the reception of texts, methods, and ideas—and did so long before the term "reception" had received anything like its common meaning.

The history of science, finally, intersected with that of ideas in the early years of both fields in ways that have become difficult to recapture. History of science, like the history of ideas, came clothed with the appeal of a new subject and one concerned with the origins of modernity itself. The most influential historians of science in the English-speaking world chiefly concerned themselves, moreover, with great episodes in the early modern history of science: the development of a mechanical world picture, the downfall of Aristotelianism, the rise of new scientific methods, and the theory of evolution and its sources. All of these subjects were intimately connected with the classic problems of the history of science, as Bury and Lovejoy, for all their differences of method and emphasis, had defined them: how the solid, timeless universe of *The Great Chain of Being* and the stable, repetitive history of the classical and medieval tradition turned into the changeable, infinite universe of modern science and the faith in infinite progress shared by capitalists and Marxists.[28]

History of science, accordingly, became a major—if not *the* major—subdivision of intellectual history in the period from the 1930s to the 1960s. Many scholars trained in history or literary history made the development of science and its impact their central concern. The *Journal* published endless inquiries, not only into such obviously central intellectual questions as the origins of heliocentrism or evolution but also into wider realms, with a social and institutional flavor to them: for example, the culture of the virtuosi who, in the seventeenth century, built the new academies and societies that first gave inquiry into nature a unique institutional base. Historians of ideas saw their work as central to understanding the old picture of the world that modern science had destroyed and replaced, the intellectual roots of modern scientific practice and ideology, and the transformation of imaginative literature under the impact of new scientific discoveries—a field in which Marjorie Nicolson and Rosalie Colie, among others, did work that remains standard to this day. It is no wonder, then, that intellectual history seemed in good health as the 1960s dawned.

Why then did Darnton—and many other observers—feel that they were witnessing a precipitous decline, only ten or fifteen years after all these streams merged in the new wave of 1960? Darnton himself identified some of the central factors—especially the rise of a challenging new social and cultural history—that operated within history departments. But other developments also mattered at least as much, and possibly more. The *Journal*, as we have seen, was unusual partly because of its uninhibited call for collaboration between disciplines. Through the 1950s—partly as a result of the common undergraduate training shared by so many professors—a historical approach continued to form part of the normal method of most of the humanistic disciplines. But challenges were emerging. Many of the literary quarterlies that in the 1940s had encouraged Panofsky, Edmund Wilson, and others to pursue largely historical approaches to art and literature now allied themselves with the New Critics. Once radical outsiders, they rapidly came to dominate some of the most influential departments of literature, and they demanded that courses on literature and the arts divest themselves of the old-fashioned apparatus of erudition in favor of direct, formal confrontation with the literary text or the work of art.[29] The literary historians, the old-fashioned "scholar-adventurers" who had once made English departments into hives of historical inquiry into the conditions of stagecraft in London, the minutiae of textual variation in manuscript and print, and the intellectual history of England and the United States found themselves more and more on the margins, dismissed as pedants. So, often, did iconologist art historians, whose work looked naïve at a time when both social history and formalist analysis seemed to give deeper insights into the visual field. Though the history of ideas continued to have practitioners and allies in the world of literary scholarship, few of them played the dominant role of a Marjorie Nicolson in the years around 1950.

Even more serious, perhaps, was the attack on history and tradition that swept almost everything before it in philosophy. Before World War II, many American philosophy departments had been eclectic, even if few could rival the pure erudition of the Hopkins Dioscuri, Boas and Lovejoy. In the 1960s and after, however, new philosophies spread from Vienna, Cambridge, and Oxford into the American university. Far more varied than their hostile observers claimed, the new approaches shared an intense hostility to many philosophical traditions. Moral philosophy and metaphysics were often dismissed as fruitless efforts to wrestle with questions that could never be answered. So was the study of most texts written before Wittgenstein's *Tractatus*—except for a few saving examples of early work technical enough to be interesting or silly enough to be fun to refute. "Just Say No to the History of Ideas"—a now-famous banner with a strange device, first sighted on a door in Princeton's long-dominant Department of Philosophy— epitomized an attitude that marginalized both the method and most of the objects of the history of ideas. Lovejoy's *Great Chain of Being,* in particular, exemplified the sort of study that most practicing philosophers wanted to abandon in every way, from its passion for untimely issues to the brevity with which it treated individual texts and thinkers.[30]

These structural changes in the humanistic disciplines called the whole notion of interdisciplinary work into question. Critics and philosophers who accepted the more radical versions of the New Critical or Wittgensteinian program could not, in principle, accept that efforts to engage in discussion with historians or historically minded humanists promised much enlightenment—much less commit themselves to cooperate with them in teaching what necessarily looked like intellectually mushy courses that gave short shrift to the most vital principles and tools of the new humanities.

Some fields—classical scholarship, for example—seemed more reluctant to adopt an unhistorical approach. But they too were expanding, and their literature was becoming an independent body of scholarship—one that historians of other fields found increasingly dense and impenetrable.

Even the history of science—once the surest support of the history of ideas—separated itself from the mother ship in the 1960s. Historians of science underwent a separate form of graduate training, wrote for the increasing number of specialized history of science journals, and turned in their research to the later periods of modern science—periods in which the work done was so technical that ordinary historians could not follow close reading of texts, much less precise reconstruction of experiments, observations, and computations. If malaise haunted many historians of ideas in the 1970s—and the present writer remembers that it did—it surely derived in large part from the feeling that what had seemed a solid intellectual continent, one in which the humanistic disciplines intersected, had turned out to be a shrinking polar ice cap. The onetime inhabitants of thriving settlements in trading zones found themselves marooned on melting floes. The history of ideas—as embodied in the *Journal* and as practiced by a larger community of humanists—suffered genuine structural problems. Combined with the larger woes of the academy at a time of rapid downsizing—and the attendant fear that a wrong choice of dissertation topic or method could condemn one to a lifetime selling secondhand books or driving a taxi—these conditions did as much as the rise of social history to make the intellectual historians feel insecure and out of sorts, and to discourage students who reasonably valued the information offered by the market from pursuing the field's traditional forms of inquiry.

And yet, in exactly this period—the late 1970s and early 1980s—a series of changes took place, all of them related but not at the same level, which enabled the field not only to survive but also to adopt new methods and attack new issues. Within the discipline of history, scholars initially made what, in retrospect, looks like an almost concerted turn toward tracing detailed internalist histories of the fields and disciplines that they had once treated deliberately as outsiders and in more general terms. In the history of philosophy, for example, Darnton noted Bruce Kuklick's dazzling recent book on philosophy at Harvard.[31] But in the same years, other historians by trade also published on philosophers—some of them, like Morris Raphael Cohen and the followers of

Hegel, long known to be unsparingly professional and technical, while others like Lorenzo Valla and Francis Bacon were rediscovered as laborers in technical vineyards.[32] Charismatic teachers like Charles Schmitt, Amos Funkenstein, and Martin Jay found many students who wanted to teach and write history, but whose interests lay in what would until recently have seemed a border zone between history and philosophy.

What looks in retrospect like a technical turn in intellectual history, moreover, attracted scholars whose interests were not primarily, or at least not only, philosophical. Historians of humanism in early modern Europe turned away from the general rediscovery of ancient eloquence that had occupied many of them in the 1950s and 1960s. They began to reconstruct, in minute and unsparing detail, the ways in which scholars centuries before their time had sorted and analyzed works of literature; translated (and distorted) philosophical texts; revived and reconfigured the ancient disciplines of grammar, rhetoric, and dialectic; and reconstructed and dated ancient objects.[33] In the 1970s, as Darnton rightly notes, a few pioneering historians devoted themselves to the history of other fields in the humanities and social sciences. But those who did so went as single spies—like George Stocking, whose pioneering investigations into the history of anthropology eventually led him to make a personal *translatio studii* and identify himself as an anthropologist. Now historians seemed to be deserting—or at least trying to gain technical mastery of other disciplines—in battalions.

If historians suddenly showed a new willingness to address past ideas in a newly rigorous way, some of the other humanists with whom they had been unable to find common ground began to find rapprochements with them. In particular, philosophers began to develop a new culture of erudition, which developed in a variety of ways. Paul Kristeller, of course, had trained students who worked systematically on Renaissance philosophy, and Richard Popkin memorably opened up the history of skepticism to philosophers and historians. Yet for all their learning and their profound impact on individuals, they remained somewhat isolated in the philosophical world of the 1950s and early 1960s. By the 1970s, however, philosophy itself was moving in new directions. Students of ancient Greek and Roman thought like Geoffrey Lloyd began to turn the study of ancient philosophy into a more historical field, one concerned with the social and political as well as intellectual conditions of inquiry that had underpinned the rise of philosophy in Greece.[34] Similar questions arose in the study of early modern, and finally even in that of modern thought. Classicists began to enlarge the canon of serious ancient thinkers, as they grasped that Stoics, Epicureans, and others deserved to be taken seriously as systematic thinkers. Students of medieval philosophy, realizing with fascination just how deft their scholastic predecessors had been at the kinds of linguistic and logical analysis that interested them most, began to master Latin and paleography.[35] More important still, students of both the ancient world and the early modern period in philosophy departments began to insist on widening the canon of texts that deserved close study.[36]

Disagreement on fundamental principles persisted, and persists. Some philosophers saw the history of philosophy as an exercise in enlarging the canon, to include doctrines and thinkers that their predecessors had dismissed. Others argued that one could not even understand the master thinkers in the canon unless one took into account everything that a given period had considered philosophy. Still others debated such difficult but unavoidable issues as why the Western canon of philosophers was exclusively male. The rapprochement between historians and philosophers—symbolized in both its powerful results and its continued propensity to cause polemics by the *Cambridge History of Early Modern Philosophy*—has restored to one form of intellectual history the interdisciplinary quality that Lovejoy sought—even if debate continues on fundamental problems of method and content.[37]

As history and philosophy began to interact again, a second intellectual transformation was also taking place—the one variously labeled "Theory" or "Postmodernism," which shook the pillars of the American house of intellect in the 1980s and 1990s, and eventually helped give rise to the culture wars whose embers are still occasionally blown into flame by grumpy scholars and desperate politicians. This movement was often represented, and sometimes represented itself, as a challenge to all traditional forms of humanistic inquiry. In fact, however, as Donald Kelley pointed out when he took the reins of the *Journal*, Theory was one in a long series of efforts to transform the enterprise of interpretation, and its presence on the intellectual scene proved helpful, not harmful, to historians of ideas. It made them take serious account of the problems and traditions of hermeneutics—the theory of interpretation itself, which had represented a major enterprise in European thought since antiquity, and to which historians of ideas had paid far too little attention, either in their capacity as historians trying to do justice to the range of Western thought or in their practice as readers of texts. In the age of theory, historians of ideas had to join their colleagues in social and cultural history and try to come to terms with the limits and problems of their disciplines. It also inspired them to tackle problems with a new kind of intellectual ambition. Michel Foucault's varied visions of history, inconsistent in themselves and faulty in application to actual sources, nonetheless inspired some of the most radical and successful efforts to reread texts that had already been interpreted many times before. The powerful, Piranesiesque vision of classificatory systems and their power that Foucault elaborated in his early works rested in part on pilfered references, and his generalizations were sometimes more distinguished by oracular force than archival foundations.[38] Nonetheless, his books repeatedly stimulated critical readers to see texts from new angles and to situate them in new contexts. Jan Goldstein and Stuart Clark both proved that critical applications of Foucault could make endlessly studied subjects take on radically new forms.[39] Ever the shape changer, Foucault approached ancient texts just as arbitrarily as modern ones in the *History of Sexuality* that occupied his later years, and in doing so helped inspire Peter Brown, Caroline Bynum, Thomas Laqueur, and others to interpret historical visions of the body and practices for its care in radically new ways.[40]

In a sense, however, the deepest impact of Theory probably lay—as that of Western Civ once did—at the level of undergraduate and graduate education. In the 1980s and after, every student in the humanities encountered courses—in language departments, history departments, and cultural studies—that emphasized the power of institutions and the practices they accepted and propagated to shape habits of mind, forms of speech and writing, and responses to other individuals and civilizations. Though honeycombed with lacunae, Edward Said's brilliant, controversial study of Orientalism inspired generations of students to deconstruct past descriptions of other societies, looking for the assumptions and practices that, much more than observed facts, gave them coherence and power—a critical enterprise that has now begun to be turned, paradoxically but fruitfully, on Islamic as well as Western intellectuals.[41] Similarly, Pierre Bourdieu's studies of high culture and the patterns of its inheritance in France led younger historians to examine the life and work of past intellectuals from radically new points of view.[42] Profoundly unhistorical itself, Theory underpinned new ways of studying history, just as Western Civ had buttressed and nourished older ones. Younger historians of ideas, whatever their divergent objects of study, converge in their fascination with the varieties of scholarly practice.[43] Like the new cultural historians—whose own practice, as William Bouwsma rightly foresaw in 1980, both incorporated elements of intellectual history and helped to expand its compass from the study of texts to the wider one of how humans make meaning in their environment—the heroes of Theory ended up not overthrowing but renewing the practices of historians of ideas.[44] Thus the older history of historiography, long dominated by an implicit teleology, was renewed when scholars connected it to a newer history of the cultural practices of memory.[45]

In the same years, the new history of political thought pioneered by Pocock and Skinner, the power and originality of which Darnton noted, metamorphosized from a modest artisanal enterprise that occupied a small number of specialists into a vast and varied network of factories in which intellectual historians of very different kinds worked at high speed. Pocock's effort to identify a coherent language of civic humanism whose speakers spanned the centuries and the continents found both adherents and critics, as his work reshaped the study of both British and American political thought.[46] Skinner's somewhat different but equally fruitful concentration on the language of politics attracted a vast range of students and colleagues, who restored forgotten masters like Justus Lipsius and Hugo Grotius to the center of attention and forged new ways to interpret such well-known texts and issues as the early modern debates over the humanity of Native Americans and the early development of Hegel's thought.[47] Cambridge University and Cambridge University Press became effective forcing houses for talented young students in the field, who produced a stately series of innovative books and articles, many in the Cambridge series that carried its central message in its title: Ideas in Context.[48] Though independent of other branches of Theory in their origins and inspiration, Laslett's and Skinner's methods attacked many similar problems—as Skinner recognized when he organized a series of lectures and articles on *The Return of Grand Theory in the Human Sciences*.[49] Criticism attended many of these efforts, of course, and continues to do so.[50]

More important than the various critiques Skinner has received—even those of his brilliant friend and occasional critic J. G. A. Pocock—are the two men's continual efforts to refine and renew their practices. Skinner's massive, erudite, and provocative study of Thomas Hobbes's place in the rhetorical tradition offers a bravura introduction to pedagogical practices and other bearers of intellectual tradition—matters for which his early work did not make much room.[51] Pocock's gargantuan study of Edward Gibbon has set the historian's vision of the past and practices of scholarship before a vast and variegated backdrop, the richest reconstruction of humanistic historiography ever attempted—and there is more to come.[52] The cumulative impact of these studies on the larger shape of intellectual history has been immense. All historians of ideas now carry, along with the other implements in their toolboxes, the methods for formal analysis of language and tradition and the intersection of linguistic fields, larger contexts, and particular individual intentions that Pocock and Skinner placed at the core of their work.

Many other developments have helped to reinvigorate the history of ideas. None of them, perhaps, has had wider effects than the so-called material turn—the rise of efforts to write history centered less on the reading of texts than on that of things—objects charged with cultural significance. The origins of this enterprise lie many years back, in the cultural histories of crops pioneered by the young William McNeil and Carl Ortwin Sauer and dramatized by younger scholars like Alfred Crosby and Donald Worster. But it really began to have an impact on intellectual history in the 1970s, when pioneering scholars began to pose the question why, at particular times, individuals decided to live in radically different ways, and to connect the newly built environments of the Renaissance palazzo and villa and the nineteenth-century apartment house with new ways of thinking about the city and its inhabitants.[53] A wave of new studies of museums revealed that the baroque antiquaries who had assembled fossils, skis, and narwhal horns in their mysterious *Kunst- und Wunderkammern* and the eighteenth- and nineteenth-century curators who had swept art, national antiquities, and natural history into their magnificent public museums had transformed Western ways of thinking about and experiencing the past.[54] A new form of history of science grew up, one that embedded scientific instruments in a broad context and showed that even the most objective-seeming of them had in fact served purposes that had been forgotten by present-minded historians.[55] And a new cultural history of death and mourning transformed monuments into unexpectedly revealing texts.[56] Five hundred years ago, Machiavelli conjured up the spirits of the mighty dead and interrogated them about their actions. Nowadays, dead objects as well as dead writers have begun to speak.

During the 1990s, moreover, intellectual history took its own material turn. In the 1980s, Darnton and other scholars, primarily Roger Chartier and Carlo Ginzburg, had created a new history of books and readers. This study used a vast range of evidence to reconstruct the ways in which the great books of a given period had actually been shaped, printed, and marketed, and in which books of lesser quality had actually been sold and read. Early historians of the book tended to argue, against the traditions of intellectual history, that numerical evidence counted for more than textual, and that the experience of large numbers of readers, to be reconstructed from the records of publishers, could shed a bright light on such endlessly debated problems as the origins of the French and English revolutions. Yet Ginzburg's pioneering study *The Cheese and the Worms* applied a very different model, inspired by the traditional, slow food methods of Italian philology and intellectual history, to interpreting the experiences of a single reader as his imagination fused disparate books and stories into a new vision of the world.[57] In the course of the 1990s, intellectual historians began to investigate systematically how the texts they studied were produced and consumed. Some of them shed new light on canonical thinkers by tracing the ways in which their texts reached the public—as scribbled clandestine manuscripts or handsomely printed books; as pamphlets or as periodical articles. The interpretation of texts now goes hand in hand with the reconstruction of intellectual and publishing communities.[58] Others have begun to ask how these canonical thinkers had read the books in their own libraries, and how their printed works in turn were read by others. Many of these have been preserved, their margins strewn with the annotations that had fallen like autumn leaves in Vallombrosa in the days when readers habitually worked pen in hand. A historian of ideas working on a sixteenth- or a nineteenth-century thinker is likely to start, now, by cataloguing books from the individual's library and investigating notebooks to see how he or she processed the material. A few professional readers have even come to light, intellectuals who read exhaustively but wrote little, and still flourished.[59] And a number of historians have argued that such readings should play a substantial part of their own in reconstructions of early modern and modern culture.[60]

Interest in these new methods, moreover, has spread not only among historians but also among literary scholars working on every field, from the classics to modernism, and to philosophers as well.[61] One reason that the history of ideas no longer seems so marginal is precisely that scholars from so many different disciplines have found that they can meet and argue productively in the margins of manuscripts and printed books, where the practices of intellectuals of all sorts have left rich deposits. The intellectual history of the 2000s has not only a newly technical character but also a new material base, which serve to distinguish it—and many of the articles that have recently appeared in the *Journal*—from earlier forms of the same pursuit. This chapter, with its emphasis on practices and material texts, clearly exemplifies these larger tendencies.

In one final respect, moreover, intellectual history has recently expanded far beyond the expectations that anyone nourished in the 1970s. It has become, increasingly, a global enterprise. Fields that were once taught and investigated in only a handful of universities have become standard fare across the English-speaking world. And a number of these have already had a tremendous impact, and will have more, on the practice of intellectual history. To give only two examples of many: every serious university in the United States and Europe supports specialists in Jewish and Chinese history. Both of these enterprises work on long cultural traditions in which the transmission and interpretation of texts has been a formative enterprise. Already in the 1960s, intellectual historians of China like Joseph Levenson, Fritz Mote, and Benjamin Schwartz attracted the attention of a few scholars outside their special areas, while Joseph Needham and Donald Lach conducted vast collaborative inquiries into the relations between the Chinese and the Western intellectual traditions. Two generations later, Chinese history established itself as one of the most profound and original fields of historical scholarship in the West. Chinese historiography offers powerful, rigorous, and elegant models for the study of ideas in their political, social, and religious contexts, as well as for the interpretation of complex, difficult texts.

In the 1960s, Jewish history was, as it had been for many years, largely in a state of primitive accumulation, as pioneering scholars continued to fix the basic outlines of the textual tradition and its larger context. Two generations later, Jewish history provided Western scholars with some of the most powerful tools in their kits for modeling the history of traditions and grasping the impact of modernity, not to mention grappling with that ancient question, a central one in the classic years of nineteenth-century intellectual history—the relations between religion and natural philosophy or science. In other fields as well—for example, the increasingly subtle and complex field of scholarship that deals with Western understandings of pre-Columbian civilization—Western scholars are showing students of the West how to think in radically new ways about their own pasts.

As historians celebrate a partial but powerful convergence with philosophers and other humanists, as intellectual history expands to confront new objects of study, both literally and metaphorically, and as new textures and styles of scholarship appear in the *Journal* and elsewhere, it has become clear that Lovejoy built extremely well—better, possibly, than he knew. The crossroads he laid out and paved remains a central and attractive meeting point for many disciplines. And the history of ideas—in the general sense of a study of texts, images, and theories that seeks to balance responsibility and precision in the formal treatment and analysis of its objects with an equally measured effort to connect them to a particular historical world—has proved resilient, even expansive, through multiple transformations of the disciplinary fields at whose borders it resides.

At least some of the structures on which Lovejoy built also survive, suitably modified to function in a changed world. Survey courses on Western civilization that still flourish at many colleges and universities, either as formal requirements for all students (as at Columbia University and Reed College) or as popular electives (as at Harvard University and the University of Chicago). Undergraduate programs in intellectual history attract many students at the University of Pennsylvania, the University of Washington and points between. The old Western Civ and the old history of ideas cannot to be restored in their pure forms. But newer versions, which combine the rigorous analysis of texts and the discriminating assay of their contents with close attention to their literary and material forms, their cultural and intellectual contexts, and their assumptions about race and gender, have proved capable of inspiring the same sorts of excitement. If the older surveys of Western or American thought lost coherence as enterprises in the 1970s, newer ones are being attempted, some of which make room for revisionist perspectives of many kinds.[62]

What, then, does the history of ideas now stand for? Ideally, it will stand for and support all of these new developments—as well as others that we cannot now predict. It will welcome investigations of texts and ideas—especially when these are located in time and space and explicated, in part, in terms of a wider historical context. But it will also be open to the investigation of books and other material objects, so long as these have a direct relation to larger questions in intellectual history and to the practices of intellectual life in all periods. It will not include positions—or invite others to debate—on questions of Theory per se, or on the much-debated status of Theory and its practitioners in literature departments. But it will certainly see providing historically informed studies of the development of hermeneutics, the work of influential theorists, and any and all other topics in the capacious realms of Theory's empire as part of its task.[63]

Many questions of method remain open. Fundamental, frequently used concepts like "context"—a term, in the end, for information somehow distilled from the same sorts of text that it is usually invoked to explicate—require far more formal analysis than they have had. Accounts of motivation—a special problem for historians of ideas, as Skinner recognized when he offered as a partial solution the notion of "intention in utterance"—remain multiple and continue to provoke considerable debate. This seems only reasonable, when one considers the anfractuosities involved in treating as forms of action complex works elaborated over decades, withheld for years from distribution, and finally made public in conditions that their authors could never have envisioned—a set of conditions that applies to Newton, Coleridge, Nietzsche, and Wittgenstein, among many others. Lovejoy himself, well aware of these problems, suggested that one reason to follow the fates of connected sets of ideas was precisely that they often appeared, in the works of a given author, combined with others that contradicted them. The seemingly impersonal and abstract paper chase for sources and unit ideas could thus shed light on the fissures and inconsistencies in a very human individual's mind. Certainly the difficulties of arriving at plausible accounts of these and other key terms and methods should not deter scholars from making the attempt.

It seems certain that the history of ideas will never again be tied to a particular political program—either the progressive ones that naturalized the field in America in the 1920s or the conservative ones with which it is sometimes bafflingly identified nowadays. But it will certainly commit itself to one current policy: globalization. In the past, a few scholars trained in traditions very distant from European and American norms have managed to enter and alter the course of debates in the English-speaking world.[64] In the decades to come, by contrast, our field should, and will, become far more cosmopolitan. Students and scholars from a wider range of countries and traditions will be writing in English on intellectual history, and their work will enrich the methods commonly used in the English-speaking world by those that have developed elsewhere. In this, as in much else, historians of ideas remain in the real tradition of Lovejoy: pursuing a lively and expansive field and making it serve again not only as a platform for specialized research but also as a place where many forms and traditions of scholarship can converge.

11

The Messrs. Casaubon

Isaac Casaubon and Mark Pattison

Mark Pattison's name calls to mind a whole lost world of Victorian learning.[1] Its locales ranged widely in character and location: from the great domed reading rooms of the British Museum, lined with its hundreds of calf-bound books, to James Murray's cramped iron Scriptorium, lined with its thousands of papers slips bearing quotations. But its inhabitants were more uniform: the bald, bearded, energetic men of letters who founded literary societies, created workingmen's colleges, taught young women to row, edited arcane texts, and wrote essays for the common reader more learned than most of what appears in modern scholarly journals. We still batten upon the rich fruits of their industry; the *New English Dictionary,* the *Dictionary of National Biography,* and the eleventh edition of the *Encyclopedia Britannica.*

Pattison occupies a peculiar niche in this gallery of sages. He was and remains the best-known Victorian defender of German culture and scholarship. Mrs. Humphry Ward's *Recollections* offers a characteristic glimpse of him talking in his library with his friend Ingram Bywater, "as they poured scorn on Oxford scholarship, or the lack of it, and on the ideals of Balliol, which aimed at turning out public officials, as compared with the researching ideals of the German universities, which seemed to the Rector the only ideals worth calling academic." One can get to know Pattison better by hunting him out in his natural habitat—the long and close-packed columns of *The Academy,* the engaging fortnightly that he helped to found, in which summaries of Richard Wagner's musicological views, reports of Heinrich Schliemann's archaeological discoveries, and descriptions of new-style pianos meant to be played with the feet, nestle invitingly side by side. Pattison appears on one page speaking in public at the Freemasons' Hall, arguing with T. H. Huxley, A. H. Sayce, Robinson Ellis, and Ray Lankester about "the low

state of learning and science in the two older universities." He reappears elsewhere, summarizing recent research on the manuscript tradition of the
Characters of Theophrastus, and castigating the German and English editors
who rearranged the text according to their fancy rather than as the manuscript evidence dictated. He pops up on yet another page out-Teutonizing the
Teutons in a review of Lucian Müller's *History of Classical Philology in the
Netherlands* (1869). In this German book, Pattison complains, "We miss . . .
the usual German virtue—*Gründlichkeit.*"

This is the Mr. Casaubon long familiar from *Middlemarch* and academic
folklore—the dry and caustic scholar who, as John Morley recalled, "was
supposed to combine boundless erudition with an impenetrable misan-
thropy." An anecdote printed just after his death by an admirer gives an idea
of his relationships with disciples:

> [Pattison] suggested that I should edit [John] Selden's *Table Talk.* The
> preparation was to be, first to get the contents practically by heart, then
> to read the whole printed literature of Selden's day, and of the genera-
> tions before him. In twenty years he promised me that I should be pre-
> pared for the work. He put the thing before me in so unattractive a way
> that I never did it or anything else worth doing. I consider the ruin of
> my misspent life very largely due to that conversation.

One begins to understand just how Pattison's learned wife managed to combine loathing for his body (which she could not bear to touch), disgust for his
character ("His screams of pain and terror," she wrote as he lay dying, "were
heard throughout the house. The moral misery is awful"), and boundless admiration for his learning and intellect.

I shall not try to penetrate the recesses of Pattison's mind and sensibility.
V. H. H. Green and John Sparrow have devoted fascinating studies to his life
and reputation, and H. S. Jones, more recently, has traced the whole arc of his
career with great learning and intelligence. My concern is not Pattison the
Oxford character but Pattison the scholar, who is still read as an authority on
two related subjects: the development of classical scholarship after the Renaissance and the transformation of the German universities after the French
Revolution. While toiling in Pattison's preferred fields of study, I have had
occasion to sample his work, to test it against his sources, and to compare it

with that of his contemporaries. The results have been disquieting. Repeated encounters with his inability to quote a document accurately, his ineptitude at establishing dates, and his incompetence at summarizing plain German accurately in English have led me to wonder whether he deserves the authority he still enjoys in the English-speaking world. This chapter—which rests on soundings in Pattison's unpublished notebooks and correspondence in the Bodleian Library as well as upon a systematic reading of his published work—is meant to subject Pattison's scholarship to something of the same critical scrutiny that his character has often received.

It is curious that Pattison became so closely identified with the quintessentially modern mental life of the German universities. His roots lay deep in rural England—in Wensleydale, where he was born in 1813. The son of an eccentric clergyman, he knew firsthand as a child the world of the crowded trout streams and unspoiled coaching inns that one reads about in *Tom Brown's Schooldays*. He went up to Oxford ignorant of the refinements of Greek and Latin and the elements of etiquette. At university he read widely and mastered the canons of upper-class civility. But he took only a second in the schools, and became a fellow of Lincoln College only thanks to the traditional system by which eligibility to compete for certain fellowships was restricted to natives of single counties.

Pattison's mental life, as it developed during the 1830s, was as limited as his academic achievements were modest. It centered on John Henry Newman and the Tractarian movement. Pattison joined in the efforts of Newman's journal, *The British Critic,* to reconstruct the doctrines and practices of the true Catholic Church of medieval England. He translated part of Thomas Aquinas's vast anthology of patristic exegesis, the *Catena Aurea,* and wrote saints' lives. In the process he became a habitué of the Bodleian and the leading expert in Oxford in out-of-the-way areas of patristic and medieval scholarship.

What Pattison seems not to have been concerned with in the 1830s and 1840s were the subjects that would inspire his best essays. Trinity College, Cambridge, and the new University of London had influential members who could read academic German with ease and even translate it into literate English with facility. B. G. Niebuhr's *History of Rome,* Karl Otfried Müller's *Dissertations* on the *Eumenides* of Aescyhlus, and other characteristic products of the historical school were published in the English versions and assimilated into the Cambridge curriculum. Cambridge classical journals, the *Museum Criticum* in the second decade of the nineteenth century and the *Philological Museum* in the fourth, carried elaborate articles on the history of scholarship and informative reports on the doings of the Germans. They published Latin and English treatises by the philologist and ancient historian August Böckh and the pioneering historian of law Friedrich Carl von Savigny—though, being English, they also published imaginary conversations among the ancients by Walter Savage Landor. Rumors of these German discoveries—and of the English discovery of Germany—reached Oxford as well as Cambridge. Thanks to the work of Thomas Arnold and other liberal Anglicans, the young Pattison was not allowed to confine his study of Roman history to reading the Roman historian Livy: "One was expected at that time to know something of Niebuhr's view"—the views of the scholar who famously subjected the traditional early history of Rome to a corrosive analysis and revealed it to be the mythical cloak of a very material social conflict. But neither Pattison nor his teachers realized that the new German scholarship was raising a challenge to the whole Oxford curriculum. Niebuhr's own complex book was less an inspiration than a nightmare to Pattison, who tried to read it rather than the potted summaries students normally used, and found it "a quagmire, a Serbonic gulf, in which I was swallowed up."

Even as a college tutor, Pattison kept his attention fixed on a narrow range of tasks and a parochial set of ideas. Since the beginning of the nineteenth century, the best Oxford tutors had been trying to give the university a serious curriculum and a responsible teaching staff. They had devised a new curriculum, instituted a system of ranking the honors degrees that students won, and convinced the fellows of a few colleges to choose future colleagues for their mental and moral gifts rather than for their attractiveness and clubbability. Above all, they tried to teach the Aristotelian and other ancient texts required for students of *literae humaniores* in a serious and systematic way, urging their pupils to grasp the philosophers' arguments per se and to see that they still bore on vital problems of morality and politics. "How can we say," Newman asked his students in his course on the *Ethics*,

> that a person by doing just actions *becomes* just, is he not just already—
> a person who performs grammatical or musical actions is a grammarian
> or musician—? . . . What three things are tests of virtuous action? What

thing *alone* is requisite for the possession of one of the arts? Is this same thing of *much* avail in the moral virtues?

Pattison soon mastered this unhistorical but philosophically illuminating approach to the texts. He became as stimulating a tutor as Oxford had, made Lincoln intellectually respectable, and soon had the pleasure of seeing that the brightest and most serious students in Oxford wished to be members of his previously obscure college. Through the 1840s, he followed these well-trodden paths without dissatisfaction. He even defended the old tutorial system of instruction as a witness before the Royal Commission that investigated Oxford in 1850–1852.

Personal disaster shook Pattison loose from tradition. In 1851 the old rector of Lincoln died. Pattison, backed by the younger, reformist fellows, hoped to succeed him and had a majority of votes pledged to him. But men changed sides at the last moment, and Thompson—a compromise candidate whom Pattison thought a "mere ruffian"—was elected in his place. "It was the return," Pattison later wrote, "to the reign of the satyrs and wild beasts—Thompson was nothing better than a satyr." He was "benumbed and stupefied—too stupefied to calculate the future." Though he managed to avoid losing his fellowship because of a technical breach of college rules, Pattison fell into despair and inactivity. He gave up his tutorship, left Oxford whenever he could, and spent his free time fishing in Scotland and walking across "large tracts of central and southern Germany, delighting in discovering nooks and corners unknown to guide-books."

During this period of misery, Pattison's mature interests finally took shape. In 1850 the Clarendon Press published in two bulky volumes the Latin diary of the sixteenth-century philologist Isaac Casaubon (1559–1614). It is a curious and compelling book, packed with interesting anecdotes, and rendered passionate and readable by Casaubon's ascetic commitment to the life of scholarship for its own sake (when friends visited and kept Casaubon from his reading, he commented "amici inimici" [my friends are my enemies]). Pattison recalled that it "immediately riveted my attention. I saw what a mine of inquiry was opened into the progress of classical learning, from the Renaissance down to Niebuhr." He reviewed the diary at length, along with a sketch of Casaubon by Charles Nisard, in the *Quarterly.*

As H. S. Jones has shown in an admirable biography, Pattison's forty-page essay marked the beginning of his immensely successful career as a writer for the educated public. It also established him as *the* English authority on the history of learning. Pattison cultivated this field with unflagging energy. He bought and read hundreds of obsolete philological treatises, worked in continental libraries and archives, and reviewed the most impressive of all nineteenth-century books in the area, Jacob Bernays's *Joseph Justus Scaliger* of 1855. Though he never wrote the vast life of Scaliger that he had planned as his great work, he did produce a solid book on Casaubon and a series of penetrating essays on the history of classical scholarship and education from the days of the sixteenth-century polymaths to the Germany of the generation just before his own.

Pattison wrote "about everything that can be known—and some other things too." He edited Pope and Milton with economical, informative commentaries. He did solid work on the history of English theology. But his studies of the classical tradition made his name. His review of Bernays brought him to the benevolent attention of that bitter, brilliant German Jew, perhaps the most learned man in Germany, with whom he corresponded for decades. His hundred-page essay on Wolf fascinated such expert and critical readers as George Eliot and Matthew Arnold. His biography of Casaubon (1875) established new standards, at least in England, for completeness of documentation. And in the course of his reading and his trips to Germany, Pattison abandoned his trust in the old Oxford system that had betrayed his hopes. He became Oxford's greatest believer in advanced research. He supported expensive, erudite projects as a delegate of the Clarendon Press. He fought to make working conditions more reasonable at the Bodleian. And he testified on behalf of endowed professorships and intellectual specialization before the second university reform commission in the 1870s. The discovery of what education and scholarship had been in Scaliger's Leiden and Wolf's Halle led Pattison to a new vision of what they should be in his Oxford. All of his historical work was written with the conditions of his own time firmly in mind; and that alone is enough to suggest that his objectivity is not complete.

To be sure, Pattison's writings on the history of learning have much to offer even now. Before most professional historians, he saw that history could no longer be an affair of drums and trumpets: "We can read anywhere of the battle-field and the council-chamber—show us, if you can, the domestic interior. We are sated with state apartments, let us have a peep into the kitchen or the housekeeper's room." Unlike the modern social historians who have followed these admonitions most closely, Pattison tried to re-create those slices of everyday life that he knew best in his own time: the day-to-day work of the teacher and scholar; the institutional, political, and economic organization of schools and universities. This he did with imagination and flair. As Jones shows, he took a special interest—highly unusual for the time—in the ways that Casaubon read and annotated his books. His detailed discussions of these points fascinated contemporary readers and had an impact on other biographers' practices. Even the essays most flawed by factual errors retain a value for Pattison's vivid reconstructions of literary life in seventeenth-century Caen or nineteenth-century Berlin. His work played a substantial role in the rise of intellectual history—a field practiced with special interest and ability in nineteenth-century England, as Arnaldo Momigliano pointed out long ago.

Pattison also managed to avoid some serious errors that his successors have fallen into. Unlike some recent historians of science and scholarship, he always evaluated the work of earlier scholars in the light of the methods and information at their disposal. After pointing out that Pierre Daniel Huet had allowed dogmatic considerations to dictate his readings in the text of Origen, he added:

> Not, be it observed, that he considers that what Origen wrote ought to be altered, but that Origen, being a Father (though not a saint) of the Church, must have written that which was orthodox. To expect him to have been emancipated from this idea, is to expect him to have been above his age.

Unlike a great many historians of education, Pattison never confused the alteration of university statutes and curricula with the real reform of education:

> You must train your masters under your own eye. No regulations can make good schools; we must have men. Even training cannot do all. To the making a successful teacher there belongs a special *charisma*. No man should dedicate himself to the profession who does not feel a special vocation to it. A zeal for his occupation, a love for youth, a genuine,

deeply-seated religious devotion to the service of the young, can alone make the toilsome occupation of school-teacher endurable.

And unlike many historians of ideas, he had a solid grasp of the content of the technical disciplines whose history he studied and an unusual ability to summarize technical points without losing clarity or brevity. No one could offer a more painless introduction to that most German of special studies, hermeneutics, than Pattison managed to slip into the beginning of his essay on the "Present State of Theology in German":

> We read a translation from the German as we would an original English book. We expect that, because the language difficulty is smoothed for us, we are to meet with no other impediment to apprehension than such as the subject itself may present. When we find that this is not the case, when we still encounter an element which eludes our grasp, and feel ourselves inhaling an atmosphere in which we do not freely breathe, we summarily condemn our book, form and matter, contents and treatment, together . . . No one expects from an English translation of the Vedas, or of Aristotle's Metaphysics, to find Hindoo or Greek philosophy lying patent before him. The whole of interpretation is to come, after translation is ended. When we have penetrated the language, there remain many integuments through which we have to make our way to the thought. The intricacies of this process may be greater for an ancient, than for any modern, literature. But they exist in all. No one, certainly, is under any obligation to undertake this labour for the Theology of Germany. But no one has any right to pronounce it "unintelligible" till he has taken the proper means to understand it.

Moreover, Pattison devoted his life to a problem of great importance that had in his time received little systematic study. Long before the foundation of the Warburg Institute or the invention of *Rezeptionsgeschichte*, he had grasped that the history of the classical tradition formed a central and a variegated thread in the fabric of the European cultural history. He summed up the great changes in the role of the classics in modern thought with breathtaking confidence and matchless brevity:

Classical Antiquity has been found in various relations to the modern mind. 1. as furnishing the highest stimulant to thought & feeling— antagonistic to popular religion, & absolute power. 2. Dropt by the innovating minds it becomes the medium of general culture—ceasing to influence *philosophy* it influences *literature,* e.g. in France . . . Racine. 3. Passing out of culture it becomes Philology, a mere antiquarianism, the occupation of a professional Class, e.g. in Germany now . . .

The 16th. cent. opened with the culte of pagan antiquity.

17th with that of Christian antiq.

18th. with the contempt of all antiquity.

Though Pattison never wrote the "History of Learning" for which these sentences are a stretch, the larger views they reveal informed and gave breadth to the monographs he managed to complete.

Pattison's gifts as a stylist also make his work attractive. He wrote concise and powerful prose, enlivening every page with quotations, anecdotes, and his unique brand of hyperbole. Nothing could be more memorable—or less fair—than his bravura description of Jesuit learning:

Jesuit learning is a sham learning got up with great ingenuity in imitation of the genuine, in the service of the church. It is related of the Chinese that when they first, in the war of 1841, saw the effect of our steam vessels, they set up a funnel and made a smoke with straw on the deck of one of their junks in imitation, while the paddles were turned by men below. Such a mimicry of the philology of Scaliger and Casaubon was the philology of the Jesuits . . . It was that caricature of the good and great and true, which the good and great and true invariably calls into being: a phantom which sidles up against the reality, mouths its favourite words as a third-rate actor does a great part, undermimics its wisdom, overacts its folly, is by half the world taken for it, goes some way to suppress it in its own time, and lives for it in history.

And he could always touch that favorite Victorian organ stop, the pathetic. Nothing could have moved Victorian readers more deeply than Pattison's often-quoted vignette of Scaliger's death: "On the 21st of January,

1609, at four in the morning, he fell asleep in Heinsius's arms. The aspiring spirit ascended before the Infinite. The most richly-stored intellect which ever spent itself in acquiring knowledge was in the presence of the Omniscient."

Yet one could ask for more than Pattison was willing to give. His analysis of Casaubon's scholarship—the life's work of the scholar he studied most closely—is insubstantial and unsatisfying. In the biography, Pattison made little direct reference to Casaubon's published works, except where they offered curious stories about Casaubon's experiences. He made even less effort to analyze the rich stock of Casaubon's working papers in the Bodleian or the many annotated books in the British Museum. Casaubon's marginal notes—so said Pattison the bibliophile—were a mere "defacement" to the books they occurred in—even his copy of *Hermes Trismegistus,* now in the British Library, the margins of which record the stages of Casaubon's discovery that this text was not a translation from ancient Egyptian sources but a work of the imperial period, originally written in Greek.

Even Casaubon's huge commentaries on classical texts, Pattison held, for all their rich marbling of erudition, lacked the lean meat of argument and ideas. Pattison did not attack Casaubon's books for their dullness. Indeed, he defended Casaubon and his fellow scholars from the attacks of De Quincey and other believers in "original thinking." But the terms of Pattison's defense are revealing. "The scholars," he wrote, "were not 'poor as thinkers,' because thinking was not their profession. They were busy interpreting their past. The fifteenth century had rediscovered antiquity, the sixteenth was slowly deciphering it. For this task memory, not invention, was the faculty in demand." Casaubon, in short, was a great man even though he had no ideas. His greatness lay in his patience and in the stock of learning he assembled, not in the finished products of his books: "The scholar is greater than his books. The result of his labours is not so many thousand pages in folio, but himself." The deficiencies of this assessment are manifest. It implies that a man without ideas can be a successful interpreter of ancient texts. It accepts that outdated works of scholarship are of merely historical interest. And it does violence to the facts.

Pattison's *Casaubon,* in fact, in some ways has as little to do with the historical Casaubon as *Middlemarch* does. The real man was not the primitive accumulator of facts that Pattison described, but an intellectual adventurer.

In learning, he matched the other polymaths of his generation, Lipsius and Scaliger. In historical insight and conjectural boldness, he sometimes surpassed them. Two examples will give some inkling of his ability as a thinker.

Early in his twenties, Casaubon published a commentary on Diogenes Laertius's *Lives of the Philosophers*. At one point in this anecdotal book, the poet and Homeric critic Aratus is represented as asking Timon of Phlius how he could obtain a sound text of Homer. Timon tells him to find an old one that no one (that is, no one like Aratus) has tampered with. This uninspired anecdote inspired Casaubon. He reconsidered everything he knew about the origin, transmission, and state of preservation of the Homeric epics. His conclusions were as revolutionary as they were concise:

> If what Josephus says is true, that Homer did not leave his poems in written form, but they were preserved by memorization and written down much later, then I do not see how we can ever have them in a correct form, even if we have the oldest MSS. For it is likely that they were written down in a form quite different from that in which they were first composed.

Twenty years later, Casaubon published a set of running notes on Dio Chyrsostom. One of Dio's orations mentions Greeks who dwelt in Asia, "taking the land to inhabit from Priam and Hector." Here, too, a passing remark led Casaubon to rework traditional accounts of a complex problem:

> From this we learn that the Greeks settled in Asia even before the Ionian, Aeolian and Dorian colonies that the historians and geographers have made famous—and, indeed, as Dio thinks, from the time of the Trojan wars. . . . We show elsewhere that the Greeks were ignorant of their origins when they wrote that the Asiatic Ionians were descended from the Europeans. On the contrary, they were the oldest of the Greeks.

Neither comment is necessarily "correct" in some ultimate, positivistic sense. Both, however, clearly reveal in Casaubon some of the very qualities that Pattison denied him: the acuity to cut to the heart of obscure problems, the audacity to jettison long-accepted views, and the capacity to call up, like a philological and sorcerer's apprentice, legions of questions that would bedevil his professional successors for centuries. Casaubon's remark about Homer sums up in advance the great set of Homeric questions that German professors and English statesmen worried over throughout the nineteenth century. His suggestion about the Ionians shows that he had already glimpsed the task that ancient historians finally took upon themselves in Pattison's day: that of writing a history of Greece distinctively different from what the Greek historians had provided. These divinations did not emerge from the faculty of memory.

Pattison would not have had to mine Casaubon's huge folios in order to turn up these gems of analysis. Both were discussed in more modern works that he knew. The note on Homer and oral poetry is explicitly recorded in one of Pattison's notebooks. Moreover, after the book came out, Bernays wrote to him about it. He praised the style and learning of the biography but regretted Pattison's inability—natural in one writing for the English public— to get into the *penetralia eruditionis* (recessed of learning). And he urged Pattison to mention Casaubon's views on Homer and the Ionians in the second edition, if he could only bring himself "to discuss Casaubon's achievements as a scholar in some depth." But Pattison paid no attention even to his admired German friend. The second edition of *Casaubon* mentions neither remark, nor does it mention the many others like them that Pattison could have turned up if he had wished to do so. Accordingly, it does no more justice than the first edition to the qualities that make Casaubon memorable.

As far as I know, only two scholars before me have collated Pattison's working notes and writings with the materials by Casaubon in the Bodleian Library. In his 1950 edition of Aeschylus's *Agamemnon*, Eduard Fraenkel showed, by direct study of Casaubon's notes and books, how profoundly his Renaissance predecessor had studied the Greek tragedians. Fraenkel noted with disappointment that Pattison had failed to appreciate this side of Casaubon's work—and, more generally, that he had evidently never studied Casaubon's notebooks with any care. More recently, A. D. Nuttall, who made his own study of Casaubon's and Pattison's materials, came to even more negative conclusions in *Dead from the Waist Down* (2003).

What all three of us have missed in Pattison is "the usual German virtue . . . *Gründlichkeit*." And that is a puzzling omission in the work of so great an admirer and so committed an imitator of the Germans. I do not think that it is too hard on Pattison to assess his famous essays as noble failures. And I do not do so merely because his slips have given me occasion more than once for gnashing of teeth. He condemned himself out of his own pen. Pattison claimed to assess the early scholars' work as well as to recapture the texture and flavor of their lives. He had the classical education and philological equipment to do so. He knew enough about editorial technique to make fun of Bywater when he compiled an inelegant critical apparatus. He knew enough about historical method to deplore Jebb's efforts to rewrite classical texts in defiance of the documentary evidence. And he knew enough about philological workmanship to appreciate a master's handiwork. What he admired above all in Bernays's work, so he wrote to his German friend, was "the ingenuity of your argumentation—the way in which, finding the allusion you want, in the most unexpected lurking place, you drag it out, and gradually prepare it for its place in the chain of proof."

Yet for all Pattison's claims to be putting an end to the "carelessness of the literary writers of the last two centuries, which has been banished from philology & history," his published works reveal far more of the stylish prose he never boasted of than they do of the rigorous erudition he was famous for. True, his working notebooks bulge with painstaking transcripts of manuscripts from Continental libraries, detailed summaries of early works of erudition, and intelligent assemblies of quotations on such once-vexed issues as the nature of New Testament Greek. One cannot confront Pattison's notes without feeling new respect for their compiler. But Pattison reserved the heady brew of this kind of learning for private consumption. Hardly any of it seeped out into what he wrote for the public; and his writings consequently look even feebler when compared with the materials he collected and did not use.

Pattison's failure as a scholar was the natural result of his upbringing and situation. He admired German professors; after his hated rival Thompson finally died, he was the head of an Oxford college. And Pattison's Oxford offered little inducement to research. Professorships were few and counted for little in the university. Major academic offices were not given out on grounds of scholarly achievement, and major scholars—like Max Müller and James Murray—found little preferment. Most dons saw their posts as little more than lucrative stopgaps, to be rested in until a pleasant college benefice became vacant and they could happily decline into a daze induced by piety or alcohol. In Germany, a single technical essay—like Bernays's famous one on the medical element in Aristotle's concept of catharsis—could make a career as well as a reputation. In Oxford, it was more likely to make trouble—as Pattison found when his harmless historical contribution to *Essays and Reviews* landed him almost as deep in hot water as his fellow contributors, whose pieces were far more challenging to the established church.

Pattison recognized the flaws in the Oxford system and detested its results. "Max Müller's election to the chair of Sanskrit," he wrote to Bernays in 1860, "is still very doubtful. [It did not take place.] He is too accomplished & too liberal for the taste of such a body of electors as our Convocation." He sent his most talented pupils on to Bernays to see real philology being practiced in Germany; he encouraged them to found an Oxonian version of the German seminar, the Oxford Philological Society. And he continually complained that "We do nothing here."

But as a writer, Pattison never rebelled against the system that had formed him. As Jones shows, he never supported research for its own sake, of the sort done in Germany, but rather called for an ascetic intellectual discipline that would form students' characters, as sports did, but in a different way. Like other dons, Pattison saw the ideal public for his work as the wide middle-class readership of the quarterlies. He published his life of Casaubon not with the Oxford University Press but with Longman's in London (disappointed when *Casaubon* received enthusiastic reviews but found few buyers, he was amused when the tax man dunned him, since the enthusiastic review in the *Times* had misled him into thinking the book must have found buyers). In some moods, Pattison criticized these assumptions about the writer's role. In his first letter to Bernays, he claimed to be ashamed of his attempt to review *Scaliger*: "Your goodness, however, makes allowance for me, & you know our English circumstances. We must write that which will pay. 'Tis yours to draw the ore from the mine, we can but coin it into sixpence & distribute to the crowd." But Pattison never fully explained why the master of an Oxford college had to "write that which will pay." When writing for English audiences, he showed little critical detachment from English ideas about the role of the man of letters. At times he abused German prose in much the terms that obscurantist Oxford dons liked to use: "All imagination, all colouring, all individuality is expelled from these dreary sentences, which average ten lines each, and of which we feel sure that no English or French readers would ever get through ten pages without nausea." This from the defender of the great scholars whose profession was not thinking; this from the advocate of hermeneutics.

Pattison admired German learning from a great distance in space and Renaissance erudition from a great distance in time. He appreciated both and wrote vividly about them, but he lacked the courage to practice the Spartan intellectual virtues that he loved to praise when there was no English public to appreciate such accomplishments. Housman dismissed Pattison's failures with a characteristic turn of phrase: he had been "a spectator of all time and all existence, and the contemplation of that repulsive scene is fatal to accurate learning." It would be much fairer to say that Pattison was never able to tear up his roots. As much as he loved the new world of German scholarship, he came from an old world of quarterlies and gentle readers; and he could never quite imagine what it would be like to write without such a public in mind, even though he did more than anyone else to build an English public for exact scholarship. That helps to explain why his sketch for a "History of Learning" not only praised the German scholars who had first aimed "at a comprehensive view of the whole life of antiquity" but also viewed with dismay the fact that German learning had become of concern only to specialists: "a mere antiquarianism, the occupation of a professional Class."

Views like these help to explain why Pattison found writing and scholarship a mournful and unpleasant set of occupations. As a writer and scholar, he was doomed to failure by the contradiction between his methods and his interests. How could he write elegant essays about a Scaliger or a Wolf and not come away with a sense of his own moral and mental inferiority?

We should not estimate Pattison's value by his flawed books—any more than we should take them at their inflated current value. As a historian of scholarship, he deserves our interest, not as an authority but as a complex, tormented figure, doomed to praise something of great value that he could not possess. He deserves our respect for his acknowledgment of the superiority of Scaliger and Bernays to him. And he deserves our attention as a witness to the vast cultural distances, far greater than geographical ones, which separated England from Germany, Oxford classics from German philology, and the knowingness of the English writer from the knowledge of the German scholar.

12

Momigliano's Method and the Warburg Institute

Studies in His Middle Period

On 22 July 1955, the *Times Literary Supplement* welcomed the appearance of a new scholarly book with an enthusiasm rarely matched in its gray, closely printed pages. Pride of place, in those days, went not to the cover but to the so-called long middle—a substantial review that normally faced the correspondence columns. On this summer Friday, Peter Green wrote with phosphorescent enthusiasm of "a trilingual collection of essays remarkable alike for their classical and humanistic erudition, their historiographical judgment, and a style equally graceful in Italian, German, or English": Arnaldo Momigliano's *Contributo all storia degli studi classici*. Green proclaimed that this work set a new standard for the history of ancient history.[1]

The fact that the *Times Literary Supplement* could feature a book printed in Italy, much of which was not in English, alerts us, if we need alerting, to a vital fact: Momigliano inhabited a world we have lost. Britain's gray, bomb-damaged cities harbored poets, novelists, and scholars whose work dominated the intellectual life of the English-speaking world. British radio, movies, theatre, literary criticism, newspapers, philosophy, and even British natural science all put their American counterparts to shame, as no one confessed more eagerly than Anglophile Americans. British universities, though as gray and underfunded as British factories and cinemas, proved cosmopolitan enough to appoint dozens of European émigrés to prominent positions, where they not only formed English students but also addressed the English public. Their presence made the English intellectual world at mid-century far livelier and more cosmopolitan than the international English-speaking intellectual world in which we now live. This rich environment not only fostered but also partly shaped Momigliano's central historical work on the classical tradition.

Yet placing Momigliano in his London milieu is not simple, as an autobiographical anecdote will illustrate: In the spring of 1973, the Fulbright Commission appointed me to a scholarship for study in England. The commission also arranged for my work to be supervised by Momigliano, then nearing the end of his time as professor at University College London. I planned to write a doctoral dissertation on Joseph Scaliger (1540–1609), the Huguenot philologist whose editions of texts and manuals of technical chronology had won him a prominent place in the pantheon of great past scholars, though no one—even Jacob Bernays or Mark Pattison, the authors of the last systematic treatments—seemed able to explain exactly what he had done, or why it mattered. My teachers at the University of Chicago—Eric Cochrane, Hanna Holborn Gray, and Noel Swerdlow—agreed that Momigliano could offer better guidance than anyone else in the world into this thorny and inaccessible part of the historical forest. In a long letter to him, I described my project and listed the works I had read to date. This song of innocence, happily, has vanished from my personal archive, and with luck it has also disappeared from that of my teacher. But I remember it all too vividly. I explained that I had read not only Momigliano's 1950 essay "Ancient History and the Antiquarian," but a number of other studies by him and others that seemed to me to have expanded usefully on points and areas that he had touched on. I noted that the Warburg Institute, which had published so many of these studies and served as a research base for most of those interested in the history of scholarship, seemed the obvious place to do my work. And I asked for further advice.

A reply, in the form of a blue air letter, turned up some two weeks later in my mailbox in Hyde Park. It too has vanished—but its memory remains fresh. Momigliano paid me the compliment, as he always did, of treating my letter with absolute seriousness. But the compliments ended there. He pointed out that other scholars already working on Renaissance scholarship—above all, Sebastiano Timpanaro and Carlotta Dionisotti—had done work of the highest level on the history of the editing of texts: "You could hardly compare with" them, he noted, unkindly but accurately. As to antiquarianism, he commented with more acerbity that I seemed to have indiscriminately studied works of very different level and value. Erna Mandowsky and Charles Mitchell's book on Pirro Ligorio, published by the Warburg Institute in 1963, had fascinated me with its effort to separate Roman antiquarians of the fifteenth and sixteenth centuries into schools and generations. He dismissed it, citing his friend Carlo Dionisotti's swingeing review in the *Rivista storica italiana.*[2] Roberto Weiss's *Renaissance Rediscovery of Classical Antiquity* had offered me what looked like a plausible model for laying out the varied pursuits of early modern antiquaries, a model that I thought I might be able to emulate in my own work. It had also tickled my fancy by emphasizing the creativity and impact of the mad but brilliant forger Annius of Viterbo, whose invented Berosus and Manetho Scaliger had denounced with enough passion to show they mattered to him. Weiss's work received an even more withering dismissal: it did not even deserve invective. Momigliano warned that this solid-seeming book represented "an outsider's first look at an unknown thing." The authors of what I had taken as standard works, Momigliano held, could offer no help in navigating the unpathed waters that I hoped to explore. Their works had little or nothing in common with his—in origin or in method.

This letter caused me some surprise. To a young American, reading in the bright new Regenstein Library in Chicago, Momigliano's essays of the 1940s and 1950s, especially "Ancient History and the Antiquarian" and the later books and articles that had emerged from the same Bloomsbury circles had looked like a collaborative study of the antiquarians' world. A number of the books Momigliano dismissed had begun life, like his article, as lectures at the Warburg Institute. In style and scale, as well as content, his essays made a natural sequel to the lectures by the Warburg's first director in England, Fritz Saxl—lectures that traced the early development of antiquarian thought in Rome and Venice, and its varied relations to politics, art, and architecture, as well as historical writing. Mitchell, Weiss and others, who analyzed at length the works of Biondo and other antiquaries, which Momigliano had mentioned but not investigated at length, seemed to me to have laid out the detailed implications of his work with great clarity and interest. Momigliano, however, saw the matter quite differently. He noted such massive differences of method and substance that he could advise me only to ignore the secondary literature, head for the British Library, and plunge in.[3]

The subsequent year's research—followed by the many years of attendance at Momigliano's lectures and seminars in Chicago, Oxford, London, and elsewhere—took me down many strange paths. The Scaliger whose life and work I reconstructed did not, in the end, look much like the protagonists of Mitchell and Mandowsky or Weiss. Like Momigliano's antiquaries, he grappled with the problems of historical method that concerned them: how to work between texts and inscriptions, for example, and how to assess the credibility, or *fides,* of attractive but wild historians like Herodotus. Like them, too, he saw some curious connections between the methods of the new science of Copernicus and that of his own new science of chronology. Momigliano had mapped the field of antiquarianism from a great height. His articles provided a schematic London Underground map of the early modern world of learning rather than an Ordinance Survey map of its details. But his cartography took me where I needed to go. Today, it still does.

This chapter records a first effort to return to Momigliano's studies of antiquarianism and historical method in early modern Europe, and to ask some questions about them. How did Momigliano himself arrive at the particular vision of the historical tradition that he espoused in these works? And how did he devise the particular form of narrative that they exemplified? What did he bring with him from Italy? What did he learn from the new environments he inhabited in Oxford, Bristol, and London—those smoky cities, gloomy and (Oxford apart) cratered, where Momigliano remade himself as scholar and teacher? What, if anything, did the Warburg Institute have to do with Momigliano's vision of the historical tradition? And why did he insist so strongly on the isolation of his own work?

First, some elementary facts: The history of the historical tradition that Momigliano articulated in the 1940s and 1950s took the form of a series of articles, most of which began as lectures. Many, but not all, of them appeared together in 1955 in Momigliano's *Contributo* and reappeared in his 1966 *Studies in Historiography.* A bold red paperback edition of this book in Harper's Torchbook series made Momigliano's work accessible to my generation of scholars in the United States. For once, the market's choice of materials was sound. The central texts include, roughly in order of original composition:

"Friedrich Creuzer and Greek Historiography" (1944)
"The First Political Commentary on Tacitus" (ca. 1947)
"Ancient History and the Antiquarian" (1949)
"George Grote and the Study of Greek History" (1952)
"Gibbon's Contribution to Historical Method" (1954)
"Perizonius, Niebuhr and the Character of Early Roman Tradition" (ca. 1957)

"The Place of Herodotus in the History of Historiography" (1957)
"Mabillon's Italian Disciples" (1958)
"Pagan and Christian Historiography in the Third Century AD"
(1958–1959)[4]

Naturally, the list is not comprehensive. By no means all of Momigliano's studies on the history of scholarship reached print in the 1960s—or ever.[5] He continued to trace the threads he had begun to follow in these pieces for many years to come—for example, in several of his Vico studies of the 1960s, in his articles on the afterlife of Polybius in the early 1970s, and in the articles on Jacob Bernays, Hermann Usener, and other German scholars of the nineteenth century that occupied him from the 1960s until his death. He also wove all the strands together early in the 1960s in his remarkable Sather lectures, the local impact of which the Berkeley anthropologist John Rowe and others have evoked, though the final text, meticulously edited by Riccardo di Donato, appeared only after Momigliano's death.[6] Nonetheless, the works in this group are clearly linked by a certain style and by their scope, themes, and methods. Momigliano continued to refer to the arguments he advanced in them over the years, as exemplary. And they represented something new in the history of historical thought and scholarship, as Green made clear in his prescient review.

All of these articles, to begin with, worked dialectically between the present—of classical studies—and their past. Momigliano consciously set out to reinvigorate the study of the ancient world by connecting it to intellectual history of a particular kind. As he formulated his plan in the programmatic article on Friedrich Creuzer: "Ancient history has now become a provincial branch of history. It can recover its lost prestige only if it proves again capable of offering results affecting the whole of our historical outlook. One of the ways is, quite simply, to regain contact with those writers of the past who treated classical subjects of vital importance to history in general."[7] Ancient history—and classical scholarship more generally—needed to develop a rich sense of what it had been, and what its professional and amateur students had been, if it hoped, in the gray world of the 1950s and 1960s, to have any sort of a future. Green put the point eloquently when he praised Momigliano for "having crystallised both past achievement and the contemporary predicament."[8]

From the start, however, Momigliano hedged his invitation to new forms of scholarship with stern warnings. One of them I have already cited: he saw the central task of the historian of scholarship as recovering the turning points in the development of the field. The historian had to identify and concentrate on those individuals and works that had made the greatest impact, both on specialists in classical studies and on the wider intellectual world. At this stage, Momigliano's approach was only incipiently sociological. True, he noted that medical men were disproportionately represented among the antiquaries of the seventeenth century. But he did not, as yet, pay much attention to the outward and visible forms of disciplines. In the 1980s, after years of exposure to Edward Shils and other social scientists at the Universities of London and Chicago, he examined the establishment of institutes, chairs, and programs in pedagogy and research.[9] In these early years, however, he took individual lives as the framework of most of his inquiries. Momigliano's history of scholarship, in its earliest phase, was vulnerable to the charge of cherry-picking—and if charged, he would have pleaded guilty. He taught, by precept as well as example, that the history of scholarship could not become profound except by concerning itself with profound scholars.

Momigliano uttered a second warning, equally charged with meaning for him, implicitly in these articles and explicitly in a number of book reviews. The history of ideas was flourishing, at least in the United States. Even in Britain, Isaiah Berlin, Herbert Butterfield, and others were doing influential work on the history of political thought and of science. Partly under their influence, a number of younger scholars had begun to turn their attention to the work of philologists and historians. Momigliano found this development repellent rather than praiseworthy. "There are now plenty of people," he warned in an otherwise favorable *Times Literary Supplement* review of Elizabeth Armstrong's *Robert Estienne, Royal Printer,* "who write about the history of historiography without ever having done a piece of plain historical research. There is also an increasing number of students (especially in America) who find it easier to write about the history of classical scholarship than about classical texts. The fact that Mrs. Armstrong is so outstandingly successful in breaking the rules of the game should not encourage the mass of D.Phil. candidates."[10] Momigliano saw the history of tradition as the preserve of a small group of classicists with broad interests and training—scholars at home both in the ancient sources and the current scholarly literature on them, and in the earlier periods in which influential interpretations and methods had taken shape. As he noted in his "Piedmontese View of the History of Ideas," he had little contact at this point with historians of science, and he apparently took no interest in the models that Butterfield, Kuhn, Medawar, and others developed in the 1940s and 1950s for re-creating the intellectual and discursive worlds of technical disciplines, any more than he did in most scholarly institutions.[11] In practice, though, he agreed with the belief of many scientists that they are better equipped than historians of science to understand the past of their field: "It is a good rule that historians should be judged by historians, classical scholars by classical scholars."[12]

Momigliano's history crystallized in a particular shape—or a particular set of shapes. Episodic in substance, it would also be episodic in form. From the start of his time in Britain—at the torturous point, in 1940 and after, when he was largely unknown and his English still fragmentary, and he was treated with patronizing superiority by some of those who meant most to him in the English academic world, such as Hugh Last and Eduard Fraenkel—Momigliano chose the lecture as his characteristic genre.[13] He would begin either with a story ("The name of Professor Friedrich Creuzer of Heidelberg University is associated with two of the most typical episodes of the Romantic period"; or "It was about twenty-five years ago that the name of Gower Street first impressed itself on my mind") or with a broad claim ("We shall not ask of Gibbon new methods in the criticism of sources"; or "When I want to understand Italian history I catch a train and go to Ravenna").[14] Then he would move, anecdote by anecdote and text by text, through a winding chain of narrative. He envisioned a public of listeners and readers who could recognize a vast range of names and milieus, possessed a broad familiarity with Western intellectual history from antiquity forward, and would not be put off by long quotations in Latin. Though these texts were continuously enlivened by Momigliano's irony and wit, he confined his rare rhetorical flights—and rarer ventures into pathos—to his conclusions ("Those who have known him [Rostovtzeff] have known greatness. They will always cherish the memory of a courageous and honest historian to whom civilization meant creative liberty").[15]

Most important, Momigliano devised a highly distinctive analytical method. At a time when Watson, Crick, Franklin, and other scientists in Cambridge and London arranged the basic material of life on what turned out to be double helices, Momigliano laid out the history of scholarship along strikingly similar sets of double axes, like sets of genetic possibilities that determined what history could become. He organized the possible modes of historical writing at a given time into two sets of possibilities and practices, and saw revolution as what took place when individuals or groups combined these. Thus, in his most famous essays, he distinguished between:

> The study of epic poetry and that of history
> Historians and antiquaries
> Philosophic and erudite historians
> Narrators and collectors of documents
> Political and intellectual historians

The Schlegels, Heyne, and Creuzer wed the first two, Mommsen and other nineteenth-century melded the second, Gibbon managed to merge the third, Eusebius—of all people—connected the fourth set, and Grote brought together the fifth. By contrast, the opposition between certain other possibilities—like history based on oral and history based on written tradition—proved so durable that they persisted in modern scholarship. Some double helices could never become single. Peter Green revealed his insight again when he called attention to the "dualisms" that recurred in Momigliano's articles. Indeed, sometimes these dualisms outlived their heuristic usefulness—as when Momigliano found it hard to accept H. J. Erasmus's demonstration, in his 1962 study of *The Origins of Rome in Historiography from Petrarch to Perizonius,* that a number of historians had found it possible in the sixteenth century to combine their pursuits and methods with those of the antiquaries.[16]

One pair of categories proved especially vital. From the start—and long before Hayden White and others had begun the revival of rhetorical analysis that amused and exasperated Momigliano in the 1970s and 1980s—he saw style as central to the history of scholarship. The antiquaries' style of collection and argument—Gibbon's august, witty prose; Eusebius's willingness to interrupt his narratives of the early church to quote extensive documents; Muret's Tacitism—all of these choices mattered to Momigliano as much as their choices of subject matter, and he paid direct and constant attention to them throughout the early part of his career as historian of scholarship (the appearance of Hayden White's books drove him to avoid such questions in later years, when he insisted that the critical use of evidence, rather than the construction of narratives, formed the core of history).[17] The antiquaries' passion for classification led them to create systematic treatises and museums; Gibbon's drive to combine reflection on causes with reflection on sources enabled him to devise the unique narrative architecture of the *Decline and Fall*—a textual Convent Garden, in which screaming Cockney vendors of macaroons and lemonade scurried about in the shade cast by splendid, ornate arches and arcades.

Momigliano's essays rested on precise and exacting study of a great many texts, but he rarely allowed the formal research he had done to peep above the waterline of his trim vessels. He did so chiefly in the essays he wrote for classical journals—especially the studies of Tacitism and Perizonius that appeared in the *Journal of Roman Studies*. Even there, detailed analysis remained more exemplary than comprehensive.[18] In the ninth volume of the *Journal of the Warburg and Courtauld Institutes*, dedicated to articles by Italian scholars, Momigliano's study of Creuzer stood out partly because it did not essay the kinds of detailed textual reading on which his fellow authors, Fausto Ghisalberti, Alessandro Perosa, and Augusto Campana, concentrated. Momigliano's style, in sum, was as distinctive as his arguments.

How then did the scholarship of Momigliano's middle period take shape?[19] It is always dangerous—as it was during Momigliano's lifetime—to suggest that he was not familiar at any given time with any given written work, from any period, or its context. He seems to have been born with an encompassing memory and a powerful interest in the history of scholarship. By the time he reached his mid-twenties, he began addressing himself to the origins and development of modern historiography. Early essays investigated the development of the notion of Hellenism, taking a special interest in Droysen's passage from the student of the Greek spirit to the analyst of Greek and Macedonian politics; the development of Roman imperial history from Tillemont and Bossuet onward; the work of Gibbon and of Creuzer; and the letters of Böckh.[20] Already, as one footnote made clear, he urged his students to carry out similar kinds of study—and, already, he insisted, with his customary irony, on his own incompetence as a student of modern intellectual history.[21] As these early essays show, Momigliano arrived in Britain steeped not only in the last two centuries and more of historiography—as well as in the larger intellectual background of Hegel and Romanticism—but also already convinced that ancient historians needed to carry on some sort of dialogue with their predecessors.

He was also already worried about the tendency of specialists in the modern world to try to assess the work of past scholars who concentrated on antiquity. With characteristic acerbity, Momigliano noted in 1937 that Meinecke did not grasp "Gibbon's contribution to the formation of a new European historiography"—an observation he developed in a characteristically mordant footnote in his essay on Creuzer: "It is perhaps evident that F. Meinecke, *Entstehung des Historismus,* 1936, though of great importance for the historiography of the 18th century, does not describe the 'Entstehung des Historismus,' which is to be found in historians and philologists whom Meinecke does not consider," and in his lifelong criticism of Meinecke's brilliant pupil, his own contemporary, Felix Gilbert.[22]

Yet most of these early essays have little in common, in structure or method, with Momigliano's later work (that of 1933 on Droysen is the most prominent exception). Bristling with extensive textual paraphrases and stuffed with long quotations, both of which dropped out of his later work, they did not adumbrate the sharp, allusive, fact-packed piece on Creuzer and its successors. More to the point, they did not anticipate Momigliano's later arguments. Steeped in the German language that he already wrote fluently, Momigliano was also committed to a German conceptual apparatus. He believed wholeheartedly, at this point, in the German historical revolution of the early nineteenth century. The young Momigliano knew the Enlightenment well enough to criticize Cassirer for his failure to engage with Jansenism in the chapter on history of his book on the Enlightenment.[23] But he had not begun to examine, in an intensive way, some of the premodern students of the ancient world who engaged him most in later years. As late as 1947, Momigliano confessed in a letter to Fritz Saxl that "I have not yet had the leisure to study the Etruscheria and the Vico tradition of the XVIII century."[24] And he did not, at this point, even suggest what became a central thesis of his later work: that "pre-critical" scholars had not only created the historical tradition, but forged many of the essential tools that modern, critical scholars still used. This may explain why he added a note, in the *Contributo,* to his early essay on Gibbon, remarking that the reader would find a "corrective" for it in his later piece on "Gibbon's Contribution to Historical Method."[25]

The shock of expulsion from Italy in 1938 and the softer blow of internment in England reshaped Momigliano's thinking about many things. So did the period he spent lecturing to a tiny public at Cambridge and his intense contacts with a small but select group of unusually cosmopolitan British scholars— Hugh Last, Beryl Smalley, Isobel Henderson, and Iris Murdoch, all of them set loose to read and talk in the midst of world war, in that strange, febrile atmosphere so well evoked in the memoir of Oxford University Press's publisher, Dan Davin.[26] So did his visits to the Warburg Institute, where Italian scholarship and culture enjoyed a respect and affection that Oxford did not always accord them—and where Fritz Saxl held open house, and an open purse, for European exiles of every sort. During these years, Momigliano learned and changed in many ways, enjoying direct contact with the German philological and historical tradition, as represented by his fellow émigrés, and learning in slow stages the terrible truth about the extinction of continental Europe's Jews, including his own parents. Momigliano's eventual biographer will have to sort out how, in this cosmopolitan world, the ferocious Italian patriot became a hater of all absolute ideologies—and a committed, if ironic, Zionist.

My interest here is much more limited. The onetime believer in the German historical revolution now devoted himself to showing that forgotten antiquaries and philologists had really laid the foundations of critical historiography. And the onetime specialist on Greek and Roman history became— as the title of his collected essays proclaimed—the preeminent historian of his own discipline. In devoting himself to the history of European scholarship, Momigliano responded to—and in some ways sought to fill—the deep fractures that exile had caused in the tradition he came from. At a very general level, one could compare his enterprise to those of other European exiles, from those he admired (notably Gershom Scholem, Felix Jacoby, and Rudolf Pfeiffer) to those he did not: an epic adventure in the collection of fragments. But how, in particular, did Momigliano's first British years shape and stamp his new scholarship?

Momigliano, after all, did not lack models as he began to use the history of scholarship to teach lessons of methodology. But none of the established ones served his need. Naturally, he could not use the old compendia of Conrad Bursian and J. E. Sandys as anything more than sources of information. Nor did he have much use for general surveys of what the classical tradition had meant in the past. Momigliano dismissed A. Bernardini and G. Righi's *Il concetto di filologia e di cultura classica nel mondo moderno* (1949) as sterile, because it dealt only with abstract programs for the study of the ancients, not with the concrete details of what scholars had done to texts and monuments. Exceptionally, for someone who never listened to his own advice for eager reviewers ("The cheapest way to get a book is to buy it"), he did not review the massive work of the scholar he dismissed as the *"compilatorio Bolgar"*: *The Classical Heritage and Its Beneficiaries from the Carolingian Age to the End of the Renaissance* (1954).[27] M. L. Clarke's tight and parochial studies of English classical scholarship, though the work of a real Hellenist, said little about the scholarly practices of their protagonists. Even Mark Pattison's classical essays and his life of Isaac Casaubon, which Momigliano cited with evident respect, generally avoided technical questions in the history of scholarship.[28] And although Jacob Bernays eventually came to have an almost talismanic value for Momigliano, Bernays's biography of Joseph Scaliger does not seem to have played a central role in his thought during this period.

Nor did Momigliano's practices resemble those of the Italian specialists on the history of humanistic scholarship whom he most admired. Between the end of World War II and the early 1960s, Carlo Dionisotti, Alessandro Perosa, Giuseppe Billanovich, and Sebastiano Timpanaro created new models for a sophisticated internal history of philological practices. They analyzed the methods that Renaissance, Enlightenment, and nineteenth-century scholars had created for assessing and collating manuscripts, editing critical texts, and explicating difficult passages. And they did so in much the same tightly focused way in which historians of science like Otto Neugebauer had long analyzed the procedures of early mathematicians and astronomers. Their rigorous, detailed historical studies of scholarship became central both for the *Journal of the Warburg and Courtauld Institutes*, which printed Billanovich's first substantial analysis of Petrarch's scholarship, and for Billanovich's own new journal, *Italia Medioevale e Umanistica*.[29] Momigliano eagerly read everything these men wrote, and he engaged in a lifelong and continually fruitful dialogue with Dionisotti. But as a historian of scholarship, he went his own way.

Moreover, Momigliano distanced himself deliberately from other intellectual possibilities and resources accessible in his new environment. He certainly knew that when he studied antiquarianism, he entered territory that well-known British scholars were actively exploring. His Bristol colleague

David Douglas, for example, had won the James Tait Black prize for biography in 1939 for a book entitled *English Scholars, 1660–1730.* Douglas dealt eloquently and at length with the polymathic nonjuror antiquaries and their successors, the men and women who forged the scholarly tools still used by everyone concerned with the British Middle Ages. The Cambridge historian Herbert Butterfield touched on similar matters in *The Whig Interpretation of History* and *The Englishman and His History,* and he was already working on the studies of German scholarship in the eighteenth and nineteenth centuries that would culminate in 1955 with the publication of his Wiles lectures, *Man on His Past.*[30] In 1950, just before Momigliano joined the staff of another great institution in Bloomsbury and just after he had completed the final draft of "Ancient History and the Antiquarian," T. D. Kendrick of the British Museum published an eloquent and witty study of what he called *British Antiquity*[31]— the first full analysis in English of how Renaissance antiquaries reconstructed and debated the British past and the texts and monuments that preserved it.

Momigliano referred to this body of work, but only to treat it as basically irrelevant to the story he had told. The British antiquaries were chiefly concerned with the past of the British Isles. Most of them had studied medieval rather than ancient history, and accordingly they had not made a sharp distinction between history, seen as elegant narrative, and antiquarianism, seen as endless compilation. Kendrick's book stood out from the rest for its engagement with the Latin scholarship of the humanists. It had, after all, emerged—as Kendrick stated—from a wider study of European antiquarianism in the Renaissance, based on the vast resources of the British Museum Library. But Momigliano seems to have felt little affinity for Kendrick, and couched his only explicit reference to *British Antiquity* in the key of irony. After arguing that the available primary documents did not support the story that the king had named John Leland his official antiquary, Momigliano noted "with pleasure" that Kendrick had arrived at the same conclusion— but also pointed out that "Mr. Kendrick does not discuss the texts mentioned above."[32] In these cases, Momigliano probably saw himself as standing with the Warburg, in favor of a historical tradition that took the study of ancient history as its core, and that connected Britain with the Mediterranean—and against the modern British scholars' tendency to treat their predecessors in isolation from continental developments, and their reluctance to enter into detailed analysis and discussion of the sources.

The decision to take this stand limited Momigliano's work in certain ways. Kendrick showed that the antiquaries' turn to material evidence did not by any means put an end to controversy or shore up the credibility of history. They regularly disagreed—in fact, they regularly flailed one another unmercifully—about what they had seen in a given church or castle and what it meant. Their disagreements showed that no drawing, woodcut, or engraving could perfectly reproduce the style and content of a site. The conventions of the artist, the assumptions of his scholarly informant, and the simple liability of humans to interpret when they mean to reproduce an object or a text all hung between the scholars and the monuments like a scrim, which no form of lighting could make transparent. For all Momigliano's belief that the study of material remains had been intimately connected with the resolution of history's skeptical crisis, he did not pursue these problems. In the end, he left the creation of a fuller and more detailed panorama of early modern antiquarianism to Francis Haskell, whose learned, depressing book on images of history praised Momigliano even as it subverted parts of his work.[33]

Momigliano's works stood out sharply from those of his contemporaries both in form and content. First of all, there was his commitment to the lecture—and, in consequence, to the biography and the episode, as the central genre of history of scholarship.[34] Here the Warburg Institute certainly played a role—and not only in the sense (obvious from "Ancient History and the Antiquarian") that it provided him with a magnificent body of primary and secondary literature, available in the open stacks—as an accessible source base that had no parallel on the Continent. Since the 1920s, when Saxl and Warburg made the original Hamburg library into a new kind of intellectual institution, lectures had played a central role in its life. They served as the occasions for polyglot international meetings and discussions; they yielded articles and monographs for the library's publication series; and they gave its programs of research and publication a unique form that united the concrete with the conceptual.[35] Warburg scholars analyzed specific texts and images in order to reveal the intellectual and emotional orders that underlay them, and visitors rapidly absorbed their method—as Ernst Cassirer notoriously found himself doing, almost involuntarily, in his Hamburg years. Momigliano joined eagerly in the library's yearly lecture series, organizing one of them and participating in others. And he regularly highlighted—in footnotes that confessed his intellectual debts—the role that discussion with an international circle had played in his work.[36] The contemplative, systematic, and argumentative thinker of the 1930s transformed himself, in these new circumstances, into an eager and intensive conversationalist as well as a more concrete and powerful writer. The Momigliano who loved to learn from others' lectures—even as he read books during them—seems to have been born in the Imperial Institute, then the Warburg's London home.[37]

Moreover, in concentrating on lectures that explored dualities and contrasts, Momigliano adopted one of the Warburg Institute's house styles. From the 1930s onward, Panofsky and Saxl began to formulate some of the Warburg scholars' major findings about the classical tradition for an English-speaking public. They found themselves at once impoverished and stimulated. Bereft of the precise but abstract German vocabulary in which they had learned to write, they had to address a public far less knowledgeable and specialized than the German one—sometimes, indeed, one that included "Chinchilla-Damen," who found Panofsky's lectures as painful to listen to as the Wagner operas they squirmed through in his presence at the Metropolitan Opera House.[38] Yet Panofsky and Saxl continued to pose and answer complex historical questions, and to insist even in their new environment on the close connections between scholarship on the one hand and art, politics, and letters on the other. They also used dualisms as narrative armatures, following Warburg—and simplifying him—as they devised sharp dilemmatic ways to present the possibilities of expression within the classical tradition. Panofsky and Saxl, for example, formulated the principle of disjunction—according to which classical form was severed from classical content in the Middle Ages and reunited with it in the Renaissance—to make the Warburg tradition of research on the classical tradition accessible and coherent to audiences in New York, Princeton, Philadelphia, and London. Furthermore, they also told stories—often familiar to a German or European public, but virtually unknown in English—from which they drew implicit morals.[39]

The Warburg Institute, finally, stood for a particular approach to the classical tradition—one that applied all the tools forged by the German philologists of the nineteenth and twentieth centuries, but that emphasized continuities rather than breaks. Well before Momigliano began to write for the *Journal,* it had published what became classical studies: by Fritz Saxl on the ways in which Renaissance scholars and artists had interpreted classical inscriptions and rituals, and by Rudolf Wittkower on the millennial tradition in Western ethnographic writing that placed monstrous races of Cynocephali and Sciapods on the edge of human habitation in India.[40] That is why Saxl reacted with such delight to Momigliano's essay on Creuzer. He liked it precisely because he knew the traditional accounts and saw at once that "It is a very unexpected contribution. I had no idea of Creuzer's importance in this respect." Frances Yates, in the same way, immediately recognized the greatness of "Ancient History and the Antiquarian": "The article is magnificent— a most deep and rich and at the same time polished and elegant piece of scholarship."[41] The Warburg circle was one of the few groups of scholars—if not the only one—in a position to appreciate and welcome the novelty of Momigliano's approach to the history of scholarship, and the revisionist character of many of his findings.

The new path that Momigliano would follow looked clear enough to him, by the late 1940s, when he announced, at a "traumatic meeting" with Dan Davin of the Oxford University Press, "that he had found a new theme for research, to which he intended to devote himself—the history of historiography."[42] In fact, however, his decision to devote himself to this new field—and the form his devotion took—had a certain element of contingency. Momigliano's early dealings with the Warburg Institute, and his exchanges with Saxl, Yates, and Bing, helped him to find his intellectual and even his stylistic way. The documents that record these discussions also clarify how early he decided not to follow certain paths as a scholar—a decision vital to understanding the nature of his enterprise as a whole.

As Oswyn Murray has shown, Saxl first brought Momigliano into contact with the Warburg Institute in the 1930s, and Momigliano submitted his article on the Ara Pacis to the *Journal* in 1942. After taking some time to read the manuscript, Wittkower accepted it with enthusiasm, and it appeared in the same year. But it was the institute's subsequent decision to produce "a volume of the *Journal* which will consist entirely of contributions from our Italian friends," in the hope of rebuilding intellectual relations between the two countries, that set Momigliano on what became his definitive way. As early as July 1945, Wittkower asked him to contribute to this project.[43] Momigliano agreed with alacrity, offering either a paper "on the study of Roman history during the Risorgimento" in Italy or one on a classical topic.[44] Wittkower, expecting the volume to "have a strong Renaissance bias," preferred the piece on the Risorgimento, which he thought might serve as a good coda.[45] Wittkower and Yates repeatedly pressed Momigliano to deliver his article through 1945, 1946, and early 1947, but to no avail.[46] Finally, on 20 March 1947, a higher authority intervened. Saxl made a direct appeal to his laggard author. The Italian manuscripts had now "come in," he wrote, "and they make quite a good number, but there is very little of outstanding merit." A piece by Momigliano would raise the quality of the whole enterprise. Without one, Saxl feared, "it will not serve the purpose, which so many people have tried to achieve."[47]

Momigliano could not resist this entreaty, but he professed his doubts about what exactly he should contribute to the *Journal.* For some time he had been badly overworked, since he was both "lecturing and tutoring like an ordinary don (though not paid like an ordinary don!)" and trying to complete two books. These primary occupations had left him little time for articles. At this point, moreover, he simply did not know enough about Vico and the eighteenth century to produce a solid piece on the Risorgimento. His work on Tacitism in Spain, France, Italy, and England, though more advanced, had stalled temporarily, until he could study manuscripts in England and Spain and clear up a number of bibliographical and textual puzzles. But he did have one old paper on a somewhat unexpected theme that he thought might serve Saxl's purposes, when revised:

> I have looked also among my mss to see whether there is anything there which I could bring together for the Journal. Two or three years ago, I wrote a paper on the pre-symbolistic phase of Creuzer—when he founded the modern study of Greek historiography. What I wrote is perhaps not unimportant, but must be re-written, because style and disposition are faulty. Besides, the subject is not Italian. If you want to see the ms, I am always happy to discuss a point with you. But you will concur with me about the necessity of re-writing it.[48]

Saxl invited him to submit the manuscript, and Momigliano duly did so, in a fair copy that he wrote himself, since he had failed to find a typist. He was still uncertain that he had done enough research, or that the work deserved publication as it stood:

> I may say that I feel that I ought to expand the introductory remarks of #2 [#3 of the paper as published]. For obvious reasons German

philology and historiography of the XVIIIth century is practically non-existing in Oxford, and I never had the leisure to complete my research in the B.M. Another spell of good sleep will do no harm to my old friend Creuzer. So it does really not matter if you cannot utilize my paper in its present form.

In the event, Saxl accepted the article on the first of May, with enthusiasm.[49]

But he also asked Momigliano to provide it with a different kind of lead-in. Evidently, the first section of the paper, as Momigliano submitted it, was the second section of the paper as printed. It began: "Friedrich Creuzer's *Historische Kunst der Griechen in ihrer Entstehung und Fortbildung* is now read in the second edition of 1845."[50] Saxl found this opening in medias res a bit forbidding and mysterious, at least for the *Journal*'s local readership, and urged a change:

> There is one thing which I feel about it. The number of English people who know the name of Creuzer is, I suppose, very small, and if they know him they know him with regard to theories of mythology. You will remember that you begin the article by saying "We are used to reading Creuzer in the second edition," and I wonder how this sounds to English ears because hardly anybody reads Creuzer either in the first or the second edition. So what I would suggest is that we type the manuscript out as it stands and have it printed. But there ought to be an introduction giving some indication of Creuzer's work to those who are quite unfamiliar with this part of German philology. I do not expect that this would give you much trouble, but I think it will help readers towards a better appreciation of the article.[51]

Momigliano saw Saxl's point. On 11 May he replied, enclosing a new introduction—section 1 of the paper, as it finally appeared. He declined to say anything about Creuzer's most famous work, his study of ancient mythology: "I should not like to have to say much more on his *Symbolik* at the present, because I have been collecting materials for the history of mythological studies for many years. When I come to it, I must do it in full." But he began the paper with a story that would grab any reader's attention—that of Caroline von

Günderode, who committed suicide out of unrequited love for Creuzer, despite his notorious ugliness. He briefly described some of Creuzer's accomplishments as a scholar. And in a second lapidary paragraph, quoted in part above, he disclosed that he now saw the study of the history of scholarship as a way to renew the study of antiquity itself. In this indirect and partly collaborative way, Momigliano created what became the distinctive intellectual style of his middle period.[52]

The story of Momigliano's contacts with the Warburg did not, of course, end here, and it sheds a new light on the limits, as well as the origins, of the historiographical studies that preoccupied him in this period. At 5:30 p.m. on Monday, 10 January 1949, Momigliano lectured at the institute on "Ancient History and the Antiquarian." His ensuing discussions with the members of the Warburg delighted him, and he submitted a revised and enlarged text of the lecture to the *Journal* at the end of 1949, to Frances Yates's great pleasure.[53] The correspondence that ensued, which lasted through 1950, shows two great scholars in their prime.[54] Only a reader with a heart of stone could fail to enjoy the lesson on copy preparation that Yates offered her brilliant author, in the hope that he would write often for the *Journal*,[55] to be amused by Momigliano's description of his heroic efforts to verify his references,[56] or to savor his assessment, in a letter to Yates, of the 1950 Paris Congress on Historical Studies: "The atmosphere was very pleasant, and the hosts were charming. But the present decline in historical research was made only too obvious. I felt like writing a ballade des historiens du temps jadis."[57]

The correspondence went well beyond editorial details and witty travel notes. Yates recognized that Momigliano's story posed a challenge to traditional versions of the origins of art history, and urged him to follow it through into the eighteenth and nineteenth centuries: "I very much hope you will find time one day to continue this fascinating story right into the 19th century when, if I understand it rightly, the Hegelians come into it in Germany and begin to claim that the Spirit of the Age can be deduced most safely from visual documents. Does not this development start already with Winckelmann?"[58] Momigliano, who always insisted on his amateur status as a student of monuments, did not take up this challenge, leaving it to Francis Haskell, Thomas Kaufmann, and others to do so two generations later.[59] This seems a pity—especially as Momigliano, in the years to come, would read and think intensively about the intellectual filiation between Jacob Burckhardt's form of cultural history and Aby Warburg's version of art history.[60] Yates's query revealed an acute sense of one of the ways in which Momigliano's story needed—and needs—to be filled in.

Another of Yates's editorial letters asked formally for a small but meaningful revision. In his discussion of the antiquaries and the history of ancient religions, Momigliano noted—a little ironically—that Athanasius Kircher, S.J. had found "even the Trinity" in Egypt. In a long, learned, and deeply intelligent letter, Yates pointed out that efforts of this kind long preceded Kircher. The Neo-Platonists of the fifteenth and sixteenth centuries had taken a serious interest in "exotic religions," even though they knew less about them than the polymaths of the of age of Kircher and Witsius, and a full study of these studies in comparative religion would have to trace their growth over several centuries.[61] Momigliano found what Yates called an "admirable" solution for the specific problem she had identified.[62] He reformulated the sentence in question to read, "The Jesuit A. Kircher satisfied himself that the *Mensa Isiaca* provided evidence for an Egyptian belief in the Trinity (1652)."[63] But although he did further work on "the discussions of the XVIII century in Italy and France between antiquarians and theologians,"[64] he never again took up the larger challenge Yates offered—that of making clear, in precise terms, exactly how the highly technical work of the seventeenth-century antiquaries differed from, and how far it grew from, the less-professionalized studies of the fifteenth- and sixteenth-century humanists. Only in the 1990s and after have Ingo Herklotz and others begun to pose this question systematically once again. One must regret that Momigliano did not return to these problems at greater length, as Yates clearly hoped he would. But this decision—like his early one not to write on the history of archaeology and art history—is entirely understandable, in light of the way he came to these subjects. Momigliano did not see himself as a member of the Warburg Institute, though he joined its committee of management, constantly advised on appointments and fellowships, worked closely with its students and younger staff members, and held his own celebrated seminars there. Rather, he was, as he had always been, a professor of ancient history, who hoped that his own field could regain the richness and cultural standing it had once enjoyed by returning to selected moments in its own tradition. The Warburg offered him a way to publish these investigations, and its members helped him find an idiom in which to couch them, so effectively that scholars in a great many fields seized upon them and made them into classics. But Momigliano never meant his work to amount to a survey of the historical tradition.

Younger scholars have recently begun to fill in the empty spaces and amend the contours of Momigliano's great map of the historical tradition. They have begun to criticize not only the details of his work but also, to some extent, his larger methods.[65] It seems only appropriate, then, to raise the sort of question that Momigliano himself would have asked first about a predecessor whom he took seriously enough to argue with: that is, to ask how Momigliano himself came to his subject, and to set his published work into its biographical and intellectual contexts. By doing so, we can learn what chances of renewal a great scholar's masterpieces may hold for the dull, provincial scholarship of our own sad time. More particularly, we can also see that Momigliano came to the history of scholarship at a particular moment and in a particular context. He regarded his salient contributions to the history of classical studies not as parts of a general survey of the historical tradition, but more modestly as "works on historical method" aimed at fellow practitioners of his own field.[66] Wide and deep though his knowledge of historiography was, he resisted many temptations, and some well-informed invitations, to attack fields outside his own. Criticism of Momigliano's work—and nothing could be more in his spirit than criticism, whether based on a renewed close reading of his sources or on wider research—can hit the mark only if it takes account, as he would have, of what the record shows.

Appendix 1: Frances Yates to Arnaldo Momigliano, 9 October 1950

Warburg Institute Archive, Journal Correspondence, typescript. Momigliano's reply is not in the archive. But Yates's letter to him of 10 November 1950, accepting his revision of the sentence on Kircher, indicates some of its contents (and reveals Momigliano's characteristic alertness to new publications of interest): "I must read the book by Schwab,[67] which you mention, which sounds most important. It certainly would be a splendid idea if we could one day have a Warburg symposium on the lines you suggest. I will mention it to the Director." See also the letter from Momigliano to Yates, printed as Appendix 2 below.

Dear Professor Momigliano,

Thank you for your letters which have been unanswered for so long because I was in Italy, whence I have just returned, and where I had—of course—a wonderful time. I am very sorry to hear of your fall, and hope that you are by now quite recovered from it. You seem to have got through a great deal of work in spite of it. I am very interested to hear that you have collected material on eighteenth century controversies between antiquarians and theologians—certainly a rich field waiting to be worked.

The various corrections to your article which you mention can certainly all be worked into the page proofs, and the point which I wanted to discuss with you would only involve a tiny adjustment somewhere about p. 309—that is if you consented to make it.

When you say (p. 309) that Kircher found "even the Trinity in Egypt" perhaps it could be indicated that this is a sixteenth century tradition (Gyraldi, Ficino, Tyard etc.). You have indeed guarded yourself by mentioning in the next sentence that there was "nothing unusual or unorthodox in the view that some pagans had known the truth," but even so one is rather left with the impression that Kircher invented the "Trinity in Egypt" idea.

It seemed to me, when trying to wrestle a little with this subject when reading for my *French Academies,* that the sixteenth century had—though in a vague way—the principles of comparative religion and had no fear of including any number of exotic religions into its scheme, though the *knowledge* of such religions which it possessed was often limited to remarks in Plutarch, or the Fathers. See for example the insistence in the sixteenth century on the truth that God is light being known to the Brahmans (quoted in my *French Academies,* p. 90) which seems to have rested on a remark in Origen. I have wondered whether, when increased knowledge of oriental religions came into the possession of scholars in the seventeenth and eighteenth centuries, the first step in their minds (so to speak) may not have been to fit their new discoveries into the framework already provided by the sixteenth century syncretistic tradition. Perhaps one could follow such a process by taking one line—for example Zoroastrianism—and tracing it through from the vague enthusiasms of Ficino and disciples for the "wise Magi" to Anquetil Du Perron. Academic debates might well provide a major source for such a study.

That the Deists seize on comparative religion as a weapon had also, of course, a pre-history. Toland derives from Giordano Bruno, who in turn derives—with only a very slightly bolder twist—from Ficino—Pico. Was it only after the Council of Trent that comparative religion began to become a badge of revolt?

But you are only touching on comparative religion in your amazingly rich and inspiring article. Please forgive this long letter, the only practical point in which is to suggest that some tiny modification of the sentence on Kircher and the Trinity on p. 309 might be made.

Yours very sincerely,

Appendix 2: Arnaldo Momigliano to Frances Yates, 20 March 1951

Warburg Institute Archive, Correspondence of Frances Yates, manuscript. Written on the occasion of the death of Frances Yates's sister Hannah, this letter also sheds light on the development of Momigliano's studies in the history of scholarship. The interest in Yates's own work and in Renaissance studies more generally that appears here is also documented elsewhere in the correspondence: for example, Momigliano to Yates, 6 April 1950, and Yates to Momigliano, 18 April 1950, Warburg Institute Archive, Journal Correspondence.

Dear Miss Yates,

I was very sorry to hear that your sister and companion died. Rubinstein who was here last week told me that you were having great anxieties. Though you are fortunate in being able to put so much of yourself into your work, there is unfortunately no remedy for personal losses. I hope you will find it possible to carry on your research on the Italian Academies which looked so promising. I was thinking of you while reading in the essay on G. Naudé by Sainte-Beuve that he gives a list of the Italian Academies in his *Mascurat*.

I am still ruminating antiquaries in my free moments and hope to elaborate into an article a paper on Gibbon which I have lately read to a "classical" audience in Reading. But it will of course take much time.

I wonder whether a review-copy of Liebeschütz's John of Salisbury would be available for the Rivista Storica Italiana. The medieval section of it is edited by my colleague Giorgio FALCO, Facoltà di lettere, Università, via Carlo Alberto, Torino, to whom any communication should be addressed. I read the book with great interest in the copy so charmingly presented to me by the author, and I should like to see the book noticed and discussed by my Italian friends who are qualified to do so.

Yours very sincerely,

Arnaldo Momigliano

13

The Public Intellectual and the American University

Robert Morss Lovett

People keep telling me two stories about American intellectual life. I encounter them over and over again: in magazines, on the literary Web sites bookmarked on my computer, and in the endless series of books and essays on the New York intellectuals of the 1930s. And I'm impressed each time I encounter them by how rich and plausible they both seem and by how precisely they contradict each other. One of them is a sad story of the deaths of kings: the fall of public man and woman, as narrated by Russell Jacoby and repeated antiphonally by many others. The other is a Horatio Alger tale of success: the rise of the public intellectual, as documented by dozens of polemical articles, satirized in a number of academic novels, and recently confirmed by the creation of professorships, research fellowships, and even a PhD program. The American university plays a central role in both narratives: that of a villainous stepmother in the first one, a nurturing birth mother in the second.

According to Jacoby, the American public intellectual belongs to a threatened species; perhaps, like the whooping crane, a disappearing one. As late as midcentury, the argument goes, critical intellectuals congregated in urban centers. There they worked outside the official culture, lived in cold-water flats, and wrote what they wanted to. Most of them had no specialized training in any single area of scholarship or science, could not count on a solid income, and followed no clear career track. But their lack of professionalism made them great. They created little magazines, like *Partisan Review*. They worked with small-scale, highly selective publishers, like James Laughlin of New Directions. They reached a small, dispersed, and bad-tempered public. And they exercised an immense influence, since they thought, wrote, and were read as generalists. They tackled the problems that their contemporaries wanted to forget about, from poverty at home and dictatorship abroad to the question of what made great American cities thrive or die. And they presented their views in clear, lucid prose that anyone could read.

After midcentury, these unofficial intellectual communities faded away even as the books their inhabitants produced became paperback best sellers. More surprisingly, many of their onetime inhabitants were swallowed up by Leviathan, that great beast: the American university, which had previously paid them little attention. Many of them, of course, had gone to college, and a few—like Lionel Trilling and Delmore Schwartz—did advanced work and stayed on to teach. But the colleges they had attended, with their fraternity-centered, anti-Semitic cultures and their conservative faculties, had offered most of them little more than access to good books and intelligent contemporaries. The official version of scholarship was backward-looking, dull, and unattractive. Most professors taught the young to count the commas in Congreve or appreciate the beauties of Wordsworth—not to explore the fragmentation of experience in the modern city with Eliot, Joyce, and Fitzgerald. The canon of texts studied formally at most universities ended decades before the present, and only Anglo-Saxon Protestants of birth and breeding could interpret them properly in any case.

In the course of their postwar expansion drive, however, university administrations offered jobs, homes, and money for periodicals. The once-proud outsiders joined faculties, but in so doing, they lost their characteristic voice, and failed to produce real successors. The voice of dissent was drowned out by the louder, jargon-clotted voices of tenure-seeking scholars. Only meticulously detailed investigations of narrowly defined questions, their results presented in impenetrable jargon, could win preferment in the new system. *PMLA* outflanked *Partisan Review*.

Outside the university, the intellectual ecology was even less welcoming to generalists and speculative thinkers. Younger writers who wanted to follow their elders' example lacked the confidence and the general culture that had empowered the Dwight Macdonalds and Mary McCarthys of an older time. The public intellectuals went through a kind of reverse pupation: bright speculative butterflies turned into dull professional grubs. Even their urban habitat, the grimy cold-water flats that intellectuals had once claimed as their own alien, bourgeois-free turf, mutated into desirable loft dwellings. The cheap pad of the 1950s, once rehabbed, could be marketed to older bourgeois couples returning to the city centers they had left when their children were small—even as the former occupants, also suitably rehabbed, were marketed to their children as distinguished professors. Between 1955 and 1980, in short, intellectuals ceded the space they had once occupied in American society and culture.

The doom and gloom sound convincing. But every coin has two sides, and in this case, the other one is bright and attractive. Externally, after all, the life of the mind has seldom seemed healthier in America than it does right now. Magazines, newspaper sections, and Web sites dedicated to the doings of scholars, publishers, and writers proliferated in the 1990s and after. In college and university towns across America, traditional and cutting-edge forms of cultural life flourish side by side. Readings, debates, and poetry slams draw hundreds. Even after college, intellectual life goes on. Membership in book groups has become as standard a life-cycle phase for the graduates of elite universities as consulting and paralegal work. Huge bookstores that sponsor evenings with poets and bring little magazines to frappacino-guzzling crowds have spread like H. G. Wells's invading Martians. They have appeared even in the suburban malls and edge cities where only a few years ago, the call of realtor to realtor was the only sound heard. Greenwich Village has come to Greenwich, Connecticut, and North Beach has spread to northern Illinois. Meanwhile, the intellectuals' NASDAQ, Amazon.com's public sales figures, shows that complex and demanding books can score high sales nationally as well as in sophisticated local markets like the larger university towns.

The American university has played a prominent and positive role in this drama of the intellectual life. It has encouraged some of its most original and productive minds to speak not only to their colleagues and students but also to the crowds outside the iron gates. Highly trained in the arcana of literary theory or Greek philosophy, prominent scholars have descended from the real but rarefied world of high ideas into the darkness and confusion of Plato's cave. Even there, it turns out, they shine, like the stars they are. Empowered, not hampered, by their up-to-date interdisciplinary academic training, they have confronted the real problems of contemporary society—from the death dance of late capitalism that so many predicted in the 1980s to the rise of a state power that invades and reports on the most secret realms of private life to the continued poverty and oppression in which most of the world's citizens live. And they have wielded sharp new intellectual tools to forge new disciplines like cultural studies. It is no wonder that deans have rewarded them with high salaries and low teaching loads, the two signs of assumption into academic heaven.

The new intellectuals have exercised a great deal of influence, since they think through and confront foreign and domestic, social and cultural problems that we would rather forget about, and publish their results for a wide public in magazines like *The Nation* and *The New Republic* and on Web sites like *Slate* and *Salon*. These buzz with lively debates of a sort that had seemed, a few years ago, almost extinct. The university-employed intellectuals are not pallid conformists confined to the belly of the whale, but powerful thinkers and writers who have found a bully pulpit and use it to good effect.

Even the story of intellectuals and real estate has ended well. Livable, politically progressive, culturally hip university towns have grown into little centers of cosmopolitanism. To the left, absentminded professors spill latte on youthful Web millionaires. To the right, black-wearing students read their way into the new public sphere. The People's Republics of Cambridge and Berkeley, Ann Arbor, and Amherst, have become the lively present-day counterparts to the Baltimore of H. L. Mencken, the New York of the young Edmund Wilson, and the Chicago of Ben Hecht. The public intellectuals who adorn their departments of philosophy, English, and biology and their programs in science and cultural studies set the tone and choose the topics for discussion. Even the generalists who have not landed in academic niches—Paul Berman, Thomas Frank, and others—find enthusiastic support and young readers in the new academic community and on its outskirts.

I'm just a historian. I have no idea which of these stories describes our present situation more precisely—any more than I can tell you whether Amazon will conquer Borders and Barnes & Noble. But I can say that neither of them does justice to the past—especially that of the American university. And I'd like to tell a story of my own, one that complicates matters in what I hope will prove a useful way.

Learned and original historians—David Hollinger, Bruce Kuklick, Dorothy Ross, James Turner, Daniel Rodgers, and Caroline Winterer—have taught us, in recent years, that the American college and university of the later nineteenth and early twentieth centuries were much livelier places than used to be believed. True, they did not look like hotbeds of modernity. A new college culture took shape in this period. It was primarily designed to produce a new, national elite of male Protestant professionals and managers and their wives, and largely financed by entrepreneurs and football fans. It served the sons and daughters of the new industrialists and those who aspired to join them. Naturally, its dominant note was nostalgia. The most ambitious colleges tried hard to camouflage their raw newness, and that of the class they were creating, by adopting traditional forms of architecture and dress and creating innumerable new forms of social and athletic ritual. But the resulting appearance of conservatism at all costs—the appearance that made Veblen want to subtitle his book on higher education in America *A Study in Total Depravity,* and Upton Sinclair entitle his book *The Goose Step*—is deceiving.

The universities became the scenes of powerful intellectual dramas, generated by professors and students who applied scientific, philosophical, and philological tools to fossils, Bibles, and society itself. They showed that what had once seemed perfect, eternal sources of truth and enlightenment were actually the contingent results of historical developments that could be reconstructed, stage by stage. They spawned expert social scientists bent on observing and reforming the new urban world that they saw around them in Chicago and New York, and gifted writers bent on expressing a new world of sexual and social experience in a new idiom. To go back, even briefly, to the university world of the turn of the century is to take part in a forgotten set of intellectual adventures—and to gain a new perspective on all the tales now being told about creativity and crisis in the American mind. It is also the historian's natural way of responding to apparent contradiction: tell another story and you may, with luck, shed light.

Turn back with me, then, to the University of Chicago in its first years of existence, the 1890s. In some ways, the institution was typical of its period. Physically, it looked as if someone had managed to drop Yale or Princeton by parachute on the midwestern flats. A monstrous outcropping of luridly carved gray stone buildings, paid for by malefactors of great wealth, rose incongruously over mud fields that had been occupied only months before by the Ferris wheels, belly dancers and Orientalist raree-shows of the Columbian Exposition. Socially and culturally, the university resembled the other colleges of what Henry Seidel Canby called the Gothic Age. Obsessed with football, Chicago students eagerly joined fraternities, invented rituals and traditions, and filled the air with the plunking of mandolins and the bleat of freshmen being paddled.

Intellectually, however, the university set itself apart from the start. William Rainey Harper, the Hebraist who served as its founding president, set out to build a great center of research in the German model. In the summer of 1891, he bought the entire stock of one of the great Berlin booksellers, S. Calvary, ordered that it be shipped to Chicago—and only then began asking benefactors for the money, which members of the board of trustees finally supplied. Harper offered top salaries to attract the greatest scientists and scholars from America and Europe. The immense sum of $7,000, then the summit of the professorial scale, attracted four great scientists from Clark University and even drew the great historian Hermann Von Holst from Freiburg. Chicago students celebrated this last acquisition with a torchlight parade—clear evidence, like the salary involved, that the academic superstar and his or her perks did not come into existence only yesterday, as even well-informed people seem to believe. Harper underlined his insistence that scholarship and science must not stand still not only by hiring productive scholars and scientists but also by continuing to take others' courses himself.

No one followed all of these developments with a more observant—or bemused—eye than Robert Morss Lovett, a young scholar of English literature who came to Chicago from Harvard. The scion of a modest Boston family—his father sold insurance, his mother was a teacher—he had distinguished himself as a student, writer, and editor while still an undergraduate. Edwin Arlington Robinson, author of "Richard Cory," felt thrilled when Lovett visited him, a lowly freshman, to ask if he could publish Robinson's poems. He described Lovett, in revealing period terms, as "perhaps the leading spirit of Harvard outside of athletics." Already as an undergraduate, Lovett plunged into the first wave of American modernism. His friends included not only Robinson but also Trumbull Stickney, who sent Lovett brilliant, eerie poems and letters during the years in Paris when he drank absinthe, visited great writers, and researched his Sorbonne thesis about Greek gnomic poetry.

Harvard's president, Charles William Eliot, who admired Lovett, hired him as his secretary. Lovett, in fact, might well have devoted his whole life to alma mater—except that when he confided his ambition to found something like the Oxford Movement in Cambridge, Massachusetts, to one of his bearded, volcano-breathed professors, this unsentimental mentor roared:

"For God's sake get away. Go anywhere; but get away." Lovett did just that by accepting, with many reservations, a position as secretary to the president of the brash new university on the Midway.

To Lovett's surprise, he flourished in Chicago. Though he saw through all of Harper's compromises and absurdities and found the city's noise, dirt, and poverty depressing, he also came to admire the energy and creativity that the hyperactive university president shared with his city. Harper worked himself to death, teaching intensively, raising money, and hiring professors. When he took a break, he rode his bicycle for exercise, so slowly that Lovett could walk beside him taking dictation. Inspired by Harper's example, Lovett taught and took courses, began to write, tutored, and lectured. He made a name for himself as an effective teacher of English, a kindly administrator, and an intellectual. He found friends among his colleagues—like the Harvard-educated playwright and novelist Robert Herrick, who shocked the staid Chicago public with a play about abortion, and the German-trained Renaissance historian Ferdinand Schevill. They drank seidels of beer in the German beer gardens that softened the austerities of Hyde Park until Prohibition was enacted. They ate together, sharing expenses to eke out their meager salaries, singing lieder after dinner while Schevill crouched tipsily on the radiator, remarking worriedly that "Je ne me sens pas bien ici." And they traveled together, spending sabbatical years in Italy, Germany, and France, where Lovett learned to see painting through the all-seeing eyes of Bernard Berenson. Walking tours took Lovett and his friends to Bavarian castles and Pius II's romantic, isolated mountain city of Pienza.

It all made a pleasant, rewarding, Bohemian life. These ill-paid young scholars enjoyed leisure of a sort a full professor can barely imagine now: sabbaticals without e-mail, in fin-de-siècle Paris, London, and Munich. But they alternated these years in paradise with longer periods of confinement at hard labor. Like the rest of America's male citizens in that frantic age of expansion and acquisition, Lovett and his friends worked fantastically hard. Though not trained in the Germanic methods of philology that would soon capture Chicago's English Department (and most others), Lovett turned out pioneering histories of English literature and studies of American fiction. He insisted—against the academic fashion of the time—that drama had been written to be performed, and could be understood only in the light of the stage conditions of the time in which it was created.

Rather like Lionel Trilling some years earlier, Lovett treated the classics of nineteenth-century English and American fiction as explorations of the intricate workings of class and money. He tried to show that each new phase in the history of the novel reflected a new phase in the evolution of society. When "the loyalty of the lower to the higher class" made way for "another loyalty—the loyalty of the workers to each other," for example, the social novel of Upton Sinclair and others replaced Thomas Mann's deep psychological exploration of the decline of the old bourgeois elite. Like many scholars in this transitional period, Lovett devoted himself more to producing synthetic works that could be used as textbooks than to writing monographs and articles. But he knew a vast amount. Even his textbooks show his mastery of technical problems in bibliography, theater history, and other fields. So do his lecture notes and letters, carefully preserved in the archives of the University of Chicago. In the first great age of American scholarship, Lovett was a distinguished scholar.

The university of the Gothic Age—even the research-oriented University of Chicago—differed in vital ways from its modern counterpart. Many faculty members—especially the younger ones—nourished a deep affection for the institutions they served and the students they worked with. Their jobs were precarious, their salaries low, and their contact with students usually took only two forms: fast-paced, fact-packed lectures that their audiences desperately tried to memorize, and pedantic, nit-picking recitation classes in which they interrogated their hearers on trivia, hoping to reveal the slackers. Nonetheless, they saw teaching as a vocation. Though he was not the son of a minister, Lovett, like many members of his academic generation, came from a deeply pious family that had made him pray three times a day as a child. One of the most affecting documents in his archive at Chicago is the pledge that he signed on 7 December 1884, with other children at the Walnut Avenue Sunday School, to abstain from drink. In leaving the church for another ideal world, that of scholarship and literature, Lovett did not abandon his sense that life must have a real end and a higher purpose.

At first Lovett seems to have found his vocation where most scholars did— in forming future scholars. He gave seminars on his fields of special interest, and had the joy of seeing great specialists emerge from them—like Joseph Q. Adams, who became a famous professor at Cornell and the influential director of the Folger Shakespeare Library. "The first course in graduate work that

I ever had," Adams wrote to him in 1918, "was at Chicago under your direction. The splendid training that you gave me in Elizabethan literature helped to determine all my subsequent work."

In time, however, undergraduates demanded something more: help and encouragement with creative writing. At first, Lovett resisted, telling a student who asked him to teach contemporary poetry, "While we could teach the history and technique of poetry I should be sorry to have academic standards applied to anything which should be so personal and spontaneous as the writing of verse." But gradually student pressure overcame Lovett's self-described "distrust of myself and my colleagues in this capacity." A student poetry club took shape under his leadership and he arranged for the members to meet Harriet Monroe, Edgar Lee Masters, Padraic Colum, and Carl Sandburg.

University teachers in England and America had been publishing collections of student verse for some time. In 1916, for example, Alfred Noyes, the author of "The Highwayman," edited *A Book of Princeton Verse,* which concluded with five short poems by Edmund Wilson. The volume of *Collected Verse by the Poetry Club of the University of Chicago,* which appeared in 1923, did not match the polish or sophistication of the Princeton collection. "Who knows," asked one young poet,

> Where my sight goes,
> What your sight shows,
> Where the peachtree blows?

Lovett himself admitted that he was too partial to judge these poems critically, and praised only their spontaneity. But the contributors included Glenway Wescott and Ivor Winters, both of whom made notable careers in literature, and Robert Redfield, who established a still more distinguished one in anthropology (amazingly, Winters wrote the verses just quoted). And where the Princeton volume was published by the Princeton University Press, the Chicago one was published by Pascal Covici—a famous, genial figure, half entrepreneur of the avant-garde and half con man, who later moved to New York, where he created scandal after scandal in later years. Covici published Radclyffe Hall's lesbian novel, *The Well of Loneliness,* and held some of the wildest parties of a wild age. The Princeton volume was the product of a country town, the Chicago one of a city; and Lovett soon made a specialty of helping his students find their way in the quintessentially urban worlds of journalism and literature. Covici was only one of the major literary figures whom Lovett mercilessly exploited on his students' behalf, and Wescott and Winters were only two of the many young writers whom he promoted relentlessly, even though their talents were in the realm of potentiality rather than of actuality.

Other colleges had charismatic writing teachers—like "Copey," Charles Townsend Copeland, who taught a famous course at Harvard, English 20, and held an even more famous salon on Monday nights, and Robert Frost at Amherst. But Lovett's practices and prejudices were unusual. He had inclusive tastes. His discoveries included the brutal, realistic Chicago novelist James T. Farrell, as well as the polished, erudite Princeton critic Edmund Wilson. The famous writing teachers of the 1920s and 1930s normally looked for their disciples among young men with the sharp nibs—and sharp elbows—that would enable them to fight their way through throngs of rivals and reach the publishers' ear trumpets. Lovett worked as hard to further the writing careers of his female students as he did those of the male ones. He was the only Chicago professor who awakened interest in the young Janet Flanner, who later became the *New Yorker*'s great European reporter, Genêt. And his papers include more than one warmly affectionate letter from female writing students who did not become famous, as Flanner did, but who never forgot what Lovett had given them: the "help and encouragement and the fire that still keeps me writing through many reject slips."

American literary modernism took shape—so many contemporaries thought, and some modern histories suggest—as part of a revolt of the highly educated against the grinding positivism of the university literature curriculum. H. L. Mencken, for example, saw no connection whatever between the social criticism of the maverick Chicago professor Thorsten Veblen and the new poetry published in the same city by Harriett Monroe. He dismissed Veblen as one more "geyser of pish-posh," a scholarly eunuch unable to express himself except in self-parodically Germanic polysyllables: "The learned professor gets himself enmeshed in his gnarled sentences like a bull trapped by barbed wire . . . He heaves, he leaps, he writhes; at times he seems to be at the point of yelling for the police." He praised Monroe, by contrast, for promoting Sandburg, Robinson, and others whose work scandalized Presbyterians in frock coats and Baptists with low foreheads. None of the dreary pedagogues and "sterile *Gelehrten*" in the universities, Mencken held, could appreciate or further writing of this kind.

Lovett, however, saw it as entirely natural to help his immigrant, urban students write bluntly and openly about the modern city, in all its sprawling, obscene, passionate life—just as he found it natural, as a critic, to break into the big time with a *New Republic* piece in which he defended the "romantic decadent" Cabell because he had "remained himself" and defied "the herd instinct" that ensured propriety in American writing. It was Professor Lovett, rather than Lovett of *The New Republic,* who read a short story by a proverbially lazy Irish student named Farrell and saw that it might become a novel. In the end, it turned into the *Studs Lonigan* trilogy, for which Lovett found a publisher.

Lovett, moreover, combined his literary radicalism with equally challenging and dangerous views about economics, politics, and society. The corruption and brutality of American politics, Chicago style, occupied Lovett's mind from the beginning of his career. He arrived in the city in the years of the panic, just after the execution of the Haymarket anarchists. During his first years of teaching, the Pullman strike split the city and the university down the middle. He and his friends watched the straggling members of Coxey's army of the unemployed make their dreary way toward Washington, where military action would scatter them.

From the start, Lovett said and wrote what he thought about Chicago politicians, police, and law courts. Gradually, his political horizons widened. After some years of living in several European countries, for example, he developed doubts about the wisdom of leaping in on the side of England and gallant little Belgium. In 1916, as the fever mounted, he agreed to chair a meeting called in opposition to American entry into World War I, even after all but he had fled the platform. Lovett did not demand that the United States stay out of war: his own son joined up, and died in France just before the Armistice. But merely providing a forum for politically challenging discussion made him detestable to many Chicagoans, including a large number of his colleagues. They held a public rally against him, at which he had the curious pleasure of seeing himself burnt in effigy. The outcry did not deter him in the least.

In the last year of the war and after, when the Palmer raids appeared to Lovett and other radicals like the beginning of a great repressive movement, he found his full vocation, which enabled him to serve the larger community as well as the collegiate one. Lovett and his wife left the academic society of Hyde Park and moved into an apartment in Jane Addams's settlement house in the slums, Hull House, which they greatly preferred to the polite suburbs. Lovett worked the switchboard two nights a week and taught classes for immigrants.

He also began spending half the year outside the university, editing first the *Dial,* a literary magazine that published Anderson, Hemingway, and Picasso, and then *The New Republic,* where he worked for ten years and contributed articles for twenty, not only on literary topics but also on educational experiments, the labor movement, and the persecution of radicals. It was here that he employed Wilson—and thus gave a start to another career more remarkable than his own. Lovett served for many years on the board of the American Civil Liberties Union. He joined and supported pacifist and pro-labor groups—many of them with Communist members—throughout the 1930s. He denounced the American government, more than once, as "fascistic" and corrupt. And he risked physical danger and public humiliation while standing up for workingmen and women as unhesitatingly as he had courted snubs while looking for publishers and producers for his students.

In 1933, for example, the *Chicago Tribune* crowed when "Robert Morss Lovett, professor of English and literature at the University of Chicago, noted as a pacifist, communist, and radical, undertook to uphold the civil liberties of a group of apron factory workers and lost his own civil liberty thereby for two hours." Lovett had been walking a picket line with black seamstresses, who wanted their ten-hour day reduced to nine and their minimum wage raised to a frightening $11 a week. The police arrested the plump, white-haired professor when he insisted that the picketers had a legal right to occupy the sidewalk. With old-fashioned courtesy, he held the door of the paddy wagon open for the policeman who booked him. In 1937 Lovett sat in with striking autoworkers in Flint, Michigan, waving his five shares of GM stock and introducing himself as a stockholder dissatisfied with management's idea of labor relations.

Lovett did not engage in these outside activities to win an endowed chair or a higher salary. Journalists and politicians regularly called for his dismissal—not a trivial threat in the university that had fired the young economist Samuel Bemis for his criticism of the Pullman Company. He lost a college deanship that meant much to him (his four assistants resigned the next day in protest). Elizabeth Dilling singled him out for attack in her massive compilation on subversives across the United States, *The Red Network* (1936). Most faculty members, and most administrators, resented his activities. One of them, Robert Maynard Hutchins, did not, and he defended Lovett with a ferocity that does credit to both men. Late in the 1930s, the Chicago papers ran a juicy story: the University of Chicago had finally decided to rid itself of its red English professor by pensioning him off. Lovett had in fact reached the retirement age of sixty-five. But that afternoon, an announcement from Hutchins reached the papers: the trustees, by a special, onetime act, had invited Professor Lovett to continue teaching as long as he wished. Hutchins, however, was an exception in this as in many other respects—he was, after all, the one president of a Big Ten university to abolish varsity football—and even he did not see Lovett's activism as desirable. For the most part, Lovett's superiors defended him only because they could do nothing else. Prominent, conservative donors and professors who agreed with Lovett on nothing, but whose wealth and prestige the university needed, threatened to resign from the board of trustees or the faculty immediately if he should be fired.

Lovett did eventually retire—to become secretary and acting governor of the Virgin Islands during World War II. And there, at the age of seventy-one, he still managed to stir up trouble. The Dies Committee, busy baiting reds while the heavens were falling, identified Lovett as a threat to national security because he had once, in a private letter, described the American government (and all others) as worthless. Congress deprived Lovett—and a couple of other officials—of their salaries, in a rider to an appropriations bill, which Roosevelt reluctantly signed. Harold Ickes insisted that Lovett and the others sue, and the federal courts eventually threw the rider out as a bill of attainder, which violated the constitution. Lovett himself did not even want to take the matter to law: as always, he had bigger fish to fry. He went off to be a professor at the University of Puerto Rico, where his old friend Schevill was also teaching. He hoped he could do something about bringing Roosevelt's Four Freedoms to that impoverished island.

Lovett was not always wise, and he certainly lacked twenty-twenty hindsight. He did not always bear in mind that the Communists who helped him defend Sacco and Vanzetti and the Scottsboro boys did not share his tolerance and humanity. And he was not always perceptive about literature. Stuart

P. Sherman, a contemporary and more conventional critic, had a point when he made gentle fun of Lovett's defense of Cabell: "The principle seems to be that any author who has succeeded in offending the Comstock Co., should be stellifed without further enquiry into the merits of the case. Or to put it in another way: If it is chivalrous to rescue a virtuous damsel in distress, how much more chivalrous it is to rescue a vicious damsel in distress?" Like Mencken, Lovett sometimes defended the shocking merely because it was shocking.

But Lovett also had a number of virtues that the standard accounts do not prepare one to find in a plump white university professor of his generation. He had no gender bias whatsoever, except an old Bostonian tendency to assume that women are morally superior to men. His hero, his personal model— as he said and wrote more than once—was Jane Addams, whose Hull House community he thought a model of what society should be. He liked and sought the company of immigrants, black people, and workingmen and workingwomen. Lovett even thought students should have rights. He wrote numerous articles encouraging American undergraduates to become autonomous and politically self-aware—to devise course evaluations, demand independent student governments, and find other ways to take responsibility for their lives.

Lovett's scholarship, as he regularly admitted, had more breadth than depth. His writing—even his articles for the *New Republic* and the *Nation*—lacked the erudition, range, and punch of Edmund Wilson's. As a lecturer, surprisingly, he could have bored for America. All that notwithstanding, he cuts a compelling—even fascinating—figure in retrospect, for he confuses and contradicts all the accepted categories. The little community of the campus, with all its rituals and its sometimes cloying conformity, remained one of his intellectual homes, and he never pulled away from it definitively. He believed absolutely that nourishing the university was an integral way to contribute to the larger community outside. Younger writers and activists would not emerge by parthenogenesis.

Yet Lovett's commitment to the campus did not make him abandon urban literary and political life—even when he split the year between New York and the magazine world and Chicago. Living in Hull House, the Lovetts naturally continued to entertain students on Sunday nights—and convinced many of them to enter careers in teaching or social work. His students admired him unreservedly. One of them, James Weber Linn, who also joined the Chicago

English Department, wrote two stirring campus novels in which admirable characters based on Lovett appeared. The shabby, old-fashioned teacher at home in the gray city of Chicago's campus and the metropolitan intellectual in New York were of a piece.

Lovett was unusual, but not unique. Christian Gauss of Princeton—another deeply cultivated intellectual and politically progressive man—resembled Lovett in many ways, as did, for all their individual differences, Scott Nearing of Pennsylvania, Edward Ross of Stanford—and, no doubt, many others. They combined strong political and civic commitments with wide-ranging scholarship, maintained their ties as long as they could to local intellectual communities and individual students, lived both in the harsh city and on the more or less idyllic campus—and played roles in the formation both of the research university and of the urban intellectual milieu of the 1930s and 1940s.

In Lovett's day, the intellectual did not have to withdraw from the great community in order to teach in the little one. And the university did not succeed in preventing some of its inhabitants from addressing the public good as well as pursuing technical forms of knowledge. Lovett's case shows that professors sometimes combined local action with global thinking, and managed to give their teaching, as well as their writing, a public orientation. Above all, it proves that both of the histories I started from—the tale of slow degradation and the tale of rapid, recent progress—oversimplify the past. Both insist on the separation between the university and modern intellectual life. But Lovett used the same social and historical method of analysis that he applied to literature as a scholar and teacher as a tool for understanding and changing the larger world as well. He reached his public in many ways—sometimes by writing for little magazines, but sometimes by crafting widely read textbooks, sometimes by thorough teaching, and always by providing the example of his own civic life. And he was not alone. The past was not as simple as some would have us believe. Perhaps the present is also more complex than we think.

Nostalgia is always the besetting temptation of the cultural historian. And nostalgia is dangerous. The elegiac tone can induce paralysis, rather than inspiring the sort of perpetual motion and creative energy that mattered most to Lovett and others like him. Still, elegy may be an appropriate tone in which to recall intellectual lives like Lovett's. No one would have been happier than Lovett to see the American university as it is now, to learn that many professors are women and that classrooms are bursting with teachers and students of different colors, cultures, and classes. We do not have much to teach Lovett about opening opportunities or furthering talent. But he—and some of his contemporaries—might have something to teach us about what we could be doing and are not, in the classroom and outside, with students and for readers. Their ability to live in the public eye while still devoting themselves to local intellectual communities inspires respect—even awe. And thus their story may serve a purpose that the two I began from do not, at least as historians usually tell them. Looking backward to the old and unfamiliar world in which Lovett and his contemporaries worked and struggled might help us understand and improve the new world that they dreamed of and that we all too comfortably inhabit.

14

The Public Intellectual and the Private Sphere

Arendt and Eichmann at the Dinner Table

The children of intellectuals confront history at the family dinner table. Over the clatter of forks on plates they hear their first discussions of the burning issues and insoluble problems, the provocative books, articles, and reviews that divide or unite communities. Their first dissections of novels and movies, plays and performances, come with the rib roast. Over salad they begin to see how the great world of ideas and ideals and the little one of personal experience and everyday life intersect. How do their parents and their friends apply what they believe to concrete practical and professional problems? How do they decide, and explain, what is right, what is wrong, what is practical? All this is served up, in the first instance, before dessert.

Or at least it all came with dinner, early in the 1960s, as I sat, a few months after my bar mitzvah, in the sunny dining nook of our apartment in New York, and listened, through long summer evenings, to my parents talk about Hannah Arendt and the banality of evil. Dinners took a long time in those days, and the world quieted down to allow the rituals of conversation and consumption to take place in peace. Cocktails preceded food, stimulating discussion. The phone remained silent on its hook. Big problems could be discussed in detail, point by point. The world looked modern in our brand-new East Side apartment house: the plain walls, low ceilings, and steel balcony railings virtually yelled "Bauhaus." But there was time for old-fashioned, serious family talk—for a kind of sociability and learning that now seem as irrevocably distant as Clarence Day's *Life with Father* did to us.

In 1963, no problem seemed bigger, or generated more serious talk, than Arendt's *New Yorker* articles on Eichmann in Jerusalem and the book she made out of them. They baffled and fascinated families like mine all over New York. The Holocaust was only then beginning its ascent to what has since become a hauntingly central place in Jewish visions and discussions of the recent past. But everyone—even children my age—had seen the newsreel footage of bodies rolling before bulldozers and the still shots of scarecrow-thin camp inmates greeting the soldiers who freed them. Everyone knew that Germans had devised and carried out this unique attack on innocent fellow citizens—and that many of those who participated in the Final Solution to the Jewish Problem still enjoyed positions of authority and wealth in the new West Germany. The horrors of modernity had not yet become the object of much close professional study. Only a few pioneers, like Raul Hilberg, had broken the academic taboos and begun to study the death camps and the system that sustained them in some depth. But even alert teenagers—to say nothing of alert adults—knew, or thought they knew, about the Six Million and the Germans. The destruction of the European Jews embodied the radical evil characteristic of totalitarian states—as Hannah Arendt had shown in what was already recognized as a classic book.

It seemed all the more amazing, then, and the more dismaying, that Arendt, of all people, had denied her own earlier insight. She was, after all, one of the most prominent and influential of the New York Jewish intellectuals. She made a brilliant career in the university, as the first woman named to a professorship at Princeton and a beloved teacher at the University of Chicago and the New School. As a writer she had done still better, escaping the little magazines to write reportage for the *New Yorker* and major books for the University of Chicago Press; Harcourt, Brace; and Viking. Against all expectation, this profound student of the darkest side of human thought and action had become the inventor of an ingenious but infuriating paradox. She now insisted that Adolf Eichmann was no monster, no hideous alien or radiation-altered mutant from a horror movie, but an ordinary, banal man, unremarkable in ideology or achievement. Worse, she claimed that the Jews themselves—or at least the Jewish leaders, the members of the councils that had rounded up their own people and helped the Nazis ship them to the East—had suffered the same moral collapse as Germans and others, and had shown the same total failure to resist totalitarianism. She described Leo Baeck, the scholarly Berlin rabbi who led and tried to save Germany's Jewish community under the Nazis, and who barely survived his own confinement in Theresienstadt, as "the Jewish Führer." In doing so she took a quotation from Hilberg out of context, as the Oxford historian Hugh Trevor-Roper pointed out, and horrified the many German Jews and others who revered Baeck and supported the scholarly institute named after him.

Perhaps worst of all, though Arendt clearly respected Eichmann's judges, she despised both his prosecutor and Ben-Gurion himself, and showed little or no admiration for the institutions of the Jewish state whose feisty glamour had so won over most middle-class Americans that even Hollywood, always embarrassed about Jews and the Jewish question, had caught the infection, as everyone my age knew from sitting through the many hours of *Exodus*. Phone lines buzzed, correspondence pages crackled, envelopes bulged, and discussions blazed in overstuffed living rooms from our own polite East Side neighborhood to the livelier West Side, and on up to Washington Heights. In the world's largest Jewish city—in the nation's most serious, best-edited magazine—Jew had apparently betrayed Jew.

Every household that belonged to a synagogue, and thousands that did not, must have asked the same angry questions: But what does she mean by the banality of evil? How can she judge the Jewish councils? Can't she put herself in their place? What would she have done? Does she like the Germans more than the Jews? But the arguments reached a special pitch in our house. My father, Samuel Grafton, was an eminent journalist in the great age of American magazines. And while everyone was talking about Arendt, he was trying as hard as he could to meet her, to thresh out the problems face to face. One of the magazines he wrote for was *Look*—a national periodical in a sense now hard to imagine, which claimed a circulation of more than 7,400,000 in the fall of 1963. Famous for its vivid photojournalism, *Look* also regularly published long articles on political and social problems. This time, the editors assigned him to explain to a wide public why Arendt's dry, concise, fact-packed book had caused such fury. In the early fall, he began to work on "The Controversy that Rocks the Jews." He sent Arendt a long, sharply worded questionnaire as preparation for an interview. She wrote even longer, sharper answers and exacted a promise that she could approve all the quotations from her that appeared in the final article. But then negotiations broke down. She refused to meet my father, and his story, which had thus lost its central character, became impossible to publish.

It is clear in retrospect that the Arendt dispute blew up at a strategic time. Intellectuals and their doings had suddenly become news, in an unfamiliar way. The Kennedys invited professors to the White House and fumed on the rare occasions when their charm did not work its seductive magic on them. The new quality paperbacks brought abstract, erudite treatises on other-directedness and the death wish to thousands of eager readers. The high-cultural magazines, like *Partisan Review* and *Commentary,* provided a sense of intellectual community for thousands of readers who loved to watch their brilliant, aggressive writers argue. Alert New York editors scanned their closely printed pages for new talent; alert New York journalists made fun of their touchy, hyperarticulate editors. "He's the man who wrote the piece on the man who wrote the piece on David Riesman"—this jingle, quoted long ago by Norman Podhoretz, conveys something of the atmosphere, congested, sensitive, and irritable, in which the banality of evil brought so many Jewish and non-Jewish readers to the boiling point.

The context seems strange. It is hard nowadays to imagine a time when American intellectuals looked so glamorous. But in another sense, the story of the Arendt debate looks very familiar. For decades, after all, we Americans have carried on all our intellectual controversies pretty much the same way. A book comes out, offering a radical new take on a painful and delicate topic— the genetic component in intelligence, the reasons for the Holocaust, or the fall of the American intellectual. Initial reviews and articles indicate that the author has something new and controversial to say, prominent writers and thinkers take positions, and quarrels break out at public forums.

All of a sudden, a story emerges: not the story of the original book, which becomes at most a sidebar and usually nothing more than a first paragraph. Rather, the conflict becomes the story. Individual positions and posturings, particular reviews and debates, generate still more publicity. The actual theses and substance of the original book lie buried and forgotten, unread or distorted, under the tons of invective hurled at the author and his or her detractors. In many cases, no one actually seems to have read the original, though everyone has read the cover article about it in the *New York Times Book Review.*

Journalists need to find a dramatic hook for every article and to summarize complex, colorful theories in stark black and white, two good ways to heap more fuel on the fires they cover. Radio, television, and the Web often do more to confuse than inform, and often give currency to falsehoods. Nuances drop away, distinctions disappear, and group divisions harden. In the end, the debate often pulls entirely free of its original moorings. Once the wheels begin to turn, the School of Athens turns into the Garden of Earthly Delights: off go the philosophical masks, out come the grimacing demons that had been hiding behind them. The Arendt debate, in short, was an early instance of a routine that is as familiar now as college sit-ins were in the 1960s. As in those days, one's stomach begins to hurt as soon as the first signs of trouble appear, for one knows only too well the whole ugly, unenlightening course that the discussion will take.

It is no wonder that Arendt and her friends, including Mary McCarthy, gave so little quarter even to the mildest of Arendt's critics when they replied. It is not surprising either that Arendt refused, in the end, to speak to my father. That eternally curious intellectual, her eyes and mind and heart always open, even to those with whom she fundamentally disagreed, had every reason to turn and seek shelter when she found herself caught in the unrelenting storm of fury and misrepresentation that her book called forth.

And yet—and yet. The story is not quite so simple. I was sitting at that dinner table, and I remember: the serious, ambitious beginning of the project; a few of the interviews and my father's descriptions of them; Arendt's engagement and her withdrawal; the article written without the conversation that should have formed its core; and the final draft—polished, corrected, and filed away, with a handwritten note on the first page recording that it had never appeared. Such were the unhappy annals of the freelance life. But I did not know the inner history of the story until recently. When my father died in the fall of 1997, my family began to look at his files. They were stuffed with documents about the story that he had tried to write. Arendt scholarship, meanwhile, has grown into something of an academic industry, and many of her letters and papers have now been published as well. The contours of the story that the documents reveal have become complex. History complements, and complicates, memory.

The unexpected turns of the story begin early: in fact, with the workings of the magazine that asked for the story in the first place. *Look*'s editors, so a memorandum in my father's files reveals, did not simply commission a piece about Arendt when the press discussion reached white heat. Betty Leavitt—Picture Editor by title, but, like *Look* itself, concerned with more than pictures—read Arendt's articles and her book, as well as the reactions these provoked. She carefully identified many of the vicious untruths and half-truths that had circulated most widely. Leavitt pointed out, for example, that

Arendt, who had worked for many years for Youth Aliyah and other Zionist enterprises, was hardly the self-hating Jew evoked by some of her opponents. An engaged and principled critic of the Zionists and their state, she had broken with them in the 1940s over their treatment of the Arabs in Palestine—a prescient position that has won her immense respect, even adoration, in liberal Israeli circles in recent years. Leavitt also supported Arendt in one of her most controversial stances. Arendt insisted, with contemptuous certainty (and, in retrospect, with considerable accuracy), that very few Germans had opposed the Nazis. *Time* and other mainstream media, committed to the Atlantic alliance and Outpost Berlin, denounced this position with special vigor. But *Look* did not buy into the received wisdom.

Leavitt also noted that most critics had failed even to mention, much less to discuss, Arendt's central arguments, such as her definition of genocide as a new kind of crime, one directed against humanity as a whole. At the same time, however, she noted some of the obviously provocative points in Arendt's book, including the attack on the Jewish councils. In many of these passages, Leavitt concluded, Arendt showed a smugness and insensitivity that naturally incensed her readers.

In other words, the editors of *Look* did far more than commission an article. They actively investigated the issues that they planned to cover, read and thought about them—and did so with a rigor and an attention to detail not found in most of the published responses to Arendt's book. Their professionalism and precision inspire respect and suggest that the Arendt affair marked something more than the beginning of a new age of recycled charges and countercharges. It was also the end of an older age—one in which national, as well as highbrow, media saw it as their task to inform the public at large, as well as they could, about major new ideas and debates, to make their readers an informed and critical community. William Shawn's *New Yorker,* now revered in memory as the one great product of immaculate, meticulous editorial care, had some surprising counterparts lower down the journalistic food chain. The public sphere of the early 1960s looks impressively thoughtful in retrospect, for all the hysteria that seized it in Arendt's case, impoverishing thought and overheating language. Certainly it was not the world of plots and cabals that Arendt herself imagined, in which Jewish organizations mysteriously seized control of national periodicals and tried to turn them against her.

If *Look* was not a modern news magazine, dragged into superficiality by the unrelenting pace of the news cycle, my father was not a modern reporter, unpracticed in confronting complex issues in a complex way. A poor Jewish boy from Philadelphia, he had excelled in the public schools and received a splendid humanistic education at Central High School and the University of Pennsylvania. He had read his way through the classics of English literature. I still have the little blue volumes from the Oxford World's Classics series, signed and dated as he bought them, one a week, at Leary's bookshop. He had modeled his fluent, complex, muscular prose on the English of Addison and Steele, Lamb and Macaulay. And by doing so, he had won the attention of H. L. Mencken, who awarded him a prize of $500 in 1929 for the best essay on "My Four Years at College," submitted in a national contest sponsored by Mencken and George Jean Nathan.

The article appeared in Mencken's *American Mercury,* with a picture of my father looking oddly like one of Walter Camp's All-Americans. It made his name, setting him on the way to a dazzling career as a reporter on the Philadelphia *Ledger,* where he learned his trade on the mean and violent city streets of the early Depression, and as an editor and syndicated columnist on the *New York Post,* where he became one of America's most prominent liberal voices. He followed the running down of the New Deal in the years before the war and wrote informed columns on labor troubles, race relations, and foreign affairs. Like Arendt, he was sometimes prescient: he infuriated President Roosevelt by denouncing the American recognition of Vichy, calling a Fascist spade a spade. Later he covered the end of the war and the fall of the free governments in Eastern Europe, once again finding his best sources in the streets. To the amazement of his fellow reporters, most of whom knew no foreign languages, my father could interview displaced persons from every country in Europe. (He was, of course, speaking to them not in Romanian or Dutch, but in what remained of the Yiddish he had spoken as a small boy.) An experienced student of America's foreign relations, a cosmopolitan who had traveled extensively and lived abroad, an unobservant Jew with many prominent Jewish friends, and a constant, passionate reader on every imaginable subject, he made a natural candidate to investigate the Arendt controversy, even though he was neither a professor nor a member of the circles nowadays referred to as the New York intellectual community. When my father set out to confront Arendt, he took the same high intellectual road that his editors had already traveled. He read her work, discussed it with her editor at Viking Books, and sent her a set of written queries that frankly reflected his response both to her work and to the reactions it had provoked. He asked straight questions:

> Do you feel that the reactions to your book throw any new light on the tensions in Jewish life and politics today?

> Do you consider that the Jews, as a whole, have learned anything from the Hitler experience?

> Have any Jewish leaders supported the book, and, if so, who are they?

He wondered if one could not defend Hausner, the prosecutor in Eichmann's trial, by reflecting that he "was under no obligation to behave with full judicial balance." He urged Arendt to reflect on Jewish collaboration and resistance, and to ponder whether the Jews could really have done more than they did. And he graphically described his own reactions to her work, as a means of inducing her to think about the way her intellectual style and arguments might affect a normal reader.

My father admitted that the demoralizing effects of totalitarianism, as Arendt had compellingly explained them, accounted for much. But was there not something monstrous, after all, "in Eichmann's devotion and dedication to his task?" Or was Arendt's clear-eyed thesis simply too hard for ordinary people to accept so soon after the event?

> I found that I accepted your explanation intellectually, and then became ruffled every time you minimized Eichmann's importance. Then I calmed down as you explained more, and became upset all over again when you down-graded Eichmann later. Is it possible that your thesis has come on the scene a little too early—that the reaction would be quite different, say twenty-five years from now? Is timing, in other words, at the bottom of the controversy, in your view?

If the controversy had become the story, my father was trying to understand it on its own terms: to see why it had burst out rather than to explain it away or to blame it, as many did, on the ignorance of Jewish history supposedly revealed by Arendt's slips on points of detail. The questionnaire posed detailed, undeferential questions. My father pushed hard, for example, on the subject of the Jewish councils, insisting that their conduct could not be understood outside its long-term historical context:

> Have not Jewish leaders worked with their Gentile overlords throughout the diaspora, cajoling, co-operating, pleading, maneuvering? Was not the method frequently successful? If the old methods had become obsolete were not Jewish leaders then guilty, at most, of an historical misinterpretation? Could they have been expected to realize that Nazism was not the final development of anti-Semitism, but the first manifestation of a new evil, complete totalitarianism, linked with genocide?

At what moment, he asked, should the Jewish leaders have said, "Cooperate no longer, but fight"?

Many of the New York intellectuals who took positions for or against Arendt knew little or nothing about the history of the Jews. Though a number of them had spoken Yiddish as children, and some would return to the study of Jewish texts and problems at a later date, few of them had written on Jewish questions or Jewish history before 1963. They had turned their faces to the warm, bright beacon of Western culture like so many flowers following the sun. Most of them knew far more about the Saint Petersburg of Gogol and Dostoyevsky, the Paris of Baudelaire and Manet, or the London of Eliot and Woolf than they did about their ancestral shtetl and its recent fate. Arendt, whose own concern with the history and tragedy of European Judaism was long established, had justice on her side when she complained that her critics in the circles around *Partisan Review* and *Dissent* seemed to take their ignorance as a qualification for denouncing her.

My father's questions, by contrast, rested on deep personal knowledge—on what he had heard as a child about life in the Russian Empire's Pale of Settlement, and what he had read as a man about the history of the ghetto (another subject he researched in the early 1960s). When he pushed Arendt, he did so after serious reading and hard thinking. Arendt pushed back just as hard in a reply that stretched over some thirteen pages. She insisted that my father's questions misrepresented the historical possibilities—and overstated the retrospective demands she herself made of the Jews and their leaders:

There never was a moment when the community leaders [could] have said "Cooperate no longer, but fight!," as you phrase it. Resistance, which existed but played a very small role, meant only: we don't want that kind of death, we want to die with honor. But the question of cooperation is indeed bothersome. There certainly was a moment when the Jewish leaders could have said: We shall no longer cooperate, we shall try to disappear.

In particular, the Jewish leaders could have done this instead of deciding which Jews should be sent to the killing centers and which allowed to remain.

Statements of this kind in Arendt's book had proved among its most explosive contents. What, many readers asked, could she possibly have meant by saying that the Jews should simply have refused to cooperate? How can one refuse to cooperate with someone who has overwhelming force at his disposal? Where could they have disappeared to?

Arendt's answers to my father do not entirely clarify her position. But they show that she had thought, and hard, about the moral dilemma with which Baeck and others found themselves confronted—that she had tried, as many of her critics thought she had not, to imagine her way into the nightmare they had lived and to find the defining moment when they had made the wrong moral decision about how to deal with it. The Jewish leaders, she argued, "fully informed of what deportation meant, were asked by the Nazis to prepare the lists for deportation." The community leaders knew what awaited those who were shipped to the extermination camps. Nonetheless, they drew up the lists; they chose those who were to go and those who were to stay. True, they followed guidelines set by the Nazis as to "the number and categories" of those they sent, but they themselves made the selection: "In other words, those who co-operated were at that particular moment masters over life and death. Can't you imagine what that meant in practice?"

To the claim that "if some of us have to die, it is better we decide it than the Nazis," Arendt firmly replied: "I disagree. It would have been infinitely better to let the Nazis do their own murderous business." She condemned with equal firmness the notion that the Jewish councils had honorably sacrificed some of the Jews under their control in order to save others. Such basically pagan expedients, she argued, had no place in the Jewish tradition as she knew it, or in her own religion, which she did not define: "This sounds to me like the last version of human sacrifice. Pick seven virgins, sacrifice them to placate the wrath of the gods. Well, this is not my religious belief, and most certainly is not the faith of Judaism." Finally, Arendt insisted that she had not meant "to bring this part of our 'unmastered past' to the attention of the public. It so happened that the Judenräte came up at the trial and I had to report on that as I reported on everything else." This portion of her work, she argued, "plays no prominent role—either in space or in emphasis. It has been blown up out of all reasonable proportion." Certainly no one reading Arendt's words could have doubted her passionate engagement with her fellow Jews and their fate. Only an anguished love could have generated such a dark and complex involvement with the decisions of those she condemned so radically.

Yet Arendt's replies did not all do full justice to my father's questions. She was right to stress that many Jewish survivors shared her view of the role of the Jewish councils. But when she argued that her critics had taken her comments out of context and blown up their importance, she showed how poorly she grasped the texture and impact of her own intellectual and literary style. Arendt wrote, as Gershom Scholem and many others complained, in an ironic, allusive style, making asides do the duty of complex arguments and using a wide range of tones, to which a careless or irritable reader could easily prove deaf. When she discussed the role of the Jewish councils so rapidly, she did not suggest that the subject had no major role in the economy of her book. Rather, she supplied many of her critics with one of their strongest grounds for attacking her: that she ignored nuance and complexity as she passed summary judgment, briefly and bitterly, on historical actors and situations of radically different kinds.

For their part, my father's questions did not do full justice to Arendt's work or to her previous life. Unlike his editors, he did not draw attention to Arendt's Zionist past. The omission is curious, especially since during the 1940s he was involved with Zionist circles and organizations in New York at the same time that Arendt and some of her friends were developing their critique of Israel's treatment of the Palestinians. They must have lectured and argued in the same synagogue halls. On the whole, however, their sharp dialogue on paper was well designed and executed. It should have prepared the ground for a discussion of the reactions to Arendt far more searching than any of those that actually took place.

Both participants thought hard. Both knew a great deal. Both spoke their minds. And neither of them, obviously, was thinking about superficial questions: they went, from their two points of view, to the heart of the matters that divided them. The conversation, however, ended with the first exchange. As Arendt told the story to Karl Jaspers, she decided that the interview would really be an inquisition—and that my father's role in the matter revealed not the seriousness of the magazine that had assigned him the story but the zeal of her Jewish enemies:

> And then one of the big illustrated magazines here, *Look,* wanted to do a report on this whole business at the end of July. They suggested a well-known, non-Jewish reporter. My publisher, as well as *The New Yorker,* thought I should agree to do it (answering written questions under certain conditions). They thought the story would be handled in a thoroughly fair way. But when *Look* came to do the story, they assigned another reporter to it, a Jew, who interviewed only people who had already spoken out against me. And he sent me a questionnaire full of loaded questions. I answered the questions, but then my publisher and *The New Yorker* thought it would be better not to cooperate. There is no question in my mind that the Jewish organizations got wind of *Look's* plans and intervened.

Read against the hard evidence of my father's drafts and notes, this letter reveals a dismaying side of Arendt's own personality—a lack of balance in her own response to the controversy she had provoked. Her self-assured assertion that my father represented "Jewish organizations" rested on no evidence. In fact, my father not only knew the subject intimately, but had sharply criticized the American government for its failure to help the European Jews at a time when this position was highly unpopular in America itself. One of his columns had even led to the creation of a small "free port" for Jews in Oswego, New York—a deeply problematic effort, but one that saved a good many lives. His files show that he went to work as a professional, open-minded and eager to collect information from many different sources, even as Arendt was deciding, on no evidence, that he would not do so.

When my father first sent Arendt his questions, he mentioned that he had already spoken about her work with her editor at the *New Yorker,* William

Shawn. He also said that he intended to interview some of her critics, notably Judge Michael Musmanno, a veteran of the Nuremberg Trials who had condemned Arendt's book in a controversial *Sunday Times* review, and "a number of Jewish leaders." These included, for example, his close friend the producer Dore Schary. Arendt urged him to see, as well, some of those who took her side, or who at least considered the harshest attacks on her unfair. The list of names she gave him included Dwight Macdonald, Jason Epstein, Hans Morgenthau, George Agree, and Norman Podhoretz—a fair sampling of the independent New York intelligentsia.

Even as Arendt and her publisher were deciding that my father intended to denounce her, he was interviewing the informants she had suggested to him. He discussed Arendt and her work in detail with several of them, meticulously sending them all the quotations that he wanted to use for their review and approval. And he found that they hardly offered unequivocal support for Arendt's analysis. Jason Epstein, for example, defended her book as a whole, but he admitted that Arendt had attacked the Jewish organizations with "excessive zeal." Morgenthau and Podhoretz both emphasized the complexity of the problem of Jewish collaboration, and Morgenthau—like many of the critics who read Arendt without any sympathy—remarked that she had done her own argument harm by presenting it so briefly, in asides. George Agree, who defended Arendt more wholeheartedly than the others, actually thanked my father for his efforts to give a more balanced treatment than previous journalists had managed. Phones must have rung on the Upper West Side and in Hyde Park, in the houses of Arendt's close friends, if not in hers, as he went the rounds. It seems impossible that she did not know that he was actually doing what she had suggested—or that he was doing so in a serious way, trying to do justice to both sides, rather than as an inquisitor set on her by mysterious Jewish organizations.

But by this point Arendt had developed a kind of paranoia about her critics, especially the Jewish ones. Walter Laqueur, with whom she had a sharp exchange in the *New York Review of Books,* and whom she described as being in effect the employee of Jews bent on her destruction, was nettled enough to assure her sarcastically that she need not fear the Elders of Zion. My father's open eyes and fair mind were lost on the apostle of the open soul. She insisted that *Look* had promised not to publish his article if she disapproved of it. In fact, as their correspondence shows, this was untrue. My father and his editors had promised only that she could approve all quotations from the intended interview. She even argued, understandably but feebly, that an article that mentioned her refusal to be interviewed would do her an injustice. Like the professional he was, my father went ahead and wrote his piece anyway: an analysis of how "a book, a single book, by a fifty-seven-year-old Jewish woman, has melted the recent Jewish past into a boiling flux, in which familiar historical landmarks have been swallowed up, and what seemed like truths have been corroded and rotted beyond recognition." He described Eichmann's arrest, his trial, Arendt's reports, and the "wave of uneasiness" that swept the Jews as these appeared: "Among Jews at the economic and cultural level which reads *The New Yorker;* Dr. Arendt's articles became dinner-table subject number one." He traced the controversy: the appearance of Arendt's book, the denunciation of it by Musmanno, and the denunciation of Musmanno, in turn, by the *New Yorker* and many individuals. He offered an acute, critical reading of Arendt's book: "As she hacks her way through dense thickets of fact, she drops numerous side remarks, usually in an abrasive style . . . This is the sort of remark that makes the average Jewish reader, and indeed many a non-Jew, rise out of his chair like a Nike rocket." He made clear that Musmanno and other angry readers often misread Arendt's irony and sarcasm. And he explained her theory: that "under totalitarianism, . . . evil becomes an everyday matter."

He was often sharply critical, sometimes insightfully so—as when he remarked that "whereas she tries to get beneath the surface in Eichmann's case, and writes about him with something like a novelist's compassion, she does no such probing in the case of leading Jews, and actually calls their role 'the darkest chapter of the whole dark story.' " And as Arendt had feared, he did describe at length the position of Jewish organizations such as the Anti-Defamation League. "There are few nuances in the Jewish reaction," he concluded. No Jewish leader he could find would go on record as supporting her book. "Several on Miss Arendt's list of impartial observers," he wrote, "felt that she did not pay enough attention to facts which contradicted her theories." Perhaps my father's most interesting suggestions, however, came toward the end of the article, where he proposed, as he had in his original questionnaire, that Arendt had literally spoken too soon. "The wounds are too recent, the graves are too fresh for that, and to most Jews and many non-Jews the cool theory that those men who operated the slaughter machine were less than evil seems a callous incitement to fury." More insightfully still, he made it clear that the affair was, in the end, a media event—a debate that threw up few new facts and shed little new light, and had become, in the end, the story, while *Eichmann in Jerusalem* itself sank from sight:

> Amazingly, according to Viking Press, the book has sold only about 10,000 copies, an extremely small number for a work about which so much has been said. Many who are discussing it have not read it; in a sense the controversy has floated loose from the book, and become a phenomenon in its own right, with a life of its own.

Media on media, white on white, the spin cycle: my father saw them all emerging from the details of the Arendt debate. It was the beginning of a new world—and one that a survivor from the older world could not view with ease.

The piece was never published: without an appearance by Arendt herself, it became *Hamlet* without the prince. And, of course, the controversy gradually died down, as Kennedy's assassination, the crises of the civil rights movement, and the war in Vietnam moved to center stage in public consciousness. The dinner table conversation at our house moved with them: blow by blow and terrible image by terrible image, into the vortex of the late 1960s, for which nothing had prepared us; and moved again, in family reunions held in later years, into the great emptiness of the 1980s and 1990s. My father, never fooled by glitz and hype, looked unhappily at the people sleeping on the streets in his once pristine New York neighborhood. He remarked that things were about as bad as they had been in his childhood in a poor, socially and racially mixed quarter of Philadelphia at the beginning of our century of progress—though at least those who died in the streets or in flophouses could now be identified, thanks to their Social Security numbers.

The wide themes of politics, as Lawrence Weschler writes in his wonderful triptych *Calamities of Exile,* "first get broached and rehearsed around the family dinner table, the place, after all, where we all receive our first gashed edges and in flight from which we all experience our first intimations of exile." It is true: even those of us who do not resemble Weschler's equivocal heroes rebel and flee. I did too. But looking backward from middle age, I see that round table in the late afternoon light not as a place of confinement but as one of warmth and excitement, a life raft for the mind in the midst of what was becoming a blinding, deafening storm of contradictory messages.

From the stories my parents told and retold, I can pick out the origins of much that has become familiar, too familiar, in subsequent years: the media covering the media; the hysteria about a single controversial book; the newspaper articles, studded with quotations pulled out of context, which dramatize and deplore. But I can also see the outlines of a social and intellectual world we no longer inhabit—a better world, in some ways, though one already in its last years. In it, intellectuals lived and worked both outside and inside the universities. Newspaper reporters and magazine editors had the training and the time—more time than professors seem to have now—to read complicated books attentively and well. Professional intellectuals could write clean, sharp, accessible English even when they were furious. There was, in short, something like an intelligentsia—one prone to hysteria and foolishness, but also committed to serious debate, to the publishing and criticism of serious books and articles, and to the long-term building of intellectual communities centered on particular magazines, big and little.

At least one central, poisonous element of our end-of-century ways of writing and reading was not there: our obsession with the trivial and the external. My father brought up only one item of personal gossip in his questions to Arendt: a rumor that in retrospect seems more than absurd, but which had been floated in some Jewish circles—that she had converted to Catholicism. And he did so only in order to assure her that he would not mention the matter in his article. Arendt herself was grimly amused by this canard. Nowhere, in my father's notes or in the published pieces I have read, have I found a reference to Arendt's looks, her clothing, or her relationships: only to what she wrote and how it should be understood and judged.

It is a shame that my father and Hannah Arendt missed their connection, that neither could respond with the wisdom and perception that the other deserved. But it is more disappointing that we would find it hard to stage, or even to imagine, such a conversation now—much less to prepare for it as they did. The noise has grown too loud; the news travels too quickly; the cell phone, the e-mail, and the instant messages are too distracting; and family dinner has gone the way of the Edsel. The conversation at those dinner tables in the early 1960s was good, even when all the i's were not dotted or all the t's crossed. It was the serious talk of serious people about serious things: it made a compelling way to encounter some of the complexities of the world and history for the first time. To contemplate the changes that have taken place since then in publishing, in writing, and in public debate and private discussion; to compare the intellectuals we have now with those we had then; and to read the documents of that first media debate against those of more recent ones is to admit that we have suffered a loss.

15

Codex in Crisis

The Book Dematerializes

Alfred Kazin began work in 1938 on his first book, *On Native Grounds*. The child of poor and diffident Jewish immigrants in Brooklyn, he studied at City College. While uninspired professors processed large classes and Stalinists and Trotskyites turned the cafeteria into a battleground, Kazin somehow developed a passion for literature and began to write reviews. He had little money or backing, yet he managed to put together an extraordinary, comprehensive book, to tell the story of the great American intellectual and literary movements from the late nineteenth century to his own time and to set them in a richly evoked historical context. One institution made his work possible: the New York Public Library at Fifth Avenue and Forty-second Street, where he spent almost five years. As Kazin later recalled:

> Anything I had heard of and wanted to see, the blessed place owned: first editions of American novels out of those germinal decades after the Civil War that led to my theme of the "modern"; old catalogues from long-departed Chicago publishers who had been young men in the 1890s trying to support a little realism; yellowing, crumbling, but intact sets of the old *Masses* (1911–1918), which was to the Stalinist *New Masses* what St. Francis is to the Inquisition.

The library's holdings taught him "what hope, élan, intellectual freshness came with those pioneer realists out of the Middle West who said there was no American literature but the one they were rushing to create." Without leaving Manhattan, Kazin read his way into "lonely small towns, prairie villages, isolated colleges, dusty law offices, national magazines and provincial 'academies' where no one suspected that the obedient-looking young reporters, law clerks, librarians, teachers would turn out to be Willa Cather, Robert Frost, Sinclair Lewis, Wallace Stevens, Marianne Moore."[1]

Kazin and his close friend Richard Hofstadter, with whom he shared quick lunches at the Automat, fast games of ping-pong, and an occasional afternoon of newsreels, were only two of the countless writers, readers, and critics who over the centuries have found themselves and their subjects in libraries. It is an old story, quiet and reassuring: bookish boy or girl enters the cool, dark library and discovers loneliness and freedom. For the last ten years or so, however, the cities of the book have been anything but quiet. The computer and the Internet have transformed reading more dramatically than anything since the printing press. In great libraries from Stanford to Oxford, pages turn, scanners hum, databases grow—and the world of books, of copyrighted information and repositories of individual copies, trembles.

Scenarios for the apocalypse have often involved books: *Revelation* mentions letters, describes a book with seven seals, and uses the closing of a book as a vivid metaphor for the end of the physical world: "And the heaven departed as a scroll when it is rolled together" (6:14). But at the beginning of the twenty-first century, the rhetorical situation has reversed itself. Great information projects, mounted by Google and rival companies, have elicited millenarian prophecies about texts as we know them: claims that the printed book, magazine, and newspaper are as dead as the trees their paper comes from, and predictions that digital repositories of human knowledge will not only replace but will also improve on them. In 2006, Kevin Kelly, the self-styled "chief Maverick" of *Wired,* published one of the more influential of these in the *New York Times.* In a thoughtful review of the intricate legal issues associated with digitizing books in copyright, Kelly vividly describes the virtual library that Google and its rivals and partners are creating. In the near future, Kelly believes, "all the books in the world" will "become a single liquid fabric of interconnected words and ideas." The user of the electronic library will be able to bring together "all texts—past and present, multilingual—on a particular subject," and by doing so gain "a clearer sense of what we as a civilization, a species, do know and don't know. The white spaces of our collective ignorance are highlighted, while the golden peaks of our knowledge are drawn with completeness."[2] Others have evoked even more millennial prospects: a universal archive that will contain not only all books and articles but also all documents everywhere: the basis for a total history of the human race.

Librarians, publishers, professors, printers—all of us are fascinated by the prospect that such prophets conjure up: a future in which readers in search of information always turn to screens rather than books, and, as e-books improve, even readers in search of pleasure begin to do the same. This prospect infuriates some acolytes of the book: for example, Jean-Noel Jeanneney, historian and former director of the Bibliothèque Nationale de France, who in 2005 published a sad little volume in which he denounced Google Books as a typical American plot, at once imperialist and boorish, rather like the war in Iraq. Google, he argued, will first fill the Web with books in English and then profit by distorting the world of learning and literature. Only energetic countermeasures—preferably sponsored by national governments rather than corporations—can save European literature and scholarship.[3]

Instinct and experience predispose me to find some substance in critiques of the new textual world. I am a lover of old libraries—the libraries of the 1960s and 1970s, in which I became a scholar. As a student in those years, I lived in what felt like a bibliomaniac's paradise and in retrospect still seems to have been an idyll. Books and journals were cheap, and library budgets were healthy. Even in the United States, the stacks of good libraries from Connecticut to California were loaded with sixteenth- and seventeenth-century tomes that no one had yet declared rare, as well as reprints of anything the library did not possess in its original form. I prowled the vast open-stack collections at the University of Chicago, where I studied, and Cornell and Princeton, where I taught, pulling books off the shelves by dozens, as fascinated by what they could tell me about nineteenth- and twentieth-century scholars and students as by what they revealed about the more distant past I studied.

As a New Yorker, like Kazin, I also loved to sit in the shabby but dignified reading rooms of the New York Public Library, waiting for the indicator to show that my books had arrived. In those days, many libraries did not have coffee shops, and those that had one were more likely to provide vending machines than fresh espresso and cappuccino. Nonetheless, they became a chosen hangout, for me and for others like me. Late in the 1970s, when I learned that the Princeton library had identified me as a "heavy user," I was not surprised, though the choice of terminology worried me a little. The love of libraries has taken me to strange and wonderful places: to the British Library in London, still housed in the 1970s under the pale blue nineteenth-century dome that sheltered Karl Marx, Colin Wilson, and other outsiders; to the Warburg Institute, also in London, whose founder and successors arranged their books by what they called the "good neighbor principle," so that readers who looked for a particular book in the stacks would be surprised and edified by the others next to it; to the Bodleian Library, the Bibliothèque Nationale in Paris, the Bibliotheek der Rijksuniversiteit te Leiden, and the Biblioteca Apostolica Vaticana. One of the many things I have learned from years misspent amid the smells of dust and noble rot is that every library embodies a perspective of its own. Their contents, the way in which manuscripts and books are catalogued and arranged on shelves, and their gaps—all tell stories to those who can listen, about writers, readers, and collectors, and the historical worlds they inhabited.

Scholars become great when they attend to what these purpose-built collections, with their distinctive systems and oral traditions, have to teach. No one has described the austerely local nature of humanistic scholarship more precisely than the historian Peter Brown, who traces his own formation to the time he spent in the Lower Reading Room of the Bodleian Library:

> It was a world of books, each deeply rooted in the landscape of a single library. They were available in one place only, for rapt readers, who, themselves, had taken on something of the quality of natural features. They were visible year after year at their desks. Over the years, from 1953 to 1978, I passed from status to status. In these years, my mind changed often. But in the Lower Reading Room of Bodley nothing seemed to change. Opposite me, for instance, there always sat a known authority on the relation between Augustine's Scriptural readings and the liturgy of Hippo. He was not a member of the university. He was a clergyman who came up regularly from his vicarage in the countryside of Oxfordshire. I observed that he wore bedroom slippers. Frequently, the slippers appeared to win out over the books, and he would fall asleep. A prim young man at that time, I wondered if I could really trust the views of so somnolent a person on the Donatist schism. But the reverend gentleman stood for a wider world of learning, open to more professions and capable of nourishing many more forms of scholarly endeavor than that which I now expect to find, among my colleagues, in a seminar room. It was for persons such as him—for persons of learning and of general culture, who were not necessarily academics—as well as for my students and colleagues at Oxford, that I wrote my Augustine of Hippo, and went

out of my way to ensure that it would be published in England by Faber's
of London and not by a University Press. Figures such as these communicated the uncanny stillness of a shared life of learning.[4]

To have known reading in this artisanal form is to distrust any plan that
treats books as interchangeable and aims—as Google does—at universality.

But it would be absurd to join Jeanneney's crusade. Enter a word or phrase
in any European language in the Google Books search field and you learn immediately that the system already contains thousands of texts in languages
other than English. As to the French government, its last great gift to the world
of books was the library that Jeanneney directed, a building that looks like the
set from some forgotten dystopian sci-fi film of the 1970s—think *Logan's
Run*—and is about as much fun to work in. As a liberal, in the current Anglo-
American sense, I believe that competent governments do many things better
than markets can, but I am not at all sure that France's statist way of providing
books for readers is a case in point. The Bibliothèque Nationale deserves
credit for its own database, Gallica, which offers a canon of carefully selected
texts, well digitized, and for its provision of up-to-date foreign books. But it
has yet to show that it can, or wants to, mobilize and make accessible to the
world a vast, disorderly mass of texts, canonical and noncanonical, for readers
to use freely. Many American and British librarians are exuberant about the
prospect of bringing the books in their custody to new publics, through new
media, and anyone can see why. After all, one thing that Google Books makes
clearer every day is that you can study many aspects of French thought and literature as deeply in New York as in Paris, and a lot more efficiently.

The Universal Library

The problem is how to understand what is happening right now, as we all try
to remain standing against the tidal waves of traditional books and new media that are breaking over us. One vital point, and an easy one to miss, is that
the Internet will not in fact bring us a universal library—much less an encyclopedic record of all human experience. None of the firms now engaged in
digitization projects claims that it will create anything of the kind. The hype
and rhetoric that reverberate around the Web make it hard to grasp what
Google and their partner libraries are actually doing, what readers will and

will not have access to in the next ten or twenty years. We have clearly reached something of a watershed, a new era in the history of text production and consumption. On many fronts, traditional periodicals and books are making way for blogs, computer databases, and other electronic formats. But magazines and books still sell a lot of copies. The current drive to digitize the written record is one of a number of critical projects in the long saga of our drive to accumulate, store, and retrieve information efficiently. It will result not in the infotopia that the prophets conjure up, but in one more in a series of new information ecologies, all of them challenging, in which readers, writers, and producers of text have learned to survive and flourish.

For centuries—for millennia—the scribes and scholars who produced books often were also the ones who organized them in collections and devised ways of helping readers find and master what they needed. As early as the third millennium BCE, Mesopotamian scribes began to catalogue the tablets in their collections. For ease of reference, they appended content descriptions to the edges of tablets, and they adopted systematic shelving for quick identification of related texts. The greatest of ancient collections, the Library of Alexandria, had, in its ambition and its methods, a good deal in common with Google's efforts. It was founded around 300 BCE by Ptolemy I, who had inherited Alexandria, a brand-new city, from Alexander the Great. A historian with a taste for poetry, Ptolemy decided to amass a comprehensive collection of Greek literature, philosophy, and science. Like Google, the library developed an efficient procedure for capturing and reproducing texts. When ships docked in Alexandria, any scrolls found on them were confiscated and taken to the library. The staff made copies for the owners and stored the originals in heaps until they could be catalogued—a fact that gives some idea of the scale of the operation. Copies of Homer obtained this way were designated "those from ships."

At the collection's height, it contained more than half a million scrolls, a welter of information that forced librarians to develop new organizational methods. For the first time, texts were shelved alphabetically. Faced with this daunting mass, the poet and scholar Callimachus drew up comprehensive bibliographies. Enterprising forgers had run up so many fake texts to satisfy the library's appetite that he had to distinguish systematically between the genuine works of the great poets and the spurious ones that the library also possessed. Gradually, the library became a center of focused scholarship, where a series of librarians—Zenodotus of Ephesus, Aristophanes of Byzantium, and Aristarchus of Samothrace—corrected and commented on classic texts. Many details of their work, only partially preserved after the destruction of the library, remain controversial. Yet it seems clear that they not only devised new philological methods but also standardized the text of Homer that circulated in Egypt during the Hellenistic and Roman periods—a major achievement in an age when every text was copied by hand.[5]

Six hundred years after Callimachus, Eusebius, a historian and bishop of the seacoast city of Caesarea in Palestine, assembled and corrected Christian sources in the local library. There he also devised a complex network of cross-references, known as "canon tables," which enabled readers to find parallel passages in the four Gospels—a system that the distinguished modern scholar James O'Donnell recently described as the world's first set of hot links. A deft impresario, Eusebius mobilized a team of secretaries and scribes to produce Bibles featuring his new tables. The emperor Constantine acknowledged that Eusebius had developed a uniquely efficient system. In the 330s, he placed an order with the bishop for fifty parchment codex Bibles for the churches of his new city, Constantinople. Constantine himself supplied the necessary skins (in the age of manuscripts, blood sacrifice was the price of beautiful books), and sent them to Eusebius by the imperial rapid delivery service. He knew that only the scriptorium in Caesarea could turn the raw materials into accurate, properly formatted bibles in the short time he allowed.[6] Throughout the Middle Ages, the great monastic libraries continued to engage in the twin enterprises of accumulating and cataloguing large holdings and, in their scriptoria, making and disseminating copies of key texts.

The rise of printing in fifteenth-century Europe transformed the regimes of librarians and readers. Into a world already literate and curious, the printers brought, within half a century, some 28,000 titles and millions of individual books—many times more than European libraries had previously held. Reports of new worlds, new theologies, and new ideas about the universe traveled faster and sold for lower prices than ever before.

Even in this period of aggressive expansion, the traditional skills of learned librarians continued to find employment in the entrepreneurial world of printing. Giovanni Andrea Bussi, librarian of the papal collection of Sixtus IV, also served as advisor to two German printers in Rome, Conrad Sweynheym and Arnold Pannartz. They printed the classics and the church fathers in handsome editions that were significantly cheaper than manuscripts. Local scholars, thrilled by the speed and economy of the new process, made the tranquil gardens of the Vatican resound with their praises. Bussi edited and corrected their copy and sometimes added eloquent prefaces to their books. Like many first movers, however, Bussi and his partners soon learned that they had overestimated the market, which could not absorb editions that ran from a few hundred to more than a thousand copies. They found themselves—as Bussi eloquently complained to pope Sixtus IV—in a Roman palace full of the drying sheets they had printed but empty of food.[7] They were not the last entrepreneurs of new information technologies to experience this kind of difficulty. Still, the model Bussi helped to establish—one in which erudite scholars advised hardheaded printers—remained standard in the sixteenth century, and some of the printers who rejected it did so only because they themselves were learned men, who could choose and correct their own copy.

Over the next three centuries, the profit-driven industry of publishing and the industrious scholarship of the libraries became separate spheres. Yet in the last few years, as sales of university press books have dwindled and journal subscription prices have gone through the roof, this ancient model has been resurgent. Through their electronic publishing programs, libraries have begun to take on many of the tasks that traditionally fell to university presses, such as distribution of PhD dissertations and reproduction of local book and document collections. Ithaka, a nonprofit consultancy that issued a report on scholarly publishing in July 2007, noted the excitement that these new possibilities had generated among librarians.[8] Ironically, neither the consultants nor the many commentators on their work realized that in regaining partial control over the ways that texts are processed and made available, great libraries were not breaking new ground but going back to the future. The new electronic library that not only stores texts but also publishes them on its Web page, is engaging in a spread of activities that Eusebius would have found perfectly natural.

Fast, reliable methods of search and retrieval are sometimes identified as the hallmark of our information age: "Search is everything" has become a proverb. But scholars have grappled for millennia with too much information, and in periods when information resources seemed to be growing especially fast, they devised ingenious ways to control and use the floods. The Renaissance, during which numbers of available texts grew at an unprecedented pace, was the great age of systematic note taking. Manuals taught students how to condense the contents of all of literature, ancient and

modern, in abstracts and extracts organized by headings. Jeremias Drexel, a
seventeenth-century Jesuit who wrote one of the standard treatments,
showed how much this art was valued by the title he chose for it, "Gold-
mine." His frontispiece was even more eloquent—it juxtaposed a group of
miners digging for gold in the ground with a single scholar taking notes on
the truer gold in his books.[9] Scholars well grounded in this regime, like
Isaac Casaubon, spun tough, efficient webs of notes around the margins of
their books and in their notebooks—hundreds of Casaubon's annotated
books and almost sixty of his copybooks survive—and used them to retrieve information about everything from the religion of Greek tragedy to
the history of Egyptian culture in late antiquity.[10]

Then, as now, attractive and costly new technologies took shape. Jacques
Cujas, a prominent sixteenth-century legal scholar, amazed visitors to his
study when he showed them the rotating barber's chair and moveable book
stand that enabled him to keep many open books in view at the same time,
moving himself or the text as the occasion required. Thomas Harrison, a
seventeenth-century English inventor who seems to have sprung from the
pages of a novel by J. G. Farrell, devised an information cabinet that he called
the "Ark of Studies." A squad of readers, he explained, could summarize and
excerpt the vast number of books being published, and arrange their notes by
subject on labeled metal hooks, somewhat in the manner of a twentieth-
century card index. The great German philosopher Leibniz—perhaps the last
man who was simultaneously at the cutting edges of history, philosophy, and
natural science—enthusiastically obtained one of Harrison's cabinets and
used it in his research.[11]

For less erudite souls, simpler techniques abridged the process of looking
for information, much as Wikipedia and Google do now. Erasmus said—and
believed—that every serious student must read the entire corpus of the classics and make his own notes on them. But he also composed a magnificent
reference work, the *Adages*, in which he laid out and explicated thousands of
pithy ancient sayings—and provided neat subject indexes to help readers
find what they needed. For centuries, thousands of schoolboys first encountered the wisdom of the ancients in this handy, predigested form. When Erasmus told the story of Pandora, he said that she did not open a jar—as in the
original version of the story by the Greek poet Hesiod—but instead a box. In
every European language except Italian, as Erwin and Dora Panofsky showed

long ago, "Pandora's box" became proverbial, as playwrights, poets, and essayists made Erasmus's collection their first port of call for a neat way to express the dangers of thoughtless action, not to mention their fear of women.[12] Like Al Gore's invention of the Internet, Pandora's box is a canard—one made ubiquitous, almost universal, by the power of a new information technology. Even the best search procedures, in other words, depend on the databases they explore, and sometimes yield factoids, rather than facts.

From the eighteenth century onward, a new pattern gradually established itself. States, universities, and academies maintained great research libraries, more or less available to the public. At their most ambitious, they offered readers books and manuscripts in encyclopedic abundance. Imperial libraries collected information on a worldwide scale, vividly symbolized by the enormous domes that covered their central reading rooms. Their staffs also pioneered in information retrieval. They not only organized the books on the shelves but also devised multiple indexes to help readers find the information they needed—including such longtime standards as the printed catalogues of the British Library and the Library of Congress.

The nineteenth and twentieth centuries also witnessed a vast democratization of general reading—a story beautifully told in part by Jonathan Rose.[13] Cheap collections like Everyman's Library and the Haldeman-Julius Little Blue Books brought solid books other than the Bible and the Book of Martyrs into working-class households. Public libraries offered little islands of peace and print among the sprawling, chaotic tenement blocks of the industrial cities. The old regimes of note taking became less important, as the dictionaries, thesauruses, encyclopedias, and collections of quotations that had been developing since the eighteenth century became more and more a part of everyday bourgeois life. The title used for one popular form of reference work in Germany and Russia, "Conversation Lexicon," gives a sense of what books like this could do for readers who, like so many Chekhov characters, wanted to converse all day on every subject under the sun.

Yet no collection, no work of reference could offer all the books or information relevant to a complex subject. In the 1940s, Fremont Rider, a practitioner of Extreme Librarianship at Wesleyan, prophesied that titles were multiplying so quickly that they would soon overflow even the biggest sets of stacks. He and his influential acolyte Verner Clapp argued that microphotography could eliminate this problem. Just photograph the books, store the images on cards, and toss the dusty, decaying originals. The card catalogue in its drawers would become the actual research library, which could survive and grow forever. Readers would be able to find anything they wanted, in a clean, accessible form, while librarians could stop building and maintaining expensive open stacks.[14] Projects multiplied. Some of them—like Eugene Power's Short Title Catalogue project, which distributed 26,000 early English books on microfilm—genuinely changed the working lives of scholars and students. Meanwhile, other companies offered texts on microfiche, or simply reprinted books that had become rare or fragile on modern, acid-free paper. From the 1950s on, libraries began to resound with the deep voices of salesmen who claimed that they could provide vast runs of material immune to decay.

The results were genuinely dramatic. As old universities expanded and new ones sprouted in the 1950s and 1960s, generous funding enabled them to buy what was available on film or microfiche and in reprint form and thus to create effective collections in ten or fifteen years—sometimes from a standing start. Many ambitious libraries devised and carried out their own schemes as well. Suddenly, you could conduct serious research on the Vatican Library's collections not only in Rome but also in St. Louis, where the Knights of Columbus assembled a vast corpus of microfilms; or study the Milanese Biblioteca Ambrosiana at Notre Dame. For the first time, you could become an expert bibliographer or paleographer, edit texts or excerpt ancient newspapers and journals, without ever leaving home in California or Kansas. (Scholars, of course, did their best to conceal these facts from the deans who funded their research travel.)

But the film- and reprint-based libraries of the 1950s and 1960s never became really comprehensive. The commercial companies that did the filming naturally concentrated on marketable materials. Nonprofit sponsors concentrated on the texts that mattered to them—Catholic institutions, for example, on medieval Latin manuscripts. No clear logic determined which texts were reprinted on paper, which were filmed, and which remained in obscurity. It all cost a great deal more than anyone had envisioned at first. Some projects—especially those that used microfiches—encountered sales resistance, and a number of the early efforts died or became dormant. Once-prosperous reprint publishers ended up, like Bussi and his associates, drowning in unsold books. Worst of all, some of the largest and best-funded projects—especially the great newspaper-filming enterprises whose history Nicholson Baker has brought to light—had tragic consequences. Thousands of original documents of great beauty and interest were physically destroyed while their contents were recorded on film. Library users who had once been able to savor the artistry of Winsor McCay's "Little Nemo in Slumberland" in the colorful pages of the *New York Herald* found themselves squinting at black-and-white images on blurry screens. In this new, Darwinian ecology, the photographic revolution dwindled—physically, in most libraries—from a sweeping project to change the way everyone read and worked to a single room where graduate students, faculty, and unusually diligent undergraduates pored over texts that they were willing to read even in an unappealing, black-and-white form. Rider's promise of a world of information on neatly filed cards yielded thousands of reels of film that must be cranked and maneuvered to be read. It is a lesson to remember as we move through a new age of rapid change and great promises.[15]

Google's Empire

The current era of digitalization unquestionably outstrips that of microfilm, in ambition and in achievement. Few individuals ever owned microfilm or microfiche readers, after all, whereas most serious readers in developed countries now have direct access to personal computers or laptops and an Internet connection. The changes wrought by all this are obvious. Even the most traditionally minded of scholars, faced with the need to look up a date, a fact, or a text, generally begins not by going to a library reference room crammed with encyclopedias and handbooks, but by consulting a search engine. "Conservatively," a cheerful editor from Cambridge University Press told me, "95 percent of all scholarly inquiries start at Google." And that makes sense: Google, the nerdiest of corporations, has roots in the world of books. According to oral tradition, Google's founders started out with a plan to create an electronic database of the books at Stanford and turned to the Web only because it offered, at that time, a smaller sample size. Google's famous search algorithm, moreover, emulates the principle of scholarly citation. By counting up and evaluating earlier links, Google steers users to the sources that others have already found helpful. In a sense, the hypermodern search engine resembles nothing more than a teeming mass of old-fashioned footnotes. Just as footnotes tell you where an author went to dig up his or her facts and quotations, so Google tells you where most people have gone before you in order to learn what you want to know.

For the last few years, Google and its competitors have been at work on staggeringly ambitious projects, designed to transform the way in which all readers go about finding books. Even the scale of this enterprise is hard to fathom. A conservative estimate of the number of books published throughout history is 32 million: currently, though, Google believes that that there could be as many as 100 million. The company collaborates with publishers—there are currently some 10,000 of these so-called Google partners around the world—to provide information about books currently in print, including text samples, to all users of the Web. So do a number of rival companies. As Google, Amazon, and Barnes & Noble compete, the Web has become a vast and vivid online bookstore. Anyone with a laptop can scan dust jackets, read blurbs, and peek between the covers of the limited group of books that can still be bought. Cambridge University Press, which became a partner in 2004, receives 500,000 page views a month from searchers who began at Google or Google Books. In other words, around two-thirds of all the potential customers for the books of the world's oldest publisher start at Google rather than the press's own Web site.

A second, even larger enterprise—the Google Library Project—has brought the company into collaboration with great libraries around the world. Drawing on the vast collections of Stanford, Harvard, Michigan, the New York Public Library, and many others, Google is digitizing as many out-of-print books as possible. It is an extraordinary effort that Google itself describes as designed to "build a comprehensive index of all the books in the world." This index, moreover, will enable readers to search all the books it contains and to see full texts of all those not covered by copyright. Google's book project is a twenty-first-century version of Fremont Rider's plan, on steroids and in your face: a list of books that will ultimately be universal in scope, accessible everywhere, and accompanied by full texts.

It is hard to exaggerate how much material is becoming accessible month by month and what will become accessible in the next few years, for those who study the distant past or the Third World as well as those primarily concerned with the present. Google is flanked by other big efforts. Some are largely philanthropic, like the old standby Project Gutenberg, which provides hand-keyboarded texts of English and American classics, plain in appearance and easy to use, and the distinctive Million Book Project, founded by Raj Reddy at Carnegie Mellon University. Reddy works with partners around the world to provide, among other things, online texts in many languages for which character-recognition software is not yet available.

Add in the hundreds of smaller efforts in specialized fields. Perseus, for example, an incredibly useful site based at Tufts, began with Greek and Latin texts and now embraces works from the English Renaissance. Readers can make direct online use of dictionaries, grammars, and commentaries as they struggle through the originals. There are also new commercial enterprises like Alexander Street, which offers libraries beautifully produced electronic collections of everything from "Harper's Weekly" to the letters and diaries of American immigrants. Even the biggest libraries are expanding faster and more vertiginously than Borges could have dreamt, thanks to the electronic resources listed, at length, on their Web pages. It has already become impossible for ordinary scholars to keep abreast of the basic sources online— though *D-Lib Magazine,* an online publication, helps by highlighting library Web pages that do an especially good job of organizing digital sources and collections, rather as material libraries used to advertise their acquisition of a writer's papers or a collection of books with fine bindings.

Many librarians view these developments with warm approval. Kristian Jensen is a dapper, hyperarticulate curator of early printed books at the British Library, who worked with Microsoft on a project, now abandoned, to digitize the library's immense holdings in nineteenth-century literature. His usual style is extremely precise and sober, but when he talks about the prospects of digital libraries, he lights up. "You can't help being enthusiastic," he says, at the thought of all this material becoming available to teachers and students at universities and schools all over the world. One way to see what he means is to visit the Web site of the Online Computer Library Center and look at their WorldMap. This imaginative application plots numbers of books in public and academic systems around the world, country by country. Ask the WorldMap to show you how many public library books the world's nations boast: you will see the relation of the Northern to the Southern Hemisphere, and of Western nations to their former colonies, all laid out in stark color. Sixty million Britons have 116 million public library books at their disposal, while the more than 1.1 billion Indians have 36 million.[16]

World poverty, in other words, is embodied in lack of print as well as lack of food—it means that citizens of many nations do not have access to their own literature and history, much less to information about other countries.

The Internet, as constituted in its short past, has not yet done much to re-dress this imbalance. In 2005, when I sat in a tin-roofed, incandescently hot West African Internet café and tried to answer questions from my students in America, I could find little high-end material on the screen, and neither, by the look of things, could my Beninese fellow users. By now it would be possi-ble to find far more, and better, digital resources, even on a slow PC in Naititingou. As the capillary spread of electrification reaches smaller and smaller cities, as Internet cafes sprout in small Asian, African, and Latin American towns, and as Google and its rivals fill the Web with solid texts, the map of knowledge will undergo a metamorphosis. Capitalism, of all things, is democratizing access to books at an unprecedented pace.

Kazin loved the New York Public Library because it admitted everyone. His fellow readers included not only neat young scholars like Hofstadter, but also wild figures from Weegee's photographs of the New York night: "the little man with one slice of hair across his bald head, like General MacArthur's . . . poring with a faint smile over a large six-column Bible in Hebrew, Greek, Latin, En-glish, French, German," and "the bony, ugly, screeching madwoman who re-minded me of Maxim Gorky's 'Boless,' the anguished old maid who had a professional scribe take down passionate letters to a lover and then asked the scribe to make up letters from the lover to her."[17] Even Kazin's democratic imagination could not have envisaged the Web's new world of information and its hordes of actual and potential users. The Internet cannot feed millions of people or protect them from AIDS or flooding. But it could feed an unlimited number of hungry minds with Paine, Gandhi, Voltaire, and Wollstonecraft—as well as the classics of other cultures, and the manuals of sciences and trades, in dozens of languages. The consequences may be seismic, bigger and louder and deeper than we can hope to predict.

Some powerful figures in the realm of books, as we have seen, fear that these projects will simply reinforce the world hegemony of English. Google did begin relatively close to home, working with English-language publishers and British and American collections. But the great American and British li-braries that first partnered with Google are stuffed with books in all the lan-guages of the world. Paul Leclerc, director of the New York Public Library (NYPL) and an enthusiastic original partner in the Google Books Project, notes that just under half of the millions of books in NYPL are in languages other than English, many of them in Asian, Slavic, and African. Richard

Ovenden, who works with Google at the Bodleian Library in Oxford, points out that the millions of books that will be digitized there are in some forty languages. Meanwhile, libraries on the Continent and elsewhere are signing Google partnership agreements of their own. The mass of old and new texts on the Web will not be an English-only zone.

The Internet's technologies, moreover, are continually developing, and many of the changes make it easier for a user to take a stand in the flood of information and fish out exactly the right book or article from the foam. Consider the search function: the hunting-gathering-connecting of information that Google or Yahoo or Ask does on our behalf. In its first age, a search engine used a "crawler"—actually a stationery entity—to look for relevant pages on a stored, and slightly out-of-date, version of the Web. No two search engines gave exactly the same results, though Google regularly found more and more useful sites than its rivals, and this accomplishment won it placement as the sole engine of choice on many official Web pages. Even Google's crawler, though, remained as fixated on surfaces as a fashion photographer. It informed the user only about the 5 percent or so of content prominently labeled as such on the top layers of Web pages. To find materials buried in such deep bodies of fact and document as the Library of Congress's Web site or JSTOR (the vast repository of scholarly journal articles), you had to carry out dynamic, focused searches: by going to the site and asking a specific question, or hiring a specialist firm like Bright Planet to ask it thousands of times for you.

In recent years, however, as anyone who regularly uses Google knows, the crawlers have become more adept at asking questions, and the search companies have apparently induced the big proprietary sites to become more responsive to the crawlers' inquiries. Specialist engines like Google Scholar can discriminate with astonishing precision between relevant and irrelevant, firsthand and derivative information. Internet tools offer not just more information every day but also more effective ways of formulating precise inquiries. One of my favorites is Amazon's list of "statistically improbable phrases," or SIPs, in any given book. Click on one of them and Amazon whisks you off to a list of other books in which the same highly unusual combination of words appears—a fast and simple way to find connections that previous buyers have not already made. Your local reference librarian still knows a lot more tricks than you do for finding information, in books or on the Web. But the powers of search keep growing, and it is hard to imagine what they will be in ten or twenty years.

For all its virtues, the Google Library Project, in its present, working form, has received mixed reviews, and that is understandable. Google shows the reader a scanned version of the page. These are generally accurate and readable—though individual pages can be blurry or obscured, and scanner operators occasionally miss pages or scan them out of order. Sometimes the copy used is imperfect. In the spirit of the movie *Office Space,* at least one scholarly acquaintance has spotted a body part, scanned with the text. Other problems are more serious. Google uses optical character recognition to produce a second version, for use by its search engine, and this process has some quirks. In a scriptorium lit by the sun, a scribe could mistakenly transcribe a "u" as an "n," or vice versa. Curiously, the computer makes the same mistakes. If you enter "qualitas"—an important term in medieval philosophy—in Google Book Search, you will find almost 2,000 appearances. But if you enter "qnalitas," a nonword, you will be rewarded with more than 600 references to "qualitas" that you would not have found using the correct term. That is a lot of "qnalitas." If you want to get a sense of the full magnitude of the problem, call up the Google version of a German book printed in the old spiky type, *Fraktur,* and ask to "view plain text"—the text used for search. In many cases, the system will show you page after page of gobbledygook. It seems significant that the German word for both science and scholarship, "Wissenschaft," often appears as "Wiffenschaft" in these random text zones. It is hard to see how errors on this scale will ever be eliminated—any more than the thousands of errors made when the catalogues of the great university and public libraries were converted into databases will ever be corrected as a whole.

Serious problems also affect the "metadata," or data about data, that Google offers its users. The cataloguing information that identifies any given item is often incomplete or confusing. Multivolume works can be very hard to use, since Google originally treated them as single items (this policy seems to have changed, perhaps in response to users' complaints: the hive mind at work). And the key terms that Google provides in order to characterize individual books are sometimes unintentionally comic. It is not all that helpful, when you are thinking about how to use an old Baedeker guide to Paris, to be told randomly that one of its central concepts is "fauteuil." The possibilities for glitches, and the pretexts for grumbling, are endless. Scholars, whose interests are minutely precise and philological, inclined by disposition and experience to look on the dark side, often concentrate on these blemishes.[18]

It is true that, thanks to Google and its rivals, social and cultural historians who work on the period from the mid-eighteenth to the early twentieth century already occupy a massive and growing intellectual sweet spot. Without ever leaving home, they can search for evidence about everything from political language to the rise of new technologies, in a database much larger than any historian has ever used before. Where details about editions matter less than sheer quantity of easily accessible, generally reliable information— or where only a single, nineteenth-century edition exists—digitization has already brought about a revolution. It is an amazing experience to teach literary texts that you know well, but not perfectly, with the Google Books text up and searchable on your laptop. And it is more than transformative to sit in your office at a small liberal arts or community college and call up, as you already can, thousands of books in dozens of languages, the nearest material copy of which is hundreds of miles away.

Still, even the sweet spot has its sour patches. Though Google claims to make full texts available for all books not protected by copyright, in fact you cannot download or even read in full many of the out-of-copyright texts. The system allows you to see only the same three wavy little banners of text (pretty much guaranteed not to contain the exact passage you need) that it offers for books in copyright. Like Erasmus, Google is both a generous and a fallible guide to the universe of books.

An analogy may help to highlight Google's accomplishments and limitations. In the 1910s and 1920s, Archibald Cary Coolidge supervised the construction and organization of Harvard University's Widener Library, the world's greatest collection of scholarly books. Like the creators of Google, he worked on a grand scale, deliberately building collections not only of rare and famous works but also of "writings which are neither great nor fashionable," since these were essential for "background and filling in." Like them, too, he emphasized the need to make books as accessible as possible, both by creating a library large enough to hold millions of them and by cataloguing them as rapidly as possible. But Coolidge, as William Bentinck-Smith recorded, "led a life of books. He was seldom without them. In his younger days he traveled across Asia with a little trunkload of them," and in later years he read as he walked in the country.[19] Accordingly, when Coolidge set out to create a universal library, he did not simply start buying books by the ton. Instead, he searched the world for integral collections that would add new fields to Widener's holdings, systematically building resources for both present and future research. His directing intelligence, and those of the helpers and donors he inspired, played a vital role in making the Widener a uniquely efficient machine for scholarly work; its catalogues were as accurate as its holdings were comprehensive. The Google Library project aims to be genuinely universal, as no material library can, even the Widener. But it lacks the governing vision of a Coolidge, and accordingly operates less as a vast, coherent ordering mechanism than as a gigantic fire hose dousing the world's readers with texts untouched by human hands or minds. Google could do much more for the world's readers if it invited Coolidge's modern counterparts—masters of both the virtual world of information and the sensuous, material world of real books—to plan and shape its virtual library. At present, though, no evidence suggests that Google sees the future of its enterprise in these terms.

In the end, moreover, general conditions set limits to what the Google project, along with its competitors, can achieve, at least in the near term. The microfilm years showed that reproduction projects on a large scale are realized when undertaken by national institutions determined to preserve a patrimony and make it available, or by companies out to make money. So far, the new Web companies have moved much faster, and unlike the Bibliothèque Nationale, they have plumped for making vast quantities of books available for others to sort and use, rather than for digitizing preselected, well known texts. But even Google's sleek, high-powered engines cannot pull books onto the Web any faster than the pots of money that fuel them will allow. In the end, Google will digitize only as much as the relevant income stream allows—a point underlined by Microsoft's recent decision to leave this field to Google. That means that they are going to leave vast numbers of important books untouched.

At every turn, technical and economic problems confront Google and its rivals and limit their freedom of action. One of the most frequently discussed difficulties is that of copyright. Google estimates, very roughly, that between 5 and 10 percent of known books are currently in print. Twenty percent more—those produced between the beginning of print in the fifteenth century and 1923—are out of copyright. The remainder—perhaps 75 percent of all books ever printed—are "orphans," still covered by the very long copy-right protections currently in force in Europe and North America, but out of print and pretty much out of mind. Rather as the Alexandrian library confiscated scrolls from ships, Google simply scans as many of these as it can, though it lacks legal permission to do so. But this part of the firm's project remains highly controversial. A number of the publishers who use Google to market their new books have sued to prevent Google from scanning books in copyright without obtaining formal permission—a daunting prospect. For the moment, accordingly, Google is not making these works fully available, and a recent legal settlement only makes it possible to show larger portions of such books to Google users.

Then, too, Google has no immediate plans to scan books from the first couple of centuries of printing. When asked why, computer people sometimes explain that the books' fragile condition makes them hard to scan. That is ridiculous: most early books are far less fragile, thanks to the fine rag paper on which they were printed and the glorious craft skills of their makers, than the nineteenth-century novels—mass-produced on wood pulp paper and now dried out and brittle—that Google's scanners are capturing by the hundreds. The real reason is commercial. Rare books require expensive special conditions for copying, and most of those likely to generate a lot of use have already been made available by companies like Chadwyck-Healey and Gale. These descendants of the microfilm houses sell massive collections to libraries and universities, for substantial fees. Early English Books Online (EEBO) offers 100,000 titles printed between 1475 and 1700, 25,000 of them searchable. Eighteenth Century Collections Online provides searchable full texts of around 150,000 books—33 million pages' worth. Massive tomes in Latin and the little pamphlets that poured off the presses during the Puritan revolution, schoolbooks, Jacobean tragedies with prompters' notes, and political pamphlets by wild-eyed Diggers are all available in their original form to any main library user in New York or London, Syracuse or Sydney. Google will not directly explore this territory.

Other vast and vital sectors of the world's book production are neither catalogued nor accessible on site, much less available for digitization. Materials from the poorest societies exert little attraction on companies that rely on subscriptions or advertising. Countries where even big city merchants do not take credit cards will not provide online advertisers with orders, or Google with cash flow. One possible outcome of the current race to digitize, then, is a new version of the existing imbalances between north and south, former metropoles and former colonies. The book-deprived inhabitants of sub-Saharan Africa and much of India may be able to read Western works of every kind on screen. It is far less certain that they will be able to find and read texts in their own languages.

Whatever happens on screen, the great libraries of the Northern Hemisphere will remain irreplaceable for a long time. One of the best things computerization will do for everyone is simply to pinpoint the location of the books people need. Astonishingly, for all the hundreds of millions of books in American college and university libraries, there are normally no more than five copies of any given book in a language other than English. Google has always described itself as a company that shows users the way to find the information they need, not as the primary provider of that information. In the carefully chosen words of Jim Gerber, director of Content Partnerships, "We want to make sure readers can find books." The company does this job very well—and we would be foolish to expect its managers to take on further tasks for no extra compensation.

A record of all history appears even more distant. In theory, repositories fall into two categories. Libraries house books and literary manuscripts, while archives preserve documents—the vast range of papers, seals, and other materials that the world's lawyers, notaries, and government officials, shops, and corporations create in the course of their work. In practice, the two categories blur, and always have. All great libraries contain lots of documents. Most archives have working libraries, some of them very large and valuable. The point to keep in mind is that if you plan to make the whole record of human experience available, as the most utopian champions of digitization imagine, you have to render both kinds of collection accessible online.

It is true that millions of documents have already appeared on-screen. The online records of the Patent and Trademark Office are a wonderland for anyone interested in exploring the brilliance and lunacy of American tinkerers. Thanks to the nonprofit Aluka archive, scholars and writers in Africa can study on the Web a growing number of African records, whose originals are stored, inaccessibly, elsewhere in the world. Historians of the papacy can read original documents without going to Rome, in a digitized collection mounted by the Vatican Secret Archive. And the Library of Congress has taken the lead at everything from digitizing the papers of major thinkers like Hannah Arendt to collecting sound and video materials systematically and making them available as well. Its Web site is already a magnificent archive open to the world.

Meanwhile, individual curiosity and passion have driven the creation of virtual archives on every imaginable subject, often unconnected with any material collection. The Web can transport you to documents on sages from Thomas and Jane Welch Carlyle to Edward Said, to vast runs of reproduced political poems and cartoons, and even into the recondite field that I cultivate: the Latin writing of the Renaissance (try the Web sites "White Trash Scriptorium" and "Philological Museum"; both are indispensable).[20]

But even the biggest of these projects is nothing more than a flare of light in the vast and still unexplored night sky of humanity's documented past. The Archive of the Indies in Simancas, a magnificent product of the Spanish monarchy's obsession with record keeping, possesses an estimated 86 million pages' worth of documents. With the help of IBM, it has now digitized more than 10 million of these. Scholars and students who go to Simancas can do much of their work on screen, saving the originals and their eyesight at one and the same time. But they cannot search or access these pages from abroad. ArchivesUSA, a Web-based guide to American archives, lists 5,500 repositories and more than 160,000 collections of primary source material. The National Archives alone contain some nine billion items. It is not likely that we will see the whole archives of the United States online in the immediate future—much less those of poorer nations.

The supposed universal library, then, and its companion universal archive, will not be a seamless mass of books, easily linked and studied together, but a patchwork of different interfaces and databases, some open to anyone with a computer and WiFi, others closed to those who lack access or money. The real challenge now is how to chart the tectonic plates of information that are crashing into one another and then to learn to navigate the new landscapes they are creating. Blaise Aguera y Arcas, until recently an architect at Microsoft Live Labs and a pioneer in computer-assisted bibliography (full disclosure: he took courses with me years ago at Princeton), suggests that the best way to think about the masses of material that are being gathered on the Web is to divide them in two.

One of them is a library and cultural archive of the present. Google and its competitors have already gathered collections far more massive than anything the world has known—collections of the books published and the music, art, and film produced after 1990 or so. Though these companies would all disclaim any ambition to serve as the world's repositories, that is what they have become. Each of them holds a sea of data, of books that have been captured and made searchable, of images and tunes—all of it washing around in multiple, redundant servers, constantly moving, continually refreshed. Over time, as more of this material emerges from protection and becomes accessible—and it will—we will be able to learn things about our culture, in the present, which we could never have known in the past. We will still be able to read books and scrutinize images as we always have, but we will also be able to interrogate this whole mass of material in new ways, using the same applied mathematical techniques that the National Security Agency uses to mine data from our telephone calls and e-mails.

Soon the present will become overwhelmingly accessible. It is a thrilling prospect, but it has some scary implications. Readers and lovers of music and the arts already attend more to the present than the past. And the second great wodge of material—the great messy assemblage of sources for earlier periods, some complete but many partial, some open to all and others for profit, that is now taking shape—will not, in the foreseeable future, coalesce into a single, accessible database. Neither Google nor anyone else will fuse the proprietary collections of early books and the local systems created by individual archives into a single accessible mass of information. Though the distant past will also be more accessible than ever before, in a technical sense, once it is captured and preserved as a vast, disjointed mosaic, it may actually recede ever more rapidly from our collective attention.

We will still need our material libraries and archives. In some ways, we have come to understand better than ever before in the last twenty years or so just what makes old-fashioned, bricks-and-mortar collections essential and distinctive. Historians, literary scholars, and librarians have realized, in the words of John Seely Brown and Paul Duguid, that information leads a "social life" of its own. The form in which you encounter a text can have a huge impact on how you use it. Take the simplest case: If you want to make people believe that a given official document—say, a letter from the commanding officer of a young Texan in the Air National Guard—is genuine, you cannot just give people its wording. You have to show that it is on the right sort of paper, entered in the standard form, and typed on the proper Selectric. The only way to know that for certain is to see the original and compare it to others, and in most cases, you can do that only in an archive where they are reliably stored. As scanning technology improves, watermarks and other vital signs are becoming more accessible to remote users. But scholarly or even forensic exactitude still requires direct consultation of original documents.

Original documents and books reward us for taking the trouble to find them by telling us things no image can. Duguid describes watching a fellow historian systematically sniff 250-year-old letters in an archive. By detecting the smell of vinegar—which had been sprinkled on letters from towns struck by cholera in the eighteenth century, in the hope of disinfecting them—he could trace the history of disease outbreaks.[21] Historians of the book, a new and growing tribe, read books as scouts read trails. Bindings—custom made, for the most part, in the early centuries of printing—can tell you who owned them and what level of society they belonged to. Marginal annotations—which abounded in the centuries when readers habitually went through books pen in hand—identify the often surprising messages that individuals have found as they read. Many original writers and thinkers—Martin Luther, Hester Thrale Piozzi, John Adams, and Samuel Taylor Coleridge—filled their books with notes that are indispensable to understanding their thought. Thousands of forgotten men and women covered Bibles and prayer books, recipe collections and political pamphlets with pointing hands, underlining, and notes that give deep insight into what their books meant to them—and how they cooked their meals, treated their illnesses, and said their prayers.

If you want to capture how a given book was packaged and what it has meant to the readers who have unwrapped it, as many scholars now do, you have to look not just at all the editions but also at all the copies you can find, from original manuscripts to cheap reprints. The databases include multiple copies of some titles, but they will never provide all the copies of, say, Adam Smith's *The Wealth of Nations* and the early responses it provoked. Sometimes, too, the processes that have turned material books into electronic texts have stripped them of the rich evidence that their original form could provide. The texts available on EEBO, for example, were not scanned from the originals, but from microfilms. Their bindings are not reproduced, and it is hard to be sure of their original sizes—two densely material sets of clues that scholars constantly use when working out who read, or was expected to read, a given book. To hear books speak, you have to interview them in their original habitat.

As companies compete for pole position, market share, and what the pioneers of the Dot Bomb laughingly called "first mover advantage," they are devising new projects with all the imaginative verve of Fremont Rider. Some of these call to mind the effort of the 1960s and 1970s to put everything on microfilm, which did a lot of harm as well as a great deal of good, because its creators and managers ignored the social life of information. Up to now, scanning has not caused a second Great Destruction of newspapers—though it has resulted in the disposal of a lot of older books and journals. But the people who are now banging at library doors seem likely to make some of the same mistakes as the microfilm mavens of the 1950s and 1960s. On the other hand, some librarians, like those at Emory University, are beginning to turn away would-be suitors whose business plans do not properly justify why a collection should surrender its intellectual property to a company—even as those at other institutions, like the Princeton Theological Seminary, say yes.

Publishing without Paper?

It is not just the conditions of research that are changing, but the whole traditional system of writing and publishing—though here, too, the situation is not easy to read. Books, magazines, daily newspapers, and scholarly journals continue to appear. R. R. Bowker, a company based in New Providence, New Jersey, compiles what was once a book and is now a database, *Books in Print.* According to Bowker, "publishers in the United States, United Kingdom, Canada, Australia and New Zealand released 375,000 new titles and editions in 2004 . . . Including imported editions available in multiple markets, the total number of new English language books available for sale in the English-speaking world in 2004 was a staggering 450,000."[22] Go to any branch of Borders or Barnes & Noble or their British counterparts, Blackwell's and Waterstone's, and torrents of brightly jacketed new books on every subject confront you—not to mention stacks of periodicals.

This tidal wave of new print, in fact, poses librarians one of their most serious current problems. In Princeton University's Firestone Library, the stacks are already full. The yearly budget cannot stretch to cover all the new books and journals that scholars demand—many of them priced in expensive pounds and euros. Electronic media, a new system for borrowing books rapidly from nearby libraries, and electronic delivery of articles all cost money that would once have been spent on traditional media. Nonetheless, every year the library adds more than a mile of new printed materials to its collection. This mass of print enters the building dynamically, like a battering ram made of paper and buckram. It forces older materials—often rare and valuable—into storage and destroys the traditional order of the collections, which served scholars for generations as a spatially defined memory theater. Like the sorcerer's apprentice, administrators and professors have conjured up so many active young scholars writing theses, articles, and books that they threaten to overwhelm libraries, and the faithful guardians of the knowledge base with them.

Journals pose even harder problems. In theory, scholarly and scientific periodicals offer the newest data and hypotheses—the very things that scholars need most urgently. But their subscription prices have risen starkly. Elsevier, said to be the world's largest for-profit scientific publisher, claims to serve "a global scholarly community of 7,000 journal editors, 70,000 editorial board members, 300,000 reviewers, and 600,000 authors." It charges as much as $21,744 per year for one of its periodicals, *Brain Research*—more than any but the very richest libraries can possibly afford. And, of course, cataloguing, binding, and finding space for this pullulating mass of new print are formidably expensive. True, new databases offer direct access to thousands of articles. A scholar in the humanities can rummage through older articles in more than 600 arts, humanities, and social sciences journals without ever leaving his or her desk, thanks to JSTOR. Project Muse, a second nonprofit collaboration based at Johns Hopkins University Press, offers full-text access to current and recent articles from almost 400 leading journals. Many libraries have solved their space problems—though not their budgetary ones—by abandoning print subscriptions for electronic ones, which enable their faculty and students to identify and read the articles they need more quickly and easily than they could in the era of print. But these databases are accessible only to those who work at research institutions. Those who remain outside these zones of privilege—including many journalists and writers—are sharply disadvantaged, and know it.

Revolutions, historians know, are often caused not by oppression and disaster, but by rising expectations. More and more, scholars and scientists expect to find everything they need on the Web. Teachers report that even advanced students refuse to trek to the library: articles available only on paper go unread, even if they are classics. Meanwhile, political authorities complain, with justice, that for-profit journals guard the gates to the kingdom of scientific research paid for by public funds, and earn massive profits by doing so. Many argue that all scholarly and scientific journals—and all university presses—should provide free full-text access to their materials to all. In the case of medical research, Congress has mandated that all 80,000 papers produced every year under the sponsorship of the National Institutes of Health be placed on an open federal database, PubMed, once a year has passed from the date of publication.

The Harvard Faculty of Arts and Sciences has gone even further. It has decided that all members of the faculty should post all of their work on an open Harvard Web page. Editors who hope to publish the work of Harvard professors will simply have to accept that a version of the piece in question is already available to the whole world, or allow the professor to post a PDF file of the work as edited and typeset for their journal. I cannot speak for journals or editors in the sciences. But I do serve as one of four editors of the *Journal of the History of Ideas,* now in its sixty-ninth year of operation. My colleagues and I receive around 200 articles a year for consideration. Two of us read each one, and those that we find original and scholarly are then submitted to further scrutiny by two specialists—or three, if the first two disagree. The referees' reports are almost always very substantive and often quite long and detailed. In many cases, they help us help authors, by suggesting exactly where and why they need to modify claims, examine further primary sources, or engage with further secondary works. Once revision has taken place, our one full-time employee who manages the flow of files, copyedits the text, as does one of the four editors. Mistakes still happen. As William Shawn explained about the *New Yorker,* "Falling short of perfection is a process that just never stops."[23] But most of our authors—and most of the readers who continue to subscribe to our journal or use it through libraries—seem to agree that we add substantial value to the articles that we accept and publish.

The four editors receive no compensation. Nor do the scores of referees who read articles at our request. But we pay all costs for the *Journal* offices in Philadelphia, since our host, the University of Pennsylvania, like many other top research universities, refuses to invest any funds in the enterprise. We pay the manager/editor who keeps the files moving, chases down referees and authors who miss their deadlines, and copyedits the articles. We pay for a yearly meeting of our full editorial board, the members of which serve as unpaid referees, advisers, and much more. And we pay the University of Pennsylvania Press, which composes, produces, and distributes the *Journal,* both on paper and electronically. Slowly, the print version of the *Journal* has been losing subscribers, but for-pay use through JSTOR and Project Muse has yielded more income each year—enough to compensate for the losses. And the entire structure that enables us to help authors produce the best work they can—the structure of refereeing and editing—depends on this stream of money.

At $40—$32 for students, $110 for institutions—the price we ask for a year's subscription to the *Journal* does not seem excessive to us, and the money all goes to the larger ends of scholarship. If we adopt an open-access model, allowing all readers to consult the entire journal without charge, or a partial one, allowing authors to publish their articles on the Web before we consider them, our income stream will certainly diminish. This could leave us unable to accept or reject most articles within three months from submission, as we do now, or to copyedit the pieces we accept, or pay for handsome, legible page composition.

True, it might be possible to create a different system that would achieve the same ends. Journals distributed to the members of a professional association can use dues to cover the costs that subscriptions do not pay, and more and more of them have adopted open-access policies. But we have no association. The university that serves as the journal's host could cover our basic costs. But major research universities nowadays consistently refuse to take on this responsibility: indeed, they do not seem to regard it as prestigious or worthwhile. Advertising revenues are supporting the large-circulation magazines as they move more and more of their offerings onto the Web: but Daimler-Benz and Dior do not regard the readers of our journal as likely sales prospects. So far as the four of us who edit the *Journal of the History of Ideas* can see, open access for us will confirm the grim prophecies of Robert Conquest and Kingsley Amis: "More will mean worse."

This little case suggests a few of the larger problems that the transformation of our media brings with it. The computer has made it possible to start writing very early—perhaps too early—in the course of research. Editors enforce a system of peer review that prevents substandard work from being published and forces all scholars, however gifted, to listen to informed advice before they give the world their work. The mass of direct publication on the

Web has created a fantastic new public sphere—and a fantastic new mass of ungainly, misspelled prose. Editors ask writers to take a second and a third look at what they have written—to clarify, polish, and correct. We form a thin-lipped gray line, protecting both readers and authors from first thoughts. And this job is more important than ever, now that scholars inhabit an environment that enables them to write on the basis of what the sociologist Andrew Abbott calls "on-time" research—that is to say, snatch-and-grab raids into what is online, carried out in the course of composition—rather than the decks of neatly written file cards that they would have compiled fifty years ago.[24] Harvard's sweeping solution to the problems faced by libraries and students may have good results in some fields. But in the humanities, satisfying the demand that every article become immediately accessible on the Web for free will force us to abandon valuable forms and standards. In this new world, journals will become something like blogs with footnotes: unedited texts, glittering with insights, but also blemished with errors that no informed eye has picked up, and succeeded by angry, scatological discussion threads. The world of humanistic scholarship needs updating, but it does not need to be transformed into one more province of the public sphere that already exists, and serves quite different needs, on the Web.

Some of the strongest advocates for digitization seem to welcome this outcome—or at least the transformation of prose forms that it would bring about. Gregory Crane, the creator of Perseus, evokes a future in which scholars cast all their information not in the traditional forms of nonfictional writing—the article and the book—but in smaller, "granular" units that can be combined and recombined by Web users in an infinite number of ways. Kristian Jensen of the British Library agrees that this may come about. When you write for the Web, he points out, you naturally tend to cast your thoughts in little textual monads rather than in the traditional linear forms. Unlike Crane, though, Jensen is concerned about the result. The flow of texts onto the Web, Jensen worries, may be accompanied by—or even help to cause—a revolution in forms of attention that will harm, or even eliminate, traditional forms of argument and writing. As the railroad threatened the cathedral, the intellectual snack pack threatens slow food.

It is not yet clear that online publication will transform writing as radically as Crane and Jensen suggest. Critics and true believers converge in emphasizing one feature of Web publication above all: its new form. The traditional book and periodical place a single story, told by a master narrator, in the fore-ground. Even the most aggressive reader has to accommodate him or herself to the given form of the text. And even the most extensive and aggressive handwritten comments wind themselves around the monumental printed text like ivy growing up a pillar.

Web sites, by contrast, place as much emphasis on images as on words and make lateral movement easier than straightforward progress. Votaries urge the reader to give up the crutches of traditional plot and argument in favor of the self-plotted curves and swoops of this new form of reading. They emphasize that the protean text of the Web, which may change hour by hour as a political crisis unrolls or a hurricane is tracked, fits the conditions of modern life, with its lack of stable beliefs and even of stable human selves. Similarly, they argue that Web sites—which can be dipped into freely for one article or image, and which encourage back talk from their readers—fit the dispersed nature of modern life better than stable print media. Others note that this new form of reading is not only dynamic but also interactive. Writers can count the num-ber of hits an article receives on a Web page; readers can use an author's name, laid out in hypertext, to send an e-mail response. Discussion strings make it possible for all involved to carry on elaborate debates about a provocative col-umn or review. At their most intense, these discussions metamorphosize into a new kind of reading and writing community—all of whose members exert pressure on the choice and treatment of topics, making the Web site itself in-teractive. Thus, *Talking Points Memo (TPM),* a liberal political site run by Josh Marshall, employs several reporters, but also depends on local information sent in by readers around the country. During Hurricane Katrina, readers who worked for the federal government, tracking climate and weather conditions, provided *TPM* with a level of precision and expertise in reporting that no newspaper or broadcast news service could match.

Critics, by contrast, heap obloquy on many features of these new texts—from the fact that some of them overemphasize design, while their words are often transcribed from out-of-copyright sources or compiled by out-of-work "content providers," to the ubiquitous presence of bright marginal strips of advertising. They insist that the prevalence of such fragmented, la-bile texts may compromise—even undermine—the print-based ability to grasp complex arguments and reason about them that seems critical to pre-serving a vital liberal democracy. And they argue that the growth of multiple tiny communities based on the Web will undermine the larger social community in which we all live.

Votaries and critics alike exaggerate the novelty of the changes the Web has wrought. The new media of the decades around 1900 transformed the presentation of texts just as radically as the Web has. Newspapers appeared regularly in multiple editions, rapidly bringing headline stories up to date. In Berlin, by the end of the nineteenth century, one of the major papers could be printed, packed, and on its way to distribution within eighteen minutes after news reached the central office. The existence of several editions each day meant that the newspaper could follow a breaking story—like the hunt for an escaped murderer—stage by stage. Sometimes, of course, editors themselves promoted, or even created, stories of this kind. The *Berliner Zeitung* sent a reporter through the city, for example, while urging readers to try to catch him—an effective way to galvanize readers' interest and commitment, brilliantly evoked by Graham Greene in *Brighton Rock*. Kiosks, pillars, and cafés made each new edition available to readers. The city itself spoke, as Peter Fritzsche has shown, spewing an endless stream of stories and sense impressions over its inhabitants.[25]

Magazines, naturally, were not as protean as newspapers: their content was fixed in each weekly or monthly edition. But their massive advertising revenue and longer lead time enabled them to experiment with even more varied ways of presenting text and advertisement. Editors self-consciously tried to make them into coherent works of art: not uninterrupted blocks of type, but artful combinations of word and image. William Dean Howells, describing the creation of a fictional magazine, *Every Other Week,* in his 1890 novel *A Hazard of New Fortunes,* showed the editor and owner realizing that they must hire an art director. He, in turn, commissioned what Howells calls "graphical comments" appropriate to each story.

Eventually, the *Gesamtkunstwerk* of the American magazine adopted a particular, commercial form. Publishers learned that they could cut subscription and newsstand prices radically, so long as they sold enough ads to recoup the loss they made on every copy of their magazine. Richard Ohmann and others have shown that as advertising itself became more professional, editors offered to work with advertisers and the makers of products, turning their magazines into *magasins* in the French sense: collections of attractive products, some to be read and others to be bought, rather like the Sears catalogue of the same period. They encouraged readers to take a serious interest in advertising by running contests for new slogans, producing series of advertising collections that could be removed from the magazines and collected in albums, and even allowing writers to mention particular products, favorably, in their stories. Most important, the form of the magazine mutated, as editors introduced the new practice of "ad-streaming." Like Web sites, magazines used advertising to generate their income stream, they adopted as their standard form a long ribbon of text that unrolled between colorful ads, and they demanded that readers develop new skills.

The experienced reader soon learned how to consume each magazine: not in a single, uniform way, like the old, learned quarterlies, which had confronted readers with immense blocks of text, but as a collection of materials useable for different purposes. Early in the 1950s, a *New Yorker* reader wrote in to the magazine that each copy was "as efficiently used up around here as the packing plants' claim for their pork. The covers go in an art scrap book, cartoons & quips clipped and sent to a brother in Korea, & the fiction & book reviews are passeled out among less fortunate acquaintances who have earned my good will."[26] Some critics deplored the fact that illustrated newspapers and magazines, designed for a world in which "the rhythm of life pounds short and hard," did not foster the "tranquil and concentrated focus" and "surrender" demanded of the true reader. They noted querulously that the new emphasis on visual information was designed to give a magazine "impact" in a life too hectic to allow the individuals to read (both remarks were made by German critics in the 1920s, lamenting the Americanization of German magazine culture.) The oddly familiar language of these critiques reminds us that our media landscape retains, and will retain, elements that would have been familiar generations ago.

The newspapers and magazines of the early years of the century did not have the near-total flexibility of the modern Web site, and their readers could not skip from one hot link to the next. But their mixture of commerce and culture, their juxtapositions of serious and trivial contents, and their ability to confront readers with the shock of the new were as widely noticed—and sometimes as forcefully deplored—by contemporaries as the similar features of the Web. Like the Web, too, the new magazines and newspapers invited their readers to see themselves as members of a single community. The evidence suggests that they often succeeded. Readership surveys collected information about audience response; readers' letters identified particular stories and articles as controversial or rewarding; and readers of magazines as diverse as the *Saturday Evening Post* and the *New Yorker* professed that they kept their subscriptions because—as readers wrote to the latter—it says "what I think and feel"; "It has to be good sense, because we agree with everything you say." Those who sent in such messages, as a study of the *New Yorker* by Mary Corey has established, included a bird curator at a museum, a UN official, an editor, doctors, enlisted men, a British war bride and a former chorus boy—about as diverse a group as have ever shared any serious interest.[27] In some ways, the world of writing has not so much been transformed as restored to a ghostly, faster-moving simulacrum of the media world of half a century ago.

By contrast, the world of serious reading does seem to be changing, in two related ways. As readers gain private, off-site access to treasures once confined to the British and New York Public Libraries, they may stay home in their pajamas rather than schlepping in, like the hard-pressed content providers in George Gissing's *New Grub Street,* to the Valley of the Shadow of the Book. Even in the great years of the nineteenth- and twentieth-century metropolitan library, after all, the greatest scholars—the historian Leopold von Ranke, for example, or the social scientist Werner Sombart—did most of their work in their own enormous collections. In Berlin, where great professors were public figures, richly paid, these might contain as many as 30,000 books. It is hard to feel anything but pleasure at the thought that Google may enable impoverished graduate students to emulate the mandarins of yesterday, and work where they like.

Yet great city and university libraries have long been America's symbolic centers of culture—the nurseries of Kazins and Hofstadters. Traditionally, they have occupied the grandest of public buildings—material, public testimony to the powers of the book. Pursuing one's studies in an environment like this was a way of learning an artisanal craft. Librarians, older scholars, and graduate students passed on informal advice. The library's own ways of collecting information—like the magnificent subject cards in the old New York Public Library catalogue—directed the reader to extraordinary finds. And a sighting of a celebrity like Frank Manuel or Barbara Tuchman could leave a young student vibrating for weeks with the sense that hard work might lift one from the Valley of the Shadow to Parnassus.

A number of great American cities have recently built big central libraries. They range in style from neo-Beaux-Arts celebrations of the traditional culture of the book to bright, glassy, open civic centers. And as Witold Rybczynski pointed out in a recent "slide-show essay" in *Slate,* the heavy facades and elegant, sterile reading rooms of the libraries in Chicago and San Francisco seem to be crying out "Books still matter! Conan the Librarian is still in charge!" to a public that shows little interest. By contrast, the newer libraries in Seattle and Kansas City are hip, appealing structures that deliberately depart from tradition. Rem Koolhaas did not even equip his ziggurat in Seattle with a reading room. These buildings pull in crowds composed of everyone, from graduate students to tourists to homeless people.[28]

The lesson Rybczynski draws is simple. Books have probably passed their sell-by date, as some prophets claim. Libraries, as such, are dinosaurs, doomed to extinction. But build a really attractive building and call it a central library—a mall with natural light, interesting spaces, and a comic book shop, like the new library in Salt Lake City—and the punters will come. Not for the books, but for the excitement and the human connections that only a great public space can generate. Libraries, in other words, can survive. But if they insist on their original mission, they will turn into enormous, handsome ghost ships, sailing along with all lights on and no passengers. On the other hand, if administrators decide that they can save libraries by sweeping all their dusty, old-fashioned books into off-site storage and filling their cavernous, loftlike spaces with the cafes and fast computers that might woo the crowds back, these treasure houses will degenerate into bigger versions of Starbucks or Barnes & Noble: splendid public spaces that people frequent to use electronic sources, most of which they could find anywhere. Neither fate seems desirable: and neither will restore the old function of the library as a training center for the crafts of scholarship.

As the books head for off-site warehouses, moreover, reading itself seems to be under threat. The newspapers and magazines of the years around 1900 coexisted with more stable forms of writing—above all the serious book—and presupposed the superiority of engaged, informed study of texts even when they did not promote it. By contrast, the hot link and the search engine seem to symbolize a particular postmodern way of approaching texts: rapid, superficial, appropriative, and individualistic. Readers do not need to master catalogues, to walk stacks, to use bibliographies—much less to work through stacks of books. All they need to do is enter a word or two into Google and compile the results. Some fear that the old-fashioned scholar's memory, stored with texts not only read, but digested and turned into marrow and bone, and the old-fashioned reader's deep play with novels and poetry studied for years, have given way to endless bricolage, mosaics assembled by students and writers who know only the bits of texts they pull from the screen.

Listen, for example, to Jonathan Barnes, a specialist on ancient philosophy, describe what the computer database of the *Thesaurus Linguae Graecae* (TLG)—a searchable, full-text archive of ancient Greek texts—has done for his field:

> Load it into your laptop, and you have instant access to virtually the whole of Greek literature. You cut and paste snippets from authors whose very names mean nothing to you. You affirm—and you're right—that a particular word used here by Plato occurs 43 times elsewhere in Greek literature. And you can write an article—or a book—stuffed with prodigious learning. (There are similar things available for Latin.) . . . The TLG is a lovely little resource (I think that's the word) and I use her all the time. But she's strumpet-tongued: she flatters and she deceives. "What an enormous knowledge you have, my young cock—why not let me make a real scholar of you?" And the young cock crows on his dung-hill: he can cite anything and construe nothing.[29]

Barnes's description of the siren song of the TLG will bring no pleasure to anyone who spends time, for example, grading papers or evaluating the work of young writers. The 200,000 titles compiled by a single entrepreneur, Philip Parker, with the aid of algorithms and a staff of programmers, offer a preview of an ugly future.

The shortcuts Barnes describes so witheringly are not confined to classics: in fact, they represent one version of what looks like a period style of approaching text. A report recently commissioned by the British Library and the Joint Information Systems Committee details the reading practices of contemporary university students, using data drawn from actual search strings. Most students begin their searches for information at Google, rather than a library Web page that lists more refined search engines. Those who consult e-book sites stay on them for an average of four minutes. True, students who consult e-journals stay longer: eight minutes, on average. But around 60 percent of them look at no more than three pages of the article in question, and the majority never return to the site. The reading that most students do on the Web takes the form of "dipping," "cross-checking," and "power skimming"—just as the traditionalists croak.

Future Reading

For now and for the foreseeable future, any serious reader will have to know how to travel down two very different roads simultaneously. No one should avoid the broad, smooth, and open road that leads through the screen into an electronic paradise of texts and images. But if you want to know what one of Coleridge's annotated books or an early "Spiderman" comic really looks and feels like, or if you just want to read one of those millions of books that are being digitized but cannot as yet be opened and read—you still have to do it the old way, and you will have to for decades to come. At Kazin's beloved New York Public Library, the staff loves electronic media. The library has made hundreds of thousands of images from its collections accessible on the Web, and Google is digitizing more than a million books from the stacks. Still, the library has done all this in the knowledge that its collections comprise 53 million items. To ensure that as many of these as possible find users, it must keep bums on pews and books and documents in front of readers.

When Paul Holdengräber, the ambassador to New York from the lost realms of European learning, organizes sellout events at Live from the New York Public Library, which thousands more hear as podcasts; or David Ferrerio, who runs the library system day to day, opens Central Branch for the first time to children, they have many ends in view. One is to provide the electronic media that New Yorkers need, in a setting that is not only disciplined and peaceful, but welcoming. Another, and no less important, is to keep the books and manuscripts alive by continuing to forge a democratic public that will come to them.

Sit in your local coffee shop and your laptop can tell you a lot, especially if you wield your search terms adeptly. But if you want deeper, more local knowledge, you will still have to take the narrower path that leads between the lions and up the stone stairs. There—as in great libraries around the world— you will use all the new sources, all the time. You will check musicians' names and dates at Grove Music Online, read Marlowe's Doctor Faustus on Google Books or EEBO, or savor the idiosyncrasies of British justice as exhibited in the online proceedings of the Old Bailey. But these streams of data, rich as they are, will illuminate rather than eliminate the unique books and prints and manuscripts that only the library can put in front of you. For now, and for the foreseeable future, if you want to piece together the richest possible mosaic of documents and texts and images, you will have to do it in those crowded public rooms where sunlight gleams on varnished tables, as it has for more than a century, and knowledge is still embodied in millions of dusty, crumbling, smelly, irreplaceable manuscripts and books.

NOTES

SOURCES

INDEX

Notes

Introduction

1. For discussion, see Martin Lowry, *The World of Aldus Manutius: Business and Scholarship in Renaissance Venice* (Ithaca, N.Y.: Cornell University Press, 1979), 196–199; Martin Davies, *Aldus Manutius: Printer and Publisher of Renaissance Venice* (London: British Library, 1995).

2. For the Platonic Academy, see the contrasting, classical treatments of Arthur Field, *The Origins of the Platonic Academy of Florence* (Princeton, N.J.: Princeton University Press, 1988), and James Hankins, "Cosimo de' Medici and the 'Platonic Academy,'" *Journal of the Warburg and Courtauld Institutes* 53 (1990), 144–162, and "The Myth of the Platonic Academy of Florence," *Renaissance Quarterly* 44 (1991), 429–475. See, more generally, Shulamit Furstenberg-Levi, "The Fifteenth-Century Accademia Pontaniana: An Analysis of Its Institutional Elements," *History of Universities* 20.1 (2006), 33–70.

3. See Michael Warner's remarkable *Publics and Counter-Publics* (New York: Zone, 2005) and *The Letters of the Republic: Publication and the Public Sphere in Eighteenth-Century America* (Cambridge, Mass.: Harvard University Press, 1990).

4. Mark Pattison, *Isaac Casaubon, 1559–1614,* 2nd ed. (Oxford: Clarendon Press, 1892), 438–439.

5. See the excellent study by H. S. Jones, *Intellect and Character in Victorian England: Mark Pattison and the Invention of the Don* (Cambridge: Cambridge University Press, 2007).

6. Pattison, *Isaac Casaubon, 1559–1614,* 364.

7. Isaac Casaubon, *Epistolae,* ed. Th. Janson van Almeloveen (Rotterdam: Fritsch and Böhm, 1709), 537–558, quoted in Isaac Casaubon, *Ephemerides,* ed. John Russell, 2 vols. (Oxford: Clarendon Press, 1850), II, 1228–1229: "Sed me non adeo collegia capiebant, ut Bodlacana Bibliotheca, opus vel Rege dignum, nedum privato. Constat Bodlaeum ducenta millia librarum Gallicarum aut vivum aut morientem contulisse ad ornatum illius bibliothecae. Locus est elegantissimus, quod figuram literae T exprimit. Partem quae stipitem erectum exprimit, olim Princeps aliquis e saxo aedificaverat, opere satis magnifico; alteram partem Bodlaeus adjecit magnificentia parem

priori. Inferior pars auditorium est theologicum, cui haud scio an sit aliquod comparandum in Europa. Opus est fornicatum, sed singulari artificio confectum. Superior pars est ipsa bibliotheca valde affabre facta, et ingenti librorum copia referta. Noli cogitare similem hic reperiri librorum Ms. copiam, atque est in Regia: sunt sane et in Anglia Mss. non pauci, sed nihil ad Regias opes. At librorum editorum admirandus est numerus, et qui incrementum quotannis est accepturus: reliquit enim Bodlaeus annuos reditus sane luculentos in eam rem. Quamdiu Oxonii fui, totos dies in bibliotheca posui, nam libri efferri non possunt, patet vero bibliotheca omnibus studiosis per horas septem aut octo quotidie. Videres igitur multos semper studiosos paratis illis dapibus cupide fruentes, quod me non parum delectabat."

8. See Paul Nelles, "The Uses of Orthodoxy and Jacobean Erudition: Thomas James and the Bodleian Library," *History of Universities* 22.1 (2007), 21–70.

9. Debora Shuger, *The Renaissance Bible: Scholarship, Sacrifice, and Subjectivity* (Berkeley: University of California Press, 1994).

10. A. D. Nuttall, *Dead from the Waist Down: Scholars and Scholarship in Literature and the Popular Imagination* (New Haven, Conn.: Yale University Press, 2003).

11. Casaubon, *Ephemerides*, II, 858: "Legi etiam hodie librum 1. epistolarum J. Camerarii in primo tomo a filiis edito. Qui liber cum sit ad summos Principes scriptus, magna ex parte non inutiliter legetur ab his, quibus necessitas invasit similium literarum exarandarum. Est enim proprius quidam stylus, maxime propter titulos Principibus dandos, et formam compellandi in tertia persona. Haec inter dolores summosque animi cruciatus scribebam, ut a cogitatione de uxore et meis omnibus animum revocarem." The notes that Casaubon took on Camerarius's letters are preserved in Bodleian Library MS Casaubon 25, 121 verso–123 verso. Cf. Rittershusius's introduction to the correspondence of Pliny with Trajan in 1609 (*Liber commentarius in epistolas Plinii et Trajani* [Amberg: Schönfeld, 1609]), 4: "Taceo, quod etiam formulae hinc sumi possunt, quas imitemur in scribendo ad Principes aliosque Magistratus superiores: nec non in relationib. sive consultationibus ad ipsos faciendis, super causis et quaestionibus arduis ac dubiis, et judicia ipsorum requirendo . . ." and 5: "Sicut etiam relationib. talibus plenus est totus liber decimus Epistolarum Symmachi ad Theodosium Imperatorem . . ."

12. Casaubon, *Ephemerides,* II, 880: "Adfui illi et coenanti, quod omne tempus positum est in vituperatione miraculorum fatuorum, stultorum, quae Rex legerat, opinor, in nono libro Plessaei. Affirmat Rex Papam vel eo nomine Anti-Christum esse, quod res tam falsas et ridiculas populo Christiano obtrudat pro veris credendas. Impie sane. Sed an sint plane omnia falsa nescio, neque item an universae Ecclesiae ea culpa sit imputanda. Sed de his alibi, si Deus volet . . ."

13. Pattison, *Isaac Casaubon, 1559–1614,* 139.

14. Casaubon, note in his copy of Joseph Scaliger, *Thesaurus Temporum* (1606), Cambridge University Library Adv.a.3.4, "Animadversiones," 161: "de hoc tempore vide Keplerum de nat. Christi. nam errat, opinor, Scal." Casaubon made his favorable view of Kepler's work public in his critique of Baronio, *De rebus sacris et*

ecclesiasticis exercitationes xvi, ad Cardinalis Baronii Prolegomena in Annales et primam eorum partem, de D.N. Iesu Christi nativitate, vita, passione, assumptione, cum prolegomenis auctoris, in quibus de Baronianis annalibus candide disputatur (Geneva: Sumptibus Ioannis Antonii et Samuelis De Tournes, 1654), 124.

15. Casaubon, *Epistolae*, 547: "Ego, etsi detestor ex animo illius perfidiam, non possum tamen non aliqua ejus tangi commiseratione, propter excellentem ipsius doctrinam."

1. A Sketch Map of a Lost Continent

1. Noelle d'Argònne, *Mélanges d'histoire et de littérature, recuillis par M. de Vigneul-Marville*, 2 vols. (Paris, 1699–1700), quoted by Paul Dibon, "Communication in the Respublica Litteraria in the 17th Century," *Res publica litterarum* 1 (1978), 43–56, at 43; for an elegant brief survey of the Republic and its institutions, see Didier Masseau, *L'invention de l'intellectuel dans l'Europe du xviiie siècle* (Paris: Presses universitaires de France, 1994). Collections of essays that help to set the scene include Herbert Jaumann, ed., *Die europäische Gelehrtenrepublik im Zeitalter des Konfessionalismus = The European Republic of Letters in the Age of Confessionalism* (Wiesbaden: Harrassowitz, 2001) and Rudolf Keck, Erhard Wiersding, and Klaus Wittstadt, eds., *Literaten—Kleriker—Gelehrte: Zur Geschichte der Gebildeten im vormodernen Europa* (Cologne: Böhlau, 1996).

2. Though the Republic, like the rest of European society, was certainly patriarchal and hierarchical, women played vital public roles in the culture of erudition. See most recently April Shelford, *Transforming the Republic of Letters: Pierre-Daniel Huet and European Intellectual Life, 1650–1720* (Rochester, N.Y.: University of Rochester Press, 2007), and more generally the pioneering study by Dena Goodman, *The Republic of Letters: A Cultural History of the French Enlightenment* (Ithaca, N.Y.: Cornell University Press, 1994).

3. For case studies in these processes of interdisciplinary scholarship, see Gianna Pomata and Nancy Siraisi, eds., *Historia: Empiricism and Erudition in Early Modern Europe* (Cambridge, Mass.: MIT Press, 2005). One of the richest full-scale studies is Nancy Siraisi, *History, Medicine, and the Traditions of Renaissance Learning* (Ann Arbor: University of Michigan Press, 2007).

4. Paula Findlen, *Possessing Nature: Museums, Collecting, and Scientific Culture in Early Modern Italy* (Berkeley: University of California Press, 1994); Horst Bredekamp, *The Lure of Antiquity and the Cult of the Machine: The Kunstkammer and the Evolution of Nature, Art and Technology*, tr. Allison Brown (Princeton, N.J.: Markus Wiener, 1995); Bredekamp, *Die Fenster der Monade: Gottfried Wilhelm Leibniz' Theater der Natur und Kunst* (Berlin: Akademie, 2004). For excellent recent surveys of the habitats of early modern savants, see *The Cambridge History of Science*, vol. III: *Early Modern Science*, ed. Lorraine Daston and Katharine Park (Cambridge: Cambridge University Press, 2006).

5. Anthony Grafton, *Bring Out Your Dead: The Past as Revelation* (Cambridge, Mass.: Harvard University Press, 2001), chap. 6.

6. Daniel Stolzenberg, ed., *The Great Art of Knowing: The Baroque Encyclopedia of Athanasius Kircher* (Stanford, Calif.: Stanford University Libraries, 2001); Paula Findlen, ed., *Athanasius Kircher: The Last Man Who Knew Everything* (New York: Routledge, 2004).

7. See esp. Wilhelm Kühlmann, *Gelehrtenrepublik und Fürstenstaat: Entwicklung und Kritik des deutschen Späthumanismus in der Literatur des Barockzeitalters* (Tübingen: Niemeyer, 1982); Mark Morford, *Stoics and Neostoics: Rubens and the Circle of Lipsius* (Princeton, N.J.: Princeton University Press, 1991); Jacob Soll, "Amelot de La Houssaye (1634–1706) Annotates Tacitus," *Journal of the History of Ideas* 61 (2000), 167–187; Soll, *Publishing the Prince: History, Reading, and the Birth of Political Criticism* (Ann Arbor: University of Michigan Press, 2005); Grafton, *Bring Out Your Dead,* chap. 12.

8. See most recently Constance Furey, *Erasmus, Contarini, and the Religious Republic of Letters* (Cambridge: Cambridge University Press, 2006).

9. Lisa Jardine, *The Awful End of Prince William the Silent: The First Assassination of a Head of State with a Handgun* (London: HarperCollins, 2005).

10. Brad Gregory, *Salvation at Stake: Christian Martyrdom in Early Modern Europe* (Cambridge, Mass.: Harvard University Press, 1999).

11. See e.g. R. J. W. Evans, *The Making of the Habsburg Monarchy, 1550–1700: An Interpretation* (Oxford: Clarendon Press, 1979).

12. For case studies, see e.g. R. J. W. Evans, *Rudolf II and His World: A Study in Intellectual History, 1576–1612* (Oxford: Clarendon Press, 1972; corrected ed., London: Thames and Hudson, 1997); Howard Louthan, *Johannis Crato and the Austrian Habsburgs: Reforming a Counter-Reform Court* (Princeton, N.J.: Princeton Theological Seminary, 1994); Louthan, *The Quest for Compromise: Peacemakers in Counter-Reformation Vienna* (Cambridge: Cambridge University Press, 1997).

13. Annie Barnes, *Jean Le Clerc (1657–1736) et la république des lettres* (Paris: Droz, 1938); Erich Haase, *Einführung in die Literatur des Refuge: Der Beitrag der französischen Protestanten zur Entwicklung analytischer Denkformen am Ende des 17. Jahrhunderts* (Berlin: Duncker und Humblot, 1959); Paul Dibon, *Regards sur la Hollande du Siècle d'or* (Naples: Vivarium, 1990); Hugh Trevor-Roper, "The Religious Origins of the Enlightenment," in *Religion, the Reformation, and Social Change* (London: Macmillan, 1967).

14. See e.g. Mordechai Feingold, ed., *Jesuit Science and the Republic of Letters* (Cambridge, Mass.: MIT Press, 2003).

15. Justin Stagl, *Apodemiken: Eine räsonnierte Bibliographie der reisetheoretischen Literatur des 16., 17. und 18. Jahrhunderts* (Paderborn: Schöningh, 1983); Stagl, *A History of Curiosity: The Theory of Travel, 1550–1800* (Chur: Harwood, 1995); Joan-Pau Rubiés, "Instructions for Travellers: Teaching the Eye to See," *History and Anthropology* 9 (1996), 139–190; Rubiés, *Travel and Ethnology in the Renaissance:*

South India through European Eyes, 1250–1625 (Cambridge: Cambridge University Press, 2000); Rubiés, "Travel Writing as a Genre: Facts, Fictions and the Invention of a Scientific Discourse in Early Modern Europe," *Journeys: The International Journal of Travel and Travel Writing* 1 (2000), 5–33; Paola Molino, "Alle origini della Methodus Apodemica di Theodor Zwinger: La collaborazione di Hugo Blotius, fra empirismo ed universalismo," *Codices Manuscripti* (forthcoming).

16. See in general M. A. E. Nickson, *Early Autograph Albums in the British Museum* (London: British Museum, 1970). For a superb example and case study, see Chris Heesakkers, ed., *Een netwerk aan de basis van de Leidse universiteit: Het Album amicorum van Janus Dousa: Facsimile-uitgave van hs. Leiden UB, BPL 1406* (Leiden: Leiden University Library, 2000).

17. Mario Biagioli, *Galileo's Instruments of Credit: Telescopes, Images, Secrecy* (Chicago: University of Chicago Press, 2006).

18. Deborah Harkness, *The Jewel House: Elizabethan London and the Scientific Revolution* (New Haven, Conn.: Yale University Press, 2007).

19. Sarah Ross, "The Birth of Feminism: Woman as Intellect in Renaissance Italy and England" (PhD dissertation, Northwestern University, 2006); Shelford, *Transforming the Republic of Letters;* see also David Norbrook, "Women, the Republic of Letters, and the Public Sphere in the Mid-Seventeenth Century," *Criticism* 46 (2004), 223–240, and Carol Pal, "Republic of Women: Rethinking the Republic of Letters, 1630–1680" (PhD dissertation, Stanford University, 2006).

20. See e.g. Otto Brunner, *Adeliges Landleben und europäischer Geist: Leben und Werk Wolf Helmhards von Hobburg, 1612–1688* (Salzburg: Müller, 1949); Manfred Fleischer, *Späthumanismus in Schlesien: Ausgewählte Aufsätze* (Munich: Delp, 1984); Morford, *Stoics and Neostoics.*

21. On the further development of the Republic, see inter alia Goodman, *Republic of Letters;* Daniel Roche, *Les républicains de lettres: Gens de culture et lumières au XVIIIe siècle* (Paris: Fayard, 1988); and Lawrence Brockliss, *Calvet's Web: Enlightenment and the Republic of Letters in Eighteenth-Century France* (Oxford: Oxford University Press, 2002).

22. For a fascinating comparative study of the similarities and differences between two provinces of the Republic, see John Robertson, *The Case for the Enlightenment: Scotland and Naples, 1680–1760* (Cambridge: Cambridge University Press, 2005).

23. The vast literature on these institutions goes back to such classics as Harcourt Brown, *Scientific Organizations in Seventeenth Century France (1620–1680)* (Baltimore, Md.: Williams and Wilkins, 1934). More recent studies include Roger Hahn, *The Anatomy of a Scientific Institution: The Paris Academy of Sciences, 1666–1803* (Berkeley: University of California Press, 1971); Stephen Shapin and Simon Schaffer, *Leviathan and the Air-Pump: Hobbes, Boyle, and the Experimental Life* (Princeton, N.J.: Princeton University Press, 1985); and David Freedberg, *The Eye of the Lynx: Galileo, His Friends, and the Beginnings of Modern Natural History*

(Chicago: University of Chicago Press, 2002). For a rapid recent review that emphasizes the connections between academies and courts, see Bruce Moran, "Courts and Academies," in *The Cambridge History of Science,* vol. III: *Early Modern Science,* 251–271.

24. See William Eamon, *Science and the Secrets of Nature: Books of Secrets in Early Modern Culture* (Princeton, N.J.: Princeton University Press, 1994); Donald Dickson, *The Tessera of Antilia: Utopian Brotherhoods and Secret Societies in the Early Seventeenth Century* (Leiden: Brill, 1998).

25. See respectively Klaus Garber, "Paris, die Hauptstadt des europäischen Späthumanismus. Jacques Auguste de Thou und das Cabinet Dupuy," in *Res publica litteraria: Die Institutionen der Gelehrsamkeit in der frühen Neuzeit,* ed. Sebastian Neumeister and Conrad Wiedemann, 2 vols. (Wiesbaden: Harrassowitz, 1987), I, 71–92; Antoine Coron, " 'Ut prosint aliis': Jacques Auguste de Thou et sa bibliothèque," in *Histoire des bibliothèque françaises,* vol. II: *Les bibliothèque sous l'Ancien Régime,* ed. Claude Jolly (Paris: Promodis, 1988), 101–125; Howard Solomon, *Public Welfare, Science, and Propaganda in Seventeenth-Century France: The Innovations of Théophraste Renaudot* (Princeton, N.J.: Princeton University Press, 1972); Simone Mazauric, *Savoirs et philosophie à Paris dans la première moitié du XVIIe siècle: Les conférences du Bureau d'adresse de Théophraste Renaudot, 1633–1642* (Paris: Publications de la Sorbonne, 1997); and Kathleen Anne Wellman, *Making Science Social: The Conferences of Théophraste Renaudot, 1633–1642* (Norman: University of Oklahoma Press, 2003).

26. For a superb case study, see Didier Kahn, "The Rosicrucian Hoax in France (1623–24)," in *Secrets of Nature: Astrology and Alchemy in Early Modern Europe,* ed. Anthony Grafton and William Newman (Cambridge, Mass.: MIT Press, 2001), 235–344.

27. On these and other technical aspects of communication in the Republic of Letters—as well as on much more—see the fine synthesis of Hans Bots and Françoise Waquet, *La République des Lettres* (Paris: Belin, 1997), as well as Bots and Waquet, eds., *Commercium litterarium, 1600–1750* (Amsterdam: APA–Holland University Press, 1994).

28. Kathy Eden, *Friends Hold All Things in Common: Tradition, Intellectual Property, and the Adages of Erasmus* (New Haven, Conn.: Yale University Press, 2001).

29. Ibid.

30. Anne Goldgar, *Impolite Learning: Conduct and Community in the Republic of Letters, 1680–1750* (New Haven, Conn.: Yale University Press, 1995); Brian Ogilvie, *The Science of Describing: Natural History in Renaissance Europe* (Chicago: University of Chicago Press, 2006).

31. On the practices of correspondents in the Republic, see Toon Van Houdt, Jan Papy, Gilbert Tournoy, and Constant Matheeussen, eds., *Self-Presentation and Social Identification: The Rhetoric and Pragmatics of Letter-Writing in Early Modern*

Times (Leuven: Leuven University Press, 2002), and the forthcoming proceedings of the conference on "Observation in Early Modern Letters, 1500–1650," held at the Warburg Institute on 29–30 June 2007, and organized by Charles Burnett and Dirk van Miert.

32. See Ann Blair, *The Theater of Nature: Jean Bodin and Renaissance Science* (Princeton, N.J.: Princeton University Press, 1997); Blair, "Reading Strategies for Coping with Information Overload, ca. 1550–1700," *Journal of the History of Ideas* 64 (2003), 11–28; Richard Yeo, "Ephraim Chambers's *Cyclopaedia* (1728) and the Tradition of Commonplaces," *Journal of the History of Ideas* 57 (1996), 157–175; Yeo, "A Solution to the Multitude of Books: Ephraim Chambers's *Cyclopaedia* (1728) as 'The Best Book in the Universe,' " *Journal of the History of Ideas* 64 (2003), 61–72. See in general Daniel Rosenberg, "Early Modern Information Overload," *Journal of the History of Ideas* 64 (2003), 1–9, and the recent mildly revisionist case study by Noel Malcolm, "William Harrison and His 'Ark of Studies': An Episode in the History of the Organization of Knowledge," *The Seventeenth Century* 19 (2004), 196–232.

33. See Goldgar, *Impolite Learning,* and Martin Gierl, *Pietismus und Aufklärung: Theologische Polemik und die Kommunikationsreform der Wissenschaft am Ende des 17. Jahrhunderts* (Göttingen: Vandenhoeck and Rupprecht, 1997). For earlier efforts to impose order, see also Wilhelm Schmidt-Biggemann, *Topica universalis: Eine Modellgeschichte humanistischer und barocker Wissenschaft* (Hamburg: Meiner, 1983) and Helmut Zedelmaier, *Bibliotheca universalis und bibliotheca selecta: Das Problem der Ordnung des gelehrten Wissens in der frühen Neuzeit* (Cologne: Böhlau, 1992); for a broader range of similar enterprises, see Frank Büttner, Markus Friedrich, and Helmut Zedelmaier, eds., *Sammeln, Ordnen, Veranschaulichen: Zur Wissenskompilatorik in der Frühen Neuzeit* (Münster: LIT, 2003).

34. See Jonathan Israel's influential *Radical Enlightenment: Philosophy and the Making of Modernity, 1650–1750* (Oxford: Oxford University Press, 2001), now somewhat revised and considerably extended in his own *Enlightenment Contested: Philosophy, Modernity, and the Emancipation of Man, 1670–1752* (Oxford: Oxford University Press, 2006).

35. Howard Goodman and Anthony Grafton, "Ricci, the Chinese, and the Toolkits of Textualists," *Asia Major* 3.2 (1990), 95–148.

36. Anthony Grafton, *Defenders of the Text: The Traditions of Scholarship in an Age of Science, 1450–1800* (Cambridge, Mass.: Harvard University Press, 1991), chap. 5.

37. Johannes Reuchlin, *Recommendation whether to Confiscate, Destroy, and Burn All Jewish Books,* tr. and ed. Peter Wortsman, critical introduction by Elisheva Carlebach (New York: Paulist Press, 2000); Erika Rummel, *The Case against Johann Reuchlin: Religious and Social Controversy in Sixteenth-Century Germany* (Toronto: University of Toronto Press, 2002).

38. Hans Guggisberg, *Sebastian Castellio, 1515–1563: Humanist and Defender of Religious Toleration in a Confessional Age,* tr. and ed. Bruce Gordon (Aldershot, U.K.: Ashgate, 2003), 73–152, esp. 88–90.

39. On the complex history of Castellio's reputation, see Hans Guggisberg, *Sebastian Castellio im Urteil seiner Nachwelt vom Späthumanismus bis zur Aufklärung* (Basel: Helbing und Lichtenhahn, 1956). For another study in late humanists' views on toleration, see Gerhard Güldner, *Das Toleranz-Problem in den Niederlanden im Ausgang des 16. Jahrhunderts* (Lübeck: Matthiesen, 1968).

40. See Chapter 6.

41. Unexpectedly, chronology has become popular again in Russia, where the polemical chronologies of the distinguished mathematician Anatoly Fomenko—in which he argues that all of world history has been falsified to make Muscovite society and culture seem younger than those of ancient Greece and Rome—are best sellers.

42. For development of the field in early modern Europe, see in general Anthony Grafton, *Joseph Scaliger,* 2 vols. (Oxford: Clarendon Press, 1983–1993); Grafton, *Defenders of the Text;* Paolo Rossi, *The Dark Abyss of Time: The History of the Earth and the History of Nations from Hooke to Vico,* tr. Lydia G. Cochrane (Chicago: University of Chicago Press, 1984); Sicco Lehmann-Brauns, *Weisheit in der Weltgeschichte: Philosophiegeschichte zwischen Barock und Aufklärung* (Tübingen: Niemeyer, 2004); and Helmut Zedelmaier, *Der Anfang der Geschichte: Studien zur Ursprungsdebatte im 18. Jahrhundert* (Hamburg: Meiner, 2003). On the wider history of scholarship in this period, see e.g. Françoise Waquet, *Le modèle français et l'Italie savante: Conscience de soi et perception de l'autre dans la République des lettres (1660–1750)* (Rome: Ecole Française de Rome; Paris: Boccard, 1989); Helmut Zedelmaier and Martin Mulsow, eds., *Die Praktiken der Gelehrsamkeit in der frühen Neuzeit* (Tübingen: Niemeyer, 2001); and C. R. Ligota and J.-L. Quantin, eds., *History of Scholarship* (Oxford: Clarendon Press, 2006).

43. Grafton, *Bring Out Your Dead,* chap. 10.

44. Grafton, *Scaliger,* II, 699, 703. For a wide-ranging study that sets another branch of late-Renaissance erudition, antiquarianism, into the context of the Republic of Letters, see Peter Miller, *Peiresc's Europe: Learning and Virtue in the Seventeenth Century* (New Haven, Conn.: Yale University Press, 2000).

45. Grafton, *Scaliger,* II, 316–322; Debora Shuger, *The Renaissance Bible: Scholarship, Sacrifice, and Subjectivity* (Berkeley: University of California Press, 1994), chap. 1.

46. For a full treatment of Casaubon's Judaic studies, see Anthony Grafton and Joanna Weinberg, *Isaac Casaubon as a Hebraist* (forthcoming).

47. Marina Rustow, "Karaites, Real and Imagined: Three Cases of Jewish Heresy," *Past and Present* 197 (2007), 35–74.

48. Gerald Geison, *The Private Science of Louis Pasteur* (Princeton, N.J.: Princeton University Press, 1995).

49. For an erudite and elegant recent treatment of the Vossius controversy and its context, see Eric Jorink, *Het "boeck der natuere": Nederlandse geleerden en de wonderen van Gods Schepping, 1575–1715* (Leiden: Primavera Pers, 2006).

50. See Claudine Poulouin, "Les érudits de l'Académie des Inscriptions et Belles-Lettres, marginaux des Lumières?" in *Les marges des Lumières françaises (1750–1789),* ed. Didier Masseau (Paris: Droz, 2004), 199–204. Cf. Mélanie Traversier, "De l'érudition à l'expertise: Saverio Mattei (1742–1795), 'Socrate imaginaire' dans la Naples de Lumières," *Revue historique* 309 (2007), 91–136, and for a radically different presentation on the grandest of scales, see J. G. A. Pocock, *Barbarism and Religion,* 4 vols. to date (Cambridge: Cambridge University Press, 1999).

51. Cf. Noel Malcolm, *Aspects of Hobbes* (Oxford: Clarendon Press, 2002); Jonathan Sheehan, "Sacred and Profane: Idolatry, Antiquarianism and the Polemics of Distinction in the Seventeenth Century," *Past and Present* 192 (2006), 35–66. Cf. more generally Martin Mulsow, *Die drei Ringe: Toleranz und clandestine Gelehrsamkeit bei Mathurin Veyssière La Croze (1661–1739)* (Tübingen: Niemeyer, 2001); Mulsow, "Practices of Unmasking: Polyhistors, Correspondence, and the Birth of Dictionaries of Pseudonymity in Seventeenth-Century Germany," *Journal of the History of Ideas* 67 (2006), 219–250.

52. Jean Le Clerc, *Parrhasiana,* 2 vols. (Amsterdam: Chez les héritiers d'Antoine Schelte, 1699–1701), I, 144.

53. Kristine Haugen, "Imagined Universities: Public Insult and the *Terrae Filius* in Early Modern Oxford," *History of Universities* 16 (2000), 1–31; Martin Mulsow, "Unanständigkeit: Zur Missachtung und Verteidigung des Decorum in der Gelehrtenrepublik der Frühen Neuzeit," *Historische Anthropologie* 8 (2000), 98–118; Mulsow, *Die unanständige Gelehrtenrepublik: Wissen, Libertinage und Kommunikation in der Frühen Neuzeit* (Tübingen: Niemeyer, 2007; English translation, Ann Arbor: University of Michigan Press, forthcoming).

2. A Humanist Crosses Boundaries

1. G. Aliotti, *Epistolae et opuscula,* ed. G. M. Scaramalli (Arezzo, 1769), I, 180–187. On the larger context of these women's visions and the way the image of the Virgin figured in them, see C. Frugoni, "Female Mystics, Visions, and Iconography," in *Women and Religion in Medieval and Renaissance Italy,* ed. D. Bornstein and R. Rusconi, tr. M. J. Schneider (Chicago, 1996), 130–164, and P. Dinzelbacher, *Heilige oder Hexen?* (Zurich, 1995; repr. Reinbek bei Hamburg, 1997). For Francesca Romana and Giovanni Mattiotti, see A. Esposito, "S. Francesca and the Female Religious Communities of Fifteenth-Century Rome," in *Women and Religion,* ed. Bornstein and Rusconi, 197–218 at 199–200; on Turrecremata, see T. M. Izbicki, *Protector of the Faith: Cardinal Johannes de Turrecremata and the Defense of the Institutional Church* (Washington, D.C., 1981).

2. Aliotti, *Epistolae et opuscula,* I, 274–276.

3. Ibid., 406.

4. Until recently, most scholars accepted the view that Alberti completed *De pictura* (the Latin form of his work) in Florence by 1435, and *Della pittura* (the Italian form) before July 1436, when he dedicated it to Filippo Brunelleschi. See C. Grayson, "Studi su Leon Battista Alberti," *Rinascimento* 4 (1953), 45–62 at 54–62, and "The Text of Alberti's *De pictura*," *Italian Studies* 23 (1968), 71–92, both reprinted in his *Studi su Leon Battista Alberti*, ed. P. Clut (Florence, 1998), 57–66, 245–269. See, however, L. Bertolini's pointed summary of later discussions, emphasizing that some internal evidence supports the priority of the Italian text, in *Leon Battista Alberti*, ed. J. Rykwert and A. Engel (Milan, 1994), 423–424. Most recently, R. Sinisgalli, *Il nuovo De pictura di Leon Battista Alberti/The New De Pictura of Leon Battista Alberti* (Rome, 2006) offers a new summary of the evidence that supports the priority of the Italian (e.g. 43–45).

5. L. B. Alberti, *De pictura*, II.41, in *On Painting and On Sculpture*, ed. and tr. C. Grayson (London, 1972), in Alberti, *Opere volgari*, ed. C. Grayson (Bari, Italy, 1960–1973), and in Sinisgalli, *Il nuovo De pictura di Leon Battista Alberti*, 207–208: "Animos deinde spectantium movebit historia . . ." Future citations are by book and section number, since these are uniform in all three editions.

6. Ibid., III.60: "Sed cum sit summum pictoris opus historia, in qua quidem omnis rerum copia et elegantia adesse debet"; cf. II.33: "Amplissimum pictoris opus historia"; II.35: "Amplissimum pictoris opus non colossus sed historia."

7. L. B. Alberti, *Kleinere Kunsttheoretische Schriften*, ed. and tr. H. Janitschek (Vienna, 1877): "Weil aber das Geschichtsbild die höchste Leistung des Malers ist . . ."

8. L. B. Alberti, *On Painting*, tr. J. R. Spencer (London, 1956; repr. with corrections, New Haven, Conn., 1966), 70, translating *Della pittura*, 33: "Grandissima opera del pittore sarà l'istoria."

9. Ibid., 23–28 at 24.

10. This approach to Renaissance art theory was first pursued by R. W. Lee, who emphasized the role of poetics in his classic article "Ut pictura poesis," *Art Bulletin* 22 (1940), 197ff., later reprinted in book form (New York, 1967); for Alberti and rhetoric, see esp. appendix 2, "Inventio, Dispositio, Elocutio." The role of ancient literary theory in Alberti's work was clarified by C. Gilbert, "Antique Frameworks for Renaissance Art Theory: Alberti and Pino," *Marsyas* 3 (1943–1945), 87–106. More recent studies, while differing on the structure and models for *On Painting*, have tended to stress rhetoric more than poetics; see esp. J. R. Spencer, "*Ut rhetorica pictura*: A Study in Quattrocento Theory of Painting," *Journal of the Warburg and Courtauld Institutes* 20 (1957), 26–44; E. H. Gombrich, "A Classical Topos in the Introduction to Alberti's *Della pittura*," *Journal of the Warburg and Courtauld Institutes* 20 (1957), 173; A. Chastel, "Die humanistischen Formeln als Rahmenbegriffe der Kunstgeschichte und Kunsttheorie des Quattrocento," *Kunstchronik* 5 (1954), 119–122, and *Art et humanisme à Florence au temps de Laurent le Magnifique* (Paris, 1959); S. L. Alpers, "*Ekphrasis* and Aesthetic Attitudes in Vasari's *Lives*," *Journal of*

the *Warburg and Courtauld Institutes* 23 (1960), 190–215; A. Ellenius, *De arte pingendi* (Uppsala, 1960); C. W. Westfall, "Painting and the Liberal Arts: Alberti's View," *Journal of the History of Ideas* 30 (1969), 487–506; L. Bek, "Voti frateschi, virtù di umanista e regole di pittore: Cennino Cennini sub specie Albertiana," *Analecta Romana Instituti Danici* 6 (1971), 63–105 at 100; M. Baxandall, *Giotto and the Orators: Humanist Observers of Painting in Italy and the Discovery of Pictorial Composition, 1350–1450* (Oxford, 1971; new ed., Oxford, 1986), and *Painting and Experience in Fifteenth-Century Italy* (Oxford, 1972); N. Maraschio, "Aspetti del bilinguismo albertiano nel 'De pictura,'" *Rinascimento*, ser. II, 12 (1972), 183–228, esp. 187–199; D. R. Edward Wright, "Alberti's *De pictura*: Its Literary Structure and Purpose," *Journal of the Warburg and Courtauld Institutes* 47 (1984), 52–71; D. Rosand, "*Ekphrasis* and the Renaissance of Painting: Observations on Alberti's Third Book," in *Florilegium Columbianum*, ed. K.-L. Selig and R. Somerville (New York, 1987), 147–163; R. Kuhn, "Albertis Lehre über die Komposition als die *Kunst* in der Malerei," *Archiv für Begriffsgeschichte* 28 (1984), 123–178; N. Michels, *Bewegung zwischen Ethos und Pathos* (Münster, 1988), esp. 1–65; P. Panza, *Leon Battista Alberti: Filosofia e teorie dell'arte* (Milan, 1994), 115–126; G. Wolf, " 'Arte superficiem illam fontis amplecti': Alberti, Narziss, und die Erfindung der Malerei," in *Diletto e Maraviglia*, ed. C. Göttler, U. M. Hofstede, K. Patz, and K. Zollikofer (Emsdetten, Germany, 1998), 10–39; M. Gosebruch, " 'Varietas' bei L. B. Alberti und der wissenschaftliche Renaissancebegriff," *Zeitschrift für Kunstgeschichte* 20 (1957), 229–238 (cf. also *Kunstchronik* 9 [1956], 301–302); H. Mühlmann, *Aesthetische Theorie der Renaissance: L. B. Alberti* (Bonn, 1981); and C. Smith, *Architecture in the Culture of Early Humanism* (New York, 1992), which concentrate on connections between rhetoric and architecture in Alberti's thought, but have much to offer students of *On Painting* as well. K. Patz, "Zum begriff der 'Historia' in L. B. Albertis De pictura," *Zeitschrift für Kunstgeschichte* 49 (1986), 269–287, and J. Greenstein, *Mantegna and Painting as Historical Narrative* (Chicago, 1992), both rightly stress Alberti's originality and eclecticism in the use of classical sources.

11. See in general G. Nadel, "Philosophy of History before Historicism," *History and Theory* 3 (1964), 291–315; R. Landfester, *Historia magistra vitae* (Geneva, 1972); M. Miglio, *Storiografia pontificia del Quattrocento* (Bologna, 1975); R. Koselleck, "Historia magistra vitae: Über die Auflösung des Topos im Horizont neuzeitlich bewegter Geschichte," in *Vergangene zukunft* (Frankfurt, 1984), 38–66; E. Kessler, "Das rhetorische Modell der Historiographie," in *Formen der Geschichtsschreibung*, ed. R. Koselleck et al. (Munich, 1982), 37–85; and, for the larger context, see E. Cochrane, *Historians and Historiography in the Italian Renaissance* (Chicago, 1981), and A. Grafton, *What Was History?* (Cambridge, 2007).

12. Alberti, *On the Art of Building in Ten Books*, tr. J. Rykwert, N. Leach, and R. Tavernor (Cambridge, Mass., 1988), 7.10, 220 (slightly altered); for the original, see *De re aedificatoria*, ed. G. Orlandi, tr. P. Portoghesi (Milan, 1966), II, 609–611:

"Et picturam ego bonam—nam turpare quidem parietem est, non pingere, quod male pingas—non minore voluptate animi contemplabor, quam legero bonam historian. Pictor uterque est: ille verbis pingit, hic penniculo docet rem; caetera utrisque paria et communia sunt. In utrisque et ingenio maximo et incredibili diligentia opus est." This passage has been quoted in a similar connection by M. B. Katz, *Leon Battista Alberti and the Humanist Theory of the Arts* (Washington, D.C., 1978), 20.

13. See Alberti, *De re aedificatoria*, II, 610n2.

14. Greenstein, *Mantegna and Painting as Historical Narrative*, chap. 2.

15. Two exceptions should be noted: Grayson dismissed the question as insignificant in his introduction to *On Painting and On Sculpture*, 13, as do C. Hope and E. McGrath in "Artists and Humanists," in *The Cambridge Companion to the Renaissance Humanism*, ed. J. Kraye (Cambridge, 1996), 161–188 at 166. The authors in question rightly point out that Alberti did not coin the term "historia"—a point on which others have repeatedly gone wrong. However, the fact that the term was not new does not imply that Alberti's usage was conventional or simple.

16. J. Schlosser Magnino, *Die Kunstliteratur* (Vienna, 1924), tr. by F. Rossi as *La letteratura artistica*, 3rd ed., ed. O. Kurz (Florence, 1977, repr. 1979), 121–129.

17. See M. Tafuri, "*Cives esse non licere.* Niccolò V e Leon Battista Alberti," in *Ricerca del Rinascimento: Principi, Città, Architetti* (Turin, 1992), 33–88.

18. For the earliest formulation and application of this rule, see L. D. Reynolds and N. G. Wilson, *Scribes and Scholars,* 3rd ed. (Oxford, 1991), 13–14.

19. See e.g. A. Grafton, *Commerce with the Classics* (Ann Arbor, Mich., 1997), chap. 2.

20. C. Hope, "Aspects of Criticism in Art and Literature in Sixteenth-Century Italy," *Word and Image* 4 (1988), 1–10 at 1–2.

21. See R. Pfeiffer, "Küchenlatein," *Philologus* 86 (1931), 455–459, reprinted in *Ausgewählte Schriften,* ed. W. Bühler (Munich, 1960), 183–187.

22. Alberti, *On the Art of Building in Ten Books,* 6.1, 154; for the original, see *De re aedificatoria*, II, 441: "Accedebat quod ista tradidisset non culta; sic enim loquebatur, ut Latini Graecum videri voluisse, Graeci locutum Latine vaticinentur; res autem ipsa in sese porrigenda neque Latinum neque Graecum fuisse testetur, ut par sit non scripsisse hunc nobis, qui ita scripserit, ut non intelligamus."

23. See esp. H. Harth, "Niccolò Niccoli als literarischer Zensor: Untersuchungen zur Textgeschichte von Poggios 'De avaritia,' " *Rinascimento,* new ser., 7 (1967), 29–53.

24. G. Ponte, "Lepidus e Libripeta," *Rinascimento* 12 (1972), 237–265.

25. M. Miglio, "Il ritorno a Roma: Varianti di una costante nella tradizione dell'antico; le scelte pontificie," in *Scritture, scrittori e storia* (Rome, 1993), II, 144.

26. See L. Goggi Carotti's note on this point in her edition of L. B. Alberti, *De commodis litterarum atque incommodis* (Florence, 1976), 42–43.

27. See e.g. the famous letter of Leonardo Dati and Tommasso Ceffi to Alberti, offering a critique of *I libri della famigilia,* in Dati, *Epistolae xxxiii,* ed. L. Mehus

(Florence, 1743), 13, 18–20, and C. Grayson's note in Alberti, *Opere volgari*, I, 380. Such exchanges, often resulting in substantial revisions, formed a normal part of the humanist system of publication before printing; see the classic study of P. O. Kristeller, "De traditione operum Marsilii Ficini," in *Supplementum Ficinianum*, ed. Kristeller, 2 vols. (Florence, 1937); Harth, "Niccolò Niccoli als literarischer Zensor"; and, more recently, A. Grafton, "Correctores Corruptores? Notes on the Social History of Editing," in *Editing Texts/Texte Edieren*, ed. G. W. Most, *Aporemata: Kritische Studien zur Philologiegeschichte* (Göttingen, 1998), II, 54–75.

28. For some of these varied senses, see e.g. Aulus Gellius, *Noctes Atticae* 1.8.1; Cicero, *Epistolae ad Atticum* 1.16.18; and Ovid, *Amores* 2.4.44.

29. "Leon Battista Alberti. *Philodoxeos fabula.* Edizione critica a cura di Lucia Cesarini Martinelli," *Rinascimento,* 2nd ser., 17 (1977), 111–234 at 144–145: "Idcirco titulus 'Philodoxeos' fabule est: namque 'philo' amo, 'doxa' vero gloria dicitur. Huius Doxe soror Phemia, quam eandem Latini proximo vocabulo famam nuncupant; has equidem, quod Romam omnes historie fuisse glorie domicilium testentur, merito ambas esse matronas Romanas fingimus."

30. See Grafton, *Commerce with the Classics,* chap. 1.

31. R. Fubini and A. Menci Gallorini, "L'autobiografia di Leon Battista Alberti: Studio e edizione," *Rinascimento,* 2nd ser., 12 (1972), 21–78, 77: "Quicquid ingenio esset hominum cum quadam effectuum elegantia, id prope divinum ducebat, et in quavis re expositam historiam <tanti> faciebat, ut etiam malos scriptores dignos laude asseveraret. Gemmis, floribus ac locis praesertim amoenis visendis nonnumquam ab aegritudine in bonam valitudinem rediit."

32. For a critical text and suggestive analysis of Lapo's letter, see M. Regoliosi, " 'Res gestae patriae' e 'res gestae ex universa Italia': La lettera di Lapo da Castiglionchio a Biondo Flavio," in *La memoria e la città,* ed. C. Bastia and M. Bolognani (Bologna, 1995), 273–305.

33. Pius II, *Memoirs of a Renaissance Pope,* ed. L. C. Gabel, tr. F. A. Gragg (New York, 1959), 323.

34. Regoliosi, " 'Res gestae patriae' e 'res gestae ex universa Italia,' " 294: "Non enim historiae una atque simplex subiecta materies nec uni tantum—ut aiunt—sectae addicta et consecrata est, sed varia, multiplex et late patens et pluribus ex artibus et studiisque colligitur."

35. Ibid., 295–296: "Hinc tanquam ex aliquo fonte uberrimo in omnes vitae partes praecepta elici possunt: quae ratio sit domesticae rei administrandae, quo pacto regenda et gubernanda respublica, quibus causis bella suscipienda, qua ratione gerenda, quousque prosequenda sint, quo modo tractandae amicitiae, ineunda foedera, iungendae societates, quo sedandi populorum motus, quo seditiones comprimendae. Hinc magnum aliquem et sapientem virum deligere possumus, cuius omnia dicta, facta, provisa, consulta imitemur."

36. Alberti, *De commodis litterarum atque incommodes,* 41: "Condant illi [the mature and perfectly learned] quidem historiam, tractent mores principum ac

gesta rerum publicarum eventusque bellorum; nos vero iuniores, modo aliquid novi proferamus, non vereamur severissima et, ut ita loquar, nimium censoria iudicia illorum, qui cum ipsi infantes et elingues sint tantum aures ad cognoscendum nimium delitiosas porrigunt, quasi doctis sat sit non pectus sed aures eruditas gerere." Cf. Cicero, *De oratore* 2.36: "Historia testis temporum, lex veritatis, vita memoriae, magistra vitae, nuncia vetustatis . . ." On the date and circumstances of Alberti's work, see L. Boschetto, "Nuovi documenti su Carlo di Lorenzo degli Alberti e una proposta per la datazione del *De commodis litterarum atque incommodis*," *Albertiana* 1 (1998), 43–60.

37. Regoliosi, " 'Res gestae patriae' e 'res gestae ex universa Italia,' " 303: "Nam et plerisque ipse, ut opinor, interfuisti rebus gerendis et quibus minus interfuisses eas investigando et percunctando ab iis apud quos gestae essent didicisti, e quibus quae locupletissimis testibus niterentur, pro veris probasti, quae vero sermonem vulgi auctorem rumoremque haberent, ut falsa ac ficta omisisti."

38. Many humanists agreed on this point. See e.g. Angelo Decembrio, *De politia literaria*, ed. Norbert Witten (Munich, 2002), 1.5.5, 162: "Contra vero historarium maria, ut aiunt, vastissima quidem asinorum opera, ac eiusdem molis immensae tres Vincentios, qui historias scripserunt magis quam historice sermonumque improprietate laxius abusi sunt?" Here Decembrio uses "historias" to mean "stories," but when he notes that Vincent of Beauvais did not write "historice," he means that proper history must have its roots in some sort of reliably transmitted facts. In a similar vein, Aeneas Silvius complains, in his *De curialium miseriis epistola*, ed. W. P. Mustard (Baltimore, Md., 1928), 40, that "Sunt qui veterum narrant historias, sed mendose atque perverse; claris auctoribus non creditur, sed fabellis inanibus fides adhibetur. Plus Guidoni de Columna, qui bellum Troianum magis poetice quam hystorice scripsit, vel Marsilio de Padua, qui translationes imperii quae nunquam fuerunt ponit, vel Vincentio Monacho quam Livio, Salustio, Iustino, Quinto Curtio, Plutarcho aut Suetonio, praestantissimis auctoribus, creditur." Here he rings a typically self-conscious change on Pliny, *Ep.* 2.5.5: "descriptiones locorum non historice tantum sed prope poetice prosequi fas est." On these points, see C. S. Celenza, "Creating Canons in Fifteenth-Century Ferrara: Angelo Decembrio's *De politia litteraria*, 1.10," *Renaissance Quarterly* 57 (2004), 43–98 at 60n79.

39. See G. Ianziti, *Humanistic Historiography under the Sforzas* (Oxford, 1988).

40. L. B. Alberti, *Opuscoli inediti di Leon Battista Alberti: "Musca," "Vita S. Potiti*," ed. C. Grayson (Florence, 1954), 86–87: "Baptistus Albertus Leonardo Dato s. Eram timida quidem in sententia, dum tecum verebar nequid eruditi viri subdubitarent hanc nostram Potiti istoriam esse fictam aliquam et puerilem fabulam. Memineram enim quam multa in istoria queritent viri non indocti quamve plene rerum causam, rem gestam, loca, tempora atque personarum dignitatem describi optent. Et videbam quoque apostolorum actus, pontificum martirumque reliquorum vitam dilucide atque plenissime a maioribus descriptam. Hanc autem Potiti

istoriam videbam ita negligenter traditam ut facile illam arbitrari potuerim esse ab imperitis non ab illis diligentissimis viris editam."

41. A. Frazier, *Possible Lives: Authors and Saints in Renaissance Italy* (New York, 2005), 67–69 at 69.

42. Alberti, *Opuscoli inediti di Leon Battista Alberti*, 87: "Hec ex epitomate martirum qui liber quoque corruptissimus est. Sed de negligentia librariorum aut de nonnullis historiarum scriptoribus quid eruditi existiment alio loco dicetur."

43. Frazier, *Possible Lives*, 69–70. On humanist efforts to produce simpler, more historical saints' lives, see also F. Bausi, "La Vita Dominici di Francesco da Castiglione: Contributo alla storia dell'agiografia umanistica," *Interpres* 25 (2006), 53–113.

44. See A. Modigliani, *I Porcari* (Rome, 1994), 495.

45. Aliotti, *Epistolae et opuscula*, I, 32–34, 44–46, 67–68.

46. Alberti, *Della pittura*, "Prologus": "Io solea maravigliarmi insieme e dolermi che tante ottime e divine arti e scienze, quali per loro opere e per le istorie veggiamo copiose erano in que' vertuosissimi passati antiqui, ora così siano mancate e quasi in tutto perdute . . ."

47. Regoliosi, " 'Res gestae patriae' e 'res gestae ex universa Italia,' " 301: "Nec est enim ullum studium praeclarius nec ocio ingenuo dignius quam hoc quo status totius orbis singulis aetatibus qui fuerit, quibus imperiis distributus quotque in eo mutationes cognoscere possumus: qui maximarum urbium conditores, qui artium inventores extiterint, quis primus hominum genus rude et agreste instruxerit, quis in civitate coegerit, quis ei leges dederit, quis cultus deorum religionesque induxerit, quis navigationem, quis agriculturam, quis litteras primus docuerit, quis rem militarem tractare coeperit."

48. See L. Barkan, *Unearthing the Past* (New Haven, Conn., 1999), chap. 2.

49. Alberti, *Della pittura*, II.26: "Ma qui non molto si richiede sapere quali prima fussero inventori dell'arte o pittori, poi che non come Plinio recitiamo storie, ma di nuovo fabrichiamo un'arte di pittura, della quale in questa età, quale io vegga, nulla si truova scritto . . ."

50. Alberti, *De pictura*, II.26: "Sed non multum interest aut primos pictores aut picturae inventores tenuisse, quando quidem non historiam picturae ut Plinius sed artem novissime recenseamus, de qua hac aetate nulla scriptorum veterum monumenta quae ipse viderim extant . . ."

51. See C. Dempsey's important note in *The Portrayal of Love* (Princeton, N.J., 1992, 29–30n24. On the debt of the humanists to Byzantine rhetoric, see esp. Baxandall, *Giotto and the Orators*, and Smith, *Architecture in the Culture of Early Humanism.*

52. Cicero, *Brutus*, 42; in fact, Cicero did not observe this distinction at all times (see e.g. *ad Atticum* 1.16.18), and in poetry, "historia" could have a sense very close to "fabula" (e.g. Ovid, *Amores* 2.4.44).

53. Alberti, *De pictura*, II.63; see Grayson's note in his edition and Goggi Carotti in her edition of Alberti, *De commodis litterarum atque incommodis.*

54. Alberti, *De pictura*, II.26 (on Narcissus): "Però usai di dire tra i miei amici, secondo la sentenza de'poeti, quel Narcisso convertito in fiore essere della pittura stato inventore; ché già ove sia la pittura fiore d'ogni arte, ivi tutta la storia di Narcisso viene a proposito"; ". . . tum de Narcisso omnis fabula pulchre ad rem ipsam perapta erit . . ."; III.53 (on the Calumny): "Quae plane historia etiam si dum recitatur animos tenet, quantum censes eam gratiae et amoenitatis ex ipsa pictura eximii pictoris exhibuisse?"; "Quale istoria se mentre che si recita piace, pensa quanto esse avesse grazia e amenità a vederla dipinta di mano d'Appelle."

55. Ibid., I.19: "Principio in superficie pingenda quam amplum libeat quadrangulum rectorum angulorum inscribo, quod quidem mihi pro aperta finestra est ex qua historia contueatur, illicque quam magnos velim esse in pictura homines determino." The Italian version of the relevant clause reads: "el quale reputo essere una finestra aperta, per donde io miri quello che quivi sarà dipinto . . ."

56. Ibid., III.61: "Caeterum cum historiam picturi sumus, prius diutius excogitabimus quonam ordine et quibus modis eam componere pulcherrimum sit. Modulosque in chartis conicientes, tum totam historiam, tum singulas eiusdem historiae partes commentabimur, amicosque omnes in ea re consulemus. Denique omnia apud nos ita praemeditata esse elaborabimus, ut nihil in opere futurum sit, quod non optime qua id sit parte locandum intelligamus"; "E quando aremo a dipignere storia, prima fra noi molto penseremo qual modo e quale ordine in quella sia bellissima, e faremo nostri concetti e modelli di tutta la storia e di ciascuna sua parte prima, e chiameremo tutti gli amici a consigliarci sopra a ciò. E così ci sforzeremo avere ogni parte in noi prima ben pensata, tale che nella opera abbi a essere cosa alcuna, quale non intendiamo ove e come debba essere fatta e collocata."

57. Ibid., III.61: "Quove id certius teneamus, modulos in parallelos dividere iuvabit, ut in publico opere cuncta, veluti ex privatis commentariis ducta suis sedibus collocentur"; "E per meglio di tutto aver certezza, segneremo i modelli nostri con paralleli, onde nel publico lavoro torremo dai nostri congetti, quasi come da privati commentari, ogni stanza e sito delle cose."

58. Ibid., III.57: "Sed cavendum ne, quod plerique faciant, ea minimis tabellis pingamus. Grandibus enim imaginibus te velim assuefacias, quae quidem quam proxime magnitudine ad id quod ipse velis efficere, accedant"; "Ma guarda non fare come molti, quali imparano disegnare in picciole tavolelle. Voglio te esserciti disegnando cose grandi, quasi pari al ripresentare la grandezza di quello che tu disegni." The whole passage reveals Alberti's preference for the large image.

59. Alberti, *On Painting*, 135n18. Cf. also F. Ames-Lewis, *Drawings in Early Renaissance Italy* (New Haven, Conn., 1981), and Rosand, "*Ekphrasis* and the Renaissance of Painting."

60. Alberti, *De pictura*, III.56: ". . . nam in historia si adsit facies cogniti alicuius hominis, tametsi aliae nonnullae praestantioris artificii emineant, cognitus tamen

vultus omnium spectantium oculos ad se rapit"; ". . . ove poi che in una storia sarà uno viso di qualche conosciuto e degno uomo, bene che ivi sieno altre figure di arte molto più che questa perfette e grate, pure quel viso conosciuto a sé imprima trarrà tutti gli occhi di chi la storia raguardi . . ."

61. Ibid., III.63: "Haec habui quae de pictura his commentariis referrem. Ea si eiusmodi sunt ut pictoribus commodum atque utilitatem aliquam afferant, hoc potissimum laborum meorum premium exposco ut faciem meam in suis historiis pingant, quo illos memores beneficii et gratos esse, ac me artis studiosum fuisse posteris predicent"; "Ebbi da dire queste cose della pittura, quali se sono commode e utili a' pittori, solo questo, domando in premio delle mie fatiche, che nelle sue istorie dipingano il viso mio, acciò dimostrino sé essere grati e me essere stato studioso dell'arte."

62. J. Pope-Hennessy, *The Portrait of the Renaissance* (London, 1963).

63. Alberti, *De pictura*, II.42. Cf. Baxandall, *Giotto and the Orators*, 129–130 and plates 3 and 5 (a).

64. Alberti, *De re aedificatoria*, 7.10, *L'architettura*, II, 609.

65. See esp. the locus classicus, Alberti, *De pictura*, II.40: "*Historia* vero, quam merito possis et laudare et admirari, eiusmodi erit quae illecebris quibusdam sese ita amenam et ornatam exhibeat, ut oculos docti atque indocti spectatoris diutius quadam cum voluptate et animi motu detineat. Primum enim quod in *historia* voluptatem afferat est ipsa copia et varietas rerum. Ut enim in cibis atque in musica semper nova et exuberantia cum caeteras fortassis ob causas, tum nimirum eam ob causam delectant, quod ab vetustis et consuetis differant, sic in omni re varietate animus et copia admodum delectatur. Idcirco *in pictura* et corporum et colorum varietas amena est. Dicam *historiam* esse copiosissimam illam, in qua suis locis permixti aderunt senes, viri, adolescentes, pueri, matronae, virgines, infantes, cicures, catelli, aviculae, equi, pecudes, aedificia, provinciaeque; omnemque copiam laudabo modo ea ad rem de qua illic agitur conveniat. Fit enim ut cum spectantes lustrandis rebus morentur, tum pictoris copia gratiam assequatur. Sed hanc copiam velim cum varietate quadam esse ornatam, tum dignitate et verecundia gravem atque moderatam. Improbo quidem eos pictores, qui quo videri copiosi, quove nihil vacuum relictum volunt, et nullam sequuntur compositionem, sed confuse et dissolute omnia disseminant, ex quo non rem agere sed tumultuare *historia* videtur. Ac fortassis qui dignitatem in primis in *historia* cupiet, huic solitudo admodum tenenda erit. Ut enim in principe maiestatem affert verborum paucitas, modo sensa et iussa intelligantur, sic in *historia* competens corporum numerus adhibet dignitatem. Odi solitudinem in *historia*, tamen copiam minime laudo quae a dignitate abhorreat. Atque in *historia* id vehementer approbo quod a poetis tragicis atque comicis observatum video, ut quam possint paucis personatis fabulam doceant. Meo quidem iudicio nulla erit usque adeo tanta rerum varietate referta *historia*, quam novem aut decem homines non possint condigne agere, ut illud Varronis huc pertinere arbitror, qui in convivio tumultum evitans non plus quam

novem accubantes admittebat. Sed in omni *historia* cum varietas iocunda est, tamen in primis omnibus grata est pictura, in qua corporum status atque motus inter se multos dissimiles sint. . . . Obscoenae quidem corporis et hae omnes partes quae parum gratiae habent, panno aut frondibus aut manu operiantur. . . . Hanc ergo modestiam et verecundiam in universa *historia* observari cupio ut foeda aut praetereantur aut emendentur . . .”; “Sarà la *storia,* qual tu possa lodare e maravigliare, tale che con sue piacevolezze si porgerà sì ornata e grata, che ella terrà con diletto e movimento d'animo qualunque dotto o indotto la miri. Quello che primi dà volutà nella *istoria* viene dalla copia e varietà delle cose. Como ne' cibi e nella musica sempre la novità e abondanza tanto piace quanto sia differente dalle cose antique e consuete, così l'animo si diletta d'ogni copia e varietà. Per questo in pittura la copia e varietà piace. Dirò io quella *istoria* essere copiosissima in quale a' suoi luoghi sieno permisti vecchi, giovani, fanciulli, donne, fanciulle, fanciullini, polli, catellini, uccellini, cavalli, pecore, edifici, province, e tutte simili cose: e loderó io qualunque copia quale s'apartenga a quella *istoria.* E interviene, dove chi guarda soprasta rimirando tutte le cose, ivi la copia del pittore acquisti molta grazia. Ma vorrei io questa copia essere ornata di certa varietà, ancora moderata e grave di dignità e verecundia. Biasimo io quelli pittori quali, dove vogliono parere copiosi nulla lassando vacuo, ivi non composizione, ma dissoluta confusione disseminano; pertanto non pare la *storia* facci qualche cosa degna, ma sia in tumulto aviluppata. E forse chi molto cercherà dignità in sua *storia,* a costui piacerà la solitudine. Suole ad i prencipi la carestia delle parole tenere maestà, dove fanno intendere suoi precetti. Così in *istoria* uno certo competente numero di corpi rende non poca dignità. Dispiacemi la solitudine in *istoria,* pure né però laudo copia alcuna quale sia sanza dignità. Ma in ogni *storia* la varietà sempre fu ioconda, e in prima sempre fu grata quella pittura in quale sieno i corpi con suoi posari molto dissimili . . . Le parte brutte a vedere del corpo, e l'altre simili quali porgano poca grazia, si cuoprana col panno, con qualche fronde o con la mano . . . Così adunque desidero in ogni *storia* servarsi quanto dissi modestia e verecundia, e così sforzarsi che in niuno sia un medesimo gesto o posamento che nell'altro.”

66. Alberti, *De pictura,* I.21: “Nam, ut ex operibus priscis facile intelligimus, eadem fortassis apud maiores nostros, quod esset obscura et difficillima, admodum incognita latuit. Vix enim ullam antiquorum historiam apte compositam, neque pictam, neque fictam, neque sculptam reperies”; “E quanto sia difficile veggasi nell'opere degli antiqui scultori e pittori. Forse perché era oscura, loro fu ascosa e incognita. Appena vedrai alcuna storia antiqua attamente composta.” Cf. F. Balters, *Der grammatische Bildhauer: Kunsttheorie und Bildhauerkunst der Frührenaissance: Alberti—Ghiberti—Leonardo—Gauricus* (Aachen, 1991).

67. Alberti, *De pictura,* II.37: “Laudatur apud Romanos historia in qua Meleager defunctus asportatur, et qui oneri subsunt angi et omnibus membris laborare videantur: in eo vero qui mortuus sit, nullum adsit membrum quod non demortuum appareat, omnia pendent, manus, digiti, cervix, omnia languida decidunt,

denique omnia ad exprimendam corporis mortem congruunt"; "Lodasi una storia in Roma nella quale Melagro morto, portato, aggrava quelli che portano il peso, e in sè pare in ogni suo membro ben morto: ogni cosa pende, mani, dito e capo; ogni cosa cade languido; ciò che ve si dà ad esprimere uno corpo morto."

68. Alberti, *De re aedificatoria*, 8.6: "Per frontes parietum locis idoneis tituli et sculptae historiae adcrustabuntur . . ."; 9.4: "sed parietem nolim affatim refertum esse aut simulachris aut signis aut penitus opertum historiaque occupatum"; 8.4: "Nostri vero Latini clarissimorum virorum gesta exprimere sculpta placuit historia"; 8.3: "Fuere qui columnae altitudinem ad pedes centenos duxerint, totamque circum asperam signis et rerum historia convestitam reddiderint."

69. A. Niehaus, *Florentiner Reliefkunst von Brunelleschi bis Michelangelo* (Munich, 1998), 22–28.

70. See K. Patz, "Zum Begriff der 'Historia,' " and P. Toynbee, "A Note on *Storia, Storiato,* and the Corresponding Terms in French and English, in Illustrations of *Purgatorio* X, 52, 71, 73," in *Mélanges offertes à M. Emile Picot par ses amis et élèves,* 2 vols. (Paris, 1913), I, 195–208.

71. Dante, *Purgatorio,* 10.52, 71, 73.

72. Leonardo Bruni to Niccolò da Uzzano, spring 1424, in R. Krautheimer and T. Krautheimer-Hess, *Lorenzo Ghiberti,* repr. of 2nd ed. (Princeton, N.J., 1982), 372: "Spectabiles etc. Io considero che le 20 historie della nuova porta le quali avete deliberato che siano del vecchio testamento, vogliono avere due cose principalmente: l'una che siano illustri, l'altra che siano significanti. Illustri chiamo quelle che possono ben pascere l'occhio con varietà di disegno, significanti chiamo quelle che abbino importanza degna di memoria . . . Bisognerà che colui, che l'ha a disegnare, sia bene instrutto di ciascuna historia, si che possa ben mettere e le persone e gl'atti occorrenti, e che habbia del gentile, si che le sappia bene ornare . . . Ma bene vorrei essere presso a chi l'harà a disegnare per fargli prendere ogni significato, che la storia importa."

73. Matteo di Paolo to the Operai of the Cathedral in Prato, 19 June 1434, in C. Guasti, *Il pergamo del Donatello di Duomo di Prato* (Florence, 1887), 19: "Karissimi etc. La chagione di questa si è, che Donatello à finita quella storia di marmo; et promettovi per gl'intendenti di questa terra, che dicono tutti per una bocha, che mai si vide simile storia. Et lui mi pare sia di buona voglia a servirvi bene . . . Lui mi priegha, che io vi scriva che per Dio non manchi che gli mandiate qualche danaio per spendere per queste feste: e io vi gravo che lo facciate; inperò che è huomo ch'ogni picholo pasto è allui assai, e sta contento a ogni cosa."

74. G. Poggi, *Il duomo di Firenze* (Florence, 1909, repr. 1988), e.g. Doc. 325: "Item locaverunt Luce Simonis delle Robbie ad faciendum storias marmoris . . ."

75. See most recently A. Cavallaro, "I primi studi dall'antico nel cantiere del Laterano," in *Alle origini della nuova Roma: Martino V (1417–1431): Atti del Convegno, Roma, 2–5 Marzo 1992,* ed. M. Chiabò, G. D'Alessandro, P. Piacentini, and C. Ranieri (Rome, 1992), 401–412.

76. See Niehaus, *Florentiner Reliefkunst von Brunelleschi bis Michelangelo.*

77. Cf. J. Bialostocki, "Ars auro potior," in *Mèlanges de littérature et philologie offertes à Miecyslaw Brahmer* (Warsaw, 1966), 55–63.

78. A. Warburg, "Sandro Botticelli's *Birth of Venus* and *Spring*," in *The Renewal of Pagan Antiquity: Contributions to the Cultural History of the European Renaissance,* ed. K. W. Forester, tr. D. Britt (Los Angeles, 1999), 95; for the original, see Warburg, *Gesammelte Schriften: Studienausgabe,* ed. H. Bredekamp, M. Diers, K. W. Forster, N. Mann, S. Settis, and M. Warnke (Berlin, 1998), I.1, 10–11.

79. See e.g. Krautheimer and Krautheimer-Hess, *Lorenzo Ghiberti,* but the argument is an old one: note e.g. H. Kaufmann, *Donatello* (Berlin, 1935), 63–66, and cf. Niehaus, *Florentiner Reliefkunst von Brunelleschi bis Michelangelo.*

80. Aliotti's testimony, cited above, confirms the view that Alberti expected to be read not only by his fellow humanists and by erudite princes of the state and church but also by artists—as he certainly was, by Filarete, Leonardo, and a number of others.

81. On the long-term consequences of this aporia in the humanistic theory of history, see U. Muhlack, *Geschichtswissenschaft im Humanismus und in der Aufklärung* (Munich, 1991).

82. L. Valla, *Gesta Ferdinandi regis Aragonum,* ed. O. Besomi (Padua, 1973), 3–5; admittedly, Valla insists that the historian is also truthful.

83. Sallust, *Bellum contra Iugurtham,* 4.5–6: "Nam saepe ego audivi Q. Maxumum, P. Scipionem, praeterea civitatis nostrae praeclaros viros solitos ita dicere, quom majorum imagines intuerentur, vehementissime sibi animum ad virtutem adcendi. Scilicet non ceram illam, neque figuram, tantam vim in sese habere; sed memoria rerum gestarum eam flammam egregiis viris in pectore crescere, neque prius sedari, quam virtus eorum famam atque gloriam adaequaverit."

84. See C. Celenza, *Renaissance Humanism and the Papal Curia* (Ann Arbor, Mich., 1999), 156, for Lapo's praise of Alberti.

85. Regoliosi, " 'Res gestae patriae' e 'res gestae ex universa Italia,' " 298–300: "Cum autem magnum quempiam laborem aut periculum, non spe commodi, non mercedis, pro libertate patriae, pro salute civium, pro incolumitate susceptum aut audivimus aut legimus, id omnes ad caelum efferimus, id stupefacti admiramur, id factum, si facultas detur, imitari cupimus; quod in fabulis picturisque perspicue intueri licet. In quibus etiam si res fictae sint, tamen variis sensibus nos ista afficiunt ut eos quorum vel aliquod praeclarum facinus proditum accepimus vel in tabula expressum aspeximus summa benivolentia complectamur. Quod si haec tantam vim habent, quos historiam stimulos ad virtutem habituram putamus, in qua non fictae personae inducuntur sed verae, non commentitiae res sed gestae, non artificii ostendendi gratia editae orationes, sed, ut feruntur habitae exprimuntur?"

86. See the important notes in Regoliosi, " 'Res gestae patriae' e 'res gestae ex universa Italia,' " and in Miglio, *Storiografia pontificia del Quattrocento,* 47–50.

87. M. Baxandall, "A Dialogue on Art from the Court of Leonello d'Este. Angelo Decembrio's *De Politia Litteraria* Pars LXVIII," *Journal of the Warburg and Courtauld Institutes* 26 (1963), 304–326. In this case, Decembrio clearly ascribed his own (and Alberti's) tastes to Leonello, who in fact eagerly collected the tapestries in question. See N. Forti Grazzini, "Leonello d'Este nell'autunno del Medioeve. Gli arazzi delle 'Storia di Ercole,' " in *Le muse e il principe: Arte di corte nel Rinascimento padano: Saggi* (Modena, 1991), 53–62 at 61–62.

88. Alberti, *De pictura*, II.40: "Fit enim ut cum spectantes lustrandis rebus morentur, tum pictoris copia gratiam assequatur."

3. A Contemplative Scholar

1. The standard life of Trithemius is Klaus Arnold's excellent *Johannes Trithemius (1462–1516)* (Würzburg: Schöningh, 1991). See also Richard Auernheimer and Frank Baron, eds., *Johannes Trithemius: Humanismus und Magie im vorreformatorischen Deutschland* (Munich: Profil, 1991), and Frank Baron and Richard Auernheimer, eds., *War Dr. Faustus in Kreuznach? Realität und Fiktion im Faust-Bild des Abtes Johannes Trithemius* (Alzey: Verlag der Rheinhessischen Druckwerkstätte Alzey, 2003). A summary of Arnold's life also appears in Johannes Trithemius, *In Praise of Scribes: De laude scriptorum*, ed. Klaus Arnold, tr. Roland Behrendt (Lawrence, Kans.: Coronado Press, 1974), 1–12.

2. Trithemius, *In Praise of Scribes*, 34–35: "Impressura enim res papirea est et brevi tempore tota consumitur. Scriptor autem membranis commendans litteras, et se et ea, que scribit, in tempus longinquum extendit."

3. Like Trithemius's actual practices in publishing, Federico's collecting practices had little to do with the rejection of print reported by Vespasiano. See Martin Davies, "The Printed Books of Federico da Montefeltro," in *Federico da Montefeltro and His Library*, ed. Marcello Simonetta (Milan: Y Press; Vatican City: Biblioteca Apostolica Vaticana, 2007).

4. Richard Southern, *Western Society and the Church in the Middle Ages* (Harmondsworth: Penguin, 1970), 237–239.

5. Trithemius, *In Praise of Scribes*, 52–53: "Ergo si manducare prohibetur, qui laborare non vult, monachi ociosi aut non manducent aut preceptorum apostoli se transgressores agnoscant."

6. On this side of Trithemius's life and work, see Noel Brann, *The Abbot Trithemius (1462–1516): The Renaissance of Monastic Humanism* (Leiden: Brill, 1981), and for the larger context see Franz Posset, *Renaissance Monks: Monastic Humanism in Six Biographical Sketches* (Leiden: Brill, 2005).

7. See Arnold in Trithemius, *In Praise of Scribes*, 3.

8. Trithemius's *Epistolae familiares* are preserved as Biblioteca Apostolica Vaticana MS Pal. lat. 730, and were printed in 1536; see Klaus Arnold, "Warum schrieben

und sammelten Humanisten ihre Briefe? Beobachtungen zum Briefwechsel des Benediktinerabtes Johannes Trithemius (1462–1516)," in *Adel—Geistlichkeit—Militär: Festschrift für Eckhardt Opitz zum 60. Geburtstag*, ed. M. Busch and J. Hillmann (Bochum: Winkler, 1999).

9. On Trithemius, Maximilian, and magic, see the classic study by Paola Zambelli, "Scholastiker und Humanisten: Agrippa und Trithemius zur Hexerei: Die natürliche Magie und die Entstehung kritischen Denkens," *Archiv für Kulturgeschichte* 67 (1985), 41–79. See also Zambelli, *White Magic, Black Magic in the European Renaissance* (Leiden: Brill, 2007), 73–112, and Noel Brann, *Trithemius and Magical Theology: A Chapter in the Controversy over Occult Studies in Early Modern Europe* (Albany: State University of New York Press, 1999).

10. James O'Donnell, "The Pragmatics of the New: Trithemius, McLuhan, Cassiodorus," in *The Future of the Book*, ed. G. Nunberg (Berkeley: University of California Press, 1996), 37–62; O'Donnell, *Avatars of the Word: From Papyrus to Cyberspace* (Cambridge, Mass.: Harvard University Press, 1998).

11. Trithemius, *In Praise of Scribes*, 62–63: "Quis nescit quanta sit inter scripturam et impressuram distantia? Scriptura enim, si membranis imponitur, ad mille annos poterit perdurare, impressura autem, cum res papirea sit, quamdiu subsistet?"

12. Ibid., 60–63: "Fuit in quodam cenobio nostri ordinis mihi non incognito frater quidam devotus, qui in scribendis ad ornatum bibliothece voluminibus magnum habebat studium, ita ut quotiescunque a divino potuisset vacare officio, ad secreta celle se conferens huic sacrato labori insisteret. Unde et multa sanctorum opuscula cum ingenti devotione excopiavit. Huius mortui ossa, cum post multos annos levarentur de terra, tres digiti dextere manus, quibus tot volumina scripserat, tam integri et incorrupti inventi sunt, ac si eodem tempore sepulchro fuissent impositi. Reliquum autem corpus ut moris est consumptum ad ossa fuit. Quo testimonio colligitur, quam sanctum hoc officium apud omnipotentem deum iudicetur, cuius ut meritum viventibus ostenderet, etiam in mortuis cadaveribus membra scriptorum honoravit."

13. Arnold in Trithemius, *In Praise of Scribes*, 15.

14. For Trithemius's early work, see Karlheinz Froelich, "Johannes Trithemius on the Fourfold Sense of Scripture: The *Tractatus de Investigatione Scripturae* (1486)," in *Biblical Interpretation in the Era of the Reformation: Essays Presented to David C. Steinmetz in Honor of His Sixtieth Birthday*, ed. Richard Miller and John Thompson (Grand Rapids, Mich.: Eerdmans, 1996), 23–60.

15. Bernd Moeller, "Religious Life in Germany on the Eve of the Reformation," in *Pre-Reformation Germany*, ed. Gerald Strauss (London: Macmillan, 1972), 13–42.

16. Trithemius, *In Praise of Scribes*, 60–61: "Denique interim, quod bonas devotasque rescribit materias, cogitaciones inanes vel turpes non patitur molestas, verba ociosa non loquitur, sevis rumoribus non maculatur, sed quietus et solitarius

sedens cum gaudio epulatur in scripturis, et bonis exerciciis ad glorificandum deum provocat intuentes. Etenim dum bonas scribit materias, scribendo in agnitionem misteriorum paulatim introducitur, et interius animo magnifice illustratur."

17. Ibid.: "Fortius enim, que scribimus, menti imprimimus, quia scribentes et legentes ea cum morula tractamus."

18. Johannes Trithemius, *Collatio de republica ecclesiae et monachorum ordinis divi patris benedicti habita colonie in capitulo annali* (n.p., 1493), Bi verso: "Longum est si velim eorum vel sola nomina transcurrere qui in ordine nostro et doctrina et sanctitate mirabiles effulserunt. Magna fervebat in eis devotio, regularis discipline inestimabilis zelus, qui nunquam sinebat esse ociosos. Semper in eorum studiis amor vigebat divinus: qui de lectione sancta conceptus ad orationem vocabat vigilantes. Nam qui se in divinis scripturis amplius exercitaverant, vacantibus a dei servicio horis earundem expositionibus intendebant. Conficiebant libros variosque tractatus, quibus fratrum suorum studia ad amorem dei provocabant. Ceteri fratres non vacabant ocio, sed operi manuum iuxta regulam post oraciones devote insistebant. Scribebant idonei libros pro bibliothece ornatu, et ex scedis ab aliis edita ad mundum importabant. Alii scriptos codices artificiose ligabant, corrigebant alii, alii rubro minio distinguebant. Gestiebant omnes sancti laboris esse participes."

19. Here and in what follows I am much indebted to the classic study of Paul Lehmann, "Nachrichten von der Sponheimer Bibliothek des Abtes Johannes Trithemius," in *Festgabe zum 7. September 1910: Hermann Grauert zur Vollendung des 60. Lebensjahres gewidmet von seinen Schülern,* ed. Max Jansen et al. (Freiburg im Breisgau: Herder, 1910), 205–220, as well as E. G. Vogel, "Die Bibliothek der Benediktinerabtei Sponheim," *Serapeum* 3 (1842), 312–328. In this case, the subscription in question appears in Munich, Bayerische Staatsbibliothek, clm 830, 60 verso (Lehmann, "Nachrichten," 212): "Complevi hoc opus epistolarum sanctissimi martyris Bonifacii . . . ego frater Franciscus Hofyrer de Kernczenheym protunc novicius iussu reverendissimi patris et scripturarum studiosissimi cultoris Joannis Tritemii abbatis secundi de reformatione Bursfeldensi anno salutis 1497, XVI. Kal. Septembris. Ora, lector devote, pro utriusque salute."

20. Stuttgart, Landesbibliothek, MS Hist. Fol. 1 (Lehmann, "Nachrichten," 214–215): "Explicit chronica fratris Roberti monachi ordinis Praemonstratensium, qui obiit anno domini MCC duodecimo, scripta per me fratrem Johanem Binguiam sacerdotem et monachum spanhemensem anno MCCCC.XCIIII. decimo Kl. Septemb."

21. Trithemius, "Nepiachus," in *War Dr. Faustus in Kreuznach?* ed. Baron and Auernheimer, 54: "Amori tamen meo et studio in scripturas sanctas propter inopiam monasterii et librorum in omni varietate multitudinem, qui impressoria iam arte in omnem diffusa terram multipliciter dietim profunduntur in lucem, nequaquam satisfacere potui. Confiteor intemperatum ad studium et libros amorem meum, quo nunquam cessare vel altero saltem fatigari potui, quo minus

animum secutus meum: quidquid in mundo scibile est, scire semper cupiebam; et libros omnes, quos vidissem vel audivissem formis excussos, quamtumlibet etiam pueriles aut inconcinnos, habere ac legere pro summis deliciis computabam. Sed non erat in mea facultate satisfacere, ut voluissem, desiderio; propterea quod vita brevis et ingenium tenue; tam multa, tam varia tamque profunda diversarum scientiarum mysteria comprehendere nullatenus queat; defuerint etiam semper pecuniae ad necessitatem, quanto magis ad librorum voluptatem comparandam. Feci tamen in utroque semper, quod potui: qui si nimius fui, creator omnipotens parce, qui hominem ab initio rectum fecisti; ipse autem infinitis se immiscuit quaestionibus."

22. Ibid., 52: "vix decem volumina, praeter Bibliam omnia parvae utilitatis. His antecessor meus 30 volumina impressa coniunxit, et ipsa communia quidem pro faciendis sermonibus ad populum et istis similia. Quod plura non comparavit, duplex causa extitit: quoniam et nimia eum paupertas in principio reformationis oppressit, et raritas librorum propter impressoriae artis novitatem pretium auxit."

23. Ibid., 52–53: "Permulta enim coenobia nostri ordinis in diversis provinciis multoties visitavi per annos viginti: omnium bibliothecas perlustravi, et ubicumque aliquid quod prius non haberem repperi duplicatum, id altero mihi dato pretio vel aliquod volumen aliud impressum, quale postulassent inventi possessores, comparans in recompensam, ut contingeret, agebam. Multa pretiosa et optandae lectionis volumina in papiro simul ac in pergameno scripta per hunc modum, non solum in nostro sed in aliquibus etiam aliis ordinibus commutando accepi. Saepius etiam contigit in diversis monasteriis et ordinibus, ut multa essent rescripta volumina in astronomia, in musica, in mathematica, in philosophia, in poesi, in oratoria, in historiis, in medicinis et in artibus, quae ipsi boni patres, qui possidebant, aut non intelligebant, aut metuentes eorum praesentia sanctam violari observantiam, me rogabant quatenus omnia illa mihi tollerem et eis alia quaedam impressa, quae magis optassent, in recompensam redderem; quod statim non invitus ut rogabar facere consuevi."

24. Johannes Trithemius, *Polygraphiae libri sex* ([Basel]: Haselberg, 1518), [q vi] recto, on a treatise describing a method of shorthand supposedly used by Cicero and Cyprian: "Rarus est codex, et a me semel duntaxat repertus, vilique precio emptus. Nam cum anno dominicae nativitatis M. quadringentesimo nonagesimo sexto bibliothecas plures librorum amore perlustrarem, reperi memoratum codicem in quodam ordinis nostri monasterio, nimia vetustate neglectum, proiectum sub pulvere atque contemptum. Interrogavi abbatem doctorem iuris quanti illum estimaret. Respondit: Sancti Anshelmi parva opuscula nuper impressa illi praeferrem. Ad bibliopolas abii, quoniam in civitate res contigit metropolitana, postulata Anselmi opuscula pro sexta floreni parte comparavi, abbati et monachis gaudentibus tradidi, et iam prope interitum actum codicem liberavi. Decreverunt enim pergameni amore illico radendum."

25. Trithemius, "Nepiachus," in *War Dr. Faustus in Kreuznach?* ed. Baron and Auernheimer, 53–54: "Comportavi itaque per hos viginti tres annos ad bibliothecam Spanheimensem non sine magno labore et multis impensis, maxima usus diligentia, circiter duo milia volumina tam scripta quam impressa in omni facultate et scientia, quae inter Christianos habetur in usu. Nec vidi in tota Germania, neque esse audivi, tam raram tamque mirandam bibliothecam; licet plures viderim, in qua sit librorum tanta copia non vulgarium neque communium, sed rarorum, abditorum, secretorum mirandorumque et talium, quales alibi vix reperiantur. In lingua etiam Graeca multa volumina tam scripta quam impressa feci mihi ex Italia afferri, quoniam et eorum mihi lectio a multis iam annis non minus iocunda quam necessaria fuit: sed Graecorum codicum numerus centenarium, ut puto, non excedit. Comparavi etiam in Hebraica lingua bibliam et quaedam alia volumina, quoniam et aliquando eius studiosus eram. Exposui autem pro libris ad bibliothecam, exceptis illis quos feci rescribi per fratres et alios non paucos, pecuniam plusquam quingentorum et mille florenorum. Quae summa etsi divitibus parva non immerito videatur, mihi tamen pro mea paupertate quasi maxima et bene intolerabilis fuit."

26. Matthaeus Herbenus Traiectensis to Jodocus Beyselius, August 1495, in Paul Lehmann, *Merwürdigkeiten des Abtes Johannes Trithemius, Sitzungsberichte der Bayerischen Akademie der Wissenschaften,* phil.-hist. Klasse (1961), Heft 2, 23–24: "Ubi (scil. in monasterio) occasio deambulandi concessa est (quod plerumque post primorum amicorum congressus atque refectiones fit) circumfert (abbas) me atque illico in admirandam bibliothecam suam introducit, ubi plurima tum Hebraea, tum Graeca volumina intueor. Nam Latinorum in omni arte, scientia et facultate ingens copia erat. Demiror itaque unius hominis in tam variis monumentis consequendis constituendisque exactam diligentiam atque vehementer obstupesco, cum in tota Germania non existimaverim tantum peregrinorum voluminum extitisse. Nam quinque linguarum, sermone et charactere a se longe distantium, libros in codicibus perantiquis illic repperi, quos Trithemii vigilans studium non sine multo sudore comportavit. Hoc igitur modo, Jodoce doctissime, fulcitam inveni Spanemensem bibliothecam: nam [non?] eam solum verum etiam et parietes totius domus abbatialis, que ampla est, et testudines camerarum Graecis, Hebraicis, Latinis versibus caracteribusque decentissime ornatas aspexi."

27. Ibid.: "Quamobrem ego ita mecum reputo, si in Germania nostra Hebraea aliqua Graecave academia sit, ea Spanhemense coenobium est, ubi plus eruditionis concipere possis ex parietibus quam multorum pulverulentis atque librorum inanibus bibliothecis. Quicquid enim antiquitatis et eruditionis Germania in libris habere potest monasterium Spanhemense Trithemio abbate procurante possidet. Mansi apud abbatem nostrum dies undecim . . ."

28. Herzog August Bibliothek, Wolfenbüttel MS 34 Aug. fol.

29. Ibid., blank 1: "liber sancti heriberti Tuicii"; [added in red] "nunc mutatus ad spanheym pro alio"; fol. 120 verso: "liber sancti Heriberti in Tuicio [erased]";

Ave maria templum
Liber sancti heriberti in tuicio
Nunc sancti Martini in
Spanheym.

30. Herzog August Bibliothek, Wolfenbüttel, MS Weissenburg 87.

31. See e.g. Paul Joachimsen, *Gesammelte Aufsätze: Beiträge zu Renaissance, Humanismus und Reformation, zur Historiographie und zum deutschen Staatsgedanken,* ed. Notker Hammerstein, 2nd ed. (Aalen: Scientia, 1983); Lewis Spitz, *Conrad Celtis, the German Arch-Humanist* (Cambridge, Mass.: Harvard University Press, 1957); Spitz, *The Religious Renaissance of the German Humanists* (Cambridge, Mass.: Harvard University Press, 1963); Gerald Strauss, *Sixteenth-Century Germany: Its Topography and Topographers* (Madison: University of Wisconsin Press, 1959); *The Renaissance and Reformation in Germany: An Introduction,* ed. Gerhart Hoffmeister (New York: Ungar, 1977); *L'humanisme allemand, 1480–1540: XVIIIe colloque international de Tours* (Munich: Fink; Pars: Vrin, 1979); Eckhard Bernstein, *German Humanism* (Boston: Twayne, 1983); Dieter Wuttke, *Humanismus als Integrative Kraft: Die Philosophia des deutschen "Erzhumanisten" Conrad Celtis: Eine ikonologische Studie zu programmatischer Graphik Dürers und Burgkmairs* (Nuremberg: Carl, 1984); Christine Johnson, *The German Discovery of the World: Renaissance Encounters with the Strange and Marvelous* (Charlottesville: University of Virginia Press, 2008).

32. Herzog August Bibliothek, Wolfenbüttel, MS Extrav 265.4 (Statius Thebais s. xii 2 [Italy]), folio 1 recto:

Qui cupit hunc librum sibimet contendere primum
hic flegetontheas satiatur sulphure flammas . . .
Stacium hunc dono Domino Ioanni De Trittenheym Abbati Spanheymensi
    bibliothecae non privatae applicandum
Iacobus V. Sletstat
Manu propria
Anno Christi mccccxciii
Rursus per fratrem venerabilem Jo. Tritemio mei iuris factus
Ja. Schenck.

33. See the synthesis by William Sherman, *Used Books: Marking Readers in Renaissance England* (Philadelphia: University of Pennsylvania Press, 2008).

34. Johannes Trithemius, *Liber de scriptoribus ecclesiasticis* (Basel: Amerbach, 1494).

35. Trithemius, *Liber de scriptoribus ecclesiasticis,* 139 verso: "Theodoricus Ulsenius homo phrysius singularis eruditionis et peritiae in carmine et oratione: inter quae extant eius: Elegiae cultae: Et alia epigrammata: Et alia plura quae ad posteritatem ventura sunt."

36. Ibid.: "comportavit et scripsit inter alia ingenii sui opuscula: ex Iacobo Pergomensi et aliis historiographis addens nonnulla maxime de rebus Germanorum opus grande et insigne quod continet: Historias temporum: De caeteris nihil vidi."

37. Ibid., 24 recto.

38. Ibid., 1 verso–2 recto: "Placuit autem mihi novo scribendi modo procedere: ut lector ipse noticiam librorum ex principiis facilius possit invenire."

39. L. D. Reynolds and N. G. Wilson, *Scribes and Scholars: A Guide to the Transmission of Greek and Latin Literature*, 3rd ed. (Oxford: Clarendon Press, 1991), 117, 269.

40. Trithemius, *Liber de scriptoribus ecclesiasticis*, 42 recto: "Fertur quaedam praeclara scripsisse opuscula. De quibus ego tantum legi volumen grande et insigne: continens ab exordio mundi usque ad nativitatem domini nostri Iesu Christi: Rerum gestarum historiam. li. vii."

41. Trithemius, *Catalogus illustrium virorum Germaniae* (Mainz: Peter von Friedberg, 1495), "Ex quibus legi centum triginta quinque. In quibus omnibus doctrina catholica relucet: que vel fidem confirmet: vel instruet disciplinam. Vidimus in eodem volumine epistolarum multas litteras Conradi tercii et Frederici primi imperatorum multorumque episcoporum . . ."

42. British Library, MS Add. 15, 102, 1 verso: "Vidi librum grande ut dixi volumen in predicto monasterio sancti ruperti de quo hec omnes que sequuntur epistole licet cum festinacione scripte sunt Anno domini millesimo cccc° octogesimo septimo per quendam monachum sancti benedicti de cenobio spanheim iubente me eiusdem monasterii abate licet indigno."

43. Trithemius, *Liber de scriptoribus ecclesiasticis,* 19 recto.

44. Herzog August Bibliothek, Wolfenbüttel, MS 78 Aug. fol., 196 verso, col. 2: "Notandum de suprascripto libro, qui beato sixto pape ascribitur, quod non ipsius sed alterius cuiusdam sixti philosophi est de quo in vita philosophorum capitulo cx sic legitur: Sixtus pitagoricus philosophus qui claruit temporibus octaviani imperatoris scripsit librum sentenciarum moralium notabilium quem enchiridion appellavit. Quem librum rufinus presbiter claro sermone ad agamani cuiusdam preces de Greco in latinum transtulit . . ."

45. British Library, MS Add. 15, 102, 1 verso: "In omnibus autem opusculis suis beata hildegardis mistice valde et obscure procedit: unde nisi a religiosis et devotis vix eius scripta intelliguntur. Nec mirum. Omnia enim que scripsit per revelacionem didicit et sensum et verba que mistica sunt et preciosa nec ante porcos i. carnales homines ponenda ne quod non intelligunt irridere incipiant et spernere."

46. Trithemius, *De scriptoribus ecclesiasticis,* 61 verso: "In omnibus opusculis suis catholica doctrina relucet: quae vel fidem confirmet: vel instruat mores: nec quicquam dixit aut scripsit unquam quod in dubium possit vocari. Et cum latini sermonis esset ignara: tamen revelante spiritu dei omnia latine et congrue dictavit: notariis excipientibus."

47. Herzog August Bibliothek, Wolfenbüttel, MS 34 Aug. fol., blank 2: "hunc librum composuit freculfus episcopus lexoviensis monachus fuldensis cenobii. Claruit Anno domini octingentesimo quadragesimo. Vide in secundo libro illustrium virorum ordinis sancti Benedicti domini Johannis Abbatis spanhemensis qualis fuerit iste freculphus episcopus."

48. Klaus Arnold, "*De viris illustribus*. Aus den Anfängen der humanistischen Literaturgeschichtsschreibung: Johannes Trithemius und andere Schriftstellerkataloge des 15. Jahrhunderts," *Humanistica Lovaniensia* 42 (1993), 52–70.

49. Trithemius, *De scriptoribus ecclesiasticis*, [141] recto: "Mirari te dicis (Alberte amantissime) quod professores saecularium litterarum: qui nihil ecclesiasticum scripserunt: inter viros illustres ecclesiasticosque scriptores posuerim."

50. Ibid.: "Non miror quod miraris: mirantur et caeteri."

51. Ibid.: "Neque enim satis eruditum in divinis scripturis quemquam dici posse arbitror: ubi saecularis litteraturae disciplinam ignorarit."

52. Ibid.: "Theologus orator animos audientium suorum in potestate sua habere dicitur."

53. Ibid.: "O utinam omnes theologi nostri temporis oratoriam colerent . . ."

54. Ibid., [141] verso: "Scientia non habet inimicum nisi ignorantem."

55. Johannes Trithemius, *Chronicon Insigne Monasterij Hirsaugiensis, Ordinis S. Benedicti* (Basel: Oporinus, 1559); Trithemius, *Tomus I [–II] Annalium Hirsaugiensium*, 2 vols. (St. Gallen: Schlegel, 1690).

56. Trithemius, *Tomus I Annalium Hirsaugiensium*, [A4] recto: "Auctorum vero de quibus auxilium habui, ista sunt nomina . . . Multa denique ex aliis diversis Chronicis et historiis Francorum, Bavarorum, Suevorum, Moguntinensium, Neometensium, Vangionum, comitumque Palatinorum Rheni dudum per Wernherum Monachum Lorissensis Coenobii comportatis, huic operi nostro inserui, quorum mihi narratio ad seriem historiae non inutilis videbatur. Ex Annalibus quoque, privilegiis, et litteris ipsius Monasterii Hirsaugiensis non mediocriter adjutus sum, quorum continentia Successione Abbatum deducantur. Plura etiam ex Legendis Sanctorum, Epistolis quoque et opusculis Patrum convenientia proposito meo non absque labore magno sum assecutus."

57. Ibid.: "Auctorum vero de quibus auxilium habui, ista sunt nomina: Megenfridus Monachus Fuldensis, qui multa scribit de prima Fundatione Hirsaugiensis Monasterii et Successionis Abbatum apud Ecclesiam S. Aurelii . . ."

58. Trithemius, *Chronicon Insigne Monasterij Hirsaugiensis.*

59. Trithemius, *Tomus I Annalium Hirsaugiensium*, 67: "Obiit autem, ut Menfridus est testis, anno aetatis suae sexagesimo tertio, regiminis vero Abbatialis septimo, mense quoque septimo, die quarto, altera die natalis sanctissimi Patris nostri Benedicti, hoc est, XI. Calendas Aprilis."

60. Konrad Peutinger, *Briefwechsel*, ed. Erich König (Munich: Beck, 1923), 88.

61. Johannes Trithemius, *Compendium sive breviarium primi voluminis annalium sive historiarum de origine regum et gentis Francorum* (Paris, 1539) sig. [; vi verso:] "Scio multos de origine Francorum et varie et diversa scripsisse, quorum nonnulli gentem contendunt indigenam, caeteri vero nescio de qua Sicambrorum urbe adventitiam. Quorum diversas opiniones neminem posse vere discernere vel concordare credimus, quem Hunibaldi compilatio non illustrat. Is enim solidus Francorum historiographus claruit in humanis Chlodovei Regis, quem sanctus

Remigius praesul Romanorum baptizavit, temporibus, anno dominicae nativitatis quingentesimo, et scripsit post Doracum philosophum, Wasthaldum philosophum, et alios plures rerum gestarum antiquissimos scriptores insigne opus, quod in libros decem et octo distinxit."

62. Ibid., sig. iii recto: "Tempus autem in his tribus voluminibus complexus sum annorum mille nongentorum quinquaginta quatuor, in quibus reges numerantur Francorum recto sibi ordine succedentes, ab ipso Marcomero iam dicto usque in vicesimum nonum annum Imperatoris Romanorum Caesaris Maximiliani Augusti, centum tres. Multi fuere collaterales . . . Per totum vero volumen primum successiones regum Francorum et gesta continuam, usque ad regem Pippinum . . ." For the origins of Bavaria, see Trithemius, DE ORIGINE GENTIS ET PRINCIPVM sive Regum Bavarorum commentarius Joannis Tritemii Abbatis Spanheymensis, Vat. lat. 7011, 214 recto–224 verso (holograph), at 214 recto: ". . . ex priscis habitatoribus admodum rudibus, et qui bestiarum more glandibus vescerentur."

63. Trithemius, *Compendium,* 12–13:

Anno regni sui vicesimo sexto, Basanus rex post multa praelia fortiter gesta, cum diversis per circuitum nationibus, volens se deorum exhibere pontificem, eorum sacra superstitione multa renovavit: Sacerdotes in cultu numinum peritissimos instituit plures, in cursu siderum curiosos, in vaticiniis, in praenotionibus, in exponendis somniis, in Ethicis, et in Physicis doctrinis, more veterum, eruditos, in carminibus quoque et historiis antiquorum regum heroumque, gentis suae duntaxat, componendis canendisque in utraque lingua exercitatissimos: inter quos praecelluit ingenio et usu scribendi caeteros Heligastus Theocali pontificis quondam filius, qui filiis ducum et nobilium instituendis praeerat, et heroum gesta carmine descripsit.

De hoc viro plura scribit miranda Hunibaldus, Francorum historiographus, quae nisi daemoniis alicuius patrata concedantur artificio, conficta potius a scriptore aliquo sunt existimanda, quam per hominem idolis deditum factitata. Multa Sicambris praedixit futura: Iovem sacerdotibus exhibuit visibilem: secreta hominum consilia deduxit in publicum: et hostium arcana in causis et negociis arduis Basano regi denudavit. Nihil eum videbatur latere omnium, quae hostes etiam secretissimo tractavissent consilio in Sicambros. Quae res amicis, securitatem: inimicis vero, desperationem incussit.

Consilio enim Heligasti rex Basan pendebat totus cum universis principibus regni: et quod ille iussit, omnes faciebant . . .

Ibid., 37: "Claruit his temporibus apud Hildericum regem, proceres quoque, et universam multitudinem Francorum gentis, magno in precio Hildegast, philosophus, consiliarius, vates, et parens regum, senior, omnium doctissimus, qui sua tempestate miranda dixit, fecit, et scripsit."

64. Cf. ibid., 18: "Mos hic erat maioribus nostris Francis atque Germanis, ut heroum facta vel dicta memoratu digna, per sacerdotes templorum, patriis commendarentur carminibus, in quibus discendis, memorandis, et decantandis, iuvenum excitarentur ingenia. Quae consuetudo multis duravit annis, donec postremo defecit."

65. Ibid., 37: "Tantaeque apud suos aestimationis et auctoritatis fuit, ut eius imperio cuncti semper obedirent."

66. Joseph Chmel, *Die Handschriften der k.k. Hofbibliothek in Wien, im Interesse der Geschichte, besonders der österreichischen, verzeichnet und excerpirt*, 2 vols. (Vienna: Carl Gerold, 1840–1841), I, 312–320.

67. Ibid., 319:

Serenissime Rex regum Cesarumque inuictissime Cesar: et Imperatorum mundi post deum unice atque gloriossime Imperator: qui has super eminentissime maiestati tue exhibebit literulas meas, Imperialis curie, ut asseruit, tue ministerialis, post discessum a me Heraldi celsitudinis metuendissime Maiestatis tue ad me venit, per quem glorie serenitatis tue, quam se aditurum dicebat, humili sugestione duxi notificandum, quod successor meus in Spanheim nunc abbas plura volumina vendidit abbati Hirsaugiensi suevo iuxta termas quae nuncupantur cellerbad. unde si Hunibald Francorum Historiographus in Spanheim non fuerit repertus, apud Hirsaugiam subtilis et cauta fiat inquisicio. Ego mores novi philobiblorum et maxime claustralium, qui nisi cautissime indicti, ne dicam circumventi, potentibus non facile libros suos communicant. Si conventus principum Vuormacie, ut phamatur, habuerit nervos et vires, cooperabor forsitan quam potuero diligenter quo Hunibald inveniatur captivus, quem ego prima die mensis aprilis anno Cristianorum Millesimo D. quinto in Spanheim egrediens cum aliis voluminibus non minus xxc in abbatia dimisi. Harum literarum potitor me rogat quo scriptis meis supremo tibi domino mundi fiat commendatus: Ecce facio, et culex murem elephanti, ceu Codrus Jovi Minervam commendo, qui te vicarium suum in terris esse voluit mundi creator deus; ipse te Maximiliane Cesar numine divitem sacro, et hic diu conservet incolumem, et faciat post fata in eternum felicem. Cui si liceret se muscam commendare divis, tritemius optaret placere. Ex meo Tugurio peapolitano xxvi die mensis aprilis anno Cristianorum Millesimo Quingentesimo Tercioque decimo. Manu mea raptiss.

E.S.Ju.Q. Majestatis cesaree

Obsequentissimus non minus quam devotissimus capellanus et orator Joannes tritemius abbas divi Jacobi Wirtzburgensis Quondam vero Spanheimensis.

68. Ibid., 320: "Serenissime Invictissime et gloriosissime omnium terrae principum. Rex Cesar et Imperator potentissime, quemadmodum tua michi celsitudo

precepit—Spanhem personaliter accessi. Hunibaldum inquisivi, sed non inveni. Suspicio mihi est, quod cum aliis plerisque pecunia sit distractus. Monasterium quod propterea venit adeundum adii. Inquisitionem subtiliter temptavi, sed bibliothecam videre non potui, quam corruisse dicebant."

69. Peutinger, *Briefwechsel*, 295 and n2.

70. Ibid., 313:

Suspicor ea que Abbas de Hunibaldo suo refert omnia ese ficta. coniecture que me ad hoc impellunt sunt iste. Iste scribit quod omnia que hic de nominibus regum et ducum ponit se ante sedecim annos ex Hunibaldo dum adhuc in Spanheim fuisset excerpsisse. asserit hic et eciam in Chronico suo quod impressum circumfertur Francos sive Sicambros ante Christi nativitatem annis 439. egressos cum universo populo de Sarmacia, venisse in Germaniam sedisseque in finibus Saxonie ad hostia Rheni, ubi nunc sunt Holandi, Frisii, Gelrenses et pars Westfalie inferioris. In aliis duabus scripturis suis, quas mox hinc subiiciam, dicit eos post Christi nativitatem anno 380. ex Sarmacia in Germaniam ad ripas Mogani penetrasse que est mirabilis differentia plusquam octingentorum annorum.

In Monasterio S. Jacobi prope Wirczburg in Abbatia sua in pariete solarii versus orientem circa picturas principum Francorum sic scripsit:

Anno Christianorum 380. Indictione octava Gens Francorum ex Sarmatia post necem Priami regis sui a Romanis in bello iuxta Sicambriam perempti, venit in Germaniam tempore Valentiniani Caesaris et a Turingis hospitibus sedes iuxta Mogani ripas acceperunt, Marcomede Priami filio et Sunnone Antemoris ex stirpe Troianorum procreatis ducibus, exercitum ducentorum sexaginta quinque milium pugnatorum in virtute magna precedentibus, quos Turingi in odium Romanorum libenter susceperunt, locum eius manendi assignantes inter Salam et Maganum fluvios. Franci ergo Turingorum amicicia freti, Thuringios accepte possessionis tempore dilatarunt magnifice.

Item scripturam subsequentem sicut ipse propria manu a tergo notavit, misit Cesaree Maiestati per Jo. de Colonia Heraldum Geldrie anno 1513 et ego habeo apud me exemplar istius Cesari missum de manu sua scriptum. ecce quam diversissima narrat in ista scriptura contra libros suos proprios et tamen eciam Hunibaldum allegat eque sicut in superioribus.

71. See Joachimsen, *Geschichtsauffassung und Geschichtsschreibung in Deutschland,* and George Huppert, "The Trojan Franks and Their Critics," *Studies in the Renaissance* 12 (1965), 227–241.

72. Andrew Jotischky, *The Carmelites and Antiquity: Mendicants and Their Pasts in the Middle Ages* (Oxford: Oxford University Press, 2002), 330.

73. See e.g. Walter Stephens, *Giants in Those Days* (Lincoln: University of Nebraska Press, 1991); Ingrid Rowland, *The Culture of the High Renaissance: Ancients*

and Moderns in Sixteenth-Century Rome (Cambridge: Cambridge University Press, 1998); Riccardo Fubini, *Storiografia dell'umanesimo in Italia da Leonardo Bruni ad Annio da Viterbo* (Rome: Storia e Letteratura, 2003); and Brian Curran, *The Egyptian Renaissance: The Afterlife of Ancient Egypt in Early Modern Italy* (Chicago: University of Chicago Press, 2007).

74. Beatus Rhenanus, *Rerum germanicarum libri tres* (Basel: Froben, 1551), 39. The adage in question was "Mulgere hircum," Erasmus, *Adagia* 1.3.51 (from Lucian). See Karl Joachim Weintraub, "Review of *Defenders of the Text,*" *Classical Philology* 88 (1993), 269–273 at 271.

75. Chmel, *Die Handschriften der k.k. Hofbibliothek in Wien,* I, 317. He also offered to exchange the manuscript of Boniface that Hofyrer had copied at his command.

76. On this aspect of Annius's work, see the classic articles of Werner Goez, "Die Anfänge der historischen Methoden-Reflexion in der italienischen Renaissance und ihre Aufnahme in der Geschichtsschreibung des deutschen Humanismus," *Archiv für Kulturgeschichte* 56 (1974), 25–48; "Die Anfänge der historischen Methoden-Reflexion im italienischen Humanismus," in *Geschichte in der Gegenwart: Festschrift für K. Kluxen,* ed. E. Heinen and H. J. Schoeps (Paderborn: Schöningh, 1972), 3–21; and the more recent treatments by C. R. Ligota, "Annius of Viterbo and Historical Method," *Journal of the Warburg and Courtauld Institutes* 50 (1987), 44–56, and Anthony Grafton, *Defenders of the Text* (Cambridge, Mass.: Harvard University Press, 1991), chap. 3.

77. Trithemius, *Compendium,* 4: "Quantas vero difficultates in itinere habuerint, quae bella cum obsistentibus sibi populis gesserint, quantaque pericula vel inciderint, vel evaserint, si quis ad plenum scire desiderat, memoratum scriptorem legat in libro historiarum gentis Francorum. Cuius initia sicuti sunt miranda, sic mihi videntur (salva pace iudicantium melius) in pluribus esse fabulosa." On the "topos of critical rejection" deployed here see Borchardt, *German Antiquity in Renaissance Myth.*

78. Ibid., 12–13: "De hoc viro plura scribit miranda Hunibaldus, Francorum historiographus, quae nisi daemonis alicuius patrata concedantur artificio, conficta potius a scriptore aliquo sunt existimanda, quam per hominem idolis deditum factitata."

79. Ibid., 111–114, esp. 111: "Et quia nunc assertionem hanc nostram magis cognovimus esse veram, ex confictis et ineptissimis literis quas in praedicto Monasterio Erphurdiano vidimus nullo munitas sigillo cuiuscunque et legimus sub nomine Dagoberti et rescripsimus, ne quis falsitatis nos argueret, operaeprecium fore duximus, si earundem litterarum exemplar cum aliis rationibus nostrae assertioni coniungamus."

80. Nikolaus Staubach, "Auf der Suche nach der verlorenen Zeit: Die historiographischen Fiktionen des Johannes Trithemius im Licht seines wissenschaftlichen Selbstverständnisses," in *Fälschungen im Mittelalter,* 5 vols. (Hannover: Hahn, 1988), I, 263–316.

81. Trithemius to Johannes Virdung on Faustus, Biblioteca Apostolica Vaticana MS Pal. lat. 730, 174 verso: "Referebant mihi quidam in oppido sacerdotes quod in multorum presencia dixit tantam se omnis sapiencie consecutum scienciam atque memoriam ut si volumina platonis et aristotelis omnia cum tota eorum philosophia in toto periissent ab hominum memoria: ipse suo ingenio velut ezras alter hebreus restituere universa cum prestanciore valeret elegancia."

82. Johannes Trithemius, *Liber octo quaestionum, quas illi dissolvendas proposuit Maximilianus Caesar* (Cologne: Impensis Melchioris Novesiani, 1534), D2 verso–D3 recto: "Cum prosequerer adolescens studia literarum, in uno lecto quatuor eramus nocte quadam dormientes, surrexit a latere meo coaevus et dormiens, ut solebant in somnis, domum oculis clausis et luna introlucente quinta decima quasi vigil circumambulabat, ascendit muros, et aelurum agilitate sua vincebat, lectum quoque secundo et tertio sopitus transcendit, calcavit nos pedibus omnes, nec magis sensimus pondus, quam si mus nos contigisset exiguus. Quocunque dormiens corpus movebatur, subito ianuarum omnes ultra aperiebantur clausurae. Altiora domus aedificia velocissime penetravit et more passeris haerebat in tectis. Visa loquor non vaga relatione audita." John Dee, marginal note in his copy, Cambridge University Library, h 15 9: "Mirandum."

83. Ibid., C4 verso–C5 recto: "Secundo facit miracula homo similitudine angelicae puritatis. Quanto enim mens nostra in fide Iesu Christi confirmata per dilectionem purior evaserit, tanto sanctis angelis effecta similior, eorum familiaritatem maiorem assequetur. Quisquis autem sanctorum angelorum omnimodam familiaritatem assecutus fuerit, cum voluerit in miraculis deo largiente coruscabit. Revelant enim sancti angeli hominibus puris et in dei amore ferventibus arcana caeteris abscondita: et multa faciunt eis mandato creatoris manifesta. Nam prope est dominus invocantibus eum in veritate." Dee, marginal note: "Hoc nobis Det Deus aliquando."

84. Trithemius, *Compendium*, [; vi] verso: "Scio multos de origine Francorum et varie et diversa scripsisse, quorum nonnulli gentem contendunt indigenam, caeteri vero nescio de qua Sicambrorum urbe adventitiam. Quorum diversas opiniones neminem posse vel discernere vel concordare credimus, quem Hunibaldi compilatio non illustrat."

85. British Library MS Add.15, 102 (Hildegard of Bingen), 1 verso: "Hec eadem virgo beata ab infancia sua divinis semper revelacionibus visitata multa scripsit non sensu humano sed quemadmodum in vera visione illa didicit videlicet li. scivias. li. vite meritorum. li. divinorum operum. li. exposicionis quorundam evangeliorum. li. simplicis medicine. li. composite medicine. ac cantica plurima cum li[n]gua ignota. et li. epistolarum cui istam premitto prefacionem vel pocius si placet commendacionem. Hec omnia scripta habentur in maximo quodam volumine et valde precioso de quo opinio vulgi est quod manu sancte hildegardis sit conscriptus. Vidi librum grande ut dixi volumen in predicto monasterio sancti ruperti de quo hec omnes que sequuntur epistole, licet cum festinacione scripte sunt,

Anno domini millesimo cccc°. octogesimo septimo per quendam monachum sancti benedicti de cenobio spanheim iubente me eiusdem monasterii abbate licet indigno. In omnibus autem opusculis suis beata hildegardis mistice valde et obscure procedit: unde nisi a religiosis et devotis vix eius scripta intelliguntur. Nec mirum. Omnia enim que scripsit per revelacionem didicit et sensum et verba que mistica sunt et preciosa. nec ante porcos i. carnales homines ponenda ne quod non intelligunt irridere incipiant et spernere."

4. The World in a Room

1. Tommaso Campanella, *The City of the Sun: A Poetical Dialogue,* ed. and tr. Daniel Donnon (Berkeley: University of California Press, 1981), 34–35: "Nel di fuora tutte maniere di pesci di fiumi, lachi e mari, e le virtù loro, e 'l modo di vivere, di generarsi e allevarsi, e a che servono, e le somiglianze c'hanno con le cose celesti e terrestri e dell'arte e della natura; sì che me stupii, quando trovai pesce vescovo e catena e chiodo e stella, appunto come son queste cose tra noi."

2. Ibid., 34–37: "Nel sesto, dentro vi sono tutte l'arte mecchaniche, e l'inventori loro, e li diversi modi, come s'usano in diverse regioni del mondo."

3. Ibid., 36–37: "e li figliuoli, senza fastidio, giocando, si trovan saper tutte le scienze istoricamente prima che abbin dieci anni."

4. Ibid., 42–43: "Onde si ridono di noi che gli artefici appellamo ignobili, e diciamo nobili quelli, che null'arte imparano e stanno oziosi e tengono in ozio e lascivia tanti servitori con roina della republica."

5. Gisela Bock, *Thomas Campanella* (Tübingen: Niemeyer, 1974); John Headley, *Tommaso Campanella and the Transformation of the World* (Princeton, N.J.: Princeton University Press, 1997); Germana Ernst, *Tommaso Campanella: Il libro e il corpo della natura* (Rome: Laterza, 2002), chap. III.

6. Francis Bacon, "New Atlantis," in *Works,* ed. J. Spedding, R. L. Ellis, and D. D. Heath, 14 vols. (London: Longman, 1857–1884; repr. Stuttgart: Frommann-Holzboog, 1963), III, 156–166.

7. Samuel Quiccheberg, *Inscriptiones vel tituli theatri amplissimi* (Munich: Berg, 1565); new ed. by Harriet Roth, *Der Anfang der Museumslehre in Deutschland: Das Traktat "Inscriptiones vel Tituli Theatri Amplissimi" von Samuel Quiccheberg* (Berlin: Akademie, 2000).

8. Rosalie Colie, "Cornelis Drebbel and Salomon de Caus: Two Jacobean Models for Salomon's House," *Huntington Library Quarterly* 18 (1954), 245–260; Colie, *"Some Thankfulnesse to Constantine": A Study of English Influence upon the Early Works of Constantijn Huygens* (The Hague: Nijhoff, 1956); William Sherman, *John Dee: The Politics of Reading and Writing in the English Renaissance* (Amherst: University of Massachusetts Press, 1995); Lorraine Daston and Katharine Park, *Wonders and the Order of Nature, 1150–1750* (New York: Zone, 1998), chap. 5.

9. Horst Bredekamp, *Antikensehnsucht und Maschinenglauben: Die Geschichte der Kunstkammer und die Zukunft der Kunstgeschichte* (Berlin: Wagenbach, 1993), tr. by Alison Brown as *The Lure of Antiquity and the Cult of the Machine* (Princeton, N.J.: Wiener, 1995); Thomas Kaufmann, *The Mastery of Nature* (Princeton, N.J.: Princeton University Press, 1993); Daston and Park, *Wonders and the Order of Nature, 1150–1750.*

10. Jean Bodin, *Colloquium heptaplomeres de rerum sublimium arcanis abditis,* ed. Ludwig Noack (Schwerin: Bärensprung; Paris: Klincksieck; London: Nutt, 1857; repr. Hildesheim: Olms, 1970), 2; see Ann Blair, *The Theater of Nature: Jean Bodin and Renaissance Science* (Princeton, N.J.: Princeton University Press, 1997).

11. Campanella, *City of the Sun,* 54–63: "e non accoppiano se non le femine grandi e belle alli grandi e virtuosi, e le grasse a' macri, e le macre alli grassi, per far temperie . . . e hanno belle statue di uomini illustri, dove le donne mirano . . . E dicono che questo abuso in noi viene dell'ozio delle donne, che le fa scolorite e fiacche e piccole: e però han bisogno di colori e alte pianelle, e di farsi belle per tenerezza, e così guastano la propria complessione e della prole." These proposals resembled those traditionally recommended in treatises on the breeding of horses.

12. Bacon, *Works,* ed. Spedding and Ellis, III, 156–157.

13. Ibid., 159.

14. For the intellectual resources Renaissance philosophers could readily muster and apply to this topic, see the classic surveys of Anthony Close, "Commonplace Theories of Art and Nature in Classical Antiquity and in the Renaissance," *Journal of the History of Ideas* 30 (1969), 467–486, and "Philosophical Theories of Art and Nature in Classical Antiquity," *Journal of the History of Ideas* 32 (1971), 163–184. Though Galileo portrayed himself as insisting that one could not trick nature, and suggested that earlier and contemporary engineers believed that one could do so, most of them in fact agreed with him, as had the author of the pseudo-Aristotelian *Mechanica.* See Markus Popplow, *Neu, nützlich und erfindungsreich: Die Idealisierung von Technik in der frühen Neuzeit* (Münster: Waxmann, 1998), 143–176.

15. See Popplow, *Neu, nützlich und erfindungsreich;* cf. Alex Keller, "Renaissance Theaters of Machines," *Technology and Culture* 19 (1978), 495–508, and Kenneth Knoespel, "Gazing on Machinery: *Theatrum Mechanorum* and the Assimilation of Renaissance Machinery," in *Literature and Technology,* ed. Mark Greenberg and Lance Schacterle (Bethlehem, Pa.: Lehigh University Press, 1992), 99–124.

16. Quiccheberg, *Inscriptiones vel tituli theatri amplissimi,* fol. B ij recto (ed. Roth, 54–57): "Animalia miraculosa & rariora: ut rarae aves, insecta, pisces, conchae ect. . . . Animalia fusa: ex metallo, gypso, luto, facticiaque materia: qua arte apparent omnia viva."

17. Ibid., fol. A iij verso (46–47): "Machinarum exempla minuta: ut ad aquas hauriendas, ligna in asseres dissecanda, grana comminuenda, palos impellendos, naves ciendas, fluctibus resistendum: ect. Pro quarum machinularum aut structurarum exemplis, alia maiora rite extrui & subinde meliora inveniri possint."

18. M. V. Adriani, ed., *Dioscorides, De materia medica libri sex* (Florence: Giunti, 1518), sig. AA iii recto.

19. Ibid., fol. 209 verso.

20. Ibid., sig. AA iii verso; cf. Paula Findlen, "The Formation of a Scientific Community: Natural History in Sixteenth-Century Italy," in *Natural Particulars,* ed. Anthony Grafton and Nancy Siraisi (Cambridge, Mass.: MIT Press, 2000), 369–400.

21. Bacon, *Works,* ed. Spedding and Ellis, IV, 66; cf. 25. Emphasis in original.

22. Ibid., 65–66.

23. Ibid., 65.

24. Guido Panciroli, *Rerum memorabilium pars prior . . . pars posterior,* ed. and tr. Heinrich Salmuth, 2 vols. (Frankfurt: Tampach, 1631), II, 125: "Hodie ad eam subtilitatem deducta est ars ista, ut Rhabarbarum, Nuces pineae, pistaceae, Cinnamonum et aliae species Saccharo condiantur, atque ita quasi recentes adserventur. Efformantur quoque ex Saccharo figurae et imagunculae pulcherrimae: necnon omnis generis fructus repraesentantur, ita ut naturales et feri videantur."

25. Ibid., II, 129, quoting Joseph Quercetanus.

26. Elizabeth Gilmore Holt, ed., *A Documentary History of Art,* 3 vols. (Princeton, N.J.: Princeton University Press, 1981), I, 164.

27. Ibid., I, 161; cf. E. H. Gombrich, *Norm and Form* (London: Phaidon, 1966).

28. H. W. Janson, "The Image Made by Chance in Renaissance Thought," in *De artibus opuscula XL: Essays in Honor of Erwin Panofsky,* ed. Millard Meiss (New York: New York University Press, 1961), 254–266.

29. Katharine Park, "Impressed Images: Reproducing Wonders," in *Picturing Science, Producing Art,* ed. C. A. Jones and P. Galison (New York: Routledge, 1998), 254–271.

30. Leon Battista Alberti, *On Painting and On Sculpture,* ed. Cecil Grayson (London: Phaidon, 1972), 120–121: "Artes eorum, qui ex corporibus a natura procreatis effigies et simulacra suum in opus promere aggrediuntur, ortas hinc fuisse arbitror. Nam ex trunco glaebave et huiusmodi mutis corporibus fortassis aliquando intuebantur lineamenta nonnulla, quibus paululum immutatis persimile quidpiam veris naturae vultibus redderetur. Coepere id igitur animo advertentes atque adnotantes adhibita diligentia tentare conarique possentne illic adiungere adimereve atque perfinire quod ad veram simulacri speciem comprehendendam absolvendamque deesse videretur. Ergo quantum res ipsa admonebat lineas superficiesque istic emendando expoliendoque institutum adsecuti sunt, non id quidem sine voluptate."

31. Ibid., 121–123: "Quemadmodum enim praestitit natura ex trunco, uti diximus, glebave, ut fieri aliquid posse a te suis operibus simile sentires, ita ab eadem ipsa natura existit promptum habileque aliquid, quo tu quidem modum mediaque habeas certa et rata, quibus ubi intenderis facile possis aptissime atque accommodatissime summum istius artificii decus attingere."

32. Ibid., 122–123: "Qualia autem statuariis a natura praestentur media commoda et pernecessaria ad opus bellissime perficiendum, exponendum est."

33. Ibid., 98–99: "Fugit enim imperitos ea pulchritudinis idea quam peritissimi vix discernunt. Zeuxis, praestantissimus et omnium doctissimus et peritissimus pictor, facturus tabulam quam in templo Lucinae apud Crotoniates publice dicaret, non suo confisus ingenio temere, ut fere omnes hac aetate pictores, ad pingendum accessit, sed quod putabat omnia quae ad venustatem quaereret, ea non modo proprio ingenio non posse, sed ne a natura quidem petita uno posse in corpore reperiri, idcirco ex omni eius urbis iuventute delegit virgines quinque forma praestantiores, ut quod in quaque esset formae muliebris laudatissimum, id in pictura referret."

34. Ibid., 98–101: "Prudenter is quidem, nam pictoribus nullo proposito exemplari quod imitentur, ubi ingenio tantum pulchritudinis laudes captare enituntur, facile evenit ut eo labore non quam debent aut quaerunt pulchritudinem assequantur, sed plane in malos, quos vel volentes vix possunt dimittere, pingendi usus dilabantur."

35. Ibid., 133–135: "Ergo non unius istius aut illius corporis tantum, sed quoad licuit, eximiam a natura pluribus corporibus, quasi ratis portionibus dono distributam, pulchritudinem adnotare et mandare litteris prosecuti sumus, illum imitati qui apud Crotoniates, facturus simulacrum Deae, pluribus a virginibus praestantioribus insignes elegantesque omnes formae pulchritudines delegit, suumque in opus transtulit."

36. Giorgio Vasari, *Lives of the Artists,* tr. J. C. Bondanella and P. Bondanella (Oxford: Oxford University Press, 1991), 277; Vasari, *Vite degli artefici, Parte terza, proemio, Opere* (Milan: Ubicini, 1840), 249: "Il disegno fu lo imitare il più bello della natura in tutte le figure così scolpite come dipinte."

37. Vasari, *Lives of the Artists,* 282; Vasari, *Vite degli artefici, Parte terza, proemio, Opere,* 250–251.

38. Cf. Valla's deliberate decision not just to rival but to surpass the ancient grammatical authorities Donatus and Priscian in his *Elegantiae.* See L. Cesarini Martinelli, "Note sulla polemica Poggio-Valla e sulla fortuna delle *Elegantiae,*" *Interpres* 3 (1980), 29–79, esp. 71–74.

39. Julius Caesar Scaliger, *Exotericarum exercitationum liber quintus decimus* (Paris: Vascosan, 1557), fols. 395 verso–396 recto: "Falsa, inquis, delectant: quia admirabilia. Delectant igitur pueros et stolidos, non senes et sapientes. Certe verum est. Sed quaeso: cur Homerica phasmata (sic enim libet appellare) delectant sapientes? . . . Illud huiusce rei caput est. Mentem nostram esse natura sua infinitam. Quamobrem et quod ad potentiam attinet, aliena appetere: et quod spectat ad intellectionem, etiam e falsis ac monstrorum picturis capere voluptatem, propterea quod exuperant vulgares limites veritatis. Aspernatur enim certorum finium praescriptionem . . . Ergo picturae quoque laudat sapiens perfectionem: tametsi fictam esse, haud ignorat. Mavultque pulchram imaginem,

quam naturali similem designatae. Naturam enim in eo superat ars. Quia multis eventis a primo homine symmetria illa depravata fuit. At nihil impedit plasten, quominus attollat, deprimat, addat, demat, torqueat, dirigat. Equidem ita censeo: nullum unquam corpus humanum tam affabre fuisse a Natura factum (duo scilicet excipio: unum primi hominis: alterum veri hominis, veri Dei) quam perfecte finguntur hodie doctis artificum manibus."

40. Erwin Panofsky, *Idea,* tr. J. J. S. Peake (Columbia: University of South Carolina Press, 1968), 222–223n20.

41. Carlo Ginzburg, *Jean Fouquet: Ritratto del buffone Gonella* (Modena: Panini, 1996).

42. Holt, *A Documentary History of Art,* I, 273–275.

43. Alberti, *On Painting and On Sculpture,* ed. Grayson, 32–33: "struttura sì grande, erta sopra e' cieli, ampla da coprire tutti 'e popoli toscani"; "Onde stimai fusse, quanto da molti questo così essere udiva, che già la natura, maestra delle cose, fatta antica e stracca, più non producea come né giuganti così né ingegni." For a full discussion of this text, see Christine Smith, *Architecture in the Culture of Early Humanism* (New York: Oxford University Press, 1992).

44. Smith, *Architecture in the Culture of Early Humanism,* 23.

45. Lorenzo Valla, *Gesta Ferdinandi regis Aragonum,* ed. Ottavio Besomi (Padua: Antenore, 1973), 195–196: "De quibus ego horologiis non loquor que et vetera sunt nec tantopere admiranda, et que ipsum per se experimentum docuit. Loquor de eo quod vere est horologium, in quo non tantum ratio horarum, sed etiam, ut sic dicam, sermo agnoscitur; utrunque enim logos significant, rationem et sermonem; quod quodammodo vitam habet, cum sponte sua cietur, et dies ac noctes pro homine opus facit. Nec solum horam oculis ostendit ac praescribit, sed etiam auribus procul et domi manentium nuntiat, campana, que superimposita est, numerum distinguente: quo nihil neque utilius neque iocundius."

46. Ibid., 194: "Et certe necesse est ut docti aliquando constituant quibus vocabulis appellande sint ee res que non ita multo superioribus temporibus sunt excogitate. Non enim exhausta sunt mortalitatis ingenia; quod haud dubie fatendum est, nisi invidemus laudes nostras proxime accedere ad solertiam antiquorum in multis, et si non omnibus, honestis atque utilibus."

47. On the origins and transmission of this text, see Alex Keller, "A Renaissance Humanist Looks at 'New' Inventions: The Article 'Horologium' in Giovanni Tortelli's *De Orthographia,*" *Technology and Culture* 11 (1970), 345–365; Ottavio Besomi, "Dai 'Gesta Ferdinandi Regis Aragonum' del Valla al 'De orthographia' del Tortelli," *Italia Medioevale e Umanistica* 9 (1966), 75–121; Brian Copenhaver, "The Historiography of Discovery in the Renaissance: The Sources and Composition of Polydore Vergil's *De Inventoribus Rerum* I–III," *Journal of the Warburg and Courtauld Institutes* 41 (1978), 192–214; Polydore Vergil, *On Discovery,* ed. and tr. Brian Copenhaver (Cambridge, Mass.: Harvard University Press, 2002).

48. Giannozzo Manetti, *De dignitate et excellentia hominis,* ed. Elizabeth Leonard (Padua: Antenore, 1975), 77: "Nostra namque, hoc est humana, sunt quoniam ab hominibus effecta cernuntur: omnes domus, omnia opida, omnes urbes, omnia denique orbis terrarum edificia, que nimirum tanta et talia sunt, ut potius angelorum quam hominum opera ob magnam quandam eorum excellentiam iure censeri debeant. Nostre sunt picture, nostre sculpture; nostre sunt artes, nostre scientie . . ."

49. Marsilio Ficino, *Platonic Theology,* ed. James Hankins and William Bowen, tr. Michael Allen, 6 vols. (Cambridge, Mass.: Harvard University Press, 2001), I, 254–255: "Quid artificium? Mens artificis in materia separata. Quid naturae opus? Naturae mens in coniuncta materia. Tanto igitur huius operis ordo similior est ordini qui in arte est naturali quam ordo artificii hominis arti, quanto et materia propinquior est naturae quam homini, et naturae magis quam homo materiae dominatur."

50. Ibid., I, 200–201: "Vidimus Florentiae Germani opificis tabernaculum, in quo diversorum animalium statuae ad pilam unam connexae atque libratae, pilae ipsius motu simul diversis motibus agebantur: aliae ad dextram currebant, aliae ad sinistram, sursum atque deorsum, aliae sedentes assurgebant, aliae stantes inclinabantur, hae illas coronabant, illae alias vulnerabant. Tubarum quoque et cornuum sonitus et avium cantus audiebantur, aliaque illic simul fiebant et similia succedebant quam plurima, uno tantum unius pilae momento. Sic deus per ipsum esse suum, quod idem re ipsa est ac intellegere ac velle quodve est simplicissimum quoddam omnium centrum, a quo, ut alias diximus, reliqua tamquam lineae deducantur, facillimo nutu vibrat quicquid inde dependet."

51. André Chastel, *Marsile Ficin et l'art* (Geneva: Droz, 1954), 105. See the subtle analysis by Stéphane Toussaint, "Ficino, Archimedes and the Celestial Arts," in *Marsilio Ficino: His Theology, His Philosophy, His Legacy,* ed. Michael Allen and Valerie Rees, with Martin Davies (Leiden: Brill, 2002), 307–326.

52. Joseph Rykwert, *On Adam's House in Paradise,* 2nd ed. (Cambridge, Mass.: MIT Press, 1981); Stephanie Moser, *Ancestral Images* (Ithaca, N.Y.: Cornell University Press, 1998).

53. Holt, *A Documentary History of Art,* I, 339.

54. T. D. Kendrick, *British Antiquity* (London: Methuen, 1950); Florike Egmond and Peter Mason, *The Mammoth and the Mouse* (Baltimore, Md.: Johns Hopkins University Press, 1997); Moser, *Ancestral Images.*

55. Pamela Long, *Openness, Secrecy, Authorship* (Baltimore, Md.: Johns Hopkins University Press, 2001).

56. Pamela Long, "Power, Patronage and the Authorship of *Ars:* From Mechanical Know-How to Mechanical Knowledge in the Last Scribal Age," *Isis* 88 (1997), 1–41.

57. Paolo Rossi, *Philosophy, Technology and the Arts in the Early Modern Era,* ed. Benjamin Nelson, tr. S. Attanasio (New York: Harper, 1970); Alex Keller, "Mathematical Technologies and the Growth of the Idea of Technical Progress in the Sixteenth

Century," in *Science, Medicine and Society in the Renaissance: Essays to Honor Walter Pagel,* ed. Allen Debus, 2 vols. (London: Science History, 1972), I, 11–27; Robert Goulding, "Method and Mathematics: Peter Ramus's Histories of the Sciences," *Journal of the History of Ideas* 67 (2006), 63–85; and, for a very different tradition, Nicholas Popper, " 'Abraham, Planter of Mathematics': Histories of Mathematics and Astrology in Early Modern Europe," *Journal of the History of Ideas* 67 (2006), 87–106. Popplow emphasizes that sixteenth-century writers rarely made contemporary technologies as such the basis for their claims of technical progress, and insists on the role of the theaters of machines in inspiring a different and more precise view in the seventeenth century.

58. Werner Gundersheimer, *Louis Le Roy* (Geneva: Droz, 1966).

59. Louis Le Roy, *De la vicissitude ou variété des choses en l'univers* (Paris: Fayard, 1988), 378: "n'ayant toute l'antiquité rien qu'elle puisse comparer à ces trois."

60. Jean Bodin, *Methodus ad facilem historiarum cognitionem,* in *Artis historicae penus,* ed. Hieronymus Wolf, 2 vols. (Basel: Perna, 1579), I, 309–310: "ac nemini dubium esse potest in eam rem penitus intuenti, quin inventa nostrorum cum maiorum inventis conferri pleraque debeant anteferri . . . omitto catapulta veterum et antiqua belli tormenta, quae si cum nostris conferantur, sane puerilia quaedam ludicra videri possint . . . una typographia cum omnibus omnium veterum inventis certare facile potest . . . habet natura scientiarum thesaurus innumerabiles, qui nullis aetatibus exhauriri possunt."

61. Henry Cornelius Agrippa, *Of the Vanitie and Uncertaintie of Artes and Sciences,* ed. Catherine Dunn (Northridge: California State University, 1974), 88; cf. Agrippa, *De occulta philosophia libri tres,* ed. V. Perrone Compagni (Leiden: Brill, 1992), II.1, 250–251: "Et Iulii Caesaris Romae iuxta Vaticanum erecta pyramis et in medio mari extructi arte montes et arces saxorumque moles, cuiusmodi ego in Britannia vidi vix credibili arte congestas. Et legimus apud fidos historicos similibus artibus olim abscissas rupes, completas valles et actos in planum montes, perfossa saxa, adaperta mari promontoria, excavata terrae viscera, diducta flumina, iuncta maribus maria, coercita aequora scrutataque maris profunda, exhaustos lacus, exsiccatas paludes, factas novas insulas rursusque alias restitutas continenti. Quae omnia, etsi cum natura ipsa pugnare videantur, tamen legimus facta et in hunc idem cernimus illorum vestigia, cuiusmodi vulgus daemonum opera fuisse fabulatur, cum eorum artes atque artifices a memoria perierint nec sint qui curent ea intelligere atque scrutari."

62. See William Eamon, *Science and the Secrets of Nature* (Princeton, N.J.: Princeton University Press, 1994).

63. Leon Battista Alberti, *L'architettura,* ed. Giovanni Orlandi, tr. Paolo Portoghesi, 2 vols. (Milan: Il Polifilo, 1966), I, 9–11: "Quid demum, quod abscissis rupibus, perfossis montibus, completis convallibus, coercitis lacu marique, expurgata palude, coaedificatis navibus, directis fluminibus, expeditis hostiis, constitutis pontibus portuque non solum temporariis hominum commodis providit, verum et aditus ad omnes orbis provincias patefecit?"

64. See the great article by Otto Mayr, "Automatenlegenden in der Spätrenaissance," *Technikgeschichte* 41 (1974), 20–32.

65. Gaspar Schott, *Magia universalis naturae et artis,* 2nd ed., 4 vols. (Bamberg: Schönwetter, 1677), III, 211: "Haec [sc. Magia thaumaturga] enim Naturae non juvat modo ac perficit, ut aliae [sc. Mathematicae disciplinae]; sed evidentissime etiam vincit, dum per machinas, quas ingeniosissime excogitat, nullam non debiliorem virtutem confirmat ac promovet, nullam non debiliorem sistit ac superat, nullum non corporibus motum, progressionem, gyrationem inducit; audax nimirum ac potentissima virium Naturae in corporibus non tam contemplatrix, quam arbitra." On the magical practices and machinery of Schott and Athanasius Kircher, see *La "Technica curiosa" di Kaspar Schott,* ed. and tr. Maurizio Sonnino (Rome: Edizioni dell'Elefante, 2000).

66. Campanella, *City of the Sun,* ed. and tr. Donno, 126–127: "Onde la costellazione che da Lutero cadavero cavò vapori infetti, da Gesuini nostri che fûro al suo tempo cavò odorose esalazioni di virtù, e da Fernando Cortese che promulgò il cristianesimo in Messico nel medesimo tempo."

67. Girolamo Cardano, *The Book of My Life,* tr. Jean Stoner (New York: Dutton, 1931; repr. New York: New York Review of Books, 2002), 189–190; *De propria vita liber, Opera,* ed. Charles Spon, 10 vols. (Lyon: Huguetan and Ravaud, 1663; repr. Stuttgart-Bad Cannstatt: Frommann-Holzboog, 1966), I, 35: "crevit opinio, minuentur et contemnentur bonae artes, et certa pro incertis commutabuntur. Sed haec alibi, interim nos florente prato gaudebimus. Nam quid mirabilius Pyrotechnia et fulgure mortalium, quod pernitiosius multo est quam Caelestium."

68. Campanella, *City of the Sun,* ed. and tr. Donno, 122–123: "E dicono che a' Cristiani questo apporterà grand'utile; ma prima si svelle e monda, poi s'edifica e piñata."

69. Ibid., 122–125.

5. Where Was Salomon's House?

1. J. Bodin, *Methodus ad facilem historiarum cognitionem* [1566], chap. vii, in *Artis historicae penus,* ed. J. Wolf, 2 vols. (Basel, 1579), I, 306 (Bodin cites the better-known examples of the compass, gunpowder, and the printing press as well; ibid., 309–310).

2. See e.g. the useful *Cambridge Companion to Bacon,* ed. M. Peltonen (Cambridge, 1996), and P. Findlen, "Francis Bacon and the Reform of Natural History in the Seventeenth Century," in *History and the Disciplines,* ed. D. R. Kelley (Rochester, N.Y., 1997), 239–260.

3. I cite the text as edited in *English Science, Bacon to Newton,* ed. B. Vickers (Cambridge, 1987), 36.

4. Ibid.

5. Ibid., 37.

6. Ibid., 42–43.

7. Cf. J. S. Freedman, *European Academic Philosophy in the Late Sixteenth and Seventeenth Centuries: The Life, Significance and Philosophy of Clemens Timpler (1563/4–1624)*, 2 vols. (Hildesheim, 1988).

8. See e.g. R.-M. Sargent, "Bacon as an Advocate for Cooperative Scientific Research," in *Cambridge Companion to Bacon,* ed. Peltonen, 146–171, and cf. the excellent articles collected in Bronwen Price, ed., *Francis Bacon's New Atlantis: New Interdisciplinary Essays* (Manchester: Manchester University Press, 2002).

9. *English Science, Bacon to Newton,* ed. Vickers, 43.

10. H. Bredekamp, *The Lure of Antiquity and the Cult of the Machine,* tr. A. Brown (Princeton, N.J., 1995); cf. T. DaC. Kaufmann, *The Mastery of Nature* (Princeton, N.J., 1993), chap. 7.

11. On Bacon and the *Kunstkammer,* see Kaufmann, *The Mastery of Nature,* 184–194. On Aldrovandi, see the complementary accounts of G. Olmi, *L'inventario del mondo: Catalogazione della natura e luoghi del sapere nella prima età moderna* (Bologna, 1992) and P. Findlen, *Possessing Nature: Museums, Collecting and Scientific Culture in Early Modern Italy* (Berkeley, Calif., 1994).

12. A. Grafton, *Joseph Scaliger,* 2 vols. (Oxford, 1983–1993), I, 120.

13. On the tradition of ecclesiastical history, see e.g. A. D. Momigliano, "Pagan and Christian Historiography in the Fourth Century AD," in *The Conflict between Paganism and Christianity in the Fourth Century,* ed. A. D. Momigliano (Oxford, 1963; repr. 1970), 79–99, and R. Wilken, *The Myth of Christian Beginnings* (Notre Dame, Ind., 1971). On the development of ecclesiastical history in the sixteenth and early seventeenth centuries, see in general E. Cochrane, *Historians and Historiography in the Italian Renaissance* (Chicago, 1981), 445–478, as well as the recent and informative works of S. Ditchfield, *Liturgy, Sanctity, and History in Tridentine Italy* (Cambridge, 1995) and S. Zen, *Baronio storico* (Naples, 1994).

14. Flacius, "Consultatio de conscribenda accurata historia ecclesiae," in K. Schottenloher, *Pfalzgraf Ottheinrich und das Buch* (Münster, 1927), 149.

15. Vienna, Österreichische Nationalbibliothek, MS 9737b, fols. 14 verso–15 recto.

16. T. Haye, "Der Catalogus testium veritatis des Matthias Flacius Illyricus— eine Einführung in die Literatur des Mittelalters," *Archiv für Reformationsgeschichte* 83 (1992), 31–47.

17. On the earlier phases of Flacius's career and its setting, see O. Olson, *Matthias Flacius and the Survival of Luther's Reform* (Wiesbaden, 2002). On his method, see in general H. Scheible, *Die Entstehung der Magdeburger Zenturien* (Gütersloh, 1966), with the more recent, detailed studies by M. Hartmann, *Humanismus und Kirchenkritik: Matthias Flacius Illyricus als Erforscher des Mittelalters* (Stuttgart: Thorbecke, 2001) and G. Lyon, "Baudouin, Flacius, and the Plan for the Magdeburg Centuries," *Journal of the History of Ideas* 64 (2003), 253–272. On the

development and use of loci by Melanchthon and other humanists, see the rich synthesis by A. Moss, *Printed Commonplace-Books and the Structuring of Renaissance Thought* (Oxford, 1996).

18. Vienna, Österreichische Nationalbibliothek, MS 9737b, fol. 3 recto.

19. *De ecclesiastica historia quae Magdeburgi contexitur narratio* (Wittenberg, 1558), EXEMPLVUM NARRATIONIS BONA FIDE EXPRESSVM DE ARCHETYPO, sig. A iij recto: "Ideam Ecclesiae Christi . . . ex vetustissimis et optimis autoribus, tum Historicis tum Patribus aliisque scriptoribus . . ."

20. Ibid., sig. A iij recto–verso: "Nam in Eusebii et in aliis plerisque Historiis personae fere tantum tractantur. De doctrina, quae anima et forma Ecclesiasticae Historiae esse debebat, fere nihil inest, de ceremoniis, de controversiarum diremptione, de gubernatione Ecclesiarum et aliis eius generis permultis, aut mutae sunt prorsus, aut valde mutilae . . ."

21. Ibid., sig. [A iiij verso]–b recto:

Facile insuper animadvertunt prudentes viri, non sufficere unum aut alterum ad res tantas comportandas et recte connectendas.

Est autem ipse processus, ut sic dicamus, tractationis, in istas quatuor quasi operas distributus. Primum alimus certis stipendiis iam septem studiosos, doctrina et iudicio mediocri praeditos, qui autores sibi propositos evolvunt summa attentione et fide, ac iuxta Methodi metas solicite [B recto] et curiose singula excerpunt, et quasi Anatomian autorum faciunt, suoque loco quaelibet adscribunt, idque faciunt semper unum seculum post aliud in manus accipientes.

Deinde alimus duos Magistros, aetate, doctrina et rectitudine iudicii praestantes, quibus quod priores sedulae ac industriae apiculae ex variis locis ac floribus convexerunt, traditur, ut rerum congestarum diiudicationem faciant, delineent ac disponant, quae in scriptionem venire debent, ac denique pertractent et connectant narratione Historica.

Tertio constituti sunt ex gubernatorum numero quidam inspectores, qui collectoribus materias distribuunt, et ea quae sunt delineata, examinant, et rerum iudicium atque partium collocationem adiuvant (Nihil enim scribitur, nisi prius hac ratione diiudicatum sit). Scripta deinde rursus sub limam vocant, ac denique etiam quaedam, pro necessitate ipsi contexunt ac scribunt.

Quarto alimus Amanuensem ut vocant, qui sic composita mundius describit.

Vltra hosce, sunt communes totius operis gubernatores et inspectores optimae fidei homines quinque, qui consiliis praesunt, et idoneas personas accersunt, non idoneas dimittunt, habent sumptuum rationem. Vnus autem ex istis, si quid contribuitur, custodit, et habet libellos acceptorum et expensorum. Singulis porro anni quadrantibus, praesente Consule, rationes subducuntur et annotantur, idque ita solicite, expresse et fideliter, ut non dubitemus cuilibet postulanti, singulorum nummorum rationem sufficientem reddere, idque non tantum bonis, sed ipsis adeo malevolis.

On sig. [B ij verso], there is a list of the "GUBERNATORES ET OPERARII Historici instituti."

22. Ibid., sig. F recto–verso: "Cogitate ipsi, si prima collectio laborat, quae est fundamentum historiae, et annalium et commentariorum instar, tota res labat. Quid enim deinceps iste bonus vir, quem non dubitamus sub opere sudare multum magnum sudorem, praesertim in hoc aestu, quid ille elaborabit atque aedificabit, si meliora omissa et deteriora collecta fuerint a collectoribus? Nimirum in hunc redundabunt alieni iudicii errata, et in vos etiam postea inspectores. Scitis autem, quam tetra res sit communicare secum aliena peccata. Profecto nemo potest melius res describendas colligere, quam is, qui collectas elaborare novit. Nam de istis per locos communes seu capita certa ex integris scriptis notationibus, praesertim quae a mediocris iudicii hominibus fiunt, ut de vestris profitemini, quid sentiendum sit, omnes intelligunt. Fieri etiam potest, ut multae praeclarae res in scriptis veterum Collectoribus vestris in locos suos non incidant."

23. Ibid.: "De hoc igitur dubitamus, an hoc recte fiat, quod septem studiosos, mediocri iudicio praeditos, corporis historici collectores constituitis, et non potius duobus Magistris iudicio praestantibus illa curatio a vobis datur. Nam vicia primae coctionis non corriguntur in secunda, ut medicus vester vos docere poterit, et helleborum dare, et adesse quando pituita molesta est. Sed profecto est res magna, et perfecti iudicii, videre et excerpere ex magna copia, quod ex usu sit, et sentietis nobiscum, ubi consideraveritis . . ."

24. Sections of these texts are available in H. Scheible, ed., *Die Anfänge der reformatorischen Geschichtsschreibung* (Gütersloh, 1966); cf. Lyon, "Baudouin, Flacius, and the Plan for the Magdeburg Centuries."

25. F. Bacon, *Advancement of Learning*, ed. Michael Kiernan (Oxford, 2000), 71.

26. Ibid., 62.

27. Ibid.

28. Bacon, *De augmentis scientiarum*, 2.4, in *Works*, ed. James Spedding, Robert Leslie Ellis, and Douglas Denon Heath, 15 vols. (Cambridge, 1863), I, 503.

29. See e.g. L. Braun, *Histoire de l'histoire de la philosophie* (Paris, 1974); G. Santinello et al., *Models of the History of Philosophy: From Its Origins in the Renaissance to the "Historia philosophica,"* ed. C. W. T. Blackwell (Dordrecht, 1993; original ed. Brescia, 1981); W. Schmidt-Biggemann, *Topica universalis: Eine Modellgeschichte humanistischer und barocker Wissenschaft* (Hamburg, 1983); Sicco Lehmann-Brauns, *Weisheit in der Weltgeschichte: Philosophiegeschichte zwischen Barock und Aufklärung* (Tübingen: Niemeyer, 2004).

30. Bacon, *Advancement of Learning*, II, sec. 4.

31. Bacon, *De augmentis scientiarum*, 2.4, in *Works*, II, 317.

32. C. Mylaeus, *De scribenda universitatis rerum historia libri quinque,* bk. 5, in *Artis historicae penus,* ed. Wolf, II, 314–392. See Donald Kelley, "Writing Cultural History in Early Modern France: Christophe Milieu and His Project," *Renaissance Quarterly* 52 (1999), 342–365.

33. See W. Sherman, *John Dee* (Amherst, Mass., 1995); O. Hannaway, "Laboratory Design and the Aim of Science: Andreas Libavius versus Tycho Brahe," *Isis* 77 (1986), 585–610; T. Nummedal, *Alchemy and Authority in the Holy Roman Empire* (Chicago, 2007).

34. D. Harkness, *The Jewel House: Elizabethan London and the Scientific Revolution* (New Haven, Conn., 2007).

35. See K. Sharpe, *Sir Robert Cotton, 1586–1631* (Oxford, 1979) and C. G. C. Tite, *The Manuscript Library of Sir Robert Cotton* (London, 1994).

36. See in general I. Philip, *The Bodleian Library in the Seventeenth and Eighteenth Centuries* (Oxford, 1983). On Bacon's exchanges with the more traditionalist Bodley, see ibid., 2–3.

37. *Letters of Sir Thomas Bodley to Thomas James,* ed. G. K. Wheeler (Oxford, 1926), xxxiii–xxxiv, 155–157, 163, 164, 198, 201, 202–203. See also Paul Nelles, "The Uses of Orthodoxy and Jacobean Erudition: Thomas James and the Bodleian Library," *History of Universities* 22 (2007), 21–70.

38. Philip, *The Bodleian Library in the Seventeenth and Eighteenth Centuries,* 15.

39. Note especially the letter in which Bodley, early in the course of the work, described his own intentions to James (*Letters,* ed. Wheeler, 155–156): "I am yet aduised, to admitte no other but suche, as will accept my allowance for their paines, lest they should assume a greater libertie then others, and not conforme themselves so strictly to that course of proceeding, which we shall determine." Interestingly, Bodley also expressed his intention of cornering the Archbishop "rather at a meale, then otherwise [155]," to win his support for the enterprise—another anticipation of a standard feature of modern academic and scientific life.

40. F. Winkelmann, "Probleme der Zitate in den Werken der oströmischen Kirchenhistoriker," in *Das Korpus der Griechischen Christlichen Schriftsteller: Historie, Gegenwart, Zukunft,* ed. J. Irmscher and K. Treu (Berlin, 1977), 195–207.

6. Chronology, Controversy, and Community in the Republic of Letters

1. Like most Germans, Mästlin and Kepler were best acquainted with the Frankfurt 1593 reprint of the first edition (Paris: Patisson, 1583).

2. Kepler 1861.

3. Kepler 1937–, 5.

4. Burke-Gaffney 1944. On Burke-Gaffney, see http://www.smu.ca/academic/science/ap/bgo.html, accessed 3 May 2007.

5. Field 1988; Stephenson 1987, 1994; Voelkel 1999, 2001.

6. Jardine 1984; Hallyn 1990; Jardine, Mosley, and Tybjerg 2003; Mosley 2007.

7. The fullest treatment is Grafton 1983–1993, II.

8. Isaak Habrecht to Wilhelm Schickard, Strasbourg, 29 February 1632; Schickard 2002, I, 661: "Et primo quidem de duobus celebratissimis authoribus Petavio et Landspergio. Quorum ille Gallus est, ordinis Jesuitici, et professor Aurelianensis, vir undique eruditissimus: scripsit is duo volumina, Calepinum magnitudine multum superantia: primum (quod 10 Impp. vaenit) est Doctrina Temporum, in quo ex observatis Ptolemaei, Hipparchi, Copernici, aliorum, exquisitissimas coelestium motuum tabulas supputavit, omnibus seculis ante et post natum Christum, praeteritis ac futuris accommodatas: easque hac dokimasia exhibet, quod omnes omnium chronologorum Eclipses ad unguem demonstrat et confert: supputando itidem complures futuras, cuius perinde aliquoties (ut et praeterito anno) in anniversariis prognosticis mentionem feci, ejusque calculum cum reliquis contuli, ut videre est: post in altera Operis parte Chronologiam extruit, a Condito mundo ad nostra usque tempora, in qua, ut reor, omnes omnium Chronicorum scrupulos ita explanat, ut nil desiderari posse ulterius, mihi persuadeam. Scaligerum acerbius tractat, reliquos moderatius, haereticos se non inspexisse fatetur, quamvis interim Buntingi frequentissima, Kepleri haud nulla fiat mentio. A Keplero in computo annorum Mundi 10 tantum annis differt, quam differentiolam si in vivis esset, procul dubio, ei vel condonasset, vel alio modo expiasset. Sed o dira fata! Unicum exemplar hic prostat, quod fere per annum in aedibus meis detineo, nam ejus lectione nunquam satior, lassor saepius, nec nisi furtivas horulas illi concedo, quoniam extra rhombum et falx in aliena messe videtur."

9. Habrecht to Schickard, Strasbourg, 23 January 1633; Schickard 2002, II, 5: "De Petavio nil respondes, propter operis prolixitatem opinor: annus vix sufficeret, homini nimirum aliis muniis destinato, evolvendo tali authori."

10. Kepler 1937–, 1, 360–361:

> At non tam necessitate meae materiae, quam peculiari quodam studio impellor ad repetendam LAVRENTII SVSLYGAE Poloni sententiam: Cupio enim hanc, ut veram meo iudicio, innotescere quam plurimis hominibus: et vero vereor, ne negligatur, quatuor potissimum de causis; prima, quod Authoris novi liber titulum praefert Chronologicum, cuius nominis artes a paucioribus excoluntur; altera, quod gravatur author praeiudicio Magnorum virorum; tertio, quod neglexit astronomiam, et in disputatione de passionis anno hanc scientiam traditionibus plane postposuit; quae res astronomos a thesi per se vera abalienare possit; denique quod ipsa solet obstare novitas et solitudo Authoris, difficulter hominum animis evelluntur usu trita multorumque consensu stabilita.
>
> Quibus incommodis etsi nonnihil prospectum iam est a POSSEVINO, qui Authorem publice commendat, facit id tamen, intacta hac quaestione, nulla significatione in ullam partem inclinans.

Itaque non abs re putavi, sententiam SVSLYGAE transscriptam in hunc libellum (quem ob materiae curiositatem in multorum manus venturum existimo), et communiorem facere, et argumentis perspicuis etiam astronomicis adiuvare, adeoque unius insuper anni subtractione in Herodis filiorumque funeribus, probatiorem et veritati propiorem reddere, ut habeant lectores pulchrum aliquid, quo frustratam inutilium divinationum expectationem solentur.

11. Kepler 1861, 153–166.

12. Jardine 1984; Grafton 1991.

13. Kepler 1937–, 10, pt. 1, 105: "De harum Aerarum intervallis deque mensium appellationibus, ordine, quantitate scripsi commentarium peculiarem, in quo omnia, quae in his foliis continentur, historiarum monumentis rationibusque idoneis demonstro et contra caeterorum Chronologorum, ipsiusque adeo SCALIGERI, authoritates, sicubi diversi a me abeunt, munio: quem alia occasione, si vita superfuerit, lectoribus communicabo. Nam materia potissimum Chronologica metas huius operis Astronomici excessura visa est."

14. Kepler 1937–, 18, 331: "Priusquam edam commentarium de aeris in Tabb: Rud: totus mihi Petavius legendus erit: adeo frequenter eandem pulsamus chordam. Mireris, idem ab utroque responderi Scaligero, nisi perpenderis, unum solum esse quod responderi possit. Sed tamen nimium alicubi detrahit ille Scaligero." See also Kepler's earlier letter to Guldin, 18, 272–273: "Inter haec tamen incommoda hoc egi: ut quod Praesidiarii nostri in Rusticos, Ego in Scaligerum susciperem. Disputationem institui luculentam de Epochis, praeclarissimas ubique notas lectio Scaliger suppeditabat, et excerpta ex plurimis authoribus laboriosissima: rarissime tamen inveni Scaligerum iis bene utentem. Perpetuus pene Elenchus est Scaligeri disputatio ista; excrevitque in tantum, ut verear partem operis facere; plus enim paginarum occuparet, quam omnia reliqua praecepta. Sed commode titulum habere poterit accessionis vel appendicis. Nam si nullo vinculo Tabulis eum tractatum annecterem plane seorsim editum; imperfectum opus videri posset. Ad tabulas vero appendicem facere de Epochis et Aeris et Annorum formulis usualibus apud Nationes varias, speciem habet necessitatis; quia nisi cognitis temporibus, computari motus coelestes non possunt. Itaque facile veniam merebor, etsi non tota Scaligeri opera interpolem. Nam eius invectivas in Clavium plane tango nuspiam, id non studio devitans, sed quia materia est jejuna et sterilis et aliena a scopo Tabularum. Vno enim verbo protestor, secundum festa mobilia nullas institui computationes siderum, quippe cum suppetat nobis fixus annus. Itaque reductio Gregorianorum temporum ad Juliana facili praecepto absolvitur. Secus est cum Anno Arabico et Graeco Hipparchi, qui seipsos regunt, non reguntur a fixo Juliano, ut nostra festa mobilia."

15. Kepler 1937–, 13, 279: "Scd finem facere necesse habeo. Es hatt schon 11. geschlagen, propediem illucescet dies 12. huius. Vale optime."

16. Kepler 1937–, 13, 277: "Dissertatio tua Chronologica mihi lectu est iucundissima. Intelligo enim quam diligenter pleraque loca, notatu digna, legeris, et me quoque de multis, quae non adeo animadverteram, admones. Porro quod ei non astipulor per omnia, rationes audi . . ."

17. Kepler 1937–, 18, 273: "Hoc pugnax scribendi genus multum mihi taedii detersit ab obsidionis incommodis et impedimentis operis . . ."

18. Salianus 1641, I, 2: "Ante mundum igitur conditum ipse sibi regia erat et palatium, nullo definitus, nedum circumscriptus loco, quippe nullus erat locus; ipse in seipso saeculis innumerabilibus et annis aeternis, sua sapientia, pulchritudine, bonitate fruebatur: intuebatur admirabiles perfectiones suas, cum inerrabili atque inaestimabili gaudio, in quarum contemplatione producebat Filium, et cum eo infinitum amorem personalem, Spiritum sanctum: cogitabat de condendo mundo in tempore suo, cum omnibus creaturis, de constituenda civitate Electorum, quos iam tum sigillatim intuens atque benedicens, summo amore complectebatur: qui aeterna quondam beatitudine, sub capite ac principe incarnato Verbo, perfruentur, de reparando mundo per peccatum perituro, et in meliorem statum revocando. Haec aliaque id genus erant opera eius, prout nos ista rudes concipere, et de iis infantes possumus balbutire: haec ipsius cogitationes antiquae, quas per *annos aeternos in mente habuit,* re nulla, quae esset extra se, neque tum, neque deinceps ad summam beatitudinem indigens: sicut nec factus est ullarum rerum creatarum accessione beatior . . ."

19. Kepler 1861, 129:

Delinivit me gaudio praecipuo Salianus, dum de mundi temporis auctore dicturus S. Johannis Evangelium enarrat; ex eo nempe in hanc cogitationem veni, Johannem Evangelistam, dum aeternitatem filii Dei ortumque eius divinum adstruit, etiam commentarium nobis edere historiae Mosaicae de creatione, et cabbalam quandam praegnantem mysteriis venerandis ex disciplina gentis Judaicae ad convincendam illius pertinaciam proferre.

Commentatorem agnoscas ex usurpatione primi verbi Mosaici, quod et Johannes primum ponit in suo Evangelio: "in principio." Cabbala vero elucet ex verbo *yhvh* etc.

20. Kepler 1861, 130: "Et ostendit sequela textus, Mosen scribere de ortu creaturarum ex ante creata massa. Sane cum W. Gilbertus demonstrat, Terram esse informatam forma magnetica per totum, haec utique forma ei non erat indita in primo ortu ex nihilo. Recte itaque informis fuisse statuitur; et si Terra caruit mineralibus, caruit et forma magnetica, id est sua propria; nihil igitur fuit nisi limus aqua mersus."

21. Mästlin 1641 includes a "thema mundi," or geniture for the universe—a widespread form of historical astrology that seems to have had its origins in Roman efforts to establish the date of the city's founding astrologically.

22. For an excellent introduction to the earlier history of this doctrine, see Smoller 1994. On its later history in the Holy Roman Empire, see Barnes 1988; Brosseder 2004.

23. See e.g. Alsted 1628.

24. Kepler 1937–, I, 11–13:

Denique levi quadam occasione propius in rem ipsam incidi . . . Igitur die 9. vel 19. Iulii anni 1595. monstraturus Auditoribus meis coniunctionum magnarum saltus per octena signa, et quomodo illae pedetentim ex uno trigono transeant in alium, inscripsi multa triangula, vel quasi triangula, eidem circulo, sic ut finis unius esset initium alterius. Igitur quibus punctis latera triangulorum se mutuo secabant, iis minor circellus adumbrabatur. Nam circuli triangulo inscripti radius est circumscripti radii dimidium. Proportio inter utrumque circulum videbatur ad oculum pene similis illi, quae est inter Saturnum et Iovem: et triangulum prima erat figurarum, sicut Saturnus et Iupiter primi Planetae. Tentavi statim quadrangulo [The text at this point contains a figure, captioned: Schema magnarum Coniunctionum Saturni et Iovis, earumque saltus per octena signa, atque transitus per omnes quatuor Zodiaci triplicitates] distantiam secundam Martis et Iovis, quinquangulo tertiam, sexangulo quartam. Cumque etiam oculi reclamarent in secunda distantia, quae est inter Iovem et Martem, quadratum triangulo et quinquangulo adiunxi. Infinitum est singula persequi.

Et finis huius irriti conatus fuit idem, qui postremi et felicis initium. Nempe cogitavi, hac via, siquidem ordinem inter figuras velim servare, nunquam me perventurum usque ad Solem, neque causam habiturum, cur potius sex, quam viginti vel centum orbes mobiles. Et tamen placebant figurae, utpote quantitates, et res coelis prior. Quantitas enim initio cum corpore creata; coeli altero die.

25. For another ingenious way of doing this, see Budovec z Budova 1616. He uses clock faces, the hand approaching midnight, to represent the course and current status of world history, adumbrating the famous cover of the *Bulletin of the Atomic Scientists*.

26. Kepler 1937–, 1, 78: "Post epulas, post fastidium ex saturitate, veniamus ad bellaria. Problemata duo pono nobilia. Primum est de principio motus; alterum de fine. Certe non temere Deus instituit motus, sed ab uno quodam certo principio et illustri stellarum coniunctione, et in initio Zodiaci, quod creator per inclinationem Telluris domicilii nostri effinxit, quia omnia propter hominem. Annus igitur Christi 1595. si referatur in 5572. mundi (qui communiter et a probatissimis 5557. censetur) veniet creatio in illustrem coniunctionem in principio Arietis."

27. See Jardine 1984; Grafton 1991.

28. Kepler 1937–, 11, pt. 2, 16.

29. Kepler 1937–, 11, pt. 2, 59: "Eclipsis Solis in 18° Cancri est in VII. domo Rudolphi, in I. Ferdinandi. Nota eclipsin anno 38. ante Christum. Contemtus atque spretus, ut tunc puer Augustus, magna audebit et efficiet et contemtum diminuet . . ."

30. Grafton 1991; Boner forthcoming.

31. See Mästlin 1641,)?(ro -)?(2 vo: "Propositiones chronologicae, methodum investigandi tempus, annum et diem creationis mundi, et connectendi potissimas historiarum sacrarum Epochas, exhibentes. Propositio I. Annorum Christi, *secundum usitatam numerationem, copulatio cum* Annis Nabonasari, *sicut ea in astronomicis tabulis Prutenicis notatur, recte habet. Illi anni, ceu a Christo nato numerati, usurpantur tanquam commune Annorum tam in politico quam Ecclesiastico usitato computo, aeque ad antecedentia ac sequentia Epochen Christi tempora, numerandorum vehiculum: Hi vero, quibus potissimum Ptolemaeus Astronomus utitur, a Nabonasaro deducti, prae omnibus maxime conducunt ad praecipuarum Epocharum et propriorum Astronomicorum Characterum Temporum veram indagationem, et certam atque exquisitam distributionem. Distantia harum Epocharum est Annorum 747. Aegyptiorum, et 130 1/2 dierum*" (emphasis in original); *Quaestiones,* 5: "Hunc Almagesti librum Ptolemaei Bessario, natione Graecus (a quo Regiomontanus eum consequutus est et in Germaniam attulit) tanti fecisse fertur, ut tota provincia aestimare non dubitaret. At nos, innumeris ejus in astronomia usibus omissis (etenim si hoc Ptolemaei Almagesto carendum esset, omnis astronomia nostri seculi, non jam adulta esset, sed in cunis recumbens, adhuc vagiret) asserere non veremur, librum illum, si nihil aliud praestitisset, ob hunc unicum characterem chronologicum, per quem transitus est ex historiis prophanis in historiam sacram, tota provincia fuisse non immerito redimendum."

32. See Herwart von Hohenburg 1612; Herwart von Hohenburg and Herwart von Hohenburg 1626.

33. Kepler 1937–, 17, 54: "Nobilis Vir Joannes Georgius Herwart, V.I.D. Cancellarius et Consiliarius Bavaricus, Vir ut nobilis, ita humanissimus et doctissimus, suis superiori anno editis novae Chronologiae Capitibus (quorum capitum aliquam partem mihi ante publicationem communicavit) me profecto dubium reddidit. Er hatt mich recht irr gemacht"; 55: "Multa tamen sic simpliciter reiicere nequeo. Expecto igitur et quaero tempus, quo sub incudem illa et mea revocem. Quod si ipse vicerit (rationes ego audire soleo, et eas quae meliores sunt prioribus, utut mihi plausibiles fuerint visae, sequor) certe ingens meae Chronologiae pars concidet. Interea inter sacrum et saxum haereo. Persuaseram mihi ipsi, mea omnia esse longe certissima. Et quidem comparatione cum aliis, cum quibus iisdem principiis utor, facta, ab illa mea sententia nondum deficerem. Atqui hic Cancellarius communia nostra fundamenta demolitur. Also das Ichs beym a b c wider muss anfangen. Quare, clarissime Vir, Ego in hac sum sententia, ut omnium primo huius Viri scriptum examinetur. Quod si recte sentit (equidem in non paucis ipsum non male sentire puto) frustra nos Helisaeo opponimus, utpote, qui aeque ac ille a vero

tramite aberraremus, ille in sinistram, nos in dextram, vel forsan uterque vel in dextram vel sinistram declinantes, neuter vero rectam viam teneret." Samuel Hafenreffer, who printed Mästlin's chronology in 1641, made it clear that his edition rested on a copy he had made just before Herwart's work reduced his teacher, always hesitant to publish, to silence: he described the work as "CHRONOLOGIAM Moestlini, a me adhuc juvene ex autographo descriptam, atque ab ipsomet postea Autore, quem hoc nomine rogaveram, accurate castigatam, jam triginta annos et quod excedit" (Mästlin 1641, [)?()?(2 vo]).

34. Kepler 1937–, 15, 206: "Scito enim ex quo primum lucem vidit opus illud, me vix tum in studiorum mathematicorum limine constitutum, commendationibus Michaelis Maestlini Praeceptoris mei instigatum in tantum desiderium totius operis cognoscendi exarsisse: ut plurimum temporis necessariis studiis ereptum, furtim isthic transtulerim. Fateor, etsi quidem vix ulla est pagina in quam transsultorio discursu non inciderim; nunquam tamen intra hoc decennium impetrare me potuisse, ut continuata et accurata lectione a capite ad calcem pervenirem, primaque cum ultimis compararem. Qua ego cogitatione si moverer, equidem tacuissem etiamnum. Ne autem ea moverer, effecit primum ipsa libri tui methodus; quae bonam partem librorum sequentium superstruit primo: itaque quantisper in primo haereo (haereo autem tenaciter) ad sequentes impeditus mihi et somnolentus erit transitus. Deinde stimulum mihi addidit ad te scribendi posthabita illa mea in absolvendo libro tuo negligentia, Magnificus D. J. Matthaeus Wackherus . . ."

35. Kepler 1937–, 15, 207: "Ex omnibus authoritatibus, quas in utraque editione allegas hoc procul dubio apparet: Annum Atticum, quem primo libro condidisti, ab ea forma quam tu es opinatus, plurimum abfuisse. Qualem autem ipse opiner fuisse primum describam, deinde argumenta vel tuam formam refellentia vel meam confirmantia, conjecturasque una nonnullas (de quibus tu rectissime judicabis) imbecilliores pro me vel contra te, itemque obiectionum solutiones promiscue subjungam."

36. Kepler 1937–, 13, 294: "Erroris S. Scripturam arguere, difficile est."

37. See *The New Grove Dictionary of Music and Musicians,* s.n. Calvisius.

38. Calvisius 1685, 3: "Cum ante haec tempora Portae in illustri Gymnasio viverem, ubi et ocio aliquo modo abundabam et Bibliotheca instructissima frui poteram, non parum temporis in historicis prolegendis ponebam, et praecipua temporum momenta tum quidem notabam: Chronologiam tamen instituere non poteram, donec libri de Emendatione temporum Iosephi Scaligeri, viri incomparabilis, Francofurti Anno 93. recuderentur, quos cum meo mihi sumtu comparassem, avide legi, et quid in quaque re sentiret, unde epochas qua[s]vis deduceret, qua ratione eas confirmaret, aut quibus fundamentis diversum sentientes refutaret, multo exantlato labore, pervigili studio, et plurima usus diligentia tandem perspexi. Est enim is Autor, ut Eruditi norunt, inprimis argutus, brevis, succinctus, subtilis et difficilis. Adhibui postea alios Chronologos omnes quotquot habere

poteram, eos omnes diligentissime contuli, et quae causa dissensionum Chronologicarum esset, anxie inquisivi, et deprehendi tandem omnem Chronologiae et temporis certitudinem ab Astronomicis legibus pendere, cum motus coelestis sit mensura temporis, et plurimum eos Chronologos inter se et cum aliis dissentire, qui neglecto astronomico calculo res ex sua opinione, conjectura et aliorum auctoritate, vel falsa, vel male intellecta adjudicarunt. Quapropter ipse aggressus rem, quae Josephus Scaliger subtilius persecutus fuerat, populari et omnibus obvio modo explicare conatus sum, omnes epochas diligentissime excussi, quae causa certitudinis earundem esset investigavi, demonstrationibus easdem munivi, et quae contradici possent, solide et evidenter refutavi." Calvisius noted that he had reckoned "ultra centum et quinquaginta eclipses, quotquot scilicet historici meminerunt, quibus res gestas, quasi certissimo charactere et nota insigniverunt" [more than one hundred and fifty eclipses, all those mentioned by historians in order to fix and mark the dates of events as certainly as possible] and drew up simple tables by which "quispiam, etiamsi alias sit astronomiae rudis" [even a novice in astronomy] can compute eclipses and equinoxes, with canons, "id quod Chronologorum ante me nemo" [which no chronologer before me has done].

39. Kepler 1937–, 17, 46: "Eclogas Chronicas ex epistolis doctorum virorum et meis mutuis habeo ad manus, cum Epitome seu indice Chronologico ex mea magna Chronologia Veteris Testamenti. Puto in forma quarta, quali est impressus libellus de Natali Christi latinus, ad 30. paginas impletum iri."

40. The text is reprinted and annotated in Kepler 1937–, 5, 221–370.

41. Kepler 1937–, 5, 10–11: "Feceram autem illi meo libello et appendicem de Christi servatoris anno Natalitio, motus hac re, quod viderem, si constaret Iesum Christum natum 4. aut 5. annis ante principium aerae nostrae quam ab Incarnatione censemus perperam, stellae novae de qua commentabar, cum illa stella quae Magis apparuit, commune hoc futurum, quod utraque cum coniunctione magna superiorum Planetarum, tali quidem, quae principium faceret novae periodi annorum Octingentorum a Trigono igneo, coincideret."

42. The best account of the episode remains Burke-Gaffney 1944.

43. Decker 1605.

44. Kepler 1937–, 15, 353: "Eadem occasione transmittam ego Mysterium Cosmographicum, et librum de stella, deque anno Christi Natalitio, ubi cum Suslyga Polono, Deckerii vestri pullo, in parte libri certo, ita ut uno anno ipsum exsuperasse videar. Dixi in parte libri: quis enim Heracles adversus illum prodigiosum cumulum lectionum, totius antiquitatis, quam ego quidem exosculor, quemque gemmam esse et haberi volui meae *bibliothêkiskês.*"

45. Decker 1605, 10 verso–11 recto.

46. Kepler 1937–, 14, 288–289: "Mihi astronomi certiores temporum Characteres in siderum aequabili motu (nisi hunc negaveris) quam historici in suis consulum Catalogis habere videntur. Quare malo propter astronomiae certitudinem

obloqui factis: quam propter turbatissimorum factorum (quicunque quantum-cunque medicati sint) fiduciam, astronomiae filum Daedaleum e manibus abi-icere. Non erat itaque inferendum, omnes observationes Ptolemaei anno uno citius contigisse, quam ab authore inscribantur, sed hoc potius, omnes impera-tores uno anno tardius coepisse, quam Ptolemaeus tradiderit: siquidem historicis credis et antiquariis, contra Ptolemaeum *autopten*. Non enim imperatores men-sura sunt motuum caelestium, sed hi imperatorum et imperiorum."

47. See the introduction to this volume.

48. Pattison 1892, 463.

49. Kepler 1937–, 15, 353: "Stylus juveniliter luxuriat, et allegoriis ludit quae re nondum persuasa, differri debuisse videntur. Res ipsa Deckerium authorem facile prodit."

50. Kepler 1937–, 15, 493: "Theologiam vellem missam faceres: cuius certe nihil intelligis."

51. Kepler 1937–, 15, 494: "Pereat igitur Josephus: et salva sit nobis scripturae tum historica, tum divina veritas: cui aliquid detrahere vel etiam permittere ut in dubitationem illa vocetur, mihi quousque vivam, religio erit. Scripseram integrum tractatum: quem rursus suppressi. In scripturae igitur sententia insistam: nihil moratus si Josephus centies obiiciatur, homo vitae et mortis Herodis imperitis-simus: nisi studiose omnia corrupit: quod proxime scribam et simul viginti Josephi contradictiones in Herodis regno et vita."

52. Kaspar Rhey to Rader, Munich, 9 January 1601; Rader 1995, 151–152: "In-terea saxum hic sanctum, non sacrum dixerim, volvo, tanto libentius, quanto iu-cundius, per diviniorem montem, quam Sisyphus ille infelix. Neque offunditur illa caligo, quae olim in Aristotelea nocte, sed lucis immensum iubar ubique expli-catur, cum sint aeterni soles. Die trium Magorum quattuor puellas in mea Catech-esi produxi, quae fraterculos suos, a Tyranno crudeliter necatos, deplanxerunt. Primae inter prima statim verba lacrymae exciderunt (nimirum omnia in lacrymas verti rogabat), truncatum caput, manus mutilatas, pedem concisum fraterculi reperit, ut osculabatur, ut alloquebatur, ut illacrymabatur. Itaque nemo erat in templo, cui non oculi rorarent. Gratum id pientissimis animis, et Deo inprimis ad cuius gloriam haec omnia referuntur. Ex quo ego mirifica in dies profundor conso-latione, cum non tantum togatos stolatasque frequentes sed etiam sagatas soc-catosque e pagis adesse et interesse conspicer."

53. Lipsius to Gerardus Buytewechius, Louvain, 26 March 1600; Burman 1727, I, 700–701 at 700: "De *Scaligero* tu nihil. Ego hoc tibi, editum esse a *M. Delrio* tertium Tomum Disquisitionum magicarum, in quo ille ex professor tangitur: et scis occa-sionem datam Societati. Sed et P. *Deckerius* in publicis lectionibus in illum dictat et sententias eius refutat: quod fortasse jam audistis." (Emphasis in original.)

54. Decker also resembled another cosmopolitan Belgian Jesuit, Andreas Schot-tus, who printed a book of his own on the lives of Aristotle and Demosthenes with

a testimonial letter from Scaliger at its head, a curious Protestant imprimatur (Schottus 1603).

55. Rader 1995, 329–330; Scaliger 1627, 396–399.

56. Rader 1995, 328n4.

57. Kepler 1937–, 16, 101: "Avocor a scriptione invitus; ergo abrumpo dulce colloquium, et claudo. Non cessemus pulsare, quaerere, orare. Christus aderit et se tandem manifestabit nobis. Sententiam D.V. expecto de exordio Annorum Nabonassaris; quo anno Iphiti et Vrbis coeperit; quo cyclo Solis et Lunae, quo die mensis; quantusque excessus sit Epochae Vrbis. Ego certe existimo aetate illa Ptolemaei sub Traiano et Hadriano, annos Nabonassaris sexennio fere integro minores esse annis Vrbis Varronianis. In quo ab aliis dissentio. Sed expecto vestrum Iudicium . . ."

58. Kepler 1937–, 16, 62: "quia satius aestimo sine cuiusquam dolore aut amaritudine discordiae in campo hoc ludere chronologico."

59. Kepler 1937–, 16, 49–50: "Obsecro pace R.V. mihi aliqua ex candore animi liceat addere. Fundamenta disputationis quae facis, omnia pulcherrime Scaliger proponit, stylo expedito, et feliciori, quam solet alias. Idem et R. Tm. et me de hoc argumenti genere admonuit: idem ex Hebraicis monumentis, quae sunt nobis utilia in hoc negotio consignavit. Esto sit haereticus, sit novator, sit SS. Patrum obtrectator, esto etiam ut stirpem sit ementitus; quid haec quaeso omnia ad praesentem quaestionem; ut tractari non possit nisi per obtrectationem eius. Haud scio an hi mores, et haec aretalogorum vindicta (ut scio vos interpretari) plus adversariis vestris prosint, an vobis obsint. Ad primum conspectum virulenti huiusmodi verbi, totus animus lectoris praeoccupatur imaginatione perpetui huius moris; quasi iam prorsus nihil utile in scripto tali insit. Video et trabem et festucam, quod multi meorum (indignantes) testari possunt, et hoc omnem imbuit pinguedinem. Oculi simulachro solet justiciae vis depingi: qui vero semel peccantem etiam cum quid recte facit, arguit et criminatur, is oculo justo carere, *prosopoleptes* esse censetur, qui facta ex persona aestimet. Non improbo ut refutes quae non placent, facio idem et ego: tantum ubi quid meritus est, id si etiam in hoste commemores, omnino fidem orationi et hic et alibi astruis. Quod si tibi vacat meum audire consilium, ubi excuderis de hoc aliquid, ipsius verba allega, non sunt nimis longa: in tua vero oratione circumcide timidiusculas allegorias et superfluas ambages: potes complecti una facie totum negotium, ubi Scaligeri verbis uti volueris. Tunc ipse suis verbis se satis excusabit."

60. Crusius 1927–1961, II, 55, where he summarizes a letter from Oseas Hala and then notes: "Addit verba haec infime: En candorem Scaligeri: qui in altera sui de emendatione temporis libri, honorificam tui mentionem, ut et in literis ad me antea, fecit."

61. Crusius 1927–1961, II, 63, 87, 95, 169.

62. Reusner 1600, 2 (for Scaliger's supposed Creation date), 51: "Supputatio haec tota pendet ex iusta annorum Nabonassaris cum sacrarum literarum annis

connexione: quorum illi ex Ptolemaeo, hi ex Ieremia Propheta petuntur. Nabonassarem autem esse Salmanassarem, qui Samariam cepit, et decem tribus in Assyriam abduxit; Nabopolassarem vero in Sacris dici Nabuchodonosorem: et historiarum series atque collatio ostendit: et ex motuum coelestium calculationibus Mathematici satis ostendunt (Hac de re vide Reinhold. in tabulis Prutenicis, Funcium in Chronologiae suae commentariis, et Bucholzerum in Isagoge Chronologica) quamvis contrarium probare conatur Iosephus Scaliger lib. 5. de emendat. Tempor. Cuius tamen rationes tanti non sunt, ut nos in suam trahant sententiam."

63. Calvisius 1685, 59: "Scribis in appendice pag. 2. *Josephum Scaligerum* a Mundo condito usque ad Christum natum, numerare annos 4712. id quod *Scaliger* nunquam nec cogitavit, nec dixit, nec scripsit. Memini te idem affirmasse in prima tui libri editione, meque te monuisse, Scaligerum si dicat Christum natum in fine anni *Periodi Julianae* 4711. non hoc velle, quod tot anni a condito mundo usque ad natum Christum numerandi sint: sed Periodum Julianam esse arte quadam concinnatum numerum, in quo perpetuo ad quemvis annum habeatur cyclus Solis, si is numerus per 28. dividatur: Cyclus item Lunae, si idem per 19. secetur, cyclus etiam indictionum, si idem numerus per quindecim dispescatur, et Scaligerum hoc suo numero 4711. nihil aliud velle, quam Christum natum eo anno, qui decurrat ad cyclum Solis 7 et ad cyclum Lunae 18. et ad indictionem primam, qui alius annus esse non potest, nisi annus mundi 3947. si Juliano more numeretur. Agnovisti tuum errorem, eumque excusasti, quod occupatissimus fueris tempore editionis libelli tui in Magistratus scholastici laboriosissimo munere, et te propterea Scaligeri sententiam in tanta festinatione Typographi vestigare non potuisse, atque ita temere aliorum fidem secutum esse. Non dubito, quin haec in memoria adhuc haereant, ideo miror, qui factum sit, quod ex re, quam agnoscis veram non esse, tanto viro, cui omnia in recte numerandis et dirigendis temporibus debemus, invidiam creare volueris." (Emphases in original.)

64. Calvisius 1685, 58: "Tuum argumentum, quod affers, leviculum est, et ex coniectura vana deductum, quando sic arguis. Ptolomeus testatur Nabonassarem praecessisse annis centum et viginti duobus Nabopollassarem. In Sacra scriptura autem invenitur, Salmanassarem praecessisse Nebucadnezarem annis 122. Ergo Salmanassar est Nabonassar et Nabopollassar est Nebucadnezar. Eodem argumento possum Ezechiam facere Nabonassarem, cum et ipse annis 122. distet a Nebucadnezare. Maiorem syllogismum ita facere debueras: Quicunque reges aequali temporis spacio ab aliquo distant, ii non sunt diversi reges, sed sunt unus et idem, at hoc tibi nemo concedet. Vides ex his tuam sententiam pugnare cum omnibus autoribus, qui aliquid de hisce circa captivitatem Babylonicam temporibus aliquid memoriae mandarunt: sive ii sint scriptores sacri, sive profani, nisi fortassis Annium monachum Viterbiensem excipias, qui Berosum et Megasthenem veracissimos historicos iam dudum amissos ex suo ingenio novos finxit et produxit mendacissimos, et plurimos secum in errores abduxit."

65. Laurentius Fabricius to Calvisius, 17 February 1606; Göttingen MS 2° Philos. 103, II, 7: "Viro undequoque perspicacissimo, Chronologico oculatissimo, Historico probatissimo, qui iudicio magnorum virorum fato excitatus est in subsidium historiae Dn. Setho Calvisio."

66. Reusner to Calvisius, 9 June 1601; Göttingen MS 2° Philos. 103, II, 4–5: "Setho Calvisio, Musico Lipsiensi Amico suo honorando. S. Ad literas tuas, Vir Ornatissime, serius respondeo, ob occupationes plurimas, quae mihi artem Stratagematicam ex historiarum monumentis colligenti et pertractanti incumbunt; quamvis ferme mihi persuaseram, nihil amplius respondere, quoniam ambigo, amicone an alio animo literae istae tuae proximae sint scriptae: quippe in quibus animadverto, te verba quaedam superiorum literarum prorsus pervertere, et in alienum sensum detorquere: Ideo ut me explicam, ipsa me cogit necessitas. Ordinem autem sequar tuarum literarum . . ."

67. Reusner 1650, 171–172: "Hinc fertur, quod cum quidam ebrietatem alteri his verbis exprobrasset, Non te ebriositatis tuae pudet? Responderit ille, Non te pudet ebrium reprehendere? Simili ratione intempestivum foret, et majori errori causam esset daturus; qui maledicum in ipso caloris impetu, et praesentibus aliis, vellet corrigere. Nec vero solum praeceptum illud sufficit: sed pro plena discretione necessum est, honesta aliqua fallacia uti, et reprehensionis amaritudinem cum laudis alicujus dulcedine miscere, aut etiam ostendere, nos alios culpare ob eosdem defectus, quibus is laborat, quem corrigere cupimus: aut vero nos ipsos arguamus, innuentes erroris nos quoque esse obnoxios. Et, ut finiam tandem, *ita corrigendus est amicus: ut et grata sit ea correctio, et magis magisque eum nobis obligatum reddat:* ut Philosophi quidam moralium suorum scriptorum monumentis prodiderunt." (Emphasis in original.)

68. Calvisius 1685, 59–60: "Potuissem quidem privatim de hisce rebus te monere, quod fortassis gratius tibi accidisset: Sed cum multi meam sententiam de tua Chronologia exquirerent, et epistolam hanc descriptam cuperent, nolui eis obluctari, cum sperem hisce demonstrationibus Juventutem erudiri, et judicium eorundem de rebus Chronologicis rectius informari posse, praesertim cum tu etiam mea, quae tamen vera, immota et demonstrata sunt; et tantum opinione tibi falsa videntur, publice proponere, ventilare et exagitare volueris"; 66: "Edidit Elias Reusnerus, professor historiarum Jenensis, superiori anno Isagoges historiae libros duos, in quibus, quo ad historias consignandas secutus est Heinricum Buntingum: in tempore vero annotando, Abrahamum Bucholcerum, celebres quidem Chronologos, sed plurimum inter se dissentientes, ideo quod alter characteres Chronologicos ut plurimum sequitur, alter vero horum rudis opinionibus tantum et coniecturis fertur. Quapropter Reusnerus etiam, quando Chronologiam suam a condito Mundo ad nostra tempora usque deducit, dum utrosque inter se inconsulte miscet, non solum in plurimis locis errat et labitur, sed etiam me, cum amicitia inter nos ex communicatione literarum coaluisset, et ipse nulla a me iniuria lacessitus esset, errorum et falsarum hypothesium coarguit. Iniuriam hanc ego tacitus mussitare

cogitaram, sed cum amici putarent, Chronologiae interesse, ut et de meis et Reusneri fundamentis Studiosi erudirentur, Epistolam ad eundem scripsi Chronologicam, in qua lenissimis verbis, absque ulla insectatione rem nude, ut est, proposui, et non me, sed illum ipsum errare et nihil ad verum suum annum in tota sua Isagoge Chronologica usque ad ducentos annos post natum Christum retulisse, evidenter, luculenter, et ad oculum demonstravi."

69. See esp. Shapin and Schaffer 1985; Shapin 1995; Serjeantson 1999, 2006.

70. On the origins of this enterprise, see Eden 2001.

71. Miller 2002; Stenhouse 2005.

72. Findlen 1994, 1999; Ogilvie 2006.

73. Jardine, Mosley, and Tybjerg 2003; Mosley 2007.

74. Visser 2004; Siraisi 2007; Pomata forthcoming; Keller 2008.

75. See more recently Lotz-Heumann and Pohlig 2007.

76. See Kühlmann 1982; Goldgar 1995; Bots and Waquet 1994, 1997; Jaumann 2001; Mulsow 2000, 2001, 2006; Grafton 2001.

77. Mout 1975; Miller 2002.

78. Grafton and Williams 2006.

79. Drexel 1641, 65–66: "Felix eram Lovanii, ubi Poetas veteres, ubi priscos Historicos omnes et omnia Lipsii opera, ubi melioris notae Philosophos et Theologos in meo museo inter ceteros numerabam. Nunc subinde vacuus in scopulis piscator haereo. Vix pauculos historicos, et quidem editionis flagitiosae, cerno; Lipsium hoc loci in Pentheum migrasse credo, adeo lacer et dissipatus est; illius pauca invenio, et editionis dissimillimae. In melioribus libris ceteris supellex curta."

80. Drexel 1641, 66: "Itaque ursum aemulor, et fructu unguium meorum victito. Excerptis meis utor."

81. Mästlin 1641, 3–33.

82. Crusius 1927–1961, I, 286, 354.

83. Crusius 1927–1961, I, 101: "M. Mich. Maestlinus mane mecum erat, interrogans aliquid ex Iosephi arcaiol. L. 3. c. 8. vel 13. Quia cogitat adhuc, tandem scriptum edere contra Gregor. Calend."

84. Mästlin 1641, 20: "20 Sic idem Plinius libr. 6. cap. 6. Megasthenem ut Authorem fide dignum, qui cum Indicis Regibus moratus sit, allegat. Veruntamen nec Scaligero, nec nobis, de iis libris sermo est, qui sub Berosi et Megasthenis [read Metasthenis: clearly someone, perhaps Hafenreffer, corrected the name here without thinking] (ipso enim nomine ridicule corrupto cum Megasthenes sit) nomine venditantur, non ita pridem opera Annii cujusdam Viterbiensis publicati, avorum memoria ab otioso seu potius malitioso quodam malitiose conficti, quia non pauca tam sacrae Scripturae, quam aliorum fide dignorum attestationibus, item hisce, quae authentica ab aliis citantur fragmentis, contraria tradunt, rectissime pro futilibus fragmentis censentur. Hac autem praesenti quaestione nos Iosephus, licet ipse aliter sentiat, et Eusebius, bearunt, qui haec fragmenta suis scriptis inserta nobis communicaverunt. Historia igitur ita se habere indubia ratiocinatione depraehenditur."

85. Crusius 1927–1961, I, 101–102: "Post H. 5am vesperi, cubans in lecto post lavationem accepi literas a Thoma Schallero, Hennenbergensi Superintendente et Pastore Ecclesiae Mayningensis. Commendat mihi adolesc. Studiosum, huc venientem: et de Beroso multos Scriptores citat, tanquam fabuloso, praesertim Goropium Becanum. Cuperet aliquid ex me scire: quia molitur ipse Franconicum aliquid, nec sine magnis sumptibus, iam diu."

86. Crusius 1927–1961, I, 103, summarizing his reply to Schaller (see note 85): "2. Quia Berosus vel Berossus (quem ego l. lib. 1. Dodec. pag. 3. pro non fictitio laudo) a multis, praesertim a Goropio, dudum reiectus est: ego in hanc sententiam respondi raptim. At extat locus in hac Epitome Berosi, de Naue Noae, apud Gordiaeum montem quiescente: qui in Graeco Iosepho Iudaeo extat. Et ambo loca ad verbum ipsi Thomae descripsi in literas. Ergo. Epitome haec non est commentitia. Berosus sine dubio copiose scripserat: sed aliquis Epitomen inde confecit olim (sicut Iustinus, ex Trogo Pompeio) non tamen usque ad Nabuchodonosorem deducens: de quo Rege Berosum Iosephus citat. Fecit Epitomen quondam aliquis Latinus vel Romanus (quia stylus satis Latinus) sicut Dictys etiam Cretensis Latine versus olim fuit. Goropium nunquam mihi videre contigit. Audivi tamen, mira in eo esse, aut etiam *allokota:* ut, quandam aliam linguam antiquiorem Hebraea esse. Clarissimi etiam viri hodie ex Beroso historias sumpserunt. Si qua in eo discrepant: etiam Iustinus *allokota:* quaedam lib. 36. de Iosepho, Mose, etc. scribit. Potuit etiam Epitome ab Amanuensibus successu temporis corrumpi. Ego denique, quia universalem de Sueuis historiam conscribendam duxeram: Beroso etiam opus habui. Conqueritur et Diodorus Siculus, apud antiquissima tempora obscuritatem, praesertim fabulis res involutas, esse, etc. Libenter tamen Goropii contra Berosum rationes scirem, etc. Ego etiam conqueror in Annalibus de paucitate et obscuritate antiquissimarum rerum Sueuicarum, etc."

87. For an important exception, see Dickson 1998.

Bibliography

Primary Sources

MANUSCRIPTS AND ANNOTATED BOOKS

Göttingen University Library
MS 2° Philos. 103

PRINTED BOOKS

Alsted, Johann Heinrich. 1628. *Thesaurus chronologiæ: In quo universa temporum & historiarum series in omni vitæ genere ponitur ob oculos, ut fundamenta chronologiæ ex S. literis & calculo astronomico eruantur, & deinceps tituli homogenei in certas classes memoriæ causâ digerantur.* 2nd ed. Herborn: heirs of Corvinus.

Budovec z Budova, Vaclav, Baron. 1616. *Circulus horologii lunaris et solaris, hoc est, brevissima synopsis, historica, typica et mystica, variis figuris et emblematis illustrata, repraesentans ex Vetere et Novo Testamento continuam seriem praecipuarum Ecclesiae et Mundi mutationum, ceu horarum quarundam praeteritarum, praesentium, et secuturarum usque ad mundi consummationem.* Hanau: Wechel, heirs of Jean Aubry.

Burman, Pieter. 1727. *Sylloges epistolarum a viris illustribus scriptarum tomi quinque*, ed. Pieter Burman. 5 vols. Leiden: Luchtmans.

Calvisius, Seth. 1685. *Appendix operis chronologici.* Frankfurt am Main: Gensch.

Crusius, Martin. 1927–1961. *Diarium*, ed. Wilhelm Göz et al. 4 vols. Tübingen: Laupp.

Decker, Joannes. 1605. *Velificato seu Theoremata de anno ortus et mortis domini, deque universa Iesu Christi in carne Oeconomia, quae ad baccalaureatus in sacra theologia lauream in Alma Gracensi Academia in disputationem adducit* REVERENDVS DOMINVS *et eruditus artium liberalium ac philosophiae Magister* LAVRENTIVS SVSLYGA POLONVS, *praeside* R.P. IOANNE DECEKERIO SOCIETATIS IESV SS. THEOLOGIAE DOCTORE AC DICTAE VNIVERSITATIS CANCELLARIO. Graz: Georgius Widmanstadius.

Drexel, Jeremiah. 1641. *Aurifodina artium et scientiarum omnium, excerpendi solertia, omnibus litterarum amantibus monstrata.* Antwerp: widow of Ioannes Cnobbarus.

Gordon, James. 1611. *Chronologia annorum seriem, regnorum mutationes, et rerum memorabilium sedem annumque ab orbe condito ad nostra usque tempora complectens.* Bordeaux: Milanges.

Gude, Marquard, et al. 1697. *Marquardi Gudii et doctorum virorum ad eum epistolae*, ed. Pieter Burman. Utrecht: Halmam and van de Water.

Herwart von Hohenburg, Joannes Georg. 1610. *Thesaurus hieroglyphicorum.* Augsburg: n.p.

———. 1612. *Novae, verae et ad calculm* [sic] *astronomicum revocatae chronologiae, seu temporum ab origine mundi supputationis, capita praecipua, quibus tota temporum ratio continetur et innumerabiles omnium chronologorum errores deteguntur.* Munich: Nicolaus Henricus.

Herwart von Hohenburg, Joannes Georg, and Joannes Fridericus Herwart von Hohenburg. 1626. *Admiranda ethnicae theologiae mysteria propalata. Vbi lapidem magnetem antiquissimis passim nationibus pro deo cultum: Et artem qua navigationes Magneticae per universum orbem instituerentur, a Veterum Sacerdotibus, sub involucris Deorum Dearumque et aliarum perinde fabularum cortice, summo studio occultatam esse noviter commonstratur. Accessit exacta temporum ratio adversus incredibiles Chronologiae vulgaris errores, opus diu desideratum.* 2 parts. Munich: Nicolaus Henricus.

Kepler, Johannes. 1627. *Tabulae Rudolphinae, quibus astronomicae scientiae temporum longinquitate collapsae restaurato continetur.* Ulm: Jonas Saur.

————. 1861. *Opera omnia,* ed. Christian Frisch, 4.1. Frankfurt: Heyder and Zimmer.

————. 1937–. *Gesammelte Werke,* ed. Max Caspar et al. Munich: Beck.

Mästlin, Michael. 1641. *Chronologicae theses et tabulae breves contractaeque ad investiganda tempora historiarum et epocharum potissimarum, praesertim sacrarum, a Creatione Mundi ad ultimam Hierosolymorum vastationem, accommodatae: Cum Exegesi Quaestionum Chronologicarum,* ed. Samuel Hafenreffer. Tübingen: Philibertus Brunnius.

Meel, Joannes Wilhelmus van. 1701. *Insignium virorum epistolae selectae.* Amsterdam: Halm.

Mercator, Gerardus. 1569. *Chronologia.* Cologne: heirs of Birckmann.

Possevino, Antonio. 1603. *Apparatus sacer.* 3 vols. in 2. Venice: Apud Societatem Venetam.

————. 1607. *Bibliotheca selecta de ratione studiorum.* 2 vols. in 1. Cologne: Gymnicus.

————. 1608. *Apparatus sacer ad scriptores Veteris et Novi Testamenti.* 2 vols. Cologne: Gymnicus.

————. 1609. *Apparatus ad studia D. Scripturae, theologiae scholasticae, et practicae, sive moralis de casibus conscientiae.* 4th ed. Ferrara: Victorius Baldinus.

Rader, Matthäus. 1995. *P. Matthäus Rader SJ. Band I: 1595–1612,* ed. Alois Schmid, with Helmut Zäh and Silvia Strodel. Munich: Beck.

Reusner, Elias. 1600. *Isagoges historicae libri duo: Quorum unus ecclesiasticam, alter politicam continet historiam: Utramque secundum cuiusque aetates exacte definitam: Quarum illa ad traditionem Domus Eliae; haec ad quatuor mundi regna, in bestiis quatuor a Daniele Propheta adumbrata, magno et pio studio est accommodata. Cum exquisitissima veterum Historicorum, tam Graecorum quam Latinorum,* CHRONOLOGIA. Jena: Tobias Steinmann.

————. 1609a. *Isagoges historicae libri duo: Quorum unus ecclesiasticam, alter politicam continet historiam: Utramque secundum cuiusque aetates exacte definitam: Quarum illa ad traditionem Domus Eliae; haec ad quatuor mundi regna, in bestiis quatuor a Daniele Propheta adumbrata, magno et pio studio est accommodata. Altera editio auctior et elaboratior. Accessit praeterea I.* PRINCIPVM *et Comitum Germanicorum Stemmatographia: II.* RECTORVM *Academiae Salanae Catalogus: III.* VIRORVM DOCTORVM *Index Chronologicus.* CUM PRIVILEGIO. Jena: Christophorus Lippold.

————. 1609b. *Stratagematographia sive Thesaurus bellicus, docens, quomodo bella iuste et legitime suscipi, recte et prudenter administrari, commode et sapienter confici debeant: Ex latissimo et laetissimo Historiarum campo Herculeo labore erutus ab Elia Reusnero Leorino, Histor. in Illustri Salana Profess. Pub. Cum eiusdem Synopsi, et gemino* INDICE *locupletissimo, altero Historiarum, altero Rerum memorabilium.* Frankfurt am Main: E Collegio Musarum Novenarum Paltheniano.

————. 1618. *Hortulus historico-politicus, coronas sex ex floribus variis variegatas complectens: Id est, lectiones historico-politicae, publice in alma* SALANA *propositae, reipublicae cuiusvis constitutionem, administrationem, conservationemque explicantes, usumque exemplis historicis demonstrantes; tam imperantibus quam obtemperantibus perutiles et necessariae*, ed. Abrahamus De La Faye. Herbornae Nassoviorum: n.p.

————, ed. 1650. Stefano Guazzo, *De civili conversatione dissertationes politicae*. Leiden: Petrus Leffen.

Salianus, Jacobus. 1641. *Annales ecclesiastici veteris testamenti*. 6 vols. in 2. 4th ed. Paris: de Heuqueville.

Samerius, Henricus. 1608. *Sacra chronologia a mundo condito ad Christum*. Antwerp: Hieronymus Verdussen.

Scaliger, Joseph. 1627. *Epistolae omnes quae reperiri potuerunt*, ed. Daniel Heinsius. Leiden: Elzevir.

Schickard, Wilhelm. 2002. *Briefwechsel*, ed. Friedrich Seck. 2 vols. Stuttgart–Bad Cannstatt: Frommann-Holzboog.

Schottus, Andreas. 1603. *Vitae comparatae Aristotelis ac Demostenis: Olympiadibus ac praeturis Atheniensium digestae*. Augsburg: Magnus.

Secondary Sources

Barnes, Robin. 1988. *Prophecy and Gnosis: Apocalypticism in the Wake of the Lutheran Reformation*. Stanford, Calif.: Stanford University Press.

Boner, Patrick. Forthcoming. "A Statesman and a Scholar: Hans Georg Herwart von Hohenburg as a Critic and Patron of Johannes Kepler." University of Cambridge, Department of History and Philosophy of Science, History of Science Workshop paper, 2 May 2007.

Bots, Hans, and Françoise Waquet, eds. 1994. *Commercium litterarium, 1600–1750*. Amsterdam: APA–Holland University Press.

————. 1997. *La République des Lettres*. Paris: Belin.

Brosseder, Claudia. 2004. *Im Bann der Sterne: Caspar Peucer, Philipp Melanchthon und andere Wittenberger Astrologen*. Berlin: Akademie Verlag.

Burke-Gaffney, M. W., S.J. 1944. *Kepler and the Jesuits*. Milwaukee, Wis.: Bruce.

Dickson, Donald. 1998. *The Tessera of Antilia: Utopian Brotherhoods and Secret Societies in the Early Seventeenth Century*. Leiden: Brill.

Eden, Kathy. 2001. *Friends Hold All Things in Common: Tradition, Intellectual Property, and the Adages of Erasmus*. New Haven, Conn.: Yale University Press.

Engammare, Max. 2004. *L'ordre du temps: L'invention de la ponctualité au XVIe siècle*. Geneva: Droz.

Field, Judith. 1988. *Kepler's Geometrical Cosmology*. Chicago: University of Chicago Press.

Findlen, Paula. 1994. *Possessing Nature: Museums, Collecting, and Scientific Culture in Early Modern Italy*. Berkeley: University of California Press.

————. 1999. "The Formation of a Scientific Community: Natural History in Sixteenth-Century Italy." In *Natural Particulars: Renaissance Natural Philosophy and the Disciplines,* ed. Anthony Grafton and Nancy Siraisi. Cambridge, Mass.: MIT Press, 369–400.

————, ed. 2004. *Athanasius Kircher: The Last Man Who Knew Everything.* New York: Routledge.

Goldgar, Anne. 1995. *Impolite Learning: Conduct and Community in the Republic of Letters, 1680–1750.* New Haven, Conn.: Yale University Press.

Grafton, Anthony. 1983–1993. *Joseph Scaliger.* 2 vols. Oxford: Clarendon Press.

————. 1991. *Defenders of the Text: The Traditions of Humanism in an Age of Science, 1450–1800.* Cambridge, Mass.: Harvard University Press.

————. 2001. *Bring Out Your Dead: The Past as Revelation.* Cambridge, Mass.: Harvard University Press.

Grafton, Anthony, and Megan Williams. 2006. *Christianity and the Transformation of the Book: Origen, Eusebius and the Library of Caesarea.* Cambridge, Mass.: Harvard University Press.

Hallyn, Fernand. 1990. *The Poetic Structure of the World: Copernicus and Kepler,* tr. Donald M. Leslie. New York: Zone.

Jardine, Nicholas. 1984. *The Birth of History and Philosophy of Science: Kepler's "A Defence of Tycho against Ursus," with Essays on Its Provenance and Significance.* Cambridge: Cambridge University Press.

Jardine, N., A. Mosley, and K. Tybjerg. 2003. "Epistolary Culture, Editorial Practices, and Tycho Brahe's Astronomical Letters." *Journal for the History of Astronomy* 34, 421–451.

Jaumann, Herbert, ed. 2001. *Die europäische Gelehrtenrepublik im Zeitalter des Konfessionalismus = The European Republic of Letters in the Age of Confessionalism.* Wiesbaden: Harrassowitz.

Keller, Vera. Forthcoming. 2008. *Cornelis Drebbel.* PhD dissertation, Princeton University.

Kolb, Robert. 1987. *For All the Saints: Changing Perceptions of Sainthood and Martyrdom in the Lutheran Reformation.* Macon, Ga.: Mercer University Press.

Kühlmann, Wilhelm. 1982. *Gelehrtenrepublik und Fürstenstaat: Entwicklung und Kritik des deutschen Späthumanismus in der Literatur des Barockzeitalters.* Tübingen: Max Niemeyer.

Lehmann-Brauns, Sicco. 2004. *Weisheit in der Weltgeschichte: Philosophiegeschichte zwischen Barock und Aufklärung.* Tübingen: Niemeyer.

Lotz-Heumann, Ute, and Matthias Pohlig. 2007. "Confessionalization and Literature in the Empire, 1555–1700." *Central European History* 40, 35–61.

Malcolm, Noel. 2002. *Aspects of Hobbes.* Oxford: Clarendon Press.

————. 2004. "William Harrison and His 'Ark of Studies': An Episode in the History of the Organization of Knowledge." *Seventeenth Century* 19, 196–232.

Mayhew, Robert. 2004. "British Geography's Republic of Letters: Mapping an Imagined Community, 1600–1800." *Journal of the History of Ideas* 65, 251–276.

———. 2005. "Mapping Science's Imagined Community: Geography as a Republic of Letters, 1600–1800." *British Journal for the History of Science* 38, 73–92.

Miller, Peter. 2002. *Peiresc's Europe: Learning and Virtue in the Seventeenth Century.* New Haven, Conn.: Yale University Press.

Mosley, Adam. 2007. *Bearing the Heavens: Tycho Brahe and the Astronomical Community of the Late Sixteenth Century.* Cambridge: Cambridge University Press.

Mout, Nicolette. 1975. *Bohemen en de Nederlanden in de zestiende eeuw.* Leiden: Universitaire Pers Leiden.

Mulsow, Martin. 2000. "Unanständigkeit. Zur Missachtung und Verteidigung des Decorum in der Gelehrtenrepublik der Frühen Neuzeit." *Historische Anthropologie* 8, 98–118.

———. 2001. *Die drei Ringe: Toleranz und clandestine Gelehrsamkeit bei Mathurin Veyssière La Croze (1661–1739).* Tübingen: Niemeyer.

———. 2006. "Practices of Unmasking: Polyhistors, Correspondence, and the Birth of Dictionaries of Pseudonymity in Seventeenth-Century Germany." *Journal of the History of Ideas* 67, 219–250.

Ogilvie, Brian. 2006. *The Science of Describing: Natural History in Renaissance Europe.* Chicago: University of Chicago Press.

Pattison, Mark, 1892. *Isaac Casaubon, 1559–1614.* 2nd ed. Oxford: Clarendon Press.

Pomata, Gianna. Forthcoming. "Sharing Cases: The Observationes in Early Modern Medicine." Paper, Conference on Cases in Science, Medicine and the Law, CRASSH, Cambridge, 20–21 April 2007.

Rothman, Aviva. Forthcoming. *Johannes Kepler and His Friends.* PhD dissertation, Princeton University.

Serjeantson, Richard. 1999. "Testimony and Proof in Early-Modern England." *Studies in History and Philosophy of Science* 30, 195–236.

———. 2006. "Proof and Persuasion." In *The Cambridge History of Science,* vol. III: *Sixteenth- and Seventeenth-Century Europe,* ed. Lorraine Daston and Katharine Park. Cambridge: Cambridge University Press.

Shapin, Steven, 1995. *A Social History of Truth: Civility and Science in Seventeenth-Century England.* Chicago: University of Chicago Press.

Shapin, Steven, and Simon Schaffer. 1985. *Leviathan and the Air-Pump: Hobbes, Boyle and the Experimental Life.* Princeton, N.J.: Princeton University Press.

Siraisi, Nancy. 2007. *History, Medicine, and the Traditions of Renaissance Learning.* Ann Arbor: University of Michigan Press.

Smoller, Laura. 1994. *History, Prophecy, and the Stars: The Christian Astrology of Pierre d'Ailly, 1350–1420.* Princeton, N.J.: Princeton University Press.

Stenhouse, William. 2005. *Reading Inscriptions and Writing Ancient History: Historical Scholarship in the Late Renaissance.* London: Institute of Classical Studies.

Stephenson, Bruce. 1987. *Kepler's Physical Astronomy.* New York: Springer.

———. 1994. *The Music of the Heavens: Kepler's Harmonic Astronomy.* Princeton, N.J.: Princeton University Press.

Van Houdt, Toon, Jan Papy, Gilbert Tournoy, and Constant Matheeussen, eds. 2002. *Self-Presentation and Social Identification: The Rhetoric and Pragmatics of Letter-Writing in Early Modern Times.* Leuven: Leuven University Press.

Visser, Arnoud. 2004. "From the Republic of Letters to the Olympus: The Rise and Fall of Medical Humanism in 67 Portraits." In *Living in Posterity: Essays in Honour of Bart Westerweel,* ed. Jan Frans van Dijkhuizen et al. Hilversum: Verloren, 299–313.

Voelkel, James. 1999. *Johannes Kepler and the New Astronomy.* New York: Oxford University Press.

———. 2001. *The Composition of Kepler's Astronomia Nova.* Princeton, N.J.: Princeton University Press.

Waquet, Françoise. 1989. *Le modèle français et l'Italie savante: Conscience de soi et perception de l'autre dans la République des lettres (1660–1750).* Rome: Ecole Française de Rome; Paris: Boccard.

———, ed. 2002. *Mapping the World of Learning: The Polyhistor of Daniel Georg Morhof.* Wiesbaden: Harrassowitz.

Zedelmaier, Helmut. 1992. *Bibliotheca universalis und bibliotheca selecta: Das Problem der Ordnung des gelehrten Wissens in der frühen Neuzeit.* Cologne: Böhlau.

———. 2003. *Der Anfang der Geschichte: Studien zur Ursprungsdebatte im 18. Jahrhundert.* Hamburg: Meiner.

Zedelmaier, Helmut, and Martin Mulsow, eds. 2001. *Die Praktiken der Gelehrsamkeit in der frühen Neuzeit.* Tübingen: M. Niemeyer.

7. The Universal Language

This chapter began as a review essay on the following volumes of the I Tatti Renaissance Library, published by Harvard University Press: Flavio Biondo, *Italy Illuminated,* ed. and tr. Jeffrey White; Francesco Petrarca, *Invectives,* ed. and tr. David Marsh; *Humanist Educational Treatises,* ed. and tr. Craig W. Kallendorf; Giannozzo Manetti, *Biographical Writings,* ed. and tr. Stefano U. Baldassarri and Rolf Bagemihl; Pius II, *Commentaries,* ed. Margaret Meserve and Marcello Simonetta; Cyriac of Ancona, *Later Travels,* ed. and tr. Edward W. Bodnar with Clive Foss; Leonardo Bruni, *History of the Florentine People,* ed. and tr. James Hankins; Marsilio Ficino, *Platonic Theology,* ed. James Hankins with William Bowen, tr. Michael J. B. Allen with John Warden; Polydore Vergil, *On Discovery,* ed. and tr. Brian P. Copenhaver; *Humanist Comedies,* ed. and tr. Gary R. Grund; Maffeo Vegio, *Short Epics,* ed. and tr. Michael C. J. Putnam with James Hankins; Angelo Poliziano, *Silvae,* ed. and tr. Charles Fantazzi; Angelo Poliziano, *Letters,* ed. and tr. Shane Butler, and a second review essay on Françoise Waquet, *Latin, or the Empire of a Sign* (London: Verso, 2001).

1. Riccardo Fubini, *Storiografia dell'umanesimo in Italia da Leonardo Bruni ad Annio da Viterbo* (Rome: Storia e Letteratura, 2003).

2. Giovanni Dominici, *Lucula noctis,* ed. Edmund Hunt (Notre Dame, Ind.: University of Notre Dame, 1940), 412, called to my attention by Alison Frazier's excellent *Possible Lives* (New York: Columbia University Press, 2005), 19.

3. See Silvia Rizzo, *Ricerche sul latino umanistico* (Rome: Edizioni di Storia e Letteratura, 2002), and Christopher Celenza, "Petrarch, Latin, and Italian Renaissance Latinity," *Journal of Medieval and Early Modern Studies* 35 (2005), 509–536.

4. See Berthold L. Ullman and Philip A. Stadter, *The Public Library of Renaissance Florence* (Padua: Antenore, 1972).

5. Ingrid Rowland, *The Culture of the High Renaissance: Ancients and Moderns in Sixteenth-Century Rome* (Cambridge: Cambridge University Press, 1998).

6. Zbigniew Herbert, "Transformations of Livy," tr. Bogdana Carpenter and John Carpenter, *New York Review of Books,* 6 November 1986.

7. John Sparrow, *Visible Words: A Study of Inscriptions in and as Books and Works of Art* (London: Cambridge University Press, 1969), 139. The unnamed historian was quoting a phrase of G. M. Trevelyan's. See also the pioneering and very important collection that Sparrow edited in collaboration with Alessandro Perosa, *Renaissance Latin Verse: An Anthology* (London: Duckworth, 1979).

8. Aldington's discussion of Poliziano appears, appropriately, in his introduction to *The Portable Oscar Wilde* (New York: Viking, 1946), 12. Poliziano's immense erudition, fostered by the study of sources few of his contemporaries knew, nourished what Aldington describes in *Wilde* as a "technique of strange erudition made poetic." This also characterized the prose of his varied, demanding, and sometimes mysterious letters, which are being edited and explicated for the I Tatti series, with great learning, by Shane Butler. Butler shows that Poliziano revised his own letters as well as those he received from friends like Pico della Mirandola. He selected, omitted, and burnished texts to assemble a vivid but sometimes deliberately deceptive mosaic of the social and cultural world in which he lived—a project that, like his scholarship, bears comparison in more than one way with his poetry.

9. In addition, many Neo-Latin texts are now available for reading or downloading on the Web. Useful sites include White Trash Scriptorium: www.ipa.net/~magreyn/ and Dana Sutton's excellent Analytic Bibliography of On-Line Neo-Latin Texts: www.philological.bham.ac.uk/bibliography/index.htm.

10. See the classic study by Michael Baxandall, *Giotto and the Orators: Humanist Observers of Painting in Italy and the Discovery of Pictorial Composition, 1350–1450* (Oxford: Clarendon Press, 1971; new ed., Oxford: Clarendon Press, 1986).

11. See Christopher Celenza, *The Lost Italian Renaissance: Humanists, Historians, and Latin's Legacy* (Baltimore, Md.: Johns Hopkins University Press, 2004), and the thoughtful review by William Stenhouse, *Bryn Mawr Classical Review,* 29 September 2004.

8. Entrepreneurs of the Soul, Impresarios of Learning

This chapter began as a review essay on John O'Malley, *The First Jesuits* (Cambridge, Mass.: Harvard University Press, 1993); W. W. Meissner S.J., M.D., *Ignatius of Loyola: The Psychology of a Saint* (New Haven, Conn.: Yale University Press, 1992); and Jean Lacouture, *Jésuites: Une Multibiographie*, vol. 1: *Les conquérants,* and vol. 2: *Les revenants* (Paris: Le Seuil, 1991).

1. The Peruvian document comes from Antonio de Egaña, S.J., ed., *Monumenta Peruana*, vol. II: *1576–1580* (Rome: Monumenta Historica Soc. Iesu, 1958), 250; see more generally the masterly study by Sabine MacCormack, *Religion in the Andes: Vision and Imagination in Early Colonial Peru* (Princeton, N.J.: Princeton University Press, 1992). On Ricci, see Jonathan Spence, *The Memory Palace of Matteo Ricci* (New York: Viking Penguin, 1984) and Jacques Gernet, *China and the Christian Impact: A Conflict of Cultures,* tr. Janet Lloyd (Cambridge: Cambridge University Press, 1985), as well as the essays and bibliography collected in Charles E. Ronan, S.J. and Bonnie B. C. Oh, eds., *East Meets West: The Jesuits in China, 1582–1773* (Chicago: Loyola University Press, 1988).

2. Albano Biondi, "La Bibliotheca selecta di Antonio Possevino: Un progetto di egemonia culturale," in *La "Ratio studiorum": Modelli culturali e pratiche educative dei Gesuiti in Italia tra Cinque e Seicento,* ed. Gian Paolo Brizzi (Rome: Bulzoni, 1981).

3. The catalog is very informative: Thomas M. Lucas, S.J., ed., *Saint, Site and Sacred Strategy: Ignatius, Rome and Jesuit Urbanism* (Rome: Biblioteca Apostolica Vaticana, 1990).

4. For the background, see the excellent book by Paul Grendler, *Schooling in Renaissance Italy: Literacy and Learning, 1300–1600* (Baltimore, Md.: Johns Hopkins University Press, 1989).

5. See Pierre Hadot, *Exercices spirituels et philosophie antique,* 2nd ed. (Paris: Etudes Augustiniennes, 1987).

6. See Mario Praz, *The Flaming Heart* (Garden City, N.Y.: Doubleday, 1958).

7. For some perspectives on casuistry, see Albert R. Jonsen and Stephen Toulmin, *The Abuse of Casuistry: A History of Moral Reasoning* (Berkeley: University of California Press, 1988) and Edmund Leites, ed., *Conscience and Casuistry in Early Modern Europe* (Cambridge: Cambridge University Press; Paris: Maison des Sciences de l'Homme, 1988).

8. See Marjorie O'Rourke Boyle, "Angels Black and White: Loyola's Spiritual Discernment in Historical Perspective," *Theological Studies* 44 (1983), 241–257.

9. See Carlo Ginzburg, "Folklore, magia, religione," in *Storia d'Italia*, vol. I: *I caratteri originali* (Turin: Einaudi, 1972), 631–633; and R. Taylor, "Ermetismo e architettura mistica nella Compagnia di Gesù," in *Architettura e arte dei gesuiti,* ed. Rudolf Wittkower and Irma B. Jaffe, tr. Massimo Parizzi (Milan: Electa, 1992).

10. See Ginzburg, "Folklore, magia, religione," 656–661.

11. Jennifer Selwyn, *A Paradise Inhabited by Devils: The Jesuits' Civilizing Mission in Early Modern Naples* (Aldershot, U.K.: Ashgate, 2004).

12. Benjamin Elman, *On Their Own Terms: Science in China, 1550–1900* (Cambridge, Mass.: Harvard University Press, 2005); Liam Brockey, *Journey to the East: The Jesuit Mission to China, 1579–1724* (Cambridge, Mass.: Harvard University Press, 2007).

13. Robert Bireley, *Religion and Politics in the Age of the Counterreformation: Emperor Ferdinand II, William Lamormaini, S.J., and the Formation of Imperial Policy* (Chapel Hill: University of North Carolina Press, 1981); Bireley, *The Counter-Reformation Prince: Anti-Machiavellianism or Catholic Statecraft in Early Modern Europe* (Chapel Hill: University of North Carolina Press, 1990); Harro Höpfl, *Jesuit Political Thought: The Society of Jesus and the State, c. 1540–1630* (Cambridge: Cambridge University Press, 2004).

14. Luciano Canfora, *Convertire Casaubon* (Milan: Adelphi, 2002); Evonne Levi, *Propaganda and the Jesuit Baroque* (Berkeley: University of California Press, 2004).

15. See e.g. Maria Teresa Borgato, ed., *Giambattista Riccioli e il merito scientifico dei gesuiti nell'età barocca* (Florence: Olschki, 2002); Mordechai Feingold, ed., *Jesuit Science and the Republic of Letters* (Cambridge, Mass.: MIT Press, 2003).

16. See the remarkable collections of articles edited by John O'Malley and colleagues: *The Jesuits: Cultures, Sciences, and the Arts, 1540–1773* (Toronto: University of Toronto Press, 1999); *The Jesuits II: Cultures, Sciences, and the Arts, 1540–1773* (Toronto: University of Toronto Press, 2006); John O'Malley and Gauvin Alexander Bailey, eds., *The Jesuits and the Arts, 1540–1773* (Philadelphia: Saint Joseph's University Press, 2005).

17. The forthcoming book by Daniel Stolzenberg will illuminate Kircher's work and world. Meantime, several excellent (and complementary) books lay out central areas of his thought. See, among others, Erik Iversen, *Obelisks in Exile*, vol. I: *The Obelisks of Rome* (Copenhagen: Gad, 1968); R. J. W. Evans, *The Making of the Habsburg Monarchy, 1550 to 1700* (New York: Oxford University Press, 1979); David Mungello, *Curious Land: Jesuit Accommodation and the Origins of Sinology* (Stuttgart: Franz Steiner, 1985); Thomas Leinkauf, *Mundus combinatus: Studien zur Struktur der barocken Universalwissenschaft am Beispiel Athanasius Kirchers SJ (1602–1680)* (Berlin: Akademie Verlag, 1993); Daniel Stolzenberg, ed., *The Great Art of Knowing: The Baroque Encyclopedia of Athanasius Kircher* (Stanford, Calif.: Stanford University Libraries, 2001); Paula Findlen, ed., *Athanasius Kircher: The Last Man Who Knew Everything* (New York: Routledge, 2004).

9. In No Man's Land

This chapter first appeared as a review essay on Adam Sutcliffe, *Judaism and Enlightenment* (Cambridge: Cambridge University Press, 2003) and Maurice Olender,

The Languages of Paradise: Aryans and Semites, a Match Made in Heaven, tr. Arthur Goldhammer (New York: The Other Press, 2003).

1. Flavius Mithridates, *Sermo de Passione Domini,* ed. with an introduction and commentary by Chaim Wirszubski (n.p.: Israel Academy of Sciences and Humanities, 1963).

2. See e.g. Joseph Dan, ed., *The Christian Kabbalah* (Cambridge, Mass.: Harvard College Library, 1997); Stephen Burnett, *From Christian Hebraism to Jewish Studies: Johannes Buxtorf (1564–1629) and Hebrew Learning in the Seventeenth Century* (Leiden: Brill, 1996).

3. See Johannes Reuchlin, *Recommendation whether to Confiscate, Destroy, and Burn All Jewish Books,* ed. and tr. Peter Wortsman; critical introduction by Elisheva Carlebach (Mahwah, N.J.: Paulist Press, 2000).

4. See David Katz, *The Jews in the History of England, 1485–1850* (Oxford: Clarendon Press, 1994), and *God's Last Words* (New Haven, Conn.: Yale University Press, 2004).

5. Noel Malcolm, "Hobbes, Ezra and the Bible: The History of a Subversive Idea," in his *Aspects of Hobbes* (Oxford: Clarendon Press, 2002), 383–431.

6. Olender's book was originally published by Harvard University Press in 1992, but it remains strikingly relevant to contemporary debates.

7. Another rich, recent, and sometimes overly polemical study nicely complements these two books: see Jonathan M. Hess, *Germans, Jews and the Claims of Modernity* (New Haven, Conn.: Yale University Press, 2002).

8. See Henk Jan de Jonge, *De bestudering van het Nieuwe Testemant aan de Noordnederlandse universiteiten en het Remonstrants Seminarie van 1575 tot 1700* (Amsterdam: North-Holland, 1980); Luciano Canfora, *Ellenismo* (Rome: Laterza, 1987).

9. Azariah de' Rossi, *The Light of the Eyes,* tr. Joanna Weinberg (New Haven, Conn.: Yale University Press, 2001), 101–111, 129. This edition is a magnificent work of scholarship. Both de' Rossi's text and Weinberg's commentary shed a flood of light on the questions raised by the books under review.

10. Daniel Heinsius, *Aristarchus sacer* (Leiden: Elzevir, 1627), 211–212.

11. For some specimens of more recent research, see Burnett, *From Christian Hebraism to Jewish Studies*; Matt Goldish, *Judaism in the Theology of Sir Isaac Newton* (Dordrecht: Kluwer Academic Publishers, 1998); Allison Coudert and Jeffrey Shoulson, eds., *Hebraica veritas? Christian Hebraists and the Study of Judaism in Early Modern Europe* (Philadelphia: University of Pennsylvania Press, 2004); Giuseppe Veltri and Gerold Necker, eds., *Gottes Sprache in der philologischen Werkstatt: Hebraistik vom 15. bis zum 19. Jahrhundert* (Leiden: Brill, 2004); Jason Rosenblatt, *Renaissance England's Chief Rabbi: John Selden* (Oxford: Oxford University Press, 2006).

10. The History of Ideas

Warm thanks to Warren Breckman and Suzanne Marchand for comments on earlier drafts of this chapter.

1. Randall Jarrell, *Pictures from an Institution: A Comedy* (New York: Knopf, 1954), 1. In the notes that follow, citations are only exemplary; to be exhaustive would be impossible.

2. Cf. the autobiographical account of Henry May, *Coming to Terms: A Study in Memory and History* (Berkeley: University of California Press, 1987), 307: "When I came to Berkeley [in 1950] intellectual history was a satisfyingly radical cause. The wise old men of the historical profession, at Berkeley and elsewhere, tended to dismiss it as impossibly vague and subjective. During the fifties, however, the vogue changed, and my kind of history became, for a short and heady few years, the rising fashion. To my surprise and slight discomfort, during my first decade at Berkeley I found myself, in writing, teaching, and university affairs, increasingly a part of the winning side."

3. Robert Darnton, "Intellectual and Cultural History," in *The Past before Us: Contemporary Historical Writing in the United States*, ed. Michael Kammen (Ithaca, N.Y.: Cornell University Press, 1980), 327–328.

4. Darnton had in mind work like that of Frank Manuel, whose Newtonian scholarship moved in the 1960s from a style of biography based on textual analysis to one that applied a more controversial psychoanalytic approach: cf. *Isaac Newton, Historian* (Cambridge, Mass.: Harvard University Press, 1963) with *A Portrait of Isaac Newton* (Cambridge, Mass.: Harvard University Press, 1968; repr. Washington, D.C.: New Republic Books, 1979). In later studies, like *The Changing of the Gods* (Hanover, N.H.: University Press of New England, 1983) and *The Broken Staff: Judaism through Christian Eyes* (Cambridge, Mass.: Harvard University Press, 1992), Manuel returned to the history of ideas in a more traditional vein, as he did in his study of *The Religion of Isaac Newton* (Oxford: Clarendon Press, 1974).

5. Quentin Skinner, "Meaning and Understanding in the History of Ideas," *History and Theory* 8 (1969), 3–53; reprinted and discussed in James Tully, ed., *Meaning and Context: Quentin Skinner and His Critics* (Princeton, N.J.: Princeton University Press, 1988), 29–67.

6. Darnton, "Intellectual and Cultural History," 338–339.

7. Ibid., 346.

8. For a fuller treatment, see Peter Burke, *What Is Cultural History?* (Oxford: Polity Press, 2004), chaps. 3–4.

9. Arnaldo Momigliano, "A Piedmontese View of the History of Ideas," in his *Essays in Ancient and Modern Historiography* (Oxford: Oxford University Press, 1977), 6.

10. Daniel J. Wilson, *Arthur O. Lovejoy and the Quest for Intelligibility* (Chapel Hill: University of North Carolina Press, 1980), chap. 5.

11. Arthur Lovejoy, "On the Discrimination of Romanticisms," *Proceedings of the Modern Language Association* 39 (1924): 229–253, reprinted in his *Essays in the History of Ideas* (Baltimore, Md.: Johns Hopkins University Press, 1948), 228–253. Here Lovejoy makes it clear how attention to what he saw as "simpler, diversely combinable, intellectual and emotional components" (253) of a sweeping term for a period style in thought and art like Romanticism could lead to great gains in conceptual clarity.

12. Arthur Lovejoy, "The Historiography of Ideas," *Proceedings of the American Philosophical Society* 78 (1928), 529–543, reprinted in his *Essays in the History of Ideas,* 1–13.

13. A. O. Lovejoy, *The Great Chain of Being; A Study of the History of an Idea* (Cambridge, Mass.: Harvard University Press, 1936).

14. Wilson, *Arthur O. Lovejoy,* 187–189.

15. Leo Spitzer, "*Geistesgeschichte* vs. History of Ideas as Applied to Hitlerism," *Journal of the History of Ideas* 5 (1944), 191–203 at 203.

16. Arthur Lovejoy, "Reply to Professor Spitzer," *Journal of the History of Ideas* 5 (1944), 204–219.

17. Rosalie Colie, " 'Method' and the History of Scientific Ideas," *History of Ideas News Letter* 4 (1958), 75–79; Crane Brinton et al., " 'Method' and the History of Scientific Ideas: Comment and Discussion," *History of Ideas News Letter* 5 (1959), 27–36; "The Editor's Column: Miss Colie Replies," *History of Ideas News Letter* 5 (1959), 50, 67–68.

18. Gilbert Allardyce, "The Rise and Fall of the Western Civilization Course," *American Historical Review* 87 (1982), 695–725.

19. For some very different cases in point, see the comments of Carl Schorske in *Thinking with History: Explorations in the Passage to Modernism* (Princeton, N.J.: Princeton University Press, 1998), 20; Richard McCormick in Michael Birkner, *McCormick of Rutgers: Scholar, Teacher, Public Historian* (Westport, Conn.: Greenwood Press, 2001), 47; and William McNeil in *The Pursuit of Truth: A Historian's Memoir* (Lexington: University Press of Kentucky, 2005).

20. Donald R. Kelley, *The Descent of Ideas: The History of Intellectual History* (Aldershot, U.K.: Ashgate, 2002).

21. Ulrich Schneider, "Teaching the History of Philosophy in 19th Century Germany," in *Teaching New Histories of Philosophy,* ed. J. B. Schneewind (Princeton, N.J.: Center for Human Values, Princeton University, 2004), 275–295. See also Schneider's book, *Philosophie und Universität: Historisierung der Vernunft im 19. Jahrhundert* (Hamburg: Meiner, 1999), which explores these issues in more depth.

22. Momigliano, "A Piedmontese View of the History of Ideas," 1.

23. J. B. Bury, *The Idea of Progress: An Inquiry into Its Origin and Growth* (New York: Macmillan, 1932).

24. See esp. Hans Baron's collected studies, *In Search of Florentine Civic Humanism: Essays on the Transition from Medieval to Modern Thought,* 2 vols. (Princeton, N.J.:

Princeton University Press, 1988), and cf. James Hankins, ed., *Renaissance Civic Humanism: Reappraisals and Reflection* (Cambridge: Cambridge University Press, 2000).

25. For part of this story, see William McGuire, *Bollingen: An Adventure in Collecting the Past* (Princeton, N.J.: Princeton University Press, 1982). Harper Torchbooks provided inexpensive editions of Lovejoy's *Great Chain of Being* and vital works on the history of ideas by Cassirer, Curtius, Garin, Rossi, and others. Beacon did the same for the works of Perry Miller.

26. See esp. Perry Miller, *The New England Mind: The Seventeenth Century* (New York: Macmillan, 1939); Samuel Eliot Morison, *The Founding of Harvard College* (Cambridge, Mass.: Harvard University Press, 1935); Morison, *Harvard College in the Seventeenth Century*, 2 vols. (Cambridge, Mass.: Harvard University Press, 1936); Morison, *The Puritan Pronaos: Studies in the Intellectual Life of New England in the Seventeenth Century* (New York: New York University Press, 1936). The great work that Miller and Morison inspired was, of course, Walter Ong, S.J., *Ramus, Method and the Decay of Dialogue* (Cambridge, Mass.: Harvard University Press, 1958). On Miller's practice, see David Hollinger, "Perry Miller and Philosophical History," in his *In the American Province: Essays in the History and Historiography of Ideas* (Bloomington: Indiana University Press, 1985), 152–166.

27. See Norman Fiering, *Moral Philosophy at Seventeenth-Century Harvard: A Discipline in Transition* (Chapel Hill: University of North Carolina Press, 1981).

28. Cf. Wilson, *Arthur O. Lovejoy*.

29. Cf. the discussion in Schorske, *Thinking with History*, 228.

30. For a useful contemporary account of the transformation of academic philosophy in Britain and its impact on America, see Ved Mehta, *Fly and the Fly-Bottle* (Boston: Little, Brown, 1962). The fullest account is now Scott Soames, *Philosophical Analysis in the Twentieth Century*, 2 vols. (Princeton, N.J.: Princeton University Press, 2003).

31. Bruce Kuklick, *The Rise of American Philosophy: Cambridge, Massachusetts, 1860–1930* (New Haven, Conn.: Yale University Press, 1977).

32. See esp. the pioneering works of David Hollinger, *Morris R. Cohen and the Scientific Ideal* (Cambridge, Mass.: MIT Press, 1975) and John Toews, *Hegelianism: The Path toward Dialectical Humanism* (Cambridge: Cambridge University Press, 1980), and the *Cambridge History of Renaissance Philosophy*, ed. Charles Schmitt, Eckhart Kessler, and Quentin Skinner, with Jill Kraye (Cambridge: Cambridge University Press, 1987).

33. See e.g. John Monfasani, *George of Trebizond: A Biography and a Study of His Rhetoric and Logic* (Leiden: Brill, 1976); James Hankins, *Plato in the Italian Renaissance*, 2 vols. (Leiden: Brill, 1990); Christopher Celenza, *The Lost Italian Renaissance: Humanists, Historians, and Latin's Legacy* (Baltimore, Md.: Johns Hopkins University Press, 2004).

34. See e.g. Geoffrey Lloyd, *Magic, Reason and Experience* (Cambridge: Cambridge University Press, 1979); Lloyd, *Science, Folklore, and Ideology: Studies in the*

Life Sciences in Ancient Greece (Cambridge: Cambridge University Press, 1983); Lloyd, *The Revolutions of Wisdom: Studies in the Claims and Practice of Ancient Greek Science* (Berkeley: University of California Press, 1987).

35. See the studies collected in *The Cambridge History of Later Medieval Philosophy: From the Rediscovery of Aristotle to the Disintegration of Scholasticism,* ed. Norman Kretzmann, A. J. P. Kenny, and Jan Pinborg, with Eleonore Stump (Cambridge: Cambridge University Press, 1982).

36. See e.g. Martha Nussbaum, *The Fragility of Goodness: Luck and Ethics in Greek Tragedy and Philosophy* (Cambridge: Cambridge University Press, 1986); Michael Frede, *Essays in Ancient Philosophy* (Minneapolis: University of Minnesota Press, 1987); John Cooper, *Reason and Emotion: Essays on Ancient Moral Psychology and Ethical Theory* (Princeton, N.J.: Princeton University Press, 1999); *The Cambridge History of Early Modern Philosophy,* ed. Daniel Garber and Michael Ayers, with the assistance of Roger Ariew and Alan Gabbey, 2 vols. (Cambridge: Cambridge University Press, 1998).

37. See the essays collected in *Teaching New Histories of Philosophy.*

38. George Huppert, "*Divinatio et Eruditio:* Thoughts on Foucault," *History and Theory* 13 (1974), 191–207; Ian Maclean, "Foucault's Renaissance Épistémé Reassessed: An Aristotelian Counterblast," *Journal of the History of Ideas* 59 (1998), 149–166. For a particularly lucid effort to clarify relations between Foucault's work and more conventional intellectual histories, see David Hollinger, "Historians and the Discourse of Intellectuals," in his *In the American Province,* 130–151.

39. Jan Goldstein, *Console and Classify: The French Psychiatric Profession in the Nineteenth Century* (Cambridge: Cambridge University Press, 1987; repr. with a new afterword, Chicago: University of Chicago Press, 2001); Stuart Clark, *Thinking with Demons: The Idea of Witchcraft in Early Modern Europe* (Oxford: Clarendon Press, 1997).

40. Peter Brown, *The Body and Society: Men, Women, and Sexual Renunciation in Early Christianity* (New York: Columbia University Press, 1988); Caroline Bynum, *Fragmentation and Redemption: Essays on Gender and the Human Body in Medieval Religion* (New York: Zone Books, 1991); Bynum, *The Resurrection of the Body in Western Christianity, 200–1336* (New York: Columbia University Press, 1995); Thomas Laqueur, *Making Sex: Body and Gender from the Greeks to Freud* (Cambridge, Mass.: Harvard University Press, 1990); Laqueur, *Solitary Sex: A Cultural History of Masturbation* (New York: Zone Books, 2003); see also Maud Gleason, *Making Men: Sophists and Self-Presentation in Ancient Rome* (Princeton, N.J.: Princeton University Press, 1995); Bernadette Brooten, *Love between Women: Early Christian Responses to Female Homoeroticism* (Chicago: University of Chicago Press, 1996); Elizabeth Clark, *Reading Renunciation: Asceticism and Scripture in Early Christianity* (Princeton, N.J.: Princeton University Press, 1999); and many more.

41. Edward Said, *Orientalism* (New York: Vintage Books, 1979). Cf. Edith Hall, *Inventing the Barbarian: Greek Self-Definition through Tragedy* (Oxford: Clarendon

Press, 1989) and Eve Troutt Powell, *A Different Shade of Colonialism: Egypt, Great Britain and the Mastery of the Sudan* (Berkeley: University of California Press, 2003). Cf. also François Hartog, *Le miroir d'Hérodote* (Paris: Gallimard, 1980).

42. For some striking cases in point, see Gadi Algazi, "Food for Thought: Hieronymus Wolf grapples with the Scholarly Habitus," in *Egodocuments in History: Autobiographical Writing in Its Social Context since the Middle Ages,* ed. Rudolf Dekker (Hilversum: Verloren, 2002), 21–44; Algazi, "Scholars in Households: Refiguring the Learned Habitus, 1480–1550," *Science in Context* 16 (2003), 9–42.

43. Cf. e.g. Ann Blair, *The Theater of Nature: Jean Bodin and Renaissance Science* (Princeton, N.J.: Princeton University Press, 1997) and Caroline Winterer, *The Culture of Classicism: Ancient Greece and Rome in American Intellectual Life, 1780–1910* (Baltimore, Md.: Johns Hopkins University Press, 2002).

44. William Bouwsma, "From History of Ideas to History of Meaning," *Journal of Interdisciplinary History* 12 (1981), 279–291, repr. in Bouwsma, *A Usable Past: Essays in European Cultural History* (Berkeley: University of California Press, 1990), 336–347.

45. See e.g. Josef Hayim Yerushalmi, *Zakhor: Jewish History and Jewish Memory* (Seattle: University of Washington Press, 1982) and Amos Funkenstein, *Perceptions of Jewish History* (Los Angeles: University of California Press, 1993).

46. J. G. A. Pocock, *The Machiavellian Moment: Florentine Political Thought and the Atlantic Republican Tradition* (Princeton, N.J.: Princeton University Press, 1975; repr. with a new afterword, Princeton, N.J.: Princeton University Press, 2003). See also Gisela Bock, Quentin Skinner, and Maurizio Viroli, eds., *Machiavelli and Republicanism* (Cambridge: Cambridge University Press, 1990).

47. See e.g. Richard Tuck, *Natural Rights Theories: Their Origin and Development* (Cambridge: Cambridge University Press, 1979); Anthony Pagden, *The Fall of Natural Man: The American Indian and the Origin of Comparative Ethnology* (Cambridge: Cambridge University Press, 1982); Anthony Pagden, ed., *The Languages of Political Theory in Early Modern Europe* (Cambridge: Cambridge University Press, 1987); Laurence Dickey, *Hegel: Religion, Economics and the Politics of Spirit, 1770–1807* (Cambridge: Cambridge University Press, 1987).

48. See more recently Eric Nelson, *The Greek Tradition in Republican Thought* (Cambridge: Cambridge University Press, 2004) and Peter Stacey, *Roman Monarchy and the Renaissance Prince* (Cambridge: Cambridge University Press, 2007).

49. Quentin Skinner, ed., *The Return of Grand Theory in the Human Sciences* (Cambridge: Cambridge University Press, 1985).

50. See James Tully, ed., *Meaning and Context: Quentin Skinner and His Critics* (Princeton, N.J.: Princeton University Press, 1993).

51. Quentin Skinner, *Reason and Rhetoric in the Philosophy of Hobbes* (Princeton, N.J.: Princeton University Press, 1996).

52. J. G. A. Pocock, *Barbarism and Religion,* 4 vols. to date (Cambridge: Cambridge University Press, 1999–).

53. See the pioneering article by Richard Goldthwaite, "The Florentine Palace as Domestic Architecture," *American Historical Review* 77 (1972), 977–1012, and Carl Schorske's influential *Fin-de-siècle Vienna: Politics and Culture* (New York: Knopf, 1979).

54. See e.g. *The Origins of Museums: The Cabinet of Curiosities in Sixteenth and Seventeenth-Century Europe*, ed. Oliver Impey and Arthur MacGregor (Oxford: Clarendon Press, 1985; repr. Kelly Bray, U.K.: House of Stratus, 2001); Paula Findlen, *Possessing Nature: Museums, Collecting and Scientific Culture in Early Modern Italy* (Berkeley: University of California Press, 1994); Suzanne Marchand, *Down from Olympus: Archaeology and Philhellenism in Germany, 1750–1970* (Princeton, N.J.: Princeton University Press, 1996); Steven Conn, *Museums and American Intellectual Life, 1876–1926* (Chicago: University of Chicago Press, 1998).

55. See the pioneering work of Steven Shapin and Simon Shaffer, *Leviathan and the Air-Pump: Hobbes, Boyle and the Experimental Life* (Princeton, N.J.: Princeton University Press, 1985); Peter Dear, *Discipline and Experience: The Mathematical Way in the Scientific Revolution* (Chicago: University of Chicago Press, 1995); and the studies collected in Lorraine Daston, ed., *Biographies of Scientific Objects* (Chicago: University of Chicago Press, 2000), and Daston, ed., *Things That Talk: Object Lessons from Art and Science* (Cambridge, Mass.: MIT Press, 2004).

56. See e.g. James Young, *The Texture of Memory: Holocaust Memorials and Meaning* (New Haven, Conn.: Yale University Press, 1993); J. M. Winter, *Sites of Memory, Sites of Mourning: The Great War in European Cultural History* (Cambridge: Cambridge University Press, 1995); Daniel Sherman, *The Construction of Memory in Interwar France* (Chicago: University of Chicago Press, 1999).

57. Carlo Ginzburg, *The Cheese and the Worms: The Cosmos of a Sixteenth-Century Miller*, tr. John Tedeschi and Anne Tedeschi (Baltimore, Md.: Johns Hopkins University Press, 1980); see Andrea Del Col, *Domenico Scandella Known as Menocchio: His Trials before the Inquisition (1583–1599)*, tr. John Tedeschi and Anne Tedeschi (Binghamton, N.Y.: Medieval and Renaissance Texts and Studies, 1996).

58. See e.g. three recent and influential approaches to the European Republic of Letters in the decades leading up to and just after 1700: Anne Goldgar, *Impolite Learning: Conduct and Community in the Republic of Letters, 1680–1750* (New Haven, Conn.: Yale University Press, 1995); Jonathan Israel, *Radical Enlightenment: Philosophy and the Making of Modernity, 1650–1750* (Oxford: Oxford University Press, 2001); Noel Malcolm, *Aspects of Hobbes* (Oxford: Clarendon Press, 2002).

59. See the provocative presentation by Kevin Sharpe, *Reading Revolutions: The Politics of Reading in Early Modern England* (New Haven, Conn.: Yale University Press, 2000), and more generally H. J. Jackson, *Marginalia: Readers Writing in Books* (New Haven, Conn.: Yale University Press, 2001).

60. See the important works of Daniel Woolf, *Reading History in Early Modern England* (Cambridge: Cambridge University Press, 2000) and Woolf, *The Social Circulation of the Past: English Historical Culture, 1500–1730* (Oxford: Oxford Uni-

versity Press, 2003), and the more recent work of Nicholas Popper, *Walter Ralegh's History of the World and the Historical Culture of the Late Renaissance* (PhD dissertation, Princeton University, 2007); and for more recent periods, Peter Fritzsche, *Reading Berlin 1900* (Cambridge, Mass.: Harvard University Press, 1996) and Jonathan Rose, *The Intellectual Life of the British Working Classes* (New Haven, Conn.: Yale University Press, 2001).

61. See e.g. Shane Butler, *The Hand of Cicero* (New York: Routledge, 2002) and Lawrence Rainey, *The Institutions of Modernism: Literary Elites and Public Culture* (New Haven, Conn.: Yale University Press, 1998).

62. See e.g. Marcia Colish, *Medieval Foundations of the Western Intellectual Tradition, 400–1400* (New Haven, Conn.: Yale University Press, 1997); William Bouwsma, *The Waning of the Renaissance, ca. 1550–1640* (New Haven, Conn.: Yale University Press, 2000); John Burrow, *The Crisis of Reason: European Thought, 1848–1914* (New Haven, Conn.: Yale University Press, 2000); and above all Maryanne Cline Horowitz, ed., *New Dictionary of the History of Ideas,* 6 vols. (New York: Scribner's, 2005).

63. Cf. Daphne Patai and Will H. Corral, eds., *Theory's Empire: An Anthology of Dissent* (New York: Columbia University Press, 2005).

64. See e.g. Andrzej Walicki, *Philosophy and Romantic Nationalism: The Case of Poland* (Oxford: Clarendon Press, 1982) and Leszek Kolakowski, *Chrétiens sans église: La conscience religieuse et le lien confessionnel au XVIIe siècle,* tr. Anna Posner (Paris: Gallimard, 1969).

11. The Messrs. Casaubon

1. This chapter rests in part on Pattison's printed works, in part on his papers in the Bodleian Library, Oxford. For a full bibliography of both, see H. S. Jones, *Intellect and Character in Victorian England: Mark Pattison and the Invention of the Don* (Cambridge: Cambridge University Press, 2007). Jones corrects standard estimates of Pattison's life, marriage, career as a writer, and views on university reform, and offers a splendid revisionist account of Pattison's career as a writer for periodicals, He also has some illuminating things to say about Pattison's work on the history of scholarship, but this part of his work is considerably shallower than the rest. He shows little grasp of the arguments of A. D. Nuttall, whose *Dead from the Waist Down* (New Haven, Conn.: Yale University Press, 2003) he cites. Jones does not even refer to Eduard Fraenkel's edition of *Aeschylus* (Oxford: Clarendon Press, 1950), I, 61–77, in which the great scholar demonstrated the brilliance of Casaubon's scholarship and the importance of his unpublished notebooks and annotated books, which, as he pointed out, Pattison did not attempt to interpret. Nuttal develops these points at length. This chapter, which has been revised to take account of Jones's work, centers on the problems on which he has the least to say. Italics and unusual spellings in quotations are reproduced from Pattison's manuscripts.

12. Momigliano's Method and the Warburg Institute

This chapter develops arguments put forward much more briefly in Grafton, "Arnaldo Momigliano e la storia degli studi classici," at 106–109, and "Einleitung." My thanks to Michael Crawford, Carlotta Dionisotti, Joseph Levine, Christopher Ligota, Anne Marie Meyer, Glenn Most, Joanna Weinberg, and above all Peter Miller, for many years of conversation on the topics discussed here; to J. B. Trapp, for a critical reading of an earlier draft and for the letter from Yates to Momigliano that appears in Appendix 2; and to Dorothea McEwan and her colleagues in the Warburg Institute archive, Susanne Meurer and Claudia Wedepohl, who enabled me to use the documents in the most pleasant imaginable working conditions.

1. Green, "Ancient History and Modern Historians." In this chapter, references to secondary sources have been kept to a minimum.

2. Dionisotti, "Review of Mandowsky and Mitchell, *Pirro Ligorio's Roman Antiquities*." Dionisotti's critique, though characteristically erudite and pointed, was overstated. Mitchell's introduction to this work offered a stimulating survey that retains some value even now.

3. For a more detailed account of this meeting and its consequences, see Grafton, "Arnaldo Momigliano: A Pupil's Notes."

4. For these articles, see Momigliano, *Contributo alla storia degli studi classici*, 233–248, 37–54, 67–106, 213–231, 195–211; *Essays in Ancient and Modern Historiography*, 231–251; *Studies in Historiography*, 127–142; *Essays in Ancient and Modern Historiography*, 277–293, 107–126.

5. Thus, on 3 November 1947, Momigliano wrote to Gaetano da Sanctis, while riding a train from Bristol to Oxford, that "oggi pomeriggio devo far lezione a Oxford per un corso di Storia dell'Umanesimo italiano, in cui siamo Dionisotti, io e altri"; to my knowledge, he did not publish this text. The notebooks that he kept during his time in Bristol, 1948–1951, include "un riassunto del saggio sull'antiquaria" in Italian. See Di Donato, "Materiali per una biografia intellettuale di Arnaldo Momigliano. 2. Tra Napoli e Bristol," 241n40.

6. Momigliano, *The Classical Foundations of Modern Historiography*. Cf. Rowe, "Ethnography and Ethnology in the Sixteenth Century."

7. Momigliano, *Contributo alla storia degli studi classici*, 234.

8. Green, "Ancient History and Modern Historians."

9. See e.g. Momigliano, "History in an Age of Ideologies [1982]" and "The Introduction of History as an Academic Subject and Its Implications [1985]." Cf. the wonderful passage on Harnack and Estienne in Momigliano, "Review of Elizabeth Armstrong, *Robert Estienne, Royal Printer: An Historical Study of the Elder Stephanus*": "It requires a great deal of worldly wisdom to get things done by other people." Of course, Momigliano referred occasionally to such institutions as the Italian academies in his early work, and his lecture on Mabillon's Italian disciples, delivered in 1958 but not published until 1966, showed a profound understanding

of the Maurists' world of learning as well as the rather different ones that flourished in the Italy of Bacchini and Muratori.

10. Momigliano, "Review of Elizabeth Armstrong, *Robert Estienne, Royal Printer: An Historical Study of the Elder Stephanus.*" Note also the remarks that led up to these: "No criticism of Mrs. Armstrong is implied if it is observed that, being neither a classical not a biblical scholar, she is less effective in assessing Robert Estienne's contribution to scholarship. She probably never intended to provide a complete assessment . . . She has prepared the way for any future study of Robert Estienne as a biblical and classical scholar. But a warning should be added even if it may seem pretentious." See also Momigliano's review of A. Bernardini and G. Righi, *Il concetto di filologia e di cultura classica nel mondo moderno* (1949), in *Contributo alla storia degli studi classici*, 393–395; his review of Domenico Maffei, *Alessandro d'Alessandro giureconsulto umanista (1461–1523)* and *Gli inizi dell'umanesimo giuridico* (1957), in *Secondo contributo alla storia degli studi classici*, 418–421; and his review of Jürgen von Stackelberg, *Tacitus in der Romania* (1963), in *Terzo contributo alla storia degli studi classici e del mondo antico*, II, 775–776. These concerns still inspired his later series of Pisan seminars on the history of historiography, on which see Cambiano, "Momigliano e i seminari pisani di storia della storiografia."

11. Cf. Momigliano, *Essays in Ancient and Modern Historiography*, 6–7: "When I became a professor at University College London more than twenty years ago, it did not take me long to realize that the best historians of ideas in the place were two practising scientists, J. Z. Young and Peter Medawar. But the fact that they talked about sciences I did not know not only paralyzed me in regard to them (which is easy to understand) but also paralyzed them in regard to me or anybody else in my position. That is, they lacked the potential public necessary for developing their scientific ideas in an historical context." In fact, this was no longer true of Medawar, at least, by the 1960s.

12. Momigliano, "Review of Elizabeth Armstrong, *Robert Estienne, Royal Printer: An Historical Study of the Elder Stephanus.*"

13. For Momigliano's reception in England and the impact of his teaching, see Dionisotti, *Ricordo di Arnaldo Momigliano;* Brown, "Arnaldo Dante Momigliano"; Oswyn Murray, "Momigliano e la cultura inglese," revised as "Arnaldo Momigliano in England"; and Crawford, "L'insegnamento di Arnaldo Momigliano in Gran Bretagna."

14. Momigliano, *Contributo alla storia degli studi classici*, 233, 213, 195; *Secondo contributo alla storia degli studi classici*, 191.

15. Momigliano, *Contributo alla storia degli studi classici*, 354.

16. Momigliano, *Terzo contributo alla storia degli studi classici e del mondo antico*, II, 769–774. More than one reviewer of *The Classical Foundations of Modern Historiography* called attention to the dualistic schemes that persisted there: see the review essays by David Konstan and Ernst Breisach. In later years—after he had laid

down the durable foundations of his work on historiography—Momigliano showed a liking for triangular schemas. See e.g. Momigliano, "History between Medicine and Rhetoric [1985]." But dualistic schemas persisted as well.

17. The locus classicus is Momigliano, "The Rhetoric of History and the History of Rhetoric: On Hayden White's Tropes [1981]."

18. I have not seen the volume by Momigliano on Seneca and Tacitus, eventually rejected by Oxford University Press, described by Riccardo Di Donato, "Materiali per una biografia intellettuale di Arnaldo Momigliano," 242.

19. For the general development of Momigliano's work in this field, and its context, see Christ, "Arnaldo Momigliano and the History of Historiography." A more detailed chronology is offered by Di Donato, "Materiali per una biografia intellettuale di Arnaldo Momigliano. 2. Tra Napoli e Bristol."

20. Momigliano, *Contributo alla storia degli studi classici,* 263–274, 165–194, 107–164, 379–382.

21. Ibid., 165n1. Momigliano's letter to D. M. Pippidi of 24 December 1933 shows him mastering these materials with his customary speed: "E stato per me un periodo molto interessante quello che ho potuto dedicare alla lettura del pensiero dei proto-romantici (Humboldt, Wolf, Niebuhr, Boeckh, etc.) che mi hanno precisato la radice del pensiero del mio Altvater Droysen (non vorrei però danneggiare presso di Lei la 'purezza' di Droysen dandogli dei discendenti semitici!)." Published in Momigliano, "L'epistolario con D. M. Pippidi," 17–18, and quoted by Di Donato, "Materiali per una biografia intellettuale di Arnaldo Momigliano," 220.

22. Momigliano, *Contributo alla storia degli studi classici,* 380, 245n32; *Essays in Ancient and Modern Historiography,* 312.

23. Momigliano, *Contributo alla storia degli studi classici,* 112–113.

24. Momigliano to Saxl, 24 March 1947, Warburg Institute Archive, Journal Correspondence.

25. Momigliano, *Contributo,* 379n.

26. See esp. Murray, "Arnaldo Momigliano in England," and Davin, *Closing Times.* For the role possibly played by Davin in the rejection of Momigliano's book on Tacitus by the Oxford University Press, see Di Donato, "Materiali per una biografia intellettuale di Arnaldo Momigliano. 2. Tra Napoli e Bristol," 242.

27. See Momigliano, "Review of R. M. Ogilvie, *Latin and Greek* (1964)," in *Quarto contributo alla storia degli studi classici e del mondo antico,* 657 (itself in some ways a curious document). Perhaps he felt that his friend Dionisotti had said what needed to be said in "Tradizione classica e volgarizzamenti," reprinted with an additional note and a massive further study of the general topic in Dionisotti, *Geografia e storia della letteratura italiana,* 103–144 (for Bolgar, see 103–109).

28. Cf. Grafton, "Mark Pattison."

29. See Most's introduction in Timpanaro, *The Genesis of Lachmann's Method.*

30. On Butterfield, see most recently Nick Jardine, "Whigs and Stories: Herbert Butterfield and the Historiography of Science."

31. Kendrick, *British Antiquity*.

32. Momigliano, *Contributo alla storia degli studi classici*, 104n61. For Momigliano's reading of Kendrick, see his letter to Frances Yates, 17 September 1950, Warburg Institute Archives, Journal Correspondence: "I have also to add at least one reference to T. D. Kendrick, *British Antiquity*—just appeared—in connection with Leland's title Antiquarius."

33. Haskell, *History and Its Images*.

34. For Momigliano's gradual decision after World War II to abandon the monograph for the public lecture, and its relation to his new environment, see esp. Dionisotti, "Commemorazione di Arnaldo Momigliano," 356–357, and *Ricordo di Arnaldo Momigliano*, 21.

35. See Giorgio Pasquali's essay of 1930, "Aby Warburg," 40.

36. Momigliano's acknowledgments, unlike most peoples', were anything but routine and normally reflected actual discussions. In "Ancient History and the Antiquarian," for example, he thanked Felix Jacoby and Carlo Dionisotti, among others, for their help. In fact, he had asked Jacoby "to read the first pages on the Greeks" in spring 1950 (Momigliano to Yates, 6 April 1950, Warburg Institute Archive, Journal Correspondence), and in the fall, he told Frances Yates, "Personally I have finished with the page proofs, but I should like them to be seen by Dionisotti, whose keen eyes will certainly catch flaws" (Momigliano to Yates, undated but after 21 September 1950, Warburg Institute Archive, Journal Correspondence).

37. On Momigliano's Warburg Institute seminar, see the fine characterization in Crawford, "L'insegnamento di Arnaldo Momigliano in Gran Bretagna," 28–29.

38. Panofsky to Gertrud Bing, 3 March 1935, in Panofsky, *Korrespondenz*, ed. Wuttke, I, 812–813.

39. See esp. Saxl, *Lectures;* Panofsky and Saxl, "Classical Mythology in Mediaeval Art."

40. Saxl, "The Classical Inscription in Renaissance Art and Politics"; Wittkower, "Marvels of the East: A Study of the History of Monsters."

41. Saxl to Momigliano, 1 May 1947; Yates to Momigliano, 4 January 1950; Warburg Institute Archive, Journal Correspondence.

42. Murray, "Arnaldo Momigliano in England," 53–54.

43. Wittkower to Momigliano, 6 July 1945, Warburg Institute Archive, Journal Correspondence (including the description of the project quoted in the previous sentence).

44. Momigliano to Wittkower, 22 July 1945, Warburg Institute Archive, Journal Correspondence.

45. Wittkower to Momigliano, 26 July 1945, Warburg Institute Archive, Journal Correspondence.

46. Wittkower to Momigliano, 1 October 1945; Wittkower to Momigliano, 26 November 1946; Yates to Momigliano, 1 January 1947, Warburg Institute Archive, Journal Correspondence.

47. Saxl to Momigliano, 20 March 1947, Warburg Institute Archive, Journal Correspondence.

48. Momigliano to Saxl, 24 March 1947, Warburg Institute Archive, Journal Correspondence.

49. Saxl to Momigliano, 27 March 1947; Momigliano to Saxl, 16 April 1947, Warburg Institute Archive, Journal Correspondence.

50. *Journal of the Warburg and Courtauld Institutes* 9 (1946 [1947]), 153.

51. Saxl to Momigliano, 1 May 1947, Warburg Institute Archive, Journal Correspondence.

52. It is not surprising that Momigliano was so willing to learn from Saxl, whom he greatly respected. See, again, his "Review of Elizabeth Armstrong, *Robert Estienne, Royal Printer: An Historical Study of the Elder Stephanus*": "The modern reader may be reminded of the skill with which Fritz Saxl got his Warburg Institute out of Germany." And cf. Momigliano to Gerturd Bing, 8 May 1957, Warburg Institute Archive, General Correspondence: "Dear Bing, as you happen to mention the fact that I did not contribute to the Saxl volume, the quite simple explanation is that I was not invited. As Gordon is a friend of mine, there is no evil intent behind the exclusion. The probable explanation is that the contributors were chosen among British subjects—*or* I may just have been forgotten."

53. Momigliano to Gertrud Bing, 12 January 1949, Warburg Institute Archive, Lecture Correspondence; Yates to Momigliano, 4 January 1950, Warburg Institute Archive, Journal Correspondence.

54. On Yates's intellectual life and scholarly career, see J. B. Trapp, ed., *Francis S. Yates, 1899–1981: In Memoriam,* and Patrizia Delpiano, " 'Il teatro del mondo': Per un profilo intellettuale di Frances Amelia Yates."

55. Yates to Momigliano, 18 May 1950, Warburg Institute Archive, Journal Correspondence: "As we all hope that you will let us have more articles for the Journal in the future, I trust you will not mind if we humbly ask you next time (a) to send us a top copy rather than a carbon; (b) to double-space your footnotes; and (c) not to continue them on the back of the page? Please forgive these petty remarks."

56. Momigliano to Yates, 17 September 1950, Warburg Institute Archive, Journal Correspondence: "I am now back from Italy, and have checked again almost all the bibliographical references and quotations on the original texts (I cannot say that I have become very popular either at the Vittorio Emanuele in Rome or in Bodley here where I performed the operation). I have discovered a considerable number of petty mistakes which usually involve only one letter or syllable. But half a dozen of them imply the addition or deletion of a word and would be better removed in the galley proofs stage. If my article is still at that stage, I should be glad to have it back. Otherwise I think we can wait for the page proofs."

57. Momigliano to Yates, 17 September 1950, Warburg Institute Archive, Journal Correspondence.

58. Yates to Momigliano, 18 May 1950, Warburg Institute Archive, Journal Correspondence.

59. Momigliano to Saxl, 16 May 1942, Warburg Institute Archive, Journal Correspondence: "Io sono non dico un dillettante—una parola che a orecchie italiane ancora suona complimento!—ma un ignorante in materia archaeologica."

60. See Momigliano to Bing, 24 July 1956, Warburg Institute Archive, General Correspondence: "Burckhardt was the first art historian to become a historian of a civilization as a whole—and this established a connection between visual studies and the Renaissance Warburg was to inherit. Then Warburg went beyond Burckhardt in emphasizing the irrational elements of the Renaissance, its anti-Flemish, anti-bourgeois reaction, its links with Antiquity through astrology and mythology. The method could be extended—it could be associated with the new trends in the psychology of the unconscious (from which it undoubtedly derived its strength) and with the new research on language. But, as far as I know, only in the study of the Renaissance the Warburg I. has produced something amounting to a reinterpretation or at least to a critical revision of a civilization. In other fields there have been contributions, suggestions, but not deep-going re-interpretations. The future will probably qualify this picture, but so far the Renaissance studies have rightly been associated with the Warburg I in the minds of the outsiders."

61. Yates to Momigliano, 9 October 1950, Warburg Institute Archive, Journal Correspondence, given in full in Appendix 1.

62. Yates to Momigliano, 10 November 1950, Warburg Institute Archive, Journal Correspondence.

63. *Journal of the Warburg and Courtauld Institutes* 13 (1950), 309.

64. Momigliano to Yates, 17 September 1950, Warburg Institute Archive, Journal Correspondence.

65. See Phillips, "Reconsiderations on History and Antiquarianism: Arnaldo Momigliano and the Historiography of Eighteenth-Century Britain," and his subsequent book *Society and Sentiment: Genres of Historical Writing in Britain, 1740–1820*. Phillips's work, which is excellent in its own terms, sheds considerable light on eighteenth-century historiography and the larger development of the historical tradition. But he does not attend to the context and documented intentions of Momigliano's studies, and this detracts from the usefulness of his important critique. William Stenhouse, "Georg Fabricius and Inscriptions as a Source of Law," incisively revises Momigliano's work in one crucial aspect.

66. Note the way in which, in a letter to D. M. Pippidi of 25 January 1950, Momigliano described the widest-ranging and most influential of all his studies in the field, "Ancient History and the Antiquarian": "Sono venuto pubblicando lavori di metodo storico—tra cui uno su "Ancient History and the Antiquarian" destinato a uscire a fine d'anno nel Journal of the Warburg Institute." Momigliano, "L'epistolario con D. M. Pippidi," 31.

67. Schwab, *La Renaissance orientale*.

Sources Cited

Breisach, Ernst. "Review of Momigliano, *The Classical Foundations of Modern His-toriography*." *Clio* 23 (1993), 81–91.

Brown, Peter. "Arnaldo Dante Momigliano." *Proceedings of the British Academy* 74 (1988), 405–442.

Butterfield, Herbert. *The Englishman and His History*. Cambridge: Cambridge University Press, 1944.

———. *Man on His Past: The Study of the History of Historical Scholarship*. Cambridge: Cambridge University Press, 1955.

———. *The Whig Interpretation of History*. London: G. Bell, 1951.

Cambiano, Giuseppe. "Momigliano e i seminari pisani di storia della storiografia." *Storia della storiografia* 16 (1989), 75–83.

Christ, Karl. "Arnaldo Momigliano and the History of Historiography." *History and Theory, Beiheft 39: The Presence of the Historian: Essays in Memory of Arnaldo Momigliano*, ed. Michael Steinberg (1991), 5–12.

Crawford, Michael. "L'insegnamento di Arnaldo Momigliano in Gran Bretagna." In *Omaggio ad Arnaldo Momigliano: Storia e storiografia sul mondo antico*, ed. Lellia Cracco Ruggini. Como: New Press, 1989, 27–41.

Davin, Dan. *Closing Times*. London: Oxford University Press, 1975.

Delpiano, Patrizia. " 'Il teatro del mondo': Per un profilo intellettuale di Frances Amelia Yates." *Rivista Storica Italiana* 105 (1993), 180–245.

Di Donato, Riccardo. "Materiali per una biografia intellettuale di Arnaldo Momigliano." *Athenaeum* 83 (1995), 213–244.

———. "Materiali per una biografia intellettuale di Arnaldo Momigliano. 2. Tra Napoli e Bristol." *Athenaeum* 86 (1998), 231–244.

Dionisotti, Carlo. "Commemorazione di Arnaldo Momigliano." *Rivista storica italiana* 100 (1988), 348–360.

———. *Geografia e storia della letteratura italiana*. Turin: Giulio Einaudi, 1967.

———. "Review of Mandowsky and Mitchell, *Pirro Ligorio's Roman Antiquities*." *Rivista Storica Italiana* 75 (1963), 890–901.

———. *Ricordo di Arnaldo Momigliano*. Bologna: Il Mulino, 1989.

———. "Tradizione classica e volgarizzamenti." *Italia Medioevale e Umanistica* 1 (1958), 427–431.

Duncan, David. *English Scholars*. London: J. Cape, 1939.

Grafton, Anthony. "Arnaldo Momigliano: A Pupil's Notes." *American Scholar* 60 (1991), 235–241.

———. "Arnaldo Momigliano e la storia degli studi classici." *Rivista storica italiana* 107 (1995), 91–109.

———. "Einleitung." In Arnaldo Momigliano, *Ausgewählte Schriften zur Geschichte und Geschichtsschreibung*, Bd II: *Spätantike bis Spätaufklärung*, ed.

Grafton, tr. Kai Brodersen and Andreas Wittenburg. Stuttgart: Metzler, 1999, vii–xx.

———. "Mark Pattison." *American Scholar* 52 (1983), 229–236.

Green, Peter. "Ancient History and Modern Historians." *Times Literary Supplement,* 22 July 1955, 412.

Haskell, Francis. *History and Its Images: Art and the Interpretation of the Past.* New Haven, Conn.: Yale University Press, 1993.

Herklotz, Ingo. *Cassiano dal Pozzo und die Archäologie des 17. Jahrhunderts.* Munich: Hirmer, 1999.

Jardine, Nick. "Whigs and Stories: Herbert Butterfield and the Historiography of Science." *History of Science* 41 (2003), 125–140.

Kendrick, T. D. *British Antiquity.* London: Methuen, 1950.

Konstan, David. "Review of Momigliano, *The Classical Foundations of Modern Historiography.*" *History and Theory* 31 (1992), 224–230.

Mandowsky, Erna, and Charles Mitchell. *Pirro Ligorio's Roman Antiquities: The Drawings in MS XIII. B7 in the National Library of Naples.* London: Warburg Institute, 1963.

Miller, Peter. *Peiresc's Europe: Learning and Virtue in the Seventeenth Century.* New Haven, Conn.: Yale University Press, 2000.

Momigliano, Arnaldo. "Ancient History and the Antiquarian." *Journal of the Warburg and Courtauld Institutes* 13 (1950), 285–315,

———. *The Classical Foundations of Modern Historiography,* ed. Riccardo Di Donato. Berkeley: University of California Press, 1990.

———. *Contributo alla storia degli studi classici.* Rome: Edizioni di Storia e Letteratura, 1955.

———. *Essays in Ancient and Modern Historiography.* Oxford: Basil Blackwell, 1977.

———. "History between Medicine and Rhetoric [1985]." In *Ottavo contributo alla storia degli studi classici e del mondo antico.* Rome: Edizioni di Storia e Letteratura, 1987, 13–25.

———. "History in an Age of Ideologies [1982]." In *Settimo contributo alla storia degli studi classici e del mondo antico.* Rome: Edizioni di Storia e Letteratura, 1984, 253–269.

———. "The Introduction of History as an Academic Subject and Its Implications [1985]." In *Ottavo contributo alla storia degli studi classici e del mondo antico.* Rome: Edizioni di Storia e Letteratura, 1987, 161–178.

———. "L'epistolario con D. M. Pippidi." *Storia della storiografia* 16 (1989), 15–33.

———. *Quarto contributo alla storia degli studi classici e del mondo antico.* Rome: Edizioni di Storia e Letteratura, 1969.

———. "Review of Elizabeth Armstrong, *Robert Estienne, Royal Printer: An Historical Study of the Elder Stephanus.*" *Times Literary Supplement,* 25 February 1955, 124.

————. "The Rhetoric of History and the History of Rhetoric: On Hayden White's Tropes [1981]." In *Settimo contributo alla storia degli studi classici e del mondo antico*. Rome: Edizioni di Storia e Letteratura, 1984, 49–59.

————. *Secondo contributo alla storia degli studi classici*. Rome: Edizioni di Storia e Letteratura, 1960.

————. *Studies in Historiography*. New York: Harper and Row, 1966.

————. *Terzo contributo alla storia degli studi classici e del mondo antico*. 2 vols. Rome: Edizioni di Storia e Letteratura, 1966.

Murray, Oswyn. "Arnaldo Momigliano in England." *History and Theory, Beiheft 30: The Presence of the Historian: Essays in Memory of Arnaldo Momigliano*, ed. Michael Steinberg. (1991), 49–64.

————. "Momigliano e la cultura inglese." *Rivista Storica Italiana* (1988), 422–439.

Panofsky, Erwin. *Korrespondenz*, ed. Dieter Wuttke. Vol. 1. Wiesbaden: Harrassowitz, 2001.

Panofsky, Erwin, and Fritz Saxl. "Classical Mythology in Mediaeval Art." *Metropolitan Museum Studies* 4 (1932–1933), 228–280.

Pasquali, Giorgio. "Aby Warburg." In *Pagine stravaganti di un filologo*, ed. Carlo Ferdinando Russo. 2 vols. Florence: Casa Editrice Le Lettere, 1994, I, 40–54.

Phillips, Mark. "Reconsiderations on History and Antiquarianism: Arnaldo Momigliano and the Historiography of Eighteenth-Century Britain." *Journal of the History of Ideas* 57 (1996), 297–316.

————. *Society and Sentiment: Genres of Historical Writing in Britain, 1740–1820*. Princeton, N.J.: Princeton University Press, 2000.

Rowe, John. "Ethnography and Ethnology in the Sixteenth Century." *The Kroeber Anthropological Society Papers* 30 (1964), 1–19.

Saxl, Fritz. "The Classical Inscription in Renaissance Art and Politics." *Journal of the Warburg and Courtauld Institutes* 4 (1941), 18–46.

————. *Lectures*. 2 vols. London: Warburg Institute, 1957.

Schwab, Raymond. *La Renaissance orientale*. Paris: Payot, 1950.

Stenhouse, William. "Georg Fabricius and Inscriptions as a Source of Law." *Renaissance Studies* 17 (2003), 96–107.

————. *Reading Inscriptions and Writing Ancient History: Historical Scholarship in the Late Renaissance*. London: Institute of Classical Studies, 2005.

Timpanaro, Sebastiano. *The Genesis of Lachmann's Method*, ed. and tr. Glenn Most. Chicago: University of Chicago Press, 2005.

Trapp, J. B., ed. *Francis S. Yates, 1899–1981: In Memoriam*. London: Warburg Institute, 1982.

Weiss, Roberto. *The Renaissance Discovery of Classical Antiquity*. Oxford: Blackwell, 1969.

Wittkower, Rudolf. "Marvels of the East: A Study of the History of Monsters." *Journal of the Warburg and Courtauld Institutes* 5 (1942), 159–197.

13. The Public Intellectual and the American University

Much of the material in this chapter derives from Robert Morss Lovett's autobiography, *All Our Years* (New York: Viking, 1948) and from the Robert Morss Lovett papers, held by the University of Chicago Library, Special Collections. For the early history of the University of Chicago, see Richard Storr, *Harper's University* (Chicago: University of Chicago Press, 1966), Robin Lester, *Stagg's University* (Urbana: University of Illinois Press, 1995), and *The Berlin Collection* (Chicago: University of Chicago Library, 1979).

14. The Public Intellectual and the Private Sphere

The primary sources for this chapter came from the papers of my father, Samuel Grafton. Reproductions of some of them can now be seen in the Hannah Arendt archive that forms part of the American Memory project at the Library of Congress (http://memory.loc.gov/ammem/arendthtml/resfold3.html, accessed August 12, 2008). See also Hannah Arendt, *The Jewish Writings*, ed. Jerome Kohn and Ron H. Feldman (New York: Schocken, 2007). For the Eichmann book and the controversies it has aroused see esp. *Hannah Arendt Revisited: "Eichmann in Jerusalem" und die Folgen*, ed. Gary Smith (Frankfurt: Suhrkamp, 2000).

15. Codex in Crisis

1. Alfred Kazin, *New York Jew* (New York: Knopf, 1978), 5–7.

2. *New York Times*, 14 May 2006.

3. Jean-Noël Jeanneney, *Quand Google défie l'Europe: Plaidoyer pour un sursaut* (Paris: Mille et une nuits, 2005).

4. Peter Brown, "A Life of Learning," Charles Homer Haskins Lecture, 2004, http://www.acls.org/op37.htm (accessed 13 August 2008).

5. Lionel Casson, *Libraries in the Ancient World* (New Haven, Conn.: Yale University Press, 2001).

6. Anthony Grafton and Megan Williams, *Christianity and the Transformation of the Book* (Cambridge, Mass.: Harvard University Press, 2006).

7. Giovanni Andrea Bussi, *Prefazioni alle edizioni di Sweynheym e Pannartz prototipografi romani*, ed. Massimo Miglio (Milan: il Polifilo, 1978); Edwin Hall, *Sweynheym & Pannartz and the Origins of Printing in Italy: German Technology and Italian Humanism in Renaissance Rome* (McMinnville, Ore.: Bird & Bull Press for Phillip J. Pirages, 1991).

8. "University Publishing in a Digital Age," http://www.ithaka.org/strategic-services/university-publishing (accessed 13 August 2008).

9. Jeremias Drexel, *Avrifodina artium et scientiarum omnium, excerpendi solertia, omnibus litterarum amantibus monstrata* (Antwerp: apud viduam Ioannis Cnobbari, 1641).

10. See Mark Pattison, *Isaac Casaubon, 1559–1614*, 2nd ed. (Oxford: Clarendon Press, 1892) and A. D. Nuttall, *Dead from the Waist Down* (New Haven, Conn.: Yale University Press, 2003).

11. Ann Blair, "Reading Strategies for Coping with Information Overload, ca. 1550–1700," *Journal of the History of Ideas* 64 (2003), 11–28; Noel Malcolm, "Thomas Harrison and His 'Ark of Studies': An Episode in the History of the Organization of Knowledge," *The Seventeenth Century* 19 (2004), 196–232.

12. Dora Panofsky and Erwin Panofsky, *Pandora's Box: The Changing Aspects of a Mythical Symbol* (New York: Pantheon, 1956).

13. Jonathan Rose, *The Intellectual Life of the British Working Classes* (New Haven, Conn.: Yale University Press, 2001).

14. Fremont Rider, *And Master of None* (Middletown, Conn.: Godfrey Memorial Library, 1955); Rider, *The Scholar and the Future of the Research Library* (New York: Hadham Press, 1944); Nicholson Baker, *Double Fold: Libraries and the Assault on Paper* (New York: Random House, 2001).

15. Baker, *Double Fold*.

16. For the OCLC WorldMap, see http://www.oclc.org/research/projects/worldmap/default.htm (accessed 13 August 2008).

17. Kazin, *New York Jew*, 7.

18. See further Robert Townsend, "Google Books: What's Not to Like?" *AHA Today*, 29 April 2007, http://blog.historians.org/articles/204/google-books-whats-not-to-like, and discussion thread.

19. William Bentinck-Smith, *Building a Great Library: The Coolidge Years at Harvard* (Cambridge, Mass.: Harvard University Library, 1976).

20. White Trash Scriptorium, http://www.ipa.net/~magreyn/ (accessed 13 August 2008); Philological Museum, http://www.philological.bham.ac.uk/ (accessed August 13, 2008).

21. John Seely Brown and Paul Duguid, *The Social Life of Information* (Boston: Harvard Business School Press, 2000), 173–174.

22. See http://findarticles.com/p/articles/mi_m0EIN/is_2005_Oct_12/ai_n15686131 (accessed 13 August 2008).

23. Ved Mehta, *Remembering Mr. Shawn's New Yorker: The Invisible Art of Editing* (Woodstock, N.Y.: Overlook Press, 1998), 338.

24. For Andrew Abbott's papers on libraries and research, see http://home.uchicago.edu/~aabbott/booksandpapers.html (accessed 13 August 2008).

25. Peter Fritzsche, *Reading Berlin 1900* (Cambridge, Mass.: Harvard University Press, 1996).

26. Mary Corey, *The World Through a Monocle: The New Yorker at Midcentury* (Cambridge, Mass.: Harvard University Press, 1999), 15–16.

27. Ibid., 15.

28. Witold Rybczynski, "How Do You Build a Public Library in the Age of Google?" *Slate*, 27 February 2008.

29. Jonathan Barnes, "Bagpipe Music," *Topoi* 25 (2006), 17–20, at 18.

Sources

The chapters gathered here began as articles written for a variety of occasions. As always, I am most grateful to the colleagues and editors who originally commissioned them, and whose criticism and counsel materially improved the original versions; also to the periodicals and publishers where they first appeared.

Chapter 1: Originally presented as a lecture at "The Republic of Letters: Between Renaissance and Enlightenment: An International Conference at Stanford University," 30 November–1 December 2007.

Chapter 2: Originally published as "*Historia* and *Istoria:* Alberti's Terminology in Context," *I Tatti Studies* 8 (1999 [2000]), 37–68; reprinted here with permission.

Chapter 3: Originally presented as one of two Rosenbach lectures at the University of Pennsylvania, April 2003.

Chapter 4: Originally published as "Renaissance Histories of Art and Nature," in *The Artificial and the Natural: An Evolving Polarity,* ed. Bernadette Bensaude-Vincent and William R. Newman (Cambridge, Mass.: MIT Press, 2007), 185–210. Reprinted by permission of the MIT Press.

Chapter 5: Originally published as "Where Was Salomon's House? Ecclesiastical History and the Intellectual Origins of Bacon's *New Atlantis,*" in *Die europäische Gelehrtenrepublik im Zeitalter des Konfessionalismus,* ed. Herbert Jaumann (Wiesbaden: Harrassowitz, 2001), 21–38.

Chapter 6: Originally presented to the departmental seminar, Department of the History and Philosophy of Science, Cambridge University, 2 May 2007.

Chapter 7: Originally published in the *New York Review of Books,* 5 October 2006, and in the *London Review of Books,* 1 November 2001, 16–18.

Chapter 8: Originally published in the *New York Review of Books,* 3 March 1994.

Chapter 9: Originally published in the *New York Review of Books,* 26 February 2004.

Chapter 10: Originally published in the *Journal of the History of Ideas* 67 (2006), 1–32. Reprinted by permission of the University of Pennsylvania Press.

Chapter 11: Originally published in *American Scholar* 52 (Spring 1983), 229–236.

Chapter 12: Originally published in *Momigliano and Antiquarianism: Foundations of the Modern Cultural Sciences,* ed. Peter N. Miller (Toronto: University of Toronto Press, 2007), 97–126. Reprinted by permission of the University of Toronto Press.

Chapter 13: Originally published in *American Scholar* 70 (Autumn 2001), 41–54.

Chapter 14: Originally published in *American Scholar* 68 (Winter 1999), 105–119.

Chapter 15: The core of this chapter was originally published in *The New Yorker* (5 November 2007), 50–54. The current, longer version was published as *Codex in Crisis* by the Crumpled Press in 2008. Reprinted with the permission of the Crumpled Press.

Index

Note: page numbers followed by *f* indicate figures.

IN THIS BOOK ANTHONY GRAFTON lets us in on one of the great secrets of scholars and intellectuals: although scholars lead solitary lives in order to win independence of mind, they also enjoy the conviviality of sharing a project sustained by common ideals, practices, and institutions. It's like Masonry, but without the secret handshakes.

Grafton reveals the microdynamics of the scholarly life through a series of essays on institutions and on scholars ranging from early modern polymaths to modern intellectual historians to American thinkers and writers. He takes as his starting point the Republic of Letters—that loose society of intellectuals that first took shape in the sixteenth century and continued into the eighteenth. Its inhabitants were highly original, individual thinkers and writers. Yet, as Grafton shows, they were all formed in some way by the very groups and disciplines that they set out to build.

In our noisy, caffeinated world it has never been more challenging to be a scholar. When many of our fellow citizens seem to have forgotten why we collect books in the buildings we call libraries, Grafton's engaging, erudite essays could be a rallying cry for the revival of the liberal arts.